MUSEUMS & GALLERIES

IN GREAT BRITAIN AND IRELAND

1993 EDITION

Editor:
DEBORAH VALENTINE

Pictured above:
MUSEUM OF THE YEAR 1992
Manx National Heritage

Cover Photographs
A twin cylinder vertical pendulous engine by Henry Maudslay of 1812 – courtesy of Brighton & Hove Engineerium, Brighton

2nd Century Mosaic Floor – courtesy of Fishbourne Roman Palace, Fishbourne

Technofix Clockwork Toy Scooter, German 1960 – courtesy of London Toy and Model Museum, London

A man's velvet suit (circa 1755) Woman's silk dress (circa 1760) Baby's printed linen gown from the 18th century – courtesy of Bath Museums Service, Bath

Vincent Van Gogh (1853–1890) Self Portrait with Bandaged Ear – courtesy of Courtauld Institute Galleries, London

Published by:
Reed Information Services Ltd
Windsor Court, East Grinstead House, East Grinstead, West Sussex RH19 1XA
Telephone: (0342) 326972 Fax: (0342) 335665 Telex: 95127 INFSER G

A Division of Reed Telepublishing Ltd.
A Member of the Reed International group

Buckingham Palace

The Queen's Gallery

A King's Purchase
George III and the Consul Smith Collection
5th March — 23rd December 1993

In 1762, King George III purchased the collection of Joseph Smith, formerly British Consul in Venice. Smith's superb collection of drawings, gems, books and engravings contains also the finest paintings by Canaletto in existence.

This exhibition, drawing on the best of this important collection, provides a rare opportunity to study the taste of this renowned collector.

Open:	Tuesday-Saturday	10.00 – 17.00
	Sunday	14.00 – 17.00
	Bank Holidays	10.00 – 17.00
Closed:	Good Friday	

The Royal Mews

The Royal Mews provides a unique opportunity to see how horse, carriage and tack combine to create the familiar pageantry associated with State Occasions.

Access and facilities for the disabled are excellent and pre-booked groups are very welcome.

Open:	1st October – 31st March	
	Wednesday	12.00 – 16.00
	1st April - mid July	
	Wednesday & Thursday	12.00 – 16.00
	Mid July – 30th September	
	Wednesday - Friday	12.00 – 16.00

The Changing of the Guard

The Changing of The Queen's Guard at Buckingham Palace usually takes place every day between 1st May and early August and every other day for the rest of the year.

In very wet weather or exceptional circumstances, the Changing of the Guard may be cancelled.

For information, including discount rates for groups, telephone 071-930 4832 ext. 3351.

24-hr Information line 071-799 2331

MUSEUMS & GALLERIES
in Great Britain & Ireland

INTRODUCTION

THIS NEW EDITION includes over 1500 museums and galleries featuring local and national collections open to the public, listed in county order, and in alphabetical order of towns within counties. Readers looking for a specific type of collection have the advantage of being able to refer to the Subject Index. There is also an alphabetical index and location index at the end of the book. Readers interested in militaria will find a separate section and index devoted to Services Museums. ·

1993 is the year of the Industrial Museum, and our introductory article is on the subject of Snibston Discovery Park, opened June 1992; the largest newly built science museum in the UK since the war.

On page X the new building for the Tate Gallery St Ives is discussed. This was designed by Eldred Evans and David Shalev, using an area of derelict ground, capitalising on the site of the old gas holder. A two tier glass gallery, and adjoining rectangular sections built along the side of the hill, reflect both 20th century art, and past generations of St Ives' artists.

The work at Wigan Pier has given new meaning to school visits. The children were given a challenge, and rose to it magnificently, adding yet another dimension to the work of the Heritage Education Trust, which is described by Martyn Dyer on page XIV.

CONTENTS

SNIBSTON DISCOVERY PARK: LEICESTERSHIRE AND ITS HISTORY

Snibston Discovery Park, Leicestershire's newest tourist attraction, opened its doors to the public on June 27th 1992. Conceived, developed and managed by Leicestershire County Council's Museums, Arts and Records Service, it is the largest newly-built Science and Industry Museum in the United Kingdom since the war.

Packwoman travelling between villages with goods for sale – early 1800s

Snibston Discovery Park

Snibston is sited on the former Snibston Colliery, in Coalville, which was the major colliery in the area until its closure in 1983. The huge head stocks are still a landmark today, forming part of the colliery trail which visitors can follow around the site, and which includes the two winding houses and the loco shed.

The Galleries

The main feature of Snibston Discovery Park is the huge new Science and Industry Museum. There are five galleries, all themed around Leicestershire's industrial heritage, but all very different.

The Science Alive Gallery explores the three themes of the Environment, the Weather, and the Human Body. There are approximately twenty-five interactive exhibits which encourage visitors to pull levers, press buttons, walk through a tornado, play with safe lightning and talk to George Stephenson.

The Transport Gallery traces the history of transport and its effect on the people of Leicestershire from 1660 to the present day. Amongst other exhibits there is a coal yard reconstruction, several horse-drawn vehicles and even a fish and chip shop!

In the Extractive Industries Gallery, the visitor can handle different kinds of rock such as granite, ironstone and coal. The emphasis is not confined to coal mining, but on the wider range of mining and quarrying industries which have helped develop Leicestershire's industrial heritage.

The successes and failures of many of Leicestershire's most famous companies are recalled in the Engineering Gallery. The focal point is the Gimson Beam Engine, which is in steam at regular times every day. There are also two other working engines, one of which powers a machine shop enabling the visitors to see conditions in which people worked in years gone by.

The fifth and final gallery, Textiles and Fashion, tells the story of the manufacturing, distribution and retailing of clothing and footwear through the ages. The present day is also well represented, with a showcase for the most recent designs in knitwear, footwear and contour fashion by the students of the De Montfort University in Leicester.

Science Play Area

The attractions are not confined to indoors. Britain's only outside Science Play area is situated at the rear of the exhibition hall. This features such unusual exhibits as the sound mirrors, the four-way seesaw and the parabola. Children's safety in this area is assured since all exhibits are on a safe play surface. The play area is based on the

Discover the 'Story of Mann' with the 'Museum of the Year'

The Story of Mann is the wide-ranging portrayal of the unique heritage of the **Isle of Man**, presented over 227 square miles of historical Manx landscape.

This exciting concept is being developed by **Manx National Heritage**, the Island's award winning unified heritage service.

Please see the 'Isle of Man' section
for further details, or contact:
Manx National Heritage,
The Manx Museum and National Trust,
Douglas, Isle of Man.
Telephone: (0624) 675522
Fax: (0624) 661899

Manx National Heritage

Eiraght Ashoonagh Vannin

same themes as the Science Alive, but the fifteen interactives are on a much bigger scale.

Workshop Complex

The 250 year old wheelwright's workshop complex is under reconstruction next to the Science Play area. Comprising a smithy, a saw mill and the workshop itself, the buildings were moved, brick by brick, from the tiny Leicestershire village of Sheepy Magna, before being painstakingly reconstructed at their new site. Upon its

The Wind Machine in Action

reconstruction in autumn 1992, the workshop will be a valuable educational as well as a leisure facility, and will enable visitors to learn about some of the smaller industries which have contributed to Leicestershire's history. Ultimately, the workshop will host woodworking and other craft demonstrations.

Leisure and Recreation

The remainder of the 100 acre site is given over to recreational facilities. An arboretum has been planted with over 30 different species of trees to provide a welcome haven from the bustle of the exhibitions hall. There is a nine-hole golf course and practice facility, the largest of its kind in Europe. There is a club house, golfers' shop and driving range, all run by an experienced professional.

The nature trail is located in the Grange area of the site, and is interpreted by ecological panels along the route, and a comprehensive brochure explaining the kinds of wildlife visitors can expect to find en route. There are two fishing lakes, for which day and season tickets are available for adults and juniors. The lakes are reclaimed colliery drainage lagoons which have been landscaped and are now stocked with roach, tench and perch.

Special Events Arena

The Special Events arena is located directly opposite the exhibition hall, and is nearly three acres in size, with a grass viewing bank around the perimeter. Events planned

The Hydroelectric cascade

for the remainder of 1992 include a Vintage Motorcycle display, Shire Horse display and a number of vehicle rallies, with a full and varied calendar being planned for 1993 and beyond. It is hoped the events will be in keeping with the exhibits on display and the whole theme of Snibston Discovery Park – Leicestershire and its history.

Accessibility has been a major concern throughout the development of Snibston. Many exhibits have braille labels; there are touch table exhibits throughout the exhibition hall, and there is parking for visitors with special needs directly outside. The nature trail follows an all weather route, and there are specially designed bays for anglers in wheelchairs. The exhibition hall is also built on one level.

Visitor Facilities

There are excellent visitor facilities within Snibston's reception area. The coffee shop serves light meals and drinks between 10am and 6pm, and there is also a comprehensively stocked gift shop, with souvenirs, confectionary and greeting cards, all competitively priced. The Tourist Information Centre, also situated in the reception area, is able to provide information about other attractions around the country, as well as accommodation both locally and further afield. The reception area carries no admission charge, similarly, visitors do not have to pay to use the nature trail facility, although there are charges for fishing.

For the benefit of visitors, there are brochures available for both the nature trail and colliery trail. There is also a group visits pack, detailing reduced rates and facilities for groups, and a full colour general brochure. All these are available by telephoning (0530) 510851, or the Tourist Information Centre on (0530) 813608.

Snibston Discovery Park is located on the A50 in Coalville, just 10 minutes from Junction 22 of the M1, or the A50/A512 Junction of the M42. It is clearly signposted from Leicester and from the M42/A42.

The opening hours are 10am–6pm every day except Christmas Day and Boxing Day. Admission charges are £3.00 for adults and £2.00 for children and concessions. There is a family ticket available, admitting two adults and up to three children, for £8.00.

Further details about Special Events, brochures and admission prices are available by telephoning (0530) 510851.

Consultancy for Management and Training

How many of these statements do you agree with:

YOUR VISITORS ARE THE MOST IMPORTANT PEOPLE ON
YOUR PREMISES AT ALL TIMES

YOU WANT THEM TO ENJOY THEIR VISIT SO MUCH
THAT THEY COME BACK AND BRING OTHERS WITH
THEM

THEY ARE NOT DEPENDENT ON
YOU — BUT YOU ARE
DEPENDENT ON THEM

THEY ARE NOT AN INTERRUPTION
TO YOUR WORK.

THEY ARE THE PURPOSE OF IT.

INSITE

YOUR SATISFIED VISITORS ARE OUR
BUSINESS

If you agree with these statements—

 CALL US ON

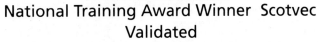 031 453 4716

National Training Award Winner Scotvec
Validated
Marista Leishman, Director.Insite, Hunter's
House, 508 Lanark Road Edinburgh EH14
5DH Tel: 031-453 4716

INSITE is a charity registered with the Inland Revenue No. ED 37/87/PLB

THE TATE GALLERY ST. IVES

by Michael Tooby

St Ives, Cornwall 1943-45 Oil and Drawing on Board, Benn Nicholson OM (1894-1982). Tate Gallery.

As I write this, in July 1992, the road above Porthmeor Beach in St Ives presents an intriguing sight. Behind screens which give onto a large circular hole, a structure of simple white rectangular forms emerges from behind towering concrete sections. Where surfers cross the road between files of schoolchildren on an environmental studies field trip, a crane lowers reinforcing sections into the rear of the circular hole. Just around the corner, a painter puts the finishing touches to the immaculate white finish of a simple doorway. A sign, revealing that the building is to be called the 'Tate Gallery St Ives' nears completion.

The New Gallery

Designed by Eldred Evans and David Shalev, the new gallery will house changing displays from the Tate's collections of paintings, sculpture and archives related to modern art associated with St Ives and West Cornwall. Its unconventional construction reflects the history of its site: a beautiful, dramatic purpose-built, brand new project, replacing a cleared area of derelict ground, the site of the town's disused gasworks. The circular hole, the foundations of the old gas holder, will become a cylinder of glass, an envelope for a two-tier curving inner gallery.

St. Ives, Oil and Drawing on Board, Alfred Wallis (1855-1942). Tate Gallery.

Moreover, gallery staff will also be engaged in projects outside the gallery, often in collaboration with other individuals and agencies in the area, whether parallel programmes with other museums and galleries, projects in institutions such as libraries, schools, colleges, worksite and residential situations, or commissions for public sites.

Green, Black and White Movement 1951. Oil on Canvas. Terry Frost (b. 1915)

quirkyness and intimate grandeur, capturing the atmosphere of the old end of St Ives which it inhabits. The scale and atmosphere of the new building will be very different from the Tate Gallery in Liverpool, with each interior space being intimate yet giving an opportunity for the best of the different generations of St Ives artists to be enjoyed in the finest modern gallery conditions.

The Tate Gallery St Ives will also present an innovative approach to programmes of displays, paralleling the developments in displays at the Tate Gallery in London. Each autumn a new annual display will be launched, describing different elements of the twentieth century art for which St Ives is famous. Within each annual cycle, three special 'study' displays will be mounted. These will generate ways of focusing on particular moments or subjects: a particular work, a moment in an artist's life, a particular theme.

The gallery will be producing for its opening a new introductory companion guide. This will provide a broad introduction to and discussion of the works on display and their background. This will be supplemented by accessible broadsheets discussing the themes of each display, including the study displays. A series of publications will also be devoted to the valuable and varied archive material related to St Ives and Cornwall in the Tate's collections.

The Hepworth Museum

The Barbara Hepworth Museum and Sculpture Garden, round the corner from the new gallery in the heart of St Ives and already a treasured special place for many visitors to Cornwall, will be run as an integral component of the new gallery. In this way visitors will be able to enjoy the contrasts between a relatively static body of work, rooted in its own setting, with the programme of changing displays designed to bring out the many and varied ways in which twentieth century art relates to the Cornish environment.

Work in this programme, "Tate Gallery St Ives Projects", will be introduced to visitors to the gallery through information displays which can then be followed up while travelling around the region.

Thus, as well as being a marvellous new building for the arts in one of the most dramatic sites anywhere in the world, the gallery will, alongside the Hepworth Museum, present a rich artistic programme firmly grounded in its region.

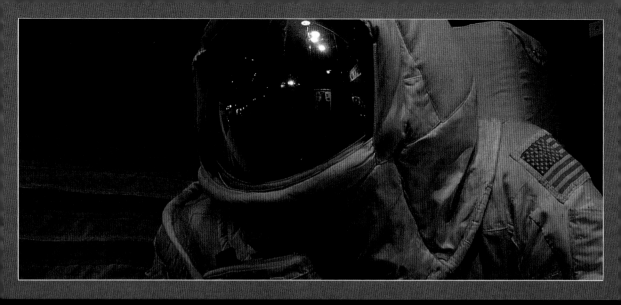

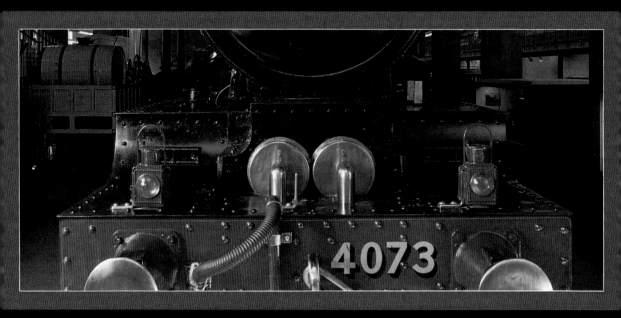

BASIC TRAINING FOR ASTRONAUTS, ENGINE DRIVERS AND CAMERAMEN.

At its three national sites, the National Museum of Science & Industry dedicates itself to furthering the public understanding of science, technology and medicine.

Not only are our collections amongst the most important in the world, but the interactive nature of many of the exhibits are specifically designed to stimulate interest amongst the widest possible audience.

The galleries of The Science Museum in London house material evidence of the emergence of modern scientific and industrial society.

The recently opened aeronautics gallery, 'Flight,' demonstrates our commitment to improvement and renewal.

In York the National Railway Museum, a unique representation of railways past, present and future, has recently re-opened at twice its former size with the inclusion of the newly designed Great Hall.

The National Museum of Photography, Film & Television in Bradford has built on its worldwide reputation in photography, and covers all aspects of film and television, including the UK's only state of the art Imax screen and the new luxury Pictureville Cinema.

The Science Museum, Exhibition Road, London. Tel: 938 8000. Admission times Mon-Sat 1000-1800 hrs, Sunday 1100-1800 hrs. National Railway Museum, Leeman Road, York. Tel: 0904 621 261. Admission times Mon-Sat 1000-1800 hrs. Sunday 1100-1800 hrs. Last admission 1700 hrs. National Museum of Photography Film & Television, Pictureville, Bradford. Tel: (0274) 727488. Admission times Tues-Sun 1030-1800 hrs.

HERITAGE EDUCATION TRUST

WIGAN IN ACTION: TRIUMPH FOR SCHOOLS CENTRE ETHA PROJECT TAKES THE STAGE AT WIGAN PIER

ETHA inspired a triumphant evening at the Mill at the Pier, Wigan on Thursday 11th June when over 120 Wigan schoolchildren from four different schools came together to demonstrate ETHA IN ACTION before a packed house of parents, friends and relations.

Heritage Education Trust Project

ETHA – Education Through Heritage and the Arts – is the Heritage Education Trust's project for putting school visits to historic properties at the centre of the curriculum in a wide range of subjects and linking them with the performing arts. It is sponsored by one of the Sainsbury Family Trusts and supported by the Ministry of National Heritage. It charts a course of development for Heritage Education which has been stimulated over the past ten years by the Sandford Awards scheme, sponsored by Reed Information Services Ltd.

Teachers and Children Challenged

Wigan's ETHA IN ACTION was the culmination of a year of co-operation between the Borough's nationally known Drumcroon Arts Centre, their performing arts advisory team led by Ken Gouge, their other advisory services and the Wigan Pier education team led by its head, Marilyn Sumner who co-ordinated the whole enterprise.

Four county primary schools took part: Britannia Bridge, Golborne, Tyldesley and Shevington. Their stimulus was a field study course entitled 'The Changing Environment' in which children re-traced the steps of a journey made in 1849 to three locations along the Leeds/Liverpool Canal, including of course the canal basin at Wigan Pier. During the field study course which included sessions on 'Kittywake', Wigan Pier's famous floating classroom, the children acted as reporters recording changes in the environment made by human influences on the landscape over the last hundred and fifty years. Thus far the children were involved in a normal, albeit highly imaginative, cross-curriculum environmental project. The unique ETHA dimension was to challenge teachers and children to mediate their work in a way which would captivate and entertain their audience: in short they had to translate their pencil and paper work into music, drama, dance and art, and put on a live stage show at Wigan Pier.

ETHA sees the 'audience challenge' as a vital element ensuring high standards in every aspect of the children's work with a key role in building self-confidence and social development and in giving new meaning and purpose to school visits.

Stage Performance Backed by Remarkable Exhibition

Using mime, dance, drama, music and puppetry the Wigan

An aspect of the preparatory art workshop organised by Sue Patterson for Tyldesley County Primary School. "We did research so that we knew what it was like before and after the Industrial Revolution".

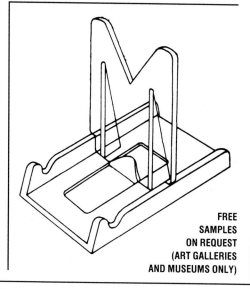

children presented a series of cameo scenes on stage in which the landscape changes were brought to life and commented on from both a contemporary and historical standpoint and with all the insight and humour that children can bring to bear. The stage performances were backed by a truly remarkable exhibition of art which represented the landscape of the Leeds/Liverpool Canal in a whole variety of ways. Shevington School produced stunning man-sized charcoal drawings; Golborne a group patchwork to tell the story of Wigan Pier today; Tyldesley Country Primary used a miscellany of items picked up from the Canalside to produce a series of individual tiles which were put together in an exhibition piece, 'Tiles of Time', depicting the ever-changing Canal environment; while Brittania Bridge worked on the notion of time and heritage, weaving and knitting together a disparate array of materials, wire and cloth to produce a beautiful 'Curtain of Time' reflecting land patterns and usages inspired by two maps dated respectively 1849 and 1951.

The Wigan evening entitled "Retracing Our Steps" was one of a series of six such events staged during the summer of 1992 by historic Sandford Award winning properties in co-operation with the Heritage Education Trust. Together they brought to a climax the first three development years of ETHA. The other five properties were all historic houses. Four-Harewood, Holdenby, Boughton and Rockingham Castle – are privately owned. The fifth, Shugborough, is administered by the National Trust on behalf of Staffordshire County Council. In this company Wigan Pier showed the flag for museums demonstrating just how much an industrial museum can do for education.

'Audience Challenge' – Key to ETHA

In the light of her experience co-ordinating Wigan's ETHA IN ACTION event, Marilyn Sumner wholeheartedly endorses the importance of the live performance and public exhibition aspect of ETHA:

> 'The whole ETHA idea provides an enjoyable way of learning necessary things to satisfy curriculum needs and much more besides, including the chance to perform in front of a large audience in a place

Creating puppets for Tyldesley School's contribution to the stage presentation which included dance and music as well as puppetry. "We decided to use puppetry because it was something new for us and an entertaining way of presenting what we wanted to say".

Britannia Bridge School's "Curtain of Time" in the making. For this part of their work the children were directed by Anne Marie Quinn, artist in residence.

different from the school hall. Their first encounter with the Mill at the Pier put the fear of God into the children – the lights, the seats, the stage. But all this up-graded their performance: they saw where all their work had been leading. They were central to a big occasion, so what they did they had to do well, justifying what they had done for a whole term.'

Enormous Benefits for the Property

ETHA is not for the faint-hearted. It requires hard work, planning and co-operation. But the benefits it delivers are enormous. Mrs Sumner's words above point to what ETHA can do for the children. What about the participating property? She has no doubts about this either:

> 'ETHA has opened new horizons at Wigan Pier by showing a wider number of ways in which the Pier can be interpreted and help teachers meet the demands of the National Curriculum in a wide range of subjects. We now have a base for spreading ETHA both inside and outside the Authority. ETHA will be included with the options available to teachers wanting to use the educational resources of Wigan Pier and if the response justifies it we shall set up an INSET course on ETHA the Wigan Way.'

The Heritage Education Trust has published a pamphlet, 'ETHA IN ACTION: Guidelines for Schools and Properties'. It is available direct from Martyn Dyer, Chief Executive, Heritage Education Trust, University College of Ripon & York St. John, College Road, Ripon HG4 2QX at £2.20 post free.

There is also a mailing list bringing regular news on the development of the Heritage Education and the work of the Trust plus an invitation to the National Presentation Ceremony for the Sandford Awards. The annual mailing list fee is £5.00. NIMROD, the periodical of the Heritage Education Trust, is published twice each year at 70p plus 30p package and postage (free to those on the mailing list). All cheques payable to the Heritage Education Trust.

Museums and Art Galleries
in Great Britain and Ireland

Collections are listed in alphabetical order of Counties, and Towns within Counties, followed by a list of Services Museums, Subject, Location and Alphabetical Indices.

AVON

BATH

AMERICAN MUSEUM IN BRITAIN
Claverton Manor, Bath   **Tel:** (0225) 460503 Education Dept (0225) 463538

The AMERICAN MUSEUM
CLAVERTON MANOR, BATH

The American Museum stands high above the Avon Valley. Eighteen furnished period rooms combine with galleries of textiles, pewter, glass and silver to illustrate the background of American domestic life between the 17th and 19th centuries. Special sections are devoted to the American Indians, Pennsylvania Germans and the Shakers. Dallas Pratt Collection of Historical Maps. American gardens, American Arboretum and teas with American cookies.

The American decorative arts from the late 17th to the mid 19th century seen in a series of furnished rooms and Galleries of special exhibits. Paintings, furniture, glass, woodwork, metalwork, textiles, hatboxes, folk art, miniature rooms. Marine room. Fire exhibit. Dallas Pratt Collection of Historical Maps. American gardens etc.
Open: Mar 27 to Nov 7. Daily (except Mon) 2-5; Bank Hol weekends Sun and Mon 11-5. During winter on application only. School tours all year by previous arrangement except in Jan. Gardens open throughout the season (except Mon) 1-6.
Admission: £4.50 child £2.50, senior citizens £4.00 (1992). Parties of children not admitted during normal opening hours. Adult parties by previous arrangement with Special Visits Secretary.
Location: 2½ miles from Bath station via Bathwick Hill; 3¾ miles south-east of Bath via Warminster road (A36) and Claverton village. Bus 18 (to University) from bus station - alight at The Avenue, 10 minutes walk to museum.
Refreshments: Teas and light refreshments at the house. Cold snack lunches Bank Hol Mons and preceding Suns.

BATH POSTAL MUSEUM
8 Broad Street, Bath   **Tel:** (0225) 460333
The story of the post, from earliest times to the present. Changing exhibitions. School and other parties welcomed. Advance bookings requested. Video.
Gift Shop.

THE BOOK MUSEUM
(Hylton Bayntun-Coward)
Manvers Street, Bath   **Tel:** (0225) 466000
Showing the craft of bookbinding, and Bath in Literature, and featuring a reconstruction of Dicken's study at Gadshill.
Open: Office hours Mon to Fri and Sat morning.
Admission: Free

MR BOWLER'S BUSINESS - BATH INDUSTRIAL HERITAGE CENTRE
Julian Road, Bath   **Tel:** (0225) 318348
The entire stock-in-trade of J.B. Bowler, Victorian brass founder, engineer and mineral water manufacturer, displayed in authentic settings - some working machinery.
Open: Easter to Oct: Daily 10-5. Nov to Easter: Weekends only 10-5. *Closed* Dec 24, 25, 26.
Admission: £2.50, chld/OAP £1.50.
Parties all year by appointment.

THE BUILDING OF BATH MUSEUM
The Countess of Huntingdon's Chapel, The Vineyards, The Paragon, Bath BA1 5NA
Tel: (0225) 333895

The Building of Bath Museum

In the 18th century Bath was transformed into one of the architectural masterpieces of the Western World. How this was achieved is the subject of a major new collection now housed at the Building of Bath Museum. Taking the craftsman as its central focus the museum explains how aesthetic, financial and technological factors affected both the city's planning and the form, shape and quality of its buildings. Exhibits, include architectural fragments, pattern books, tools and the fabulous city model, and are presented in such a way as to interest the expert and passerby alike.

Open to the public:
Tuesdays – Sundays 11.30am – 5.00pm

Open Bank Holidays
Closed 16th December – 28th February
Open for educational and group visits by prior arrangement

For further details and information about the Exhibition and any of the Museum's activities, please contact:

The Curator
The Building of Bath Museum
The Countess of Huntingdon's Chapel
The Vineyards, The Paragon Bath BA1 5NA
Telephone: (0225) 333895

Admission: £2, concessions £1.50, Group rates on application.
Contact: Christopher Woodward

FASHION RESEARCH CENTRE
(Bath City Council)
4 Circus, Bath   **Tel:** (0225) 461111 Ext. 2752
Facilities for study and research, including extensive reference library and study collection of costume.
Open: Mon to Fri 9.30 - 5, by appointment.
Admission: Free

GEORGIAN GARDEN
(Bath City Council)
Gravel Walk, Bath   **Tel:** (0225) 461111 Ext. 2760
Authentic 18th century town garden layout, discovered by excavation and recreated using plants of the period.
Open: May to Oct: Mon to Fri 9 - 4.30.
Admission: Free

GUILDHALL
(Bath City Council)
High Street, Bath   **Tel:** (0225) 461111 Ext. 2785
18th century Banqueting Room.
Open: Mon to Thurs 8.30 - 5; Fri 8.30 - 4.30. Subject to bookings.

HOLBURNE MUSEUM AND CRAFTS STUDY CENTRE
Great Pulteney Street, Bath   **Tel:** (0225) 466669

The Holburne Museum, Bath, is a successful combination of ancient and modern. Set in an elegant 18th century building the collection of decorative and fine art which it contains was made by Sir Thomas William Holburne (1793-1874) and includes superb English and continental silver and porcelain. Italian maiolica and bronzes, together with glass, furniture, miniatures and old master paintings. Fine examples of work by British 20th century artist craftsmen are also on view in the Crafts Study Centre. This collection and archive embraces printed and woven textiles, pottery, furniture and calligraphy. Study facilities by appointment. Temporary exhibitions and events throughout the year.
Open: Mon to Sat 11-5, Sun 2.30-6. Open Bank Holidays except Christmas. *Closed* mid Dec to end Feb and Mons Nov to Easter.
Admission: £2.50, Chld £1, OAP/Students £2.
Refreshments: Licensed teahouse in lovely garden.
Free Parking. Coaches welcome by prior appointment.

SALLY LUNN'S HOUSE
4 North Parade Passage, Bath   **Tel:** (0225) 461634
The oldest house in bath. A cellar museum shows the ancient kitchen and excavations of Roman, Saxon and Medieval buildings on the site. In this building was created the famous Sally Lunn bun, a bread based on the French brioche. 1990 museum visitors in excess of 43,000.
Open: Daily except Christmas and New Year's Day 10-5; Sun 12-6.
Admission: 30p; Chld/OAPs Free.
Parties by arrangement. Not suitable for disabled.

MUSEUM OF COSTUME
(Bath City Council)
Assembly Rooms, Bennett Street, Bath   **Tel:** (0225) 461111 Ext. 2785
The Museum of Costume is one of the largest and most prestigious in this country and is housed in Bath's famous 18th century Assembly Rooms, designed by John Wood the Younger in 1769. The Museum's extensive collections are devoted to fashionable dress for men, women and children from the late 16th century to the present day.
Open: Daily Mar to Oct: 9.30-6 (Sun 10-6); Nov to Feb: 10-5; (Sun 11-5). Last tickets half and hour before closing.
Admission: £2.40, Chld £1.50, reduction for parties.

THE MUSEUM OF EAST ASIAN ART
Circus Lodge, 12 Bennett Street, Bath B1 2QL   **Tel:** (0225) 464640

A representative collection of East Asian Art displayed in a restored Georgian house close to Bath's famous Circus and opposite the Assembly Rooms. The Museum houses a wide range of Chinese ceramics (2500BC to 1820AD), jades (5000BC TO 1800AD), metalwares (1900BC to 1881AD) and decorative arts. Art objects from Japan, Korea, Thailand, Indochina, Tibet and Mongolia are also represented in the collection.
Open: April 1993
Admission: Group and educational visits are welcome by arrangement.
Facilities for the disabled. Wheelchair lift access to all floors. For further information please telephone above number.

MUSEUM OF ENGLISH NAIVE ART
(Andras Kalman)
Countess of Huntingdon Chapel, The Vineyard, Paragon, Bath BA1 5NA
Tel: (0225) 446020

MUSEUM OF ENGLISH NAIVE ART

The Countess of Huntingdon Chapel
The Vineyard/Paragon, Bath BA1 5NA

The Museum was opened in 1987 and houses the Crane Kalman Collection, a wonderful selection of 18th and 19th century paintings depicting ordinary people, pursuits and incidents with a direct simplicity that is both revealing and entertaining.
Open: Easter to Christmas daily, 10.30 to 5, Sun 2-6.
Admission: £2. Family and group tickets available.
Location: Just a three minute walk from the top of Milsom Street, along the Paragon, next door to the Countess of Huntingdon's Chapel in what was the Old School House, you will find the Museum of English Naive Art.
There is also an excellent shop on the ground floor selling a delightful range of crafts,

books, postcards, reproductions of paintings from the collection and much more. A calendar of events, concerts, workshops etc is available from the Museum.

ROMAN BATHS MUSEUM
(Bath City Council)
Abbey Church Yard, near Bath Abbey, Bath   **Tel:** (0225) 461111 Ext. 2785
Adjoins the extensive remains of the Roman Baths and includes material from that and other Roman sites, including architectural fragments, inscriptions, metalware and offerings from the sacred spring.
Open: Winter: Mon to Sat 9-5 Sun 10-5. Summer: Daily 9-6 (Aug late opening 8-10)
Admission: £3.80, Chld £1.80 (including entrance to Pump Room, Roman Baths and Temple Precinct). Reductions for parties.

NO. 1 ROYAL CRESCENT
(Bath Preservation Trust)
Bath BA1 2LR   **Tel:** (0225) 428126

No. 1 ROYAL CRESCENT
BATH, BA1 2LR
Museum telephone Bath (0225) 428126

Number 1 was presented to the Bath Preservation Trust in 1968 and has been restored to its original position as one of the grandest and most beautiful houses in the Heritage City of Bath. The Royal Crescent, started in 1767 by John Wood the Younger, is a perfect example of Palladian architecture. Visitors to Number 1 can enjoy a house redecorated and furnished so that it appears as it might have been soon after the house was completed.

A Georgian Town House in Bath's most magnificent crescent; redecorated and furnished to show the visitor how it might have appeared in the late 18th century.
Open: Mar 1 to Mar 31 and Oct 1 to Dec 13: 11-4. Closed Mons. Apr 1 to Sept 30: 11-5 daily. Last admission 30 minutes before closing time.
Admission: £3, concessions £2.

THE ROYAL PHOTOGRAPHIC SOCIETY
Milsom Street, Bath   **Tel:** (0225) 462841
Five Galleries with changing exhibitions, museum, restaurant and shop.

VICTORIA ART GALLERY
(Bath City Council)
Bridge Street, Bath   **Tel:** (0225) 461111 Ext. 2772
Exhibitions from permanent collections and temporary exhibitions frequently changed. Paintings, prints and drawings, glass, ceramics and watches. Local topography.
Open: Mon to Fri 10-6; Sat 10-5.30. Closed Sun and Bank Holidays.
Admission: Free

BRISTOL

ARNOLFINI GALLERY
16 Narrow Quay, Bristol

ASHTON COURT VISITORS CENTRE
(City of Bristol)
Ashton Court Stable Block, Bower Ashton, Bristol   **Tel:** (0272) 639174

BLAISE CASTLE HOUSE MUSEUM
(City of Bristol)
Henbury, Bristol
Collections in an 18th century house, dealing with objects illustrating English domestic, urban and rural life in former days.

BRISTOL INDUSTRIAL MUSEUM
(City of Bristol)
Princes Wharf, Bristol
Collections of manufacturing equipment and of transport - air, land and sea. Unique items - the Grenville Steam Carriage (1875), believed to be the oldest self-propelled passenger-carrying road vehicle still in working order; the Wanderer Caravan, built by the Bristol Wagon and Carriage Works in 1880 for the first president of the Caravan Club; the definitive collection of Bristol-built aero-engines and the world's oldest tug 'Mayflower'.

BRISTOL MUSEUM AND ART GALLERY
(City of Bristol)
Queen's Road, Bristol BS8 1RL
Collections of Egyptology, ancient glass, British archaeology, ethnography, technology, natural history and geology,'ceramics & glass' with special reference to the Bristol region and the West Country. Oriental, European paintings.

THE EXPLORATORY HANDS-ON SCIENCE CENTRE
Bristol Old Station, Temple Meads, Bristol   **Tel:** (0272) 252008

GEORGIAN HOUSE
(City of Bristol)
7 Great George Street, Bristol
The late 18th century town house of a Bristol sugar merchant, which contains many of its original architectural features. Basement includes complete kitchen, laundry and plunge-bath and reconstructed house-keeper's room.

GUILD GALLERY
68 Park Street, Bristol BS1 5JY   **Tel:** (0272) 265548
Monthly exhibitions by mainly, but not exclusively, West Country artists and craftspeople.
Open: Mon to Sat 9.30-5. Closed Bank holidays.
Admission: Free.
Not suitable for the disabled.

HARVEYS WINE MUSEUM
12 Denmark Street, Bristol   **Tel:** (0272) 277661
Unique collection of wine-related exhibits in medieval cellars.
Open: Daily 10-1 & 2-5 weekdays; 2-5 weekends. *Closed* bank holidays.
Admission: £2.50; £1.50 concessions.
Guided tours and tastings by arrangement, please phone for details.

MARITIME HERITAGE CENTRE
(City of Bristol)
Gas Ferry Road, Bristol
Houses the collections of the 18th and 19th century shipbuilders Charles Hill and Sons. The displays feature a full size replica of Isambard Kingdom Brunel's scraper dredger and incorporates the original engine.

THE RED LODGE
(City of Bristol)
Park Row, Bristol
An Elizabethan house with early 18th century alterations and furnishings of these periods. The only surviving 16th century domestic interior in Bristol.

CLIFTON

DAVID CROSS GALLERY
7 Boyces Avenue, Clifton BS8 4AA   **Tel:** (0272) 732614
Specialists in traditional British paintings and drawings.
Open: Mon to Sat 9-6.
Please telephone for details of forthcoming exhibitions.

WESTON-SUPER-MARE

WOODSPRING MUSEUM
Burlington Street, Weston-Super-Mare   **Tel:** (0934) 621028
A friendly local museum for all the family. Set around a palm-lined courtyard, in the old Gaslight Co's workshops are displays of the Seaside Holiday, local industries, Mendip mining, local archaeology, costume, camera collection and natural history. Also the Peggy Nisbet collection of costume dolls and frequent temporary exhibitions. Clara's Cottage adjoining, is displayed as seaside lodgings of the 1900 period.
Open: Tues to Sun 10-5; Open Bank Hol Mon.
Admission: Free.
Refreshments: Tea, coffee, soft drinks and biscuits are available.

BEDFORDSHIRE

BEDFORD

BEDFORD MUSEUM
(North Bedfordshire Borough Council)
   Castle Lane, Bedford   **Tel:** (0234) 353323
The Museum for North Bedfordshire with displays of local material including archaeology, local and social history, natural history and geology. Programme of temporary exhibitions, children's activities and other events.
Open: Tues to Sat 11-5; Sun and Bank Hol Mons 2-5.

BROMHAM MILL
(Bedfordshire County Council Leisure Services)
   Bromham, Bedford   **Tel:** (0234) 228330
Restored water mill and machinery. Milling demonstrations on the last Sunday of each month during the open season and by arrangement. Natural history room, special exhibitions, art gallery and craft cabinets. Nature sanctuary and adjoining picnic area.
Open: Apr to Oct: Wed to Fri 10-4.30. Sat, Sun and Bank Hol 11.30-6.
Admission: (1992 rates) 60p, Chld and OAPs 30p. Party rates on application.
Car parking for 30 cars. Some parts of this property are not suitable for disabled.

THE BUNYAN MEETING LIBRARY AND MUSEUM
(Trustees of Bunyan Meeting)
   Mill Street, Bedford

ELSTOW MOOT HALL
(Bedfordshire County Council Leisure Services)
   Elstow, Bedford   **Tel:** (0234) 228330
Medieval market hall containing 17th century artefacts furniture and craftwork. John Bunyan grew up locally and the Hall has many ties with Bedford's most famous son.
Open: Apr to Oct: Tue to Sat and Bank Hol Mon 2-5; Sun 2-5.30
Admission: (1992 rates) 60p, Chld/OAP 30p; party rates on application.
Some parts of this property are not suitable for disabled.

CECIL HIGGINS ART GALLERY AND MUSEUM
   Castle Close, Bedford   **Tel:** (0234) 211222
Changing displays of English watercolours from the Gallery's outstanding collection. English and Continental ceramics and glass which are particularly rich in 18th century pieces. Award-winning Victorian Mansion displayed in room settings to create a 'lived-in' atmosphere, including bedroom with furniture designed by William Burges. Some objets d'art, metalwork and jewellery. Permanent display of Bedfordshire lace.
Open: Tues to Fri 12.30-5; Sat 11-5; Sun 2-5 and Bank Holiday Mon 12.30-5. *Closed* Mon, Good Friday and Christmas.
Admission: Free.
Refreshments: Lunches/suppers for visiting groups in booking in advance.
Sandford Award winner, 1989. Quizzes and jigsaws available for children. Special arrangements for group visits and evening parties to the Gallery.

LUTON

JOHN DONY FIELD CENTRE
(Luton Museum Service)
   c/o Bushmead Community Centre, Hancock Drive, Luton   **Tel:** (0582) 422818
Interpretation of local environment and educational facility.
Please telephone for further information. Educational enquiries telephone Dr T. Tween at the above number.

LUTON MUSEUM AND ART GALLERY
(Luton Museum Service)
   Wardown Park, Luton LU2 7HA   **Tel:** (0582) 36941-2
Collections/displays archaeology, costume, dolls and toys, fine and decorative art, local history, social history, military (Beds and Herts Regiment), natural history/geology, lace, straw plait, changing exhibitions.
Open: Weekdays and Sat 10-5, Sun 1-5. For Christmas/New Year closures and further details please phone museum.
Study access to reserve collections by appointment only. Educational group visits welcome by prior booking.

STOCKWOOD CRAFT MUSEUM AND GARDENS HOME OF THE MOSSMAN COLLECTION
(Luton Museum Service)
   Stockwood Park, Farley Hill, Luton LU1 4BH   **Tel:** (0582) 38714
The largest collection, on public display of horse-drawn vehicles and carriages in the UK. Collections/displays rural crafts and trades including thatching, saddlery, shoemaking, rushwork, blacksmithing, wood crafts, wheelwrighting and agriculture, wheeled vehicles. Also to be seen: craft workshops, regular weekend craft demonstrations, period gardens and sculptures by Ian Hamilton Finlay.
Open: Mar-Apr to Oct: Weekdays and Sat 10-5; Sun 10-6. *Closed* Mon and Tues (except Bank holiday Mondays). Open Nov to Mar: Fri, Sat, Sun 10-4.
Location: Near M1 exit 10.
Educational group visits welcome by prior booking (0582) 36941 x 221.

OLD WARDEN

THE SHUTTLEWORTH COLLECTION
   Nr Biggleswade, Old Warden

BERKSHIRE

COOKHAM-ON-THAMES

STANLEY SPENCER GALLERY
   King's Hall, Cookham-on-Thames   **Tel:** (062 85) 20890/20043
Major Spencer collection (The Last Supper 1920, Christ Preaching at Cookham Regatta 1959, etc) in village immortalized by the artist.
Open: Easter-Oct: daily, 10.30-5.30. Nov-Easter: Sat, Sun and Bank Holidays 11-5.
Admission: Fee charged.
Gallery shop. Enquiries, telephone on the above number.

CECIL HIGGINS ART GALLERY AND MUSEUM, BEDFORD

"Faust in his Study", by Rembrandt Van Ryn, c.1652, etching.

Rare soup tureen in the shape of a swan, Chelsea porcelain, about 1752-56.

The Gallery's outstanding collections of watercolours, ceramics, glass and furniture are all displayed in an award-winning Victorian Mansion and a modern extension, opened in 1976. It is situated in pleasant gardens leading down to the River Embankment.

"Helmet Head I", by Henry Moore, 1950, bronze.

LUTON MUSEUM SERVICE

WARDOWN PARK

Luton Museum and Art Gallery

Bedfordshire archaeology, social history, natural history, social & domestic life. Doll & toy collection. Bedfordshire and Hertfordshire Regimental museum display. Set in beautiful parkland. Free admission, ample free parking.

STOCKWOOD PARK

Stockwood Craft Museum and Gardens

Rural crafts and trades of Bedfordshire with displays including reconstructed workshops, dioramas and wheeled vehicles. Craft demonstrations most weekends, see the reconstructed timber framed building and the beautiful period gardens. Free admission to craft museum & gardens. Home of the Mossman Collection.

FOR FURTHER DETAILS OF THE ABOVE MUSEUMS AND THE JOHN DONY FIELD CENTRE–*see editorial reference.*

MAIDENHEAD

COURAGE SHIRE HORSE CENTRE
Maidenhead Thicket, Maidenhead **Tel:** (0628) 824848

See the prize winning Shires at the

COURAGE

SHIRE HORSE CENTRE

On the A4 two miles west of Maidenhead (M4 Exit 8/9)

- Free guided tours • Prize Winning Shire Horses
- Display of Harness • Saddler's Shop
- Small animal and bird area • Audio visual presentation
- Souvenir Shop • Tea room and picnic area • Dray rides

OPEN DAILY · 10.30am to 5pm (last entry 4pm)
1st March to 31st October

Enquiries Tel: Littlewick Green (062882) 4848
Cherry Garden Lane, Maidenhead Thicket, Berkshire SL6 3QD

No animal on earth can match the Shire Horse's unique combination of size, strength, grace and beauty and nowhere will you get a better chance to see Shires in their home environment than at the Courage Shire Horse Centre. Knowledgeable trained guides offer free tours and a rare insight into the world of the 'Gentle Giants' or you can wander around the Centre at your own pace. Every horse has its own stable, looking out across a communal courtyard, where the horse's names are displayed to help visitors to get to know each horse individually. The Courage Shire Horse Centre is a working stable and the care and preparation that prize-winning Shires demand is evident wherever you look. Daily grooming and harnessing and polishing the harnesses and brasses calls for hard work and devotion, but the reward is displayed for visitors to see in the shape of hundreds of prize rosettes. The farrier's workshop is normally in use on three days a week and a saddler is at work in the saddlers shop every day.
Open: Daily from 10.30-5 from Mar 1 to Oct 31.
Location: The Centre is situated on the A4, 2 miles west of Maidenhead and within a few miles of junction 8/9 of the M4.
Refreshments: The Centre's tea rooms sell a range of hot and cold food and drinks. If you prefer to take your own food, there are several picnic areas inside the Centre.
Additional attractions at the Centre include a free audio visual presentation, a well-stocked souvenir shop, children's playground, a small animal and bird area and dray rides. Suitable for disabled visitors. Car parking is free.

HENRY REITLINGER BEQUEST
Oldfield, Guards Club Road, Maidenhead SL6 8DN **Tel:** (0628) 21818

NEWBURY

NEWBURY DISTRICT MUSEUM
The Wharf, Newbury **Tel:** (0635) 30511

NEWBURY DISTRICT MUSEUM

The Museum is situated in two picturesque and adjoining Historic Buildings, the 17th century Cloth Hall and 18th century Granary. Displays include Local History, K & A Canal, Costume, Traditional Crafts and Pastimes. Ballooning and Civil War displays incorporate audio-visual presentations.

Frequent temporary exhibitions.

Admission Free
Open:
10–5 daily, 1–5 Sundays & Bank Holidays.
Closed:
Weds (except during school hols.), and 4pm and Suns from 1 Oct to 31 March.

The Wharf, Newbury, Berks.
Tel: (0635) 30511

In picturesque 17th and 18th century buildings. Displays: Ballooning; Kennet & Avon Canal; Traditional Crafts; Costume; Civil War battles of Newbury (with audio-visual). Local collections: archaeology, history, geology and birds. Also pewter and pottery.
Open: Apr to Sept: Mon to Sat 10-5; Sun and Bank Hol 1-5. Oct to Mar: Mon to Sat 10-4. *Closed* Wed (except during school hols.)

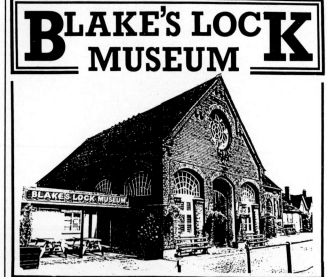

READING'S WATERWAYS, TRADES & INDUSTRIES

Main Museum and Art Gallery closed for major restoration.
The re-opening date, during 1993, of the new Musuem of Reading will be announced.

Reading
BOROUGH COUNCIL

READING

BLAKE'S LOCK MUSEUM
(Reading Borough Council)
   Gasworks Road, off Kenavon Drive, Reading   **Tel:** (0734) 390918
Displays the history of the industrial and commercial life of Reading and the development of its waterways.
Open: Tues to Fri 10-5, Sat and Sun 2-5. Bank Hol Mon 2-5.

THE COLE MUSEUM OF ZOOLOGY
(The University of Reading)
   Whiteknights, Reading   **Tel:** (0734) 875123
A specialist collection which surveys the animal kingdom and contains some fine dissections, skeletons and models.
Open: Weekdays 9-5.

MUSEUM AND ART GALLERY
(Reading Borough Council)
   Blagrave Street, Reading   **Tel:** (0734) 390918
Closed for major refurbishment and extension of gallery space. During 1993 a re-opening date of the new **Museum of Reading** will be announced. It will include displays on Reading Abbey and the Story of Reading. Important fine and decorative art collection, archaeology and natural history.

MUSEUM OF ENGLISH RURAL LIFE
(The University of Reading)
   Whiteknights, Reading   **Tel:** (0734) 318660
A national collection of material relating to the history of the English countryside, including agriculture, crafts, domestic utensils and village life. There is a permanent exhibition open to the general public and, in addition, study collections of objects and documentary material which may be consulted on application to the Secretary.
Open: Tues to Sat 10-1, 2-4.30. *Closed* Sun, Mon and Public Hols.

NATIONAL DAIRY MUSEUM
   Wellington Country Park, Riseley, Reading   **Tel:** (0734) 326444
Exhibits and displays showing the growth of the dairy industry from a small rural activity to a large countrywide industry.
Open: Mar 1 to Oct 31: Daily 10-5.30; also weekends in winter.
Admission: (includes entry to Country Park) £2.75, Chld £1.25 (under 5's free). Party reduction for 20 or more £2.20, each chld £1.10 (1992 charges.)

THE URE MUSEUM OF GREEK ARCHAEOLOGY
(The University of Reading)
   Whiteknights, Reading   **Tel:** (0734) 318420
Greek pottery.
Open: Mon to Fri 9-5.
Advisable to telephone. Parties by appointment.

BUCKINGHAMSHIRE

AYLESBURY

BUCKINGHAMSHIRE COUNTY MUSEUM
(Buckinghamshire County Council)
   Church Street, Aylesbury   **Tel:** (0296) 88849
Open galleries: Displays illustrating local history and temporary exhibitions.
Open: Mon to Sat 10-1.30 and 2-5. *Closed* Bank Holidays, Christmas Day, Boxing Day, New Year's Day and Good Friday.
Undergoing major refurbishment.

CHALFONT ST. GILES

CHILTERN OPEN AIR MUSEUM
   Newland Park, Gorelands Lane, Chalfont St Giles   **Tel:** (0494) 871117

CHILTERN OPEN AIR MUSEUM

BUILDINGS THROUGH THE AGES

Newland Park, Gorelands Lane,
Chalfont St Giles, Buckinghamshire
Tel: (0494) 871117

Open April to October
Wednesday – Sunday, plus Bank Holidays

Historic buildings and rural life of the Chilterns from the Iron Age to the Victorian era. Barns, granaries, stables, cartsheds, toll house, cottages, public convenience and furniture factory rescued from demolition and re-erected in 45 acres of beautiful countryside.
Open: Apr to Oct: Wed to Sun and Bank Holidays 2-6.
Admission: Fee charged.
Refreshments: Available.

Special events are held during the season. School parties welcome all year round. Free car park. Gift Shop.

MILTON'S COTTAGE
Chalfont St Giles   **Tel:** (0494) 872313
Personal and contemporary relics. Library includes first editions of 'Paradise Lost' and 'Paradise Regained'. Portraits and busts of Milton. Objects of local interest, several old maps.
Open: Mar 1 to Oct 31: Tues to Sat and Bank Holiday Mons 10-1, 2-6; Sun 2-6. *Closed* Mon and Nov, Dec, Jan and Feb.
Admission: £1.50, Chld (under 15) 60p. Parties of 20 or more £1.20.

HIGH WYCOMBE

THE DISRAELI MUSEUM
(The National Trust)
Hughenden Manor, High Wycombe   **Tel:** (0494) 32580
Home of Benjamin Disraeli, Earl of Beaconsfield (1847-81). Disraeli relics, furniture, pictures and books.

WYCOMBE LOCAL HISTORY AND CHAIR MUSEUM
(Wycombe District Council)
Castle Hill, Priory Avenue, High Wycombe   **Tel:** (0494) 421895
Attractive 18th century house built on a medieval site and set in Victorian gardens with a nature trail. Exhibitions on the crafts and history of the local people highlighting the importance of the furniture industry. Displays on archaeology, art and much more.
Open: All year Mon to Sat (closed Bank Holidays)
Admission: Free.

MILTON KEYNES

MILTON KEYNES EXHIBITION GALLERY
(Buckinghamshire County Council)
Milton Keynes Library, 555 Silbury Boulevard, Milton Keynes   **Tel:** (0908) 835025
Programme of exhibitions changing monthly, covering art, craft, social and local history.
Open: Mon to Wed 9.30-6, Thurs & Fri 9.30-8, Sat 10-5. *Closed* Christmas Day, Boxing Day, New Year's Day and Good Friday.

MILTON KEYNES MUSEUM OF INDUSTRY & RURAL LIFE
Stacey Hill Farm, Southern Way, Wolverton, Milton Keynes MK12 5EJ   **Tel:** (0908) 319148 or 316222
An extensive collection of industrial, agricultural and domestic items including tractors, implements, stationary engines, lawnmowers, and photographic, printing and telephone equipment. Exhibitions include Wolverton & Stony Stratford Tram, Salmons-Tickford, E & H Roberts.
Open: Apr 28 to Oct 31: Wed to Sun 1.30-4.30; Bank Holiday Mon 1.30-4.30; also Easter Sun and Easter Monday 1.30-4.30.
Admission: £1.25, concessions 75p. Special Events: May 16, July 18, Aug 15, Sept 19, 11-5.30 (Special exhibits, demonstrations and craft displays). Admission £2, concessions £1.25. Schools and group visits at other times by arrangement. Special party rates available on request.
Location: Access off MK Grid Road H2, Millers Way, or off Southern Way.
Refreshments: Available.
Free car park. Souvenir shop.

OLNEY

COWPER & NEWTOWN MUSEUM
Market Place, Olney   **Tel:** (0234) 711516
Home of poet William Cowper and Rev. John Newton. Lace exhibitions. Costume Gallery. Gardens.

SLOUGH

SLOUGH MUSEUM
23 Bath Road, Slough SL1 3UF **Tel:** (0753) 526422
Did you know that 3 famous 18th century astronomers lived in Slough? Just one of the surprising facts we tell in Slough's story from mammoths to modern town.
Open: Wed to Fri 12-4; Sat and Sun 2-5; Bank Holidays 2-5.
Admission: Free.
Parties free by arrangement. Free parking at weekend. Access by wheelchair possible but no disabled toilet.

WEST WYCOMBE

WEST WYCOMBE MOTOR MUSEUM
Chorley Road, West Wycombe

CAMBRIDGESHIRE

CAMBRIDGE

CAMBRIDGE AND COUNTY FOLK MUSEUM
2 and 3 Castle Street, Cambridge
Museum occupying the former White Horse Inn, contains domestic and agricultural bygones, toys, pictures, trade exhibits illustrating the life of the people of the County covering three centuries.

DUXFORD AIRFIELD
Duxford Airfield, Duxford, Cambridge CB2 4QR   **Tel:** (0223) 835000 (information line)
Once a famous RAF station which played a vital role in the Battle of Britain, Duxford Airfield is now home to the finest collection of military and civil aircraft in Britain - from First World War fighters to Concorde. Also on display are military vehicles, artillery and large naval exhibits. Among the other attractions are a ride simulator, an adventure playground, a 1940's pre-fab furnished in Utility style and many special exhibitions including one based on the development of Trans-Atlantic flight.
Open: Daily: Summer (mid-Mar to end-Oct), 10-6, Winter (Nov to mid-Mar) 10-4 (or dusk if ealier). *Closed* 24-26 Dec and 1 Jan.
Location: Junction 10 off the M11.
Refreshments: Restaurant, picnic areas.
Souvenir shop. Ample free parking.

FITZWILLIAM MUSEUM
Trumpington Street, Cambridge
Picture gallery of old and modern masters. Collections of antiquities, ceramics, applied arts, coins, drawings and prints, historical and Medieval manuscripts, special exhibitions.

KETTLES YARD
(University of Cambridge)
Castle Street, Cambridge CB3 0AQ   **Tel:** (0223) 352124
A unique permanent collection of modern art and craft and a challenging gallery dedicated to experimental art.
Open: Gallery: Tues to Sat 12.30-5.30, Sun 2-5.30. House: Tues to Sun 2-4.

THE SCOTT POLAR RESEARCH INSTITUTE
Lensfield Road, Cambridge CB2 1ER   **Tel:** (0223) 336540
Current scientific work in the Arctic and Antarctic. Expedition relics and equipment. Eskimo and general polar art collections.

SEDGWICK MUSEUM OF GEOLOGY
Downing Street, Cambridge   **Tel:** (0223) 333456
One million fossils and subordinate collections of minerals, building stones and ornamental marbles.
Open: Mon to Fri 9-1, 2-5; Sat 10-1 throughout the year. *Closed* one week at Christmas also Good Friday and Easter Monday.

UNIVERSITY COLLECTION OF AERIAL PHOTOGRAPHS
Mond Building, Free School Lane, Cambridge CB2 3RF   **Tel:** (0223) 334578
A collection of aerial photographs illustrating different aspects of agriculture, archaeology, geography, geology, history, vegetation, and the social and economic past and present of the United Kingdom.
By appointment only. Curator: D.R. Wilson M.A.

UNIVERSITY MUSEUM OF ARCHAEOLOGY AND ANTHROPOLOGY
Downing Street, Cambridge   **Tel:** (0223) 337733
Archaeological collections illustrating world prehistory and Britain from the earliest period until post-Medieval times. Anthropological galleries exhibits material from all parts of the world.
Open: Mon to Fri 2-4; Sat 10-12.30.

UNIVERSITY MUSEUM OF CLASSICAL ARCHAEOLOGY
Sidgwick Avenue site, Cambridge   **Tel:** (0223) 335153
Representative collection of casts of Greek and Roman sculpture.
Open: Mon to Fri 9-5.

WHIPPLE MUSEUM OF THE HISTORY OF SCIENCE
Free School Lane, Cambridge   **Tel:** (0223) 334540
Collection of historic scientific instruments from the 16th to 19th century.
Open: Mon to Fri 2-4. During vacations the museum may be closed.
Special exhibitions.

ELY

ELY MUSEUM
High Street, Ely   **Tel:** (0353) 666655
Displays covering the social and natural history of the Isle of Ely. Collections include local archaeology, Fenland farm and craft instruments, the bicycle which won the

world's first bicycle race, video films of Fenland life and much more besides. Something for everybody!
Admission: Party reductions.
Limited access for disabled.

THE STAINED GLASS MUSEUM
North Triforium, Ely, Ely Cathedral **Tel:** (0353) 778645
Stained glass from medieval to modern times, including important 19th century collection, mainly rescued from redundant churches and now displayed at eye level. Models of a modern workshop, origins and history of the craft.
Open: Mar to Oct, Mon to Fri 10.30-4, Sat and Bank Hols 10.30-4.30, Sun 12-3, plus every weekend throughout the year.
Admission: Party reductions.

HUNTINGDON

THE CROMWELL MUSEUM
(Cambridgeshire County Council)
Grammar School Walk, Huntingdon **Tel:** (0480) 425830

Oliver Cromwell was born in Huntingdon in 1599, and spent his early life in the town. The Museum illustrates the life of Oliver Cromwell and the Parliamentary side of the Puritan Revolution 1642-1660.
Open: All year round. Apr-Oct: 11-1, 2-5 Tues to Fri; 11-1, 2-4 Sat & Sun, Nov-Mar: 1-4 Tues to Fri; 11-1, 2-4 Sat; 2-4 Sun.
Admission: Free.
Location: The Museum is in Cromwell's old school in the centre of the town.

Refreshments: Available nearby.
Party bookings are welcome. Coach parking. For further details and leaflet write or telephone above number.

PETERBOROUGH

RAILWORLD
Oundle Road, Peterborough PE2 9NR **Tel:** (0733) 344240
'Railworld: Exhibition of modern train travel; Museum of World Railways; opening soon.'

SACREWELL FARM AND COUNTRY CENTRE
Sacrewell, Thornhaugh, Peterborough PE8 6HJ **Tel:** (0780) 782222
Large open air museum on attractive farm site. Working 18th century watermill on Domesday site. Very large collection of hand implements, tools, and equipment relating to farming, and the Mill's history, housed in 18th century farm buildings; traditional building materials.
Open: Always.
Location: Easily accessible from A47, 8m W of Peterborough.
Refreshments: Available
Ample parking, toilets and gift shop. Farm, nature and general interest trails. Aviary, maze and other entertainments for children.

ST. IVES

NORRIS MUSEUM
(St. Ives Town Council)
The Broadway, St. Ives **Tel:** (0480) 465101
Local history of Huntingdonshire: fossils, archaeology, bygones, crafts, research library.
Open: Mon to Fri 10-1, 2-5 (winter closes at 4); Sat 10-12. May to Sept also open 2-5 Sat and Sun.

WISBECH

WISBECH AND FENLAND MUSEUM
Museum Square, Wisbech **Tel:** (0945) 583817
Local history, archaeology, natural history, geology, ceramics, bygones, (library by appointment only).
Open: Tues to Sat 10-5 (closes at 4 in winter).

CHANNEL ISLANDS

GUERNSEY

All enquiries to Guernsey Museum & Art Gallery (0481) 726518, education service (0481) 723688. Joint ticket available to all three museums £6.50.

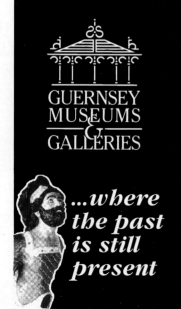

CASTLE CORNET
St. Peter Port, Guernsey   **Tel:** (0481) 721657
Medieval castle with important Elizabethan, Georgian, Victorian and Second World War additions. Major new maritime museum; museums with military, CI Militia, RAF, German Occupation collections; picture galleries; refectory and shop.
Open: Apr to Oct: daily 10.30-5.30. Noon-day Gun, conducted parties at 10.45 and 2.30.
Admission: £4, Chld £1.50, OAPs £2.

FORT GREY SHIPWRECK MUSEUM
Rocquaine Bay, St. Peter's, Guernsey   **Tel:** (0481) 65036
Napoleonic fort restored as a maritime museum specialising in west coast shipwrecks.
Open: Apr to Oct: Daily 10.30-12.30, 1.30-5.30.
Admission: £1.50, Chld 50p, OAPs 75p.

GERMAN OCCUPATION MUSEUM
Forest, Guernsey
Maritime Street; occupation kitchen, bunker rooms.
Open: Apr to Oct: Daily 10.30-5.00. Winter: Sun and Thurs afternoons 2-4.30.
Admission: £2, Chld £1.
Refreshments: Tearoom and garden.
Also Pleinmont Tower and fortifications (summer only).

GUERNSEY MUSEUM & ART GALLERY
St. Peter Port, Guernsey   **Tel:** (0481) 726518
Guernsey's new museum tells the story of the island and its people. It also includes an art gallery and audio-visual theatre. Frequent special exhibitions.
Open: Daily: 10.30-5.30 (4.30 winter).
Admission: £2, Chld 75p, OAPs £1.
Refreshments: Tea-room.

JERSEY

SIR FRANCIS COOK GALLERY
(Jersey Museums Service)
Route de la Trinité, Augrès, Jersey   **Tel:** (0534) 63333
Converted methodist chapel - permanent collection of work of Sir Francis Cook.
Open: As advertised locally.
Admission: Free.
Car parking. Director of Museums Michael Day B.A., A.M.A.

ELIZABETH CASTLE
(Jersey Museums Service)
St. Aubins Bay, Jersey   **Tel:** (0534) 23971
Elizabethan fortress built on an islet about one mile from shore. Eighteenth century garrison buildings with interpretive displays and museum of Jersey militia, refortified by the German occupying forces in 1940-44. New permanent exhibition 'In War and Peace' opened in the officers' quarters July 1989.
Open: Apr to Oct: Daily 9.30-6 including Bank Hols.
Admission: £2; Chld, OAPs £1. Children under 10 free.
Refreshments: Available.
Parties by arrangement. Director of Museums Michael Day B.A., A.M.A.

HAMPTONNE
Rue de la Patente, St Lawrence, Jersey   **Tel:** (0534) 30511)
Jersey's Country Life Museum, opening Summer 1993. Restored and furnished medieval and later buildings, exhibition, farm trail.
Open: (provisionally) June to October.
Admission: (provisionally) £1.50; Chld 75p; children under 10 free.
Refreshments: Picnic area
Car parking. Parties by arrangement. Director of Museums Michael Day BA AMA.

JERSEY MUSEUM
(Jersey Museums Service)
Weighbridge, St. Helier, Jersey   **Tel:** (0534) 30511

JERSEY MUSEUM
Weighbridge, St Helier. Tel 30511.
Open throughout the year.
Monday - Saturday 10am - 5pm.
Sunday 2pm - 5pm.

LA HOUGUE BIE MUSEUM
Grouville. Tel 53823.
Open April - October.
Daily 10am - 5pm.

ELIZABETH CASTLE
St Aubin's Bay. Tel 23971.
Open April - October.
Daily 9.30am - 6.00pm.

MONT ORGUEIL
Gorey. Tel 53292.
Open April - October.
Daily 9.30am - 6.00pm.

HAMPTONNE
St Lawrence. Tel 30511.
First year of opening, summer 1993.

Purpose built museum opened spring 1992. Permanent exhibition 'Story of Jersey'. A.V. Theatre, art gallery, temporary exhibition gallery.
Open: Mon to Sat 10-5, Sun 2-5 throughout the year.
Admission: £2; Chld, OAPs £1. Children under 10 free.
Refreshments: Available
Parties by arrangement. Car parking at nearby multi-storey in Pier Road. Director of Museums Michael Day B.A., A.M.A.

LA HOUGUE BIE MUSEUM
(Jersey Museums Service)
Grouville, Jersey   **Tel:** (0534) 53823
3,850 B.C. Neolithic tomb - open to the public, two Medieval chapels, museums of archaeology, geology, agriculture and the German occupation. Site excavation in progress.
Open: Mar to Nov: seven days a week 10-5.
Admission: £1.50; Chld, OAPs 75p. Children under 10 free.
Parties by arrangement. Car parking. Director of Museums Michael Day B.A., A.M.A.

MONT ORGUEIL CASTLE
(Jersey Museums Service)
Gorey, St. Martins, Jersey   **Tel:** (0534) 53292
Medieval fortress. Small archaeological museum of local finds. Tableaux illustrating the Castle's history.
Open: Apr to Oct: Daily 9.30-6.
Admission: £2; Chld, OAPs £1. Children under 10 free.
Refreshments: Available.
Parties catered for. Director of Museums Michael Day B.A., A.M.A.

CHESHIRE

CHESTER

CHESTER HERITAGE CENTRE
St. Michael's Church, Bridge Street Row, Chester   **Tel:** (0244) 317948
New displays in this converted church on the Historic Rows illustrate Chester's history and architecture.
Open: 11-7 Mon to Sat, 12-5 Sun (Apr to Oct), 11-5 Mon to Sat, 12-5 Sun (Nov to Mar).
Admission: Fee charged.
Access: steps to entrance and stairs to upper floor.

GROSVENOR MUSEUM
Grosvenor Street, Chester   **Tel:** (0244) 321616

KING CHARLES TOWER
City Walls, Chester   **Tel:** (0244) 318780
Built c.13th or 14th centuries: heavily damaged during the Civil War and subsequently rebuilt in its present form. From the roof King Charles I watched the defeat of his army at the Battle of Rowton Moor in 1645. Displays on the Civil War and the Siege of Chester.
Open: (Apr to Oct): Mon to Fri 11-5, Sat 10-5, Sun 2-5. (Nov to Mar): weekends only, Sat 10-5, Sun 2-5 (or dusk).

Admission: Fee charged.
Access: steps to upper chamber.

ST OLAVES
Lower Bridge Street, Chester   **Tel:** (0244) 312378
Centre for exciting new programme of crafts and contemporary art exhibitions.
Open: Mon to Sat 10.30-5, Sun 2-5. (*Closed* between exhibitions).
Admission: Free.
Access: steep steps to entrance.

WATER TOWER
City Walls, Chester   **Tel:** (0244) 311610
Built around 1321, it retains much of its medieval character. Its use is thought to have been to monitor and protect shipping on the River Dee. Camera Obscura gives panoramic view of the area. Audio guide scenes from local history.
Open: (Apr to Oct): Mon to Fri 11-5, Sat 10-5, Sun 2-5; (Nov to Mar): open weekends only, Sat 10-5, Sun 2-5 (or dusk).
Admission: Fee charged.
Access: many steep steps within Tower.

ELLESMERE PORT

THE BOAT MUSEUM
(Britains Premier Canal Museum)
Dockyard Road, Ellesmere Port L65 4EF   **Tel:** (051 355) 5017
A working museum in the old docks at the junction of the Shropshire Union and Manchester Ship Canals. Over 50 historic canal boats, steam driven pumping engines; exhibitions, including worker's cottages, and blacksmith's forge; craft workshops; The Tom Rolt education conference centre.
Location: Access from junction 9 of M53.
Tel for bookings and information. **Winner Sandford Award**

FRODSHAM

CASTLE PARK ARTS CENTRE
Castle Park Estate, Frodsham
Created from the repair and conversion of the 1852 clock tower building of the Castle Park Estate, the Arts Centre is run as a charitable trust for display of the visual arts, classes and meetings of local groups, and a garden designed for the disabled. Exhibitions of art works are normally changed monthly - nominal charge except for members and children.
Open: All year except Christmas week, Tues to Sat 10-12.30, 2-4.30; Sun 2-5. Nov to Feb *closed* 4 each day.
Refreshments: Coffee shop.
Gift shop.

KNUTSFORD

TABLEY HOUSE COLLECTION
(Tabley House Collection Trust)
Knutsford   **Tel:** (0565) 750151
A great Regency picture collection in its splendid gallery and adjacent rooms of Tabley House, the exceptionally fine series of English paintings, including *Taley: Windy Day,* by J.M.W. Turner (1808), and works by Dobson, Lely, Reynolds, Cotes, Northcote, Thomson, Ward, Calcott, Fuseli, Lawrence, Opie, Martin and Danby, are part of those assembled by Sir John Leicester, Bt., (1st Lord de Tabley) during the first decades of the 19th century, ultimately with the intention of establishing a National Gallery of British Art.

MACCLESFIELD

JODRELL BANK SCIENCE CENTRE & ARBORETUM
Macclesfield SK11 9DL   **Tel:** (0477) 71339
Marvel at the 76m Lovell telescope, a landmark in astronomy and Cheshire. See displays on astronomy, space and communications. Experience hands-on exhibits and a journey through the Solar system in the Planetarium. Explore the Environmental Discovery Centre. Follow trails through the beautiful Arboretum.
Open: Winter weekends and Christmas holidays 12-5; Easter to Oct 31: Daily 10.30-5.30.
Admission: Adult £3.20, Chld £1.80, OAPs £2.40. Family Ticket (two adults, up to 3 children) £10. Schools - child rate + 1 adult free with every 10 children. 10% discount with 20 or more in the party.
Free car parking. Suitable for the disabled.

MACCLESFIELD SILK MUSEUM AND HERITAGE CENTRE
(Trustees of Macclesfield Museums Trust)
Roe Street, Macclesfield   **Tel:** (0625) 613210

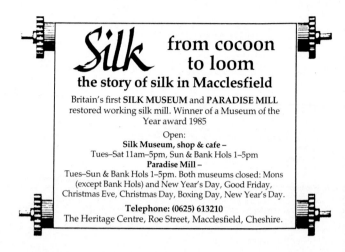

Silk Museum (Britain's first) - The story of silk in Macclesfield, audio visual, models and costume displays, silk shop. *Heritage Centre* - Free exhibitions on the history of the Sunday School building.
Open: Tues to Sat 11-5; Sun 1-5. *Closed* Mon (except Bank Hols 1-5), Christmas Eve, Christmas Day, Boxing Day, New Year's Day and Good Friday.
Admission: Fee charged.
Refreshments: Tea room.
Parties at other times by arrangement. *Victorian Schoolroom* - Educational parties by appointment only. Director: Moira Stevenson.

PARADISE MILL
(Trustees of Macclesfield Museums Trust)
Old Park Lane, Macclesfield   **Tel:** (0625) 618228
26 silk hand looms with Jacquards, demonstrations of hand weaving, room settings of 1930s, design and card cutting rooms, Manager's office. Silk Shop.
Open: Tues-Sun 1-5. *Closed* Mon (except Bank Hols 1-5), Chritmas Eve, Christmas Day, Boxing Day, New Year's Day, Good Friday.
Refreshments: Tea room in Heritage Centre, 5 minutes walk.
Parties by arrangement, mornings and evenings. 1985 Museum of the Year Award for achievement with limited resources. Director: Moira Stevenson.

WEST PARK MUSEUM
(Trustees of Macclesfield Museum Trust)
Prestbury Road, Macclesfield   **Tel:** (0625) 619831
Fine and decorative art, Egyptology. Work by C.F. Tunnicliffe, A.R.A.
Open: Tues to Sun 2-5. *Closed* Mon (except Bank Holiday 2-5) Christmas Eve, Christmas Day, Boxing Day, New Year's Day and Good Friday.
Admission: Free.
Director: Moira Stevenson.

NANTWICH

NANTWICH MUSEUM
(Nantwich Museum Trust Ltd)
Pillory Street, Nantwich CW5 5BQ   **Tel:** (0270) 627104
Local history, cheese making and temporary exhibitions.

NORTHWICH

LION SALT WORKS
(Vale Royal Borough Council)
Ollershaw Lane, Marston, Northwich CW9 6ES   **Tel:** (0606) 40555

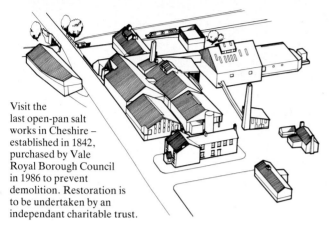

Visit the last open-pan salt works in Cheshire – established in 1842, purchased by Vale Royal Borough Council in 1986 to prevent demolition. Restoration is to be undertaken by an independant charitable trust.

Site may be visited daily: temporary exhibition/shop
Open 1.30pm – 4.30pm.

Marston, Northwich, Cheshire CW9 6ES Tel: (0606) 40555
(also on Trent and Mersey Canal)

LION SALT WORKS PROJECT

Admission: Free.
Temporary exhibition and shop. Car parking. Parties prior booking.

SALT MUSEUM
(Cheshire County Council)
London Road, Northwich   **Tel:** (0606) 41331
Museum of the Cheshire Salt Industry from Roman times to the present day. Displays include Audio-Visual programmes, models and reconstructions as well as old salt-working tools and equipment. Temporary exhibitions.
Open: Daily (except Mon) 10-5. Open bank holiday Mondays.
Admission: Charge.
Refreshments: Coffee Shop.
Shop.

RUNCORN

NORTON PRIORY MUSEUM
(Norton Priory Museum Trust)
Tudor Road, Runcorn   **Tel:** (0928) 569895
A fulfilling place for a family visit - two sites: at the first are the excavated remains of the medieval priory set in 16 acres of beautiful and peaceful woodland gardens. Indoor displays on the life and work of the canons who moved to Norton in 1134 and the Brooke family who bought the estate in 1545. The second site is the attractive and colourful Georgian walled garden which once belonged to the Brookes. Events throughout the year.
Open: From 12 noon. *Closed* Dec 24-26 and Jan 1. Walled Garden: as above, but closed Nov to Feb.
Admission: Fee charged.
Refreshments: Available, picnic area.
Special packages for school and party visits. Gift shop, facilities for disabled people, free car park.

STYAL

QUARRY BANK MILL
(Quarry Bank Mill Trust Ltd as tenants of The National Trust)
Styal   **Tel:** (0625) 527468

QUARRY BANK MILL, STYAL.

The Mill, founded 1784   *The Apprentice House & Garden.*

Award-winning textile museum set in 275 acre estate complete with village, school, chapel and pub. Large restaurant and shop. Mill meadow and riverside walks.
Exhibitions cover social life, printing, dyeing and technology; the looms are water-powered using England's most powerful water wheel. The organic garden at the Apprentice House grows 1830's varieties and fruits and vegetables are used in the restaurant in season.
3 Function rooms may booked for weddings and business functions.
Open all year: 2 miles from Manchester Airport: full details under listing.

A property of
The National Trust.

Enquiries: (0625) 527468

The Only Working Water-powered
Cotton Mill in the World

QUARRY
BANK MILL

18th century cotton mill, fully restored and producing cloth by water power, now an award-winning working museum of the cotton industry housed in a 200 year-old spinning mill. Skilled demonstrators operate vintage machinery showing cotton processes from carding and spinning to weaving on Lancashire looms. Display on water power, the lifestyle of the mill-owning Greg family plus the millworkers' world at home and at work in the 19th century. Giant 1850 waterwheel restored to working order. Renovated Apprentice House. The millworkers' village of Styal and the mill are set in the 250 acre Styal Country Park. Mill shop.
Open: *Mill:* All year. Apr-Sept: Daily 11-5. Oct-Mar: Tues-Sun 11-4. Open all Bank Hols. Pre-booked parties from 9.30 throughout the year (not Sun or Bank Holidays) and specified evenings May to Sept. *Apprentice House and Garden:* as Mill opening times during school holidays. Tues-Fri: 2 to Mill closing time during term time. Sat, Sun: as Mill opening times.
Admission: (No dogs) Prices not available at time of going to press. Advance booking essential for all groups of 10 or more, one in 20 free, but not in June or July; please apply for booking form at least 3 weeks in advance. Guides, fee per guide per 20 persons, may be booked at the same time.
Refreshments: Licensed restaurant.
Please note that due to fire and safety regulations a maximum of 30 people can be accommodated in the house at one time. Admission is by timed ticket ONLY available from Mill Reception. Members wishing to avoid crowds are advised not to visit on Bank Holidays and Sun afternoons in spring and summer. Shop, newly sited and refurbished, open as Mill. Stocks goods made from cloth woven in mill. *Disabled access:* Exterior and special route through part of interior using step-lift. Please telephone for access details and leaflet. Cars may set down passengers in Mill yard. Disabled lavatory by Styal Workshop. Mill unsuitable for guide dogs.

WARRINGTON

MUSEUM AND ART GALLERY
(Warrington Borough Council)
Bold Street, Warrington WA1 1JG   **Tel:** (0925) 444400 or 30550

WARRINGTON MUSEUM AND ART GALLERY
BOLD STREET, WARRINGTON

Toy Shop Front c. 1940 with 19th and 20th century items displayed in a new Social History Gallery.

Rich collections of Art, Natural History and Curiosities displayed in a period Museum. Of particular interest are the rare Roman Actor's Mask, the Egyptian Coffin and 'Still Life' by Van Os. Of appeal to specialists are the extensive ceramic and geology collections while examples of an early fire-engine, stocks, gibbet iron and bicycles mean there is something here for everyone.

General collections of natural history, geology, ethnology and Egyptology. Local history is well represented in the Prehistory, Roman and Medieval periods. Good collections of pottery, porcelain, local glass and clocks. Recently refurbished art galleries now house special exhibitions and a selection of the town's fine collection of oil paintings and watercolours. A new Social History Gallery reflects on life in Victorian times in a most dramatic way. Museum Education service operates.
Open: Mon to Fri 10-5.30, Sat 10-5. *Closed* Sun and Bank Hols.

WALTON HALL
(Warrington Borough Council)
Walton Lea Road, Warrington, Higher Walton WA4 6SN   **Tel:** (0925) 601617
Victorian Hall, formerly home of Greenall Family (well known local brewers). Situation in attractive parkland. Permanent displays and A.V. show illustrate family history. Two rooms furnished with fine antiques from L.J. Gibson bequest. Imposing staircase with oils by Luke Fildes R.A., Henry Woods R.A. and James Charles. Small temporary exhibition space.
Open: Easter-Sept, Thurs, Fri, Sat, Sun and Bank Hols 1-5. Winter: Sun only 12.30-4.30.
Admission: 60p, Chld/OAPs 30p.

WIDNES

CATALYST: THE MUSEUM OF THE CHEMICAL INDUSTRY
(Halton Chemical Industry Museum Trust)
Gossage Building, Mersey Road, Widnes WA8 0DF   **Tel:** 051-420 1121
Catalyst is where science and technology come alive! It offers a feast of hands-on exhibits and demonstrations exploring the chemical industry and its effect on our lives. Designed to be different, there's fun and stimulation for all the family. 'Scientrific' is Catalyst's stunning new experience. Over 30 hands-on exhibits allow you to explore how chemicals are made and test out products of the industry. Travel to 100 feet above the River Mersey in an external glass lift to the 'Observatory'. Floor to ceiling glass walls give unrivalled and breathtaking views over the surrounding panorama. Voted North West Museum and Visitor Attraction of the Year 1992.
Open: Tues to Sun 10-5 and Bank Holiday Mons, except Christmas Eve, Christmas Day, Boxing Day and New Year's Day.
Admission: Charge
Car park adjacent. Suitable for disabled.

CLEVELAND

HARTLEPOOL

GRAY ART GALLERY AND MUSEUM
(Hartlepool Borough Council)
Clarence Road, Hartlepool   **Tel:** (0429) 268916
Nineteenth and 20th century paintings. Oriental antiquities including Japanese gallery. Displays illustrating archaeology, social history and natural history of the district. Changing programmes of temporary exhibitions. Reconstructed buildings in grounds including Hart Smithy, Tram Office, Brine Pump and local cottage.
Open: Mon to Sat 10-5.30; Sun 2-5. *Closed* Christmas Day, Boxing Day, New Year's Day and Good Friday.

MARITIME MUSEUM
(Hartlepool Borough Council)
Northgate, Hartlepool   **Tel:** (0429) 272814
Maritime history of the town including fishing, ship-building, marine engineering etc. Displays include simulated fisherman's cottage and ship's bridge and an early gas-lit lighthouse lantern, net store and boat builder.
Open: Mon to Sat 10-5. *Closed* Sun, Christmas Day, Boxing Day, New Year's Day and Good Friday.

HARTLEPOOL MUSEUMS & ART GALLERY

Hartlepool Lighthouse lantern, 1846, Maritime Museum.

GARY ART GALLERY
Nineteenth and 20th century paintings, Oriental antiquities including Japanese gallery. Displays illustrating archaeology, social history and natural history of the district. Changing programme of temporary exhibitions. Reconstructed buildings in grounds including Hart Smithy, Tram Office, Brine Pump and local cottage.

MARTIME MUSEUM
Housed in a building overlooking the docks. The museum contains ship models and displays relating to all aspects of Hartlepool's maritime history, including one of the World's first gas-lit lighthouse lanterns.

KIRKLEATHAM

KIRKLEATHAM 'OLD HALL' MUSEUM
(Langbaurgh on Tees Borough Council)
Redcar, Kirkleatham   **Tel:** (0642) 479500
Restored Queen Anne building dating from 1709, once a free school endowed by Sir William Turner, now housing displays reflecting the life and industry of the area and recalling the history of the Turner family.
Open: Thurs to Mon 10-5 (*Closed* Tues & Weds & also Dec 25 & 26, Jan 1 & Good Friday.
Admission: Free.
Refreshments: Cafe
Playground and Car Park. Curator: Mr. P. Philo.

MIDDLESBROUGH

CAPTAIN COOK BIRTHPLACE MUSEUM
(Middlesbrough Borough Council)
Stewart Park, Middlesbrough   **Tel:** (0642) 311211 or 813781

CAPTAIN COOK BIRTHPLACE MUSEUM   MIDDLESBROUGH

This award winning Museum traces the story of James Cook R.N., F.R.S. (1728–1779) and illustrates the ethnography and natural history of the many countries he visited.

Illustrating Captain Cook's early life and voyages of exploration; Cook personalia; natural history and ethnography of Australia, New Zealand, North America and Pacific Islands.
Open: Tues to Sun 10-6 (summer), 9-4 (winter).
Admission: £1.00p, Chld/OAPs 50p, Family £2.50.(Last tickets 0¾ hour before).
Refreshments: Cafeteria.
Changing exhibitions. Souvenir Shop. Full access for the disabled.

CLEVELAND CRAFTS CENTRE
57 Gilkes Street, Middlesbrough TS1 5EL

CLEVELAND CRAFTS CENTRE

Gilkes St., Middlesbrough   Tel: (0642) 226351

A Walter Keeler Teapot – Salt-glazed stoneware 1983.

The Cleveland Crafts Centre houses a major collection of contemporary ceramics with fine examples representing the entire period, from work by the pioneer potters to the masters of the 1970s and 1980s. The ceramics are on open display. There is also a national and international collection of contemporary jewellery.

CLEVELAND GALLERY
(Libraries & Leisure Dept)
Victoria Road, Middlesbrough TS1 3QS
Exciting range of temporary exhibitions which change every four to six weeks. The Gallery houses the County's permanent collection of modern drawings and paintings, decorative art from the seventeenth century to the present day, and collections of antique maps and lace, all of which are exhibited from time to time.

DORMAN MUSEUM
(Middlesbrough Borough Council)
Linthorpe Road, Middlesbrough   **Tel:** (0642) 813781
Local, social, industrial and natural history. Permanent display of regional and Linthorpe pottery. Exhibition on History of Middlesbrough. Temporary exhibition programme.
Open: Tues to Sat 10-6.
Admission: Free.

MIDDLESBROUGH ART GALLERY
(Middlesbrough Borough Council)
Linthorpe Road, Middlesbrough   **Tel:** (0642) 247445
Exhibitions of regional and national importance. Permanent collection of British 20th Century art and 17th to 19th Century collection. Both shown through temporary exhibitions. Outdoor Sculpture Court.
Open: Tues-Sat 10-6. *Closed* for lunch (1-2).
Admission: Free.

SALTBURN

MARGROVE SOUTH CLEVELAND HERITAGE CENTRE
Margrove Park, Boosbeck, Saltburn TS12 3BZ
A new facility, the Centre promotes the upland valley and coastal landscapes of South Cleveland, charting man's impact on the environment. Also changing exhibitions. Shop, local walks and picnic areas.

STOCKTON-ON-TEES

BILLINGHAM ART GALLERY
(Stockton Borough Council)
Queensway, Billingham, Stockton-on-Tees   **Tel:** (0642) 555441
A purpose built modern art gallery with a constantly changing programme of exhibitions.
Open: Mon to Sat 9-5 during exhibitions *Closed* Sun and Bank Holidays.

GREEN DRAGON MUSEUM AND TOURIST INFORMATION CENTRE
(Stockton Borough Council)
Finkle Street, Stockton-on-Tees   **Tel:** (0642) 674308
Local history museum showing the development of Stockton. Experience the sights, sounds and smells at the dawn of the railway era in an exciting new audio/visual show '1825 - the birth of railways', the story of the Stockton and Darlington, the world's first public railway built for steam power. Other exhibits include an extensive display of local pottery, an exhibition showing the life of John Walker, the inventor of matches, and a rebuilt nineteenth century print shop, showing examples of contemporary printing methods.
Open: Mon to Sat 9-5. *Closed* Sun and Bank Holidays.

PRESTON HALL MUSEUM
(Stockton Borough Council)
Yarm Road, Stockton-on-Tees   **Tel:** (0642) 781184

Preston Hall Museum

Return to a bygone age at Preston Hall Museum, stroll down a recreated Victorian high street with period shops and working craftsmen or explore over 100 acres of picturesque parkland overlooking the River Tees.

Extensive galleries throughout the museum show life as it was in Victorian times, with the highlight, a recreated high street featuring period shops and working craftsmen. Among the museum's other exhibits are collections of arms and armour, costume and fine art which includes Georges de la Tour's enchanting painting 'The Dice Players'. The Museum stands in over 100 acres of picturesque parkland with picnic areas, a tropical bird aviary, riverside walks, children's play area with 'safety surfaces' and a historical walk along a length of original Stockton & Darlington Railway trackbed - the world's first railway built for passenger travel.
Open: Summer: (Easter to Sept 30), Mon-Sun 10-6; Winter: (Oct 1 to Easter), Mon-Sun 10-4.30. Last admission ½ hour before closing. *Closed* New Year's Day, Good Friday, Christmas Day, Boxing Day.
Party bookings Tel: (0642) 602474 ext 2778

CORNWALL

BODMIN

BODMIN TOWN MUSEUM
Bodmin
Local history collection.
Enquiries to Bodmin Town Council, Shire House, Mount Folly Square, Bodmin.

BOLVENTOR

POTTERS MUSEUM OF CURIOSITY
Jamaica Inn, near Launceston, Bolventor   **Tel:** (0566) 86838
Life work of Victorian naturalist and taxidermist, plus numerous curiosities from all over the world.
Open: Apr 1 to Oct 31: 9.30-4 low season, 9.30-6 high season.
Refreshments: Available.
Party bookings by request during winter months by telephoning above number. Toilets, shop and partially disabled facilities.

CAMBORNE

CAMBORNE SCHOOL OF MINES GEOLOGICAL MUSEUM AND ART GALLERY
Pool, Camborne, Redruth   **Tel:** (0209) 714866
Collection of minerals and ores. Art exhibition, cornish gallery with National Trust and Mineral Tramways project.
Open: Mon to Fri 9-5. Closed Bank Hols.
Admission: Free.

CORNISH ENGINES
(The National Trust)
East Pool Mine, Camborne, Pool
The 30-in. rotative beam winding engine (1887) and the 90-in. beam pumping engine (1892) both stand complete in their houses.

CAMELFORD

NORTH CORNWALL MUSEUM AND GALLERY
The Clease, Camelford   **Tel:** (0840) 212954
A privately owned museum of rural life in North Cornwall from 50 to 100 years ago. Two wagons and a dog cart; sections on agriculture, cidermaking, slate and granite quarrying, blacksmith's and wheelwright's tools, cobbling, the dairy and domestic scene. Pilgrim Trust award 1978.
Open: Apr to Sep: Mon to Sat 10-5. *Closed* Sun.

FALMOUTH

FALMOUTH ART GALLERY
(Falmouth Town Council)
The Moor, Falmouth   **Tel:** (0326) 313863
Programme of regularly changed exhibitions throughout the year, comprising one-man shows by contemporary artists, travelling exhibitions, and subjects of local interest, in addition to one exhibition of major artistic importance each year. Permanent collection includes works by Waterhouse, Munnings and Tuke and fine 18th and 19th century maritime paintings and prints.
Open: Mon to Fri 10-4.30 and some Sats/Bank Holidays. *Closed* between Christmas and New Year.
Admission: Free.
All enquiries to the Curator.

FALMOUTH MARITIME MUSEUM
c/o Hon Secretary, Higher Penpol House, Mawnan Smith, Nr. Falmouth
Tel: (0326) 250507
Cornwall's Maritime History.

HELSTON

FLAMBARDS
Culdrose Manor, Helston   **Tel:** (0326) 573404/574549
Three major award-winning all-weather exhibitions set in magnificient prize-winning gardens together with many exciting attractions and family rides. **Flambards Victorian Village.** An authentically reconstructed life-size village of over 50 shops, traders and dwellings, with cobbled streets, carriages, and fashions. **Britain in the Blitz.** A recreated wartime street with the authentic atmosphere of air-raids, blackouts, and rationing. Opened by Dame Vera Lynn D.B.E., LL.D. **Cornwall Aero Park.** Aircraft, helicopters and special exhibitions paying tribute to men and machines from the earliest days to Concorde. Plus 'Hall of Miscellany', The famous Chemist Shop Time Capsule, Cornwall's Exploratorium, Live entertainment, Adventure playgrounds, and plenty more to interest every taste and age.
Open: Easter to end Oct every day 10am, last admissions 4pm, extended opening hours last week July and whole Aug.
Admission: Pay-at-the-gate, price includes all exhibitions and rides.
Infoline (0326) 564093.

HELSTON FOLK MUSEUM
Old Butter Market, Helston
Folk Museum dealing with all aspects of local life in the Lizard Peninsula.

POLDARK MINE AND HERITAGE COMPLEX
Wendron, Helston

ISLES OF SCILLY

THE VALHALLA FIGUREHEAD COLLECTION
Tresco
Abbey Gardens, Tresco, Isles of Scilly   **Tel:** (0720) 22849 **Fax:** (0720) 22807
Figureheads and ships' carvings from wrecks around the Isles of Scilly. A National Maritime Museum Outstation.
Open: Daily Apr to Oct, 10-4.

LISKEARD

THORBURN MUSEUM AND GALLERY
Liskeard   **Tel:** (0579) 20325/21129
World's first audio-visual gallery. Nationally important collection of Archibald Thorburn;'s (1860-1935) celebrated wildlife paintings in series of 'live' cameos.
Open: Easter to end Oct: Daily 10-6 (last adm 4.30). *Closed* in winter.
Wheelchair access. Braille pads. Soundalive record tours (special versions for blind/handicapped). Limited Edition Thorburn prints. 'One of the most remarkable galleries conceived.' Simon Tate. *The Times.* Winner of Sotheby's Award. Best Fine Art Museum in Britain 1987.

MEVAGISSEY

MEVAGISSEY FOLK MUSEUM
East Quay, Mevagissey

NEWLYN

NEWLYN ART GALLERY
   Newlyn   **Tel:** (0736) 63715
Exhibitions of contemporary works by leading West Country artists. Supported by South West Arts.
Open: Mon to Sat 10-5.

PENZANCE

PENZANCE AND DISTRICT MUSEUM AND ART GALLERY
Penzance Town Council
   Morrab Road, Penzance   **Tel:** (0736) 63625
Local antiquities and Natural History. Exhibition of paintings, including some fine examples of the Newlyn school.

ST. AUSTELL

MID CORNWALL GALLERIES
   St. Austell PL24 2EG   **Tel:** (0726) 81 2131
The gallery is a Victorian School converted to well lit modern gallery showing a very comprehensive range of contemporary arts and crafts. Approximately 8 Exhibitions/Group Shows a year.
Location: On A390 at St. Blazey, 3 m E of St. Austell on A390.

ST. AUSTELL CHINA CLAY MUSEUM
   Carthew, St. Austell

ST. IVES

THE BARBARA HEPWORTH MUSEUM
(The Tate Gallery)
   Barnoon Hill, St. Ives   **Tel:** (0736) 796226
The house, studio, sculpture garden and workshops of the famous sculptor.
Open: Mon to Sat: Spring/Summer 10-5.30; Autumn/Winter 10-4.30. *Closed* Sun, Good Friday, Christmas and Boxing Days.
Admission: Charge

OLD MARINERS CHURCH
(St. Ives Society of Artists)
   Norway Square, St. Ives
Exhibitions by members.

TATE GALLERY ST IVES
   Porthmeor Beach, St.Ives
This new, purpose-built gallery will show changing groups of work from the Tate Gallery collection of St Ives painting and sculpture, dating from about 1925 to 1975. Artists include Wallis, Nicholson, Hepworth, Gabo, Lanyon, Frost, Wynter, Heron and Hilton.
Open: Spring 1993.
See introductory article for further details.

SALTASH

COTEHELE QUAY AND SHAMROCK - NATIONAL MARITIME MUSEUM OUTSTATION
(with The National Trust)
   Saltash   **Tel:** (0579) 50830
Display on shipping and trade of the River Tamar. Home of the NMM/NT restored Tamar sailing barge *Shamrock*.
Open: Daily Apr to Oct, 11-4.
Location: Off A388 near St. Dominick. (Follow Cotehele House signs). Resident NMM staff.

TRURO

ROYAL CORNWALL MUSEUM
(Royal Institution of Cornwall)
   River Street, Truro   **Tel:** (0872) 72205
Local antiquities and history. Ceramics and art. World famous collections of Cornish minerals.
Open: Mon to Sat 9-5. *Closed* Sun and Bank Hols.
Refreshments: New cafe.
Shop. Full facilities for disabled.

ZENOR

WAYSIDE MUSEUM
   Old Millhouse, Zenor

CUMBRIA

BEETHAM

HERON CORN MILL AND MUSEUM OF PAPERMAKING
(Beetham Trust)
   c/o Henry Cooke Makin, Waterhouse Mills, Beetham, nr. Milnthorpe LA7 7AR
   Tel: (05395) 63363
Working, 18th century lowder water driven corn mill. All machinery driven by a 14ft high breast shot water wheel. Some 18th century machinery still in use but the mill as a whole represents a mill of the early 20th century. Demonstrations of milling given regularly. Mill products on sale as well as various information pamphlets and other goods. **Museum of Papermaking**. Established in 1988 to commemorate 500 years of papermaking in Britain. Displays try to tell the story of papermaking from early times to the present highly mechanised process. Various displays show different aspects of the industry, and are changed regularly. (Still in development stage) Housed in a renovated Carter's Barn on the same site as the Corn Mill.
Open: Apr 1/Easter to end of Sept: Tues to Sun; Bank Hols.
Admission: £1.25, Chld/OAPs 80p. 10% discount for parties over 20 prebooked. Teachers with school parties allowed free entry.
Location: 1 mile S of Milthorpe on A6.
Free car park. Parts of mill not suitable for disabled. Paper museum accessible to disabled. Open to prebooked parties, especially schools, during October. Many aspects of the Mill and Museum of Papermaking are very applicable to various aspects of the National Curriculum. Evening parties welcome by prior arrangement.

POTTER'S MUSEUM OF CURIOSITY
One of the last truly Victorian Museums in England, consisting of assembled items of curiosity worldwide.
Jamaica Inn Courtyard, Bolventor, Nr. Launceston, Cornwall.   Tel: (0566) 86838.

Come browse round the Museum of Walter Potter, the famous Victorian Naturalist and Taxidermist's lifetime's work and collection of curios - his taxidermed tableaux 'The Original Death and Burial of Cock Robin', 'The House that Jack Built', 'The Kittens' Wedding' and others, plus over 10,000 unusual items - a piece of Zeppelin, General Gordon's autograph, a mummified cat, a 3-legged pig, a native shield decorated with human hair, smoking memorabilia and many more. Then take refreshment at Jamaica Inn, made immortal by the lateDame Daphne du Maurier's famous book 'Jamaica Inn' and once owned by the late Alistair Maclean. Visit the Dame Daphne du Maurier Memorial Room, Joss Merlyn's Bar and the Gift Shop. All this will undoubtedly give recreational enjoyment to visitors from all areas and all ages.

Cumbria

CARK-IN-CARTMEL

HOLKER HALL - LAKELAND MOTOR MUSEUM
Cark-in-Cartmel

Set in the peaceful surroundings of Holker Hall the Lakeland Motor Museum houses a fine collection of over 100 cars, motorcycles, bicycles and engines against a background of displays of automobilia including mascots, badges, early motoring accessories, toys and pottery.

Open: 1st April to end October: Daily (except Sat) 10.30-5. Last admission 4.30.

CARLISLE

THE GUILDHALL MUSEUM
(Carlisle City Council)
Greenmarket, Carlisle   **Tel:** (0228) 34781

Early 15th century half-timbered house. Displays of Guild, Civic and local history, including medieval items.

Open: For hours contact Tullie House.

Admission: Adults 50p; children/OAP 25p price includes the use of sound guide.

TULLIE HOUSE
(Carlisle City Council)
Castle Street, Carlisle   **Tel:** (0228) 34781

Museum and Art Gallery, reopened January 1991. Tracing the history and Natural History of the border City, many interactive exhibits, an audio-visual show on the Reivers, Environment Gallery complete with changing sky dome, reconstruction of Hadrian's Wall, Carlisle's past as a railway city and much more. New fully equipped Art Gallery displaying all kinds of contemporary works of art.

Open: Museum and Art Gallery 364 days a year from 10 a.m.(12.00 Sun) 5.00pm. Old Tullie House open 11-3, 364 days a year.

Admission: Ground floor free. Admission charge to upper floor other than residents of Carlisle using their Tullie card.

Refreshments: Garden restaurant

Allow 2-3 hours for your visit. Shop. Facilities for the disabled.

COCKERMOUTH

THE CUMBERLAND TOY AND MODEL MUSEUM
Bank's Court, Market Place, Cockermouth   **Tel:** (0900) 827606

Mainly British toys from 1900 to present including Hornby, Meccano, Triang, Sutcliffe etc. Visitor operated Hornby layouts, Scalextric, Lego and other toys.

Open: Feb to Nov inclusive: Daily 10-5; winter by appointment

Admission: Fee charged. Reduction for parties.

Free educational quiz, opportunity to handle some toys, small play area for young children. Special exhibitions each year.

CONISTON

THE RUSKIN MUSEUM
Coniston   **Tel:** (053 94) 41387

GRASMERE

DOVE COTTAGE AND WORDSWORTH MUSEUM
Grasmere   **Tel:** (05394) 35544/35547/35003

Combined ticket gives access to Dove Cottage (home of Wordsworth during his most creative years, 1799-1808) and the museum which has an extensive display of verse manuscripts, paintings and special exhibitions providing a context for the poet's life and work.

Open: 9.30-5.30 (last admission 5).

Admission: Reductions for parties.

Refreshments: Restaurant

Educational visits welcome. Book and gift shop.

THE HEATON COOPER STUDIO
(John Heaton Cooper)
The Studio, Grasmere LA22 9SX   **Tel:** (05394) 35280

In the centre of the village is an exhibition of original watercolour paintings and a unique collection of colour reproductions by W. Heaton Cooper R.I. and A. Heaton Cooper (1863-1929) who through their paintings of mountains and lakes are recognised as the foremost artists of the area. There are also many examples of sculpture by Ophelia Gordon Bell. Reproductions and originals may be purchased from The Studio at Grasmere or Bowness together with books, art materials and greetings cards.

Open: Easter to end Oct: Daily 9-6 (Sun 12-6); Nov to Easter: Mon to Sat 9-5, (Sun 12-5). Open Bank Hols *(except Christmas).*

Parties welcome. Car park. Suitable for disabled.

HAWKSHEAD

BEATRIX POTTER GALLERY
(The National Trust)
Main Street, Hawkshead LA22 0NS   **Tel:** (05394) 36355

Admission: Charge payable. Parties by pre-arrangement only. Car parking in village.

KENDAL

ABBOT HALL ART GALLERY
Kendal, Cumbria

Impressive Georgian house with comprehensive collections of work by Romney and Gardner and a new gallery of Lake District art over 250 years. Furniture by Gillows displayed in recently restored rooms. Lively programme of temporary exhibitions. Access for disabled throughout the Gallery. Adjacent Museum of Lakeland Life recaptures flavour of everyday social and industrial life in the Lakes. Arthur Ransome Room and John Cunliffe Room (Postman Pat). Also visit award-winning Kendal Museum of Natural History and Archaeology on Station Road.

Open: Daily except Dec 25, 26 and Jan 1. Mon-Sat 10.30-5.30, Sunday 2.00-5.00. Reduced hours during winter/spring.

Admission: Charge, concessions for OAPs, families, children and students.

Location: Off Kirkland near Kendal Parish Church. Leave M6 at J.36. Disabled access. Free parking.

KESWICK

KESWICK MUSEUM AND ART GALLERY
  Station Road, Keswick
Contains original Southey, Wordsworth and Walpole manuscripts. Local geology and natural history.
Open: Easter to Nov: Sun to Fri 10-12, 1-4. Open Bank Holiday Monday.
Admission: 80p, Chld/OAPs 40p. Group reductions.

RAILWAY MUSEUM
(Derwent Railway Society)
  28 Main Street, Keswick
Railwayana and relics mainly associated with railways of Cumbria.

MARYPORT

MARITIME MUSEUM
(Allerdale District Council)
  Senhouse Street, Maryport   **Tel:** (0900) 813738
Maritime and local history. Steamship section in adjacent harbour.

MILLOM

MILLOM FOLK MUSEUM
(Millom Folk Museum Society)
  St. Georges Road, Millom
Unique full-scale model of a Hodbarrow iron mine drift, miner's cottage, smithy and many other items.

PENRITH

PENRITH MUSEUM
(Eden District Council)
  Robinson's School, Middlegate, Penrith   **Tel:** (0768) 64671
Local history, archaeology and geology. The museum building, dating from 1670, was a charity school.
Open: Jun 1 to Sept 30: Mon to Sat 10-7; Sun 1-6. Oct 1 to May 31: Mon to Sat 10-5.
Admission: Free.

ULVERSTON

THE LAUREL AND HARDY MUSEUM
  4c Upper Brook Street, Ulverston   **Tel:** (0229) 52292

WHITEHAVEN

WHITEHAVEN MUSEUM AND ART GALLERY
(Copeland Borough Council)
  Civic Hall, Lowther Street, Whitehaven CA28 7SH   **Tel:** (0946) 693111, Ext. 307
Local History including coal and iron mining, maritime history, archaeology, pottery etc. Programme of temporary exhibitions throughout the year. Lecture programme and wide range of museum publications - lists available.
Open: Mon to Sat 10-4.30. *Closed* Sun and Bank Holidays.

WINDERMERE

WINDERMERE STEAMBOAT MUSEUM
  Rayrigg Road, Windermere LA23 1BN   **Tel:** (905394) 45565

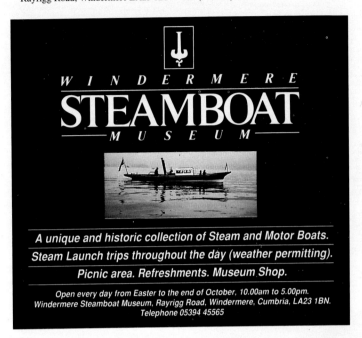

A unique and historic collection of Steamboats and Motorboats in the Heart of Lakeland. Elegant and beautiful Victorian and Edwardian steam launches, including the S.L. 'Dolly' - the oldest working steamboat in the world - plus many other historic craft. Steam launch trips each day (weather permitting). Museum displays.
Open: Every day, from Easter to end of October 10am to 5pm.
Refreshments: Available.
Shop, picnic area.

WORKINGTON

HELENA THOMPSON MUSEUM
(Allerdale District Council)
  Park End Road, Workington   **Tel:** (0900) 62598
Costumes and applied art; local history collection.
Open: Mon to Sat Apr 1 - Oct 31: 10.30-4; Nov 1 - Mar 31: 11-3.

DERBYSHIRE

BAKEWELL

THE OLD HOUSE MUSEUM
(An Independent Museum)
  Cunningham Place, Bakewell   **Tel:** (0629) 813647
An early Tudor house with original wattle and daub interior walls and open-timbered chamber. Victorian kitchen, costumes on models, craftsmen's tools, lace, toys etc.
Open: Apr 1 to Oct 31: Daily 2-5.
Admission: £1, Chld 50p. (1992 rates).
Parties mornings or evenings by appointment.

BUXTON

BUXTON MUSEUM AND ART GALLERY
(Derbyshire Museum Service)
  Terrace Road, Buxton SK17 6DU   **Tel:** (0298) 24658
Journey through time into the geology, archaeology and history of the Peak District in seven unusual settings ranging from a prehistoric Coal Forest to a Victorian Petrification shop. Complementing the Wonders of the Peak gallery is the period study of Sir William Boyd Dawkins and an extensive display of local history and ephemera. Temporary exhibition programme and an intriguing shop complete an unforgettable visit.
Open: Tues to Fri 9.30-5.30; Sat 9.30-5.
Admission: Free.
Wonders of the Peak received the BBC History and Archaeology Unit's Award for **Best Museum of Archaeological and Historical Interest** in the Museum of the Year Awards, July 1990.

Derbyshire

CHESTERFIELD

PEACOCK HERITAGE CENTRE
(Chesterfield Borough Council)
Low Pavement, Chesterfield   **Tel:** (0246) 207777
Sixteenth century timber-framed building with first floor room open to the timber frame; fully restored in 1981.
Open: Mon to Sat 11-4.
A continuous programme of changing exhibitions and a short video on Chesterfield.

REVOLUTION HOUSE
(Chesterfield Borough Council)
Old Whittington, Chesterfield   **Tel:** (0246) 453554/231224
Originally an alehouse where three conspirators met to plot the Revolution of 1688. Temporary exhibition of local material, video available of the events of 1688.
Open: Sat and Sun throughout the year, daily Easter to end Oct, 10-4.

CRICH

THE NATIONAL TRAMWAY MUSEUM
(The Tramway Museum Society)
Crich, near Matlock   **Tel:** (0773) 852565
Unique collection of about 50 restored horse, steam and electric trams built 1873-1953. Tram services regularly operated over one mile scenic track. Large new display area.
Open: Weekends and Bank Hols Apr to Nov 10-6.30; also mid Apr to end Sept: Mon to Thurs 10-5.30, plus selected Fris in summer holidays. Dates subject to confirmation.

CROMFORD

ARKWRIGHT'S MILL
Cromford, near Matlock   **Tel:** (0629) 824297
The world's first successful water powered cotton spinning mill. The Arkwright Society are in the process of restoring the mills.
Open: Tel above No.
Admission: Tel above No.
Refreshments: Cromford Mill Restaurant.
Exhibitions, audio-visual slide display, craft shops, mill shop. Guides available any time.

HIGH PEAK JUNCTION WORKSHOPS AND HIGH PEAK TRAIL
Cromford
Location: Railway Workshops at High Peak Junction, the junction of the railway with the Cromford Canal, approx 1½ miles from Cromford village, signposted from Cromford to Crich Road.

DERBY

DERBY INDUSTRIAL MUSEUM
The Silk Mill, off Full Street, Derby   **Tel:** (0332) 255308
Displays form an introduction of the industrial history of Derby and Derbyshire. They also include a major collection of Rolls-Royce aero engines ranging from an Eagle of 1915 to an RB211 from the first TriStar airliner. New railway engineering gallery now open.
Open: Mon 11-5, Tues to Sat 10-5, Sun and Bank Hols 2-5.
Admission: 30p, concessions 10p.

DERBY MUSEUMS & ART GALLERY
The Strand, Derby   **Tel:** (0332) 255586
Museum. Archaeology, military history, natural history, geology. **Art Gallery.** Major works by 18th century painter Joseph Wright of Derby, including examples of his unusual scientific and industrial subjects. The art collection also specialises in works by other local artists and topographical views of Derby and Derbyshire. The Derby porcelain gallery displays an unrivalled collection.
Open: Mon 11-5, Tues to Sat 10-5, Suns and Bank Hols 2-5.
Admission: Free.
Museum shop. Temporary exhibitions. School service: term-time lessons and holiday activities for children. **Regimental Museum of the 9th/12th Royal Lancers (Prince of Wales), Derbyshire Yeomanry** and material of the **Sherwood Foresters.**

DONNINGTON MOTOR MUSEUM *SEE* LEICESTERSHIRE

PICKFORD'S HOUSE MUSEUM
41 Friar Gate, Derby   **Tel:** (0332) 255363
A Georgian town house opened in late 1988 as a social history museum interpreting domestic life in the late 18th and early 19th centuries, both above and below stairs. Displays of Georgian and later period rooms, and historic costumes.
Open: Mon 11-5, Tues to Sat 10-5, Sun and Bank Hols 2-5.
Admission: 30p, concessions 10p.
Period garden.

ROYAL CROWN DERBY MUSEUM
Osmaston Road, Derby   **Tel:** (0332) 47051
The only factory allowed to use the words 'Crown' and 'Royal', a double honour granted by George III and Queen Victoria. The museum, opened by the Duchess of Devonshire in 1969, traces the development of the company from 1748 to the present day.
Open: Weekdays 9.30-12.30, 1.30-4.
Factory tours, factory shop. *Closed* factory holidays.

ELVASTON

ELVASTON CASTLE MUSEUM
(Derbyshire Museum Service)
The Working Estate, Elvaston Castle Country Park, Borrowash Lane, Elvaston DE7 3EP   **Tel:** (0332) 571342
This unusual museum re-creates the past through displays and demonstrations in and around the original workshops and cottage providing visitors with opportunities to experience and involve themselves in the life and work of the craftsmen, tradesmen, labourers and their families about 1910. The site includes gipsy caravans, agricultural machinery, livestock, corn mill, machines for the preparation of timber, estate craft workshops - wheelwright, blacksmith, farrier, plumber, joiner, saddler and cobbler and an estate cottage with gardens, laundry and a dairy.
Open: Easter Saturday to Nov 1. Wed to Sat 1-5; Sun and Bank Hols 10-6.
Admission: Fee charged.
School and organised parties by prior arrangement.

ILKESTON

EREWASH MUSEUM
(Erewash Borough Council)
High Street, Ilkeston   **Tel:** (0602) 440440, Ext. 331.
Eighteenth century town house, set in pleasant gardens, housing local history collections in room settings and galleries.

Open: All year Tues, Thurs, Fri, Sat 10-4; Bank Holidays 10-4, but *Closed* Jan, Christmas and New Year.

MATLOCK

CAUDWELL'S MILL
   Rowsley, Matlock DE4 2EB   **Tel:** (0629) 734374
This 19th century water turbine powered flour mill with precision roller mills is still producing quality wholemeal flour for sale. See four floors of machinery and exhibitions. Crafts-people in the Stable Yard.
Open: Daily 1st Mar to end Oct 10-6, weekends only in winter.
Refreshments: Cafe.
Car Park.

MIDDLETON-BY-WIRKSWORTH

MIDDLETON TOP ENGINE HOUSE
(Derbyshire County Council)
   Middleton-by-Wirksworth
Beautifully restored Beam Winding Engine dating from 1830 when the railway was built to link the Cromford Canal with the Peak Forest Canal.
Location: Signposted from the B5036 Cromford to Wirksworth Road.

REPTON

REPTON SCHOOL MUSEUM
   Repton   **Tel:** (0283) 702375
Open: By appointment.

SUDBURY

MUSEUM OF CHILDHOOD
(The National Trust)
   Sudbury Hall, Sudbury DE6 5HT **Tel:** (0283) 585305
Displays of aspects of childhood - costume, toys, the child at work, education etc. Related activities and special exhibitions. Charles II house with outstanding plasterwork and woodcarvings. Lakeside lawns and 17th century village. Displays incorporate the Betty Cadbury 'Playthings Past' Collection into The Toy Box gallery.
Open: Apr to Oct: Wed to Sun and Bank Hol Mons 1.00-5.30 (last adm 5.00).
Admission: Fee charged. National Trust members free.
Parties by pre-arrangement only.

DEVON

ASHBURTON

ASHBURTON MUSEUM
   1 West Street, Ashburton
Local antiquities, implements, bronze age flints, geology, lace. American Indian antiques.
Open: Mid May to end Sept: Tues, Thur, Fri and Sat 2.30-5.

BARNSTAPLE

THE MUSEUM OF NORTH DEVON INCORPORATING THE ROYAL DEVON YEOMANRY MUSEUM
(North Devon District Council)
   The Square, Barnstaple EX32 8LN   **Tel:** (0271) 46747
Headquarters of North Devon Museums Service. A major new museum displaying and interpreting the natural and human history of North Devon and its environs. The museum includes fascinating old collections dating as far back as the museum of the Barnstaple Literary and Scientific Institution founded in 1845 but many of the displayed collections have been assembled over the last five years. The museum is the regional museum for the Natural History, Archaeology, Militaria and Pottery Industry of Northern Devon. It features the collections of the Royal Devon Yeomanry, spectacular displays of North Devon Pottery, a seventeenth century pottery kiln, a Victorian Library, West Country Pewter, Fine Art, Fossils, Marine Life and displays on the History of Science and the Victorian Fern Craze. New displays include 'Rural Pursuits' and 'Settlement, Invasion and Defence in Northern Devon'.There is an active temporary exhibition programme.
Open: All year Tuesday-Saturday 10-4.30. *Closed* Sun, Mon and Public Holidays.
Admission: Free.
All correspondence to Museums Officer, North Devon Service (see above).

NORTH DEVON MUSEUMS SERVICE
(North Devon District Council)
   Museum of North Devon, The Square, Barnstaple EX32 8LN   **Tel:** (0271) 46747
All correspondence to Museums Officer at above address.

ST. ANNE'S CHAPEL AND OLD GRAMMAR SCHOOL MUSEUM
(North Devon District Council)
   St. Peter's Churchyard, High Street, Barnstaple   **Tel:** (0271) 78709 (when open) or (0271) 46747
St. Anne's Chapel is probably 14th century in origin but housed Barnstaple Grammar School from 1550 until 1910 and was used by Huguenot refugees for their Sunday worship from 1686 until 1750. The museum has been re-displayed to reflect the history of the building. It features an atmospheric recreation of the school room (with its original unique oak furniture) as it would have been at the end of the 17th century when the poet John Gay was a pupil there. Saint Cuthbert Mayne was a pupil at the school in the mid 16th century. The newly cased museum in the crypt describes the history of schooling in North Devon and contains displays of 16th-20th century social history items.
Open: Late May-Oct, Tuesday to Saturday, 10am-1pm and 2pm-4.30pm and at other times by appointment.
Admission: Free.
All correspondence to Museums Officer, North Devon Museums Service (see above).

BIDEFORD

BURTON ART GALLERY
(Torridge District Council)
   Victoria Park, Kingsley Road, Bideford
Contains the Hubert Coop Collection of paintings and other objects of art.

BRIXHAM

BRIXHAM MUSEUM
(The Brixham Museum and History Society)
Bolton Cross, Brixham TQ5 8LZ   **Tel:** (0803) 856267
Local and Maritime History. H.M. Coastguards' Museum.
Open: Easter to end Oct: Mon to Sat 10-5
Admission: Modest admission charges. Concessions Chld/OAPs/Family.
Central car park 100 yds.

BUDLEIGH SALTERTON

FAIRLYNCH ARTS CENTRE AND MUSEUM
(Trustees)
27 Fore Street, Budleigh Salterton   **Tel:** (0395) 442666
Emphasis on local material, local history, archaeology and geology, natural history. Period costume, especially Victorian. Lace. Lace making demonstrations.
Open: Easter to mid Oct 2-4.30, mid July to end Aug additionally 11-1. *Closed* Sun mornings, 3 weeks from Boxing Day 2.30-4.30.
Admission: 80p, Chld/OAP/Students 50p.
Parties by arrangement. Car parking on sea front. Suitable for disabled persons on ground floor only. Curator Mrs P.M. Hull.

OTTERTON MILL CENTRE AND WORKING MUSEUM
Budleigh Salterton
Water mill museum; wholemeal flour production using water power. Gallery with fine art and craft exhibitions (Easter to Dec). Workshops.
Open: Daily: summer 10.30-5.30; winter 11.30-4.30.
Admission: Fee charged.
Location: Otterton (off the A376 between Newton Poppleford and Budleigh Salterton).
Refreshments: Restaurant and bakery, picnic area.
Shop. Christmas hol activities.

CAPTON

PREHISTORIC HILL SETTLEMENT
Capton, Near Dittisham, Dartmouth TQ6 0JE   **Tel:** (080 421) 452
Stone age hill settlement. Reconstructed neolithic roundhouse.
Open: Mar to end Sept: Daily 10-5.
Admission: Free.
Parking for 40 cars. Not suitable for coaches.

DARTMOUTH

DARTMOUTH MUSEUM
(Friends of Dartmouth Museum)
The Butterwalk, Dartmouth
Housed in former merchant's house built 1640. Original panelling and ceilings. Historic and maritime exhibits.

NEWCOMEN ENGINE HOUSE
(Newcomen Society)
adjacent to The Butterwalk, Dartmouth   **Tel:** (0803) 832281
Contains one of Newcomen's original atmospheric pressure/steam engines circa 1725. May be seen working.
Open: Easter - Oct 31.

DAWLISH

DAWLISH MUSEUM
Brunswick House, Brunswick Place, Dawlish

EXETER

THE BRUNEL ATMOSPHERIC RAILWAY
(The Brunel Atmospheric Railway Trust)
Brunel Pumping House, Starcross, Nr. Exeter

GUILDHALL
(Exeter City Council)
High Street, Exeter

QUAY HOUSE INTERPRETATION CENTRE
(Exeter City Council)
The Quay, Exeter

ROUGEMONT HOUSE MUSEUM OF COSTUME AND LACE
(Exeter City Council)
Castle Street, Exeter   **Tel:** (0392) 265213

ROYAL ALBERT MEMORIAL MUSEUM AND ART GALLERY
(Exeter City Council)
Queen Street, Exeter

ST. NICHOLAS PRIORY
(Exeter City Council)
The Mint, Fore Street, Exeter

UNDERGROUND PASSAGES
(Exeter City Council)
High Street, Exeter

HARTLAND

HARTLAND QUAY MUSEUM
Hartland, near Bideford
A museum devoted to the Hartland coastline displaying four centuries of shipwreck, natural history, geology, Harland Quay and coastal trades and activities.
Open: Easter week then Whitsun to Sept 30: Daily 11-5.
Admission: 50p, Chld 20p.

HONITON

ALLHALLOWS MUSEUM
High Street (next to St. Paul's Church), Honiton   **Tel:** (0404) 44966
Comprehensive exhibition of Honiton Lace with frequent demonstrations of lace making. Local history.
Open: Easter then mid May to end Oct: Weekdays 10-5 *(During Oct 10-4).*
Admission: 60p, Chld 25p.

ILFRACOMBE

ILFRACOMBE MUSEUM
Wilder Road (opposite Runnymeade Gardens), Ilfracombe
Collections: Natural History, Victoriana, Costume, China, Maritime, Railway, Engravings, Pictures and Brass Rubbing Centre.
Open: From 10, all year.
Admission: 50p, Chld 10p, OAPs 30p.

KINGSBRIDGE

COOKWORTHY MUSEUM OF RURAL LIFE IN SOUTH DEVON
The Old Grammar School, 108 Fore Street, Kingsbridge
A lively local museum with everything from costumes to carts. Complete walk in Victorian kitchen and Edwardian pharmacy, large farm gallery in a walled garden, toys and dolls-house. Programme of craft demonstrations.
Open: Easter to Sept: daily 10-5 (except Sun). Oct: Mon to Fri 10.30-4.
Admission: Fee charged.

MORWELLHAM QUAY

MORWELLHAM QUAY MUSEUM AND 19TH CENTURY PORT AND COPPER MINE
(Morwellham and Tamar Valley Trust)
Morwellham Quay   **Tel:** (0822) 832766; Information only: (0822) 833808
A charming riverside village hidden away in 150 acres of Tamar valley woodland. Founded by Monks 1000 years ago, it grew to become by 1868, 'the greatest copper port in Queen Victoria's empire'. Researched and restored for over 20 years by Morwellham Trust and vividly brought to life. Ride underground into a copper mine and enjoy a heavy horsedrawn wagonette ride along the Duke of Bedford's carriageway. Unspoilt country, riverside and woodland trails, slide shows and other exhibits will help in discovering a thousand years of history.
Open: Daily (except Christmas week) summer: 10-5.30 (last adm 3.30); winter: 10-4.30 (last adm 2.30).
Admission: All inclusive adm charge.
Location: Off A390 between Tavistock and Gunnislake.

NEWTON ABBOT

TUCKERS MALTINGS
Teign Road TQ12 4AA   **Tel:** Malt (0364) 52403 Visitor Attraction (0626) 334734
Preserving our heritage. 'See, touch, smell and taste!' The only traditional working malthouse open to the public in England.
Open: Daily, except Saturdays 10-5 Easter to end October
Guided tours

OKEHAMPTON

MUSEUM OF DARTMOOR LIFE
West Street, Okehampton **Tel:** (0837) 52295

The North Dartmoor Museums Trust

MUSEUM of DARTMOOR LIFE

West Street, Okehampton, Devon
Tel. (0837) 52295

Set in a Regency mill with working waterwheel.
Discover Dartmoor's unique past in galleries
showing its geology, prehistory and social,
industrial and agricultural history.

Temporary exhibitions, research & education facilities. The courtyard features a National
Park Visitor Centre, craft and gift shops and cottage tea rooms.

MUSEUM of WATERPOWER FINCH FOUNDRY

Sticklepath,
Nr. Okehampton, Devon.
Tel. (0837) 840046

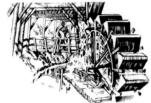

A unique, restored 19th century edge tool
works with primitive machinery powered by
three waterwheels. Museum galleries house
a display of tools and show the development
of waterpower. Also: gift shop, refreshments, picnic area and country walks.

Both museums open: March – Mid November, Mon-Sat. (+ Suns June – Sept.), 10am – 5pm
Both are well signposted from the A30 and have free car parks.

Set in a large Regency mill with a working waterwheel alongside attractive cobbled
courtyard and cottages to the front. Displays cover many aspects of the geology,
archaeology and social, industrial and agricultural history of Dartmoor and its
borderland.
Open: March to mid-Nov, Mon to Sat (+ Suns June to Sept), 10-5.
Admission: £1, OAPs 80p, Chld 60p. Reductions for groups (please book in advance).
Refreshments: Cottage tea rooms.
The courtyard with its unspoilt and friendly atmosphere also offers a National Park
Visitor Centre, Opal Studio, craft & gift shops. Free car park.

PAIGNTON

TORBAY AIRCRAFT MUSEUM
(Mr Keith Fordyce)
Higher Blagdon, Paignton TQ3 3YG **Tel:** (0803) 553540

PLYMOUTH

CITY MUSEUM AND ART GALLERY
(Plymouth City Council)
Drake Circus, Plymouth **Tel:** (0752) 264878
Local and natural history; fine ceramics, silver, old master paintings; lively changing
exhibitions of contemporary art.
Open: Tues to Sat 10-5.30; Bank Holiday Mon 10-5.

ELIZABETHAN HOUSE
(Plymouth City Council)
32 New Street, Plymouth
Authentic furnished Elizabethan merchant's house.
Open: Apr to Oct: Tues to Sat 10-5.30; Bank Holiday Mon 10-5. *Closed* lunchtimes
1-2.
Admission: Small charge

MERCHANT'S HOUSE
(Plymouth City Council)
33 St. Andrew's Street, Plymouth **Tel:** (0752) 264878
Plymouth's rich history packed into a fine 16th century house.
Open: Apr to Oct: Tues to Sat 10-5.30. Bank Holiday Mon 10-5; *Closed* lunchtimes
1-2.
Admission: Small charge.

SALCOMBE

OVERBECKS
(The National Trust)
Sharpitor, Salcombe **Tel:** (054 884) 2893
A museum of local interest of special appeal to children: Salcombe ships and
shipbuilding, a good collection of 19th century local photographs, agricultural bygones
from the South Hams of Devon and a modestly good collection of natural history

subjects. Children's room with dolls and dolls' house furniture. Gulbenkian Award
winners 1991 'Best provision for young children'.
Gardens always open.

SOUTH MOLTON

SOUTH MOLTON MUSEUM
(South Molton Town Council)
Town Hall, South Molton
Local trades, agricultural implements, fire engines, pewter collection.
Open: Mar to Nov: Tues, Thurs, Fri 10.30-1, 2-4; Wed and Sat 10.30-12.30. *Closed*
Sun, Public Hols and Mons.
Admission: Free

STICKLEPATH

MUSEUM OF WATERPOWER
Finch Foundry, Sticklepath, Nr Okehampton **Tel:** (0837) 840046
The highly regarded museum was founded in 1966 around an ingenious, waterpowered
edge tool works which had produced high quality hand tools from 1814 until its closure
in 1960. Three waterwheels can be seen driving the restored machinery which includes
massive trip hammers, shears, air fan and grindstone. There is also a comprehensive
display of tools and an exhibition of waterpower.
Open: Mar to mid-Nov, Mon to Sat (+ Suns June to Sept) 10-5.
Admission: £1.60, OAPs £1.20, Chld 50p (1992 rates), reductions for groups (please
book in advance).
Refreshments: Available, kiosk and a picnic area.
Gift shop. Delightful country walks lead off from the site. Free car park.

TIVERTON

THE TIVERTON MUSEUM
St. Andrew Street, Tiverton **Tel:** (0884) 256295
Award-winning ('Museum of the Year 1977') large local museum. Railway Gallery and
Lace Machine Gallery.

TOPSHAM

TOPSHAM MUSEUM
25 The Strand, Topsham

TORQUAY

TORBAY MUSEUM
Babbacombe Road, Torquay **Tel:** (0803) 293975.
Exciting archaeology gallery featuring important finds from Kents Cavern. Special
summer exhibitions, resources of museum available during visits for National
Curriculum work in History and Science for Primary schools, school room, Information
packs.
Open: Mon to Fri 10-4.45, also Sats Easter to Oct, Sun afternoons in July/Aug. *Closed*
Good Fri and Christmas holidays.
Admission: Fee charged.

TORQUAY MUSEUM
Babbacombe Road, Torquay, Devon **Tel:** (0803) 293975
Exciting archaeology gallery featuring important finds from Kents Cavern. Victorian
Doll's House. Local history. Natural history and geology gallery. Special summer
exhibitions, resources of museum available during visits for National Curriculum work
in History and Science for Primary Schools, school room, information packs.
Open: Mon-Fri 10.00-4.45, also Sats Easter to October. Sun afternoons in July/Aug.
Closed Good Fri and Christmas Holidays.
Admission: Fee charged

TORRE ABBEY
(Torbay Borough Council)
   The Kings Drive, Torquay   **Tel:** (0803) 293593

TORRE ABBEY
TORQUAY

A 12th Century Monastery converted for use as a private residence after the dissolution in 1539 and extensively remodelled by the Cary Family between 1700 and 1750.

Contains furnished period rooms, family chapel and extensive collection of paintings and other works of art. Ruins of medieval Abbey also on show.

Formal gardens contain tropical palmhouse and rose beds.
Tennis, bowls and other recreational facilities in adjoining grounds.

Various exhibitions in Torre Abbey throughout the summer.

ADMISSION – See editorial reference

Purchased by the local authority in 1930 and redesigned to house the town's art collections, including fine paintings, silver, porcelain etc. Agatha Christie Room. Various exhibitions throughout the summer.
Open: Apr to Oct: Daily 10-6.
Admission: Fee charged.
Refreshments: Tearooms in Victorian kitchens.
Extensive grounds and formal gardens.

TOTNES

DEVONSHIRE COLLECTION OF PERIOD COSTUME
   Bogan House, 43 High Street, Totnes
Exhibitions from the Collection, changed annually, on show in historic house.
Open: Spring Bank Hol to Oct 1: Mon to Fri 11-5, Sun 2-5.
Admission: Fee charged.

MOTOR MUSEUM
   Steamer Quay, Totnes TQ9 5AL

TOTNES (ELIZABETHAN) MUSEUM
(Charitable Trust)
   70 Fore Street, Totnes   **Tel:** (0803) 863821.

UFFCOLME

COLDHARBOUR MILL WORKING WOOL MUSEUM
   Uffcolme, Nr Cullompton   **Tel:** (0884) 840960

DORSET

BLANDFORD

BLANDFORD FORUM MUSEUM
   Old Coach House, Bere's Yard, Market Place, Blandford

BOURNEMOUTH

BOURNEMOUTH NATURAL SCIENCE SOCIETY'S MUSEUM
   39 Christchurch Road, Bournemouth   **Tel:** (0202) 553525
History, archaeology, botany, geology, physics, chemistry, zoology, geography, horticulture and astronomy.
Open: By arrangement.

RUSSELL-COTES ART GALLERY AND MUSEUM
(Bournemouth Borough Council)
   East Cliff, Bournemouth

TERRACOTTA WARRIORS
(World Heritage)
   Bournemouth Exhibition Centre, Old Christchurch Lane, Bournemouth
Travel back in time to the Third Century BC and meet the unifier of China and its first emperor - Qin Shi Huang. See the actual size reconstruction of part of the excavations of the terracotta army at Xian.

TRANSPORT MUSEUM
(Bournemouth Borough Council and Bournemouth Passenger Transport Association)
   Mallard Road, Bournemouth   **Tel:** (0202) 551009

BOVINGTON CAMP

THE TANK MUSEUM
(Royal Armoured Corps and Royal Tank Regiment)
   Bovington Camp, Nr Wool   **Tel:** (0929) 403463 or 403329 or 463953 ansafone

One of the world's largest collections of armoured fighting vehicles. Six Exhibition Halls with many new displays and major exhibits. Costume Collection and new 'Past & Presents'.
Open: Daily 10-5. Closed for two weeks over the Christmas and New Year period.
Admission: Fee charged.
Refreshments: Large restaurant, picnic area.
Gift shop in addition to our usual military gift shop. Video theatres, Astro Jet simulator, remote controlled cars. Free parking. Facilities for disabled.

BRIDPORT

BRIDPORT MUSEUM
(West Dorset District Council)
   South Street, Bridport   **Tel:** (0308) 22116

CHRISTCHURCH

CHRISTCHURCH TRICYCLE MUSEUM
   Quay Road, Christchurch
World's first museum devoted to multi-wheeled cycles. Approx. 40 exhibits.

RED HOUSE MUSEUM AND GARDENS
(Hampshire County Council Museums Service)
   Quay Road, Christchurch   **Tel:** (0202) 482860
Museum of the outstanding heritage of the Christchurch area, particularly domestic and social history, natural history, and archaeology. New archaeology gallery opened 1991. Permanent exhibition of fashionable dress and an active programme of temporary exhibitions and events. The house was formerly the local workhouse and is a fine example of mid-Georgian architecture. It is set in a beautiful garden featuring scarce and old-fashioned herbaceous plants and roses and a superb walled herb garden.
Open: Tues to Sat 10-5, Sun 10-5, Sun 2-5. Bank Holiday Mondays.
Admission: Charge in summer.
Parties welcome by appointment. Curator: Ms. A J Carter, BA, MA, AMA.

DORCHESTER

THE DINOSAUR MUSEUM
(World Heritage)
    Icen Way, Dorchester

At Britain's only dinosaur museum four life-size dinosaur reconstructions are begging to be touched by tiny hands and here that is encouraged. Visitors can 'feel' into the past by handling fossils and bones. Computers, audio-visual, and interactive displays help to recreate the prehistoric past. Owen the live iguana lizard makes a truly 'living' museum and fascinating fun for all ages.
Open: 9.30-5.30, seven days a week, all year. *Closed* Dec 24-26.
Admission: Fee charged.

DORSET COUNTY MUSEUM
(Dorset Natural History and Archaeological Society)
    Dorchester   **Tel:** (0305) 262735
A Regional Museum whose collections cover Dorset geology, natural history, prehistory, bygones and history with Thomas Hardy Memorial room. Temporary exhibitions each month.
Open: Mon to Sat 10-5. *Closed* Christmas Day, Boxing Day and Good Friday.
Admission: £2, Chld (5-16 years) and OAP, £1.

DORSET MILITARY MUSEUM
    The Keep, Bridport Road, Dorchester   **Tel:** (0305) 264066
Exhibits of Dorset Regiment, Dorset Militia and Volunteers, Queen's Own Dorset Yeomanry and Devonshire and Dorset Regiment.
Open: Mon to Sat 9-1, 2-5; (Oct to June, *closed* Sat afternoon).
Admission: £1, Chld 50p.
Free car park.

THE TUTANKHAMUN EXHIBITION
(World Heritage)
    High West Street, Dorchester

The only exhibition of its kind on the boy king outside Egypt - Tutankhamun's tomb and treasures are superbly recreated through sight, sound and smell. Be there at the discovery of the tomb, walk through the ante-chamber filled with its fabulous treasures, and enter the burial chamber to witness the raising of the golden coffins. Finally marvel at the exact facsimiles of Tutankhamun's greatest treasures.
Open: 9.30-5.30, seven days a week, all year. *Closed* Dec 24-26.
Admission: Fee charged.

LANGTON MATRAVERS

COACH HOUSE MUSEUM
    Behind Parish Church, Langton Matravers

LYME REGIS

DINOSAURLAND
    Coombe Street, Lyme Regis, Dorset
Fossils, models and live animals. Come and meet Peter Langham featured in Lost Worlds, Vanished Lives and Blue Peter.
Guided Walks. Shop.

THE LYME REGIS MUSEUM
    Bridge Street, Lyme Regis   **Tel:** (0297) 443370
Old prints and documents, fossils and lace; an old Sun fire engine of 1710.

POOLE

THE OLD LIFEBOAT HOUSE
    East Quay, Poole
Poole's 1938 lifeboat *Thomas Kirk Wright*, veteran of Dunkirk. On loan from the National Maritime Museum.
Open: Times fluctuate, Easter to end Sept.
Volunteer staff.

SCAPLEN'S COURT
(Poole Borough Council)
    High Street   **Tel:** (0202) 683138.
One of the finest examples of a 15th century town house to be seen on the south coast. This medieval merchants house provides the setting for a range of displays which cover everday life in Poole throughout the ages.
Open: Mar to Oct, Mon to Sat 10-5; Nov - Feb, Sat and Suns only 2-5. *Closed* Christmas Day, Boxing Day, New Year's Day and Good Friday.
Admission: 75p, Chld 30p. Prices subject to alteration.

WATERFRONT MUSEUM, POOLE QUAY
(Poole Borough Council)
   4 High Street   **Tel:** (0202) 683138.   **Fax:** (0202) 660896.

Listen
to the
Smuggler's
Tale

Victorian
Street
Scene

The
Story
of
Scouting

Admission price now includes
SCAPLEN'S COURT Museum of Domestic Life
Telephone (0202) 683138

Set in the medieval town cellars and 18th century, five floored Oakley's Mill, the museum offers an exciting insight into the history of the town and port. Displays cover underwater archaeology, the trades and crafts of the local people, the history of scouting, and a Victorian street. Modern audio visual techniques are used alongside traditional museum displays.
Open: Mar to Oct, Mon to Sat 10-5; Sun 2-5. Nov to Feb, Sat and Suns only, *Closed* Christmas Day, Boxing Day, New Year's Day and Good Friday.
Admission: £2.95, Chld £1.50, Family ticket £7.25, OAP/Student £2.25. Price includes admission to Scaplen's Court Museum.
Lift, toilet and shop.

PORTLAND

PORTLAND MUSEUM
(Weymouth and Portland Borough Council)
   Wakeham, Portland   **Tel:** (0305) 821804

SHAFTESBURY

LOCAL HISTORY MUSEUM
   Goldhill, Shaftesbury   **Tel:** (0747) 52157
Five galleries illustrating local history, archaeology, industry, farming, shopping and schooling, coin and costume displays and 1744 fire engine.
Open: Easter to end Sept: Mon to Sat 11-5, Sun 2.30-5.
Admission: 60p, Chld 20p.

SHAFTESBURY ABBEY RUINS AND MUSEUM
(Shaftesbury Abbey and Museum Preservation Trust Company Ltd)
   Shaftesbury, Dorset   **Tel:** (0747) 52910
Ruins of 9th century Abbey founded by Alfred the Great set in an attractive and peaceful garden. Museum displays finds from the site.
Open: Easter to Oct, daily 10-5.30.
Admission: 80p, Consessions 50p, Chld 30p.
Location: 100 metres West of Shaftesbury Town Centre. Map G3.

WAREHAM

WAREHAM TOWN MUSEUM
(Wareham Town Council)
   East Street, Wareham   **Tel:** (0929) 553448 or (0929) 552454
Local history. Archaeology. Pictorial collection 'Lawrence of Arabia'.
Open: Easter-mid Oct: daily except Sun 10-1, 2-5.
Admission: Free.
Max 12 persons in parties. Car parking nearby. Suitable for disabled.

WEYMOUTH

DEEP SEA ADVENTURE AND TITANIC STORY
(Mr Brian Cooper)
   Custom House Quay, Weymouth   **Tel:** (0305) 760690

NOTHE FORT
(Weymouth Civic Society and Weymouth and Portland Borough Council)
   Nothe Gardens, Weymouth   **Tel:** (0305) 787243

WEYMOUTH MUSEUM, TIMEWALK & BREWERY MUSEUM
(Devenish and Weymouth and Portland Borough Council)
   Brewer's Quay, Hope Square, Weymouth DT4 8TR   **Tel:** (0305) 777622 **Fax:** (0305) 760715

WIMBORNE MINSTER

PRIEST'S HOUSE MUSEUM
   23-27 High Street (opposite the Minster), Wimborne Minster   **Tel:** (0202) 882533
Award winning museum set in beautiful walled garden. Features a working Victorian kitchen, reconstructed stationers and ironmonger's shops, period rooms and special exhibitions.
Open: April 1 to end-Oct: everyday (not July 28). Nov 1 to Christmas: weekends only plus Christmas exhibition. Mon to Sat 10.30-4.30, Sun 2-4.30.
Refreshments: Tea room.
Gift shop.

COUNTY DURHAM

BARNARD CASTLE

THE BOWES MUSEUM
(Durham County Council)
   Barnard Castle   **Tel:** (0833) 690606
The main collections are representative of European art from the late Medieval period to the 19th century. They comprise paintings, tapestries, furniture, porcelain, glass, jewellery, sculpture and metalwork. Paintings by Italian, Spanish, Flemish, Dutch, French and English artists.
Open: Mon to Sat 10-5.30 (Oct, Mar, Apr 10-5; Nov to Feb 10-4); Sun 2-5 (winter 2-4).
Admission: £1.75, Chld/OAPs 85p (at time of going to press).
Refreshments: Tea room in the building (Apr to Sep).
Free parking. Good facilities for the disabled. Attractive gardens.

BEAMISH

BEAMISH, THE NORTH OF ENGLAND OPEN AIR MUSEUM
   Beamish   **Tel:** (0207) 231811
This open air museum shows how the people of the North of England lived and worked early this century. Buildings from the region have been rebuilt and furnished as they once were and costumed staff demonstrate the way of life. The Town has Co-operative Shops, a Victorian pub with stables, town houses, printers workshop and park. At the Colliery Village visitors can go down a 'drift' mine, see Colliery buildings, visit furnished pit cottages, a school and a chapel. Home Farm with traditional farm house also has animals, poultry and exhibitions. Locomotives can often be seen in steam at Rowley Station, the centrepiece of the Railway area. Also electric tramway and fairground.
Open: Apr to Oct: Daily 10-6. Nov to Mar: Daily (*closed* Mondays), 10-5. Last admission always 4pm.
British Museum of the Year 1986, European Museum of the Year 1987).

BISHOP AUCKLAND

BINCHESTER ROMAN FORT
   Bishop Auckland

DARLINGTON

DARLINGTON ART GALLERY
(Borough of Darlington)
   Crown Street, Darlington   **Tel:** (0325) 462034
Loan exhibitions, local exhibitions.
Open: Mon to Fri 10-8; Sat 10-5.30.

DARLINGTON MUSEUM
(Borough of Darlington)
   Tubwell Row, Darlington   **Tel:** (0325) 463795 (Curator)
Social history of Darlington. Natural history of Teesdale. Historic fishing tackle. Observation beehive during summer months.
Open: Mon to Fri 10-1, 2-6 (except Thur 10-1 only); Sat 10-1, 2-5.30.

DARLINGTON RAILWAY CENTRE AND MUSEUM
(Darlington Borough Council)
North Road Station, Darlington DL3 6ST   **Tel:** (0325) 460532

See Stephenson's 'Locomotion' and many other exhibits on display in the restored North Road Station. ¾ mile north of town centre, on A167. Free car and coach parking. B.R. train service nearby. For further details see editorial entry. Steam locomotive operating days and special events–please enquire.

Tel: Darlington (0325) 460532

A leisure facility provided by Darlington Borough Council

Based on the restored 1842 station of the Stockton & Darlington Railway and associated buildings. Engines and rolling stock from 1825, including 'Locomotion', the first locomotive to run on a public railway. Models, documents, pictures and other exhibits relating to the railways of north-east England.
Open: Daily 9.30-5 (except Christmas/New Year). Last admission 4.30.
Admission: £1.50, OAP £1.10, Chld 75p. Party rates available on application. Pre-booked school groups free.
Most areas suitable for the disabled. Hours and charges subject to revision.

DURHAM

THE CATHEDRAL TREASURY
Durham   **Tel:** 091-384 4854
The relics of St. Cuthbert, Medieval seals, vestments, manuscripts, church plate, the Sanctuary knocker.
Open: Weekdays 10-4.30; Sun 2-4.30.
Admission: £1, Chld (under 14) 20p. Entry free to Friends of Durham Cathedral.

DURHAM HERITAGE CENTRE
(The Bow Trust (Durham) Ltd)
St. Mary-le-Bow, North Bailey, Durham
Medieval church with fine 17/18th century woodwork. Exhibits history, antiquities, architecture, industries of city and county. Audio visual programmes. Brass replica rubbing.
Open: Apr to Sept 2-4.30.
Admission: Fee charged.
Limited Car parking 100 yards. Partly suitable for disabled.

DURHAM LIGHT INFANTRY MUSEUM AND DURHAM ART GALLERY
Durham   **Tel:** 091-384 2214
Museum: uniforms, medals, weapons and illustrations tell the story of the County Regiment's 200 years of history. **Art Gallery:** Changing exhibitions of art and craft.
Open: Weekdays (except Mon) 10-5; Sun 2-5. Open Bank Holiday Mons. *Closed* Christmas Day to New Year's Day.
Admission: 75p, Chld/OAPs 35p. (subject to alteration).
Location: Near Railway Station and County Hall.
Refreshments: Coffee Bar.
Car Park. Suitable for the disabled (including lift and toilet facilities).

DURHAM UNIVERSITY ORIENTAL MUSEUM
Elvet Hill, South Road, Durham   **Tel:** 091-374 2911

OLD FULLING MILL, MUSEUM OF ARCHAEOLOGY
The Banks, Durham   **Tel:** 091-374 3623
Permanent archaeological collections of local and national importance and varied programme of temporary exhibitions.
Open: Daily Apr to Oct 11-4; Nov to Mar 12.30-3.
Admission: Adults 80p, Schoolchildren 20p, OAPs, Students and UB40s 40p.

ESSEX

BILLERICAY

BARLEYLANDS FARM MUSEUM
(H.R. Philpot & Son (Barleylands) Ltd.)
Barleylands Farm, Barleylands Road, Billericay

BURNHAM-ON-CROUCH

THE BURNHAM MUSEUM
Providence, Burnham-on-Crouch

CASTLE HEDINGHAM

COLNE VALLEY RAILWAY
Halstead, Castle Hedingham   **Tel:** (0787) 61174

DURHAM LIGHT INFANTRY MUSEUM AND DURHAM ART GALLERY

Museum
Raised in 1758, disbanded in 1968; the Durham Light Infantry served in almost every major campaign from the West Indies to Borneo.

The Museum, through uniforms, weapons, medals, photographs and other Regimental relics, tells the story of the D.L.I. at war and at peace and also of the Durham Militia and Volunteers.

Exhibits include the 2-pounder anti-tank gun on which Private Adam Wakenshaw won his posthumous V.C. in 1942; a 17-pounder anti-tank gun; and a Bren-Gun Carrier.

Art Gallery
The Art Gallery runs a programme of major temporary exhibtions relating to all aspects of the visual arts.

D.L.I. Museum & Durham Art Gallery
Aykley Heads, Durham City DH1 5TU
Tel. Durham (091) 3842214

Tuesday to Saturday 10–5; Sunday 2–5. Closed Mondays.
except Bank Holidays. Admission charge.
Free Car Park. Sales Desk. Coffee Bar.

Fully accessible to disabled and wheelchair bound visitors (including lift and toilet facilities)

CHELMSFORD

CHELMSFORD AND ESSEX MUSEUM, ESSEX REGIMENT MUSEUM
Oaklands Park, Moulsham Street, Chelmsford CM2 9AQ **Tel:** (0245) 353066 & 260614
The history of Chelmsford, costume, bygones, ceramics, geology, birds, glass, coins and Victorian Room displayed in an Italianate Victorian mansion. Also the history of the Essex Regiment.
Open: Mon to Sat 10.00-5.00pm. Sundays 2.00-5.00pm.
Admission: Free

COLCHESTER

CASTLE MUSEUM
(Colchester Borough Council)
Colchester **Tel:** (0206) 712939

COLCHESTER CASTLE MUSEUM

MAGNIFICENT NEW ROMAN DISPLAYS IN THE LARGEST NORMAN CASTLE KEEP EVER BUILT

COLCHESTER

OPEN: Mon-Sat 10 - 5.00
Sun (Mar-Nov) 2 - 5.00
Tel: (0206) 712931/2
for more details

Colchester Castle is unique. It is the largest Norman Castle keep in Europe, built over the remains of the magnificent Roman Temple of Claudius. Colchester was the first capital of Roman Britain, and the archaeological collections which have been totally re-displayed are among the finest in the country. Many new 'hands-on' exhibits for children.
Open: Mon to Sat, 10-5; Sun (Mar to Nov) 2-5. Tours of vaults and prisons.
Admission: £1.50, Chld/OAPs/Students 75p. Tours of vaults and prisons; £1, Chld 50p. Prices subject to alteration. Pre-booked groups at reduced rates.

COLCHESTER MUSEUMS
(Colchester Borough Council)
Museum Resource Centre, 14 Ryegate Road, Colchester CO1 1YG **Tel:** (0206) 712931/2
Colchester Borough Council's Museum Service administers five museums, see *(Colchester Borough Council)*.
All enquiries and correspondence should be sent to the Curator and Head of Museum Services at the Museum Resource Centre, address above.

HOLLYTREES MUSEUM
(Colchester Borough Council)
High Street, Colchester **Tel:** (0206) 712940
Two centuries of fascinating toys, costume and decorative arts displayed in an attractive Georgian town house of 1718.
Open: Mon to Sat 10-5.
Admission: Free.

NATURAL HISTORY MUSEUM
(Colchester Borough Council)
All Saints Church, High Street, Colchester **Tel:** (0206) 712941
Recently updated interactive displays of the distinctive natural history of N.E. Essex, including impressive dioramas, housed in the former All Saints Church.
Open: Mon to Sat 10-5.
Admission: Free.

SOCIAL HISTORY MUSEUM
(Colchester Borough Council)
Holy Trinity Church, Trinity Street, Colchester **Tel:** (0206) 712942
Town and country life in the Colchester area over the last two hundred years displayed in the fourteenth century former church of Holy Trinity.
Open: Mon to Sat 10-5
Admission: Free.

TYMPERLEY'S CLOCK MUSEUM
(Colchester Borough Council)
Trinity Street, Colchester **Tel:** (0206) 712943
A fine collection of Colchester clocks displayed in Tymperley's, a restored sixteenth century house.
Open: Apr to Oct only. Mon to Sat 10-5.
Admission: Free.

DEDHAM

THE SIR ALFRED MUNNINGS ART MUSEUM
(Castle House Trust)
Castle House, Dedham **Tel:** (0206) 322127

EAST TILBURY

COALHOUSE FORT
East Tilbury **Tel:** (03752) 4203

GRAYS

THURROCK MUSEUM
(Thurrock Council)
Thameside Complex, Orsett Road, Grays **Tel:** (0375) 390000

THURROCK MUSEUM GRAYS
TEL: (0375) 390000 Ext. 2414

Local History and Archaeology.

Social, Agricultural and Industrial History.

Topographical Pictures and the work of local artists.

Now incorporates the maritime collections of the former Riverside Museum.

ADMISSION FREE

A LOCAL SERVICE PROVIDED BY THURROCK COUNCIL

'The Old High Street Grays'
An etching by Christopher Shiner in the Thurrock Museum Collection.

Over 50 cases of exhibits demonstrating Thurrock's rich archaeological, social and industrial history.
Open: Mon to Sat 9-8. *(Closed* Bank holidays).

HARLOW MUSEUM

HARLOW, ESSEX

Passmores House. Georgian Wing built 1727.

MARK HALL CYCLE MUSEUM & GARDENS

Courtyard with 52″ penny-farthing.

HARLOW

HARLOW MUSEUM
(Harlow District Council)
Passmores House, Third Avenue, Harlow   **Tel:** (0279) 446422
A Tudor and Georgian farmhouse set in pleasant landscaped grounds. Local archaeology and history collections including Roman and Post-Medieval, Folk Life and Farming plus Geology and Natural History.
Open: Sun to Thurs 10-5; *closed* 12.30-1.30 on Sun; *closed* Fri and Sat.
Admission: Free.
Ground floor only suitable for the disabled.

MARK HALL CYCLE MUSEUM AND GARDENS
(Harlow District Council)
Muskham Road, off First Avenue, Harlow   **Tel:** (0279) 439680
A converted 19th century stable block housing a fine collection of bicycles from the 1818 Hobby Horse to the 1982 Plastic Itera incorporating the Collins Collection. The large accessory collection includes lamps of all types, tools, saddles, pumps and a wide range of components.
Open: Sun to Thurs *closed* 1-2; *closed* Fri and Sat
Admission: Free.
The grounds include three walled period gardens. Suitable for the disabled.

HARWICH

HARWICH REDOUBT
(The Harwich Society)
Main Road, Harwich

Courtesy ECC

180ft diameter circular fort built 1808 to defend port against Napoleonic invasion. Now being restored by Harwich Society, and part is museum. Eleven guns on battlements.
Open: Daily 2-5 in July and Aug; Suns 10-12, 2-5 all year. Parties at any time by prior arrangement (with 52 Church St).
Admission: £1. Family accompanied chld free. No unaccompanied chld. Schools 50p per person.
Refreshments: Light drinks available.
Car parking in Harbour Crescent. Shop. Curator: A. Rutter.

PORT OF HARWICH MARITIME MUSEUM
(The Harwich Society)
Harwich Green, Harwich
Housed in a disused lighthouse on the edge of Harwich Green with specialised displays on RNLI, RN and commercial shipping.
Open: Sun 10-12, 2-5, Easter to Oct. Parties at any time by prior arrangement (to 52 Church St).
Admission: 50p. Accompanied chld free; no unaccompanied chld.
Car parking in Harbour Crescent. Curator: P. Gates.

SAFFRON WALDEN

SAFFRON WALDEN MUSEUM
Museum Street (near Church), Saffron Walden   **Tel:** (0799) 522494
Collections of archaeology, local history, ceramics, glass, costume, furniture, dolls and toys, ethnography and ancient Egyptian room. Castle ruins in grounds.
Open: Apr to Oct: Mon to Sat 10-5. Sun and Bank Holidays 2.30-5. Nov to Mar: Tues to Sat 11-4, Sun 2.30-4.30.
Admission: £1, Discounts 50p. Chld (under 18) free.

SOUTHEND-ON-SEA

BEECROFT ART GALLERY
(Borough of Southend-on-Sea)
Station Road, Westcliff-on-Sea, Southend-on-Sea   **Tel:** (0702) 347418
Contains the Municipal, Thorpe Smith and Beecroft Collections. Picture loan scheme. Exhibitions changed monthly.
Open: Mon to Sat 9.30-5. *Closed* Sun.

CENTRAL MUSEUM: SOUTHEND MUSEUM SERVICE
(Borough of Southend-on-Sea)
Victoria Avenue, Southend-on-Sea   **Tel:** (0702) 330214

SOUTHEND-ON-SEA MUSEUMS

PRITTLEWELL PRIORY MUSEUM
BEECROFT ART GALLERY, Westcliff-on-Sea
SOUTHCHURCH HALL MUSEUM
SOUTHEND CENTRAL MUSEUM & PLANETARIUM

Telephone: 0702 330214

Administrative headquarters. The human and natural history of south-east Essex. The only Planetarium in south-east England, outside London. Temporary exhibitions throughout the year.
Open: Mon 1-5, Tues to Sat 10-5. *Closed* Sun. Planetarium Wed to Sat only.

PRITTLEWELL PRIORY MUSEUM
(Borough of Southend-on-Sea)
Priory Park, Southend-on-Sea   **Tel:** (0702) 342878
Originally a Cluniac Monastery, now a museum of local history and natural history with a large collection of radios, televisions, gramophones and printing equipment.
Open: Tues to Sat 10-1, 2-5. *Closed* Sun and Mon.
Parties in the mornings by arrangement, guide-lecturer available.

SOUTHCHURCH HALL
(Borough of Southend-on-Sea)
Southchurch Hall Close, Southend-on-Sea   **Tel:** (0702) 467671
Moated timber-framed manor house, early 14th century, with small Tudor wing, the open hall furnished as a Medieval hall; with exhibition room.
Open: Tues to Sat 10-1, 2-5. *Closed* Sun and Mon.
Parties in the mornings by arrangement, guide-lecturer available.

UPMINSTER

UPMINSTER TITHE BARN AGRICULTURAL AND FOLK MUSEUM
(London Borough of Havering and Hornchurch & District Historical Society)
Hill Lane, Upminster   **Tel:** (0708) 744297
Collections of agricultural implements, craft and farm tools, local bricks and domestic bygones, displayed in 15th century timber and thatched barn.
Open: First full weekend of each month Apr to Oct, 2-6.

WALTHAM ABBEY

EPPING FOREST DISTRICT MUSEUM
39/41 Sun Street, Waltham Abbey EN9 1EL

EPPING FOREST DISTRICT MUSEUM
WALTHAM ABBEY

Local history Museum

Temporary exhibition programme.

Collection of contemporary work by Essex artists.

Shop – souvenirs, booklets, replicas etc.

Herb garden

Refreshments

SEE EDITORIAL ENTRIES FOR FURTHER DETAILS.

Epping Forest District Museum opened November, 1981.

The Museum is situated in two timber framed houses dating from c1520 -c1760. Permanent displays illustrate the social history of the Epping Forest District from the Stone Age to the 20th century, including magnificent oak panelling carved for the Abbot of Waltham during the reign of Henry VIII and a spectacular display of 19th century life featuring a recreation of Victorian shops. There are also changing temporary exhibitions ranging from historical subjects to contemporary arts and crafts, often complemented by workshops, demonstrations, lectures and other events. Outreach and educational programmes include oral history sessions, holiday activities for children, living history workshops and much more.
Open: Fri, Sat, Sun, Mon, 2-5. Tues 12-5. Wed & Thurs closed (except for party bookings). Open all Bank Holidays except Christmas Day, Boxing Day and New Year's Day.
Admission: Free.
School parties are welcome. Museum shop sells local history publications, souvenirs and gifts.

GLOUCESTERSHIRE

CHELTENHAM

CHEDWORTH ROMAN VILLA
(The National Trust)
Yanworth GL54 3LJ   **Tel:** (0242) 890256
Remains of a large Romano-British villa: excavations have revealed underfloor heating, fine mosaics, and a water shrine. Museum and introductory video.

Gloucestershire

CHELTENHAM ART GALLERY AND MUSEUM
(Cheltenham Borough Council)
Clarence Street, Cheltenham   **Tel:** (0242) 237431

Cheltenham Art Gallery and Museums
A wealth of interest for everyone

Art Gallery & Museum
Clarence Street

Holst Birthplace Museum
4 Clarence Road

Pittville Pump Room Museum
Pittville Park

For further information Telephone: (0242) 237431

Foremost Arts and Crafts collection inspired by William Morris. The story of Edward Wilson, a famous son of Cheltenham, and his explorations with Scott of the Antarctic. Collection of rare Oriental porcelain and English ceramics. Social history of Cheltenham, Britain's most complete Regency town. Archaeological treasures of the Cotswolds. Special exhibitions throughout the year.
Open: Mon to Sat 10-5.20, Sun (June, July & Aug) 2-5.20. *Closed* Bank Hols.
Admission: Free.
Refreshments: Cafe.
Museum shop. Access for disabled people.

HOLST BIRTHPLACE MUSEUM
(Trustees: administered by Cheltenham Borough Council)
4 Clarence Road, Pittville   **Tel:** (0242) 524846.
The World of Gustav Holst, composer of *The Planets*. The story of the man and his music; his original piano and manuscripts. Hear his music on compact disc. A Regency terrace house showing the 'upstairs-downstairs' way of life in Victorian and Edwardian times, including working kitchen, elegant drawing room, and children's nursery.
Open: Tues to Sat 10-4.20. *Closed* Sun, Mon and Bank Hols.
Admission: Free.
Guided tours, by prior arrangement.

PITTVILLE PUMP ROOM MUSEUM
(Cheltenham Borough Council)
Pittville Park, Cheltenham   **Tel:** (0242) 512740
Housed in the magnificent Pump Room, overlooking its own beautiful lake and gardens. Imaginative use of original costumes, bringing to life the history of Cheltenham, from its Regency heyday to the Swinging Sixties. Jewellery showing changing taste and fashion from Regency to Art Nouveau including a spectacular collection of tiaras.
Open: Spring Holiday Sunday-end Sept; Tues-Sat 10.00-4.20; Sun 11.00-4.20; Spring & Summer Bank Holiday Mondays 11.00-4.20.
Admission: Fee charged.
Guided tours, by prior arrangement. Free car park.

CINDERFORD

DEAN HERITAGE CENTRE
Soudley, Royal Forest of Dean, Cinderford GL14 7UG   **Tel:** (0594) 822170
Regional Museum for Forest of Dean with industrial, social and natural history displays plus nature trails, craft workshops.
Open: Daily Apr to Oct 10-6, Nov to Mar 10-5, (*closed* Christmas Day and Boxing Day).
Admission: Fee charged.
Refreshments: Cafe, pjcnic/barbeque area.
Shop, adventure playground, art and craft events. Suitable for disabled.

CIRENCESTER

CIRENCESTER LOCK-UP
(Cotswold District Council)
Trinity Road, Cirencester   **Tel:** (0285) 655611
Newly-restored two-cell town lock-up dating from 1805 and incorporating interpretative displays on lock-up and workhouse history plus exhibition of architectural conservation in the Cotswolds. Details from Corinium Museum.

Open: Daily by arrangement.
Admission: Free.

CORINIUM MUSEUM
(Cotswold District Council)
Park Street, Cirencester   **Tel:** (0285) 655611
A regional museum for Cirencester and the Cotswolds displaying one of the finest collections of antiquities from Roman Britain from the site of Corinium (modern Cirencester). Full-scale reconstructions of kitchen, dining room and mosaic craftsman's workshop bring Corinium to life. New gallery of Cotswold prehistory. Special exhibitions programme of local history and archaeology.
Open: Throughout the year: Apr to Oct: Daily 10-5.30, Sun 2-5.30; Nov to Mar: Tues to Sat 10-5, Sun 2-5. Open all Bank Hols, *closed* Christmas.
Admission: Adults £1, Chld 50p, OAPs/Students/Party groups 75p.
Award winning displays; in the Good Museums Guide 'Top Twenty'.

FILKINS

SWINFORD MUSEUM
Filkins, nr Lechlade   **Tel:** (0367) 860376
Local domestic bygones, rural trade tools etc.

GLOUCESTER

CITY EAST GATE
(Gloucester City Council)
Eastgate Street, Gloucester
Roman and medieval gate towers and moat in an underground exhibition chamber.
Open: May to Sept: Sat 10-12, 2.15-5
Admission: 40p, Chld/OAP 10p.

CITY MUSEUM AND ART GALLERY
(Gloucester City Council)
Brunswick Road, Gloucester   **Tel:** (0452) 524131
The Marling bequest of 18th century walnut furniture, barometers and domestic silver. Paintings by Richard Wilson, Gainsborough, Turner etc. supplemented by art exhibitions throughout the year. Local archaeology including mosaics and sculptures; natural history including a freshwater aquarium.
Open: Mon to Sat 10-5. Open Bank Holidays.
Admission: Free.

FOLK MUSEUM
(Gloucester City Council)
99-103 Westgate Street, Gloucester   **Tel:** (0452) 526467
A group of half-timbered houses, Tudor and Jacobean, furnished to illustrate local history, domestic life and rural crafts. Civil War armour, Victorian toys. Severn fishing traps, wooden ploughs etc. Reconstructed Double Gloucester dairy, ironmongers, carpenter's and wheelwright's shop. Pin factory with 18th century forge.
Open: Mon to Sat 10-5. Open Bank Holidays.
Admission: Free.

NATIONAL WATERWAYS MUSEUM
Llanthony Warehouse, The Docks, Gloucester   **Tel:** (0452) 307009 or 25524
An enthralling collection portraying the history of Britain's canals and inland waterways in the beautiful setting of Gloucester's remarkable inland docks. The Museum itself is centred on the magnificent Victorian Llanthony Warehouse where three floors of innovative displays and fascinating exhibits bring to life the long history of our canals. Voted Best Museum of Industrial or Social History - National Heritage Museum of the Year Awards 1991.
Open: Daily, except Christmas Day. Access to all.

NATURE IN ART
(The International Centre for Wildlife Art)
Wallsworth Hall, Gloucester   **Tel:** (0452) 731422
A unique collection of fine wildlife art from all parts of the world, and all historical periods, including porcelain, mosaic, furniture, etc. Displayed in a Georgian building c.1750, with interesting features. Constantly changing exhibits.
Open: Tues to Sun 10-5, Bank holiday Mon 10-5. *Closed* Mon and Dec 24, 25, 26.
Admission: £2.50, Chld/OAPs £1.75, Family £7.50.
Refreshments: Licensed coffee shop and restaurant.
Winner of a Special Commendation in the National Heritage Museum of the Year Awards. Parties welcome by arrangement. Free parking. Suitable for disabled people. Artist in residence from Feb-Oct, and art course programme. Art shop, play area, outdoor sculptures.

REGIMENTS OF GLOUCESTERSHIRE MUSEUM
Custom House, The Docks, Gloucester GL1 2HE   **Tel:** (0452) 522682
The story of the Glosters and the Royal Gloucestershire Hussars. Life-size displays with sound effects show how soldiers lived in a First World War trench, in the North African desert and in the jungle of Burma during World War II. Fascinating photographs from the last 100 years. Archive film of the Korean War.
Open: Tues to Sun and Bank Hol Mons 10-5.
Admission: Fee charged.
Shop. Facilities for disabled visitors. Voted the Museum achieving the most with the least - National Heritage Museum of the Year Awards 1991.

Cotswold Museums
bringing history alive

– the Museums Service of
Cotswold District Council –
"Caring for the Cotswolds"

CORINIUM MUSEUM

Roman Britain comes alive

One of the finest collections of antiquities
from Roman Britain ...
Full-scale reconstructions of a Roman
dining room, kitchen and mosaic
craftsman's workshop recreate life
in Corinium, Roman Cirencester.
Permanent displays of Cotswold
archaeology and local history
and special exhibitions.

Open daily throughout the year except
winter Mondays; open all Bank Holidays –
closed Christmas.

In Park Street, CIRENCESTER.
☎ (0285) 655611

COTSWOLD COUNTRYSIDE COLLECTION

A Museum of Rural Life

Award-winning displays of Cotswold rural
life and farming history, displayed in the
former House of Correction at Northleach.
Preserved cells and court room offer plenty
of atmosphere! 'Below Stairs' gallery or
laundry, dairy and kitchen.
Special exhibitions each season.
Open daily April to October incl.
10.00 to 5.30 and Sundays 2.00 to 5.30
including Bank Holidays.
Plus bookshop, tourist information,
refreshments and free parking.
On the Fosseway at NORTHLEACH.
☎ (0451) 860715

GLOUCESTER MUSEUMS AND ART GALLERY

*Left:
puppets at the
City Museum*

*Right:
wheelwright's
shop at the
Folk Museum*

The City Museum collections cover the archaeology and natural history of the city and county of Gloucester. On the first floor is the art gallery (temporary exhibitions throughout the year) and collections of English furniture, pottery, silver, glass and costume.
The Branch Museum at the Folk Museum contains collections illustrating the post-medieval history of Gloucester and the trades, crafts and industries of the surrounding countryside.

NATURE IN ART
THE INTERNATIONAL CENTRE FOR WILDLIFE ART

Only a few minutes from exit 11 M5 on A38

AN IMPORTANT AND UNIQUE COLLECTION OF THE FINEST WILDLIFE ART IN ANY MEDIA FROM ALL PARTS OF THE WORLD AND ALL PERIODS

Artists in residence. Garden. Outdoor Sculptures.
Licensed Coffee Shop. Art Shop.

Open – Tuesday to Sunday 10am–5pm
Bank Holiday Mondays 10–5
Closed – other Mondays & Dec. 24, 25, 26

Admission charges: £2.50. Children & OAP's £1.75.
Reduced rates for parties. Disabled visitors welcome.

**WALLSWORTH HALL, TWIGWORTH,
GLOUCESTER GL2 9PA**
Telephone: Gloucester (0452) 731422

WINNER OF SPECIAL COMMENDATION IN THE NATIONAL HERITAGE MUSEUM OF THE YEAR AWARDS

Gloucestershire

TRANSPORT MUSEUM
(Gloucester City Council)
Bearland, Gloucester
Horse-drawn vehicles visible from the road at all times.

NEWENT

THE ROBERT OPIE COLLECTION, MUSEUM OF ADVERTISING AND PACKAGING
Albert Warehouse, Gloucester Docks, Newent GL1 2EH   **Tel:** (0452) 302309
A nostalgic journey back through the memories of one's childhood, brought vividly to life by this unique collection of packaging and advertising material.

THE SHAMBLES MUSEUM
16-20 Church Street, Newent   **Tel:** (0531) 822144
A complete Victorian town of shops, cobbled streets, gas lamps and alley ways, rural and town trades and crafts, approached through a fully furnished four storey house.
Open: Mid-Mar to Dec: Tues to Sun and Bank Holiday Mon 10-6.
Admission: Fee charged.
Refreshments: Available (seasonal).
Parties by arrangement. Gift shops.

NORTHLEACH

COTSWOLD COUNTRYSIDE COLLECTION
(Cotswold District Council)
Fosseway, Northleach   **Tel:** (0451) 860715
Opened in 1981 this museum of rural life displays the Lloyd-Baker Collection of agricultural history including wagons, horse-drawn implements and tools, exhibited in a 'seasons of the year' display. A Cotswold gallery records the social history of the area. New 'Below Stairs' exhibition of laundry, dairy and kitchen. The museum's home is a House of Correction and its history is displayed in a restored cell-block and court-room. Audio and visual sequences.
Open: Daily Apr to Oct inc: 10-5.30 and Sun 2-5.30.
Admission: Adults £1, Chld 50p, OAPs/Students/Party rate 75p.
Location: Easy access from A429 Fosse Way.
Refreshments: Available weekends.
Award-winning displays: Civic Trust 1982, Museum of the Year Award commendations 1983 and 1985, Come to Britain Trophy certificate of distinction 1984. No additional charge for events programme. Free car parking. Tourist information.

STROUD

STROUD DISTRICT (COWLE) MUSEUM
(Stroud District Council)
Lansdown, Stroud   **Tel:** (0453) 763394
Also in Lansdown hall. Collections cover geology, archaeology, crafts and industries, farming and household equipment, ceramics, dolls etc. Records of local houses and mills.
Open: Weekdays 10.30-1, 2-5.

TEWKESBURY

THE JOHN MOORE COUNTRYSIDE MUSEUM
41 Church Street, Tewkesbury
Countryside collections and natural history. Also The Little Museum, restored Medieval merchant's cottage.

THE MUSEUM
Barton Street, Tewkesbury
In an old half-timbered building, items concerning the history of the town. Small heritage centre display. Model of Battle of Tewkesbury.
Open: Apr to Oct: Daily 10-1, 2-5. Also open during winter months.
Admission: Small fee charged.

WINCHCOMBE

HAILES ABBEY MUSEUM
(English Heritage)
Hailes Abbey   **Tel:** (0242) 602398
Medieval sculpture and other architectural fragments found in the ruins of the Abbey. Fine collections of 13th century roof bosses, one depicting Samson and the Lion (selected for the Age of Chivalry exhibition). Also medieval floor tiles, manuscripts, pottery and iron work. Exhibition and site information illustrates the history of the Abbey, and recent excavations.
Open: Apr 1 to Sept 30 daily 10-6. 1 October-31 March, Tues-Sun 10am-4pm. *Closed* 24-26 Dec and 1 January.
Admission: £1.60, Concessions £1.20, Chld 80p (1992 prices).

WINCHCOMBE FOLK AND POLICE MUSEUM
Old Town Hall, Winchcombe   **Tel:** (0242) 602925
A comprehensive display of artefacts illustrating the history of Winchcombe, together with a collection of British and international police uniforms.
Open: Apr 1 to end Oct: Mon to Sat 10-5.

Admission: 50p, Chld/OAP/Students 30p (1992 rates).
Parties - maximum 12. Parking nearby. Not suitable for people in wheelchairs.

WINCHCOMBE RAILWAY MUSEUM
(T.R Petchey)
23 Gloucester Street, Winchcombe
A collection of items of British Railway interest, from tickets and labels to horse-drawn railway road vehicles.

GREATER MANCHESTER

ASHTON-UNDER-LYNE

THE MUSEUM OF THE MANCHESTERS: A SOCIAL AND REGIMENTAL HISTORY
(Tameside Metropolitan Borough)
Ashton Town Hall, The Market Place, Ashton-under-Lyne   **Tel:** 061-344 3078
The history of the Manchester Regiment, displayed with the social history of the community in which it was based.
Open: Mon-Sat 10-4. *Closed* Sun and Bank Hols.
Admission: Free.
Full access and facilities for disabled.

PORTLAND BASIN INDUSTRIAL HERITAGE CENTRE
(Tameside Metropolitan Borough)
Portland Place, Portland Street South, Ashton-under-Lyne   **Tel:** 061-308 3374
200 years of Tameside's social and industrial history displayed in a former canal warehouse with a waterwheel on the wharf.
Open: Oct to Mar: Tues to Sat 10-4, Sun 12-4. Apr to Sept: Tues to Sat 10-6, Sun 12-6. *Closed* Mon (but open Bank Holiday Mon).
Admission: Free.
Full access and facilities for disabled.

BOLTON

BOLTON MUSEUM AND ART GALLERY
(Bolton Metropolitan Borough Council)
Le Mans Crescent, Bolton   **Tel:** (0204) 22311, Ext. 2191
Collections of archaeology, local and industrial history, natural history, geology and Egyptology. Art gallery containing collection of 18th century watercolours; sculpture, ceramics; temporary exhibitions gallery.
Open: Mon, Tues, Thurs and Fri 9.30 - 5.30; Sat 10-5. *Closed* Wed, Sun and Bank Hols.

HALL I'TH' WOOD MUSEUM
Green Way, off Crompton Way, Bolton   **Tel:** (0204) 301159
Open: Apr to Sept: Tues to Sat 11-5; Sun 2-5. *Closed* Mons except Bank Hols 11-5. Oct to Mar (inclusive). *Closed* to the general public.
Admission: £1.55, concessions 75p.
Location: Bus 546 from Town Centre.
Open to pre-booked educational parties and evening party tours.

MUSEUM OF LOCAL HISTORY
Little Bolton Town Hall, St. George's Street, Bolton   **Tel:** (0204) 22311, Ext. 2192
The museum displays various aspects of the social history of the region.
Open: Wed to Sat 12-4. *Closed* Sun, Mon, Tues and Bank Holidays.

SMITHILLS HALL MUSEUM
off Smithills Dean Road, Bolton   **Tel:** (0204) 841265
Open: As for Hall i'th' Wood Museum.
Admission: As for Hall i'th' Wood Museum.
Location: Bus 526 from Town Centre.

TONGE MOOR TEXTILE MUSEUM
The Library, Tonge Moor Road, Bolton   **Tel:** (0204) 21394/22311, Ext. 2195
Houses a collection of important early textile machines including Crompton's Mule, Hagreaves' Jenny and Arkwright's Water Frame.
Open: Mon and Thurs 9.30-7.30; Tues and Fri 9.30-5.30; Sat 9.30-12.30. *Closed* Wed, Sun and Bank Hols.

LEIGH

TURNPIKE GALLERY
(Wigan Metro.Borough)
Leigh   **Tel:** (0942) 604131
Contemporary art works, changing exhibition programme including major touring exhibitions.
Open: Mon to Fri 10-5.30 (Wed 10-5), Sat 10-3.

HALL I'TH' WOOD MUSEUM
Greenway, off Crompton Way, Bolton

Dating from the latter half of the 15th century and furnished throughout in the appropriate period. The Hall itself, built in the post and plaster styles, dates from 1483, a further extension was added in 1591 in the form of a north west wing, the last addition being made in 1648 during the Civil War. Home of Samuel Crompton in 1779 when he invented the Spinning Mule. House contains Crompton relics.

SMITHILLS HALL MUSEUM
off Smithills Dean Road, Bolton

One of the oldest manor houses in Lancashire, a house has stood on this site since the 14th century. The oldest part of Smithills, the Great Hall, has an open timber roof. Smithills has grown piece by piece over the centuries and such irregularly planned buildings, with the cluster of gables at the west end, gives the hall its present day picturesque effect. Furnished in the styles of the 16th and 17th centuries. Withdrawing room contains linenfold panelling. Grounds contain a nature trail and trailside museum which is open to the public between Easter and October.

Autumn Leaves
Sir John Everett Millais

Manchester City Art Galleries

Mosley Street and Princess Street

Monday–Saturday 10.00–5.45
Sunday 2.00–5.45

Admission Free

Tel: 061-236 5244

MANCHESTER

CITY ART GALLERIES
Mosley Street and Princess Street, Manchester   **Tel:** 061-236 5244
The City Art Galleries on Mosley Street were designed by Charles Barry in an imposing neo-classical style. It houses one of the greatest collections of paintings and decorative arts in the North. The outstanding group of Pre-Raphaelite paintings are in one of a series of galleries displaying 19th century art in lavishly decorated and furnished settings typical of the period. There are also good collections of 17th-18th century art by British and continental artists including Stubbs, Claude, Lorrain, Bellotto. The decorative arts are shown throughout the galleries but an exciting new development is A New Look at Decorative Art, a challenging display from the permanent collections exploring the theme of taste. Fine art and decorative art exhibitions take place in the City Art Galleries on Molsey Street but the adjacent City Art Galleries on Princess Street is the principal venue for an ambitious programme of temporary exhibitions.
Open: Mon to Sat 10-5.45; Sun 2-5.45.
Admission: Free
Refreshments: Cafe Gallery
Gallery Shop

GALLERY OF ENGLISH COSTUME
(Manchester City Art Galleries)
Platt Hall, Rusholme, Manchester   **Tel:** 061-224 5217
One of the finest costume collections in the country. Displays include clothes and fashions from 16th century embroidered garments to present day designs by Zandra

Rhodes and Caroline Charles. Changing programmes of special displays. The costume library and study collection is open to students on request.
Open: Open daily except Tues 10.00-5.45; Sun 2.00-5.45. Note from 1 Nov - 28 Feb the Gallery closed at 4.00 and weekend opening Apr-Aug is subject to change: telephone to check current opening.
Admission: Free

GREATER MANCHESTER POLICE MUSEUM
(Greater Manchester Police)
Newton Street, Manchester   **Tel:** 061-856 3287
Set in a Victorian Police Station, the Police Museum features a reconstructed Charge Office of the 1920's, the station cells and in three other rooms collections of uniforms, equipment, forgery exhibits and photographic displays.
Open: By appointment only, throughout the year. *Closed* weekends, Public and Bank Hols.
Admission: All visits free of charge.
Parties - no minimum number, but a maximum size of 20 persons only per visit. Curator: Mr Duncan Broady. Assistant: Mrs Christine Watkins.

HEATON HALL
(Manchester City Art Galleries)
Heaton Park, Prestwich, Manchester   **Tel:** 061-236 5244
'The finest house of its period in Lancashire and one of the finest in the country' (Pevsner). Designed for the Earl of Wilton by James Wyatt in 1772, the house has

superbly restored, painted and gilded interiors with fine furniture, plasterwork and paintings. Special featues include the music room with a famous 18th century organ by Samuel Green and a unique 'Pompeian' style cupola room with decorations by Biagio Rebecca. Set in 650 acres of parkland with panoramic views, the Heaton Gallery shows temporary exhibitions.
Open: Easter to September, please telephone for details of opening times.
Admission: Free

MANCHESTER JEWISH MUSEUM
(Trustees of Manchester Jewish Museum)
190 Cheetham Hill Road, Manchester M8 8LW   **Tel:** 061-834 9879 or 832 7353
The museum is in a former Spanish and Portuguese synagogue built in 1874. Downstairs the synagogue has been restored to its original condition whilst upstairs, in the former ladies gallery, there is an exhibition on the history of Manchester's Jewish community over the last two hundred years.
Open: Mon to Thurs 10.30-4; Sun 10.30-5. *Closed* Fri, Sat and Jewish holidays.
Admission: £1, concessions 50p, family ticket £3. No charge for teachers with school parties or on preliminary visits.
Temporary exhibition area and programme of trails, talks and concerts. Car parking on street nearby. Suitable for disabled persons on ground floor only. All parties **must** be booked in advance with the Administrator.

MANCHESTER MUSEUM
The University, Oxford Road, Manchester M13 9PL **Tel:** 061-275 2634
Important collections of geology, botany, zoology, entomology, archaeology, Egyptology, ethnology, numismatics, the Simon Archery Collection and the Cannon Aquarium and Vivarium; museum education service and frequent temporary exhibitions.

Open: Mon to Sat 10-5. *Closed* a few days at Christmas and on Good Friday and May Bank Holiday.
Museum shop. Frequent bus services from Albert Square and Piccadilly stopping near the front entrance of the Museum. Car parking. **Museum of the Year 1987.**

THE MUSEUM OF SCIENCE AND INDUSTRY IN MANCHESTER
Liverpool Road, Castlefield, Manchester   **Tel:** 061-832 2244
Museum of the Year 1990. Opened in 1983 and based on the site of the oldest passenger railway station in the world. Recent developments include the 'Out of this World' space gallery, the 'Energy for the Future' exhibition and the National Gas Gallery. Other permanent exhibitions include Xperiment! the interactive science centre, the Air and Space Gallery, 'Underground Manchester' and the 'Making of Manchester'. Temporary exhibitions and special events programme.
Open: Daily 10-5. Last admission 4.30. *Closed* Dec 23-25.
Refreshments: Available.
Museum shop.

MUSEUM OF TRANSPORT
Boyle Street, Cheetham, Manchester   **Tel:** 061-205 2122
A working museum, specialising in preserved buses with a collection of over 60 large vehicles.
Open: Wed, Sat, Sun and Bank Holidays (except Christmas) 10-5.
Admission: £1.25, Chld/OAPs 75p, Family ticket £3.00
Location: Situated behind Queen's Road bus garage; near junction of A6010/A665, 3m S of M62, junction 17, and 1m N of city centre.
Parties by arrangement. Vintage bus services, special events, annual rally in September. Education Talks service. Visits, disabled persons weekend. Contact 061-205 2122.

THE
MANCHESTER MUSEUM
The University, Oxford Road M13 9PL.

Museum of the Year 1987. Superb collections of Botany (living plant display), Geology (Stratigraphical Hall with fossil Ichthyosaur), Entomology and Zoology (Cannon Aquarium and observation beehive). New Mammal Gallery including human evolution and interactive displays. Prize winning Ancient Egyptian Galleries. Large Ethnographic collections; Simon Archery collection and Numismatics. New Mediterranean archaeology gallery opening for 1993.

Museum education service and frequent temporary exhibitions. Museum shop.

Monday to Saturday 10—5. Closed a few days at Christmas and on Good Friday and May Day Bank Holiday.

For further information telephone: 061 275 2634. Admission free.

A Peruvian textile circa A.D. 600-900.

WHITWORTH ART GALLERY
(University of Manchester)
Oxford Road, Manchester   **Tel:** 061-273 4865; information line 061-273 5958

The Whitworth Art Gallery

University of Manchester, Oxford Road
(opposite the Royal Infirmary), Manchester
Open : Mon-Sat 10am-5pm, Thurs 10am-9pm

Admission free

Exhibitions
Displays
British watercolours
Prints
Textiles
Wallpapers
Contemporary art
Bistro
Shop

Information line : 061-273 5958

Portion of a wallpaper frieze, early 20th century

Outstanding collections of British watercolours; historic and modern prints; textiles, ranging from Coptic weaves to contemporary fabrics; wallpapers; contemporary art and sculpture. Major exhibitions.
Open: Mon to Sat 10-5, Thurs 10-9. *Closed* Sun and Christmas to New Year, also Good Friday.
Admission: Free.
Location: Buses 40-47, 143, 157, 191, P11, B5, B6.
Award winning Bistro, and Shop. Car parking. Disabled access.

WYTHENSHAWE HALL
(Manchester City Art Galleries)
Wythenshawe Park, Northenden, Manchester   **Tel:** 061-236 5244
A black and white half-timbered country house dating partly from Tudor times, with panelled interiors, Tudor wall paintings, a recently restored early 19th century library, collections of paintings and oak and walnut furniture. Temporary exhibition programme. Set in beautiful gardens with an aviary, kitchen garden and horticultural centre.
Open: Easter to September, please telephone for details & opening times.
Admission: Free

OLD TRAFFORD

MANCHESTER UNITED MUSEUM AND TOUR CENTRE
Old Trafford M16 0RA   **Tel:** 061-877 4002

MANCHESTER UNITED FOOTBALL CLUB

Covers the history on Manchester United in words, pictures, sound and vision.
More than 300 exhibits on display.
See editorial reference for further details

The first purpose built Museum in British Football. Over 300 exhibits including shirts, trophies, pennants, caps and programmes. Special exhibitions.
Open: Tues to Sun 9.30 to 4.00
Admission: Charge with concessions for children, senior citizens and families.
Refreshments: Coffee shop.
The Museum includes a trophy room, video show, souvenirs are available. Free car parking, ground tours available.

OLDHAM

ART GALLERY
(Oldham Leisure Services)
Union Street, Oldham   **Tel:** 061-678 4651
Frequently changed exhibitions of contemporary art and photography. Also Oldham collections comprising early English watercolours, British 19th and 20th century paintings, modern prints, English ceramics and glass, plus small Oriental collection.
Open: Mon, Wed, Thurs and Fri 10-5; Tues 10-1; Sat 10-4; *Closed* Sun.

Oldham Art Galleries and Museums

Oldham Art Gallery – contemporary art, photography and historical thematic exhibitions. Also arts-related events and activities and a community loan exhibition service.

Museum: The Green Room.

Husband and Wife by Howard Hodgkin.

Bellizona–The Bridge over the Ticino c. 1843 by J.M.W. Turner.

The Local Interest Museum – Going up Town – Shopping in Oldham – a major exhibition on the history and development of Oldham town centre. Includes videos, activity guide, worksheets.
Also natural history displays in The Green Room. New Education Service Phone 633 2392

SALFORD MUSEUMS AND ART GALLERIES

Endless Chain Haulage, 'Buile Hill No. 1 Drift Mine' – Salford Mining Museum

SALFORD MUSEUM AND ART GALLERY: Chief features: L. S. Lowry collection of paintings and drawings; temporary art exhibitions; 'Lark Hill Place', a 19th century 'street' of shops and period rooms; Gallery of Victorian Art.

SALFORD MINING MUSEUM: History and technology of Coalmining; reproduction of underground mine and drift mine.

ORDSALL HALL MUSEUM: Manor House with fine 16th century spere truss in Great Hall; collections of furniture, kitchen equipment and local history items.

VIEWPOINT PHOTOGRAPHIC GALLERY (City of Salford) The Old Fire Station, Crescent, Salford (just across the road from the Museum and Art Gallery). The Gallery shows a wide range of exhibitions including major national and international shows in addition to thematic exhibitions which use archival material and the work of regionally based photographers.

Bramham Hall: Victorian Kitchen

Stockport Museum: Air Raid Shelter Tours

Stockport Art Gallery: Art & craft items for purchase or hire from 'Artlink'.

STOCKPORT MUSEUMS AND ART GALLERY SERVICE

LOCAL INTEREST MUSEUM
(Oldham Leisure Services)
  Greaves Street, Oldham   **Tel:** 061-678 4657
Two floors devoted to changing exhibitions of local interest.
Open: Mon, Wed, Thurs and Fri 10-5; Tues 10-1; Sat 10-4. *Closed* Sun.
Local studies library and tourist information point in adjacent building.

SADDLEWORTH MUSEUM & ART GALLERY
  High Street, Uppermill, Oldham   **Tel:** (0457) 874093 or 870336
The history of a unique Pennine Parish. Textile machinery, vintage vehicles. Victorian rooms. Art Gallery.
Open: Daily.
Shop. Parties welcome.

ROCHDALE

ROCHDALE ART GALLERY
  Esplanade, Rochdale

ROCHDALE MUSEUM
Rochdale Metro.Borough)
  Sparrow Hill, Rochdale

ROCHDALE PIONEERS CO-OPERATIVE MUSEUM
  Toad Lane, Rochdale
Houses the original store of the Rochdale Co-operative Pioneers containing documents, pictures and other material of British and international co-operative interest.

SALFORD

MUSEUM AND ART GALLERY
(City of Salford)
  Peel Park, The Crescent, Salford   **Tel:** 061-736 2649
The main museum exhibit is that of a period street typical of a northern industrial town at the time of the turn of the century. The Art Gallery permanently displays a comprehensive collection of the works of L.S. Lowry and holds frequently exhibitions by artists of this region. A Gallery of Victorian Art has recently been opened.
Open: Mon to Fri 10-4.45; Sun 2-5.

ORDSALL HALL MUSEUM
(City of Salford)
Taylorson Street, Salford   **Tel:** 061-872 0251
This largely 15th to 17th century building has been restored for use as a museum and apart from its architectural interest it contains period rooms and local history displays.
Open: Mon to Fri 10-12.30, 1.30-5; Sun 2-5.

SALFORD MINING MUSEUM
(City of Salford)
Buile Hill Park, Eccles Old Road, Salford   **Tel:** 061-736 1832
The museum is devoted to the history and technology of coal-mining and reproductions of an underground mine and a drift mine illustrate this theme.
Open: Mon to Fri 10-12.30, 1-5; Sun 2-5.
Organised school parties on pre-arranged visits are welcome.

VIEWPOINT PHOTOGRAPHIC GALLERY
(City of Salford)
The Old Fire Station, Crescent, Salford
The Gallery shows a wide range of exhibitions including major national and international shows in addition to thematic exhibitions which use archival material and the work of regionally based photographers.
Open: Tues to Fri 10-5, Sun 2-5. *Closed* Mon and Sat.
Location: Opposite Museum & Art Gallery.

STALYBRIDGE

THE ASTLEY CHEETHAM ART GALLERY
(Tameside Metropolitan Borough)
Trinity Street, Stalybridge   **Tel:** 061-338 2708/3831
The Cheetham Collection of paintings; 14th century Italian gold ground paintings to Burne-Jones. Monthly exhibition programme covering fine art, craft and photography.
Open: Mon, Tues, Wed and Fri 1-7.30; Sat 9-4. *Closed* Sun and Thur.
Admission: Free.

STOCKPORT

LYME HALL AND PARK
(Metropolitan Borough of Stockport)
Disley, Stockport   **Tel:** (0663) 62023
Fine house dating from the 16th century, remodelled in early 18th century in Palladian style.
Open: Hall: Easter to Sept: Tues to Sun 2-4.30. *Closed* Mon and Oct to Easter except for special Christmas opening. Park open all year 8 to dusk.
Admission: To Park and Gardens: per car and occupants £12.50 (second car £5); To Hall: £1.95, Chld/OAPs £1, Party (max 5 people) £4.95 (Subject to revision.) NT members free.
Location: 7m from town centre.
Extensive gardens and 1,320 acre park. Maintained by Stockport Metropolitan Borough Council on behalf of the National Trust.

STOCKPORT ART GALLERY
War Memorial Building, Wellington Road South, Stockport   **Tel:** 061-474 4453
Changing exhibitions of contemporary art, photography and craft with emphasis on complementary events - practical workshops for children and adults, lectures etc. 'Artlink' scheme for purchasing or borrowing contemporary works of art including paintings, sculpture, photographs and craft work. Small permanent collection of 19th and 20th century British paintings.
Open: Mon to Fri 11-5 (Wed 11-7); Sat 10-5. *Closed* Sun.

STOCKPORT MUSEUM
Vernon Park, Turncroft Lane, Stockport   **Tel:** 061-474 4460
Displays on the history of Stockport from Pre-historic times to the present, and the 'Green Gallery' - a display on the local environment.
Open: Apr to Oct: Daily 1-5. Nov to Mar: Sat and Sun only 1-5. Open Bank Holiday Mons.
Schools and organised parties all year, by appointment. Tours of Stockport's unique system of underground World War II air raid shelters by arrangement. Telephone for details.

STOCKPORT MUSEUMS AND ART GALLERY SERVICE
BRAMALL HALL
(Metropolitan Borough of Stockport)
Bramhall, Stockport   **Tel:** 061-485 3708
Fine 14th to 16th century half-timbered Hall originally the home of the Davenport family.
Open: Apr to Sept: Daily 1-5; Oct to Mar: 1-4, *closed* Mon and all of Jan (except New Years Day). *Closed* Dec 25 & 26.
Admission: £2.50, Chld/OAP £1.50, Group ticket (2 adults/2 children) £7. (subject to revision).
Location: 4m from town centre.
Schools and organised parties all year, by appointment.

WIGAN

WIGAN PIER
(Wigan Metropolitan Borough Council)
Wigan Pier, Wigan WN3 4EU
Step back in time and live the life of 1900. Experience the actors bringing the history to life. Shop in the market, work down the mine, drink in the pub, go to school, journey to Blackpool - all without leaving Wigan! At Trencherfield Mill marvel at what is probably the largest working mill steam engine in the world. See the working mill, colliery and ropemaking machinery.
Open: All year except Christmas Day and Boxing Day 10-5.
Admission: Generous group discounts.
Refreshments: Cafe, pub, restaurant.
Other attractions include gift shop, concert, conference and exhibition hall, waterbuses. Full education service. Free parking. Suitable for disabled persons. Phone for further information. Piermaster - Chris Abram.

HAMPSHIRE

ALTON

THE CURTIS MUSEUM AND ALLEN GALLERY
(Hampshire County Council Museums Service)
High Street, Alton   **Tel:** (0420) 82802
The Curtis Museum contains the new 'Story of Alton' display and includes a fascinating collection of children's toys, dolls and games. The Allen Gallery displays a comprehensive collection of English pottery, paintings from the W.H. Allen bequest, and an exciting programme of temporary exhibitions.
Open: Tues-Sat, 10-5. *Closed* Sun and Mon.
Admission: Free.
There is also a garden for visitors to enjoy. Parties welcome. Curator: T. Cross.

ANDOVER

THE ANDOVER MUSEUM AND MUSEUM OF THE IRON AGE
(Hampshire County Council Museums Service)
Church Close   **Tel:** (0264) 366283
Extensive new local history displays opened in 1992. Natural History Gallery, fresh water aquaria and geology room. Temporary exhibitions changed monthly. Also, Museum of the Iron Age, a major exhibition of the nationally important excavations at Danebury Hillfort.
Open: Tues to Sat 10-5; Museum of the Iron Age also Apr to Sept: Sun 2-5.
Admission: Andover Museum Free, Museum of The Iron Age small charge.
Parties welcome; pre-booked schools free. Curator: D.W.H. Allen, Bsc.,FSA.

BASINGSTOKE

WILLIS MUSEUM
(Hampshire County Council Museums Service)
Old Town Hall, Market Place, Basingstoke   **Tel:** (0256) 465902
The museum occupies one of Basingstoke's finest buildings, once the Town Hall. There are magnificent displays of clocks, watches, embroideries and toys dating from the 16th to the 20th century. The Basingstoke Story illustrates the history of the area from 2,500 BC to the present day. Natural history and geology displays can be found on the ground floor, together with the exhibition gallery and Tourist Information Centre.
Open: Tues to Fri 10-5, Sat 10-4, Mon (Tourist Information Centre only) 9.30-5. *Closed* Sun.
Admission: Free.
Curator: T. Evans.

BEAULIEU

BEAULIEU ABBEY & EXHIBITION OF MONASTIC LIFE
Beaulieu
Voted Best Museum Educational Initiative - National Heritage Museum of the Year Awards.

MARITIME MUSEUM
Buckler's Hard, Beaulieu   **Tel:** (0590) 616203
Collection of models and exhibits of ships built at Buckler's Hard for Nelson's Fleet. Also the 18th century homes of a master shipbuilder. Shipwright and labourer and an Inn Scene have been re-created in the village in the original cottages. This is open to the public as part of the Buckler's Hard restoration programme.
Open: Daily: Easter to May, 10-6; June to Sept, 10-9; Oct to Easter, 10-4.30.
Admission: Fee charged.
Location: 87 miles from London.

NATIONAL MOTOR MUSEUM

Beaulieu   **Tel:** (0590) 612345

One of the finest and most comprehensive Museums in the world, the National Motor Museum has grown from the Montagu Motor Museum, founded by Lord Montagu in memory of his father, a motoring pioneer. Many special displays and over 250 historic vehicles present the story of motoring from 1894 right up to modern times, with record breaking cars, commercial vehicles, motorcycles and bicycles. 'Wheels' a major feature in the Museum, takes visitors on a ride in space-age 'pods' from 1895 to way beyond the year 2000, past moving displays showing how motoring has developed in Britain over the last 100 years and how it might be in the future.

Open: Daily: 10-6 (10-5 in winter).

Admission: Fee charged.

Location: 85 miles from London.

Refreshments: Licensed restaurant.

BURSLEDON

BURSLEDON WINDMILL
(Hampshire County Council Museums Service)

Windmill Lane, Bursledon   **Tel:** (0703) 643026 (Eastleigh Museum)

Early 19th century brick tower mill restored to full working order by Hampshire buildings Preservation Trust.

Open: May to Sept: Fri & Sat 10-4; Oct to Apr: Wed & Thurs 10-4.

Admission: Small fee charged.

Parties welcome by arrangement. Curator: G.G.S. Bowie, BA MA PhD.

CHAWTON

JANE AUSTEN'S HOUSE
(Jane Austen Memorial Trust)

Chawton   **Tel:** (0420) 83262

JANE AUSTEN'S HOUSE

CHAWTON ALTON HAMPSHIRE

Seventeenth-century house where Jane Austen wrote or revised her six great novels. Contains many items associated with her and her family, documents and letters, first editions of the novels, pictures, portraits and furniture. Pleasant garden, suitable for picnics. Bakehouse, with brick bread oven and washtub, houses Jane's donkey carriage. Bookshop, Refreshments available in village. See editorial for details

Jane Austen's home containing many personal relics of herself and her family.

Open: Daily 11-4.30 (incl. Sun and Bank Hols). *Closed* Mon and Tues Nov, Dec, Mar and Christmas and Boxing Days. Jan and Feb open Sat and Sun only.

Admission: Fee charged.

Location: Road A31, 1 mile S.W. of Alton, signpost 'Chawton'.

EASTLEIGH

EASTLEIGH MUSEUM
(Hampshire County Council Museums Service)

High Street, Eastleigh   **Tel:** (0703) 643026

Displays reflecting the history, life and culture of the Eastleigh area from the arrival of the railway in about 1840. Video presentations including archive film. Temporary exhibitions changed regularly.

Open: Tues to Fri 10-5; Sat 10-4. Parties welcome by arrangement.

Admission: Free.

Museum shop selling local gifts and publications. Fully accessible to disabled. Curator: G.G.S. Bowie, BA, MA,PhD.

FAREHAM

FORT NELSON

Portsdown Hill, Fareham PO17 6AN   **Tel:** (0329) 233734

The Royal Armouries museum of artillery, housed in an 1860's Palmerston Fort overlooking Portsmouth Harbour, displays the nation's collection of artillery through the ages, including Tudor cannon, Victorian field guns, a firing Armstrong gun and sections of the Iraq 'Supergun'.

Open: Easter to Oct 31: 12-4.30, weekends and Bank Holidays only. Firing dates 10 Apr, 9 May, 20 June, 18 July, 15 Aug, 19 Sept, 31 Oct.

Admission: £2, Chld/OAP £1,with a supplementary charge on firing and special theme days.

Group reductions on application. Guided tours only. Education service available by appointment. Curator: N. Hall.

WESTBURY MANOR MUSEUM
(Hampshire County Council Museums Service)

West Street, Fareham   **Tel:** (0329) 824895

Museum displays on all aspects of natural and local history in the Fareham area in fully restored 18th century town house. Completed in 1990.

Open: All year except Christmas. Mon to Fri 10-5, Sat 10-4.

Admission: Free.

Location: From M27 take exit off for A32 Gosport and Fareham Town Centre. 3rd exit from roundabout into Hartlands Road and marked 'Fareham Town Centre'. Turn left at 'T' junction into West Street.

Parking in Hartlands Road. Please telephone for party booking details. Access for people in wheelchairs limited to ground floor only. Curator: A. Penfold.

FORDINGBRIDGE

ROCKBOURNE ROMAN VILLA
(Hampshire County Council Museums Service)

Rockbourne, near Fordingbridge   **Tel:** (072 53) 541

Site Museum displaying finds from the Roman Villa, totally refurbished in 1988. Foundations with mosaics, open to view.

Open: Early Apr to early Oct: Mon to Fri 2-6; Sat, Sun and Bank Hols 10.30-6. July & Aug daily: 10.30-6.

Admission: Small charge.

Parties by arrangement. Curator: D.W.H. Allen, BSc., FSA.

GOSPORT

GOSPORT MUSEUM
(Hampshire County Council Museums Service)

Walpole Road, Gosport   **Tel:** (0705) 588035

An interesting an unusual Art Nouveau building (1901). Completely re-displayed in 1992. Tells the story of the Borough of Gosport, high-lighting the aspects which make it unique. Regular temporary exhibitions.

Open: Tues to Sat 10-5. Suns (May-Sept only) 1-5. *Closed* Mon.

Admission: Free.

Curator: Ian Edelman.

HAVANT

THE HAVANT MUSEUM
(Hampshire County Council Museums Service)

East Street, Havant   **Tel:** (0705) 451155

Five rooms of recently completed local history displays; a major collection of sporting firearms from wheel-locks to automatics, the Vokes Collection; and a new Temporary Exhibition Gallery showing a wide range of art, photography and other exhibitions.

Open: Tues to Sat 10-5. *Closed* Sun and Mon.

Admission: Free.

Parties by arrangement welcome. Curator: C Palmer, BSc,PhD.

LYNDHURST

NEW FOREST MUSEUM AND VISITOR CENTRE

High Street   **Tel:** (0703) 283914

Audio-visual show and museum displays telling the story of the New Forest, its history, traditions, characters and wildlife. Includes life-sized models, computer data banks, children's quizzes and the New Forest Embroidery.

Open: 10am daily throughout the year.

Admission: On application. Special reductions.

Parties welcome. Free car parking. Suitable for disabled visitors.

THE NATIONAL MOTOR MUSEUM AT BEAULIEU

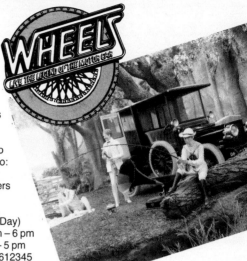

The National Motor Museum featuring over 250 historic vehicles tells the exciting story of Britain's motoring heritage.

The collection is complemented by 'Wheels' an automated ride through the history of motoring, where visitors are transported through a series of displays depicting motoring from 1895 to fantasies of the future.

'Wheels' is included in the admission to the Museum which also covers entry to: Palace House; Beaulieu Abbey and Monastic Life Exhibition plus vouchers for additional Rides and Drives

OPEN DAILY (Except Christmas Day)
EASTER to SEPTEMBER 10 am – 6 pm
OCTOBER to EASTER 10 am – 5 pm
Tel: (0590) 612123 (24 hrs) or 612345

MIDDLE WALLOP

MUSEUM OF ARMY FLYING
Stockbridge, Middle Wallop ' **Tel:** (0264) 384421

Middle Wallop,
Stockbridge, Hants.
Tel: Andover (0264) 384421

On the A343 between Andover and Salisbury. The story of Army Flying from the 19th Century to the present day; Balloons, Kites and Airships, World War I and II Aircraft, unique collection of Military Gliders and Experimental Helicopters. More recent campaigns

also represented including The Falklands and the Gulf. All brought vividly to life by means of photographs, displays and dioramas. New audio stereo guide available.

Includes a licensed 1st floor restaurant and coffee shop overlooking active military airfield – conference facilities and cinema.

Open throughout the year– except Christmas and New Year period 10am-4.30pm. (Last admission 4pm).

Reasonable prices, reductions for OAPs, students and children.

Groups and Schools welcomed.

Admission: Adults £3.50, OAP £2.50, Chld/Student £2. (1992 prices). Group reductions on application.
Refreshments: Licensed restaurant and coffee shop.
Free cinema, full disabled facilities.

PETERSFIELD

FLORA TWORT GALLERY AND RESTAURANT
(Hampshire County Council Museums Service)
Church Path, Petersfield **Tel:** (0730) 260756
The Flora Twort Gallery commemorates the life and work of the artist Flora Twort (1893-1985) in the refurbished cottage which was her home and studio.
Open: Tues to Sat 9.30-5.
Admission: Free.
Managers: Richard and Gaye Bartlett, Curator: T. Cross.

JOHN SPARROW BEAR MUSEUM
38 Dragon Street, Petersfield GU31 4JJ **Tel:** (0730) 265108
Britain's first bear museum houses an internationally renowned collection of teddy's and other bears in charming settings. Alongside the bears are displayed antique dolls in an Edwardian nursery scene. A miniature teddy bears house and a life size teddy bears picnic are among the attractions. The museum shop stocks exclusive hand made teddy bears.
Open: Mon-Sat inc. 10.00-5.00
Admission: Free

PORTSMOUTH

CITY MUSEUM
(Portsmouth City Council)
Museum Road, Old Portsmouth PO1 2LJ **Tel:** (0705) 827261
Permanent displays on the history of Portsmouth. These include domestic life in Portsmouth and a local picture gallery. Also gallery of decorative art, contemporary craft and temporary exhibitions.
Open: Daily 10.30-5.30. *Closed* Christmas Eve, Christmas Day and Boxing Day.

D-DAY MUSEUM AND OVERLORD EMBROIDERY
(Portsmouth City Council)
Clarence Esplanade **Tel:** (0705) 827261
The museum incorporates the Overlord Embroidery, the modern counterpart of the Bayeux Tapestry, depicting the allied invasion of Normandy on June 6 1944. It consists of 34 panels measuring a total of 272ft. in length. The displays then bring the D-Day action to life with realistic sound and visual effects and some of the vehicles, including a Sherman tank and a DUKW, which took part.
Open: Daily 10-5.30. *Closed* Christmas Eve, Christmas Day and Boxing Day.

CHARLES DICKENS' BIRTHPLACE MUSEUM
(Portsmouth City Council)
393 Old Commercial Road, Portsmouth **Tel:** (0705) 827261
A house of 1805 in which the famous novelist was born and lived for a short time, now restored and furnished to illustrate the middle class taste of the early 19th century. Small display of items pertaining to his work.
Open: Daily 10.30-5.30. *Closed* Nov 1 to Feb 29.
Please telephone for details of the special Birthday Event on Feb 7, 1993 to mark the anniversary of Dickens' birth.

HMS VICTORY
HM Naval Base, Portsmouth **Tel:** (0705) 819604 (Group visits: 839766)
Centrepiece of the Naval Heritage Area at Portsmouth is HMS *Victory*, flagship of Vice Admiral Lord Nelson at the Battle of Trafalgar. His cabin, the 'cockpit' where he died and the sombre gundecks where his men lived and fought can all be visited in a memorable and moving history tour. Visitors can also see the painstaking and highly skilled work, currently being carried out to restore the splendid old ship to her Trafalgar condition. But the *Victory* is more than just a preserved warship. She is the flagship of the Commander in Chief, Naval Home Command and is manned by officers and ratings of the Royal Navy, so each visit has a unique naval flavour.
Open: Daily 10-5, but during July and Aug, late opening until 7. Telephone (0705) 839766.
Admission: Entry price includes access to the Royal Naval Museum.
All tours of the ship are guided.

HMS WARRIOR 1860
(Warrior Preservation Trust)
HM Naval Base, Portsmouth **Tel:** (0705) 291379. Group visits: (0705) 839766
During her heyday in the 1860s *HMS Warrior* was the pride of Queen Victoria's Navy, one of the most influential warships in the world. The last survivor of the once 45-strong Black Battlefleet, she takes her place in history as the world's first iron-hulled, armoured battleship. Now beautifully and accurately restored, she is back in Portsmouth for everyone to see and enjoy. There are four vast decks available for visitors to explore,

all filled with restored Victorian naval artefacts and the personal possessions of the crew. The restoration recaptures one day in the 1860s when the ship was first commissioned. The officers' table is set for formal dinner; whilst on the mess deck pewter plates and bowls are laid out for the seamen; in case of French attack the cannon are awaiting action; the Colt 45's and rifles are ready to load. The domestic life of the 700-strong crew is also displayed, from the washroom complete with mangles; to the hammocks in which you slept and were buried. It is a living exhibition where visitors can sit at the mess tables, touch the cannon, wander down to the Engine Room, see the prison cells - and even examine a cat-o-nine tails at close quarters.
Open: Every day except Christmas Day. Mar to Oct 10.00-5.30; but during July and Aug late opening until 7; Nov to Feb 10.00-5.00.
Admission: Fee charged.

MARY ROSE SHIP HALL AND EXHIBITION
(Mary Rose Trust)
   H.M. Naval Base, College Road PO1 3LX   **Tel:** (0705) 750521 (Group visits: 839766)
In October 1982, thousands watched as Henry VIII's favourite warship, *Mary Rose*, was recovered from the Solent seabed, where she had lain for 437 years. The ship workshop in No.3 Dry Dock is open to visitors while work continues to restore and preserve the hull. Nearby, an exhibition features a reconstruction of a section of the gun deck and many of the important objects recovered during the excavations. Clothing, weapons, medical equipment are used to illustrate sixteenth Century social and military history, and an audio visual presentation helps the visitor relive the exciting years of underwater exploration and salvage.
Open: Daily 10-5.30; but during July and Aug, late opening until 6.45; winter 10.30-5. *Closed* Christmas Day.
Admission: Fee charged.
Refreshments: Available in the Naval Base, Victory Buffet, hot and cold snacks and drinks. Seats 125.
Gift shop adjacent to exhibition features exciting range of souvenir items. No car parking in Naval Base. Historic Ships car park nearby. Suitable for disabled persons. *Wheelchairs are available. *NB. In the Ship Hall, access for wheelchairs is limited to a single gallery.

NATURAL SCIENCE MUSEUM AND BUTTERFLY HOUSE
(Portsmouth City Council)
   Eastern Parade, Portsmouth   **Tel:** (0705) 827261
Geology and natural history of the Portsmouth area including a full-size reconstruction of the dinosaur Iguanodon, fresh water aquaria and displays of local woodland, chalk downland and marshland, also a Butterfly House where British butterflies can be seen in free flight.
Open: Daily 10.30-5.30. *Closed* Christmas Eve, Christmas Day and Boxing Day.

ROYAL MARINES MUSEUM
   Southsea (entry via sea front entrance), Portsmouth   **Tel:** (0705) 819385
Considered one of the finest military museums in Britain. It is located in spacious grounds adjacent to Southsea beach and outdoor exhibits include a Whirlwind helicopter and Falklands Landing Craft into which visitors can walk. The museum tells the story of the Royal Marines from 1664 to the present day in a lively and fascinating way. Popular exhibitions include dynamic Falklands audio visual and a chilled Arctic display. A new early history gallery featuring a talking head of Hannah Snell, the first female Marine and live maggots. Plus one of the greatest medal collections in the country.
Open: Daily Whitsun to Aug 10-5.30; Sept to May 10-4.30.
Admission: Fee charged.
Refreshments: Light only.
Free car parking and seafront entrance. Well stocked shop offers a wide range of quality goods for all ages. Junior Commando assault course.

THE ROYAL NAVAL MUSEUM, PORTSMOUTH
   H.M. Naval Base, Portsmouth   **Tel:** (0705) 733060 (Group visits: 839766)
YOU'VE SEEN THE SHIPS, NOW MEET THE MEN. Alongside *HMS Victory*, the *Mary Rose* and *HMS Warrior 1860* stands the Royal Naval Museum, the only museum in Britain devoted to the overall history of the Royal Navy. Here the ghosts of past seamen are brought vividly to life in a series of exciting, modern displays that tell the story of our Senior Service from earliest times right up to the present day. Exhibits include figureheads, ship models, uniforms, medals, relics of personnel and ships, paintings and prints, and commemorative silverware and pottery. Pride of place is given to the possessions of ordinary officers and seamen and the displays concentrate on the social history of the Royal Navy.
Open: Sept to June 30th - 10.30-17.30; July and Aug - 10.30-19.00.
Admission: Fee charged.
Within the Museum complex there is a buffet and a well-stocked souvenir and book shop.

SOUTHSEA CASTLE AND MUSEUM
(Portsmouth City Council)
   Clarence Esplanade, Portsmouth   **Tel:** (0705) 827261
Fort built in 1545 by King Henry VIII as part of his national coastal defences. Contains displays illustrating Portsmouth's development as a military fortress, aspects of naval history and local archaeology.
Open: Daily 10.30-5.30 Mar-Oct 10.00-4.30 *Closed* Christmas Eve, Christmas Day and Boxing Day.

ROMSEY

THE MOUNTBATTEN EXHIBITION
(Lord Romsey)
   Broadlands, Romsey

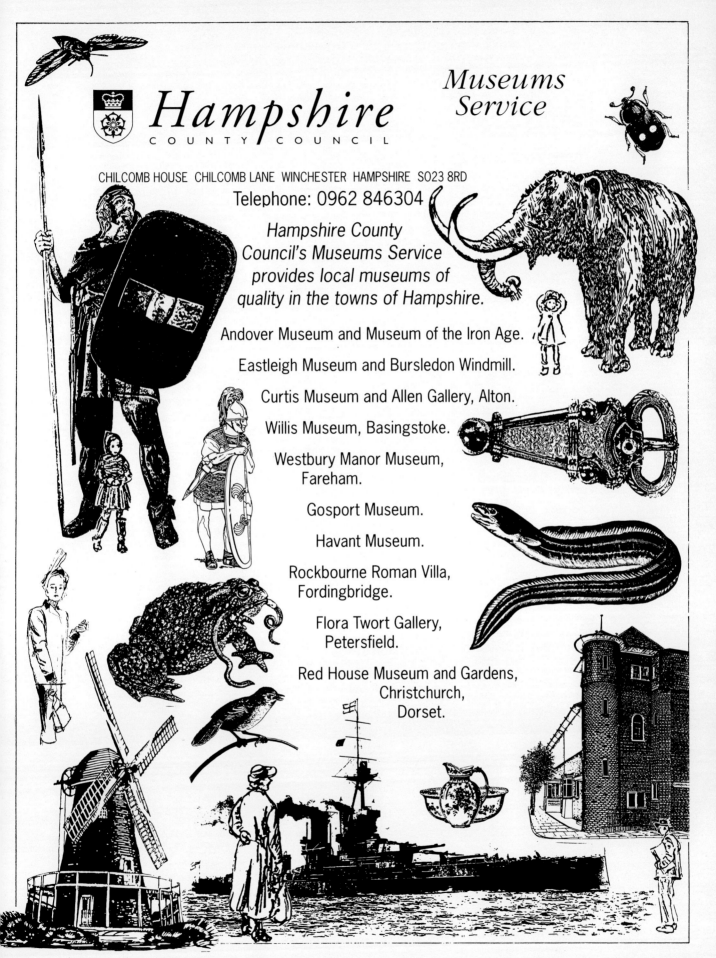

Hampshire
COUNTY COUNCIL

Museums Service

CHILCOMB HOUSE CHILCOMB LANE WINCHESTER HAMPSHIRE SO23 8RD

Telephone: 0962 846304

Hampshire County Council's Museums Service provides local museums of quality in the towns of Hampshire.

Andover Museum and Museum of the Iron Age.

Eastleigh Museum and Bursledon Windmill.

Curtis Museum and Allen Gallery, Alton.

Willis Museum, Basingstoke.

Westbury Manor Museum, Fareham.

Gosport Museum.

Havant Museum.

Rockbourne Roman Villa, Fordingbridge.

Flora Twort Gallery, Petersfield.

Red House Museum and Gardens, Christchurch, Dorset.

Hampshire

SELBORNE

GILBERT WHITE'S HOUSE & GARDEN AND THE OATES EXHIBITIONS
The Wakes, Selborne, Alton **Tel:** (042 050) 275

SELBORNE
ALTON, HAMPSHIRE.

GILBERT WHITE'S HOUSE & GARDEN
Home of Rev. Gilbert White,
author of 'The Natural History of Selborne'
★ Historic house with furnished rooms ★
★ Glorious 5 acre garden ★
★ Oates Exhibitions ★
★ Come and enjoy a day out in Selborne ★

Historic home and glorious tranquil garden of the 18th century naturalist and ecologist. The Rev. Gilbert White, author of 'The Natural History of Selborne'. Furnished rooms and displays on White and Selborne. Events to commemorate the bicentenary of his death. Also exhibitions on Captain Lawrence Oates of the Scott Antarctic expedition and Frank Oates, Victorian explorer and naturalist.
Open: 11-5.30 (last adm 5) Tues to Sun & Bank Hols from 13th March to 31st Oct. Saturday & Sunday from 6th Nov to 2nd Jan. (Not 25th & 26th Dec)
Admission: £2 adults, £1.50 OAPs and Students, £1 Children (first child free). Free admission to shop.
Refreshments: In village, picnic area.
Parties by arrangement.

SILCHESTER

CALLEVA MUSEUM
c/o Cherry Tree Cottage, Silchester Common, Silchester **Tel:** (0734) 700450
Completely redesigned in 1976. Providing a pictorial graphical display of life in Roman Silchester.
Open: Daily 10-dusk.
Admission: Voluntary donations.

SOUTHAMPTON

MARITIME MUSEUM
(Southampton City Council)
Wool House, Bugle Street, Southampton **Tel:** (0703) 223941
Fourteenth century wool store now a museum of shipping.

MUSEUM OF ARCHAEOLOGY
(Southampton City Council)
Town Quay, Southampton **Tel:** (0703) 220007
Early 15th century fortification now a museum of local archaeology.

SOUTHAMPTON CITY ART GALLERY
(City Council)
Civic Centre, Southampton **Tel:** (0703) 223855
Specialising in British painting, particularly 20th century; a good collection of Old Master paintings and Impressionist and Post-Impressionist works.

TUDOR HOUSE MUSEUM
(Southampton City Council)
St. Michael's Square, Southampton **Tel:** (0703) 332513
Tudor mansion, built in the 16th century, containing exhibitions of Victorian and Edwardian life with a reconstructed sixteenth century garden.

WINCHESTER

GUILDHALL GALLERY
(Winchester City Council)
Broadway, Winchester **Tel:** (0962) 52874
Programme of changing exhibitions.
Open: Tues to Sat 10-5; Mon and Sun 2-5 (summer). *Closed* Mon in winter.
Admission: Free.

THE WESTGATE MUSEUM
(Winchester City Council)
High Street, Winchester **Tel:** (0962) 848269
Medieval west gate of the city. Sixteenth century painted ceiling from Winchester College.
Open: Mon to Sat 10-5; Sun 2-4 (winter), 2-5 (summer). *Closed* Mon in winter.
Admission: 30p, Chld 20p.

WINCHESTER CATHEDRAL TRIFORIUM GALLERY
c/o The Cathedral Office, 5 The Close, Winchester **Tel:** (0962) 853137
This new gallery is spectacularly situated in the Triforium of Winchester Cathedral's South Transept. It comprises stone sculpture, woodwork and metalwork surviving from eleven centuries of the Cathedral's history. The strength of the display is the late 15th century stone images from the Great Screen, portrait sculpture without any parallel in this country. The Museum of the Year Award judges described it as 'an exemplary gallery, beautifully carried out to a well-considered plan'. Visitors to the gallery will also see the Cathedral Library, a complete 17th century bookroom and the Winchester Bible, a 12th century illuminated manuscript of incomparable quality.
Open: Easter to end Sept: Mon 2-4.30; Tues to Fri 10.30-1, 2-4.30; Sat 10.30-4.30.
Admission: Fee charged.
National Heritage Museum of the Year Awards 1990 - **winner, Best Fine/Applied Art Museum.**

WINCHESTER CITY MUSEUM
(Winchester City Council)
The Square, Winchester **Tel:** (0962) 848269
Archaeology and history of Winchester and central Hampshire. 19th century shops.
Open: Mon to Sat 10-5; Sun 2-4 (winter), 2-5 (summer). *Closed* Mon in winter.
Admission: Free.
19th century shops.

THE WINCHESTER GALLERY
(Winchester School of Art)
Park Avenue, Winchester **Tel:** (0962) 852500
Changing exhibitions of contemporary painting, sculpture, printmaking, crafts, design.
Open: Tues to Fri 10-4.30.

HEREFORD & WORCESTER

BEWDLEY

BEWDLEY MUSEUM
(Wyre Forest District Council)
The Shambles, Load Street, Bewdley **Tel:** (0299) 403573

Housed in the town's 18th century Shambles the museum offers a fascinating insight into the past trades of the Wyre Forest area.
Open: Mar to Nov: Mon to Sat (and Bank Hols) 10-5.30; Sun 2-5.30. At other times by appointment.
Admission: 60p, OAPs 30p, Chld free.

BROBURY

BROBURY HOUSE GALLERY & GARDEN
Brobury   **Tel:** (0981) 500299
The largest provincial antique print gallery in Britain, set in 8 acres of semi-formal gardens on the banks of Wye.
Open: Daily all year (except Suns, Christmas and New Year) 9-4.30; (winter 9-4).
Admission: £1.50, OAPs £1, Chld 50p, Parties £1. Gallery free and also garden to purchasing customers.
Ample parking.

BROMSGROVE

AVONCROFT MUSEUM OF BUILDINGS
Stoke Heath, Bromsgrove B60 4JR   **Tel:** (0527) 31363/31886

An open-air museum containing buildings of great interest and variety, from a fully-operational Windmill to a 15th century Merchant's House; from the 18th century, an ice house, earth closet and a cider mill, and also a 19th century toll house. Recent exhibits include the 14th century Guesten Hall Roof from Worcester and now a 19th century lock up.
Open: June, July, Aug: Daily 11-5.30. Apr, May, Sept, Oct: Daily 11-5.00. (later at weekends). *closed* Mon; open Bank Hols. Mar & Nov: Tues, Wed, Thurs, Sat & Sun 11-4.30. *Closed* Mon and Fri: *Closed* Dec to Feb.
Admission: £3.00, Chld £1.50, OAPs £2.10, Family ticket (2 adults, 2 chld) £8.00. Reductions Mar and Nov. Parties at reduced rates welcome by arrangement.
Refreshments: Available.
Souvenir and book shop. Free car park and picnic site.

BROMSGROVE MUSEUM
(Bromsgrove District Council)
26 Birmingham Road, Bromsgrove   **Tel:** (0527) 77934
Past industries and crafts; Victorian and Edwardian shops displaying costume, haberdashery, toys, chemists, hairdressing, radios, millinery, shoes, gramophones, cameras, tobacconists, stationers and newsagents.
Open: Mon to Sat 10-5; Sun 2-5. (Opening times under review please telephone before visit)
Admission: (1991 charges) £1, OAPs and Students 50p, Chld 25p.
Public car park opposite.

DROITWICH SPA

DROITWICH HERITAGE CENTRE
Droitwich Spa   **Tel:** (0905) 774312 (24 hours)

Originally the St Andrew's Brine Baths, the building has been carefully converted into a local history museum, exhibition hall and tourist information centre. The town's history display depicts the fascinating development of Droitwich from Iron Age salt town to present day luxury spa resort. Incorporated in the display are finds from some of the most significant archaeological excavations of recent times, including Iron Age salt making containers, skeleton, preserved brain with a reconstruction of the owner's face from the skull, and other Roman artefacts, an Elizabethan salt bushel and many items connected with the salt and spa industries of the town. The centre also has an extensive programme of temporary exhibitions and is also an established brass rubbing centre offering a wide selection of brasses.
Open: Summer: Mon to Fri 9.30-5. Winter: Mon to Fri 9.30-4; Sat 10-4.
Admission: Free.
Parties welcome, information sheets and guides available. Free car parking space, suitable for disabled visitors.

EVESHAM

ALMONRY MUSEUM
Abbey Gate, Evesham   **Tel:** (0386) 446944
Romano-British, Anglo-Saxon, Medieval and monastic remains. Agricultural implements and exhibits of local historic interest.
Open: Mon to Sat 10-5; Sun 2-5 (Aug, Sun 10-5); Bank Holiday 10-5.
Admission: £1, OAPs and Chld free.

HARTLEBURY

HEREFORD AND WORCESTER COUNTY MUSEUM
(Hereford and Worcester County Council)
Hartlebury Castle, Hartlebury, near Kidderminster

HEREFORD

CHURCHILL GARDENS MUSEUM
(Hereford City Council)
Venn's Lane, Hereford   **Tel:** (0432) 267409
Part of the extensive costume collection is always on show, also fine furniture, choice water-colours and paintings by local artists. Period rooms including Victorian kitchen, Parlour and Nursery. The Brian Hatton Gallery is an extension of the museum and is devoted to the work of this local artist.
Open: Tues to Sat 2-5; Sun (Apr to Oct) 2-5. *Closed* Mon but open Bank Hol Mons.
Admission: 75p, Chld/OAPs 40p. Joint adm to The Old House £1.40, Chld/OAP 70p. Charges subject to review.
Party visits welcome by appointment.

CIDER MUSEUM AND KING OFFA DISTILLERY
(Hereford Cider Museum Trust)
Pomona Place, off Whitecross Road, Hereford HR4 0LW   **Tel:** (0432) 354207
Originally a cider works, where the story of traditional farm cidermaking is told up to the growth of modern factory methods. Working Cider Brandy Distillery.
Location: A438 to Brecon.

Hereford & Worcester

HEREFORD CITY MUSEUM AND ART GALLERY
(Hereford City Council)
  Broad Street, Hereford   **Tel:** (0432) 268121, Ext. 207
Collections of archaeology and natural history, embroidery, textiles, military equipment and agricultural bygones. Pictures by local artists and examples of applied art, silver, pottery and porcelain in the Art Gallery Collection. Changing exhibitions monthly. Temporary Exhibition Programme.
Open: Tues, Wed, Fri 10-6; Thurs and Sat 10-5 (winter *closes* at 4 on Sat). *Closed* Mon but open Bank Hol Mons.
Admission: Free.
Party visits welcome by appointment. Major gallery changes under way in 1993.

THE OLD HOUSE
(Hereford City Council)
  High Town, Hereford   **Tel:** (0432) 268121, Ext. 207
The Old House is preserved as a Jacobean period museum and is furnished accordingly.
Open: Apr to Sept: Mon to Sat 10-1, 2-5.30. Oct to Mar: Mon 10-1 (*closed* p.m.). Open Bank Hol Mons. Tues to Fri 10-1, 2-5.30; Sat 10-1 (also 2-5.30, Summer only).
Admission: 75p, Chld/OAPs 40p. Joint adm to Churchill Gardens Museum: £1.40, Chld/OAP 70p. Charges subject to review.
Parties welcome by appointment.

HEREFORD MUSEUMS
& ART GALLERY

The Museum and Art Gallery in Broad Street ilustrates the Natural History and Early History of Hereford and its environs and has extensive reserve collections. The Natural History collections include an observation hive and bee-keeping displays. The Archaeology exhibits include finds from Iron Age Hill Forts and the Roman town of Magna (Kenchester). The Museum is especially rich in Folklore material. The Art Gallery has an important collection of early English Water Colours and the works of modern artists and local painters are well represented. Changing exhibitions each month.

The Hall, The Old House

The Old House, High Town, built in 1621, is a branch museum and contains 17th century furniture on three floors including a Kitchen, Hall and Bedrooms.
The Churchill Gardens Museum is set in a park on the outskirts of the City and this branch Museum contains displays of Costume, Furniture and Paintings, chiefly of the 18th and 19th centuries together with a Victorian Nursery, Butler's Pantry and Parlour. Displays of 18th and 19th century costumes and furniture are completed. New Victorian Kitchen now open. Open Bank Holiday Mondays.
The Brian Hatton Gallery at Churchill Gardens shows work by Brian Hatton, the local artist killed in the First World War as well as changing exhibitions of work by local artists.

LEOMINSTER

LEOMINSTER FOLK MUSEUM
  Etnam Street, Leominster

MALVERN

MALVERN MUSEUM
  The Abbey Gateway, Abbey Road, Malvern WR14 3ES   **Tel:** (0684) 567811
A museum of local history situated at the foot of the Malvern Hills. Sections on geology, Elgar, the Water Cure, Morgan cars, radar research, and medieval and Victorian Malvern.
Open: Easter to Oct 10.30-5. *Closed* Weds in school term.
Admission: 50p, Child 10p.

OMBERSLEY

OMBERSLEY GALLERY
  Church Terrace, Ombersley, Nr Droitwich Spa WR9 0EP   **Tel:** (0905) 620655
A well established Gallery, situated in a beautiful Worcestershire village. Housed in one of the oldest buildings, carefully renovated to display paintings and craft by Britain's leading contemporary artists and crafts-persons.

REDDITCH

FORGE MILL NEEDLE MUSEUM AND BORDESLEY ABBEY VISITOR CENTRE
  Needle Mill Lane, Riverside, Redditch B97 6RR   **Tel:** (0527) 62509
The only needle museum in Britain is sited in a restored 18th century needle mill, complete with a working water-wheel. Celebrates nearly four centuries of

needle-making in the Redditch area. The newly opened Visitor Centre exhibits some of the unique archaeological finds from the nearby 12th century abbey ruins.
For details of admission charges and opening times, contact above address.

WORCESTER

CITY MUSEUM AND ART GALLERY
(Worcester City Council)
  Foregate Street, Worcester WR1 1DT

THE COMMANDERY
(Worcester City Council)
  Sidbury, Worcester

THE DYSON PERRINS MUSEUM OF WORCESTER PORCELAIN
(Dyson Perrins Museum Trust)
  Worcester Royal Porcelain Works, Severn Street, Worcester   **Tel:** (0905) 23221
The finest and most comprehensive collection of old Worcester in the world.

THE ELGAR BIRTHPLACE
  Crown East Lane, Lower Broadheath, Worcester

TUDOR HOUSE MUSEUM
(Worcester City Council)
  Friar Street, Worcester

HERTFORDSHIRE

ASHWELL

ASHWELL VILLAGE MUSEUM
(Trustees)
  Swan Street, Ashwell
Illustrates life and work in the village from the Stone Age to the present day.

HATFIELD

MILL GREEN MUSEUM AND MILL
(Welwyn Hatfield District Council)
  Mill Green, Hatfield   **Tel:** (0707) 271362
Working mill producing flour. Adjoining former Miller's house has local history displays and a small temporary exhibition gallery.
Open: Tues to Fri 10-5; weekends and Bank Hols 2-5.
Suitable for the disabled. Car parking.

HERTFORD

HERTFORD MUSEUM
(Trust)
  18 Bull Plain, Hertford   **Tel:** (0992) 582686
Fine collections from Hertford, Hertfordshire and beyond: archaeology, social history, natural history, geology, fine art and photographs. Changing exhibition and events programme.
Open: Tues to Sat 10-5. *Closed* Sun and Mon.
Attractive Jacobean Garden. Ground floor suitable for disabled. Museum Shop.

HITCHIN

HITCHIN MUSEUM AND ART GALLERY
(North Herts. District Council)
  Paynes Park, Hitchin   **Tel:** (0462) 434476
Displays of social history, costume, Hertfordshire Yeomanry Regimental Museum. Pharmaceutical gallery with reconstructed Victorian chemist's shop, complemented by physic garden of medicinal plants adjoining building, open same hours. Art exhibitions changed monthly.
Open: Mon to Sat 10-5; Sun 2-4.30. *Closed* Bank Hols.
Admission: Free.

LETCHWORTH

FIRST GARDEN CITY HERITAGE MUSEUM
(Letchworth Garden City Corporation)
  296 Norton Way South, Letchworth   **Tel:** (0462) 482424
Exhibition of items relating to the Garden City movement and the development and social history of Letchworth Garden City, displayed in the former office and home of the architect Barry Parker. Temporary exhibitions.
Open: Mon to Fri 2-4.30; Sat 10-1, 2-4. *Closed* Sun, Christmas and Boxing Day.
Admission: Free.

Hertfordshire

VERULAMIUM

The museum of everyday life in Roman Britain

- Lively new displays
- Recreated Roman rooms, including artefacts, costumes and wallpaintings
- Hands-on discovery areas
- Excavation videos

Open: Mon-Sat 10.00-5.30
(4.00 Nov-Feb),Sun 2.00-5.30
(4.00 Nov-Feb)

Verulamium Museum,
St. Michaels, St Albans
Tel: (0727) 819339
(0727) 59919

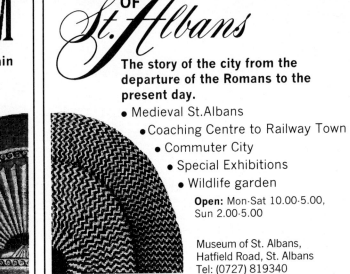

MUSEUM OF St. Albans

The story of the city from the departure of the Romans to the present day.

- Medieval St.Albans
- Coaching Centre to Railway Town
- Commuter City
- Special Exhibitions
- Wildlife garden

Open: Mon-Sat 10.00-5.00,
Sun 2.00-5.00

Museum of St. Albans,
Hatfield Road, St. Albans
Tel: (0727) 819340

LETCHWORTH MUSEUM AND ART GALLERY
(North Herts. District Council)
   Broadway, Letchworth   **Tel:** (0462) 685647
Displays on the archaeology of North Hertfordshire. Major natural history gallery in the county. Monthly art exhibitions.
Open: Mon to Sat 10-5. *Closed* Bank Hols.
Admission: Free.

LONDON COLNEY

THE MOSQUITO AIRCRAFT MUSEUM
   Salisbury Hall, London Colney, St. Albans, Hertfordshire   **Tel:** (0727) 822051
Display of de Havilland Aircraft, aircraft and memorabilia, featuring the de Havilland Mosquito Prototype.
Open: Thursdays 2.00-5.30, Saturdays, Sundays and Bank Holidays 10.30-5.30. 1st March to 31st October.
Admission: £2, Children £1. Parties by appointment.

ROYSTON

MUSEUM
(Royston Town Council)
   Lower King Street, Royston   **Tel:** (0763) 242587
Local and social history and paintings by E.H. Whydale. Temporary exhibitions (changing every 4-5 weeks). Postal history collection.
Open: Wed, Thurs & Sat 10-5, other times by appointment.
Admission: Free.
Small Shop. Parties by arrangement. Parking at Town Hall, 5 mins walk. Ground floor suitable for disabled.

ST. ALBANS

CLOCKTOWER
(St. Albans District Council)
   Market Place, St. Albans
Erected in 1402-11; restored by Sir Gilbert Scott in 1866. The tower stands 77ft. high with five storeys.
Open: Good Friday to Mid Sept: Sat, Suns and Bank Hols only.
Admission: 20p, Chld 10p.

HERTFORDSHIRE COLLEGE OF ART AND DESIGN: ST. ALBANS MARGARET HARVEY GALLERY
   7 Hatfield Road, St. Albans AL1 3RS   **Tel:** (0727) 45544   **Fax:** (0727) 46293
Various exhibitions of contemporary painting, drawing, sculpture, design, crafts. Tel the above number, or write to be put on mailing list.

THE MUSEUM OF ST. ALBANS
(St. Albans District Council)
   Hatfield Road, St. Albans   **Tel:** (0727) 819340
The impressive Salaman collection of craft and trade tools has been redisplayed for 1993.
Open: Mon to Sat 10-5, Sun 2-5.
Admission: 70p, Chld/student/OAPs 35p, Family £1.50. (residents free).

ST. ALBANS ORGAN MUSEUM
   320 Camp Road, St. Albans   **Tel:** (0727) 51557/873896
A permanent working exhibition of mechanical musical instruments. Organs by Decap, Bursens, and Mortier; Mills Violano-Virtuoso; reproducing pianos by Steinway and Weber; musical boxes; Wurlitzer and Rutt theatre organs.
Open: Every Sun (except Christmas Day) 2.15-4.30.
Admission: £1.50, Chld 60p.
Refreshments: Light only.
Parties by arrangement. Souvenirs. Shop.

THE VERULAMIUM MUSEUM
(St Albans District Council)
   St. Michael's, St. Albans   **Tel:** (0727) 819339 Recorded information (0727) 59919
The museum has been completely re-displayed. New displays include recreated Roman rooms, 'hands-on' Discovery Areas, excavation videos - the museum of everyday life in Roman Britain. Stands on the site of the Roman City of Verulamium and houses material from the Roman and Belgic cities including several of the finest mosaics in Britain, one of which is preserved *in situ* in the 'Hypocaust annexe'.
Open: Summer: Mon to Sat 10-5.30; Sun 2-5.30. Winter: Mon to Sat 10-4; Sun 2-4.
Admission: (incl. Hypocaust) £2, Chld/Students/OAPs £1, Family ticket (2 adults, 2 Chld) £5 (residents free).

STEVENAGE

STEVENAGE MUSEUM
   St. George's Way, New Town Centre, Stevenage SG1 1XX   **Tel:** (0438) 354292
A local museum which tells the story of Stevenage through its displays. There is also a natural history and geology display. The temporary exhibition area houses up to six exhibitions each year. A comprehensive education service provides talks and loans material to Hertfordshire schools.
Open: Mon to Sat 10-5 *Closed* Sun.
Admission: Free.
Suitable for disabled. Multi-storey car park 100 yds.

TRING

ZOOLOGICAL MUSEUM, BRITISH MUSEUM (NATURAL HISTORY)
   Akeman Street, Tring   **Tel:** (044 282) 4181
Mounted specimens of animals from all parts of the world.

WARE

TRADING PLACES GALLERY
   11 New Road, Ware SG12 7BS   **Tel:** (0920) 469620

WATFORD

WATFORD MUSEUM
(Watford Council)
   194 High Street, Watford   **Tel:** (0923) 232297
Local history with special emphasis on printing, brewing and wartime, plus an art gallery and a temporary exhibition gallery with displays changing monthly.

Open: Mon to Sat 10-5. *Closed* Sun.
Admission: Free.

WELWYN GARDEN CITY

WELWYN ROMAN BATHS
(Welwyn Hatfield District Council)
Welwyn By-pass, Old Welwyn   **Tel:** (0707) 271362
A third century AD bath house, the one visible feature of a villa complex, preserved in a specially constructed vault under the A1 (M).
Open: Thurs to Sun and Bank Holidays 2-5 (or dusk if earlier).
Admission: Fee charged.
Telephone to arrange party visits. Suitable for the disabled. Car parking.

HUMBERSIDE

BARTON-ON-HUMBER

BAYSGARTH HOUSE MUSEUM
(Glanford Borough Council)
Baysgarth Leisure Park, Caistor Road, Barton-on-Humber   **Tel:** (0652) 32318
An 18th century town house and park with displays of porcelain, local history, archaeology and geology. Adjacent cottage and stable block house rural craft and industrial displays.
Open: Thurs, Fri and most Bank Holidays 10-4; Sat and Sun 10-5.
Admission: Free.
Car park free.

BEVERLEY

BEVERLEY ART GALLERY AND MUSEUM
(Beverley Borough Council)
Champney Road, Beverley   **Tel:** (0482) 882255
Art Gallery includes paintings by the Beverley artist F.W. Elwell, R.A. Museum of local antiquities.
Open: Weekdays 10-12.30, 2-5 (Thurs 10-12 noon; Sat 10-12, 2-4).

SKIDBY WINDMILL AND MUSEUM
(Beverley Borough Council)
Skidby, Beverley   **Tel:** (0482) 882255
Restored windmill and museum relating to milling and corn production.
Open: May to Sept: Tues to Sat 10-4; Sun and Bank Hols 1.30-4.30. Operated alternate Suns commencing first Sun in May. Open Oct to Apr: Mon to Fri 10-4.

BRIDLINGTON

BRIDLINGTON ART GALLERY AND MUSEUM
(Borough of East Yorkshire)
Sewerby Hall, Bridlington   **Tel:** (0262) 677874
Wide range of temporary exhibitions. Permanent Amy Johnson exhibition. Local and natural history and archaeology. Old farm implements.
Open: Easter to end Sept: Sun to Fri 10-6; Sat 1.30-6. Also open Christmas, Feb/ Mar, Oct/Nov 11.00am-4.00pm (subject to confirmation) 7 days per week
Enquiries tel above number.

city of hull
MUSEUMS & ART GALLERIES

TOWN DOCKS MUSEUM
Queen Victoria Square.
Sumptuous Victorian building including magnificent Court Room of former Dock Co. Displays cover Whales and Whaling, with extensive collection of scrimshaw; Fishing and Trawling; Hull and the Humber; Ships and Shipping.

SPURN LIGHTSHIP
Hull Marina.
Built in 1927 and originally positioned S.E. of Spurn Point until transferred to Bull Station in 1959. Restored and berthed in Hull Marina 1986. Visitors can see the Master's Cabin, crew's quarters and light mechanism etc.

WILBERFORCE HOUSE & GEORGIAN HOUSES
24-25 High Street, Hull.
Built in c1656, Wilberforce House is a museum with unique collections relating to its most famous resident, William Wilberforce (1759–1833) and his fight to abolish slavery. The house, together with the neighbouring Georgian Houses, also contains furnished rooms of different periods, costume, militaria and a variety of items of local interest including the famous Hull silver.

FERENS ART GALLERY
Queen Victoria Square.
The Gallery extended during 1990/91, has the latest facilities for educational and Live Art activities with a new cafe-restaurant, La Loggia. The extension houses a busy programme of exhibitions. The old building continues to show the permanent collections of Old Masters, Dutch Portraits, Marine Paintings and Contemporary Arts, and features 'Hull Through the Eyes of the Artist', a fresh look at local views.

HULL & EAST RIDING MUSEUM
36 High Street, Hull.
Come and see the ways our ancestors lived: 'A Celtic World' – the sights and sounds of the Iron Age, the astonishing Iron Age Hasholme Boat, magnificent Roman mosaics and other treasures of the past are all on show. Other new galleries for archaeology and environmental history are in preparation.

'STREETLIFE' – HULL MUSEUM OF TRANSPORT
26 High Street, Hull.
Hull's newest museum illustrates how different forms of transport have changed our lives – beginning in the first phase with public transport. Visitors can experience a busy inn courtyard in the days of the stage coaches, step inside Britain's oldest tram and other vehicles, all brought to life with period conversation and sounds.

Future phases will explore other aspects of road transport, starting in Phase 2 (opening 1992) with the social history of cycling, from boneshakers to BMX's.

OLD GRAMMAR SCHOOL
South Church Side, Hull
The story of Hull and its People, Part One. Using objects, photographs, people's memories and other historical evidence, Hull's Social History Museum explores the lives of the people of Hull through the centuries. The Old Grammar School also contains Hull Museums' archive and photograph collections, which will be open for local history research in the future. 'Hull in the Forties' is the current temporary exhibition on display.

Sales area. Wheelchair access to ground-floor exhibitions.

Percy Wyndham LEWIS (1882-1957)   Mr. Wyndham Lewis as a Tyro, c1920-21.

GOOLE

GOOLE MUSEUM AND ART GALLERY
(Humberside County Council)
    Goole Library, Market Square, Goole DN14 5AA   **Tel:** (0405) 762187
Collections illustrating the early history of the area and the formation and development of Goole as a port. Maritime paintings. Temporary exhibitions.
Open: Mon to Fri 10-5; Sat 9.30-12.30, 2-4.
Admission: Free.

GREAT GRIMSBY

WELHOLME GALLERIES
(Great Grimsby Borough Council)
    Welholme Road, Great Grimsby

HORNSEA

HORNSEA MUSEUM
    Burns Farm, 11 Newbegin, Hornsea   **Tel:** (0964) 533443
19th century home and village life. Period rooms, local history, farming, rural trades. Occasional craft displays.
Open: Easter to Nov: Daily.
Large garden. Small gift shop. Parties by arrangement all year.

HULL

FERENS ART GALLERY
(Hull City Council)
    Queen Victoria Square, Hull   **Tel:** (0482) 593912
The Gallery extended during 1990/1991, has the latest facilities for educational and Live-Art activities with a new cafe-restaurant, La Loggia. The extension houses a busy programme of exhibitions. The old building continues to show the permanent collections of Old Masters, Dutch Portraits, Marine Paintings and Contemporary Arts, and features 'Hull Through the Eyes of the Artist', a fresh look at local views.

HULL AND EAST RIDING MUSEUM
(Hull City Council)
    36 High Street, Hull   **Tel:** (0482) 593902
'A Celtic World' displays of East Yorkshire archaeology, the iron-age Hasholme Boat and spectacular Romano-British mosaics. Also a collection of horse-drawn vehicles and early motorcars.
Open: Mon to Sat 10-5, Sun 1.30-4.30.

HULL MUSEUM OF TRANSPORT - STREETLIFE
(Hull City Council)
    26 High Street, Hull   **Tel:** (0482) 593902
A new museum, opened 1989, showing public transport from horse-drawn vehicles, including the rare Ryde Pier Tram, to the Kitson steam tram and the newly restored Hull Tram; new displays for 1993: the history of cycling from bone shaker to BMXs.

OLD GRAMMAR SCHOOL
(Hull City Council)
    South Church Side, Hull   **Tel:** (0482) 593902
Hull's oldest secular building, 1583-5, shows the first phase of The Story of Hull and its people, with videos, visitor participation etc in displays from childhood to parenthood over 700 years. The ground floor 1992/3 has a special exhibition of Hull in the 40's, years of the blitz and the following austerity.

SPURN LIGHTSHIP
(Hull City Council)
    Hull Marina, Hull   **Tel:** (0482) 593902
Built 1927 and restored 1985/6, visitors can see the master's cabin, crew's quarters and light mechanism etc.
Open: Mon-Sat 10-5, Sun 1.30-4.30. *Closed* Mon and Tues Winter months.

TOWN DOCKS MUSEUM
(Hull City Council)
    Queen Victoria Square, Hull   **Tel:** (0482) 593902
Whales and Whaling with collection of Scrimshaw; Fishing and Trawling; Court Room of the former Docks Board; Hull and the Humber; Ships and Shipping.
Open: Mon to Sat 10-5; Sun 1.30-4.30. Cafe 11-4 (Mon to Sat).

UNIVERSITY OF HULL ART COLLECTION
(University of Hull)
    The Middleton Hall, University of Hull, Cottingham Road, Hull   **Tel:** (0482) 465192
Specialising in art in Britain 1890-1940. Painting, sculpture and drawings including work by Sickert, Steer, Lucien Pissarro, Augustus John, Stanley Spencer, Gill, Epstein and Moore. Also the Thompson Collection of Chinese Ceramics (chiefly 17th century) and temporary exhibitions.
Open: Mon-Fri 2-4; (Wed 12.30-4) except public holidays.
Admission: No charge.
Parties welcome. Limited car parking. Access for disabled persons. Hon. Curator: John G. Bernasconi.

WILBERFORCE HOUSE AND GEORGIAN HOUSES
(Hull City Council)
    23-25 High Street, Hull   **Tel:** (0482) 593902
Birthplace of the slave emancipator with slavery collections. 17th and 18th century Merchants' houses with collections of furniture, silver and costume.
Open: Mon to Sat 10-5; Sun 1.30-4.30.

SCUNTHORPE

MUSEUM AND ART GALLERY
(Scunthorpe Borough Council)
    Oswald Road, Scunthorpe   **Tel:** (0724) 843533

NORMANBY HALL
(Scunthorpe Borough Council)
    Scunthorpe   **Tel:** (0724) 720215

NORMANBY PARK FARMING MUSEUM
(Scunthorpe Borough Council)
    Scunthorpe

ISLE OF MAN

CASTLETOWN

CASTLE RUSHEN
(Branch of Manx National Heritage)
    Castletown
This finely preserved medieval castle, on the site of a Viking stronghold, was developed as a fortress by successive Kings and Lords of Man between the thirteenth and sixteenth centuries. Major redevelopment, completed in 1991, recreates castle life at important phases in its history.
Open: Easter to end of Sept: Daily 10am-5pm

THE NAUTICAL MUSEUM
(Branch of Manx National Heritage)
    Bridge Street, Castletown
Across the harbour from Castle Rushen, the displays centre on the late 18th century armed yacht 'Peggy' in her contemporary boathouse. Part of the original building is constructed as a Cabin Room of the Nelson period and the museum also displays many nautical exhibits, ship models etc, a fine range of photographs of Manx vessels in the days of sail and a reconstruction of a sailmaker's loft.
Open: Easter to end of Sept: Daily 10am-5pm

ST. MARY'S CHAPEL, LATER THE GRAMMAR SCHOOL
(Branch of Manx National Heritage)
    Castletown
The former capital's first church built around 1200 AD. It was also used as a school from at least 1570 and served exclusively in that capacity from 1702 until its closure in 1930. The interpretive displays include a Victorian school-room.
Open: Easter to end of Sept: Daily 10am-5pm

DOUGLAS

THE MANX MUSEUM
    Douglas   **Tel:** (0624) 675522
The headquarters of the Trust and the National Museum of the Island with displays of Manx Archaeology, History, Folk Life and Natural Sciences. The building also houses the National Art Gallery with works of Manx interest and the Island's National Archive and Reference Library.
Open: All year round Mon to Sat 10-5.
Admission: Free.

LAXEY

LAXEY WHEEL AND LEAD MINES
(Branch of Manx National Heritage)
    Laxey
The spectacular focus to this historic mining valley is the Great Laxey Wheel. Completed in 1854, the 'Lady Isabella' is the largest wheel of its kind in the world and was built to operate the pumping system which cleared water from the lead mines. Enjoy the mines trail and even venture underground!
Open: Easter to end of Sept: Daily 10am-5pm

PEEL

ODIN'S RAVEN
(Branch of Manx National Heritage)
    Peel
In 1979, in celebration of the Island's Millenium, this two-thirds scale replica Viking ship was sailed by a mixed Norwegian and Manx crew over 1500 miles from Norway to the Isle of Man. The story of the voyage is presented in the boathouse that now preserves this magnificent ship.
Open: Easter to end of Sept: Daily 10am-5pm

PEEL CASTLE
(Branch of Manx National Heritage)
    Peel
St. Patricks Isle is surrounded by the imposing walls of Peel Castle which also enclose the eleventh century church of St. Patrick and the round tower, the thirteenth century Cathedral of St. German and the later apartments of the Lords of Man.
Open: Easter to end of Sept: Daily 10am-5pm

PORT ST. MARY

THE CREGNEASH VILLAGE FOLK MUSEUM
(Branch of Manx National Heritage)
    Near Port St. Mary
Illustrates, in situ, the life of a typical Manx upland crofting/fishing community at the turn of the century. Many of the buildings are thatched and include a crofter-fisherman's home, a weaver's shed with handloom, a turner's shed with treadle lathe, a thatched farmstead and a smithy. Church Farm is being developed as a traditional working farm, and other demonstrations, including spinning, are given on certain days each week. The property adjoins the Manx National Trust lands of the Spanish Head area.
Open: Apr to Sept: Mon to Sat 10-1, 2-5; Sun 2-5.

RAMSEY

THE GROVE MUSEUM
(Branch of Manx National Heritage)
    Near Ramsey
A small, pleasantly-proportioned early Victorian house with associated range of outbuildings. The house displays a series of Victorian period rooms, a costume room and general museum displays. The outbuildings contain early agricultural equipment and vehicles and include a horse-powered threshing mill restored to a working condition. The pleasant garden is being brought back to its Victorian state, with ornamental pool and fish pond, and waterfowl on the duckpond.
Open: Apr to end of Sept: Daily 10am-5pm

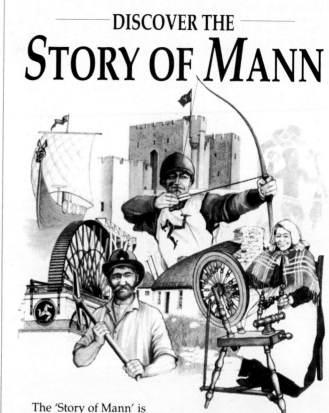
ISLE OF WIGHT

BEMBRIDGE

BEMBRIDGE MARITIME MUSEUM
(Martin J. Woodward)
    Sherborne Street, Bembridge   **Tel:** (0983) 872223 or 873125
Six galleries plus a shop. Ship models, wreck items. Our discovery of the missing WW2 submarine HMS Swordfish.

THE RUSKIN GALLERY
    Bembridge School, Bembridge   **Tel:** (0983) 872101
Large collection of pictures and manuscripts by Ruskin and his contemporaries. By appointment only.

BRADING

ISLE OF WIGHT WAX MUSEUM
Brading

Cameos of Island history with authentic costume, wax figures and period furniture, cleverly brought to life with sound, light and motion.

Open: All the year - May to Sept: Daily 10-10; Oct to Apr: Daily 10-5.

LILLIPUT MUSEUM OF ANTIQUE DOLLS AND TOYS
High Street, Brading

THE ROMAN VILLA
Brading **Tel:** (0983) 406223

COWES

SIR MAX AITKEN MUSEUM
The Prospect, 83 High Street, Cowes **Tel:** (0983) 293800

COWES MARITIME MUSEUM
(Isle of Wight County Council)
Beckford Road, Cowes **Tel:** (0983) 293341

Models, paintings and an extensive photographic archive illustrate the former shipbuilding industry which serviced the Navy with vessels for several centuries. Also a collection of boats representing the modern yacht building industry, including Prince Philip's 'Coweslip'.

Open: All year.
Admission: Free.

EAST COWES

OSBORNE HOUSE
(English Heritage)
East Cowes **Tel:** (0983) 200022

Queen Victoria's seaside home was built at her own expense in 1845 and designed by Thomas Cubitt. Here, she and Prince Albert sought peace and solitude, away from the affairs of state. At the request of their son, King Edward VII, this wonderful monument to Victorian family life has been preserved almost unchanged. The house itself is an Italianate villa with two tall towers. The apartments and rooms contain mementoes of royal travel abroad, sometimes incorporated into the decor. You will see intricate Indian plaster decoration, furniture made from deer antlers and over 400 works of art, pictures and pieces of furniture. There is even a fascinating glimpse into the early years of the royal children in the newly restored Royal Nursery.

Open: Apr 1 to Oct 31, daily 10-5.00.
Admission: £5.00, concessions £4.00, Chld £3.00 (1992 prices)

NEWPORT

CARISBROOKE CASTLE MUSEUM
(Trustees of the Museum)
Newport **Tel:** (0983) 522107

Isle of Wight Museum - collection illustrating the history of the castle and the imprisonment of Charles I together with items relating to Tennyson's home on the island. Various other aspects of island history are also shown.

Open: Apr 1 to Sept 30, daily 10-6. Oct 1 to Mar 31, daily 10-4. *Closed* Dec 24 to 26, Jan 1.
Admission: £3.00, Concessions £2.30, Chld £1.50 including admission to Castle. (1992 prices)

ROMAN VILLA
(Isle of Wight County Council)
Cypress Road, Newport **Tel:** (0983) 529720

Hidden beneath the soil of surburban Newport lies a 3rd century Roman Villa uncovered by archaeologists. The well preserved baths are displayed and the rooms in which the family lived reconstructed. The newly refurbished exhibition includes: objects recovered from the excavations; an audio-visual presentation on Roman Wight; a Roman garden and a Resource Room for use by schools.

Open: Easter to Sept: Sun to Fri 10-4.30.
Admission: Fee charged.

RYDE

NATIONAL WIRELESS MUSEUM
'Lynwood', 52 West Hill Road, Ryde **Tel:** (0983) 67665

Exhibits at Arreton Manor and Puckpool Park, Seaview from Easter to Oct.

SANDOWN

GEOLOGY MUSEUM
(Isle of Wight County Council)
Sandown Library, High Street, Sandown **Tel:** (0983) 404344

Houses an extensive collection of fossils and rocks. A special feature has been made of recently excavated Dinosaurs. Reconstructions help visitors to understand these fascinating animals and modern displays interpret millions of years of prehistory of the Isle of Wight.

Open: All the year.
Admission: Free.

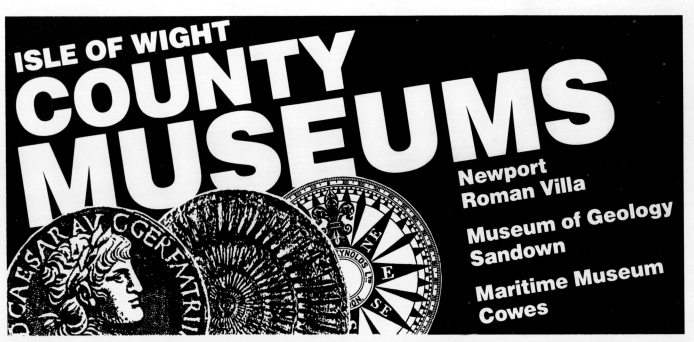

ISLE OF WIGHT COUNTY MUSEUMS

Newport Roman Villa

Museum of Geology Sandown

Maritime Museum Cowes

KENT

BIRCHINGTON

QUEX MUSEUM, HOUSE AND GARDENS
Quex Park, Birchington   **Tel:** (0843) 42168

QUEX MUSEUM, HOUSE AND GARDENS,

QUEX PARK, BIRCHINGTON, KENT

Unique collections of African and Asian fauna and native artefacts, firearms, E. Kent archaeological material, superb Oriental Fine Arts and beautifully furnished Regency Mansion provide something for everyone at Quex Park.

OPEN: 2.15–6.00
House and Museum
April 1 – Sept 30: Weds, Thurs & Sundays + Bank Holidays & Fridays in August.
Museum Only
Oct – March: Sundays only.
Pre-booked Parties at other times.

Contact: Curator ☎ (0843) 42168
A.H. ☎ (0843) 45088

Combine a morning visit to Canterbury with a never to be forgotten afternoon at Quex House, set in 250 acres of beautiful gardens & woodland. The fine Regency house was built in 1805 by John Powell Powell, High Sheriff of Kent and is still the Powell-Cotton family home. Seven of the rooms are on view with superb family collections - fine furniture, porcelain, pictures, silver, clocks etc. Of unique importance is the Museum built adjoining the House by Maj. P.H.G. Powell-Cotton, Naturalist, Explorer, Photographer. Author and Collector Extraordinary. Words cannot do justice to the amazing collections housed in this remarkable private museum of nine large galleries. The African and Asian animals in their huge natural landscape dioramas look so alive that visitors have claimed to have seen them move; one of the most important ethnographical collections is housed here together with a very large weapons and cannon collection, African butterflies, local archaeological material, treasures from the Orient, including a unique series of Chinese Imperial and Export porcelain and English and European pottery and porcelain.
Open: House and Museum. 2.15-6 April 1 to Sept 30: Wed, Thurs and Sun, Bank Hols and Fri in Aug. **Museum only:** Oct to Mar: Sun only. Pre-booked parties booked at other times; contact Curator (0843) 42168. After hours (0843) 45088.
Admission: Museum only: Adults £1 child under 16 and Sen. Cits. 75p. House & Museum: Adults £2 child under 16 and Sen. Cits. £1.50. Garden only 50p.
Location: A28 12 miles east of Canterbury; signposted St. Nicholas-at-Wade and Prospect Roundabouts and Birchington Square.
Refreshments: Tea room open in season.
Free parking for cars & coaches.

BROADSTAIRS

CRAMPTON TOWER MUSEUM
High Street, Broadstairs
Dedicated to the work of Broadstairs resident, Thomas Russell Crampton.
Open: (1993) Apr-Sept: 2.30-5 (*Closed* Wed and Weekends except Bank Holiday Suns)

DICKENS' HOUSE MUSEUM
(Thanet District Council)
Victoria Parade, Broadstairs

DICKENS HOUSE MUSEUM
BROADSTAIRS
ON THE MAIN SEA FRONT

" The house on the cliff " immortalised by Dickens as the home of Miss Betsey Trotwood, "David Copperfield's" Aunt.

Dickens letters and personal belongings. Local and Dickensian prints, Costume and Victoriana. The parlour is furnished in the style described and illustrated in "David Copperfield".

OPEN DAILY: April to October 2.30–5.30 p.m.

Parties by arrangement with Hon. Curator. Tel: Thanet 862853.

Admission: Fee charged.

CANTERBURY

THE CANTERBURY CENTRE
(The Canterbury Urban Studies Centre)
St. Alphege Lane, Canterbury CT1 2EB   **Tel:** (0227) 457009

CANTERBURY HERITAGE MUSEUM
(Canterbury City Council)
Poor Priests' Hospital, Stour Street, Canterbury

ETHNIC DOLL & TOY MUSEUM
(Mr & Mrs L Pickering)
Castlegate House, 1 Tankerton Road, Whitstable, Canterbury CT5 2AB
Tel: (0227) 771456/769877
Britain's only Ethnic Doll Museum, displaying unique dolls from all parts of the world, ethnic model houses, dolls houses, miniature rooms, shops, a 27 room Victorian London Town House, working model railway layout, teddy bears and other toys.
Open: Feb to Christmas: Seven days a week; Christmas to end Jan *closed* but open to groups by appointment.
Admission: Fee charged.

THE ROMAN MOSAIC
(Canterbury City Council)
Butchery Lane, Canterbury

THE ROYAL MUSEUM & ART GALLERY AND BUFFS REGIMENTAL MUSEUM
(Canterbury City Council)
High Street, Canterbury

THE WEST GATE
(Canterbury City Council)
Canterbury

WHITSTABLE MUSEUM
(Canterbury City Council)
Oxford Street, Canterbury

CHATHAM

FORT AMHERST
off Dock Road, Chatham

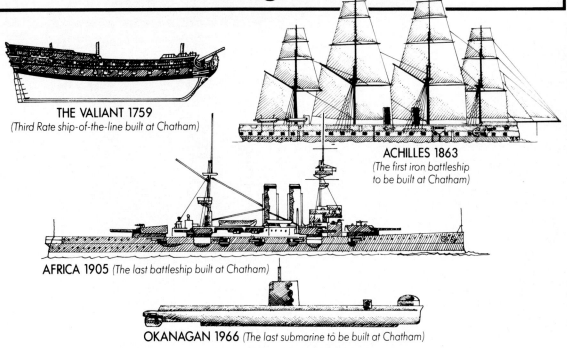

51

THE HISTORIC DOCKYARD, CHATHAM
(Chatham Historic Dockyard Trust)
   Chatham ME4 4TE   **Tel:** (0634) 812551 **Fax:** (0634) 826918
An 80 acre living, working museum with 47 Scheduled Ancient Monuments forming the most complete surviving Georgian/early Victorian dockyard. Eight museum galleries, covering 400 years of shipbuilding history, include award winning 'Wooden Walls' which recreates through animated scenes the building of a wooden warship in the dockyard of 1758.
Open: to Mar 27 1993: Wed, Sat, Sun 10-4.30; from Mar 28 1993; Wed to Sun and all Bank Holidays 10-6. *Closed* Christmas Day.
Admission: £5.20, students/OAPs £4.50.
Further information: Sue Hudson, Information Officer, telephone above number.

MEDWAY HERITAGE CENTRE
   Dock Road, Chatham

DARTFORD

DARTFORD BOROUGH MUSEUM
(Dartford Borough Council)
   Market Street, Dartford   **Tel:** (0322) 343555
A lively and interesting 'local' museum. Archaeology, natural and local history, geology. 'The Darenth Bowl' (c.450 A.D.), reconstruction Draper's Shop with working 'Cash Railway'. Temporary exhibitions. School Loans Service.
Open: Mon, Tues, Thur and Fri 12.30-5.30; Sat 9-1, 2-5. *Closed* Wed and Sun.

DOVER

DOVER CASTLE
(English Heritage)
   Dover   **Tel:** (0304) 201628
One of the most powerful medieval fortresses in Western Europe. Included in admission to Dover Castle is Hellfire Corner, the secret war tunnels concealed in the white cliffs from where Vice Admiral Ramsay masterminded the evacuation of Dunkirk in 1940.
Open: Apr 1 to Sept 30, daily 10-6. Oct 1 to Mar 31, daily 10-4. *Closed* Dec 24 to 26, Jan 1.
Admission: £4.50. Concessions £3.40 and Chld £2.50 (1992 prices) Hellfire Corner - extra charge.

DOVER MUSEUM
(Dover District Council)
   Ladywell, Dover CT16 1DQ
Dover's history and natural history with other items of interest.

DOVER OLD TOWN GAOL
(Dover District Council)
   Biggin Street, Dover   **Tel:** (0304) 242766
Courtroom, cells and Victorian prison experience brought to life by actors and animated figures.
Open: Phone 24 hour ansaphone for opening times.
Admission: Phone 24 hour ansaphone for charges.

GRAND SHAFT
(Dover District Council)
   Snargate Street, Dover
Unique Napoleonic triple staircase cut through the cliffs of Dover.

ROMAN PAINTED HOUSE
   New Street, Dover   **Tel:** (0304) 203279
Exceptionally preserved Roman Town House with in situ wall paintings and hypocausts; Roman defensive wall and bastion, major displays on Roman Dover.
Open: Apr to Oct: Daily 10-5. *Closed* Mon.
Admission: £1, Chld and OAPs 50p

TIME-BALL TOWER
   Beach Street, Dover
Nineteenth century Semaphore House converted to a Time-ball Tower in 1855.

FAVERSHAM

FLEUR DE LIS HERITAGE CENTRE
(The Faversham Society)
   13, Preston Street, Faversham ME13 8NS   **Tel:** (0795) 534542

FLEUR DE LIS HERITAGE CENTRE

**Preston Street, Faversham
ME13 8NS
(Faversham 534542)**

In one of Britain's finest Heritage Towns . . .

* 1,000 years of history, industry and architecture vividly brought to life * Colourful displays, bygones and audio visual * Only 1 mile M2, 400 yards mainline station * Housed in historic 15th century building * Created and staffed by local volunteers * Any profits ploughed back for conservation of area * Well-stocked Kentish Bookshop.

OPEN ALL YEAR
Daily 10-4 *(closed Sundays from November to March inclusive).*

Admission £1.00. Children (under 15). Students Pensioners and other concessions 50p.

. . . and after your visit make sure you explore our wonderful town!

Audio-visual, bygones and colourful displays on 1,000 years of life in one of Britan's finest Heritage Towns with over 400 listed buildings. Housed in a 15th century inn, where the plot to murder 'Arden of Faversham' was hatched in 1551, this is the first Heritage Centre in the South.
Open: Daily 10-4 *Closed* Sundays from Nov to Mar inclusive.
Admission: £1, Chld/OAPs and other concessions 50p.

FOLKESTONE

FOLKESTONE MUSEUM AND ART GALLERY
(Kent County Council)
   Grace Hill, Folkestone   **Tel:** (0303) 850123

METROPOLE ARTS CENTRE
   The Leas, Folkestone CT20 2LS   **Tel:** (0303) 255070
Art exhibitions, chamber/jazz/piano recitals, lectures, workshops, children's events. Children's Festival - April. Kent Literature Festival - Oct. Paintings, cards, books and craft works for sale.
Open: Apr to Oct: Mon to Sat 10-5, Sun 2.30-5. Nov to Mar: Tues to Sat 10-4, Sun 2.30-5.
Refreshments: Coffee shop open daily.
Telephone the Gallery reception as above for further information.

GOUDHURST

FINCHCOCKS, LIVING MUSEUM OF MUSIC
   , Goudhurst   **Tel:** (0580) 211702
Magnificent collection of historical keyboard instruments in 18th century manor. Played whenever the house is open. Many musical events.
Open: Season: Apr to Oct

GRAVESEND

GRAVESHAM MUSEUM
(Kent County Council and Gravesham Borough Council)
   High Street, Gravesend   **Tel:** (0474) 323159

NEW TAVERN FORT
   Gravesend   **Tel:** (0474) 535027

HERNE BAY

HERNE BAY MUSEUM
(Kent County Council)
High Street, Herne Bay   **Tel:** (0227) 374896
New displays telling the story of Herne Bay.
Open: Mon, Tues and Fri 9.30-7; Wed 9.30-1; Thurs and Sat 9.30-5. *Closed* on public holidays.
Admission: Free.

HYTHE

HYTHE LOCAL HISTORY ROOM
(Hythe Town Council and Kent County Council)
Oaklands, Stade Street, Hythe   **Tel:** (0303) 266152
Local history.
Open: Mon to Sat when Library is open.

MAIDSTONE

MUSEUM AND ART GALLERY
(Maidstone Borough Council)
St. Faith's Street, Maidstone   **Tel:** (0622) 754497
House in 16th century Chillington Manor, the museum (extended considerably in the 19th century) contains outstanding collections, some of national importance. These include ceramics, natural history, costume, furniture, Japanese decorative art, local history and, in the recently refurbished Art Gallery, 17th & 18th century Dutch & Italian oil paintings. Also on display is the museum of the Queen's Own Royal West Kent Regiment. Following redisplay work, galleries of Pacific Ethnography and Kentish Archaeology will be opened.
Open: Mon to Sat 10-5.30, Sun 2-5, Bank Hol Mon 11-5.
Admission: Free.

MUSEUM OF KENT LIFE
(Kent County Council)
Lock Lane, Sandling, Maidstone
The history of the Kent Countryside explained through displays on farming history, exhibits of agricultural tools and machinery and outside planting of crops important to Kent, including orchard fruits, hops, arable, pasture and market garden crops, and livestock typical to the county, especially Romney Marsh Sheep. New themed display on H.E.Bates & Darling Buds of May.

Kent

TYRWHITT-DRAKE MUSEUM OF CARRIAGES
(Maidstone Borough Council)
Archbishop's Stables, Mill Street, Maidstone   **Tel:** (0622) 754497
Housed in the stable block of the nearby Archbishops Palace, the Carriage Collection is thought to be the finest and most wide-ranging in Britain. Most types of carriages are represented, all in superbly original condition, alongside a number of Royal vehicles.
Open: 10.30-5.30 7 days
Admission: Charge

MARGATE

OLD TOWN HALL MUSEUM
(Thanet District Council)
Market Place, Margate   **Tel:** (0843) 225511 ext. 2520
Margate's development as a seaside resort; also old Court Room and Victorian Police cells.
Open: (1993) May-Sept: 10-5 (except Sun).
Admission: Fee charged. Discounts for chd, groups and school parties.
Small selection of souvenirs.

MINSTER

AGRICULTURAL AND RURAL LIFE MUSEUM
Bedlam Court Lane, Minster   **Tel:** (0843) 225511 ext 2155
Farming through the ages, including machinery and craft demonstrations.

PADDOCK WOOD

WHITBREAD HOP FARM
Beltring, Paddock Wood   **Tel:** (0622) 872068
Award winning tourist attraction set in the heart of beautiful Kent countryside. Largest collection of Victorian Oasthouses in the world, New Hop Story Exhibition, extended Shire Horse Centre, Owl Flying Displays (weather permitting), Working Pottery, Animal Village, Nature Trail, Weekend Special.
Admission: Adults £4.25. Children, OAPs, Reg Disabled £3.00
Refreshments: Restaurant
Gift Shop

RAMSGATE

MARITIME MUSEUM COMPLEX
Royal Harbour, Ramsgate   **Tel:** (0843) 587765
National and local maritime history Museum with adjacent Dry Dock and historic vessels.
Open: All year: Winter Mon to Fri, Summer 7 days
Admission: Small charge. Concessions. Groups welcome(booking advisable)

RAMSGATE MOTOR MUSEUM
Westcliff Hall, The Paragon, Ramsgate
Exotic and exciting vintage and classic cars plus motorcycles, bikes and related memorabilia.

RAMSGATE MUSEUM
(Kent County Council)
Ramsgate Library, Guildford Lawn, Ramsgate   **Tel:** (0843) 593532
The story of bygone Ramsgate; watercolours, photos, archaeology, holiday souvenirs.
Open: Mon to Thurs 9.30-6; Fri 9.30-7; Sat 9.30-5 *Closed* on public holidays.
Admission: Free.
Limited car parking nearby. Suitable for disabled persons.

SPITFIRE AND HURRICANE PAVILION
(R.A.F. Manston)
Ramsgate

RICHBOROUGH

RICHBOROUGH CASTLE
(English Heritage)
Richborough   **Tel:** (0304) 612013
Objects found during excavation of the site, Roman pottery, coins and other small objects.
Open: Apr 1 to Sept 20, daily 10-6. 1 Oct-31 Mar, Tues-Sun 10am-4pm. *Closed* 24-26 Dec and 1 Jan.
Admission: £1.40, Concessions £1, Chld 70p (1992 prices)

ROCHESTER

CHARLES DICKENS CENTRE
(City of Rochester-upon-Medway)
Eastgate House, High Street, Rochester   **Tel:** (0634) 844176
'Step back into Dickensian England and experience the reality of Victorian Life'.
Open: All year 10-5.30. Last admission 4.45. *Closed* Dec 25, 26, but open Jan 1.

GUILDHALL MUSEUM
(City of Rochester-upon-Medway)
Guildhall, High Street, Rochester   **Tel:** (0634) 848717
Local history, archaeology, arms and armour, costumes, Victoriana, models of ships and aircraft.
Open: Daily 10-5.30, except Christmas Day, Boxing Day and Good Friday.

ROLVENDEN

THE C.M. BOOTH COLLECTION OF HISTORIC VEHICLES
Falstaff Antiques, 63-67 High Street, Rolvenden

SANDWICH

THE GUILDHALL MUSEUM
(Sandwich Town Council)
Sandwich
Collection of ancient and interesting items.
Open: Tues to Fri.

THE PRECINCT TOY COLLECTION
38 Harnet Street, Sandwich
Dolls' houses, Noah's Arks, dolls, clockwork toys etc.
Open: Easter to end Sept: Mon to Sat 10.30-4.30; Sun 2-4.30. Oct: Sat and Sun only 2-4.30.
Admission: £1; Chld/OAPs 50p.

SEVENOAKS

SEVENOAKS MUSEUM
(Kent County Council)
Buckhurst Lane, Sevenoaks   **Tel:** (0732) 452384 & 453118

STAPLEHURST

BRATTLE FARM MUSEUM
Staplehurst TN12 0HE   **Tel:** (0580) 891222
Vast collection of Vintage Cars, Tractors, Engines, Bikes, domestic bygones, Blacksmith's and wheelwright equipment. Pair working oxen.
Open: Every Sunday & Bank Holidays, Easter to end of Oct.
Admission: £1.50, Child/OAP £1.
Groups any time

TENTERDEN

TENTERDEN AND DISTRICT MUSEUM
Station Road, Tenterden   **Tel:** (058 06) 3350 and 4310
Townscape and history of Tenterden, Limb of the Cinque Ports. Local trades and industries, building materials; bygones, agricultural implements, hop gardens. The Col. Stephens Railway Collection.
Open: Apr to Oct: Daily 2-5 (Aug weekdays 11-5). Special arrangements for groups

TONBRIDGE

THE MILNE MUSEUM
The Slade, Tonbridge   **Tel:** (0798) 831370

TUNBRIDGE WELLS

THE BROADWATER COLLECTION
Broadwater Court, Tunbridge Wells

TUNBRIDGE WELLS MUSEUM AND ART GALLERY
(Tunbridge Wells Borough Council)
Civic Centre, Mount Pleasant, Royal Tunbridge Wells   **Tel:** (0892) 526121
Local history, Tunbridge ware, dolls, toys, bygones, natural history and regularly changing art exhibitions.
Open: Mon to Sat 9.30-5. *Closed* Sun and Bank Holidays.
Admission: Free.

WYE

AGRICULTURAL MUSEUM
(University of London)
Wye College, Court Lodge Farm, Brook, Wye

Blackburn Museums & Art Galleries

Scene in the South Asian Gallery.

Sekiya on the Sumida River, by Hokusai, from the large collection of Japanese prints bequeathed by the late T.B. Lewis.

LANCASHIRE

ACCRINGTON

HAWORTH ART GALLERY
(Hyndburn Borough Council)
Haworth Park, Accrington   **Tel:** (0254) 33782
Collection of works of the early English watercolour period. One of the finest collections of Tiffany glass in the world. Special exhibitions throughout the year.

BACUP

BACUP NATURAL HISTORY SOCIETY'S MUSEUM
24 Yorkshire Street, Bacup
Collection of natural history subjects; a local geology collection and domestic bygones.

BARROWFORD

PENDLE HERITAGE CENTRE
Park Hill, Nelson, Barrowford BB9 6JQ
A regional centre for heritage education and interpretation. The Centre is based in a 17th century farmhouse, the former home of the Bannister family and features displays about the Pendle area, its buildings and its witches.

BLACKBURN

BLACKBURN MUSEUM AND ART GALLERY
(Blackburn Borough Council)
Museum Street, Blackburn   **Tel:** (0254) 667130
The R.E. Hart collection of coins, illuminated manuscripts, and printed books; Japanese prints, oil paintings, English watercolours, British and Oriental ceramics and decorative art, icons and newly opened gallery of South Asian art and culture. The museum of the East Lancashire Regiment is currently undergoing renovation.
Open: Tues to Sat 10-5.
Children's activity, questionnaire and colouring sheets are available on request.

LEWIS TEXTILE MUSEUM
(Blackburn Borough Council)
Exchange Street, Blackburn   **Tel:** (0254) 667130
The ground floor display of textile machinery is at present undergoing renovation. Constantly changing art exhibitions in first-floor gallery.
Open: Tues to Sat 10-5.

SUNNYHURST WOOD VISITOR CENTRE
(Blackburn Borough Council)
Sunnyhurst Wood, Darwen, Blackburn   **Tel:** (0254) 71545
Changing displays on the history of Darwen; a full programme of changing art exhibitions.
Open: Tues, Thur, Sat, Sun and Bank Hol Mons 2-4.30.

WITTON COUNTRY PARK VISITOR CENTRE
(Blackburn Borough Council)
Witton Country Park, Preston Old Road, Blackburn   **Tel:** (0254) 55423
Located in the stables with displays of harness and agricultural machinery and a natural history room. A fresh section is the newly opened wildlife centre.
Open: Thurs, Fri and Sat 1-5; Sun and Bank Hol Mons 11-5.

BLACKPOOL

GRUNDY ART GALLERY
(Blackpool Borough Council)
Queen Street, Blackpool   **Tel:** (0253) 751701
Permanent collection of paintings and drawings by outstanding 19th and 20th century British artists, also regular one man shows and travelling exhibitions.
Open: Mon to Sat 10-5.

BURNLEY

TOWNELEY HALL ART GALLERY AND MUSEUMS AND MUSEUM OF LOCAL CRAFTS AND INDUSTRIES
(Burnley Borough Council)
Burnley   **Tel:** (0282) 24213

TOWNELEY HALL ART GALLERY & MUSEUMS
Burnley, Lancashire

The former home of the Towneley family, dating originally from the 14th Century, has been an Art Gallery & Museum since 1903. A separate Museum of Local Crafts & Industries is housed in the brew-house, and there is a Natural History Centre with Nature Trails in the grounds.

Fine collection of oil paintings and early English watercolours. Large collections of period furniture, and decorative arts. Major summer exhibitions and temporary loan exhibitions. There is a Natural History Centre with a modern aquarium and nature trails

in the ground. A separate museum of local crafts and industries is housed in the brew-house.
Open: Hall and Natural History Centre: Mon to Fri 10-5; Sun 12-5 all year. **Natural History Centre only:** Apr to Sept: Sat 10-5.
Admission: Free.
Refreshments: Cafe in grounds in Summer.
Parties by appointment.

WEAVERS' TRIANGLE VISITOR CENTRE
Wharfmaster's House, 85 Manchester Road, Burnley
Textile Heritage Centre in a Victorian industrial area astride Leeds & Liverpool Canal.
Open: Easter to Sept, Sat to Wed 2-4; Oct: Suns 2-4. Parties by arrangement.

CHORLEY

ASTLEY HALL
Astley Park, Chorley   **Tel:** (0257) 262166
Charming Tudor/Stuart building set in beautiful park. A lovely manor house combined with museum and art gallery.
Open: Daily Apr 1 to Oct 31: 11-5. Winter Nov 1 to Mar 31: Fri, Sat, Sun 11-5. *Closed* Mon to Thur except for party bookings.
Admission: £2 (£1 concessions). Family ticket £4. Party bookings and prices (evening or day) on enquiry.
Free car park.

COLNE

BRITISH IN INDIA MUSEUM
Newtown Street, Colne BB8 0JJ
Paintings, photographs, coins, stamps, medals, diorama, model railway and other items.
Open: Mon to Sat 10-4 (*except* Tues). *Closed* Jan and Dec, July 5 to July 15, Sept 13 to Sept 18 and all Bank Holidays.

HELMSHORE

HELMSHORE TEXTILE MUSEUMS
(Lancashire Council)
Holcombe Road, Helmshore
Two mill museums showing many aspects of the history of Lancashire's textile industry. One a woollen fulling mill with working water wheel and fulling stocks. The other a cotton mill where spinning mules are demonstrated daily.
Open: Mar to Oct.
Admission: Fee charged.
Refreshments: Cafe.
Parking, shop.

LANCASTER

CITY MUSEUM
(Lancaster City Council)
Market Square, Lancaster   **Tel:** (0524) 64637
Prehistoric, Roman and Medieval archaeology and local history. Museum of the King's Own Royal Regiment.
Open: Mon to Sat 10-5.

MARITIME MUSEUM
(Lancaster City Council)
St. George's Quay, Lancaster   **Tel:** (0524) 64637
Ship models, the Port of Lancaster, inshore fishing, the Lancaster canal, Morecambe Bay. AV show.
Open: Easter to Oct: Daily 11-5; Nov to Easter; Daily 2-5.
Admission: Fee charged.
Refreshments: Cafe.
Shop.

PERIOD COTTAGE
(Lancaster City Council)
15 Castle Hill, Lancaster   **Tel:** (0524) 64637
Dwelling furnished in style of c1820 artisan.
Open: Easter to Sept: Daily 2-5.
Admission: Fee charged.

LEYLAND

SOUTH RIBBLE MUSEUM AND EXHIBITION CENTRE
(South Ribble Borough Council)
The Old Grammar School, Church Road, Leyland   **Tel:** (0772) 422041
Timber framed Tudor Grammar School housing Borough's Museum collection. Local history and archaeology. Monthly exhibitions by local artists.
Open: Tues 10-4; Thurs 1-4; Fri 10-4; Sat 10-1. *Closed* Bank Hols.
Admission: Free.
Car parking 200m from main town centre car park. Not suitable for disabled persons.

PADIHAM

GAWTHORPE HALL
(A National Trust House, leased to Lancashire County Council and administered by the County Museum Service)
Gawthorpe Hall, Padiham, Nr Burnley BB12 8UA   **Tel:** (0282) 78511
Displays include a wide range of needlecraft from R.B.K. Shuttleworth Collection, furniture and portraits from National Portrait Gallery.
Open: House open Good Friday to end-Oct daily except Mon and Fri. Open Bank Holidays.
Admission: Fee charged.

PRESTON

HARRIS MUSEUM AND ART GALLERY
(Borough of Preston)
Market Square, Preston PR1 2PP   **Tel:** (0772) 58248
Magnificent Greek Revival building housing fine collections of British paintings, ceramics, glass and costume. Story of Preston gallery. Lively programme of contemporary art and social history exhibitions with accompanying events and activities. During 1993 special exhibitions and events to mark centenary of opening.
Open: Mon to Sat 10-5. *Closed* most Bank Holidays.
Refreshments: Cafe.
Shop.

RIBCHESTER

MUSEUM OF CHILDHOOD
Church Street, Ribchester
A museum of childhood, toys, models, dolls, miniatures, curios, 54 dolls houses and model fairground.
Special Teddy Bear Collection, museum shop.

Just one of the great
Maritime Museum
Lancaster City Museums

ROSSENDALE

ROSSENDALE MUSEUM
(Rossendale Borough Council)
  Whitaker Park, Rawtenstall, Rossendale **Tel:** (0706) 217777/226509

ROSSENDALE MUSEUM
RAWTENSTALL, LANCASHIRE
TELEPHONE: (0706) 217777/226509

Former home of the textile manufacturing Hardman family, set in Whitaker Park. The building houses a wide variety of collections including fine and decorative arts, natural history and local history. There are displays on the family and a small collection of late 19th century wallpapers.

Admission free.

For further details see editorial entry.

Former Victorian mill owner's mansion housing displays of fine and decorative arts and furniture, including a reconstruction of a Victorian drawing room. Natural history collections include William Bullock's tiger and python. Local history; temporary exhibitions.
Open: Mon to Fri 1-5; Sat 10-12, 1-5; Sun 1-5 (Apr to Oct); 1-4 (Nov to Mar). Groups at other times by arrangement.

RUFFORD

RUFFORD OLD HALL
(The National Trust)
  Rufford, nr Ormskirk **Tel:** (0704) 821254
A superb example of a medieaval hall of half-timber and plaster panels. Interesting collection of local bygones in the stable.

TURTON

TURTON TOWER
(Lancashire County Council)
  Chapeltown Road, Turton, Bolton **Tel:** (0204) 852203
Medieaval Pele Tower with later extensions, 17th century furniture, Civil War arms and armour, temporary exhibitions.
Open: May to Sept: Mon to Fri 10-12, 1-5; Sat and Sun 1-5. Mar, Apr, Oct: Sat to Wed 2-5. Nov and Feb: Sun 2-5. Open Bank Holidays. *Closed* Dec, Jan.
Admission: Fee charged.
Refreshments: Tea rooms.
Parties, guided tours by appointment. Car parking. Shop, nine acres of woodland gardens.

LEICESTERSHIRE

ASHBY-DE-LA-ZOUCH

ASHBY-DE-LA-ZOUCH MUSEUM
  North Street, Ashby-de-la-Zouch LE6 5HU **Tel:** (0530) 560090
Small museum with local material; including model of Ashby Castle under attack, and early 20th century shop.
Open: Mon to Fri 10-12, 2-4; Sat 10-4; Sun 2-4 (Easter to Aug). For winter opening ring first.
Admission: 25p, OAPs 20p, Chld 15p. No reductions. Parties (max. 20) can book for evenings.
Parking. Charity status - voluntarily run.

CASTLE DONINGTON

THE DONINGTON MOTOR MUSEUM
  Donington Park, Castle Donington

DONINGTON-LE-HEATH

THE MANOR HOUSE
  Hugglescote near Coalville, Donington-le-Heath **Tel:** (0530) 31259

LEICESTER

BELGRAVE HALL
  Church Road, Belgrave, Leicester
Small Queen Anne house of 1709-1713, with period room settings from late 17th to late 19th century. Coaches in stable block. Outstanding period and botanic gardens with over 6,500 species of plants.
Open: Weekdays 10-5.30, Sun 2-5.30. *Closed* Good Friday, Christmas Day and Boxing Day.
Access for disabled to all gardens, but ground floor only of three storey house. Unrestricted street parking outside.

JOHN DORAN GAS MUSEUM
(British Gas East Midlands)
  Aylestone Road, Leicester **Tel:** (0533) 535506
Museum devoted to the history of the gas industry, mainly in the East Midlands, with a wide range of exhibits, reflecting all aspects of the industry's heritage.
Open: Tues to Fri 12.30-4.30. *Closed* Sat to Mon, Good Friday, Bank Hols and Tues following.

JEWRY WALL MUSEUM
  St. Nicholas Circle, Leicester **Tel:** (0533) 473021
Museum of Leicestershire Archaeology from earliest times to AD1500 in modern building looking over Roman Baths site and the massive 2nd century Roman Jewry Wall.
Open: Weekdays 10-5.30, Sun 2-5.30. *Closed* Good Friday, Christmas Day and Boxing Day.
Access for disabled via rear entrance in Holy Bones; public parking in centre of St. Nicholas Circle by Holiday Inn.

THE LEICESTERSHIRE MUSEUM AND ART GALLERY
  New Walk, Leicester **Tel:** (0533) 554100
Rutland Dinosaur and other geology and natural history displays. Ancient Egypt Gallery; major regional Art Gallery with European art collection from 15th century including German Expressionists and French Impressionists; important decorative arts collection, especially ceramics.
Open: Weekdays 10-5.30; Sun 2-5.30. *Closed* Good Friday, Christmas Day and Boxing Day.
Full access for disabled. Very limited car parking. Multi storey car park in East St. 200 yards.

LEICESTERSHIRE RECORD OFFICE
  Long Street, Wigston Magna, Leicester LE8 2AH **Tel:** (0533) 571080 **Fax:** (0533) 571120
One of the largest County Record Offices, with extensive collections of official and private archives, both urban and rural, relating to Leicestershire. Now combined with the LEICESTERSHIRE COLLECTION, the local studies library, to include large holdings of published local material; including newspapers, maps and sound recordings.
Open: Mon, Tues & Thurs 9.15-5; Wed 9.15-7.30; Fri 9.15-4.45; most Sats 9.15-12.15. *Closed* Bank Hol Weekends, Mon-Tues and for annual stocktaking week in October. Visitors' car park.

MUSEUM OF COSTUME
  Wygston's House, Applegate, St. Nicholas Circle, Leicester **Tel:** (0533) 554100

MUSEUM OF TECHNOLOGY
  Corporation Road, Abbey Lane, Leicester **Tel:** Curatorial enquiries: (0530) 510851
Housed in 1891 Abbey Pumping station formerly used as part of Leicester's sewer and draining system. Original four giant beam engines, built by Gimson of Leicester. Other engines, transport collection, 64 ton Steam Navvy. Regular programme of steam and other special events. Direct access from Riverside walk, extensive grounds.
Open: Weekdays 10-5.30; Sun 2-5.30. *Closed Good Friday, Christmas Day, Boxing Day.*
Admission: Free except on Special Event days.
Location: Bus 54 from Railway Station or Charles Street.
Access for disabled except to Beam Engines. Visitors' car park.

MUSEUM OF THE ROYAL LEICESTERSHIRE REGIMENT
  The Magazine, Oxford Street, Leicester **Tel:** (0533) 555389
History of the Royal Leicestershire Regiment (late 14th Foot) including mementos, battle trophies and relics, housed in early 15th century Newarke Gateway.
Open: Weekdays 10-5.30; Sun 2-5.30. *Closed* Christmas, Boxing Day and Good Friday.
Wheelchair access impossible. Multi-storey car park in Newarke St, 150 yards.

NEWARKE HOUSES MUSEUM
  The Newarke, Leicester **Tel:** (0533) 554100
Social history collections of Leicestershire from late 15th century to present day. Features include 19th century street scene. Fine collection of clocks, and feature on Leicester's 19th century giant Daniel Lambert. Quiet period garden leads to Castle Close.

Open: Weekdays 10-5.30; Sun 2-5.30. *Closed* Good Friday, Christmas Day and Boxing Day.
Access for disabled very limited for wheelchairs. Multi-storey car park in Newarke St, 200 yards.

SNIBSTON DISCOVERY PARK

Ashby Road, Coalville, Leicester LE5 2LN   **Tel:** (0530) 510851 **Fax:** (0530) 813301

snibston
Leicestershire

Leicestershire's newest and largest attraction - covering over 100 acres just 10 minutes drive from J22 of the M1.

- Purpose built science and industry museum with 'hands-on' approach.
- Country park with nature trail, fishing and golf course.
- Science Play Area.
- Special events.

Open daily 10am-6pm except 25/26 December.

Admission
Adults £3.00, Children and Concessions £2.00.
Group rates available.

Ashby Road, Coalville, Leicestershire LE6 2LN
Tel: 0530 510851 Fax: 0530 813301

Makes finding out a great day out . . .

LEICESTERSHIRE
COUNTY COUNCIL

Major new Science and Industry Museum with the emphasis on 'hands on' participation, working wheelwrights workshop dating from 1742. Country park with trails and lakes.
Open: 10am -6pm daily. *Closed* Christmas Day and Boxing Day.
Admission: £3.00, children and OAP's £2.00
Refreshments: Coffee shop
Free parking. Gift shop and Tourist Information Centre. Telephone for free colour brochure and more details. All areas fully accessible for disabled.

LOUGHBOROUGH

THE BELL FOUNDRY MUSEUM
(John Taylor Bell Founders Ltd)
Freehold Street   **Tel:** (0509) 233414

THE BELL FOUNDRY MUSEUM
FREEHOLD STREET
LOUGHBOROUGH, LEICESTERSHIRE

THE ONLY MUSEUM OF BELLS & BELLFOUNDING IN GREAT BRITAIN.

Fascinating and educational displays set in scheduled historic premises containing good industrial archaeology, yet part of a well-equipped working foundry.

Open Tuesday–Saturday 9.30am–12.30pm and 1.30pm–4.30pm, other times and Bellfounding tours by appointment.

Ideally placed for access from M1, A6, A46 and A60. Regular train services. Ample free parking.

Phone: (0509) 233414

Unique exhibition of the bellfounder's craft. Original material relating to bells, their history and fittings. Industrial archaeology and historic furnace area.
Open: All year Tues to Sat and Bank Hol Mons 9.30-12.30, 1.30-4.30.

Admission: Museum only 75p, Chld 50p. Pre-booked combined museum visit and bell foundry party visits £2.50, Chld (under 16) £1.50; School party rate Chld £1, two supervising teachers free, other adults at Chld rate.
Ample free parking.

LOUGHBOROUGH CARILLON AND WAR MEMORIAL TOWER
(Charnwood Borough Council, Borough Surveyor's Department)
Queens Park, Loughborough   **Tel:** (0509) 263151 Ext 2652
On three levels a collection of militaria and associated memorabilia relating to service of the crown since 1900 to the present. Housed in a unique carillon bell tower where 47 bells are played via a clavier keyboard. Recitals twice weekly - Easter to Sept 30, Thur and Sun.
Open: Good Friday to Sept 30: daily 2-6.
Admission: 60p, Chld 30p (1992 prices).

LUTTERWORTH

STANFORD HALL MOTORCYCLE MUSEUM
Lutterworth   **Tel:** (0788) 860250
Outstanding collection including unique racing and other motorcycles, most in running order, housed in the Stables at Stanford Hall.
Open: Easter to end Sept: - Sat, Sun, 2.30-6; Bank Hol Mons and Tues following and Event days, 12-6.
Admission: £2.50, Chld 90p (1993 charges) including Stanford Hall grounds.
Location: 6 miles NE Rugby near Swinford. M1 exits 18 and 20 M6 Exit 1.

MARKET BOSWORTH

BOSWORTH BATTLEFIELD VISITOR CENTRE AND COUNTRY PARK
(Leicestershire County Council)
Battlefield Visitor Centre, Sutton Cheney, Market Bosworth CV13 0AD
Tel: (0455) 290429
Site of the famous Battle of Bosworth Field, 1485, between Richard III and the future Henry VII. Comprehensive interpretation of the Battle with Visitor Centre including exhibitions, models, film theatre. Illustrated Battle Trails around Battle site. Series of Special Medieval attractions during summer months.
Open: Battlefield Visitor Centre: Easter to Oct 31 Mon to Sat 1-5.30; Sun and Bank Hol Mon 1-6. Country Park and Battle Trails: All year during daylight hours.
Admission: £1.50, Chld/OAPs £1. Pre-booked parties of 20 or more: £1.30, Chld/OAPs 80p. Parties taken throughout the year by appointment.
Refreshments: Cafeteria.
Car parks 30p. Coaches £1.50. Suitable for disabled persons. Special charges apply on main special event days. Book and gift shops.

SHACKERSTONE RAILWAY MUSEUM
(Shackerstone Railway Society Ltd)
Shackerstone Station, Shackerstone CV13 6NW   **Tel:** (0455) 880754
Museum of RAILWAYANIA, much of it 19th century with special emphasis on railways of WEST LEICESTERSHIRE.
Admission: 50p, Chld free (Suns and Bank Hols); No reductions for parties.
Free car parking. Suitable for disabled. Cafe.

MARKET HARBOROUGH

HARBOROUGH MUSEUM
(Leicestershire County Council)
Council Offices, Adam and Eve Street, Market Harborough   **Tel:** (0858) 432468
Fax: 9862766
Museum of the town of Market Harborough and its surrounding area illustrating the Medieval planned town and its role as a market, social and hunting centre and a stagecoach post. Displays from the Symington Collection of Corsetry and a local bootmaker's workshop.
Open: Mon to Sat 10-4.30; Sun 2-5. *Closed* Good Friday, Christmas Day and Boxing Day.
Access for disabled via lift in Council offices (on Sat, Sun and Bank Hols please contact museum staff). Visitors' car park.

MELTON MOWBRAY

MELTON CARNEGIE MUSEUM
(Leicestershire County Council)
Thorpe End, Melton Mowbray   **Tel:** (0664) 69946
Local museum of the history and environment of the Borough of Melton (which includes the famous Vale of Belvoir); sporting paintings and local exhibitions.
Open: Mon to Sat 10.00-5.00. Easter to Sept 2-5. *Closed* Good Friday, Christmas Day and Boxing Day.
Full disabled access. Street parking nearby.

OAKHAM

OAKHAM CASTLE
(Leicestershire County Council)
Market Place, Oakham   **Tel:** (0572) 723654
12th century Great Hall of Norman Castle in castle grounds with earlier motte. Unique collection of horseshoes presented by visiting Peers of the Realm.
Open: Castle Grounds: Apr to Oct 10-5.30 daily. Nov to Mar 10-4 daily. Great Hall: Apr to Oct, Tues to Sat and Bank Hol Mon 10-1, 2-5.30. Sun 2-5.30. Nov to Mar, Tues to Sat 10-1, 2-4, Sun 2-4. *Closed* Good Friday, Christmas Day and Boxing Day.
Access for disabled to Great Hall. Parking only for disabled visitors on request.

RUTLAND COUNTY MUSEUM
(Leicestershire County Council)
Catmos Strteet, Oakham   **Tel:** (0572) 723654
The Museum of Rutland Life, including agricultural equipment, implements and wagons, local crafts and domestic items, local archaeology. All housed in a splendid 18th century Cavalry Riding School. Special gallery on the Volunteer Soldier in Leicestershire and Rutland.
Open: Mon to Sat 10-5, Sun (Apr to Oct) 2-5, (Nov to Mar) 2-4. *Closed* Good Friday, Christmas Day and Boxing Day.
Access for disabled throughout except balcony displays. Public car park adjacent.

RUTLAND WATER

NORMANTON CHURCH MUSEUM, RUTLAND WATER
(Anglian Water Services Ltd)
Rutland Water, Nr. Oakham

LINCOLNSHIRE

ALFORD

MANOR HOUSE FOLK MUSEUM
West Street, Alford

BOSTON

GUILDHALL MUSEUM
(Boston Borough Council)
South Street, Boston   **Tel:** (0205) 365954

The museum houses the original prison cells in which the early Pilgrim Fathers were imprisoned in 1607 after their abortive attempt to leave England for religious freedom in Holland. Pictures and prints of local interest. Local archaeological material. Collection of firemarks and maritime exhibits. Monthly exhibition programme.
Open: Mon to Sat 10-5. Also Sun *(Apr to Sept only)* 1.30-5.
Admission: Charge includes the use of a personal audio guided tour. Children free. Shop.

CONINGSBY

BATTLE OF BRITAIN MEMORIAL FLIGHT
Royal Air Force, Coningsby LN4 4SY   **Tel:** (0526) 44041
One hour conducted tour of the flying aircraft, five Spitfires, one Hurricane and one of the only two flying Lancasters in company of expert guide. A memorabilia exhibition and souvenir shop.
Open: Mon-Fri 10.00-5.00pm. (Last conducted tour 3.30pm) *Closed* weekends, Bank Holidays and over Christmas.
Admission: Charge.

GAINSBOROUGH

GAINSBOROUGH OLD HALL
(Lincolnshire County Council and English Heritage)
Parnell Street, Gainsborough **Tel:** (0427) 612669

FROM A MEDIEVAL HALL TO AN AWARD WINNING
SOCIAL HISTORY MUSEUM COME AND DISCOVER
LINCOLNSHIRE'S HISTORY FROM 140,000 BC ONWARDS.

Gainsborough Old Hall   Church Farm Museum
Grantham Museum   Stamford Museum
Lincoln – Usher Gallery
City & County Museum   Museum of Lincolnshire Life

For an information Pack ring (0522) 552809.
Lincolnshire County Council, Recreational Services Dept.

15th century manor house with great hall, medieval kitchen, displays on Richard III and life in the Old Hall.
Open: Mon-Sat 10.00-5.00, Summer Suns 2-5.30 Visitors at other times by arrangement.
Admission: Charge. Reduced rates for parties booked in advance.
Refreshments: Light only available.
Winner of Gulbenkian Catering Award 1990. Visits at other times by arrangement.

RICHMOND PARK EXHIBITION CENTRE
Richmond Park, Gainsborough

GRANTHAM

GRANTHAM MUSEUM
(Lincolnshire County Council)
St. Peters Hill, Grantham **Tel:** (0476) 68783
Collection of local prehistoric, Roman and Saxon archaeology, Grantham local history, trades and industries and a collection devoted to Isaac Newton and to Prime Minister Margaret Thatcher.
Open: Apr to Sept: Mon to Sat 10-5, Sun 2-5; Oct to Mar: Mon to Sat 10-12.30, 1.30-5.
Admission: Fee charged.

LINCOLN

CITY AND COUNTY MUSEUM
(Lincolnshire County Council)
Broadgate, Lincoln **Tel:** (0522) 530401
Shows the natural history and geology of the country and the Story of man in Lincolnshire from prehistoric times to 1750.
Open: Mon to Sat 10-5.30, Sun 2.30-5.
Admission: Charge.

THE LAWN
(Lincoln City Council)
Union Road, Lincoln **Tel:** (0522) 560330
Former psychiatric hospital converted into Conference and Visitor Centre with extensive grounds. Various attractions: Sir Joseph Banks Conservatory and aquarium, with shop and information centre; Lincoln Archaeology Centre explains the work of the City's archaeologists with hands-on displays; Charlesworth Centre describing history of the Lawn Hospital and psychiatric treatment in general. Also conference and function rooms. entre explains
Open: Daily all year round.
Admission: Free
Refreshments: Pub and restaurant.
Shops. Extensive grounds, picnic areas and children's play area.

LINCOLN CASTLE
Castle Hill, Lincoln LN1 3AA **Tel:** (0522) 511068
Built by William the Conqueror in 1068, the Castle has impressive towers, walls and gatehouses, which enclose beautiful gardens. Unique Victorian 'Silent System' prison chapel. Events take place throughout the summer.
Open: BST 9.00-5.30 Mon to Sat; 11.00-5.30 Sunday; GMT 4.00 closing. Last admission 30 minutes before closing.
Admission: Charge.

LINCOLN CATHEDRAL LIBRARY
Lincoln **Tel:** (0522) 544544
Medieval MSS and early printed books. Wren Library by appointment only.

LINCOLN CATHEDRAL TREASURY
The Cathedral, Lincoln **Tel:** (0522) 544544
Gold and silver plate from the Diocese.
Open: Weekdays 11-3.

LINCOLNSHIRE ARCHIVES
St Rumbold Street, Lincoln LN2 5AB **Tel:** (0522) 525158 (Search room) (0522) 526204 (Enquiries)
Established in 1948 to preserve Lincolnshire's documentary heritage for the benefit of present and future generations. The service is provided by Lincolnshire County Council and includes: document storage and conservation, research facilities, Archives Education, Genealogical Research and reprographics. Free leaflets are available on request.
Open: Students' hours: Mon 2.00-7.45pm; Tues-Fri 9.00-5.00pm; Sat 9.00-4.00pm (prior notice of visit advisable)
Admission: Charge.
Free car parking.

MUSEUM OF LINCOLNSHIRE LIFE
(Lincolnshire County Council)
Burton Road, Lincoln **Tel:** (0522) 528448
Displays illustrate the social, domestic, commercial, agricultural and industrial life of Lincolnshire over the last 200 years. New display of the Royal Lincolnshire Regiment and First World War tank.
Open: May-Sept daily 10-5.30, Oct-April Mon-Sat 10-5.30, Sun 2-5.30. By appointment.
Admission: Fee charged.
Refreshments: Light only.

USHER GALLERY
(Lincolnshire County Council)
Lindum Road, Lincoln **Tel:** (0522) 527980
The major Lincolnshire venue for all aspects of the fine and decorative arts. Usher collection of watches, porcelain and miniatures; Peter de Wint watercolours; local topographical works; Tennyson memorabilia and coin gallery. Continuous programme of temporary exhibitions.
Open: Mon to Sat 10-5.30; Sun 2.30-5.
Admission: Charge.

SKEGNESS

CHURCH FARM MUSEUM
(Lincolnshire County Council)
Church Road South, Skegness **Tel:** (0754) 766658
Houses the Bernard Best collection of agricultural and domestic equipment in a 19th century farm complex. Reconstructed timber-framed cottage and brick barn now open. Temporary exhibitions and regular craft demonstrations.
Open: Apr to Oct: Daily 10.30-5.30.
Admission: Fee charged.
Refreshments: Light only.

SPALDING

AYSCOUGHFEE HALL AND GARDENS
(South Holland District Council)
Churchgate, Spalding   **Tel:** (0775) 725468

AYSCOUGHFEE HALL

Churchgate, Spalding

Ayscoughfee

Displays in the renovated 15th century merchants house are on land-reclamation, agriculture and horticulture with particular emphasis on the bulb industry. Also displayed are birds from the collection of the Spalding Gentlemen's Society and visitors can see the beautifully restored panelled Library, as well as galleries on village history and the history of Ayscoughfee Hall. There are changing displays in the temporary exhibtions gallery.

March–October	Open daily
November–February	Weekends Closed
Admission Free	Enquiries 0775 725468

Recently established museum. Displays on land reclaimation, agriculture, horticulture and social history.
Open: Gardens open all year.Museum Mar to Oct open daily: Nov to Feb *closed* weekends.

THE PINCHBECK ENGINE HOUSE
(South Holland District Council & Welland & Deeping Internal Drainage Board)
West Marsh Road, Spalding   **Tel:** (0775) 725468/722444

THE PINCHBECK ENGINE

The steam beam engine driving a scoop wheel was erected in 1833 to drain Spalding and Pinchbeck.
It ceased operations in 1952 when it was the last of its type working in The Fens.
Newly open to the public is this fine example of early 19th Century industrial engineering and architecture.
Displays tell the story of the evolution of The Fens by embanking and Draining and contain a unique collection of the tools and equipment used to undertake the works.
A joint venture by the Welland and Deepings Internal Drainage Board and the South Holland District Council at West Marsh Road, Spalding.
Admission Free. Open daily April-October. Other times by appointment:
Tel: Spalding 0775 725468 0775 722444

This restored steam beam engine driving a scoop wheel was erected in 1833 to drain Spalding and Pinchbeck. It ceased operations in 1952 when it was the last of its type working in The Fens. Newly open to the public is this fine example of early 19th Century industrial engineering and draining. Displays tell the story of the evolution of The Fens through embanking and draining.
Open: Daily Apr to Oct, other times by appointment.
Admission: Free.

SPALDING MUSEUM
(Spalding Gentlemen's Society)
Broad Street, Spalding   **Tel:** (0775) 4658
Good collection of bygones, ceramics, glass, coins, medals and prehistoric relics. By appointment only.

STAMFORD

BROWNE'S HOSPITAL
Broad Street, Stamford PE9 1PD   **Tel:** (0780) 63746 and 51226

STAMFORD BREWERY MUSEUM
All Saints Street, Stamford   **Tel:** (0780) 52186
Set in attractive stone buildings the Museum is a complete Victorian steam brewery with steam engine, coppers, coopered vats, boiler, boot and flogger and welly warmer. Displays features Victorian working life in a cooperage, brewer's office, laboratory and in-home brewing.
Souvenir shop.

STAMFORD MUSEUM
(Lincolnshire County Council)
Broad Street, Stamford   **Tel:** (0780) 66317
A museum of local archaeology and history. Exhibits include Daniel Lambert's clothing.
Open: Apr to Sept: Mon to Sat 10-5, Sun 2-5. Oct to Mar: Mon to Sat 10-12.30, 1.30-5.
Admission: Fee charged.

TATTERSHALL

TATTERSHALL CASTLE
(The National Trust)
Tattershall
Museum in Guard House contains many interesting exhibits, including a model of the Castle as it used to be in the seventeenth century.
Open: Every day except Christmas Day and Boxing Day.

GREATER LONDON

ACCADEMIA ITALIANA DELLE ARTI E DELLE ARTI APPLICATE
24 Rutland Gate, London SW7 1BB   **Tel:** 071-225 3474

The museum space for the presentation in Bratain of Italian artistic achievement. Past exhibitions include Giorgio Morandi, Old Master Drawings by Giambattista Tiepolo, Italy by Moonlight (Italian Nocturnal Landscapes 16th-19th centuries). Exhibitions being planned for 1993 are Ruskin and Tuscany, Ricardo Cinali, the sculpture of Antonio Canova, and Francesco Guardi. Also concerts, debates and lectures on all aspects of Italian Art, Design and style.
Open: Tues to Sat 10-5.30, Wed 10-8, Sun 2-5.30.
Admission: £3; Students, OAPs, UB40s, WCC res £1.50. No discounts unless by prior arrangement.

Metered parking in Rutland Gate, public parking at Metrostore, Kensington Road. Suitable for disabled persons (no wheelchairs available).

APSLEY HOUSE (WELLINGTON MUSEUM)
(A branch of the Victoria and Albert Museum)
Hyde Park Corner, London W1V 9FA   **Tel:** 071-499 5676
Closed for essential work to maintain the fabric and security of the building. Visitors are advised to telephone the House for up to date information towards the end of 1993.

BADEN-POWELL HOUSE
(The Scout Association)
Queen's Gate, London SW7 5JS   **Tel:** 071-584 7031
Mementoes of Baden-Powell and historical records.
Open: Daily 9-5.

BANK OF ENGLAND MUSEUM
Threadneedle Street (entrance in Bartholomew Lane), London EC2R 8AH
Tel: 071-601 5545

BANK OF ENGLAND MUSEUM

THREADNEEDLE STREET
(entrance in Bartholomew Lane)
LONDON EC2R 8AH
Telephone: 071-601 5545
Nearest Underground:
BANK

OPENING TIMES:
Monday to Friday 10.00–5.00
Sunday (Easter to end of September) and Public Holidays 11.00–5.00

ADMISSION FREE

Located in the Bank of England itself, the Museum tells the history of the Bank from its foundation in 1694 to its role today as the nation's central bank. Displays include banknotes, coins, gold bullion, interactive videos and a reconstructed 18th century banking hall.
Open: Monday to Friday 10-5; Sunday (Easter to end-September) and Public Holidays 11-5. *Closed* Saturday, 25 & 26 December and 1 January. Also open on the day of the Lord Mayor's show.
Admission: Free
Location: Underground: Bank

BANKSIDE GALLERY
(Blackfriars tube), 48 Hopton Street, Blackfriars, London SE1 9JH
Royal Watercolour Society and the Royal Society of Painter-Printmakers. Spring and Autumn exhibitions plus open exhibitions and contemporary and historical exhibitions from Britain and abroad.

BANQUETING HOUSE
(Historic Royal Palaces)
Whitehall, London SW1A 2ER
Designed by Inigo Jones for James I in 1619, with a magnificent Rubens ceiling. Site of Charles I's execution.

BARBICAN ART GALLERY
(Corporation of the City of London (Libraries, Art Galleries Dept)
Level 8, Barbican Centre, London EC2Y 8DS   **Tel:** 071-638 4141 Extension 306
Large temporary exhibition gallery with a varied programme of changing exhibitions. Telephone 071-588 9023 (recorded information) for details of current exhibitions and opening times.
Admission: Charges vary with each exhibition. Half price for chld, students, OAPs, registered disabled and unemployed. Reduced rates for pre-booked parties.
National car park in Barbican Centre; further parking in NCP car parks, London Wall and Finsbury Square. Suitable for disabled persons. Wheelchairs available from Red Cross. Restaurants in Barbican Centre.

BARNET MUSEUM
(Barnet and District Local History Society)
31 Wood Street, Barnet EN5 4BE   **Tel:** 081-440 8066
Archaeological and historical exhibits relating to the area.
Open: All year, Tues, Wed and Thurs 2.30-4.30; Sat 10-12 and 2.30-4.30.

BEN URI ART SOCIETY AND GALLERY
21 Dean Street, London W1V 6NE   **Tel:** 071-437 2852
The aim of the Society, which is a registered charity founded in 1915, is to promote Jewish Art as part of the Jewish cultural heritage. The gallery provides a showcase for exhibitions of contemporary art by Jewish artists, as well as for the society's own permanent collection of over 500 works by artists including Bomberg, Auerbach and Gertler.
Open: Mon to Thurs 10-5, some Sun afternoons. *(Closed* Fri, Sat, Jewish Hols and Bank Hols.
Admission: Free.
Group visits welcome. NCP car park opposite. Suitable for disabled persons.

BETHNAL GREEN MUSEUM OF CHILDHOOD
(A branch of the Victoria and Albert Museum)
Cambridge Heath Road, London E2 9PA   **Tel:** 081-980 3204
The National Museum of Childhood. Outstanding collection of toys, dolls, doll's houses, games, puppets. Also children's costume, nursery antiques; new galleries on the history of childhood in preparation. New gallery; 'Trash or Treasure', the Renier Collection of historic and contemporary children's books.
Open: Mon to Thurs and Sat 10-6. *Closed* Fri, also Christmas Eve, Christmas Day, Boxing Day, New Year's Day, Good Friday and May Day Bank Holiday.

BEXLEY MUSEUM
Hall Place, Bourne Road, Bexley   **Tel:** (0322) 526574
Historic house, permanent and temporary exhibitions, general and local. Local Studies Centre. Visitor Centre.
Open: Mon to Sat 10-5 (dusk in winter); Sun (in summer) 2-6. Beautiful gardens open daily. Visitor Centre open daily in Summer.

BEXLEY MUSEUMS

The north wings of Hall Place, Bexley, 1537–40.

Bexley Museum, Hall Place, Bourne Road, Bexley.
The Local History Museum of the Borough of Bexley, housed in a Tudor and Jacobean Mansion. Permanent archaeology and natural history displays with temporary exhibitions of social history.

Erith Museum, Erith Library, Walnut Tree Road, Erith.
The history of Erith, including displays on Lesnes Abbey, The Great Harry, Maxim's flying machine and an Edwardian kitchen.

BOURNE FINE ART
14 Mason's Yard, Duke Street, St. James's, London   **Tel:** 071-930 4215/6

BRITISH DENTAL ASSOCIATION MUSEUM
(Smith Turner Historical Collection)
63-64 Wimpole Street, London W1M 8AL   **Tel:** 071-935 0875
Collection illustrating the history of dental surgery.
Open: Mon to Fri 9-5.

THE BRITISH LIBRARY
Great Russell Street, London WC1   **Tel:** 071-636 1544
The British Library is the UK's national library and its exhibitions, lectures and seminars are based on its vast collections, world famous for their richness and variety. Many of the most outstanding items in the Library's collections are on permanent display. They include Magna Carta, the first folio edition of Shakespeare's works (1623), the Lindisfarne Gospels and the Gutenberg Bible, 1455 (the first book printed in movable type).
Open: Mon to Sat 10-5, Sun 2.30-6.

The Priory
Church Hill
Orpington
BR6 0HH
Tel: 0689 873826

Free Admission

THE LONDON BOROUGH

Find out about the archaeology of the London Borough of Bromley - from the earliest times to Domesday - and Sir John Lubbock, 1st Lord Avebury, the man responsible for giving this country its Bank Holidays.

Open **9.00am - 5.00pm** (closed Thursday, Sunday and Bank Holidays)

BRITISH MUSEUM
Great Russell Street, London WC1B 3DG   **Tel:** 071-636 1555
Comprising the national collection of antiquities and Prints and Drawings. The Museum departments are: Greek and Roman, Egyptian, Pre-historic and Romano-British, Western Asiatic, Oriental, Japanese, Coins, Medals and Bank Notes, Medieval and Later, Prints and Drawings and Ethnography (see under Museum of Mankind).
Open: Weekdays 10-5; Sun 2.30-6.
Admission: Free
Location: Underground stations: Tottenham Court Road, Holborn, Russell Square.

BROMLEY MUSEUM
The Priory, Church Hill, Orpington BR6 0HH   **Tel:** (0689) 873826
The archaeology of the London Borough of Bromley from earliest times to Domesday, and Sir John Lubbock, 1st Lord Avebury, the man responsible for giving this country its Bank Holidays.
Open: 9-5 except Thurs, Sun and Bank Holidays.
Admission: Free.

BRUCE CASTLE MUSEUM
(London Borough of Haringey)
Lordship Lane, Tottenham, London N17 8NU   **Tel:** 081-808 8772
Local history. Postal history.
Open: Tues to Sun: 1-5. *Closed* winter Bank Hols and Good Friday.

BUCKINGHAM PALACE, THE QUEEN'S GALLERY
Buckingham Palace Road, London SW1   **Tel:** 071-799 2331
Exhibition for 1993.'A King's Purchase: George 111 and the Consul Smith Collection'
Open: 5th March-23rd December
Admission: Fee charged.

BUCKINGHAM PALACE, THE ROYAL MEWS
Buckingham Palace Road, London SW1W 0QH   **Tel:** 071-799 2331
The Royal Mews provides a unique opportunity to see how horse, carriage and tack combine to create the familiar pageantry associated with State Occasions.
Open: Every Wed 12-4 all year with additional days during the Summer.
Admission: Fee charged

CABINET WAR ROOMS
Clive Steps, King Charles Street, London SW1A 2AQ   **Tel:** 071-930 6961
Take a step back to the dark days of the Second World War when Churchill and his Chiefs of Staff masterminded Britain's war effort from a complex of underground rooms beneath Whitehall. A fascinating personal sound tour takes you through 21 historic rooms which have been preserved exactly as they were fifty years ago. See the Cabinet Room, the Map Room, Churchill's bedroom and the Transatlantic Telephone Room which allowed Churchill to speak directly to the President in the White House.
Open: Daily: 10 (last admission 5.15). *Closed* 24-26 Dec and 1 Jan.
Location: Nearest tube station: Westminster
Information: 071-930 6961.

CANADA HOUSE GALLERY
(Michael Regan - Visual Arts Officer)
Trafalgar Square, London SW1Y 5BJ   **Tel:** 071-629 9492, Ext 2229
Changing exhibitions of Canadian art, craft and design.
Open: Mon to Fri 11-5. *Closed* Bank Hols.

Admission: Free.
Suitable for disabled persons.

CAREW MANOR AND DOVECOTE
(London Borough of Sutton)
Church Road, Beddington
This building, formerly known as Beddington Park or Beddington Place, contains a late-medieval Great Hall, with an arch-braced hammer-beam roof, which is listed Grade I. The house is used as a school, but the Hall is now accessible every Sunday from Easter until Nov, together with the interior of the restored early 18th century Dovecote, with its 1,288 nesting boxes and potence, which is a scheduled ancient monument. Guided tours available of the Dovecote, the Great Hall and the ancient cellers of the house which contain medieval, Tudor, and later features (cellars accessible on guided tours only). Some tours take in the late 14th century Church of St Mary, Beddington, with its Norman font and its 15th century Carew Chapel containing important Carew memorials (the Carews of Beddington were lords of the manor for over four hundred years). Carew manor and Beddington Church stand on the edge of Beddington Park, the landscaped home park of the Carews, through which a Heritage Trail has been established giving details of the history, historic buildings, garden features, and wildlife of this important conservation area.
Open: Suns & Bank Holiday Mons from Easter to Nov 1 (telephone Sutton Heritage Service 081-773 4555 for details).
Admission: Fee charged.
Location: Church Road, Beddington. Off A232 ¾m E of junction with A237.
Guide book, trail leaflet and other publications and souvenirs available.

CARLYLE'S HOUSE
(The National Trust)
24 Cheyne Row, Chelsea SW3   **Tel:** 071-352 7087
Portraits, furniture, prints, 'personal relics' and a small library of books belonging to Thomas Carlyle.

CARSHALTON HOUSE
(Daughters of the Cross)
Pound Street, Carshalton (St. Philomena's)
An important listed building, built by about 1707 around the core of an older house and with grounds originally laid out by Charles Bridgeman. Carshalton House is open on a limited number of occasions each year. Its garden buildings include the unique Water Tower, now in the care of the Carshalton Water Tower Trust. The house contains principal rooms with 18th century decoration, including the important Blue Room and the Painted Parlour (attributed to Robert Robinson). Openings are organised by Sutton Heritage Service in conjuction with the Water Tower Trust and the Daughters of the Cross. Tours of the house and grounds and a programme of short talks on the house and its people are given during the day (included in entrance fee); Publications are available. Carshalton House is close to Sutton's Heritage Centre at Honeywood, in the Carshalton conservation area.
Open: Dates for 1993 are Easter Bank Holiday Mon Apr 12 Sat Sept 12 10am-5pm (last adm 4.15)
Admission: Fee charged.
Location: Pound Street, Carshalton, at junction with Carshalton Road, on A232.
Refreshments: Available
For further details telephone Sutton Heritage Service on 081-773 4555.

CENTURY GALLERY
100/102 Fulham Road, Chelsea SW3 6HS   **Tel:** 071-581 1589 **Fax:** 071-589 9468
Gallery deals in 20th century art from the USSR - also 20th century French paintings.
Open: Mon to Sat 10-6.

Admission: Free.
Suitable for disabled persons.

CHARTERED INSURANCE INSTITUTE'S MUSEUM

20 Aldermanbury, London EC2V 7HY   **Tel:** 071-606 3835
Collection of Insurance Companies' firemarks, firefighting equipment, helmets, medals indicating the part played by insurance companies in lessening the dangers of fire.
Open: During office hours, Mon to Fri.

CHELSEA COLLEGE OF ART AND DESIGN (THE LONDON INSTITUTE)

London   **Tel:** 071-351 3844
Summer Shows. Foundation, B'TEC National Diploma, and BA Degree shows are held in late June/early July. MA Degree shows are held in the first week of September.
Please telephone college for details. See above

CHISWICK HOUSE

(English Heritage)
Burlington Lane, Chiswick W4   **Tel:** 081-995 0508
Villa designed by the Earl of Burlington 1725 and derived from villas by Palladio and Scamozzi. William Kent assisted with the interior decoration. New exhibition covering the development of House and Grounds.
Open: Apr 1 to Sept 30, daily 10-6. 1 October-31 March, daily 10-4. *Cosed* 24,25 December.
Admission: £2.00, Concessions £1.50, Chld £1.(1992 prices). Adm price includes a free personal stereo guided tour.

CHURCH FARM HOUSE MUSEUM

(London Borough of Barnet)
Greyhound Hill, Hendon NW4 4JR   **Tel:** 081-203 0130
Local history, furnished rooms in period style. Special exhibitions throughout the year.
Open: Mon to Thurs 10-5, Sat 10-1, 1-5.30, Sat 2-5.30. *Closed* Fri

CITY & GUILDS OF LONDON ART SCHOOL

124 Kennington Park Road, London SE11 4DJ **Tel:** 071-735 2306
Degree Show for Restoration & Conservation Studies, Painting, Sculpture, Decorative Arts, Illustrative Arts, Lettering, Stonecarving, Wood Carving & Gilding held annually at the end of the Summer Term.

CLOCKMAKERS' COMPANY MUSEUM

Guildhall Library, Aldermanbury

COMMONWEALTH INSTITUTE

Kensington High Street, London W8 6NQ   **Tel:** 071-603 4535 **Fax:** 071-602 7374

Why just come to London when you can visit the Caribbean, see Canada from a skidoo, climb Mount Kenya or take a rickshaw across Bangladesh?

Discover the history, landscapes, wildlife and crafts of the Commonwealth on 3 floors of magical galleries in a spectacular listed building.

There are also cultural events and exhibitions, and special events for children.

Visit the Commonwealth Shop and be tempted by the stunning collection of crafts and books or enjoy a meal with a difference at Flags Restaurant.

Open Monday to Saturday 10.00 until 17.00, Sunday 14.00 until 17.00.

Admission free.

Commonwealth Institute
Kensington High Street, London W8 6NQ. Tel: 071-603 4535

Visit the spectacular tent-shaped building next to Holland Park. Programmes include visual art and craft exhibitions, live gallery events, childrens' holiday activities, and the Schools' Programme with workshops, seminars and conferences for teachers and students. Facilities include the Commonwealth Resource Centre for multi-media resources on the Commonwealth countries, Compix a slide loan service, the Conference and Event Centre with a range of venues for hire, the Commonwealth Shop for postcards, gifts, food and wine from around the world, and Flags Restaurant. A free copy of *What's On* can be obtained from Marketing and Publicity.

Open: *Closed* Christmas Eve, Christmas Day, Boxing Day, New Years Day, Good Friday and May Day.
Location: High Street Kensington, Earl's Court, Olympia, Holland Park. Bus 9,10,27,28,31,49, C1 Hoppa.
Refreshments: Licensed Flags Restaurant.

THE THOMAS CORAM FOUNDATION FOR CHILDREN

(Foundling Hospital Art Treasures)
40 Brunswich Square, London WC1   **Tel:** 071-278 2424
About 150 paintings, prints etc., including works by Hogarth, Gainsborough and Reynolds; historical records; musical scores by Handel; furniture and clocks; mementoes from the Foundling Hospital (founded 1739).
Open: Mon to Fri 10-4. *Closed* at weekends, Public Hols when the rooms are in use for conferences etc. Before visiting, it is advisable to check by telephone that the rooms are open.
Admission: £1, OAPs/registered art students and Chld 50p.
Location: Underground stations: Russell Square, King's Cross. Buses to Russell Square.

COURTAULD INSTITUTE GALLERIES

Somerset House, Strand, London WC2R ORN   **Tel:** 071-873 2526
The Galleries of the University of London; including the Lee Collection, the Gambier-Parry Collection, the important Princes Gate Collection of Old Master paintings and drawings, the famous Courtauld Collection of Impressionist and Post-Impressionist paintings, and the Fry and Hunter collection of modern art.
Open: Weekdays 10-6; Sun 2-6. *Closed* Dec 24, 25, 26, Jan 1.

THE CRAFTS COUNCIL

44a Pentonville Road, London N1 9BY   **Tel:** 071-278 7700

Crafts Council
National centre for the crafts

Crafts Council
44a Pentonville Road
Islington London N1
Tel 071 278 7700

Open Tues to Sat
11am – 6pm
Sundays 2 – 6pm
Closed Mondays

Free entry to
● The Crafts Council Gallery
  Britain's major public gallery
  for contemporary crafts
● Gallery Shop
● The Crafts Council Collection
● Information centre
● Picture library of 33,000 slides
● Reference library
● Café

The national centre for the crafts. Gallery with changing exhibitions, information centre, slide library, reference library.
Open: Tues to Sat 11-6, Sun 2-6. *Closed* Mon.
Admission: Free.
Cafe, gallery shop.

CUMING MUSEUM

(London Borough of Southwark)
155-157 Walworth Road, London SE17 1RS   **Tel:** 071-701 1342
The Museum of Southwark's History. The worldwide collections of the Cuming family joined with the local history of Southwark, from Roman times to the present. Special displays of Medieval Southwark, Dickens and George Tinworth's sculpture.
Open: Tues to Sat 10-5. *Closed* Sun, Mon.
Admission: Free

UNIVERSITY OF LONDON
COURTAULD INSTITUTE
GALLERIES

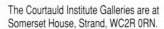

The Courtauld Institute Galleries are at Somerset House, Strand, WC2R 0RN.

The magnificent neo-classical "Fine Rooms" in the North Block of Somerset House were built by the royal architect Sir William Chambers, in 1776-80, to house the three learned societies: The Royal Society, The Society of Antiquaries, and The Royal Academy of Arts, as part of an ambitious scheme to accommodate government offices on the site of the former royal palace. The Courtauld Institute of Art (E.Entrance) and the Courtauld Institute Galleries (W.Entrance) are now re-united here, after an extensive programme of refurbishment and adaptation was completed 1987-90.

The range and quality of the Courtauld collections can now be enjoyed in a splendid architectural setting, which has been decorated in the original

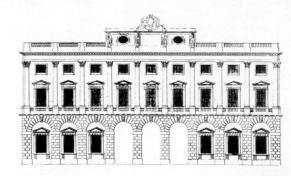

colours specified by Chambers. Furniture and carpets give warmth and intimacy to the rooms.

Many more works of art are now on show: from Bernardo Daddi alterpieces of the 14th C. to paintings by Ben Nicholson and contemporary living artists. The famous Courtauld collection of Impressionist and Post-Impressionist paintings, and the superb Princes Gate, Lee of Fareham, and Gambier-Parry collections of old masters, are complemented by 20th C. art from the Fry, Hunter and Browse collections.

There is a special exhibition room for prints, drawings and watercolours. Prints and drawings not on show may be seen in the Study Room by prior appointment.

A bookshop and cafeteria are also provided.

CUTTY SARK CLIPPER SHIP
(The Maritime Trust)
 King William Walk, Greenwich SE10 9HT   **Tel:** 081-858 3445 **Fax:** 081-858 2698

**CLIPPER
SHIP
CUTTY SARK**

Open all year
(closed Dec.
24,25,26)
For Admission
details see
editorial reference

The last of the China Tea Clippers, built 1869, *Cutty Sark* used to race home to London with the new season's tea. Later she brought wool from Australia and made many record-breaking voyages. *Cutty Sark* was famous for her speed and beauty and survived storms and hurricanes, losing her rudder and dismasting. Displays and audio visual on board tell her story. 1993 programme of restoration work in the ship - shipwrights and riggers may be seen practising their traditional skills (weekdays) on repairs to the masts and rigging, deck and keel. In the lower hold the 'Long John Silver' collection of merchant ships' figureheads, the biggest collection in the country, is on display.
Open: Mon to Sat 10-5.30, Sun 12-5.30. Winter close 4.30. *Closed* Dec 24, 25, 26.
Admission: £3,25 concessions £2.25 Family £8.00 (from 1/4/93). Handicapped free. Parties 20% discount, booked in advance Mon to Fri. Also **Gipsy Moth IV**, Sir Francis Chichester's Round the World yacht, small charge.
Car park and coach parking alongside. Only partly suitable for disabled.

DARWIN MUSEUM
 Down House, Downe, Kent

DE MORGAN FOUNDATION - OLD BATTERSEA HOUSE
 Vicarage Crescent, Battersea, London SW15 6HL   **Tel:** 071-788 1341

DE MORGAN FOUNDATION
OLD BATTERSEA HOUSE

Paintings and drawings by Evelyn De Morgan, Spencer Stanhope, Strudwick, Cowper; Ceramics by William De Morgan – all in a fine Wren style building.
Admission by appointment only – see editorial reference.
Works from the Foundation's collection are also on public display at Cardiff Castle, Cragside House Cumbria, Knightshayes Court, Tiverton, Devon.
The St. John portraits are at Lydiard Park, Swindon.

The ground floor of this elegantly restored Wren style building provides the setting of a private home for a substantial part of the De Morgan Foundation Collection which has been here since the early 1930s. Paintings and drawings by Evelyn De Morgan, her uncle Roddam Spencer Stanhope, J.M. Strudwich and Cadogan Cowper are displayed with ceramics by William De Morgan.
Open: By appointment only - usually Wed afternoons.
Admission: £1, optional catalogue £1.50. No special reductions. Parties maximum 30 (split into two groups of 15).
Write in advance to: De Morgan Foundation, 21 St Margaret's Crescent, Putney, London SW1 6HL. Car parking in Vicarage Crescent. No special facilities for disabled but front steps are the only minor obstacle (no wheelchairs available). Visitors often also arrange a visit to Old Battersea Church nearby.

THE DESIGN MUSEUM AT BUTLERS WHARF
 Shad Thames, London SE1 2YD   **Tel:** 071-403 6933

DESIGN MUSEUM

The Design Museum is a museum of everyday things: the first to explain why and how mass-produced consumer objects work and look the way they do, and how design contributes to the quality of our lives.

Directions:	The Design Museum is beside Tower Bridge opposite St Katherine's Dock.
Tube	Tower Hill (Circle and District Line). London Bridge (Northern Line).
BR	London Bridge.
DLR	Tower Gateway.
Buses	15,78 to Tower Hill. 42,47, P11 to Tooley Street. Ample parking.

Design Museum, Shad Thames, Butlers Wharf, London SE1 2YD.

The Design Museum provides visitors, design professionals and students with a lively analysis of everyday products. It contains a study collection of 20th century, mass-produced consumer objects, an international review of new products, temporary exhibitions and graphics gallery, and operates an extensive education programme. Facilities include a library, lecture theatre for films and talks, members scheme.
Open: Tues to Sun 11.30-6.30. *Closed* Mon (open Bank Holidays).
Admission: £3.50, concessions £2.50, free admission to members.
Cafe, restaurant. Disabled access.

THE DICKENS HOUSE MUSEUM
 48 Doughty Street, London WC1N 2LF   **Tel:** 071-405 2127
A tribute to the novelist, was his home from 1837 to 1839 where he finished 'The Pickwick Papers' and worked on 'Oliver Twist', 'Barnaby Rudge' and 'Nicholas Nickleby'. Displays include manuscripts, first editions, letters, quill pens, original drawings, and the grandfather clock which belonged to Mosses Pickwick.
Open: Mon to Sat 10-5.00
Admission: £2.00

ANTHONY D'OFFAY GALLERY
 9, 21 & 23 Dering Street, off New Bond Street, London W1R 9AA   **Tel:** 071-499 4100 **Fax:** 071-493 4443

DR. JOHNSON'S HOUSE
 17 Gough Square, London EC4   **Tel:** 071-353 3745
Where he lived 1749-59 and compiled his Dictionary, Relics and prints.
Open: Mon to Sat 11-5.30 (Oct to Apr, 11-5). *Closed* Sun and Bank Hols.
Admission: Fee charged.

DULWICH PICTURE GALLERY
 College Road, London SE21 7AD   **Tel:** 081-693 5254; Recorded information 081-693 8000
'London's most perfect Gallery' *The Guardian*, England's oldest public art gallery was designed by Sir John Soane especially for the unique collection of Old Masters which includes works by Rembrandt, Rubens, Claude, Poussin, Van Dyck, Reni and a

particularly fine Dutch collection.
Open: Tues to Sun.
Admission: Fee charged.
Free guided tours Sat and Sun 3. Pre-booked group visits with guide; extended tour to include Dulwich College. Idyllic setting for corporate entertaining fifteen minutes from City and West End.

DUNCAN R. MILLER FINE ARTS
17 Flask Walk, Hampstead NW3 1HJ   **Tel:** 071-435 5462
Leading gallery in modern Scottish painting. Specialising in the Scottish Colourists - Peploe, Fergusson, Hunter, Cadell.
Open: Mon to Sat 10-5, Sun 1.30-4.30.

EAST HAM NATURE RESERVE
(Governors of the Passmore Edwards Museum/Newham Leisure Services)
Norman Road, London E6 4HN   **Tel:** 081-470 4525

The Churchyard of St Mary Magdalene, East Ham, the largest in London, managed with care to provide a variety of wildlife habitats. New trails with wheelchair access and tapping board. Visitor Centre has displays with handling table, shop and teaching facilities (including audio-visual equipment for visitors with impaired vision or hearing). Winner of Gulbenkien Award 1991 for provision for people with disabilities.
Open: Reserve open daily: Mon to Fri 9-5 (or until dusk), Sat, Sun 2-5. Visitor Centre open Sat, Sun 2-5.
Admission: Free. Party visits must be booked in advance.

EPPING FOREST MUSEUM
(Corporation of London)
Queen Elizabeth's Hunting Lodge, Chingford E4
The museum and the Tudor hunting grandstand are closed for extensive repairs and refurbishment. They are expected to re-open in the Autumn of 1993.

ERITH MUSEUM
Erith Library, Walnut Tree Road, Erith   **Tel:** (0322) 526574
Local history, including archaeology, industry and famous events.
Open: Mon and Wed 2.15-5.15; Sat 2.15-5.

THE FAN MUSEUM
12 Crooms Hill, Greenwich SE10 8ER   **Tel:** 081-858 7879/081-305 1441
The world's only museum of fans with its own unsurpassed collection housed in beautifully restored, listed Georgian houses. Changing exhibitions, shop, workshops, study facilities. Orangery and landscaped garden. Special tours and private functions.
Open: Tues to Sat 11-4.30. Sun 12-4.30. *Closed* Mon.
Admission: £2.50, concessions chld/OAP/disabled/concessions family rates
Gold and silver tours on request. Car park adjacent to museum. Lift, ramp, and lavatory for disabled. Fan making classes.

MICHAEL FARADAY'S LABORATORY AND MUSEUM
(The Royal Institution)
The Royal Institution of Great Britain, 21 Albemarle Street, London W1X 4BS   **Tel:** 071-409 2992
The Laboratory, where many of the most important discoveries were made, has been restored to the form it was known to have in 1845. An adjacent museum houses a unique collection of original apparatus arranged to illustrate the more significant aspects of Faraday's contribution to the advancement of science.
Open: Mon to Fri 1-4. Parties at other times by arrangement.
Admission: £1, Chld 50p.

FENTON HOUSE
(The National Trust)
Hampstead Grove, Hampstead NW3   **Tel:** 071-435 3471

The Benton-Fletcher collection of early musical instruments and the Binning collection of porcelain and furniture in a William and Mary House.

FORTY HALL MUSEUM
(London Borough of Enfield)
Forty Hill, Enfield, London EN2 9HA   **Tel:** 081-363 8196   **Fax:** 081-367 9095

FREUD MUSEUM
20 Maresfield Gardens, Hampstead, London NW3   **Tel:** 071-435 2002/435 5167
The museum contains Sigmund Freud's extraordinary collection of antiquities, his library and furniture, including the famous couch. The founder of psychoanalysis transferred his entire domestic and working environment here from Nazi-occupied

GEFFRYE MUSEUM

Kingsland Road, Shoreditch E2 8EA   Tel: 071-739 9893

This is one of London's most friendly and enjoyable Museums. Set in elegant 18th century almshouses with delightful gardens, the Museum presents the changing style of the domestic interior.

The displays take you on a walk through time, from the 17th century, with oak furniture and panelling, past the refined splendour of the Georgian period, the high style of the Victorians, to 20th century art deco and post war utility. A personal sound guide offers background information, and the Museum has a comprehensive reference library and furniture trades archive.

School and adult groups are always welcome, but must book in advance. The Museum has a lively programme of temporary exhibtions and events, and there are special activities for children and families most weekends and during school holidays. For recorded information telephone 071-739 8543.

Books, guides and souvenirs available from the shop, and refreshments from the coffee bar. A lovely walled herb garden is open from April through October during museum hours.

Admission Free.

Hours of Opening: Tuesdays to Saturdays 10.00 – 5.00
    Sundays and Bank Holiday Mondays 2.00 – 5.00

Nearest Stations: Liverpool St, then buses 22A, 22B, 149.
    Old St (exit 2), then bus 243, or fifteen minutes walk.

For disabled access, please telephone in advance. Parking available in nearby streets.

THE GEFFRYE MUSEUM TRUST

Vienna, and resumed work. Interpretive displays; archive films; shop.
Open: Wed-Sun 12-5 all year.
Admission: 2, OAPs and students £1, Chld under 12 free.
Location: Finchley Road Underground Station.
Group tours booked in advance.

GEFFRYE MUSEUM
Kingsland Road, Shoreditch, London E2 8EA **Tel:** 071-739 9893
A unique presentation of the changing style of the domestic interior, set in elegant 18th century almshouses with delightful gardens. Fine collections of furniture, paintings and

decorative arts. Reference library and furniture trades archive. Full programme of exhibitions, events, weekend and holiday activities. New walled herb garden.
Open: Tues to Sat 10-5, Sun and Bank Hol Mons 2-5.
Admission: Free.
Location: Stations: Liverpool Street, then buses 22A, 22B, 149, or Old Street, then bus 243 or 15 minute walk.
School and adult groups welcome, but please book in advance.

JILL GEORGE GALLERY LTD
38 Lexington Street, Soho W1R 3HR **Tel:** 071-439 7343/7319 **Fax:** 071-287 0478
Contemporary Art Gallery specialising in paintings, drawings, small sculpture and limited edition prints by British artists, from the established artist to the recent graduate.

Monthly exhibition programme.

GOETHE-INSTITUT LONDON
50 Princes Gate, Exhibition Road, London SW7 **Tel:** 071-411 3400
Exhibitions of German Art.
Open: Mon to Thurs 10-8; Fri 10-4; Sat 9.30-12.30; please check first.

Admission: Free.
Location: Underground: South Kensington.

GOLDSMITHS' HALL
Foster Lane, London EC2

GRANGE MUSEUM OF COMMUNITY HISTORY
(London Borough of Brent)
Neasden Lane, London NW10 **Tel:** 081-452 8311

The Grange Museum Neasden NW10

Opened in 1977, one of London's newest community history museums tells the story of the last two hundred years of the area we know today as Brent, its people and communities.

London Borough of Brent

Community history museum housed in the stable block of a large farm built in the early 1700s and converted into a gothick cottage in about 1810. The permanent displays cover aspects of life in the area and includes a Victorian Parlour, a 1930s Lounge and an Edwardian draper's shop as well as a display of souvenirs of the British Empire Exhibition held at Wembley in 1924-5. The museum also has a programme of temporary displays during the year. The Grange houses the borough's archives and local history library collection (library by appointment only).
Open: Mon-Fri 11.00-5.00; Wed 11-8; Sat 10-12, 1-5; Sun (June-Aug) 2.00-5.00
Admission: Free. Parties by arrangement only.
Location: Nearest station: Neasden (Jubilee Line)
Parking available on roundabout. Garden open for picnics. Conservatory with drinks vending machines.

GREENWICH BOROUGH MUSEUM
(London Borough of Greenwich)
   232 Plumstead High Street, London SE18   **Tel:** 081-855 3240
Local museum of archaeology, history and natural history. Also temporary exhibitions, children's activities and sales point.
Open: Mon 2-7; Tues, Thur, Fri & Sat 10-1, 2-5. *Closed* Wed and Sun.

GREENWICH PRINTMAKERS GALLERY
   1a Greenwich Market, Greenwich SE10 9HZ   **Tel:** 081-858 1569
Gallery of contemporary, original, limited-edition prints and water colours by 45 artists.
Open: Tues to Sun 10.30-5.30.

MARTYN GREGORY
   34 Bury Street, St. James's, London SW1Y 6AU   **Tel:** 071-839 3731
British watercolours and paintings. Pictures relating to China and the Far East.

GROB GALLERY
   4th Floor, 20 Dering Street, London W1R 9AA   **Tel:** 071-493 6732

GUNNERSBURY PARK MUSEUM
(London Boroughs of Ealing and Hounslow)
   Gunnersbury Park, London W3 8LQ   **Tel:** 081-992 1612

GUNNERSBURY PARK MUSEUM

GUNNERSBURY PARK, LONDON W3 8LQ

Easy access from Central London

The Museum from the South

Fine local history collections in the decorative rooms of the Rothschilds' first English country house bought by Nathan Mayer in 1835. Originally built for Alexander Copeland, Architect, 1801. Extensively altered by Sidney Smirke 1835-36.
Set in extensive parkland with sporting facilities.

Local history museum for the London Boroughs of Ealing and Hounslow. Collections cover archaeology, social history, local views, domestic life, toys and dolls, new costume gallery, transport (including Rothschild carriages), crafts and industries, especially laundry. Housed in part of an early 19th century former Rothschild country house set in a large park. Programme of temporary exhibitions. Victorian kitchens, open on weekends during the summer.
Open: Nov to Mar: daily 1-4; Apr to Oct: daily 1-5, (6pm weekends and Bank Holidays).
Admission: Free.
Location: Underground: Acton Town. Bus: E3 (daily), 7 (Suns only).
Special facilities for schools by arrangement with interpretative officer.

H.M.S. BELFAST
   Morgans Lane, off Tooley Street, London SE1 2JH   **Tel:** 071-407 6434
Visit Europe's largest preserved Second World War battleship and discover how sailors lived, worked and fought aboard this impressive cruiser, which helped sink the *Scharnhorst* and saw action on D-Day and later in the Korean War. She is now permanently moored on the Thames, close to the Tower of London. Visitors can explore all seven decks from the Bridge to the Boiler and Engine Rooms, including the gun turrets, mess decks, galley, punishment cells and more. Special exhibitions and the latest A/V displays recreate the conditions of life on board. Recorded guided tours are available.
Open: Daily. Summer: Mar 20-Oct 31, 10 (last adm 5.20), Winter: Nov 1 - Mar 19, 10 (last adm 4). *Closed* Dec 24-26 and Jan 1.
Location: Nearest tube station - London Bridge.
Information: 071-407 6434.

HACKNEY MUSEUM
   Central Hall, Mare Street, London E8
Displays on the history of Hackney and the world-wide roots of Hackney people. Programme of unusual and interesting exhibitions and events.
Admission: Free

HAM HOUSE
(The National Trust)
   at Petersham, Richmond, on bank of River Thames, London   **Tel:** 081-940 1950
Built 1610 and altered at various times in 17th century. Set in beautifully restored garden. Fine collection of late Stuart furniture.
Open: Garden open all year daily (except Mon) 11-5.30.
Closed for restoration throughout 1992.

HAMPSTEAD MUSEUM
(Burgh House Trust (Registered Charity))
   Burgh House, New End Square, London NW3 1LT   **Tel:** 071-431 0144
1703 house, museum of local history. Constable Room, Allingham collection. Buttery.
Open: Wed to Sun 12-5; Bank Hols 2-5.
Admission: Free
Bookstall.

HAMPTON COURT PALACE
(Historic Royal Palaces)
   Hampton Court, East Molesey, Surrey KT8 9AU
Royal Palace begun in 1514 by Wolsey, additions by Henry VIII and later by Wren for William and Mary. Staterooms, tapestries, pictures.

THE HAMPTON HILL GALLERY LTD
(Robert Crewdson)
   203 & 205 High Street, Hampton Hill, London TW12 1NP   **Tel:** 081-977 1379

HARROW MUSEUM AND HERITAGE CENTRE
(Harrow Arts Council)
   Headstone Manor, Pinner View, London   **Tel:** 081-861 2626
Based in 16th century Tithe Barn, with associated moated manor house dating back to 14th century. Purpose to reflect the history and heritage of Harrow.
Open: Wed to Fri 12.30-5, Sat, Sun and Bank Holidays 10.30-5. *Closed* Mon, open Tues afternoons for lectures. Parties by arrangement, morning and evening.
Car parking. Easy access and toilet for disabled persons. Catering, books and souvenir shop.

HAYES AND HARLINGTON MUSEUM
(Hayes and Harlington Local History Society and London Borough of Hillingdon)
   Golden Crescent, Hayes, Middlesex   **Tel:** (0895) 231218

HAYWARD GALLERY, SOUTH BANK CENTRE
   Belvedora Road, South Bank, London SE1   **Tel:** 071-928 3144. Recorded information: 071-261 0127. Advance Bookings: 071-928 8800.

HAYWARD GALLERY

Tel: 071-928 3144 · London SE1 8XZ

1993

21 January - 14 March
Gravity and Grace:
The Changing Condition of Sculpture, 1965 - 1975

8 April - 27 June
Georgia o'Keefe: American and Modern
James Turrell (Upper Gallery)

22 July - 10 October
Aratjara: Australian Aboriginal Art

4 November - 6 February 1994
Bonnard at la Villa le Bosquet

Since 1968 the Hayward has been the originator or host of many of the world's most influential exhibitions. Historical and contemporary exhibitions have included Art in Latin America, Magnum Photographers, Chinese Paintings from the British Museum, Twilight of the Tsars, Doubletake: Collective Memory and current Art as well as exhibitions devoted to the work of Leonardo da Vinci, Andy Warhol, Jasper Johns, Richard Long, Toulouse Lautrec and Magritte. The Hayward is now part of the

Sutton Heritage Service
A unique collection of Historic Houses

HERITAGE CENTRE
HONEYWOOD WALK, CARSHALTON

Opened in 1990, in a 17th century listed building, with later additions. Permanent displays outline the history of the Borough and its people plus a changing programme of exhibitions on varied subjects. Features include magnificent Edwardian billiard room. Tea room and gift shop. For details, telephone 081-773 4555.

LITTLE HOLLAND HOUSE
40 BEECHES AVENUE, CARSHALTON

The Living Room and part of the Sitting Room

The home of Frank Dickinson (1874-1961), follower of the Arts and Crafts movement; artist designer and craftsman in wood and metal who built the house himself to his own design and in pursuance of his philosophy and theories. Features his interior design, painting, hand-made furniture and other craft objects.
Guide book and other publications available.

WHITEHALL
1 MALDEN ROAD, CHEAM

This unique timber-framed, continuous jettied house dates back to about 1500. Originally built as a farm house, Whitehall with its many additions has associations with Henry VIII's Nonsuch Palace, the English Civil War and Cheam School. Whitehall features revealed sections of original fabric and displays including Medieval Cheam Pottery, Nonsuch Palace, timber-framed buildings and Cheam School.
Refreshments and appropriate publications are available.

CARSHALTON HOUSE
ST. PHILOMENA'S SCHOOL, CARSHALTON

Built about 1707 around the core of an older house, with grounds laid out originally by Charles Bridgeman, Carshalton House contains principal rooms with 18th century decoration. Garden buildings include the unique Water Tower. Tours of the grounds and a programme of short talks are included in the entrance fee. Refreshments, publications and souvenirs available. Open Days for 1993: Easter Mon, 12th April and Sat 12th Sept. Carshalton House is close to the Carshalton conservation area.

CAREW MANOR & DOVECOTE
CHURCH ROAD, BEDDINGTON

This building contains a late-medieval Great Hall, with an arch-braced hammer-beam roof, listed Grade 1. The Hall is open every Sunday from Easter until 1 November, together with the recently-restored early 18th century Dovecote, with its 1.288 nesting boxes and potence (circular ladder). Guided tours available which include the cellars of the house with their medieval, Tudor and later features and the 15th century Carew Chapel in the nearby St. Mary's Church.
A Heritage Trail around Beddington Park features the history, historic buildings, garden features and wildlife of this important conservation area. Guide book, trail leaflet, books and souvenirs available.

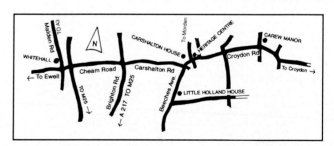

For information, call 081-773 4555

Sutton
Leisure Services

international arts centre - the South Bank Centre.
Open: Daily 10-6pm, late night Tues & Wed until 8pm. Closed between exhibitions.
Admission: Fee charged to all shows.
Location: Underground: Waterloo/Embankment. Buses: Waterloo. Riverbus: Festival Pier.
Refreshments: Cafeteria
We welcome people with disabilities and to ensure that your visit is as straightforward as possible please telephone the Gallery Superintendent first. Advanced booking available.

HERITAGE CENTRE
(London Borough of Sutton)
   Honeywood Walk, Carshalton   **Tel:** 081-773 4555
Honeywood is a 17th century listed building with later additions. Discover the fascinating history of the area and its people. (The London Borough of Sutton includes Beddington, Carshalton, Cheam, Sutton and Wallington). Permanent displays plus a changing programme of exhibitions cover many aspects of local life. Honeywood stands at the head of Carshalton's picturesque town ponds, one of the sources of the River Wandle, and at the heart of a conservation area.
Open: Tues to Sun and Bank Hol Mons, 10-5.30.
Admission: Fee charged.
Location: Honeywood Walk, Carshalton. By Carshalton Ponds, opp. Greyhound Inn. Station: Carshalton ¼ mile.
Refreshments: Tearoom
Free entry to tearooms and gift shop. Telephone Sutton Heritage Service 081- 773 4555 for further information.

HOGARTH'S HOUSE
(London Borough of Hounslow)
   Hogarth Lane, Great West Road, Chiswick, London W4   **Tel:** 081-994 6757

Open: Mon to Sat 11-6 (winter 11-4); Sun 2-6 (winter 2-4). *Closed* Tues all year; also for first two full weeks of Sept, and last three weeks in Dec for staff holidays.
Admission: Free.
Use Chiswick House Grounds' car park.

HORNIMAN MUSEUM
   London Road, Forest Hill, London SE23 EPQ   **Tel:** 081-699 1872/2339/4911
Museum dealing with the study of man and his environment. Ethnographical, natural history collections and aquarium. There is a large collection of musical instruments from all parts of the world. Special exhibitions throughout the year. Extensive library (*closed* Mon). Education centre for schools and children's leisure activities. Free lectures and concerts (autumn and spring).
Open: Weekdays 10.30-5.30; Sun 2-5.30. Open Good Friday. *Closed* Christmas Eve, Christmas Day and Boxing Day. Café open Mon to Fri 11-4.30, Sat 11-5.30, Sun 2.30-5.30.
Pleasantly located with gardens, picnic area, nature trails and animal enclosures. Free parking in Sydenham Rise (opp. museum).

HUNTERIAN MUSEUM
Royal College of Surgeons, Lincoln's Inn Fields, London WC2A 3PN   **Tel:** 071-405 3474
Comparative and morbid anatomy collection, mainly 18th century material. Admission normally restricted to members of the medical and veterinary professions and to scientists. By written application to the Curator.

IMPERIAL WAR MUSEUM
(A National Museum)
Lambeth Road, London SE1 6HZ   **Tel:** 071-416 5000
See thousands of imaginatively displayed exhibits from art to aircraft, from Utility clothes to U-boat, in the Museum of the Year 1990. Special features include: interactive videos, the walk through Trench Experience with soldiers going over the top, the dramatic Blitz Experience - complete with sound, smells and other effects, and 'Operation Jericho' - a chance to find out what it was like to fly with the RAF on a daring bombing raid over Occupied Europe.
Open: Daily 10-6. *Closed* Dec 24-26, Jan 1.
Location: Nearest tube station - Lambeth North.
Information: 071-416 5000 or 071-820 1683 (recorded information).

MALCOLM INNES GALLERY
172 Walton Street, London SW3 2JL   **Tel:** 071-584 0575
19th and 20th Century Scottish, landscape, sporting and military pictures - oil paintings, watercolours and prints.
Open: Mon to Fri 9.30-6, most Sats 10-1. *Closed* Bank Holidays.
Not suitable for disabled persons.

WILLIAM JACKSON GALLERY
28 Cork Street, London W1X 1HB   **Tel:** 071-287 2121
Contemporary British and European paintings and sculpture.

JEWISH MUSEUM
Woburn House, Tavistock Square, London WC1H OEP   **Tel:** 071-388 4525
Collection of antiquities illustrating Judaism and Jewish history.
Open: Tues to Thurs (and Fri and Sun, Apr to Sept) 10-4; Fri and Sun Oct to Mar 10-12.45. *Closed* Mon, Sat, Bank and Jewish Hols.
Admission: Fee charged
Group visits by arrangement with the Secretary.

KEATS HOUSE (WENTWORTH PLACE)
(Camden Borough Council)
Keats Grove, Hampstead, London NW3 2RR   **Tel:** 071-435 2062
Keats's Regency home where he spent the greater part of his five creative years. Relics and manuscripts of the famous poet.
Open: Apr to Oct: Mon-Fri 10-1, 2-6; Sat 10-1, 2-5; Sun and Bank Holidays 2-5. Nov 1 to Mar 31: Mon-Fri 1-5; Sat 10-1, 2-5; Sun 2-5. *Closed* Christmas Eve, Christmas Day, Boxing Day, New Year's Day, Good Friday, Easter Eve and May 3. Please telephone to confirm opening times.
Audio tours, English, French, German and Japanese, conducted tours for parties by prior arrangement. Shop.

KENSINGTON PALACE, COURT DRESS COLLECTION AND STATE APARTMENTS
(Historic Royal Palaces)
London W8
Unique collection of Court Dress depicting the colour and glitter of 200 years of Society.

KENWOOD - THE IVEAGH BEQUEST
(English Heritage)
Hampstead Lane, London NW3   **Tel:** 081-348 1286
The paintings include a fine Rembrandt self-portrait, Vermeer's 'Guitar Player' and works by Van Dyck, Hals and Cuyp, as well as English 18th century paintings by Reynolds, Gainsborough and Romney. Important collection of English neo-classical furniture, housed in Robert Adam mansion.
Open: Apr 1 to Sept 30, daily 10-6. 1 October-31 March, daily 10-4. *Closed* Dec 24,25.
Admission: Free.

DAVID KER GALLERY
85 Bourne Street, London SW1W 8HF   **Tel:** 071-730 8365
Small gallery in Belgravia specialising in Decorative English Paintings, water-colours and drawings from the 18th, 19th and 20th centuries - prices from a modest £40 to £500,000.
Open: Mon to Fri 9.30-5.30. *Closed* Bank Holidays.
Suitable for disabled persons. Easy parking. Browsers welcome!

KEW BRIDGE STEAM MUSEUM
(Kew Bridge Engines Trust)
Green Dragon Lane, Brentford, London   Tel: 081-568 4757

KEW BRIDGE STEAM MUSEUM

GREEN DRAGON LANE, BRENTFORD, MIDDLESEX

Unique giant beam engines operating under steam! The earliest built in 1820, these are the largest of their kind in the world, the "dinosaurs" of the Industrial Revolution come to life. As well as these 5 engines, which pumped London's water supply for over 100 years, 4 other major engines have been added and there is a steam railway, vintage diesels plus memorabilia.

Tea Room (weekends only) – Souvenir & Bookshop – Free Car Park.

OPEN DAILY 11–5p.m. In steam every weekend and Bank Holiday Monday. Closed at Christmas.

Admission charge. Family and party rates. We are 10 minutes walk from Kew Gardens, 5 minutes walk from the Musical Museum.

Grand Junction 90" Beam Engine.   **Tel: 081-568 4757**

Working forge, steam railway, models.
Admission: Fee charged. Family and party rates.
Suitable for the disabled.

KEW PLACE
(Historic Royal Palaces)
Royal Botanic Gardens, Kew TW9 3AB
Collections reflect domestic lives of George III and his family.

KINGSTON MUSEUM AND HERITAGE CENTRE
Wheatfield Way, Kingston upon Thames KT2 5PE   **Tel:** 081-547 6755
Local History library open at North Kingston Centre, Room 46, Richmond Road, Kingston upon Thames, Surrey, KT2 5PE. Telephone 081-547 6738.
Open: Museum closed for refurbishment until early 1993.

FRANCIS KYLE GALLERY
9 Maddox Street, London W1R 9LE   **Tel:** 071-499 6870/6970 **Fax:** 071-495 0180
Regular exhibitions of paintings and drawings by contemporary artists from Europe and America including: Barnden, Dael, Fisher, George, Hillier, Hughes, Keon, Milton, More Gordon, Sartorius, Stone, Sutton, Toulgouat, Woodruff.

LEIGHTON HOUSE ART GALLERY AND MUSEUM
(The Royal Borough of Kensington and Chelsea Libraries and Arts Service)
12 Holland Park Road, Kensington, London W14 8LZ   **Tel:** 071-602 3316
Leighton House, the home of Frederic Lord Leighton P.R.A. designed for him 1864-66 by George Aitchison R.A. Leighton lived here until his death in 1896. His unique collection of Islamic tiles is displayed in the walls of the Arab Hall and the Victorian interiors, now restored to their original appearance, are hung with paintings by Leighton, Millais, Watts and Burne-Jones. Fine 'New Sculpture' by Leighton, Brock, Thorneycroft in the house and garden. Study collection of Leighton drawings may be seen by appointment. Temporary exhibitions of modern and historic art throughout the year.
Open: Mon to Sat 11-5.30. Garden open Apr to Sept, *closed* Bank Hols.
Chld under 16 to be accompanied by an adult. All parties and tours of the house by arrangement with the Curator.

LEIGHTON HOUSE
MUSEUM AND ART GALLERY

High Victorian paintings and sculpture by Lord Leighton and his contemporaries, who created the remarkable Artists' Colony of studios centred around Leighton House. It is the earliest and most opulent aesthetic interior in London, and is now restored to its original splendour. Open free throughout the year. Monday to Saturday 11 a.m.–5.30 p.m.

Administered by The Royal Borough of Kensington and Chelsea Libraries and Arts Service, 12 Holland Park Road W14 8LZ. Tel. 071-602 3316.

LINLEY SAMBOURNE HOUSE
(The Victorian Society)
18 Stafford Terrace, London W8   **Tel:** 081-994 1019

LINLEY SAMBOURNE HOUSE

18 STAFFORD TERRACE, W.8

A fascinating survival of a late 19th century 'artistic' interior. The original decorations, furniture and pictures have been preserved almost unchanged from the time of the first owner, Linley Sambourne (1844–1910) chief political cartoonist at 'Punch'. An interesting collection of photographs taken by Sambourne in the 1890s is now on display.

Open: Mar 1 to Oct 31: Wed 10-4; Sun 2-5. Parties admitted at other times by prior arrangement. Apply to The Victorian Society, 1 Priory Gardens, London W4 1TT. **Admission:** £3.

LITTLE HOLLAND HOUSE
(London Borough of Sutton)
40 Beeches Avenue, Carshalton, Surrey   **Tel:** 081-773 455
The home of Frank Dickinson (1874-1961), follower of the Arts and Crafts movement; artist, designer and craftsman in wood and metal, who built the house himself to his own design and in pursuance of his philosophy and theories. Features his interior design, painting, hand-made furniture and other craft objects.
Open: Mar to Dec: first Sun in month plus Sun and Mon of Bank Hol weekends 1-6.
Location: Few minutes from Carshalton Beeches B.R. Station.
Further information from Sutton Heritage Service on 081 773 4555.

LIVESEY MUSEUM
(London Borough of Southwark)
682 Old Kent Road, London SE15 1JR   **Tel:** 071-639 5604
Southwark's family museum holds a lively programme of hands-on exhibitions for children up to 12 years, their schools, families and careers.
Open: Mon to Sat 10-5.
Admission: Free

LOCAL HISTORY LIBRARY
(London Borough of Greenwich)
90 Mycenae Road, Blackheath SE3   **Tel:** 081-858 4631
Open: Mon, Tues 9-5.30; Thurs 9-8; Sat 9-5. *Closed* Wed and Fri.

LONDON BRASS RUBBING CENTRE
(Andrew and Patricia Dodwell)
The Crypt, St. Martin-in-the-Fields Church, Trafalgar Square, London WC2   **Tel:** 071-437 6023
Unusual combination of workshop/gallery with 90 brasses for making rubbings. Knights, Kings, Heraldic Animals, Scholars and Celtic designs, with specialist materials and friendly help mean instant success and fun. Entry to the exhibition of Brass Rubbings is free, charges for making rubbings start at only £1.50, varying with size.
Open: Daily 10-6, Mon-Sat (12-6 Sun). *Closed* Christmas Day, Boxing Day, Good Friday and Jan 1.
Admission: Free.
Refreshments: Restaurant/Cafe available.
Pre-booked parties of 10 or more get a 10% discount. Car parking Trafalgar Square Underground NCP park. Suitable for disabled. Art gallery, bookshop & market all on church site, open same hours.

THE LONDON GAS MUSEUM
Bromley-By-Bow, London   **Tel:** 071-987 2000
The London Gas Museum, Bromley-By-Bow, is a small museum illustrating the history of the gas industry with particular emphasis on London. It contains many examples of gas memorabilia and items of interest are constantly being discovered and sent to the museum for classification and display. The Museum was created by British Gas North Thames in 1982, 170 years after the establishment of a gas supply in London. On this large site a gasworks was constructed in 1870 by the Imperial Gas Light Company in an attempt to maintain its commercial position against the competition from an even larger gasworks at Beckton, established by the Gas Light and Coke Company which commenced gas production the same year.
Parking available. Organised parties are welcome by arrangement with the museum.

THE LONDON MUSEUM OF JEWISH LIFE
(The Sternberg Centre)
80 East End Road, London N3 2SY   **Tel:** 081-346 2288/349 1143
Permanent display on Jewish immigration and settlement. Reconstruction of tailoring workshop, immigrant home, and east London bakery. Changing exhibitions, travelling displays, walking tours and educational programmes.
Open: Mon to Thurs 10.30-5; Sun (except in Aug and on Bank Holiday weekends) 10.30-4.30. *Closed* Fri and Sat, Jewish Festivals, Public Holidays and Dec 25 to Jan 2.
Curator: Rickie Burman, MA, M.Phil.

THE LONDON GAS MUSEUM
Bromley-by-Bow

A small Museum illustrating the history of the gas industry with particular emphasis on London.

Parking available. Organised parties are welcome by arrangement. Individuals must telephone first to check the Museum is open. Nearest Underground station, Bromley-by-Bow.

British Gas
North Thames

The London Gas Museum, British Gas North Thames, Twelvetrees Crescent, Bromley-by-Bow, London E3 3JH Telephone: 071-987 2000

THE LONDON TOY AND MODEL MUSEUM
23 Craven Hill, (entrance 21 Craven Hill), London W2 **Tel:** 071-262 7905/9450

A UNIQUE MUSEUM IN THE HEART OF LONDON

The London Toy & Model Museum

FOR ALL GENERATIONS AND ALL SEASONS.

INCLUDING:- TRAINS, DOLLS, PLANES, BEARS AND JUVENILIA AND PENNY SLOT MACHINES.

ADMISSION CHARGE:

OPEN MONDAY TO SATURDAY 10-4.30. SUNDAYS AND ALL BANK HOLIDAY MONDAYS 11-4.30.

AT: 21-23 CRAVEN HILL, LONDON W2 3EN   071-262 7905

'Museum of the Year Award'
Best museum in the South, overall runner-up in the UK.
1986

Illustrated London News National Heritage.
'Museum of the Year' Special Judges Award.
1985

The English Tourist Board.
The first London Museum Project to be supported by the Board.
1984

British Tourist Authority.
'Come to Britain Trophy'
1982

Extensive display of many trains, planes, cars, boats, Dinky toys, dolls, animals and teddy bears. In the large garden there is a running dislay of electric trains, a full-size open double decker bus, a vintage carousel and also a ride on a train.
Open: Mon to Sat 10-4.30, Sun and Bank Hols 11-4.30.
Admission: Fee charged. Group rates by arrangement.
Gift shop and cafe.

LONDON TRANSPORT MUSEUM
Covent Garden, London WC2E 7BB

MCC MUSEUM
(Marylebone Cricket Club)
Lord's Ground, London NW8 8QN **Tel:** 071-289 1611
Contains new displays illustrating the history of cricket.
Open: All match days Mon to Sat 10.30-5. Open match days on Sun 1-5.
Admission: Fee charged. Ground adm also payable on most match days.
For details of Gestetner tour of Lords, on match days and on other occasions, telephone 071-266 3825.

MALL GALLERIES
(Federation of British Artists)
The Mall, London SW1Y 5BD **Tel:** 071-930 6844

MARBLE HILL HOUSE
(English Heritage)
Richmond Road, Twickenham, London **Tel:** 081-892 5115
A perfect example of an English Palladian villa. Early Georgian paintings and furniture.
Open: Apr 1 to Sept 30, daily 10-6. Oct 1 to Mar 31, daily 10-4. *Closed* Dec 24,25.
Admission: Free.

MARK GALLERY
9 Porchester Place, Marble Arch, London W2 2BS **Tel:** 071-262 4906
Specialises in Russian 16th to 19th century icons and modern and contemporary lithographs and etchings by Chagall, Dali, Mirò, Moore, Picasso, Buffet and others.
Open: Mon to Fri 10-6, Sat 11-1.

MARKFIELD BEAM ENGINE AND MUSEUM
(Markfield Beam Engine and Museum Ltd, Charitable Company, Limited by Guarantee)
Markfield Road, South Tottenham, London N15 4RB **Tel:** 081-800 7061 or 071-387 331

MARKFIELD BEAM ENGINE and MUSEUM
MARKFIELD ROAD, SOUTH TOTTENHAM
LONDON N15 4RB 081-800 7061

1886 Beam Pumping Engine restored to working order in original building. Steaming certain weekends and by arrangement. Small exhibition to illustrate aspects of public health engineering for which the large pumping engine was developed.

See editorial for further details.

Open: Apr to Nov. Parties by arrangement - can include special steaming on weekdays. Car parking not on site. Trains and buses, Tottenham Hale and Seven Sisters station. Suitable for disabled persons. Technical Director: A.J. Spackman, MSc, DIC, CEng, FRSA.

BRITAIN AT WAR

10am to 6pm daily

Visit Britain's war museums and you'll see, feel and even smell what life was really like in the two world wars.

Walk the trenches of the First World War at London's Imperial War Museum.

Sit behind the guns of a real battleship aboard HMS *Belfast.*

See where Churchill planned Hitler's downfall, deep within the vaults of the Cabinet War Rooms.

And get a pilot's eye view of war in the air at Duxford Airfield, near Cambridge.

We'll also show you what life was like for the families at home. After all, the experience of war was shared by everyone. And now we'd like to share it with you.

Open for visitors from 10am to 6pm every day at: the Imperial War Museum, Lambeth North ⊖; Cabinet War Rooms, Westminster ⊖; HMS *Belfast,* Tower Hill ⊖; Duxford Airfield, Junction 10, M11, near Cambridge. For more details call **071-416 5000.**

Part of your family's history IMPERIAL WAR MUSEUM

MARTINWARE POTTERY COLLECTION
(London Borough of Ealing)
   Southall Public Library, Osterley Park Road, Southall, Middlesex **Tel:** 081-574 3412
Martinware Pottery was made by the Martin brothers at their factory in Southall from 1877-1915. The display is open on request during Library hours, Tues-Sat.
Admission: Free.
Please telephone for an appointment.

MATTHIESEN FINE ART
   7-8 Mason's Yard, Duke Street, St. James's, London SW1 **Tel:** 071-930 2437 **Fax:** 071-930 1387

Specialising in Italian, Spanish and French Old Master paintings, 19th century paintings and sculpture.
Open: 10.00 to 5.00pm By Appointment.

MEDICI GALLERY
   7 Grafton Street, London W1X 3LA **Tel:** 071-629 5675
Changing display of original paintings by contemporary artists, original prints, limited editions and antique prints. Greetings cards and larger reproductions in lower gallery.
Open: Mon to Fri 9-5.30. *Closed* Bank Holidays.
Admission: Free.
Not suitable for disabled persons.

WILLIAM MORRIS GALLERY
(London Borough of Waltham Forest)
   Water House, Lloyd Park, Forest Road, Walthamstow, London E17 4PP **Tel:** 081-527 3782
The Frank Brangwyn collection of pictures and sculpture by 19th century and other artists and by the donor. Study collection and reference library by appointment.
Open: *Closed* Mon and all Public Hols.
Admission: Free.
Location: *Nearest tube station: Walthamstow Central (Victoria Line).*
Group visits by prior appointment. Guided tours available (charge), by prior appointment. Schools' activities by arrangement. Access for disabled to ground floor and gardens. Shop.

MUSEUM OF GARDEN HISTORY
(The Tradescant Trust)
   Lambeth Palace Road, London SE1 7JU **Tel:** 071-261 1891 **Fax:** 071-401 8869

Permanent exhibition of aspects of garden history including a collection of antique garden tools. Lectures; Concerts; Exhibitions; Tombs of the Tradescants and Admiral Bligh of the *Bounty* in the replica 17th century garden.
Open: Daily Mon-Fri 11-3, Sun 10.30-5. *Closed* Sat and *Closed* from the second Sun in Dec to the first Sun in Mar.
Location: Nearest underground: Victoria or Waterloo, then 507 or C10 buses.
Refreshments: Available.
Gift shop. Groups welcomed, but prior arrangement essential.

THE MUSEUM OF LONDON
   London Wall, London EC2Y 5HN **Tel:** 071-600 3699
Opened in December 1976 (Museum of the Year - 1978) - presents the visual biography of the London area from 250,000 years ago. Exhibits (based on collections of former Guildhall and London Museums) arranged chronologically include the Lord Mayor's Coach, models and room reconstructions, everyday tools and rich men's extravagances, Mithraic treasure, the Great Fire experience, 18th century prison cells, 19th century shops, Selfridge's lifts. Education Department, Print Room, Library, by appointment.
Open: Tues to Sat 10-6; Sun 12-6. *Closed* Mons, (except Bank Hols), Dec 24-26 incl, and New Year's Day.
Parties must book in advance.

MUSEUM OF MANKIND
   6 Burlington Gardens, London W1X 2EX **Tel:** 071-437 2224
(Ethnography Department of the British Museum).
Open: Weekdays 10-5; Sun 2.30-6.
Admission: Free.
Location: Underground stations: Piccadilly Circus, Green Park.

THE MUSEUM OF METHODISM
   49 City Road, London EC1Y 1AU
The house in which John Wesley lived and died.
Location: In the crypt of Wesley's Chapel, with John Wesley's House.

MUSEUM OF RICHMOND
   Old Town Hall, Whittaker Avenue, London **Tel:** 081-332 1141
This new independent museum deals with Richmond's rich and colourful history in a lively and informative way. Varied collection, models, dioramas and audio visual displays.
Open: Tues-Sat: 11 to 5; Also Suns May to Oct: 1.30-4. *Closed* Bank Hols.
Admission: £1, annual pass £3, Chld/OAPs and UB40s 50p, annual pass £1.50. Pre-booked school parties admitted free. Parties welcome weekday mornings by arrangement.
Public car park nearby. Suitable for disabled persons, no wheelchairs available.

MUSEUM OF THE MOVING IMAGE (MOMI)
   BF1 South Bank, Waterloo, London SE1 8XT **Tel:** 071-401 2636
The award-winning Museum of the Moving Image (MOMI) vividly brings to life the history and magic of cinema and TV. Some fifty exhibit areas take the visitor on a journey from the earliest pre-cinema experiments to the technical wizardry of a modern TV studio. In between there are hundreds of film and TV clips, a fine collection of movie props and memorabilia and a cast of actor-guides. There is even the opportunity to read the 'News at Ten', be interviewed by Barry Norman, or animate a cartoon.
Open: Daily 10-6, (except Dec 24-26).
Admission: Fee charged.

THE
NATIONAL
GALLERY

Trafalgar Square London WC2

Admission Free

Open Monday – Saturday
10am–6pm, Sunday 2pm–6pm
Closed 24, 25 and 26 December,
1 January, Good Friday & May Day

Telephone 071 839 3321
Recorded Information 071 839 3526

Location: Under Waterloo Bridge next to Royal National Theatre.
Refreshments: At adjacent National Film Theatre
Gift and book shops. Information Telephone above.

MUSEUM OF THE ROYAL PHARMACEUTICAL SOCIETY OF GREAT BRITAIN
1 Lambeth High Street, London SE1 7JN   **Tel:** 071-735 9141
Collection of crude drugs of vegetable and animal origin used in the 17th century; early printed works, manuscripts and prints relating to pharmacy; English delft drug jars, leech jars, bell-metal mortars, medicine chests, dispensing apparatus etc.
Open: By appointment.

THE MUSICAL MUSEUM
(A Charitable Trust)
368 High Street, Brentford, London   **Tel:** 081-560 8108

THE MUSICAL MUSEUM
BRENTFORD

A LIVE DEMONSTRATION OF THE MILLS "VIOLANO VIRTUOSO" WHICH PLAYS AUTOMATICALLY A VIOLIN AND PIANO.

Alive with the sound of music, a museum which takes you back to a bygone age to hear and see a marvellous working collection of automatic musical instruments. From small musical boxes, reproducing grand pianos, and orchestrions to a mighty Wurlitzer theatre organ, this museum will appeal to both those old enough to remember the age of the pianola and those young enough to learn that modern computer techniques played instruments in 1913!
Open: Working demonstrations every Sat and Sun 2-5, Apr to Oct inclusive, additional days during the summer holidays.
Admission: £2, Concessions £1.50. Party visits by arrangement.

NARWHAL INUIT ART GALLERY
(Ken & Tija Mantel)
55 Linden Gardens, Chiswick, London W4 2EH   **Tel:** 081-747 1575 **Fax:** 081-742 1268
Narwhal Inuit Art Gallery - a permanent exhibition of Canadian and Russian, Greenlandic contemporary Inuit (Eskimo) art. Carvings in stone, bone and horn plus graphics.
Open: By appointment 7 days a week.
Admission: Free.
Unsuitable for disabled.

NATIONAL ARCHAEOLOGICAL RECORD *SEE* ROYAL COMMISSION ON THE HISTORICAL MONUMENTS OF ENGLAND

NATIONAL ARMY MUSEUM
(a National Museum)
Royal Hospital Road, London SW3 4HT   **Tel:** 071-730 0717
The only museum dealing with the British Army in general during the five centuries of its existence, it includes the story of the Indian Army to 1947. Paintings, uniforms, weapons, equipment, regimental and personal mementoes and colours.
Open: Daily 10-5.30.*Closed* Jan 1, Good Fri, May Bank Holiday, 24-26 Dec. The reference collections of prints, photographs, books and archives are open Tues to Sat (except Sats of Bank Hol weekends) 10-4.30.
Admission: Free. Admission by Reader's ticket, obtainable by written appl
At the Royal Military Academy, Sandhurst, items from the museum's collections are displayed in the Indian Army memorial Room. They may normally be viewed by appointment, Mon to Fri. Written applications giving at least seven days' notice to National Army Museum, RMA, Sandhurst, Camberley, Surrey GU15 4PQ. Tel: (0276) 63344 Ext. 457.

NATIONAL BUILDINGS RECORD *SEE* ROYAL COMMISSION ON THE HISTORICAL MONUMENTS OF ENGLAND.

NATIONAL FILM ARCHIVE
(British Film Institute)
21 Stephen Street, London W1P 1PL   **Tel:** 071-255 1444
Collection of cinematograph films and recorded television programmes, both fiction and non-fiction, illustrating history of cinema and television as art and entertainment and as a record of contemporary life and people, ethnography, transport, exploration etc. Also a large collection of film stills, posters and set designs.
Open: Daily (by appointment only) 10.30-5.30.

THE NATIONAL GALLERY
Trafalgar Square, London WC2N 5DN   **Tel:** 071-839 3321 National Gallery Info: 071-389 1785
The Nation's outstanding permanent collection of Western painting from c.1260-1920, including works by Leonardo, Rembrandt, Constable and Cézanne. Exhibitions centred on specific aspects of the Collection, plus an excellent Education service offering quizzes, audio-visual shows and lectures for adults. The Sainsbury Wing opened in July 1991 and provides galleries for the Early Renaissance collection, together with galleries for temporary exhibitions, a large auditorium for lectures, the Micro Gallery computer information room, a restarant and shop.
Open: Mon to Sat 10-6; Sun 2-6. *Closed* Good Friday, May Day, Dec 24, 25, 26 and Jan 1. Shop Mon to Sat 10-5.40; Sun 2-5.40.

NATIONAL MARITIME MUSEUM
THE QUEEN'S HOUSE ◆ OLD ROYAL OBSERVATORY
──── GREENWICH ────

THE STORY OF BRITAIN & THE SEA ◆ A ROYAL PALACE FROM THE TIME OF CHARLES I
THE HISTORY OF ASTRONOMY & TIME
Outstanding collections & magnificent buildings within a Royal Park.

081-858 4422

Admission: Free. (Charges for major exhibitions in the Sainsbury Wing)
Refreshments: Restaurants open Mon to Sat 10-5 (last orders 4.30); Sun 2-5. Shop and restaurant.

NATIONAL LIBRARY OF AIR PHOTOGRAPHS *SEE* **ROYAL COMMISSION ON THE HISTORICAL MONUMENTS OF ENGLAND.**

NATIONAL MARITIME MUSEUM
(a National Museum)
   Romney Road, Greenwich, London SE10 9NF   **Tel:** 081-858 4422
Galleries here and in the Old Royal Observatory in Greenwich Park, part of the Museum, show many aspects of maritime history in paintings and prints, ships models, relics of distinguished sailors and events, navigational instruments and charts, history of astronomy, medals, a large library with a reference section and information service and a fine collection of manuscripts. See the new 20th century Seapower Gallery; new time and space exhibition at the Royal Observatory (opens Mar) and the beautifully restored Queen's House.
Open: Mon-Sat 10-6 (10-5 in winter); Sun 12-6 (2-5 in winter). *Closed* Christmas Eve, Christmas Day, 26 December.
Admission: (1992): Each site £3.50; Child/OAP/Student £2.50. Passport to all sites including Cutty Sark £6.95; Child/OAP/Student £4.95. Family £13.95.
Location: Greenwich. Station: Maze Hill (BR); Island Gardens (Docklands Light Railway); River buses.
Refreshments: Restaurant: Licensed
For NMM Outstations see Saltash, and Tresco (Isles of Scilly).

NATIONAL MONUMENTS RECORD *SEE* **ROYAL COMMISSION ON HISTORICAL MONUMENTS OF ENGLAND.**

NATIONAL PORTRAIT GALLERY
   St. Martin's Place, London WC2H 0HE   **Tel:** 071-306 0055

NPG
NATIONAL PORTRAIT GALLERY
St. Martin's Place London WC2H 0HE
☎ 071-306 0055
Admission free
Open daily
See entry for details
◆

VIRGINIA WOOLF BY G C BERESFORD

Portraits of famous men and women in British history and culture: poets and princesses, statesmen and sportsmen, artists and actresses, explorers and astronomers, on display in paintings, sculpture, drawings, miniatures and photographs. The Gallery has constantly changing displays, with a programme of special exhibitions, acquisitions, commissions and four outstations; Montacute House, Beningbrough Hall, Gawthorpe Hall and Bodelwyddan Caste (see separate entries).
Open: Mon to Fri 10-5; Sat 10-6; Sun 2-6. *Closed* Dec 24-26, Jan 1, Good Friday, May Day Bank Holiday.
Admission: Free.
Location: Nearest tube: Charing Cross, Leicester Square.

NATIONAL POSTAL MUSEUM
King Edward Building, King Edward Street, London EC1A 1LP **Tel:** 071-239 5420

Reginald M. Phillips and Post Office Collections of British postage stamps, and related material. Frank Staff collections of postal history. UPU collection of world stamps since 1878. Special exhibitions each year. Philatelic correspondence archives of Thos. de la Rue and Co., covering postage and/or revenue stamps of 200 countries or states 1855-1965 on microfilm. Research facility available by prior arrangements.
Open: Mon to Fri 9.30-4.30.
Admission: Free.

THE NATURAL HISTORY MUSEUM
Cromwell Road, South Kensington, London SW7 5BD   **Tel:** 071-938 9123

NORTH WOOLWICH OLD STATION MUSEUM
(Governors of the Passmore Edwards Museum/Newham Leisure Services)
Pier Road, London E16 2JJ   **Tel:** 071-474 7244

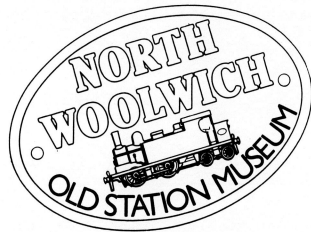

Discover the history
of the Eastern Counties Railway
the Great Eastern LNER
and BR Eastern Region

Photos, tickets and posters, railway models, equipment, a 1920s booking office, 1876 coffee pot locomotive and much more in a dignified Victorian station. Education Service, holiday activities. Engines in steam first Sunday of summer months and special events (phone for details).
Open: Mon to Wed and Sat 10-5, Sun and Bank Hols 2-5.
Admission: Free.
Shop.

OLD SPEECH ROOM GALLERY, HARROW SCHOOL
(Governors of Harrow School)
High Street, Harrow-on-the-Hill, London   **Tel:** 081-869 1205 or 081-422 2196

Situated in the Old Schools at Harrow School, Old Speech Room Gallery was designed by Alan Irvine in 1976. It houses the School's collections: Egyptian and Greek antiquities, watercolours, some Modern British pictures, printed books, Harroviana, natural history. Exhibitions average 3 a year.
Open: On most days during term (except Wed), weekdays at other times. Times of opening and enquiries telephone the above number.
Admission: Free.
Tour parties can be arranged. Curator: Carolyn Leder MA.

ORLEANS HOUSE GALLERY
(London Borough of Richmond upon Thames)
Riverside, Twickenham, London   **Tel:** 081-892 0221

ORLEANS HOUSE GALLERY
RIVERSIDE, TWICKENHAM

In this beautiful riverside setting by the Thames stands the remains of Orleans House, James Gibb's splendid baroque Octagon Room, c.1720. The adjacent Art Gallery shows temporary exhibtions.

Remains of Orleans House, James Gibbs's baroque Octagon Room c. 1720 in a beautiful riverside setting. The adjacent art gallery shows temporary exhibitions on a range of subjects, and houses the Ionides Collection, 18th and 19th century oil paintings, water-colours and prints of Richmond and Twickenham (this collection is not on permanent display).
Open: Tues to Sat 1-5.30 (Oct to Mar, 1-4.30); Sun 2-5.30 (Oct to Mar, 2-4.30); Bank Hols 2-5.30, New Year's Day 2-4.30. *Closed* Mon (except Hols) and Dec 24-26 and Good Friday.
Admission: Free.
Free parking. WCs. Access for disabled: W,S.

OSTERLEY PARK HOUSE
(The National Trust)
near Osterley Station, London   **Tel:** 081-560 3918

An 18th century villa set in a landscaped park. Elegant neo-classical interior decoration and furnishings designed by Robert Adam for the Child family.
Location: Isleworth, ½ mile North of Great West Road, near Osterley Station.

PASSMORE EDWARDS MUSEUM
(Governors of the Passmore Edwards Museum/Newham Leisure Services)
Romford Road, London E15 4LZ   **Tel:** 081-534 2274/0276
New displays on local history, archaeology and natural history, and a lively temporary exhibitions programme in a recently refurbished purpose-built museum of 1900. Education Service, holiday activities.
Open: Wed to Fri 11-5, Sat 1-5, Sun and Bank Hols 2-5.
Admission: Free.
Location: *Buses* 25, 86, 69, and 238. *Tube:* BR and DLR, Stratford.
Shop. New wheelchair access to lower levels.

THE MUSEUM GOVERNORS & NEWHAM LEISURE SERVICES
PRESENT
THE
PASSMORE EDWARDS MUSEUM

ROMFORD ROAD, STRATFORD, LONDON E15

STEP BACK IN TIME & SEE

EVERYDAY OBJECTS from the Stone Age to the 20th Century

MAMMOTH'S TUSKS *from the* **ICE AGE** in East London

FOSSILS *from the* **TROPICAL SEA** that once covered NEWHAM

RECONSTRUCTION *of* **VICTORIAN DISPLAYS** from the original museum

The products of local industries including **BOW PORCELAIN**

WILDLIFE that lives in Newham Parks, Gardens, Rivers & built up areas

MANY SPECIMENS NEVER BEFORE DISPLAYED

PARTIES BY ARRANGEMENT PLEASE
ADMISSION FREE

PERCIVAL DAVID FOUNDATION OF CHINESE ART
(University of London, School of Oriental and African Studies)
53 Gordon Square, London WC1H 0PD   **Tel:** 071-387 3909 **Fax:** 071-383 5163

UNIVERSITY OF LONDON
PERCIVAL DAVID FOUNDATION OF CHINESE ART
53 Gordon Square, London WC1H 0PD

The Collection comprises some 1,700 items consisting of ceramics of the Song, Yuan, Ming and Qing dynasties, and a Reference Library of some 5,000 books and periodicals dealing with the art and culture of the Far East. It was presented to the University of London in 1950 by Sir Percival David and the Foundation is administered and financed on behalf of the University by the School of Oriental and African Studies.

OPENING HOURS:
MONDAY TO FRIDAY
10.30am – 5pm
CLOSED WEEKENDS
& BANK HOLIDAYS

Blue and white Temple Vase inscribed and dated 1351

The Foundation comprises the collection of Chinese ceramics and a library of Chinese and other books dealing with Chinese art and culture presented by Sir Percival David to the University of London in 1950.

PETRIE MUSEUM OF EGYPTIAN ARCHAEOLOGY
University College, Gower Street, London WC1E 6BT   **Tel:** 071-387 7050, Ext. 2884
Contains the collections of the late Miss Amelia Edwards and of the late Professor Sir Flinders Petrie.
Admission: Parties are requested to make an appointment.

PITSHANGER MANOR MUSEUM
(London Borough of Ealing)
Mattock Lane, Ealing, London   **Tel:** 081-567 1227

PITSHANGER MANOR MUSEUM

MATTOCK LANE EALING

Built 1800–04 by the architect Sir John Soane, Pitshanger Manor is set in an attractive park. A Victorian room holds a changing and extensive display of Martinware pottery including a unique chimney-piece of 1891.

The Breakfast Room, Pitshanger Manor Museum.

Set in an attractive park, Pitshanger Manor was built 1800-04 by the architect Sir John Soane (1753-1837) as his family home. The house incorporates a wing of the late 1760s by George Dance. The interiors are being restored. All rooms are open to the public every afternoon. If viewing required mornings, please enquire in advance. A Victorian room holds a changing and extensive display of Martinware pottery including a unique chimney-piece of 1891. Extensive exhibition and cultural programme. **Martinware**

Pottery Collection at Southall Public Library *see under M.*
Open: Tues to Sat 10-5. *Closed* Sun, Mon, Easter, Christmas and New Year.
Admission: Free. Parties by arrangement in advance.
Refreshments: Tea and coffee vending machine.
Partial access for the disabled. **Martinware Pottery Collection at Southall Public Library** *see under M.*

PLUMSTEAD MUSEUM
232 Plumstead High Street, London SE18

POLLOCK'S TOY MUSEUM
1 Scala Street, London W1

PUBLIC RECORD OFFICE MUSEUM
Chancery Lane, London WC2

QUEEN CHARLOTTE'S COTTAGE
(Historic Royal Palaces)
Royal Botanic Gardens, Kew, Surrey TW9 3AB
Picturesque cottage served as summer house for George III.

RAFAEL VALLS LIMITED
(Mr. Rafael Valls)
11 Duke Street, St. James's, London SW1Y 6BN **Tel:** 071-930 1144 **Fax:** 071-976 1596
An Art Gallery specialising in Dutch and Flemish 17th century painting, and other European and English painting from 16th, 17th, 18th and 19th centuries. Some watercolours, gouaches and drawings.
Open: Mon to Fri 10-6, Weekends by appointment only. *Closed* Bank Holidays.
Admission: Free.
Occasional exhibitions.

RANGER'S HOUSE
(English Heritage)
Chesterfield Walk, Blackheath, London SE10 **Tel:** 081 853 0035
A long Gallery of English Portraits from the Elizabethan to the Georgian period in the famous 4th Earl of Chesterfield's house at Blackheath, including the Suffolk collection of paintings. Dolmetsch collection of musical instruments on the first floor.
Open: Apr 1 to Sept 30, daily 10-6. Oct 1 to Mar 31, daily 10-4. *Closed* Dec 24,25.
Admission: Free.

ROYAL ACADEMY OF ARTS
Piccadilly, London W1V 0DS **Tel:** 071-439 7438
The Royal Academy of Arts is world famous for its exciting programme of international art exhibitions. The exhibitions, held in some of Europe's most beautiful galleries including the new, highly acclaimed, Sackler Galleries, cover all aspects of art. A varied programme is planned for 1993 including **British Watercolours: The Great Age (1750-1880), Camille Pissarro** and **American Art in the 20th Century** as well as the popular annual **Summer Exhibition** (see national press for details).
Open: Daily, including weekends 10-6.
Admission: Fee charged.
Location: Underground Piccadilly Circus, Green Park. Bus 9, 14, 19, 22, 25, 38, 55.

ROYAL AIR FORCE MUSEUM
(a National Museum)
Grahame Park Way, Hendon, London NW9 5LL **Tel:** 081-205 2266
Britain's only National Museum of aviation, telling the story of flight from the early days to the present time. Some 60 aircraft are now on show, with galleries depicting aviation history from the Royal Engineers of the 1870s up to the RAF of the 1990s.

ROYAL ARMOURIES
(The National Museum of Arms and Armour)
HM Tower of London, London EC3N 4AB **Tel:** 071-480 6358

Britain's Heritage will knock you out.

Britain's oldest museum is a treasure trove where you'll see the arms and armour of our sovereigns, from Henry V to Edward VIII. There's a fascinating range of bizarre and beautiful weapons on show, including, amongst many others, ingenious axe-pistols and superbly decorated swords. There's plenty of terror and torture too. You'll shiver as you survey Tiger's Claws, executioners' axes, maces and sinister gun-shields with hidden pistol barrels.
This wealth of heritage will make your imagination soar across the centuries.
Don't miss one of the world's great historical collections - it's the next best thing to time travel!

ROYAL ARMOURIES
AT THE TOWER OF LONDON

Britain's oldest national museum, the Royal Armouries, still in its original home at the Tower of London, houses one of the finest collections of arms and armour in the world. The White Tower houses European armours and weapons from the Dark Ages to the 17th century, including the armours of Henry VIII, Charles I, and Charles II. The Waterloo Barracks houses the Oriental Armoury, including fine Japanese and Indian armours and the famous elephant armour. The New Armouries houses the British Military Armoury, and a new display bringing the story of arms and armour up to the present century. The Lower Martin Tower houses the block and axe and other instruments of torture and punishment.
Open: Mar 1 to Mar 22: Mon to Sat 9-5; Sun 2-5; Mar 23 to Oct: Mon to Sat 9.30-5; Sun 10-5. Nov to Feb: Mon to Sat 9.30-4. *Closed* Sun.
Location: Underground: Circle and District lines to Tower Hill. Bus routes: 15, 42, 78. Riverboat: to Tower Pier.

ROYAL ARTILLERY REGIMENTAL MUSEUM
Royal Military Academy, Academy Road, Woolwich, London SE18 **Tel:** 081-854 2242, Ext. 3128
Location: Bus: 161, 161a, 122.

ROYAL BOTANIC GARDENS (KEW GARDENS)
London
The most famous botanic gardens in the world with glasshouses, art galleries and the Thread of Life exhibition in the new Sir Joseph Banks building.
Open: Gardens and glasshouses open at 9.30. Closing time for gardens varies according to season but the galleries and houses are never open later than 4.30 on weekdays or 5.30 on Sun and Bank Hols. *Closed* Christmas Day and New Year's Day.
Admission: To Gardens £3.30; OAPs/Students/Unemployed £1.70; Chld £1.10.
Refreshments: Refreshments available.

ROYAL COLLEGE OF MUSIC DEPARTMENT OF PORTRAITS
Prince Consort Road, South Kensington, London SW7 2BS **Tel:** 071-589 3643
An extensive collection of portraits of musicians, comprising some 280 original portraits and many thousands of prints and photographs. Also houses the College's important collection of concert programmes.
Open: During term-time: Mon to Fri by appointment. Parties by arrangement.
Admission: Free.
Keeper of Portraits: Oliver Davies.

ROYAL COLLEGE OF MUSIC MUSEUM OF INSTRUMENTS
Prince Consort Road, South Kensington, London SW7 2BS **Tel:** 071-589 3643
One of the world's most important collections of musical instruments. Over 500 keyboard, stringed and wind instruments from c. 1480 to the present, including the Donaldson, Tagore, Hipkins and Ridley Collections.
Open: Wed during term-time, 2-4.30 (subject to review).
Admission: Fee charged.
Parties and special visits by appointment with the Curator.

ROYAL COMMISSION ON THE HISTORICAL MONUMENTS OF ENGLAND
(National Monuments Record)
    Fortress House, 23 Savile Row, London W1X 2JQ   **Tel:** 071-973 3500
National archive of photographs, documents and information on archaeological sites and historic buildings in England. Organized in three sections: National Buildings Record, National Archaeological Record, National Library of Air Photographs (now at Swindon (0793) 414100). Arranged topographically for reference and study. It is expanding continually.
Open: Mon to Fri 10-5.

ROYAL HOSPITAL MUSEUM
(Commissioners Royal Hospital)
    Royal Hospital Road, Chelsea, London SW3 4SL
Pictures, plans and maps, medals and uniforms, connected with Royal Hospital.
Open: Daily 10-12, 2-4. *Closed* Bank Hol weekends (Sat to Mon) and Sun from Oct to Mar.

ROYAL SOCIETY OF PAINTER-PRINTMAKERS
    Bankside Gallery, 48 Hopton Street, Blackfriars, London SE1 9JH
Contemporary Print Exhibitions. Spring (Open Exhibition) and Summer (Members' Exhibition).

ROYAL SOCIETY OF PAINTERS IN WATERCOLOURS
    Bankside Gallery, 48 Hopton Street, Blackfriars, London SE1 9JH
Contemporary Watercolour Exhibitions. Spring and Autumn plus Summer.

ST. BRIDE'S CRYPT MUSEUM
(Rector and Churchwardens of St. Bride's Church)
    St. Brides Church, Fleet Street, London EC4   **Tel:** 071-353 1301
During excavations made prior to rebuilding over 1,000 years of unrecorded history were revealed. Roman pavement and remains of seven previous churches (dating from 6th century) on site can be seen together with permanent display of history of print etc.
Open: Daily 9-5.

ST. JOHN'S GATE, THE MUSEUM OF THE ORDER OF ST. JOHN
(The Headquarters of the Order of St. John)
    St. John's Lane, Clerkenwell, London EC1M 4DA   **Tel:** 071-253 6644

ST. JOHN'S GATE

CLERKENWELL, LONDON

THE MUSEUM OF THE ORDER OF ST. JOHN

Early 16th century gatehouse containing silver, furniture, pictures and other treasures of the Knights of St. John.
Tours of the building include the Grand Priory Church and Norman Crypt.

Open: Mon to Fri 10-5; Sat 10-4, with tours at 11 and 2.30 on Tues, Fri and Sat.

SCIENCE MUSEUM
    Exhibition Road, South Kensington, London SW7   **Tel:** 071-938 8000/8080/8008
The outstanding collections at the Science Museum form an unparalleled record of mankind's greatest inventions and achievements. There are nearly a thousand working exhibits. Carry out your very own experiments in 'Launch Pad', the interactive galley for children of all ages, or test your skill at flying a model jump jet in 'Flight Lab', the hands-on gallery themed on flight. From Stevenson's Rocket to the Apollo 10 space capsule you can discover what technology is, how it works and what it can do for you. Discover them for yourself seven days a week at the Science Museum, South

Kensington.
Open: 10.00-18.00 Mon-Sat, 11.00-18.00 Sun
Admission: Charged

SERPENTINE GALLERY
(Arts Council)
    Kensington Gardens, London W2 3XA   **Tel:** 071-402 6075 **Fax:** 071-402 4103

SERPENTINE GALLERY
LONDON'S MOST BEAUTIFUL VENUE FOR CONTEMPORARY ART

TALKS
WORKSHOPS
EXHIBITIONS
changing throughout the year
PERFORMANCES
BOOKSHOP

Talks about the exhibition every Sunday at 3pm
OPEN DAILY
(except when closed for installation)
ADMISSION FREE
Kensington Gardens, London, W2 3XA
Recorded information 071 723 9072
Underground: South Kensington, Lancaster Gate • Buses 9, 10, 12, 52

Monthly exhibitions of British and international twentieth century and contemporary art.
Open: Daily 10-6, except when installing exhibitions. School and other group visits are welcomed and can be arranged on request.
Admission: Free.
Location: Underground: Lancaster Gate/South Kensington. Bus 9, 10, 12, 52.
The gallery is easily accessible by public transport. Disabled access. Toilets for disabled visitors nearby.

THE SHAKESPEARE GLOBE MUSEUM AND ROSE THEATRE EXHIBITION
    Bear Gardens, London SE1   **Tel:** 071-928 6342

SHERLOCK HOLMES MUSEUM
    221b Baker Street, London NW1   **Tel:** 071-935 8866

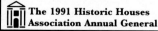

Sherlock Holmes and Doctor Watson are believed to have resided in lodgings at 221b Baker Street from about 1881-1904. The rooms at this address have been faithfully maintained to preserve their Victorian atmosphere and are open to the public as a museum. Seventeen steps lead up to the familiar 1st floor study overlooking Baker Street and convey visitors back a hundred years into the world of Sherlock Holmes. Memorabilia from the stories and personal possessions of the great detective are on display and visitors can also read some of the letters written to Mr Holmes by admirers from around the world. His autograph is given free to every visitor and exclusive souvenirs are available from the gift shop. The Museum is run by the Sherlock Holmes International Society and is a member of the Historic Houses Association.
Open: Every day 10-6.
Admission: £5, Chld £3.
Location: Underground: Baker Street.

SILVER STUDIO COLLECTION
Middlesex Polytechnic, Bounds Green, London N11

SIR JOHN SOANE'S MUSEUM
13 Lincoln's Inn Fields, London WC2A 3BP **Tel:** 071-405 2107; Information line: 071-430 0175
The museum was built by Sir John Soane, R.A., in 1812-13 as his private residence and contains his collection of antiquities and works of art.
Open: Tues to Sat 10-5 (Lecture tours Sat 2.30, maximum 25 people, no groups). Late evening opening on the first Tues of each month 6-9. Groups welcome at other times, please book. *Closed* Bank Hols.

SOUTH LONDON ART GALLERY
(London Borough of Southwark)
65 Peckham Road, London SE5 8UH **Tel:** 071-703 6120
Annual programme of 6/7 temporary exhibitions, mainly of contemporary British art. Permanent collection, including reference collection of 20th century prints shown in special exhibitions.
Open: Tues, Wed, Fri 10-5; Thurs 10-7; Sun 2-5; *Closed* Sat Mon and Bank Hol weekends.
Admission: Free

SPENCER HOUSE
27 St. James's Place, London SW1 **Tel:** 071-409 0526
Spencer House, built 1756-66 for the first Earl Spencer, an ancester of HRH The Princess of Wales, is London's finest surviving private palace.
Open: Its nine state rooms are open to the public on Sun (except during Aug and Jan) from 11.30-5.30. Access is by guided tour (last tour 4.45). Tickets may be purchased on the door from 10.30. To avoid disappointment, visitors are advised to purchase tickets early in the day or use the advance reservation system (tel: 071 499 8620, Mon to Fri 10-1 only)
Admission: £5.00, Concessions: £4.00 (senior citizens and students with cards, Friends of the V & A and National Trust members with cards, children under 16. No children under 10 admitted). Prices are valid until end March 1993.
Location: Underground: Green Park.
Also available for private and corporate entertaining. Access for disabled visitors.

ST BARTHOLOMEW'S HOSPITAL PATHOLOGICAL MUSEUM
West Smithfield, London EC1 **Tel:** 071-601 8537
Pathological specimens. Sherlock Holmes connection. Available for meetings. Visitors welcome by appointment.

THE STORY OF TELECOMMUNICATIONS
145 Queen Victoria Street, London EC4V 4AT **Tel:** 071-248 7444. Information Line:(0800) 289 689
BT's Museum of telecommunications, traces over 200 years of social and industrial history. A hands on display which leads you from the first telegraph machine through the inventions of the telephone to todays world of digital information. New displays in 1992 have brought the story up to date.
Open: Mon to Fri 10-5, except Bank Hols. Special opening each year on Lord Major's Show day.
Location: Near Blackfriars Underground

TATE GALLERY
Millbank, London SW1P 4RG **Tel:** 071-821 1313; Recorded Information 071-821 7128; Education Department 071-828 1456; Friends of the Tate Gallery 071-834 2742

THAMES BARRIER VISITORS' CENTRE
Unity Way, Woolwich, London SE18 5NJ **Tel:** 081-854 1373
A multi-media show and exhibition of photographs, models, video film and information display tubes about the history of the Thames Barrier.
Open: Daily except Christmas.
Admission: Fee charged.
Refreshments: Self-service cafeteria. Function room and evening carvery for pre-booked groups.
Round Barrier Cruises. (Tel: 081-854 5555.) Car park. Free coach park. Evening booking by arrangement. Disabled access.

THEATRE MUSEUM
(A branch of the Victoria & Albert Museum)
Old Flower Market, Covent Garden, London **Tel:** 071-836 7891
The Theatre Museum in the old Flower Market in London's Convent Garden - Britain's first national museum of the performing arts - houses one the the world's richest collections of theatrical material. As well as the permanent gallery which traces the history of theatre, puppetry and pop, ballet and dance, circus and opera from the time of Shakespeare to the present day, there are also two temporary exhibition galleries. The museum has a theatrical paintings gallery, its own studio theatre and its own Box Office where tickets for London shows, concerts and other events may be purchased. Library and study facilities are available by appointment.
Open: Galleries Tues to Sun 11-7. Shop, Cafe and Box Office Tues to Sat 11-8, Sun 11-7. *Closed* every Mon, also Christmas Eve, Christmas Day, Boxing Day, New Year's Day, Good Friday, May Bank Holiday.
Admission: £3.00, Students/OAPs/UB40 holders and Chld aged 5 to 14 £1.50, Chld under 5 and Friends of the V&A free. School parties (pre-booked only) free.
Refreshments: Licensed cafe.
Shop.

Thames Barrier Visitors Centre

The Barrier and its Visitors Centre have now taken their place as **the** technological attraction for visitors to London

Souvenir Shop ● Riverside Self-Service Cafeteria ● Function Room and
Evening Carvery for groups

Barrier Centre
A major audio-visual presentation and exhibition illustrates the important and historic role of London's River Thames and the construction and function of the Thames Barrier.

Riverside Walkway
Riverside promenades with Viewing Terraces offer wide panoramic views of the Barrier and river. Children's Play Area

Barrier Gardens Pier
Barrier cruises lasting 25 minutes. Regular sailings to Greenwich and Westminster.

Car/Coach Parking
Parking for over 200 cars and 30 coaches is available, with a special set-down point between the buffet and exhibition buildings. Coaches FREE.

Opening Times
The centre is open 7 days a week all year round, except Christmas. Admission charge, with concessions for children, OAPs, school parties, groups and families.

**The Thames Barrier Visitor Centre
Unity Way, Woolwich,
London SE18 5NJ
Tel: 081-854 1373**

The Thames Barrier

British Rail Charlton Station 15 mins walk.
Bus nos: 177 & 180. Off A206 Woolwich Road between Greenwich & Woolwich. ON THE SOUTH SIDE OF THE RIVER.

TOWER BRIDGE
(Corporation of London)
London SE1 2UP   **Tel:** 071-403 3761
The tour inside the bridge is closed in 1993 until July, when an all-new exhibition, 'The Celebration Story' opens. Taking visitors back to Victorian times, when the bridge was built, the new exhibition will tell the story of the bridge and explain how it works in an exciting and imaginative new way.
Open: The bridge is open daily Apr 1 to Oct 31: 10-6.30. Nov 1 to Mar 31: 10-4.45. Last ticket 45 mins before closing. *Closed* Dec 24, 25, 26, Jan 1, Good Friday.
Admission: £2.50, Chld (5-15)/OAPs £1. Parties of 10 or more 20% off normal rates Jan to June, Sept to Dec. 10% off normal rates July and Aug. Admission prices from 1/7/93 adults £3.50; child £2.50.
Location: Tube: Tower Hill and London Bridge. Bus: 15, 42, 70, 78. Riverboat: Tower Pier (4 mins walk). Further information 071-407 0922.
Prior booking details on request. Lifts in Tower, and toilet in Museum. Bags are subject to a security search at entry points.

TOWER OF LONDON
(Historic Royal Palaces)
Tower Hill, London EC3N 4AB
Mediaeval Fortress begun by William the Conqueror. Crown jewels, historic relics, armouries, torture instruments, ravens.
Open: The Tower and all its buildings are *closed* on Dec 24, 25, 26; Jan 1 and Good Friday.

UNITED GRAND LODGE OF ENGLAND LIBRARY & MUSEUM
Freemason's Hall, Great Queen Street, London WC2

UNIVERSITY COLLEGE MUSEUM OF ZOOLOGY AND COMPARATIVE ANATOMY
Gower Street, London WC1E 6BT   **Tel:** 071-387 7050, Ext. 3564
Specialised teaching collection of Zoological material. By arrangement only.

VALENCE HOUSE MUSEUM AND ART GALLERY
(London Borough of Barking and Dagenham)
Becontree Avenue, Dagenham, Essex   **Tel:** 081-592 4500, Ext. 4293
A 17th century manor house still partly moated, devoted exclusively to local history, including Fanshawe portraits.
Open: Mon to Fri, 9.30-1, 2-4.30.

VESTRY HOUSE MUSEUM
(London Borough of Waltham Forest)
Vestry Road, Walthamstow E17 9NH   **Tel:** 081-509 1917

WILLIAM MORRIS GALLERY
**Forest Road, Walthamstow, London E17 4PP
081-527 3782**

Boyhood home of William Morris, containing displays of textiles, wallpapers, furniture etc. by Morris and his firm and by members of the Arts and Crafts Movement. Also pictures by the Pre-Raphaelites and contemporaries.

**ADMISSION FREE
Tues-Sat 10–1, 2–5. 1st Sunday of month 10–12, 2–5
See listing for details.**

VESTRY HOUSE MUSEUM
**Vestry Road, Walthamstow, London E17 9NH
081-509 1917**

The local community history museum and archive for Waltham Forest. Housed in an early eighteenth century workhouse in Walthamstow Village conservation area, with excellent displays on Victorian domestic life, toys and costume. A changing programme of temporary exhibitions help bring the story up to date.

**ADMISSION FREE
Mon-Fri 10–1, 2–5.30. Sat 10–1, 2–5.00**

A local history museum housed in an early eighteenth century workhouse in the Walthamstow Village Conservation Area. The permanent displays illustrate aspects of past life in Waltham Forest and include displays of costume and local domestic life, a reconstructed Victorian parlour, a nineteenth century police cell, the Bremer Car, c.1894, etc. Temporary exhibition programme throughout the year. Vestry House also serves as the base for Waltham Forest's Archives and Local History Library.
Open: Mon to Fri 10-1, 2-5.30; Sat 10-1, 2-5. Group visits by prior appointment.
Admission: Free.
Location: Nearest station: Walthamstow Central (Victoria Line).
Special facilities for schools by arrangement.

New at the V&A for 1993

V&A

Three new galleries are opening at the end of 1992:-

The Frank Lloyd Wright Gallery
This new Gallery contains the most comprehensive Frank Lloyd Wright collection this side of the Atlantic. The focal point of the Gallery is the Edgar Kaufmann Office of 1937, the only complete Wright room to be exhibited outside the United States, an important example of the work of this famous and influential architect.

A new Twentieth Century Gallery
From domestic lighting to "vegetarian" shoes, from radios to rugs, significant art and design objects from 1900 to 1992 are shown in context in the innovative Twentieth Century Gallery.

The Samsung Gallery of Korean Art
The new gallery provides a permanent home for the V&A's collection of Korean artefacts, including ceramics, metalwork, lacquer and a set of ceremonial costume, and constitutes the most comprehensive collection of Korean Art on display in Britain

Exhibitions for 1993
We have an exciting programme of exhibitions planned for 1993. Our 24 hour recorded information lines are listed below, which give general information on the V&A, including opening times, as well as details of current exhibitions.

The V&A has some of the finest collections of fine and decorative arts in the world, furniture, ceramics and glass, jewellery and metalwork, dress and textiles, sculpture and paintings, galleries devoted to the arts of India, China, Japan, and the Middle East – as well as a licensed restaurant and an exciting shop. You can relax by the fountain in the Pirelli Garden while you write your postcards or admire the V&A's magnificent architecture. Just two minutes walk from South Kensington Underground Station, or take the C1, 14 or 74 bus – all stop right outside.

24 Hour Recorded Information Lines

071-938 8441 – general information on the V&A
071-938 8349 – current exhibitions

THE WALLACE COLLECTION

Hertford House, Manchester Square, London W1M 6BN

Rembrandt
The Artist's Son

An opulent and remarkable collection of fine and applied art formed in the nineteenth century in London and Paris, principally by the 3rd and 4th Marquesses of Hertford and by Sir Richard Wallace, whose widow bequeathed it to the Nation in 1897.

Includes paintings by Titian, Rubens, Van Dyck, Rembrandt, Velázquez, Canaletto, Guardi, Watteau, Boucher and Fragonard; French Royal furniture from Versailles and outstanding arms and armour.

Velazquez *Lady with a Fan*

Admission Free: Weekdays 10-5, Sundays 2-5; closed New Years Day, Good Friday, May Day and 24-26 December

VICTORIA AND ALBERT MUSEUM
Cromwell Road, South Kensington, London SW7 2RL **Tel:** 071-938 8500; Recorded information on 071-938 8441 (general); 071-938 8349 (exhibitions).
Some of the world's finest collections of furniture, ceramics and glass, jewellery and metalwork, dress and textiles, as well as paintings and sculpture, prints and drawings, posters and photographs. Superb galleries devoted to China, Japan, India and the Middle East. Opening winter 1992/1993 - new 20th Century Gallery, Samsung Gallery of Korean Art, Frank Lloyd Wright Gallery.
Open: Museum Mon to Sat 1025.50, Sun 2.30 5.50. Open to Patrons and Friends of the V&A on Wednesday evenings. *Closed* Christmas Eve, Christmas Day, Boxing Day, New Year's Day, Good Friday, May Day Bank Holiday.
Admission: Free although visitors are invited to make a voluntary donation. Some temporary exhibitions carry an admission charge.
Refreshments: Restaurant.
Shop.

THE WALLACE COLLECTION
Hertford House, Manchester Square, London W1M 6BN **Tel:** 071-935 0687
This unique collection of superb paintings, beautiful French eighteenth century furniture, porcelain, clocks and objects d'art, plus the largest array of arms and armour outside the Tower of London, is displayed in the luxurious setting of the original family home which was left to the nation by Lady Wallace at the end of the last century.
Open: Weekdays 10-5, Sun 2-5.
Admission: Free.
Location: Tube: Bond Street. Buses: Selfridges, Oxford Street.
Contact: Bunty King

WANDSWORTH MUSEUM
(London Borough of Wandsworth)
Putney Library, Disraeli Road, Putney SW15 2DR **Tel:** 081-871 7074

Wandsworth Museum

1745

Visit the Wandsworth Museum and you'll
be surprised by the story it has to tell!

Wandsworth

Wandsworth Museum tells the fascinating story of the Thames-side towns of Battersea, Putney and Wandsworth, the water-powered industries of the river Wandle, the farms and country villas of Balham, Tooting and Roehampton - and their transformation into bustling London suburbs.
Open: Mon, Tue, Wed, Fri and Sat 1-5. Group visits welcome but please book in advance.
Admission: Free.
Location: Nearest stations: Putney (BR) and East Putney (Underground).

WESLEY'S CHAPEL
London **Tel:** 071-253 2262

WESTMINSTER ABBEY MUSEUM
(Dean and Chapter of Westminster)
London **Tel:** 071-222 5152

Westminster Abbey Museum

EXHIBITS INCLUDE THE ABBEY'S SPECTACULAR COLLECTION OF ROYAL AND OTHER EFFIGIES

Open daily 10.30–16.00
Modest charge
(includes admission to
Chapter House and
Treasury)

Museum housed in magnificent Norman Undercroft. The Abbey's famous collection of Royal and other effigies forms centrepiece of the exhibition. Other items on display include replicas of Coronation regalia and surviving panels of medieval glass.

Open: Daily 10.30-4.
Admission: Fee charged (includes adm to Chapter House and Treasurey).

WESTMINSTER GALLERY
Westminster Central Hall, Storey's Gate, Westminster, London SW1H 9NH
Tel: 071-222 2723
Spacious new Gallery in the heart of London opposite Westminster Abbey. Annual exhibitions include: Botanical artists, women artists, Yorkshire water colours, Britain's painters.
Open: Daily 10-5 (except Sun).
Suitable for disabled persons (no wheelchairs available). Telephone 071-222 2723 for exhibition details.

WHITECHAPEL ART GALLERY
80-82 Whitechapel High Street, London E1 7QX **Tel:** 071-377 0107
A purpose-built gallery opened 1901 to the design of Charles Harrison Townsend. Organises major exhibitions, generally of modern and contemporary art; no permanent collection. An extensive community education programme for adults and children - public tours, lectures, workshops, audio-visual programmes and studio visits. Lecture theatre.
Open: Tues to Sun 11-5 (Wed to 8). *Closed* Mon and Bank Hols.
Admission: Free.
Refreshments: Cafe
Bookshop. Full access for people with disabilities.

WHITEHALL
(London Borough of Sutton)
1 Malden Road, Cheam, Surrey **Tel:** 081-643 1236
Timber-framed house built c.1500. Features revealed sections of original fabric and displays including medieval Cheam pottery, Nonsuch Palace, timber-framed buildings and Cheam School. Changing exhibition programme.
Open: Apr to Sept: Tues-Fri 2-5.30; Sat 10-5.30. Oct to Mar: Wed, Thurs and Sun 2-5.30; Sat 10-5.30. Open Bank Holiday Mons 2-5.30. *Closed* Christmas Eve to Jan 2 (incl).
Location: On A2043 just N of junction with A232. *Station:* Cheam (¼m).
Refreshments: Tea room.
Further information from Sutton Heritage Service on 081-773 4555. Party bookings, guided tour facilities available. Please ring in advance. Gift shop.

THE WIMBLEDON LAWN TENNIS MUSEUM
All England Club, Church Road, Wimbledon, London SW19 5AE **Tel:** 081-946 6131

THE WIMBLEDON LAWN TENNIS MUSEUM
ALL ENGLAND CLUB, CHURCH ROAD, WIMBLEDON, SW19 5AE
081-946 6131

Fashion, trophies, replicas and memorabilia are on display representing the history of lawn tennis. An audio visual theatre shows films of great matches and the opportunity is now given to observe the famous Centre Court from the Museum. The Museum shop offers a wide range of attractive souvenirs. Tea Room serves light lunches and teas.

Open. Tuesday–Saturday 11am–5pm. Sunday 2pm–5pm.

Closed Mondays, Public & Bank Holidays and on the Friday, Saturday, and Sunday prior to the Championships.

During the Championships. Admission to the Museum is restricted to those attending the tournament.

Admission. Adults £2.00p, Students, Children & O.A.P.'s £1.00

Limited facilities are available for disabled visitors who are most welcome.

Admission: 10% reduction for parties of 20 or more booked in advance.
Curator Miss Valerie Warren.

WIMBLEDON SOCIETY'S MUSEUM
Village Club, Ridgway, Wimbledon, London
History and natural history of Wimbledon. Photographic survey 1900-14 containing 900 prints. Good collection of watercolours and prints.
Open: Sat 2.30-5.

WIMBLEDON WINDMILL MUSEUM
Windmill Road, Wimbledon Common, London SW19 **Tel:** 081-947 2825
The history of windmills and windmilling told in pictures, models and the machinery and tools of the trade.

Open: Easter to Oct: Sat, Sun and Public Hols 2-5.
Admission: 50p, Chld 25p. Group visits by arrangement.

WOODLANDS ART GALLERY
(London Borough of Greenwich)
90 Mycenae Road, Blackheath SE3   **Tel:** 081-858 4631
Open: Mon, Tues 9-5.30, Thurs 9-8; Sat 9-5. *Closed* Wed and Fri.

ZELLA NINE GALLERY
2 Park Walk, London SW10 0AD   **Tel:** 071-351 0588
Over 5,000 watercolours, etchings, lithographs and other works on paper by major and new British artists.
Open: Daily including Sun and Bank Hols 10-9.
Admission: Free.
Not suitable for disabled persons.

MERSEYSIDE

BIRKENHEAD

BIRKENHEAD PRIORY
Priory Street, Birkenhead
Remains of Benedictine Monastery established 1150 AD.
Open: Tues to Sat 10.30-1.30, 2-5; Sun 2-5. Open Bank Holidays.

HISTORIC WARSHIPS
Birkenhead   **Tel:** 051-650 1573
The Submarine ONYX and Frigate PLYMOUTH are both Falklands Veteran Warships, now on public display for you to explore -watever the weather! It's unique!
Open: Daily from 10am.

ST. MARY'S TOWER
Priory Street, Birkenhead   **Tel:** 051-666 1249
Tower of the 1st Parish Church of Birkenhead restored with original Knox bell and clock.
Open: Tues to Sun 2-5. Open Bank Holidays.

SHORE ROAD PUMPING STATION
Shore Road near Woodside, Birkenhead
Home of the giant restored steam engine - 'The Giant Grasshopper'.
Open: Tues to Sat 10.30-1.30, 2-5; Sun 2-5. Open Bank Holidays.

WILLIAMSON ART GALLERY & MUSEUM
(Wirral Borough Council, Department of Leisure Services & Tourism)
Slatey Road, Birkenhead   **Tel:** 051-652 4177
Fourteen galleries display valuable collections of British watercolours, British oil paintings including artists of the Liverpool School, Liverpool porcelain, Birkenhead Della Robbia Pottery. Museum displays include maritime and local history. Temporary exhibition programme presents constantly changing displays of all types.
Open: Mon to Sat 10-5 (Thurs 10-9); Sun 2-5. *Closed* Good Friday and Christmas Day.
Admission: Free.
Car parking. Suitable for disabled persons. One wheelchair available.

WOODSIDE VISITOR CENTRE
Woodside, Birkenhead
Birkenhead Tram display.
Open: Mon to Sun 11-5.
Refreshments: Available
Information Office. Metropolitan Borough of Wirral, Department of Leisure Services and Tourism, Tel: 051-647 2366.

LIVERPOOL

DENTAL HOSPITAL MUSEUM
(School of Dental Surgery, Liverpool University)
Pembroke Place, Liverpool L3 5PS   **Tel:** 051-709 2000 **Fax:** 051-706 5807

LIVERPOOL MUSEUM
William Brown Street, Liverpool L3 8EN   **Tel:** 051-207 0001
One of Britan's finest museums with collections from all over the World, from the wonders of the Amazonian rain forests to outer space. Located in the centre of the city, the Liverpool Museum contains over a million specimens. Outstanding items on display include Egyptian mummies, masks, weapons, classical sculpture and land transport exhibits. The Museum also contains a Planetarium, Aquarium, Vivarium and an award-winning Natural History Centre. Major exhibitions are shown on the ground floor.
Open: Mon to Sat 10-5; Sun 12-5. *Closed* Christmas Eve, Christmas Day, Boxing Day, New Year's Day and Good Friday.
Admission: Free, a small charge is made for the Planetarium.
Refreshments: A coffee bar serving hot and cold snacks, is open 7 days a week, and special facilities are available for educational groups.

MERSEYSIDE MARITIME MUSEUM
(National Museums and Galleries on Merseyside)
Albert Dock, Liverpool L3 4AA   **Tel:** 051-207 0001
Set in the historic heart of Liverpool's magnificent waterfront at the Albert Dock, this large award-winning museum provides a unique blend of floating exhibits, craft demonstrations and working displays. The Merseyside Maritime Museum has captured the romance, the day-to-day atmosphere of working on the docks and aboard ship while tracing the changes and development of Liverpool from a small hamlet to a major international port. A gallery entitled 'Art & Sea' shows an inspiring display of work by painters who worked in the port from the late 18th century until about 1900 and who specialised in ship portraits. Other major displays include World of Models, Emigrants to a New World, Builders of Great Ships, Safe Passage and The Evolution of the Port.
Open: Daily 10.30-5.30 (last ticket sold at 4.30). *Closed* Dec 24, 25, 26, Jan 1 and Good Friday.
Admission: Fee charged.
Refreshments: The Museum has a Smorgasbord restaurant and Waterfront Cafe.
Gift shop and car parking facilities.

SPEKE HALL
(National Trust and grant aided by the National Museums and Galleries on Merseyside)
Liverpool
An extremely fine half-timbered building, originally the home of the Norris family and dating from the 15th century. The house is fully furnished and includes the Great Hall with its magnificent 'Great Wainscot' and the Great Parlour with fine Jacobean stucco ceiling. There are also a number of priest holes.
Location: 7 miles from city centre.

SUDLEY
(National Museums and Galleries on Merseyside)
Mossley Hill Road, Liverpool L18 8BX
Sudley, a fine house overlooking the Mersey, was formerly the home of a wealthy 19th century shipowner who bought paintings of the taste of that period. On display is a fine collection of late 18th and 19th century British paintings including Turner, Bonnington, Cox, Copley, Fielding and Landseer.
Open: Mon to Sat 10-5, Sun 12-5. Sudley Tea Rooms open Sat and Bank Hols 10-4.30, Sun 12-4.30. *Closed* Dec 24, 25, 26, Jan 1 and Good Friday.
Admission: Free.

TATE GALLERY LIVERPOOL
Albert Dock, Liverpool L3 4BB   **Tel:** 051-709 3223; Information line 051-709 0507
Opened in May 1988 by His Royal Highness The Prince of Wales, Tate Gallery Liverpool offers a unique opportunity to see the best of the National Collection of twentieth century art. The Gallery, a converted Victorian warehouse, has a changing programme of displays, providing visitors with a rare opportunity to see international exhibitions not previously seen outside London.
Open: Tues to Sun 10-6; *closed* Mon but open Bank Holidays.
Admission: Free.

UNIVERSITY OF LIVERPOOL ART GALLERY
3 Abercromby Square, Liverpool   **Tel:** 051-794 2347/8
The Gallery contains a selection from the University's collections: sculpture; paintings, including works by Audubon and Wright of Derby; watercolours, including works by Turner; contemporary prints; furniture; porcelain and silver.
Open: Mon, Tues and Thurs 12-2; Wed and Fri 12-4 or by appointment *Closed* Public Hols and Aug.

WALKER ART GALLERY
(National Museums and Galleries on Merseyside)
William Brown Street, Liverpool L3 8EL   **Tel:** 051-207 0001
One of the finest galleries in Europe with outstanding collections of European art from 1300 to the present day. The gallery is especially rich in European old masters by Rubens, Rembrandt and Poussin. The French impressionists include Monet, Seurat and Degas. The Medieval and Renaissance gallery which has recently been redecorated, houses the internationally important Medieval and Renaissance collections.
Open: Mon to Sat 10-5, Sun 12-5.
Refreshments: Cafeteria
Baby change facilities. Disabled access.

PORT SUNLIGHT

LADY LEVER ART GALLERY
(National Museums and Galleries on Merseyside)
Port Sunlight Village, Wirral L62 5EQ   **Tel:** 051-207 0001
An outstanding collection of English 18th century paintings and furniture, Chinese porcelain, Wedgwood pottery and Victorian paintings, formed by the first Viscount Leverhulme at the turn of the century as the centrepiece of his model village, Port Sunlight. Of special note is the series of superb carved and inlaid cabinets, some by Chippendale, and paintings by Reynolds, Wilson, Sargent, Burne-Jones and Leighton.
Open: Mon to Sat 10-5, Sun 12-5. *Closed* Dec 24, 25, 26, Jan 1 and Good Friday.
Refreshments: Restaurant

PRESCOT

PRESCOT MUSEUM OF CLOCK AND WATCH-MAKING
(National Museums and Galleries on Merseyside and Knowsley Metropolitan Borough Council)
    34 Church Street, Prescot L34 3LA   **Tel:** 051-430 7787

ST. HELENS

MUSEUM AND ART GALLERY
(St. Helens Metropolitan Borough Council. Community Leisure Department)
    College Street, St. Helens   **Tel:** (0744) 26429
Museum of the history and culture of the people of St Helens, the glassmaking capital of Britain. Lively and imaginative programme of changing exhibitions on local themes. The Art Gallery features the permanent collections and displays by local artists.
Open: Tues-Fri 10-5; Sat 10-4.
Admission: Free.

PILKINGTON GLASS MUSEUM
(Pilkington P.L.C.)
    Prescot Road, St. Helens   **Tel:** (0744) 692014
The museum shows the evolution of glassmaking techniques.
Open: Mon to Fri 10-5; Evenings for groups by appointment. Sat, Sun and Bank Hols 2-4.30. *Closed* Christmas to New Year.
Admission: Free.
Schools and organised parties by prior arrangement with the Curator.

SOUTHPORT

ATKINSON ART GALLERY
(Merseyside-Sefton Borough Council)
    Lord Street, Southport   **Tel:** (0704) 533133, Ext. 2110
Permanent collections include British art of the 18th, 19th and 20th centuries. Oils, watercolours and sculpture. Contemporary prints. Old English glass and Chinese porcelain. Continuous programme of temporary exhibitions.
Open: Mon, Tues, Wed and Fri 10-5; Thurs and Sat 10-1.
Admission: Free.

BOTANIC GARDENS MUSEUM
(Merseyside-Sefton Borough Council)
    Churchtown, Southport   **Tel:** (0704) 27547
A small museum with interesting displays of local history (The Growth of Southport), natural history, Victoriana, dolls and Liverpool porcelain.
Open: All year Tues to Fri: 11-3; Sat and Sun 2-5. *Closed* Mon. Open Bank Hol Mons but *closed* Fri following.
Admission: Free.

BRITISH LAWNMOWER MUSEUM
    106-114 Shakespeare Street, Southport   **Tel:** (0704) 535369
Open: All year daily 9.00-5.30. Except Sundays.

STEAMPORT TRANSPORT MUSEUM
    Derby Road, Southport

WALLASEY

WALLASEY MUSEUM & EXHIBITION CENTRE
    Central Library, Earlston Road, Wallasey

NORFOLK

BRESSINGHAM

BRESSINGHAM STEAM MUSEUM AND GARDENS
(Bressingham Steam Preservation Co. Ltd)
    Diss, Bressingham IP22 2AB   **Tel:** (0379 88) 386 and 382
Live Steam Museum. Containing hundreds of steam related exhibits including Standard Gauge locomotives from all over Europe. Three different narrow gauge railways. Road and Static Steam Engines, Victorian Steam Roundabout. The Norfolk Fire Museum - a collection of exhibits including engines, uniforms and equipment. Adjoining the internationally famous gardens and nurseries of the Museum's founder, Alan Bloom.
Open: Between Easter and Oct on application.
Admission: Between Easter and Oct on application. Special reductions children and parties.
Location: 2½ miles west of Diss on the A1066
Ample and free car parking. Suitable for disabled persons. Wheelchairs available if advised in advance.

CROMER

THE CROMER MUSEUM
(Norfolk Museums Service)
    East Cottages, Tucker Street, Cromer NR27 9HB   **Tel:** (0263) 513543
Row of cottages with displays about the people, natural history and geology of the area. Furnished 1890's home o local fishing people.

FAKENHAM

THE THURSFORD COLLECTION
(J.R. Cushing)
    Fakenham   **Tel:** (0328) 878477
Live musical shows each day from nine mechanical organs and one Wurlitzer cinema organ; there are road rollers, showmen's engines, traction engines, barn/oil engines, and a Savage Venetian Gondola switchback ride.
Open: Apr 1 to Oct 31: 1-5; June, July and Aug: 11-5; Christmas as per programme during Dec.
Admission: £4.20, Chld £1.80, OAPs £3.80.
Refreshments: Self-service dispensing light snacks.
Free car parking. Suitable for disabled persons. Small Norfolk village of gift shops.

GREAT YARMOUTH

ELIZABETHAN HOUSE MUSEUM
(Norfolk Museums Service)
    4 South Quay, Great Yarmouth NR30 2QH   **Tel:** (0493) 855746
16th century merchant's house with period rooms including Victorian kitchen and scullery.

EXHIBITION GALLERIES
(Norfolk Museums Service)
    Central Library, Tolhouse Street, Great Yarmouth NR30 2SH   **Tel:** (0493) 858900
Travelling and local exhibitions.

MARITIME MUSEUM FOR EAST ANGLIA
(Norfolk Museums Service)
    Marine Parade, Great Yarmouth NR30 2EN   **Tel:** (0493) 842267
Once a home for shipwrecked sailors, now a museum with displays which include wrecks and rescues, herring fishing and artefacts associated with Nelson.

NELSON'S MONUMENT
(Norfolk Museums Service)
    South Beach Parade, Great Yarmouth   **Tel:** (0493) 858900
217 steps to the top of 144ft. Monument erected in 1819 as a memorial to Nelson.

OLD MERCHANT'S HOUSE, ROW 111 HOUSES AND GREYFRIARS' CLOISTERS
(English Heritage)
    Great Yarmouth   **Tel:** (0493) 857900
Two 17th Century town houses of a type unique to Great Yarmouth, containing original fixtures and displays of local architectural fittings salvaged from bombing in 1942-43.
Open: (Entry by tour only) Apr 1 to Sept 30, daily 10-6.
Admission: £1.10 Concessions 85p, Chld 55p (1992 prices).

THE TOLHOUSE MUSEUM AND BRASS RUBBING CENTRE
(Norfolk Museums Service)
    Tolhouse Street, Great Yarmouth NR30 2SQ   **Tel:** (0493) 858900
Yarmouth's oldest civic building which once served as courtroom and town gaol. Dungeons with their originals cells. Local history museum and brass rubbing centre.

GRESSENHALL

NORFOLK RURAL LIFE MUSEUM AND UNION FARM
(Norfolk Museums Service)
    Beech House, Gressenhall, Dereham NR20 4DR   **Tel:** (0362) 860563
Displays illustrating history of the County of Norfolk over the past 200 years housed in 1777 Union Workhouse. Reconstructed village shop, saddlers, wheelwrights and basket makers' workshops; farmworker's home and garden. Union Farm is a working 1920s farm.

KING'S LYNN

THE LYNN MUSEUM
(Norfolk Museums Service)
    Old Market Street, King's Lynn PE30 1NL   **Tel:** (0553) 775001
Natural history, archaeology and local history relating to NW Norfolk.

THE TOWN HOUSE - MUSEUM OF LYNN LIFE
46 Queen Street, King's Lynn PE30 5DQ   **Tel:** (0553) 773450
Museum opened in 1992 which illustrates the history of King's Lynn. Historic room displays including costume, toys, a working Victorian kitchen and a 1950s living room.

NORWICH

BRIDEWELL MUSEUM OF LOCAL INDUSTRIES
(Norfolk Museums Service)
Bridewell Alley, Norwich NR2 1AQ   **Tel:** (0603) 667228
Exhibits illustrating Norwich crafts, industries and aspects of city life.

COLMAN'S MUSTARD MUSEUM
The Mustard Shop, 3 Bridewell Alley , Norwich   **Tel:** (0603) 627889
The Mustard Shop sells a large selection of mustards, many of which are unique to the Shop. The Shop also houses a mustard museum which traces the history of the Colman Family and indeed the story of mustard.
Open: 9.30-5.15pm

NORWICH CASTLE MUSEUM
(Norfolk Museums Service)
Norwich   **Tel:** (0603) 223624

NORWICH CASTLE MUSEUM

Once a royal castle, then a prison, now one of the finest museums in East Anglia.

- Stone Keep built about 1120
- Norwich School paintings
- World's largest teapot display
- Important archaeological collections
- Natural history displays
- Guided tours of battlements & dungeons
- Shop and cafeteria

10am-5pm Monday to Saturday; 2-5pm Sunday

Norfolk Museums Service

Large collections of art (particularly of the Norwich School), local archaeology and natural history (Norfolk Room dioramas), social history and ceramic display. Important loan exhibitions.

ROYAL NORFOLK REGIMENTAL MUSEUM
(Norfolk Museums Service)
Shirehall, Castle Meadow, Norwich   **Tel:** (0603) 223624
A museum displaying the history of the Royal Norfolk Regiment and the Norfolk Yeomanry since 1685.

SAINSBURY CENTRE FOR VISUAL ARTS
University of East Anglia, Watton Road, Norwich NR4 7TJ   **Tel:** (0603) 592470 (office hours), (0603) 56060 (24 hrs)   **Fax:** (0603) 259401
The Robert and Lisa Sainsbury Collection is wide-ranging, remarkable and of international importance. With the recent addition of Sir Norman Foster and Partners' superb new Crescent Wing seven hundred paintings, sculptures and ceramics are on permanent display with Picasso, Moore, Bacon and Giacometti shown alongside art from Africa, the Pacific and the Americas. The Centre also houses the Anderson Collection of Art Nouveau. Three special exhibitions a year.
Open: Galleries open daily (except Mon) 12-5.
Admission: £1, concessions 50p.
Refreshments: Restaurant, buffet and coffee bar.
Accessible to disabled people.

ST. PETER HUNGATE CHURCH MUSEUM
(Norfolk Museums Service)
Princes Street, Norwich   **Tel:** (0603) 667231
15th century church used for display of ecclesiastical art and East Anglian antiquities.

STRANGERS' HALL
(Norfolk Museums Service)
Charing Cross, Norwich NR2 4AL   **Tel:** (0603) 667229
Late medieval mansion furnished as a museum of urban domestic life 16th-19th centuries.

STRUMPSHAW OLD HALL STEAM MUSEUM
(W.S. Key)
Strumpshaw, Norwich   **Tel:** (0603) 712339
This museum is undercover and has over 15,000 sq ft filled with exhibits including working beam engines and mechanical organs, plus narrow gauge railway.
Open: May 14 to Oct 2 every day (except Sat) 2-5.
Admission: £2, Chld £1, OAP £1.50.
Location: Off the A47 between Great Yarmouth and Norwich - follow brown tourist signs.
Parties by arrangement. Car parking. Suitable for disabled persons.

THETFORD

THE ANCIENT HOUSE MUSEUM
(Norfolk Museums Service)
White Hart Street, Thetford IP24 1AA   **Tel:** (0842) 752599
Early Tudor half-timbered house with collections illustrating Thetford and Breckland life, history and natural history.

WALSINGHAM

SHIREHALL MUSEUM
(Norfolk Museums Service)
Common Place, Little Walsingham NR22 6BP   **Tel:** (0263) 513543 or (0328) 820510
The principal exhibit is the Georgian court room which may be seen with its original fittings including the prisoners' lock-up. The museum contains many items illustrating the history of Walsingham including a display on the history of pilgrimage.

WELLS-NEXT-THE-SEA

BYGONES AT HOLKHAM
Holkham Park, Wells-next-the-Sea   **Tel:** (0328) 710806/710277

A unique and comprehensive collection of Victorian and Edwardian agricultural and domestic items displayed in the restored 19th century stables adjacent to Holkham Hall in Holkham Park.
EXHIBITIONS INCLUDE: Craft Tools, Cars, Carriages, Fire Engines, Sewing Machines, a Working Pump Room, Laundry, Victorian Cottage Kitchen, Brewery, Dairy, Harness Room, Engineerium. **ALSO:** Holkham Hall, Holkham Pottery, Holkham Garden Centre. Teas in a modern complex adjoining the Bygones Collection.
Holkham Park, Wells next the Sea, Norfolk.
On the A149: Fakenham 8 miles, King's Lynn 30 miles, Norwich 34 miles.

A unique and comprehensive collection of the Victorian and Edwardian era. Housed in the magnificent 19th century stable buildings in Holkham Park the exhibition includes: Fire Engines, Cars, Craft Tools, Harness, a Victorian Cottage Kitchen, Brewery, Dairy, Shoe Shop, Engineerium, Carriages, Veterinary items, Laundry, Sewing Machines.
Open: May 30 to Sept 30: daily except Fri and Sat 1.30-5; Easter, May, Spring and Summer Bank Holidays Sun & Mon 11.30-5.
Admission: £2.70, Chld £1.20, pre-paid parties 20+ 10% reduction.
Location: On the A149: Fakenham 10 miles, King's Lynn 30 miles, Norwich 34 miles.
Refreshments: Tea rooms.
Also visit Holkham Hall, Holkham Pottery and Holkham Garden Centre.

NORTHAMPTONSHIRE

KETTERING

ALFRED EAST GALLERY
   Sheep Street, Kettering   **Tel:** (0536) 410333 Ext 381
An exciting programme of temporary exhibitions of fine art, craft and photography. Permanent collection of works by Sir Alfred East RA and Thomas Cooper Gotch on view by appointment.
Open: Mon to Sat 9.30-5.
Admission: Free.

MANOR HOUSE MUSEUM
   Sheep Street, Kettering   **Tel:** (0536) 410333 Ext. 381
Displays reflecting the growth of the town and borough of Kettering.
Open: Mon to Sat 9.30-5.
Admission: Free.

NORTHAMPTON

ABINGTON MUSEUM
(Northampton Borough Council)
   Abington Park, Northampton   **Tel:** (0604) 39415
The museum will be closed until further notice.

CENTRAL MUSEUM & ART GALLERY
(Northampton Borough Council)
   Guildhall Road, Northampton   **Tel:** (0604) 39415

CENTRAL MUSEUM AND ART GALLERY
Guildhall Road, Northampton

Discover Northampton's boot and shoe heritage – and much more – at the Central Museum and Art Gallery.
Monday - Saturday 10.00 am - 5.00 pm
Thursday until 8.00 p.m.
Sunday 2.00 p.m. - 5.00 p.m.
ADMISSION FREE
Phone (0604) 39415 for further information.

Northampton's History: Objects, sound and film combined to tell the history of the town from the Stone Age to the present. Decorative arts - priceless Chinese and English ceramics. The Art Gallery - a fine collection of Italian 15th-18th century paintings, and British art. Special temporary exhibitions.

MUSEUM OF LEATHERCRAFT
(Northampton Borough Council)
   The Old Blue Coat School, Bridge Street, Northampton   **Tel:** (0604) 39415
Displays tell the story of leather's use throughout history from ancient Egyptian times to the present day.
Open: Mon to Sat 10-5.

MUSEUM OF THE NORTHAMPTONSHIRE REGIMENT
(Northampton Borough Council)
   Abington Park, Northampton
Open: Opening hours as for Abington Museum, see above.

MUSEUM OF THE NORTHAMPTONSHIRE YEOMANRY
(Northampton Borough Council)
   Abington Park, Northampton
Open: Opening hours as for Abington Museum, see above.

NASEBY BATTLE AND FARM MUSEUM
   Purlieu Farm, Northampton

STOKE BRUERNE

THE CANAL MUSEUM
   Stoke Bruerne   **Tel:** (0604) 862229
Visit Stoke Bruerne with its famous Canal Museum and discover 200 years of colourful canal history and traditions. There are guided tours available, traditional 'Roses and Castles' painting demonstrations, a shop, Blisworth Tunnel, flight of seven locks, boat trips and countryside walks.
Open: Easter to Oct daily 10-6; Oct to Easter daily (except Mon) 10-4.
Admission: Fee charged.
Refreshments: Pub, restaurants, tea rooms.

NORTHUMBERLAND

ALNWICK

ALNWICK CASTLE MUSEUM
(Duke of Northumberland)
   Alnwick Castle, Alnwick NE66 1NQ   **Tel:** (0665) 510777
This is one of the oldest private museums in England, open to public viewing since 1826. Prehistoric, Roman, Celtic and Viking artefacts collected by the Third and Fourth Dukes, 1817-65. Items from Pompeii and items of Percyana.
Admission: Charge for museum is included in charge for admission to Alnwick Castle. Organised party rates by arrangement.
Free car parking at castle.

BAMBURGH

THE GRACE DARLING MUSEUM
(Royal National Life-boat Institution)
   Bamburgh   **Tel:** (0665) 720 039
Grace Darling relics.
Open: Easter to Oct: Daily 11-6. Other times be arrangement with Hon. Curator (Mr. D.W.N. Calderwood).
Admission: Free but voluntary donations to R.N.L.I. invited.

BERWICK-UPON-TWEED

BERWICK BOROUGH MUSEUM & ART GALLERY
(Berwick-upon-Tweed Borough Council)
   The Clock Block, Berwick Barracks, Berwick-upon-Tweed TD15 1DQ
Tel: (0289) 330933

Situated in the first ever purpose built Barracks, come and peer through a Window on Berwick, or enter the dragon and step into Cairo Bazaar where some of the 800 pieces donated to Berwick by Sir William Burrell are displayed. The art treasures comprise 42 important paintings, including a Degas and many fine items of porcelain, glass and metalware. With a changing programme of art exhibitions, this is a most unconventional museum.

Open: Easter to Oct: Mon to Sat 10-12.30, 1.30-6; Sun 10-1, 2-6. Oct to Easter: Tues to Sat 10-12.30, 1.30-4; Sun 10-1, 2-4, *closed* Mon.
Admission: £1.80, Chld 90p, OAPs £1.40. Fee is for the whole Barracks complex and includes two other museums, the Kings Own Scottish Borderers Regimental museum and By Beat of Drum, English Heritage are custodians.
Car parking. Suitable for disabled on ground floor only (no wheelchairs available).

THE CELL BLOCK MUSEUM
(Berwick-upon-Tweed Corporation (Freemen) Trustees)
  The Town Hall, Marygate, Berwick-upon-Tweed   **Tel:** (0289) 330900
A Georgian town hall and former town jail situated in the town centre, this magnificent building with its 150ft spire now houses the Cell Block Museum, Guild Hall, Council Chamber and Mayor's Parlour. Guided tours are arranged twice daily when visitors can learn of bygone Berwick, see civic artefacts and cells in their original state and also ring out tunes on the town hall bells, the only town hall in England where this is possible. Learn some of the history that makes Berwick-upon-Tweed so unique, sign the old visitors book and find out who spent a night locked in the cells.
Open: Weekdays only Easter to end Sept. *Closed* Bank Holidays.
Admission: £1, Chld 30p. Special reductions for school groups. Parties by arrangement.
Car parking nearby. Guided tours only at 10.30 and 2, several flights of stairs are involved.

CAMBO

WALLINGTON HOUSE, GARDEN AND GROUNDS
(The National Trust)
  Cambo
Fine porcelain collection, needlework, pictures and dolls' houses as well as a museum.

CHESTERS

CHESTERS MUSEUM
(English Heritage)
  Hadrian's Wall near Chollerford, Chesters   **Tel:** (0434) 681379
Roman inscriptions, sculpture, weapons, tools and ornaments from the forts at Chesters, Carrawburgh, Housesteads, Greatchesters and Carvoran.
Open: Apr 1 to Sept 30, daily 10-6. Oct 1 to Mar 31, daily 10-4. *Closed* Dec 24 to 26, Jan 1.
Admission: £1.80, Concessions £1.40, Chld 90p (1992 prices).

CORBRIDGE

CORBRIDGE ROMAN STATION
(English Heritage)
  Corbridge   **Tel:** (0434) 632349
Roman pottery, sculpture, inscribed stones and small objects.
Open: Apr 1 to Sept 30, daily 10-6. Oct 1 to Mar 31, Tues to Sun 10-4. *Closed* Dec 24 to 26, Jan 1.
Admission: £1.80, Concessions £1.40, Chld 90p (1992 prices).

FORD & ETAL ESTATES

HEATHERSLAW CORN MILL
  Cornhill-on-Tweed, Ford & Etal Estates   **Tel:** (089 082) 338
A rare chance to visit a restored and working 19th Century water powered corn mill.

LADY WATERFORD HALL AND MURALS
  Ford Village, Berwick-upon-Tweed, Ford & Etal Estates   **Tel:** (089 82) 224
A beautiful Hall and Murals by Louisa, Marchioness of Waterford.

HEXHAM

MIDDLEMARCH CENTRE FOR BORDER HISTORY
  The Old Gaol, Hallgate, Hexham

HOUSESTEADS

HOUSESTEADS MUSEUM
(English Heritage)
  Bardon Mill, Hexham, Housesteads   **Tel:** (0434) 344363
Roman pottery, inscribed stones, sculpture and small objects.
Open: Apr 1 to Sept 30, daily 10-6. Oct 1 to Mar 31, daily 10-4. *Closed* Dec 24 to 26, Jan 1.
Admission: £1.80, Concessions £1.40, Chld 90p (1992 prices).

LINDISFARNE

LINDISFARNE CASTLE
(The National Trust)
  Holy Island, Lindisfarne
Built about 1550, the Castle was converted into a comfortable home by Sir Edwin Lutyens in 1903. Flemish and English oak furniture of the 17th century and some pieces designed for the Castle by Lutyens. Interesting collection of Ridinger and other prints.

LINDISFARNE PRIORY
(English Heritage)
  Holy Island, Lindisfarne   **Tel:** (028 989) 200
The fascinating story of Lindisfarne is told in an exhibition which gives an impression of life for the monks, including a reconstruction of a monk's cell. (Tide times restrict access to island).
Open: Apr 1 to Sept 30, daily 10-6. Oct 1 to Mar 31, Tues to Sun 10-4, *Closed* Dec 24 to 26, Jan 1.
Admission: £1.80, Concessions £1.40, Chld 90p (1992 prices).

MORPETH

MORPETH CHANTRY BAGPIPE MUSEUM
  The Chantry, Bridge Street, Morpeth   **Tel:** (0670) 519466
Set in a restored 13th century church building, the museum has one of the largest and best collections of its kind in the world. The infra red sound system allows each visitor (including the deaf) a unique musical experience.
Open: Mon to Sat: Jan to Feb, 10-4; Mar to Dec, 9.30-5.30. *Closed* Bank Holidays and between Christmas and New Year.
Admission: 65p; Chld/OAPs 35p; parties 10p; MA free.
Free disc parking in Morpeth.

ROTHBURY

CRAGSIDE HOUSE AND COUNTRY PARK
(The National Trust)
  Rothbury
Designed by Richard Norman Shaw and built for the first Lord Armstrong. It contains much of his original furniture designed by Shaw, pictures and experimental scientific apparatus made by Lord Armstrong.
Open: House open: Apr to end Oct daily except Mon (open Bank Holiday Mon) 1-5.30. Last adm 5. Country Park open daily except Mon (open Bank Holiday Mon). Apr to Oct 10.30-7, (or dusk if earlier); Nov to Dec: Tues, Sat and Sun 10.30-4.

STOCKSFIELD

CHERRYBURN, BEWICK MUSEUM
(The National Trust)
  Mickley, Nr. Stocksfield NE43 7DB   **Tel:** (0661) 843276
Birthplace of Northumbria's greatest artist, wood engraver and naturalist, Thomas Bewick, in 1753. His family cottage is restored and there are animals in the adjacent farmyard. The small museum explores his famous works and life and in the Printing House. Demonstrations of hand printing from wood blocks can be seen.
Open: Apr 1 to end Oct: daily except Tues 1-5.30. Last adm 5.
Admission: £2.50. No party rates.
Wheelchair access, WC. No dogs please. Small shop selling Thomas Bewick mementoes and prints.

NOTTINGHAMSHIRE

MANSFIELD

MANSFIELD MUSEUM AND ART GALLERY
(Mansfield District Council)
  Leeming Street, Mansfield   **Tel:** (0623) 663088
Exhibitions; Images of Mansfield Past and Present; The Nature of Mansfield; William Billingsley Porcelain; Watercolours of Old Mansfield.
Open: Mon to Sat 10-5.
Admission: Free

NEWARK-ON-TRENT

THE CASTLE STORY
(Newark and Sherwood District Council)
  Gilstrap Centre, Newark NG24 1BG   **Tel:** (0636) 611908
The rich history of Newark Castle, colourfully told. Adjacent to Castle ruins and picturesque town wharf.
Open: Daily 10-6 (summer), 10-5 (winter).
Admission: Free

BIRTHPLACE

EASTWOOD NOTTINGHAMSHIRE

The Lawrence museum opens daily:
10.00 a.m. to 5.00 p.m. April to October
10.00 a.m. to 4.00 p.m. November to March
Open Bank Holidays, but closed 24th Dec. to 1st Jan. inclusive.

BROXTOWE
Borough Council

VINA COOKE MUSEUM OF DOLLS & BYGONE CHILDHOOD
The Old Rectory, Cromwell, Newark-on-Trent   **Tel:** (0636) 821364
Fine house built c1685, now home of the Vina Cooke collection of dolls, costumes, toys and items evoking the magic of golden days. Also unique handmade portrait dolls.
Open: All year daily (except Christmas Day and Boxing Day); 10.30-12, 2-5. Parties catered for by appointment day and evening.
Admission: £1.50, Chld 50p,OAP £1. Reduction for parties of more than 10.
Refreshments: Available during normal opening hours.
Picnic area and interesting gardens. Souvenirs and crafts for sale. Car parking free. Unsuitable for disabled persons.

MILLGATE FOLK MUSEUM
(Newark & Sherwood District Council)
Millgate, Newark-on-Trent NG24 4TS
The social and folk life of Newark from Victorian times until the second World War.

NEWARK AIR MUSEUM
(Registered Charity, run by Committee, Chairman Mr. R. Bryan)
The Airfield, Winthorpe, Newark-on-Trent NG24 2NY   **Tel:** (0636) 707170
Nearly half of the collection of 40 aircraft are now displayed undercover. Undercover artefacts and engine displays.
Open: Everyday except Christmas Eve, Christmas Day and Boxing Day. Apr to Oct Weekdays 10-5, Weekends 10-6; Nov to Mar everyday 10-4.
Admission: £2.50, concessions £1.50, parties of 10+ £2 and concessions £1.
Free car parking. Suitable for the disabled.

NEWARK MUSEUM
(Newark and Sherwood District Council)
Appleton Gate, Newark-on-Trent NG24 1JY   **Tel:** (0636) 702358
Collections are of local archaeology, history and some natural history.
Open: Weekdays 10-1, 2-5; Sat 10-1, 2-5. Sun (Apr to Sept) 2-5. *Closed* Thurs.

NOTTINGHAM

BREWHOUSE YARD MUSEUM
(Nottingham City Council)
Nottingham   **Tel:** (0602) 483504

CANAL MUSEUM
(Nottingham City Council)
Canal Street, Nottingham   **Tel:** (0602) 598835

GREENS MILL AND SCIENCE CENTRE
(Nottingham City Council)
Windmill Lane, Nottingham NG2 4LF   **Tel:** (0602) 503635

INDUSTRIAL MUSEUM
(Nottingham City Council)
Wollaton Park, Nottingham NG8 2AE   **Tel:** (0602) 284602

THE LACE CENTRE NOTTINGHAM
Severns Building, Castle Road, Nottingham NG1 6AA   **Tel:** (0602) 413539

D.H. LAWRENCE BIRTHPLACE MUSEUM
(Broxtowe Borough Council)
8a Victoria Street, Eastwood, Nottingham   **Tel:** (0773) 763312
David Herbert Lawrence - novelist, playwright, poet and artist - was born at 8a Victoria Street, Eastwood, on Sept 11 1885. After careful restoration and furnishing the house now provides both an insight into the author's early childhood and an accurate example of working class life in Victorian times. Supplement a visit to the museum by purchasing a personal guided tour cassette and a series of maps; both pin-point buildings of Lawrence significance and suggest walks in the nearby 'country of my heart'. New extended exhibition areas.
Gift shop.

MUSEUM OF COSTUME AND TEXTILES
(Nottingham City Council)
51 Castlegate, Nottingham NG1 6AF   **Tel:** (0602) 483504

NATURAL HISTORY MUSEUM
(Nottingham City Council)
Wollaton Hall, Nottingham NG8 2AE   **Tel:** (0602) 281333/281130

NEWSTEAD ABBEY
(Nottingham City Council)
Linby, Nottingham NG15 3GE   **Tel:** (0623) 793557

NOTTINGHAM CASTLE MUSEUM
(Nottingham City Council)
Nottingham   **Tel:** (0602) 483504

UNIVERSITY OF NOTTINGHAM ART GALLERY
The Arts Centre, University Park, University of Nottingham NG7 2RD
Tel: (0602) 484848 Ext. 3457
The Art Gallery is housed in the newly opened Arts Centre at the south entrance of the university campus. Temporary exhibitions of contemporary and historical art will be mounted throughout the year, accompanied by a programme of educational activities, musical events and poetry readings. The Department of Art History is also sited in the Arts Centre.
Open: 10-7 Mon to Fri, Sat 11-7. *Closed* Sunday.
Admission: Free.
Refreshments: Cafe
Bookshop. Car park, access for disabled.

OLLERTON

RUFFORD CRAFT CENTRE
Rufford Country Park, Mansfield, Ollerton   **Tel:** (0623) 822944

RETFORD

THE BASSETLAW MUSEUM
(Bassetlaw District Council)
   Amcott House, Grove Street, Retford   **Tel:** (0777) 706741
Archaeology, local history, bygones, decorative arts. Opened Dec 1986.
Open: Mon to Sat 10-5. *Closed* Sun. (See also Worksop, Nottinghamshire.)
Admission: Free.

RUDDINGTON

FRAMEWORK KNITTERS' MUSEUM
   Chapel Street, Ruddington   **Tel:** (0602) 846914
Unique complex of frameshops - working handframes and allied machinery with
cottages restored for 1850 and 1900. NEWLY purchased adjacent primitive Methodist
Chapel: All buildings 1829. Range of educational facilities - video, exhibitions, research
etc.
Open: Apr to end Dec: Tues to Sun. inc. and Bank Hol Mons. Advance bookings all
year.
Admission: Charged, concessions.
A Museum of the Year Award and AIA Dorothea Award for Conservation - 1984.
Registered museum no 525.

WORKSOP

WORKSOP MUSEUM
(Bassetlaw District Council)
   Memorial Avenue, Worksop
Items of local interest. Pilgrim Fathers' exhibition. Part of the Bassetlaw Museum (see
Retford, Nottinghamshire).
Open: Mon to Wed, Fri 10-5; Thurs, Sat 10-1. *Closed* Sun.
Admission: Free.

OXFORDSHIRE

ABINGDON

ABINGDON MUSEUM
(Oxfordshire County Council with Abingdon Town Council)
   The County Hall, Market Place, Abdingdon   **Tel:** (0235) 523703
The museum is housed in the Old County Hall, built in 1677 (to designs by Sir
Christopher Kempster) when Abingdon was the county town of Berkshire. The display
will combine contemporary crafts with traditional craftsmanship from the town.
Open: Tues to Sun 1-5 (Summer), 1-4 (Winter). The museum is currently undergoing
refurbishment and opening hours in 1993 are likely to be extended; from 11am. Ring
to confirm opening hours.
Admission: Free.
Shop/car park nearby.

BANBURY

BANBURY MUSEUM
(Oxfordshire County Council with Cherwell District Council)
   8 Horsefair, Banbury   **Tel:** (0295) 259855
The museum overlooks Banbury Cross, and is housed in the old boardroom of the Poor
Law Guardians. There is an exciting programme for the temporary exhibition gallery.
The comprehensive collection of photographs and glass plate negatives of the region
can be viewed on microfiche by appointment with the Senior Museum Officer, who
welcomes enquiries and the opportunity to identify local finds.
Open: Apr to Sept: Mon to Sat 10-5; Oct to Mar: Tues to Sat 10-4.30.
Admission: Free.
Refreshments: Available
Shop, guided tours by arrangement. Tourist Information Centre, toilets, car park nearby.
Access for the disabled.

EDGEHILL BATTLE MUSEUM
(Edgehill Battle Museum Trust)
   The Estate Yard, Farnborough Hall, Banbury, Farnborough OX17 1DU
   Tel: (0295) 89593 (Wed & Sat pm only). (0926) 428109 (Office). (0926) 313677
   (Evenings).
The Museum contains some dramatic displays of Arms, Armour and Costumes of the
period together with models, dioramas and maps of the Battle. Appropriate 17th century
music helps create the mood and the whole is attractively set against the historical
backdrop of Farnborough Hall. On Oct 23 1642 The Army of Parliament commanded
by Robert Devereaux 3rd Earl of Essex clashed at Edgehill with a Royalist Army
commanded by King Charles I. 30,000 Englishmen fought this, the first major battle
of the English Civil Wars. The Museum commemorates the events of that day, and of
those items.
Open: Apr to Sept inclusive: Wed and Sat 2-6; also Sun, Mon May Day Bank Holiday.
School visits available outside visiting times.
Admission: £1, Chld 50p. Free if dressed in 17th century style costume.
Parties welcome (Battlefield tours by prior arrangement). Car parking (and coaches).
Marginally suitable for disabled persons (cobbled floors - no wheelchairs available).

BURFORD

TOLSEY MUSEUM
   High Street, Burford

DIDCOT

DIDCOT RAILWAY CENTRE
(Great Western Society Ltd)
   Didcot   **Tel:** (0235) 817200
Re-creating the Golden Age of the Great Western Railway. Steam trains in the engine
shed, reconstructed station, Brunel broadgauge demonstration. Train rides on steaming
days. Small exhibits museum.
Open: All year: Sat, Sun and Bank Hols (*not Christmas or Boxing Day*) 11-5; also
daily Easter to end Sept. Steaming Days: first and last Sun each month from Mar, Bank
Hols, all Suns June to Aug and Weds during Aug.
Refreshments: Meals, snacks and drinks
Car parking. Adjoining Didcot Parkway B.R. Souvenir shop. General Manager: M.
Dean.

PENDON MUSEUM OF MINITURE LANDSCAPE AND TRANSPORT
   Long Wittenham, Nr Didcot

DORCHESTER-ON-THAMES

DORCHESTER ABBEY MUSEUM
(The Rev. John Crowe)
   The Monastery Guest House, Dorchester-on-Thames OX10 7HZ   **Tel:** (0865)
   340007

FARINGDON

BUSCOT PARK
(The National Trust)
   Faringdon
Classical late Georgian house in park, containing Faringdon Collection of the English
and Continental schools including Rembrandt, Murillo and Reynolds. Burne-Jones'
'Legend of the Briar Rose' series occupies one room. Fine furniture.
Location: Near Faringdon on A417.

HENLEY-ON-THAMES

BOHUN GALLERY
(Patricia Speirs)
   15 Reading Road, Henley-on-Thames   **Tel:** (0491) 576228
Specialising in 20th century British paintings, prints and sculpture. Ten exhibitions a
year.
Open: 9.30-1.15, 2.15-5.30. *Closed* Wed, Sun and Bank Holidays.

HISTORIC HOUSE AND MUSEUM
Marian Fathers, Fawley Court, Henley-on-Thames

HISTORIC HOUSE & MUSEUM
MARIAN FATHERS, FAWLEY COURT
HENLEY-ON-THAMES, OXON

Fawley Court, designed by Sir Chrisopher Wren, was built in 1684 for Col. William Freeman as a family residence.

The Mansion House, decorated by Grinling Gibbons and later by James Wyatt, is situated in a beautiful park designed by Lancelot "Capability" Brown.

The museum consists of the library, the Polish kings' various documents, very rare and well preserved collection of historical sabre and many memorable military objects of the Polish Army, Navy and Air Force. Furniture and paintings illustrate the past ages. Coach parties welcome!.

Open: Mar to Oct: Wed, Thur and Sun 2-5. *Closed* Easter, and Whitsuntide weeks.
Admission: £2, Chld £1, OAPs £1.50.
Refreshments: Available July and Aug.
Car park. Dogs not allowed. Coach parties welcome.

OXFORD

THE ASHMOLEAN MUSEUM OF ART AND ARCHAEOLOGY
Beaumont Street, Oxford   **Tel:** (0865) 278000
British, European, Mediterranean, Egyptian and Near Eastern archaeology. Italian, Dutch, Flemish, French and English oil paintings; Old Master and modern drawings, watercolours and prints; miniatures; European ceramics; sculpture and bronzes; English silver; objects of applied art. Coins and medals of all countries and periods. Casts from the antique. Chinese and Japanese porcelain, painting and lacquer. Chinese bronzes, Tibetan art, Indian sculpture and painting, Islamic pottery and metalwork.
Open: Tues to Sat 10-4; Sun 2-4. *Closed* Mons and Sept 6, 7 and 8, and a period over Christmas, the New Year and Easter, but open Bank Hol Mons, Easter to late summer 2-5.
Admission: Free.
Guided tours available. Education Service, temporary exhibition programme. School and adult party advanced bookings (0865) 278015. Gift shop.

BATE COLLECTION OF HISTORICAL INSTRUMENTS
Faculty of Music, St. Aldate's, Oxford

CHRIST CHURCH LIBRARY
Peckwater Quadrangle, Oxford   **Tel:** (0865) 276169
Statuary, Carrolliana, manuscripts and printed books.
Open: Mon to Fri (by special appointment only).

CHRIST CHURCH PICTURE GALLERY
Oxford   **Tel:** (0865) 276172
Important Old Master paintings and drawings.
Open: Mon to Sat 10.30-1, 2-4.30 (5.30 Easter to end Sept); Sun 2-4.30 (5.30 Easter to end Sept). *Closed* for one week at Christmas and Easter.
Admission: 80p, Chld 40p. Reduced rates for parties by arrangement.
Location: Enter by Canterbury Gate.
Free guided tours of the collections each Thurs 2.15-3.

EAST MEETS WEST
50 High Street, Oxford OX1 4AS   **Tel:** (0365) 242167
Conceptional comparisons between Oriental (particularly Chinese) and 'Western' painting. Reproductions, books, jewellery, painting materials, etc.
Open: Weekdays 10-4.30, Suns 11.30-4.30 in summer.

MUSEUM OF MODERN ART
30 Pembroke Street, Oxford   **Tel:** (0865) 722733 recorded information: (0865) 728608

MUSEUM OF OXFORD
(Oxfordshire County Council)
St. Aldates, Oxford   **Tel:** (0865) 815559
The museum tells the story of the City and the University: history, archaeology, architecture and environment, and is the starting point for anyone who wants to learn more about Oxford. Situated opposite the Information Centre, it is housed in the historic Town Hall, also the meeting point for Oxford Walking Tours. In addition to ancient, medieval and later objects, there are maps, plans, many excellent models and reconstructed Oxford interiors from the 16th century to the present day.
Open: Tues to Sat 10-5.
Admission: Free.
Shop/guided tours by arrangement.

MUSEUM OF THE HISTORY OF SCIENCE
Broad Street, Oxford
Collection of early scientific instruments (astrolabes, armillary spheres, sundials, microscopes, astronomical, electrical, medical and chemical apparatus), photographic apparatus, clocks and watches; also library, manuscripts and photographic records.

THE OXFORD STORY
(Heritage Projects Oxford Ltd)
Broad Street, Oxford OX1 3AJ   **Tel:** (0865) 728822

The Oxford Story - a brilliantly imaginative presentation of key aspects of The University's story, devised in conjunction with the University itself. The Oxford Story skillfully blends scholarship, technology and audio-visual techniques to bring the University's past to life. From your moving scholar's desk you experience eight centuries of the sights, sounds and personalities encountered by Oxford students. Witness great events, the Martyrdom of Cranmer in Broad Street, the University as a seat of the Royalist cause during the Civil War and the creation of *Alice's Adventures* by Oxford Don, Lewis Carroll. Above all you encounter great men and women who shaped both the University and the world.
Open: Daily (except Christmas Day).
Admission: £3.95, Chld £2.75, OAP/Student, family and group reductions available all year.
Parties are advised to book in advance. Gift shop.

OXFORD UNIVERSITY MUSEUM
Parks Road, Oxford   **Tel:** (0865) 272950   **Fax:** (0865) 272970
Natural history collections In historic Victorian gothic-style building.
Open: Mon to Sat 12-5 (check opening times for Easter and Christmas).
Admission: Free (donations box).

THE PITT RIVERS MUSEUM
South Parks Road (entrance through University Museum), Oxford   **Tel:** (0865) 270927
Oxford's Museum of Mankind - Ethnology and prehistoric archaeology of the peoples of the world. (includes the Balfour Building, entrance beside no. 60 Banbury Road, Tel. (0865) 274726. Hunter-gatherer societies; musical instruments - unique headphone system).
Open: Mon to Sat 1-4.30. *Closed* for a period over Christmas, the New Year and Easter.
Admission: Free.
Education Service (0865) 270927. Temporary exhibition programme. Gift shop.

THE ROTUNDA MUSEUM OF ANTIQUE DOLLS' HOUSES
Grove House, Iffley Turn, Oxford
Dolls' Houses 1700-1900 and contents (silver, dinner services, dolls etc).
Open: Sun afternoons from May 1 to Mid-Sept and for parties of 12 or more by written appointment.
Admission: Fee charged.
No children under 16.

SWALCLIFFE

SWALCLIFFE BARN
Swalcliffe, nr Banburry   **Tel:** (0295) 788127 or 78562. Schools: Contact Sibford Gower School (0295) 78270.
Known locally as the Tythe Barn, Swalcliffe Barn was built for the Rectorial Manor of Swalcliffe by New College, who owned the manor. Constructed between 1400 and 1409, it is one of the dozen best barns in the country, with much of its medieval timber half-crick roof intact. The Oxfordshire Building Trust owns it and repaired it with a great from English Heritage. Oxfordshire County Museums lease the barn as 'display storage' and visitors may see some of the collection of agricultural and trade vehicles.
Open: April: Easter Sun & Mon 2-5; Sundays in May & Sept 2-5; Sat & Sun in June, July & Aug; Bank Hol Mons May & Aug 2-5. Other times & from Oct to Mar: by arrangement in advance with the Swalcliffe Society (see above) or Oxfordshire County Museum (0993) 811456.
Admission: Free
Disabled access; toilet.

WALLINGFORD

WALLINGFORD MUSEUM
Flint House, High Street, Wallingford   **Tel:** (0491) 35065
Permanent display, regularly updated, illustrating the span of local history; changing exhibitions.

WANTAGE

VALE AND DOWNLAND MUSEUM CENTRE
(Vale and Downland Museum Trust, Oxon County Council)
The Old Surgery, Church Street, Wantage   **Tel:** (02357) 66838
Housed in a converted 16/17th century cloth merchant's house with modern extensions and a reconstructed barn, the museum has permanent displays showing the geology, local history and archaeology of Wantage and the Vale of the White Horse, and a programme of temporary exhibitions. Local community groups are invited to exhibit on local issues. As a branch museum of the County service, schools are warmly invited to use the museum and education room.
Open: Tues to Sat 10.30-4.30, Sun 2.30-5.
Admission: Free.
Contact the curator or the education officer, County Museum, Woodstock. Car park nearby. Shop, access for the disabled, picnic area, guided tours on request, toilets.

WITNEY

COGGES MANOR FARM MUSEUM
Church Lane, Cogges, Witney   **Tel:** (0993) 772602
The manor house and farm buildings close to the church and the river are an open-air museum of farming and the countryside, telling the history of Cogges village over 1,000 years. The house, dairy, farm buildings, walled garden and orchard show what life there was like at the turn of the century.
Open: Mar to Nov: Tues to Fri, Bank Hol Mon 10.30-5.30, Sat and Sun 12-5.30, *closes* at 4.30 from Oct. Mon reserved for booked educational groups.
Admission: Fee charged.
Refreshments: Available
Special rates for parties. Season tickets. Shop, car park.

COMBE MILL BEAM ENGINE AND WORKING MUSEUM
(An Independent Museum)
Witney, Nr. Long Handborough   **Tel:** (0993) 891785
19th century sawmill, featuring: a restored beam and two smaller steam engines, a working forge and a display of 19th century artifacts.
Open: In steam third Sun in May (16), Aug (15) and Oct (17) 10-5.
Admission: £1, Chld/OAPs 60p.
Free parking, picnic area.

WOODSTOCK

OXFORDSHIRE COUNTY MUSEUM
(Oxfordshire County Council, Department of Leisure and Arts)
Fletcher's House, Woodstock   **Tel:** (0993) 811456
The County Museum, in a fine town house with a pleasant garden, has permanent display galleries which tell the story of Oxfordshire - its people, buildings and landscapes, from early times to the present day, and a changing programme of temporary exhibitions.
Open: May to Sept: Mon to Fri 10-5, Sat 10-6, Sun 2-5; Oct to Apr: Tues to Fri 10-4, Sat 10-5, Sun 2-5.
Admission: Free.

University of Oxford

Pitt Rivers Museum
Parks Road

One of the great Ethnographic Museums, this Aladdin's cave of treasures, ranging from a 40ft totem pole to a witch in a bottle, draws its collections from all over the world and all periods of history.
In the nearby Balfour Gallery can be found hunter-gatherers (past and present) and musical instruments.

The Ashmolean Museum
Beaumont Street

The oldest Museum in Britain, open to the public since 1683, the Ashmolean's treasures range in time from the earliest implements of Man to 20th century Art.
They include curiosities like Guy Fawkes' lantern; Antiquities from Egypt, Greece and Rome; Oriental Art; British and European paintings from the Renaissance to the present day, including works by Giorgione, Poussin, Van Dyck, Gainsborough, Corot, Van Gogh, Pissarro and Picasso.

University Museum
Parks Road

The University Museum is Oxford's natural history Museum and houses the University's entomological, geological, mineralogical and zoological collections in its magnificent Victorian Gothic building in Parks Road.

Admission to all of these Museums is free.

Refreshments: Available
Car park nearby. Shop, picnic area, guided tours by arrangement, toilets.

SHROPSHIRE

ACTON SCOTT

ACTON SCOTT HISTORIC WORKING FARM
(Shropshire County Council)
   Wenlock Lane, near Church Stretton, Acton Scott   **Tel:** (0694) 781306/7
A working farm museum using heavy horses and machinery to demonstrate agriculture as it was at about the turn of the century. Crafts demonstrated regularly, programmes available on application.
Open: Apr to Nov: Daily except Mons, but open Bank Holiday Mons.
Admission: Fee charged.
Refreshments: Cafe
Car park, picnic area, shops. Suitable for disabled visitors.

BRIDGNORTH

BRIDGNORTH MUSEUM
(Bridgnorth and District Historical Society)
   North Gate, High Street, Bridgnorth

CLUN

CLUN TOWN TRUST MUSEUM
   Clun   **Tel:** (058 84) 576
Local geology, prehistoric, flints, local history, early photographs etc.
Open: Easter to Nov: Tues and Sat 2-5; also Hols: Sat, Mon and Tues 11-1, 2-5; also by appointment.
Admission: Free.

LUDLOW

THE BUTTERCROSS MUSEUM
(Shropshire County Council)
   Church Street, Ludlow   **Tel:** (0854) 873857
A new museum featuring the history of the town will be developed during 1993/4 in the Assembly Rooms, The Square, Ludlow.
Open: Apr to end Sept: Mon to Sat; June to Aug: daily.
Admission: Fee charged.

MUCH WENLOCK

MUCH WENLOCK MUSEUM
(Shropshire County Council)
   High Street, Much Wenlock   **Tel:** (0952) 727773
The geology, natural history and local history of the area of the parish.
Open: Apr to end Sept: Mon to Sat; June to Aug: daily.
Admission: Fee charged (adults only).
Suitable for disabled visitors.

SHIFNAL

THE AEROSPACE MUSEUM
   Cosford, Shifnal TF1 8UP
Four Museums in One! 1) The Missile Collection 2) The Warplane Collection 3) The Transport Aircraft Collection 4) The Research and Development Aircraft Collection

SHREWSBURY

CLIVE HOUSE
(Borough of Shrewsbury and Atcham)
   College Hill, Shrewsbury   **Tel:** (0743) 354811
Fine Georgian House briefly associated with Clive of India containing outstanding collection of Shropshire porcelain and art, in room settings which reflect eighteenth and nineteenth century life above and below stairs.

COLEHAM PUMPING STATION
(Borough of Shrewsbury and Atcham)
   Old Coleham, Shrewsbury   **Tel:** (0743) 361196
Preserved beam engines.
Open: By appointment only.

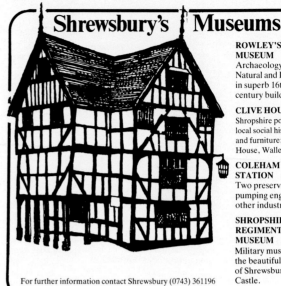

Shrewsbury's Museums

ROWLEY'S HOUSE MUSEUM
Archaeology, Geology, Natural and Local History in superb 16th–17th century buildings.

CLIVE HOUSE
Shropshire porcelains, local social history, art and furniture; Georgian House, Walled garden.

COLEHAM PUMPING STATION
Two preserved steam pumping engines with other industrial exhibits.

SHROPSHIRE REGIMENTAL MUSEUM
Military museum in the beautiful setting of Shrewsbury Castle.

For further information contact Shrewsbury (0743) 361196

THE RADBROOK CULINARY MUSEUM
   Radbrook College, Radbrook Road, Shrewsbury SY3 9BL   **Tel:** (0743) 232686
A unique collection of domestic utensils and examples of household crafts covering the late Victorian and Edwardian era and tracing the early years in the formation of Shropshire Technical School for Girls.
Open: Visitors welcome by appointment. Parties welcomed.
Admission: Free.
Ample car parking. Suitable for disabled persons.

ROWLEY'S HOUSE MUSEUM
(Borough of Shrewsbury and Atcham)
   Barker Street, Shrewsbury   **Tel:** (0743) 361196
Set in the 16th century warehouse and 17th century mansion of the Rowley family. Wealth of archaeology, including material from Wroxeter (Viroconium), costume, geology, natural and local history.

SHROPSHIRE REGIMENTAL MUSEUM
(Borough of Shrewsbury and Atcham and Regimental Trustees)
   Shrewsbury Castle, Shrewsbury   **Tel:** (0743) 358516
Military museum containing fine displays of the history of the Shropshire regiments. In the superb historic setting of Shrewsbury Castle.

TELFORD

BLISTS HILL
   Telford
A working Victorian industrial community set at the turn of the century. Exhibits incl. fully operational Foundry, Candle Factory, Saw Mill, Printing Shop, Pit Head Winding Engine and the only wrought iron works in the western world. Also many shops, cottages and Hay Inclined Plane. 42 acre site. Various catering outlets including the 'New Inn'.

COALPORT CHINA MUSEUM
   Telford
Magnificent display of Coalport and Caughley china. Displays on the history of the Works and its people. Housed in the original Coalport factory buildings, and used until 1926. Slide-and-tape show. Working demonstrations and pottery workshops.

IRON BRIDGE AND INFORMATION CENTRE
   Telford
The world's first iron bridge. A small exhibition in the adjacent Tollhouse tells its history, and tells visitors more about the whole museum.

IRONBRIDGE GORGE MUSEUM
(Ironbridge Gorge Museum Trust)
Telford   **Tel:** (0952) 433522   **Fax:** (0952) 432204

THE IRONBRIDGE GORGE MUSEUM

★ Blists Hill: A working Victorian Industrial community set in the 1890's
★ Museum of the River ★ The World's first Iron Bridge ★ Museum of Iron
★ Rosehill House ★ Coalport China Museum ★ Jackfield Tile Museum
Open Daily from 10a.m.–5p.m. (For winter openings please telephone) Free
Coach Parking. Good food and drink. Group Discounts. PASSPORT to all sites
available. Just 10 minutes from the M54 (junction 4).

Come early to see it all!

Contact: Visitor Information
Ironbridge Gorge Museum Trust, Ironbridge, Telford, Shropshire.
Tel: Ironbridge (0952) 433522 or 432166 Fax: (0952) 432204

A major museum based on a unique series of industrial monuments in the Ironbridge Gorge, now a World Heritage Site.
Open: Daily 10-5 (10-6 in June, July, August). Some small sites close in winter.
Admission: Admission to all the museum sites is by 'passport' ticket, valid until all sites have been visited once. Adult passport £7.80, Chld £5, family ticket £23½0, OAP £6.80, Student £5 (1992 rates). Ticket admits to all sites.
For further information and party bookings write to: Ironbridge Gorge Museum Trust, Ironbridge, Telford, Shropshire TF8 7AW telephone above number.

JACKFIELD TILE MUSEUM
Telford
Housed in the former Craven Dunmill Tileworks, this is the Trust's latest addition. Beautiful display of tiles. Buildings in the process of being restored. Tile manufacture may be seen.

MUSEUM OF IRON AND FURNACE SITE
Telford
Opened in 1979, this museum is close to Abraham Darby's blast furnace and tells the story of iron and steel and the history of Coalbrookdale. The Darby Furnace has multi-lingual panels.
Refreshments: Coffee Shop

MUSEUM OF THE RIVER
Telford
Housed in the restored Severn Warehouse the centre outlines the tory of the Gorge in the words and pictures of people who visited it over two centuries. Slide-and-tape show in a special auditorium. Special emphasis on the use of water.

ROSEHILL HOUSE
Telford
A restored ironmaster's home, set in the early 19th century, typical of the Darby family houses.
Refreshments: Tea room.

TAR TUNNEL
Telford
An 18th century mining tunnel from which natural bitumen was extracted and where visitors may go underground wearing hard hats.
Open: Daily 10-5 *Closed* Nov-Mid Feb

WROXETER

WROXETER ROMAN CITY
(English Heritage)
Wroxeter   **Tel:** (074 375) 330
The excavated centre of the forth largest city in Roman Britain, with impressive remains of the 2nd century municipal baths. The museum has pottery, coins and other objects from the town.

Open: Apr 1 to Sept 30, daily 10-6. 1 October-31 March, Tues-Sun 10am-4pm *Closed* 24-26 December and 1 January.
Admission: £1.50, Concessions £1.10, Chld 75p (1992 prices).

SOMERSET

AXBRIDGE

AXBRIDGE MUSEUM: KING JOHN'S HUNTING LODGE
(The National Trust administered by Sedgemoor District Council
The Square, Axbridge   **Tel:** (0934) 732012
Built c. 1500. Museum of local history, archaeology, geology, ceramics and glass.

BRIDGWATER

ADMIRAL BLAKE MUSEUM
Blake Street, Bridgwater   **Tel:** (0278) 456127
The birthplace of Admiral Blake, containing Blake relics, exhibits relating to the Battle of Sedgemoor. Archaeology and local history.
Open: Mon to Sat 11-5; Sun 2-5 including Bank Holidays.
Admission: Free. Parties by arrangement.

WESTONZOYLAND PUMPING STATION
(Westonzoyland Engine Trust)
Hoopers Lane, Westonzoyland, Bridgwater   **Tel:** (0823) 412713
Earliest land drainage station on Somerset levels. Steam and drainage exhibits, plus working forge and narrow gauge railway.
Open: In steam - first Sun in month Apr to Oct, plus Bank Hol Suns and Mon 2-5. Static - other Suns Apr to Oct.
Admission: £2, OAPs £1.50, Chld £1.
Car park free. Suitable for disabled but no special toilet, no wheelchairs available.

CASTLE CARY

CASTLE CARY MUSEUM AND PRESERVATION SOCIETY
The Market House, Castle Cary

CHARD

CHARD AND DISTRICT MUSEUM
High Street, Chard   **Tel:** (0460) 65091
Displays on the History of Chard, John Stringfellow pioneer of powered flight, early artificial limbs made in Chard, cider making and agriculture, with a complete blacksmith's forge, carpenter's workshop, kitchen, laundry, childhood and costume galleries and barn with agricultural machinery, garage and wagons.
Open: May 3 to Oct 9 Mon to Sat 10.30-4.30 (also Sun in July and Aug).

CHEDDAR

CHEDDAR SHOWCAVES MUSEUM
Cheddar Gorge, Cheddar   **Tel:** (0934) 742343

GLASTONBURY

GLASTONBURY LAKE VILLAGE MUSEUM
The Tribunal, High Street, Glastonbury
Collection of late prehistoric antiquities from Glastonbury Lake Village and items of local interest.
Admission: Fee charged.

SOMERSET RURAL LIFE MUSEUM
(Somerset County Council)
Abbey Farm, Chilkwell Street, Glastonbury   **Tel:** (0458) 831197
Museum interpreting Somerset's rural history with award winning permanent exhibitions and a lively programme of events and demonstrations throughout the summer. Temporary exhibitions and magnificent 14th century Abbey Barn.
Open: Easter to Oct 31: weekdays 10-5, weekends 2-6; Nov 1 to Easter: weekdays 10-5, Sat 11-4. *Closed* Good Friday, Christmas Day and Boxing Day.
Admission: Fee charged.
Refreshments: Tea room (summer only)
Large car park.

SHEPTON MALLET

SHEPTON MALLET MUSEUM
(Shepton Mallet Town Council)
Great Ostry, Shepton Mallet

Visit Somerset County Museums

Somerset County Council

County Museum
Taunton Castle Telephone: (0823) 255504

Rural Life Museum
Glastonbury Telephone: (0458) 831197

SPARKFORD

HAYNES MOTOR MUSEUM IN SPARKFORD
Sparkford BA22 7LH

STREET

THE SHOE MUSEUM
C. & J. Clark, High Street, Street **Tel:** (0458) 43131

THE SHOE MUSEUM
C. & J. CLARK, STREET, SOMERSET

Housed in the oldest part of the factory of C. & J. Clark, the museum contains shoes from Roman times to the present; Georgian shoe buckles; caricatures and engravings of shoemakers; costume illustrations and fashion plates; shoe machinery from the 1860s until 1920; advertising material from 1850 and 19th century documents and photographs which illustrate the early history of C. & J. Clark from the founding of the firm in 1825 by Cyrus Clark.

Easter Monday to 31st October:
Monday to Friday 10 a.m.–4.45 p.m.
Saturdays 10 a.m.–4-30 p.m.
During winter months by appointment only.

Phone Mrs. Brook on Street (0458) 43131.

Old shoe machines and hand tools, 19th century documents.

TAUNTON

SOMERSET COUNTY MUSEUM
(Somerset County Council)
Taunton Castle, Taunton **Tel:** (0823) 255504
Set in the medieval castle where Judge Jeffreys held the 'Bloody Assize', the museum displays collections relevant to the county of Somerset, including archaeology, geology and palaeontology, natural history, ceramics, costume, dolls and military gallery. Temporary exhibitions.
Open: Mon to Sat 10-5.
Admission: Fee charged.

WELLS

WELLS MUSEUM
8 Cathedral Green, Wells **Tel:** (0749) 673477
Samplers, local bygones, prehistoric cave finds, natural history, Mendip rocks, fossils and minerals, Roman lead pigs.
Open: Apr to Oct: Weekdays 10-5.30, Suns 11-5.30. Nov to Mar: Wed to Sun 11-4.
Admission: £1, Chld/over 60 50p.

WOOKEY HOLE

WOOKEY HOLE CAVES AND MILL
Wookey Hole
The most spectacular caves in Britain presided over by the famous Witch of Wookey.

YEOVIL

THE MUSEUM OF SOUTH SOMERSET
(South Somerset District Council)
Hendford, Yeovil **Tel:** (0935) 24774

The Museum was completely refurbished in 1991, and now has exciting new gallery displays. Friendly Societies and Petters-Westland story on the ground floor. Upstairs are artefacts displayed within a Roman villa from the Westland, Lufton and Ilchester

Mead sites, as well as samples from the 'Stiby' gun collection. Items from the museum's costume and glassware inventory are also on display and changed regularly in a period room setting.
Admission: Free - donations welcome.

YEOVILTON

FLEET AIR ARM MUSEUM AND CONCORDE EXHIBITION
Yeovilton   **Tel:** (0935) 840565
The development of naval aviation is presented in a display of over 40 historic aircraft, many ship and aircraft scale models, photographs, uniforms, medals, documents, photographs and paintings all housed under one roof. The interior of Concorde is open to the public. Many special exhibitions including the KAMIKAZE SUICIDE BOMBERS, the WRENS, the FAIREY SWORDFISH STORY, the HARRIER JUMP JET, the RNAS IN WORLD WAR 1.
Open: Daily (inc Bank Hols) 10-5.30; Mar to Oct; 10-4.30 Nov to Feb. *Closed* Dec 24, 25, 26.
Admission: Charge (party rates, Child half price, OAPs etc reduced adm)
Refreshments: Licenced restaurant
Free parking, coaches and caravans welcome. Picnic and flying viewing areas. Open cockpits. Children's adventure playground. Facilities for the disabled.

MONTACUTE HOUSE
(The National Trust)
Montacute, Yeovilton TA15 6XP   **Tel:** (0935) 823289
National Portrait Gallery Exhibitions of Elizabethan and Jacobean portraits. Heraldic glass, tapestries, panelling, furniture in a magnificent Elizabethan mansion.

STAFFORDSHIRE

BURTON-UPON-TRENT

BASS MUSEUM, VISITOR CENTRE AND SHIRE HORSE STABLES
Horninglow Street, Burton-upon-Trent   **Tel:** (0283) 511000

BASS MUSEUM
Bass Visitor Centre & Shire Horse Stables

7,000 years of ales and beers.
A museum of
Industrial and Social
History.

Open 7 days a week
Mon-Fri 10.00 am
Sat-Sun 10.30 am
Last Admission 4.00pm

Licensed bar.
Souvenir Shop.
Restaurant.
Shire Horse Stables.
Lively displays bring the story of
Burton and beer to life.
Education service and Brewery
Tours by arrangement.
Shire horse drawn tour of the town
everyday (exc. Mon)

Bass Museum, Horninglow Street, (A50) Burton upon Trent.
Tel (0283) 511000.

The Museum adjoins the Bass Burton Brewery complex and is housed in buildings formerly occupied by the joiners, wheelwrights and engineers, dating from the mid 19th century. Three floors are devoted to the story of Bass in Burton and the transport of beer. Special displays include a working railway model of Burton in 1921, fine glass and ceramics associated with beer drinking, an Edwardian bar and display of pumping engines. External exhibits include the stables of the prize-winning Bass Shires and their drays, vintage vehicles including a 1920s bottle shaped car. An experimental brewhouse is used for special brews several times a year and a 1905 Robey horizontal cross compound engine is steamed some weekends. A reconstructed railway ale dock is used to exhibit a steam locomotive and items associated with the Bass Private Railway.
Open: 7 days a week Mon-Fri 10, Sat & Sun 10.30, last admission 4. *Closed* 25, 26 Dec, 1 Jan.
Admission: Fee charged.
Location: A50.
Refreshments: Bar and refreshments
Free parking. Brewery tours and/or Education Service by arrangement. The museum has completed major extensions featuring a gallery on the process of brewing, and also a gallery in 1990 - Bass - The Company Story. Horse drawn tours of Burton upon Trent (available daily except Mon, unless a Bank Holiday).

HERITAGE BREWERY MUSEUM
Anglesey Road, Burton-upon-Trent DE14 3PF   **Tel:** (0283) 69226

LEEK

BRINDLEY WATER MILL AND MUSEUM
(Brindley Mill Preservation Trust)
Mill Street, Leek
Operational corn mill built by James Brindley.
Open: Information on opening times and private visits: (0538) 381000

CHEDDLETON FLINT MILL
(Cheddleton Flint Mill Industrial Heritage Trust)
Leek

Cheddleton Flint Mill

A Museum of
Industrial Archaeology
at Cheddleton,
Near Stoke-on-Trent,
North Staffordshire.

It specialises in the
preparation of the raw
materials used in the
Pottery Industry.

Associate Member,
North Staffordshire Museums Association

Twin water-wheels on the River Churnet operate flint grinding pans. The South Mill foundations date back to the 13th century when it ground corn and was a fulling mill. Converted to grinding flint in about 1800 after it was joined by The North Mill which was built specially in the late 18th century to grind flint. The Museum collection includes a Robey 100hp steam engine, model Newcomen engine, rare 1770 haystack boiler, and the narrow boat 'Vienna' moored on the Caldon Canal. The miller's cottage is furnished as it would have looked in the 19th century.
Open: Buildings open Sat and Sun afternoons throughout the year and on most weekdays.
Admission: Free. Donations welcome.
Location: Between Stoke-on-Trent and Leek on A520.
Books, postcards and wallchart on sale; also guides to the Mill in English, French, German and Italian.

LICHFIELD

SAMUEL JOHNSON BIRTHPLACE MUSEUM
(Lichfield City Council)
Breadmarket Street, Lichfield   **Tel:** (0543) 264972
Relics and pictures of Dr. Johnson and his contemporaries.
Open: Throughout the year 10-5.
Admission: 90p, Chld/OAPs 50p, Family £2.30, joint ticket with Lichfield Heritage Exhibition £1.50 (concessions 80p).

LICHFIELD HERITAGE EXHIBITION, TREASURY AND MUNIMENT ROOM
Market Square, Lichfield   **Tel:** (0543) 256611
Audio-visual presentation of the Civil War. Civic, Church and Regimental Plate, Maces, State Sword, Ashmole Cup. Superb tapestry of the Bower Procession of 1795. Superb views from tower.
Open: Daily 10-4.30. *Closed* Christmas Day, Boxing Day, New Year's Day and Spring Bank Holiday Monday.
Admission: £1.00, Chld/OAPs and Students 50p; joint ticket Samuel Johnson Birthplace Museum £1.50, concessions 80p.

LICHFIELD
STAFFORDSHIRE

SAMUEL JOHNSON BIRTHPLACE MUSEUM
Lichfield (0543) 264972

HERITAGE EXHIBITION, TREASURY AND MUNIMENT ROOM
Lichfield (0543) 256611

In the heart of Lichfield's Market Square

Open throughout the year

Coffee and Gift Shop

NEWCASTLE-UNDER-LYME

BOROUGH MUSEUM AND ART GALLERY
Brampton Park, Newcastle-under-Lyme   **Tel:** (0782) 619705

free admission

BOROUGH MUSEUM
• & ART GALLERY •

Brampton Park Newcastle-under-Lyme Staffs
Telephone: (0782) 619705

Permanent & Temporary Exhibitions of Fine Art, Social History, Ceramics & Militaria

Set in eight acres of parkland

OPENING TIMES
Monday - Saturday 10am - 5.30pm
Sunday 2pm - 5.30pm

NEWCASTLE
UNDER·LYME
YOU'LL NOTICE THE DIFFERENCE

The Museum & Art Gallery has permanent displays of Staffordshire pottery and glass, weapons, toys and social history, including a recreated Victorian street scene. There is also a frequently changing temporary exhibition programme of fine art and crafts, drawn both from the gallery's permanent collection and touring exhibitions. Set in the 8 acres of Brampton Park, there is an aviary and wildlife garden adjacent to the Museum and a safe children's play area.
Open: Mon to Sat 10-5.30, Sun 2-5.30. *Closed* Bank Holidays except Spring Bank Holiday Monday.
Admission: Free.
Free car and coach parking, access for the disabled.

SHUGBOROUGH

MANSION HOUSE, STAFFORDSHIRE COUNTY MUSEUM, AND PARK FARM
(National Trust property administered by Staffordshire County Council)
Milford, Shugborough, Nr. Stafford   **Tel:** (0889) 881388
Mansion: 18th century ancestral home of the Earls of Lichfield, containing furniture, paintings, porcelain, silver etc. **Museum:** housed in the servants' quarters with estate interiors (working brew-house, laundry, kitchen, Victorian School room, coach houses) displays of domestic costume and craft material. Fine collection of horse drawn vehicles. **Working Farm Museum and restored Corn Mill:** Georgian farmstead with

agricultural galleries, mill, rare breeds of livestock and traditional farm activities.
Parkland and Gardens: with neoclassical monuments, beautiful Victorian terraces and rose garden.
Open: Walks and Trails: Mar 27 to Oct 31: Daily including Bank Holiday Mon 11-5. Site open all year to booked parties from 10.30.
Admission: Reduced rates for children, senior citizens, registered unemployed and coach parties. Special rates and activities for schools/colleges. Site access for parking, picnic area, park and garden £1 per vehicle.
Refreshments: Cafe.
Coach and School parties welcome. National Trust Shop. Visitor Centre. Special events throughout the year, programme available. For further information, including admission charges, please telephone as above.

STAFFORD

STAFFORD ART GALLERY AND CRAFT SHOP
(Staffordshire County Council)
Lichfield Road, Stafford ST17 4ST   **Tel:** (0785) 57303

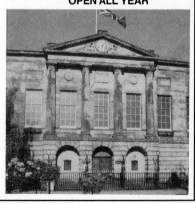

Lichfield Road·Stafford·ST17 4ST·Tel (0785) 57303
STAFFORD ART gallery

OPENING HOURS
Tuesday – Friday 10-5
Saturday 10-4
Admission Free

A Crafts Council Selected Gallery

OPEN ALL YEAR

A major gallery for the visual arts with temporary exhibitions of painting, craft and photography throughout the year.

CRAFT SHOP
Largest Midlands craft venue for quality work by British craftsmen, jewellery, glass, ceramics, wood, toys, textiles, cards and giftwrap.

Art Gallery showing lively programme of temporary exhibitions of contemporary art, craft and photography with related events. Craft Shop selected for quality by the Crafts Council selling high quality work by outstanding British craftsmen.
Open: Tues to Fri 10-5; Sat 10-4. *Closed* Mondays.
Admission: Free

Shugborough

ANCESTRAL HOME OF LORD LICHFIELD
MILFORD, STAFFORDSHIRE

18th century Mansion House
Original Servants' Quarters and Museum
Newly restored working Brewhouse
Working Park Farm and Restored Corn Mill
Beautiful Gardens and Parkland
Neo-classical Monuments
Tearooms and National Trust Shop
Coach and School parties welcome

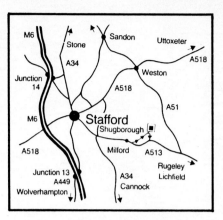

Admission

Single site tickets. 'All-in' tickets and Family tickets available. Reduced rates for children, OAP's and the unemployed. Charges on Special Events days may vary.

March 27 to Oct 31: open daily including Bank Holiday Monday 11–5. Site open all year round to booked parties from 10.30 am.

For further information about opening times, admission charges and special events at Shugborough, telephone Little Haywood (0889) 881388.

IZAAK WALTON'S COTTAGE
Shallowford, Stafford
Author of The Compleat Angler.

STOKE-ON-TRENT

CHATTERLEY WHITFIELD MINING MUSEUM
(Chatterley Whitfield Mining Museum Trust)
Tunstall, Stoke-on-Trent ST6 8UN **Tel:** (0782) 813337
Visit Chatterley Whitfield Mining Museum. Ride the Cage to the underground workings. See how the miners of yesteryear worked, with ex-miner guides whose stories bring to life the history and progress of coal mining. Climb aboard the underground train used by miners of today to travel to the coal 'Face'. Tour the site's many attractions.
Open: All year round.
Refreshments: Relax with a miner's cup of tea or coffee in the 1930's Whitfield Kitchen.
Free parking for coach or car. Sandford Award Winning Education Services.

CITY MUSEUM AND ART GALLERY
(Stoke-on-Trent District Council)
Bethesda Street, Hanley, Stoke-on-Trent ST1 3DW **Tel:** (0782) 202173

CITY MUSEUM & ART GALLERY
STOKE·ON·TRENT

for Superb Ceramics – Colourful Costume – Lively Local History
· · · · · and a comprehensive programme of exhibitions.

BETHESDA STREET, HANLEY. 0782 202173 – all enquiries.

Facilities for disabled people – Shop – Cafe and Bar
Branch Museums at:
Ford Green Hall (Smallthorne) – Beautiful Timber Framed Farmhouse and
Etruria Industrial Museum – the last steam-powered Potters Mill in Britain

ALL ADMISSION FREE

An award winning purpose built museum all about 'the Potteries'. Archaeology, Social History and Natural History displays celebrate the unique nature of the area and are complimented by other galleries and exhibits which range from costume to a LF XVI

Spitfire (the latter the centre-piece of a display about its designer - Reginald Mitchell, born locally). In addition the museum is internationally renowed for housing one of the largest and most important collections of English pottery and porcelain (primarily from Staffordshire) in the world. Regular exhibitions range across the whole spectrum from Art to Social History.
Open: Mon to Sat 10-5, Sun 2-5. Please telephone for opening times at Bank Holidays and Christmas week.
Admission: Free.

ETRURIA INDUSTRIAL MUSEUM
(Stoke-on-Trent City Council)
Lower Bedford Street, Etruria, Stoke-on-Trent **Tel:** (0782) 287557
Britain's sole surviving steam-powered Potters Mill, 'Jesse Shirley's Etruscan Bone and Flint Mill' was built to grind materials for the agricultural and pottery industries. The mill contains a gear room, grinding pans, boiler and 1820s Beam Engine, 'Princess' - in steam one weekend a month. There is also a working forge.
Open: Wed to Sun 10-4.
Admission: Free.

FORD GREEN HALL
(Stoke-on-Trent District Council)
Ford Green Road, Smallthorne, Stoke-on-Trent ST6 1NG **Tel:** (0782) 534771
A timber-framed yeoman's farmhouse built c. 1624 with eighteenth century brick additions. Contains appropriate period furnishings. Regular events including performances of Early Music are held at the Hall.
Open: Daily 1-5.
Admission: Free.
Refreshments: Tea Room.
Shop. Facilities for school parties/small groups.

MUSEUMS & GALLERIES

For further details on editorial listings or display advertising contact:

Editor:
Deborah Valentine
Windsor Court, East Grinstead House
East Grinstead, West Sussex RH19 1XA
Tel: (0342) 335794   Fax: (0342) 335665

Staffordshire

GLADSTONE POTTERY MUSEUM
Uttoxeter Road, Longton, Stoke-on-Trent **Tel:** (0782) 319232

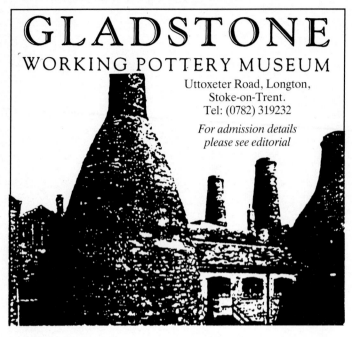

GLADSTONE
WORKING POTTERY MUSEUM

Uttoxeter Road, Longton,
Stoke-on-Trent.
Tel: (0782) 319232

*For admission details
please see editorial*

A typical working 'potbank' set in a restored Victorian pottery factory complete with cobbled yard, bottle ovens, workshops and steam engine. Galleries include Staffordshire Pottery History; Tiles; Loos and Baths; Colour and Decoration. Live demonstrations daily in the original workshops. Gift shop; bookshop.
Open: Mar to Oct: Mon to Sat (including Bank Hols) 10-5, Sun 2-5; Nov to Feb: Tues to Sat 10-5
Admission: £2.75, Students and Senior Citizens £2, Child £1.50
Refreshments: Available
Group bookings: please enquire.

MINTON MUSEUM
London Road, Stoke-on-Trent **Tel:** (0782) 744766
Minton was founded in 1793 and the museum features the many aspects of the company's world famous artistry - parian, majolica, acid gold, pate-sur pate and fine bone china.
Open: Weekdays 9-1, 2-4.30. Closed factory holidays.
Factory shop

THE SIR HENRY DOULTON GALLERY
Nile Street, Burslem, Stoke-on-Trent **Tel:** (0782) 575454
Sir Henry Doulton was recognised by his contemporaries as the greatest potter of his time. This gallery traces the story of Doulton from its foundation in 1815. The gallery also includes the world famous Royal Doulton collection of over 300 rare figures.
Open: Weekdays 9-4.15. Closed factory holidays.
Factory tours, factory shop.

The Sir Henry Doulton Gallery
Nile Street, Burslem
Stoke-on-Trent
Telephone 0782 575454

Royal Crown Derby MUSEUM
Osmaston Road, Derby
Telephone 0332 47051

MINTON MUSEUM
London Road, Stoke-on-Trent
Telephone 0782 744766

Open 9.00am to 4.30pm Monday to Friday
Factory Tours can be arranged

WEDGWOOD MUSEUM
(Josiah Wedgwood and Sons Limited, Barlaston)
Barlaston, Stoke-on-Trent ST12 9ES **Tel:** (0782) 204218/204141

Wedgwood
Welcomes Visitors

Award-winning museum and art galleries

Cinema video on 230 years of history and craftsmanship

Highly skilled potters and decorators producing tableware and giftware

Extensive souvenir shop

Refreshments lounge

Ample free parking for cars and coaches

VISITOR CENTRE OPENING TIMES
Mon-Fri 9.00am-5.00pm (inc Bank Holidays)
Saturdays 10.00am-5.00pm. Summer Sundays
10.00am-5.00pm (Easter to October)
Closed Christmas week and New Year's Day

**OPEN SUNDAYS
EASTER TO OCTOBER**

**Barlaston, Stoke-on-Trent ST12 9ES
Telephone: (0782) 204141 &
(0782) 204218 (24 hrs)**

A 'Living Museum' displaying the most comprehensive collection of Wedgwood ceramics and art over two centuries, with craft manufacturing centre adjacent.
Open: Mon to Fri 9-5; Sat 10-5 all year, and Summer Sundays (Easter to October) 10-5
Admission: Adults £2.50, Chld £1.25 Special reductions senior citizens and students.
Refreshments: Available
Parties welcome. Factory connoisseur tours. Car Parking. Suitable for disabled persons. Curator: Gaye Blake Roberts.

TAMWORTH

TAMWORTH CASTLE AND MUSEUM
The Holloway, Tamworth **Tel:** (0827) 63563

TAMWORTH CASTLE
STAFFORDSHIRE

Built in the 1180's, Tamworth's sandstone Norman Castle is one of the country's few remaining Shell-Keeps. Within its walls are the square Tower, mid 15th century timber-framed Gt. Hall, Tudor Warder's Lodge, 17th century brick wings housing magnificent period room settings spanning eight centuries, including a Norman exhibition & Victorian suite, plus local history collections & A.V.

Norman castle with later additions houses local history museum. Audio-visual presentation on the history of the town and castle, plus 15 period room settings showing castle life spanning 800 years.

WALL

WALL ROMAN SITE (LETOCETUM)
(English Heritage/National Trust)
Wall **Tel:** (0543) 480768
Finds from the excavated Roman station called Letocetum.
Open: Apr 1 to Sept 30, daily 10-6. 1 Oct-31 March, Tues-Sun 10am-4pm. *Closed* 24-26 Dec and 1 January.
Admission: £1.10, Concessions 85p, Child 55p (1992 prices)

SUFFOLK

BUNGAY

BUNGAY MUSEUM
Waveney District Council
Council House, Bungay **Tel:** (0986) 2176
local history museum.

BURY ST. EDMUNDS

THE GERSHOM-PARKINGTON MEMORIAL COLLECTION OF CLOCKS AND WATCHES
(The National Trust and St Edmundsbury Borough Council)
8 Angel Hill, Bury St. Edmunds **Tel:** (0284) 757072

MOYSE'S HALL MUSEUM
(St Edmundsbury Borough Council)
Cornhill, Bury St. Edmunds **Tel:** (0284) 757072

CAVENDISH

NETHER HALL MUSEUM AND ART GALLERY
Cavendish **Tel:** (0787) 280221
Painting and bygones in 15th century listed Manor House and period barn. Vineyard wine tastings.
Open: Daily, 11-4.
Admission: £2, OAP's £1.50, Child free

THE SUE RYDER FOUNDATION MUSEUM
(The Sue Ryder Foundation)
Sue Ryder Home, Cavendish **Tel:** (0787) 280252

THE SUE RYDER FOUNDATION MUSEUM
SUE RYDER HOME, CAVENDISH, SUFFOLK

This small Museum is set in beautiful surroundings. It depicts the remarkable story of how the Foundation was established, its work today and its hopes for the future.
Location: On A1092 Long Melford−Cambridge. (Long Melford 4 miles: Sudbury 8 miles: Bury St. Edmunds 16 miles: Cambridge 29 miles). Open daily: Mondays to Sundays 10 am to 5.30 pm. GIFT SHOP also COFFEE SHOP providing lunches and light meals. Parties welcome. Menu on request. For special bookings, please write to:– The Sue Ryder Foundation, Cavendish, Sudbury, Suffolk CO10 8AY.
Tel: Glemsford (0787) 280252.

COTTON

MECHANICAL MUSIC MUSEUM
(An independent Museum)
Blacksmith Road, Near Stowmarket, Cotton **Tel:** (0449) 781354
A large collection of musical items.

DUNWICH

DUNWICH MUSEUM
St. James's Street, Dunwich
History of the lost Medieval town and local wild life.
Open: Easter to Sept 11.30-4.30; Oct 12.00-4.00; Mar Sat & Sun 2-4.30

EASTON

EASTON FARM PARK **Tel:** (0728) 746475
Wickham Market, Easton
Large collection of old farm machinery, country bygones, laundry. Farm animals including some rare breeds. Food and farming exhibition.
Open: 21 Mar - 30 Sept 10.30-6.00
Refreshments: Country style tea room.
Car parking free. Suitable for disabled persons. Curator: Farm Park Manager

IPSWICH

CHRISTCHURCH MANSION AND WOLSEY ART GALLERY
(Ipswich Borough Council)
Christchurch Park, Ipswich IP1 3QH **Tel:** (0473) 253246
Country house collection of furniture, pictures and ceramics. Works by Gainsborough, Constable and other Suffolk artists. Lively temporary exhibition programme in the Wolsey Art Gallery.
Open: Tues to Sat 10-5; Sun 2.30 to 4.30 (closing at dusk in winter). Open Bank Holiday Mons.
All written enquiries to: The Curator, Ipswich Museum, High Street, Ipswich, IP1 3QH

IPSWICH MUSEUM AND HIGH STREET EXHIBITION GALLERY
(Ipswich Borough Council)
High Street, Ipswich **Tel:** (0473) 213761
Geology , natural history, archaeology of Suffolk from earlier times to the medieval period, including the Roman Villa gallery and Mankind Gallery - Africa, Asia, Pacific and the Americas.
Open: Tues to Sat 10-5; (Gallery 4.45).
All written enquiries to: The Curator as above.

LAVENHAM

LAVENHAM GUILDHALL
(The National Trust)
Market Square, near Sudbury, Lavenham
Used for community purposes and exhibitions of local history (especially the Taylor family, one of whom wrote 'Twinkle, twinkle,little star'), cooperage and wood manufacture. The Guildhall, built c. 1528 houses a display about the cloth industry, farming and local industry.

LEISTON

LONG SHOP MUSEUM
Main Street, Leiston

LOWESTOFT

LOWESTOFT MARITIME MUSEUM
Sparrows Nest Park, Lowestoft
Fishing etc. through the ages.

LOWESTOFT MUSEUM
(Lowesoft Archaeological and Local History society and Waveney District Council)
Broad House, Nicholas Everitt Park, Oulton Broad, Lowestoft
Lowestoft porcelain, archaeology, local and domestic history, toys.
Open: Apr 3 to 17, May 22 to Oct 3, Mon to Sat 10.30-1, 2-5, Sun 2-5; Apr 24 to May 16 : Sat and Sun 2-5; Oct 9 to Oct 31: Sat and Sun 2-4.
Admission: Fee charged.

DISCOVER THE MUSEUMS
AND GALLERIES
OF IPSWICH

CHRISTCHURCH MANSION

A fine Tudor house set in beautiful parkland.
Period rooms in styles from 16th – 19th century;
outstanding collections of china, clocks, and glass.
Paintings by Gainsborough, Constable and other
Suffolk artists. Attached Wolsey Art Gallery shows
contemporary works.

Open Tuesday – Saturday, 10am – 5pm
Sunday 2.30 – 4.30pm
For further information tel. Ipswich (0473) 213761

IPSWICH
BOROUGH
COUNCIL

IPSWICH MUSEUM

Life in Roman Suffolk, rare and beautiful
objects from Africa, Asia and the Pacific, the
geological origins of our region, the best collection
of British birds in the country, the Victorian
Natural History Gallery, temporary exhibition
programme in the the Exhibition Gallery.

Open Tuesday – Saturday 10am – 5pm
Exhibition Gallery closes at 4.45pm
For further information tel. Ipswich (0473) 213761

NEWMARKET

THE NATIONAL HORSERACING MUSEUM
99 High Street, Newmarket   **Tel:** (0638) 667333

NATIONAL HORSERACING MUSEUM,
Newmarket

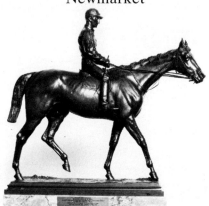

NEWMARKET EQUINE TOURS
These tours offer the museum visitor a unique chance to see both faces of Newmarket;
the modern thoroughbred working on the historic gallops, the famous stallions at the
studs, the training grounds and the racecourses. The historic side is beautifully
explained in the museum. BOOKING ESSENTIAL. Details on request.

THE NATIONAL HORSERACING MUSEUM
99 High Street, Newmarket, Suffolk CB8 8JL   Phone: (0638) 667333

The National Horseracing Museum, which is housed in the Regency Subscription
Rooms on the Newmarket High Street, was opened by The Queen on April 30 1983.
In the Museum's five permanent galleries the great story of the development of
Horseracing in this Country is told. Each year, with changing loans and fresh exhibits,
the display varies. Another display of fine paintings belonging to the British Sporting
Art Trust. A video programme of classic races and a walled garden are added attractions
to the museum.
Open: Mar to Dec: Tues to Sat 10-5, Sun 2-5. July and Aug: Mon to Sat 10-5, Sun
12-5.
Admission: Fee charged. Reductions for groups of 20 or more.
Refreshments: Licensed coffee shop
Gift Shop

SOUTHWOLD

SOUTHWOLD MUSEUM
  Bartholomew Green, Southwold
Local archaeology, history, natural history and bygones.

STOWMARKET

MUSEUM OF EAST ANGLIAN LIFE
  Stowmarket   **Tel:** (0449) 612229

MUSEUM OF EAST ANGLIAN LIFE
STOWMARKET, Suffolk

EAST ANGLIA'S OPEN AIR MUSEUM

Extensive site with riverside picnic
areas. Displays on agriculture,
crafts, social life and industry in
East Anglia. Reconstructed buildings including Boby Building
containing craft workshops,
steam gallery, video displays,
working machinery and
Industrial Heritage exhibition.
Programme of special events and
craft demonstrations (send SAE).
Museum shop.

Open April to October
  Weekdays 10.00 - 5.00
  Sundays 10.00 - 5.00
Admission charged:
  Party reductions.
  Tel: Stowmarket (0449) 612229
Museum entrance in centre
of Stowmarket

Engine No 776 of 1879.
One of a unique pair of Burrell steam
ploughing engines owned by the Museum.

Large open air museum on attractive riverside site in centre of Stowmarket.
Reconstructed buildings including Smithy, Watermill and Windpump. Boby Building
houses steam gallery, craft workshops and East Anglian industrial heritage museum.
Working Suffolk Punch horse. Displays on domestic, agricultural and industrial life,
steam traction engines.
Admission: Fee charged. Reductions for parties.
Location: Two minutes walk from Stowmarket market place.
Refreshments: Restaurant available.
Shop

SUDBURY

GAINSBOROUGH'S HOUSE
  46 Gainsborough Street, Gainsborough, Sudbury   **Tel:** (0787) 372958
Birthplace of Thomas Gainsborough R.A. Delightful house with paintings and
drawings by Gainsborough in 18th century setting. Exhibitions of contemporary and
historic art and craft. Attractive garden. Active print workshop in converted coach
house.
Open: Easter to Oct 31: Tues to Sat 10-5; Suns, Bank Hol Mons 2-5. Nov to Maundy
Thursday close 4. Closed Mon (except Bank Hols), Good Fri and Christmas to New
Year.
Admission: £2, OAPs £1.50, students, children £1
Parties by arrangement.

SURREY

CAMBERLEY

SURREY HEATH MUSEUM
(Surrey Heath Borough Council)
 Surrey Heath House, Knoll Road, Camberley GU15 3HD
An attractive museum combining permanent displays on local history and environment with a lively programme of temporary displays of local and regional interest.

CARSHALTON

HERITAGE CENTRE
(London Borough of Sutton)
See entry under Greater London

CATERHAM

EAST SURREY MUSEUM
 1 Stafford Road, Caterham CR3 6JG
Changing displays of local history, archaeology, natural history, crafts and local artists.
Open: Wed to Sat 10-5; Sun 2-5
Admission: 20p, Child and OAPs 10p.

CHERTSEY

CHERTSEY MUSEUM
(Runnymede Borough Council)
 The Cedars, Windsor Street, Chertsey   **Tel:** (0932) 565764
The museum contains 18th and 19th century costume, furniture, ceramics, clocks, glass, local history and archaeology.
Open: Tues to Thurs 2-5; Wed, Fri and Sat 10-1, 2-5

COBHAM

COBHAM BUS MUSEUM
(London Bus Preservation Trust)
 Redhill Road, Cobham   **Tel:** (0932) 864078
A collection of preserved omnibuses dating from the 1920's to recent times. A 'working garage' environment with vehicles in various stages of restoration.

EGHAM

THE EGHAM MUSEUM
(The Egham Museum Trust)
 Literary Institute, High Street, Egham
Local history and archaeology exhibits from Egham, Englefield Green, Thorpe and Virginia Water.
Open: Tues, Thurs 10.00-12.30 2-4.30 and Sats 10.30-12.30 and 2.30-4.30
Admission: Free

FARNHAM

JOHNSON WAX KILN GALLERY
 Farnham Maltings, Bridge Square, Farnham GU9 7QR   **Tel:** (0252) 726234

MUSEUM OF FARNHAM
(Waverley Borough Council)
 Willmer House, 38 West Street, Farnham   **Tel:** (0252) 715094
Early Georgian (1718) front of cut and moulded brick; fine carvings and panelling. Local history and archaeology. William Cobbett, decorative arts. Walled gardens.
Open: Tues to Sat 10-5

RURAL LIFE CENTRE
 Reeds Road, Tilford, Farnham   **Tel:** (025 125) 2300/5571
Collection includes wagons, farm implements, hand tools, Dairy, Kitchen, Forge, Wheelwright's shop and Arboretum.
Open: Apr to Sep: Wed to Sun and Bank Hols 11-6.
Suitable for disabled visitors. Rustic Sunday July 25, 1993.

GODALMING

GODALMING MUSEUM
(Godalming Museum Trust/Waverley Borough Council)
 109A High Street, Godalming   **Tel:** (0483) 426510
Medieval Building; Local history and people; Lutyens-Jekyll room; Garden; shop; Exhibitions.
Open: Tues to Sat, 10-5

GUILDFORD

BRITISH RED CROSS MUSEUM AND ARCHIVES
(British Red Cross)
 Barnet Hill, Wonersh, Guildford   **Tel:** (0483) 898595
History of the Red Cross movement, particularly British Red Cross from 1870. Features uniform, medals and badges, nursing equipment and other material depicting work of the Society in peace and war. Reference and photgraph library and research facilities available.
Open: Appointment only
Admission: Free
Parties maximum 20 people. Car parking available

GALLERY 90
(Guildford Borough)
 Ward Street, Guildford   **Tel:** (0483) 444740
Exhibition gallery in coverted 19th century church. Varied monthly art exhibitions of paintings in all media, craftwork and sculpture.
Open: Mon to Fri 10-4.30; Sat 10-12.30, 1.30-4.30.
Admission: Free

GUILDFORD MUSEUM
(Guildford Borough Council)
 Castle Arch, Guildford   **Tel:** (0483) 444750
Archaeological and historical museum for the county, especially West Surrey and Guildford Borough. Needlework collection of general interest.
Open: Mon to Sat 11-5.

THE WATTS GALLERY
 Compton, near Guildford, Guildford   **Tel:** (0483) 810235
Paintings by G.F.Watts, O.M.,R.A.
Open: Daily (except Thurs) 2-6 (Oct to Mar, 2-4); also Wed and Sat 11-1.
Location: 3 miles from Guildford
No dogs.

HASLEMERE

HASLEMERE EDUCATIONAL MUSEUM
 High Street, Haslemere   **Tel:** (0428) 642112
Fine collection of British birds, geology, zoology, local industries etc.

REDHILL

ROYAL EARLSWOOD HOSPITAL MUSEUM
 Redhill   **Tel:** (0737) 768511, Ext 8325

WESTCOTT

THE WESTCOTT GALLERY
(Anthony and Barbara Wakefield)
 4 Guildford Road, Westcott RH4 3NR   **Tel:** (0306) 876261
Specialise in contemporary Surrey artists. At least three major exhibitions per year. Browsers welcome.
Open: Mon to Fri, 9-5; Sat 10-5 *Closed* Bank holidays.
Admission: Free
Car parking around Village Green opposite Gallery. Suitable for disabled persons (no wheelchairs available).

WEYBRIDGE

ELMBRIDGE MUSEUM
 Church Street, Weybridge   **Tel:** (0932) 843573
Changing displays of local archaeology, social history, natural history and costume. Special exhibition 'Victorian Times' runs until Summer 1993.
Open: Mon, Tues, Thurs, Fri 2-5; Sat 10-1, 2-5. *Closed* Wed, Sun.
Admission: Free
Special exhibitions throughout the year telephone for details.

EAST SUSSEX

BATTLE

BATTLE MUSEUM
(Battle and District Historical Society)
 Langdon House, Battle

BEXHILL-ON-SEA

BEXHILL MUSEUM OF COSTUME AND SOCIAL HISTORY
Manor House Gardens, Old Town, Bexhill   Tel: (0424) 215361 or 211711
Open: Easter to Sept.

BRIGHTON

Opening times for museums and galleries in the case of Brighton Borough Council are subject to variation. Visitors are advised to telephone to check opening times in advance.

THE BOOTH MUSEUM OF NATURAL HISTORY
(Brighton Borough Council)
Dyke Road, Brighton   **Tel:** (0273) 552586
A comprehensive display of British birds, mounted in settings that re-create their natural habitats. Galleries on vertebrate evolution, butterflies of the World and Sussex geology. Frequent temporary exhibitions. Reference collections of insects, osteology, palaeontology, bird and mammal skins, eggs and herbaria.
Open: Mon to Sat 10-5; Sun 2-5. *Closed* Thurs, Christmas Day, Boxing Day, Jan 1 and Good Friday.
Admission: Free

BRIGHTON MUSEUM AND ART GALLERY
(Brighton Borough Council)
Church Street, Brighton   **Tel:** (0273) 603005
The collections include the Willett Collection of English pottery and porcelain; fine and applied art of the Art Nouveau and Art Deco periods; old master paintings, watercolours, furniture, fashion, musical instruments, ethnography, archaeology and Brighton history. Frequent special exhibitions.
Open: Mon, Tues, Thurs to Sat 10-5.45. Sun 2-5, *closed* Wed, Good Friday, Christmas Day, Boxing Day.
Admission: Free
Refreshments: Cafe open Tues to Sat.

PRESTON MANOR
(Brighton Borough Council)
Preston Park, Brighton   **Tel:** (0273) 603005, Ext 3239
Preston Manor was rebuilt in 1738, with further additions in 1905, and houses a collection of English and Continental furniture and decorative art from the 16th to the 19th century, including the Macquoid bequest. Servants' quarters now open.
Open: Tues to Sat 10-5, Sun 2-5. *Closed* Mons (except Bank Hols), Good Friday, Christmas Day and Boxing Day. Please telephone for details.
Admission: Fee charged.

THE ROYAL PAVILION
(Brighton Borough Council)
Brighton   **Tel:** (0273) 603005
The seaside palace of the Prince Regent (King George IV), containing some of the most dazzling and magnificent interiors in the world, now in final phase of restoration. Decorations in a fantastic version of 'The Chinese taste', Regency and other contemporary furniture and works of art, including many original pieces returned on loan from H.M. The Queen.
Open: Daily 10-5 (June to Sept, 10-6). *Closed* Christmas Day and Boxing Day.
Admission: Fee charged, reduced for child and parties.
Refreshments: Queen Adelaide tea room newly opened.
Guided tours by appointment. Pavilion Shop. £10 million structural restoration now complete. For further information on guided tours, special events and room hire, please call Public services on (0273) 603005.

EASTBOURNE

ROYAL NATIONAL LIFEBOAT INSTITUTION MUSEUM
Grand Parade, Eastbourne   **Tel:** (0323) 30717
Many types of lifeboats from the earliest date to the present time. Various items used in lifeboat service.

SUSSEX COMBINED SERVICES MUSEUM - REDOUBT FORTRESS
Royal Parade, Eastbourne   **Tel:** (0323) 410300
Built 1805-10. A circular ten-gun fort with barrack room casemates for a garrison of 350 men. Restored to house the Military Museum for the three services in Sussex. Also contains the Regiment museum of the Royal Sussex Regiment, and The Queen's Royal Irish Hussars. Collection of cannons on the battlements.
Open: Easter to Oct: Daily 10-5.30 (last adm 5). Other times by arrangement.

TOWER NO. 73 (THE WISH TOWER)
King Edwards Parade, Eastbourne   **Tel:** (0323) 410440
A restored Napoleonic War Martello Tower housing part of the National Collection of the British Model Soldiers society. Displays include model military miniatured as well as an extensive collection of antiques toy soldiers. Contemporary firearms and

illustrations are also on display.
Open: Daily, Whitsunday to September, 10-5.30.

TOWNER ART GALLERY AND LOCAL HISTORY MUSEUM
Manor Gardens, High Street, Old Town, Eastbourne   **Tel:** (0323) 411688

THE TOWNER ART GALLERY

The Towner Art Gallery is situated in Eastbourne's Manor House, dating from the 1770s. The Gallery, opened in 1923 following the generous bequest of Alderman John Towner, has an important collection of mainly 19th and 20th century British art, a selection from which is on show at any one time. Eric Ravilious, Edward Burra, Christopher Wood and Graham Sutherland are among the artists represented. The Gallery runs a lively temporary exhibition programme. Workshops, lectures, talks and other events are organised to complement the exhibitions. The South East Arts Association collection of contemporary art is housed at the Gallery.

THE LOCAL HISTORY MUSEUM
The history and development of Eastbourne and district is depicted from early prehistoric times with artefacts, models, reconstructions and photographs. Highlights include a life-size model of a Neolithic flint-miner at work, a Saxon skeleton and the Victorian cooking ranges from the kitchen of the Manor House.

ADMISSION FREE Tues-Sat: 10-5, Sun & Bank Holidays: 2-5

MANOR GARDENS, HIGH STREET, OLD TOWN, EASTBOURNE, E. SUSSEX
Tel: (0323) 411688

Elegant 18th century Manor House in public gardens. **Gallery:** Collection of mainly 19th and 20th century British art, a selection from which is on show at any one time. Lively programme of temporary exhibitions, workshops, talks, concerts and other events (see local press for details). **Local History Museum:** The Eastbourne area from Prehistoric times. Also reconstructed Victorian kitchen. Photographic archives.
Open: Tues to Sat 10-5; Sun and Bank Holidays 2-5.
Admission: Free

HAILSHAM

MICHELHAM PRIORY
(Sussex Archaeological Society)
Upper Dicker, Hailsham   **Tel:** (0323) 844224

MICHELHAM PRIORY
near Hailsham, East Sussex

Founded in 1229, this Augustinian Priory is surrounded by one of the largest moats in England. Medieval building with Tudor wing with 17-18th century furnishings, exhibition about the history of the Priory, temporary exhibitions, musical instruments. Art exhibitions in Great Barn, 14th century Gatehouse, Sussex Wagons, working Watermill, Blacksmiths' and Wheelwrights' Museum, Rope Museum. Licensed Restaurant.
Large gardens, physic garden, picnic area and children's playground. Replica Iron Age round house.

A property of the Sussex Archaeological Society

Open: Daily Mar 25 to Oct 31, 11-5.30; Suns only, Nov, 11-4
Admission: Adults £3.30, child £1.90.
Refreshments: Licensed restaurant.

HASTINGS MUSEUMS

OLD TOWN HALL MUSEUM
OF LOCAL HISTORY

DURBAR HALL
MUSEUM & ART GALLERY

HASTINGS

MUSEUM AND ART GALLERY
(Hastings Borough)
Cambridge Road, Hastings   **Tel:** (0424) 721202
Paintings, ceramics, Sussex ironwork, new wildlife and dinosaur displays opening 1992, Oriental, Pacific and American Indian Art, The Dunbar Hall (Indian Palace). Temporary exhibitions.
Open: Mon to Fri 10-5; Sat 10-1, 2-5; Sun 3-5
Admission: Free

MUSEUM OF LOCAL HISTORY
(Hastings Borough)
Old Town Hall, High Street, Hastings
Displays on maritime history, the Cinque Ports, smuggling, fishing, local personalities such as John Logie Baird.
Open: Easter to end Sept: Tues to Sun 10-1, 2-5; Oct to Easter Sun: 3-5.
Admission: Free

SHIPWRECK HERITAGE CENTRE
Rock-a-Nore Road, Hastings TN34 3DW   **Tel:** (0424) 437452
3,000 years of treasures from shipwrecks and the S.E. Coast. Videos and audio visual show 'A Shipwreck Adventure'. Live RADAR and live satellite pictures showing the weather.
Open: Open Easter to end of September

HEATHFIELD

SUSSEX FARM MUSEUM
(Sussex Farm Museum Trust)
Horam Manor, Heathfield TN21 0JB
Nature Trails. Countryside interpretation.
Refreshments: Available
Free parking and picnic. Camping and caravan visitors welcome.

HOVE

THE BRITISH ENGINEERIUM
Nevill Road, Hove   **Tel:** (0273) 559583

The majestic Eastons & Anderson Beam Engine of 1876.

at the **BRITISH ENGINEERIUM** Off Nevill Road Hove BN3 7QA.

Telephone: 0273-559583

A unique working steam museum telling the story of Britain's engineering heritage within the building of the fully restored Goldstone Pumping Station. See the huge Eastons & Anderson beam engine of 1876, plus hundreds of models and full size engines depicting the history of steam power on land, sea road and rail. Conservation and restoration projects of industrial archaeological material for national and private collections worldwide, can be seen under way in the period workshops.
Open: Daily 10-5. Engines in steam Sun and Bank Holidays.
Admission: £3.00, Conc £2.00, Family £8 (1992)
Access for disabled.

HOVE MUSEUM AND ART GALLERY
(Hove Borough Council)
19 New Church Road, Hove BN3 4AB   **Tel:** (0273) 779410

HOVE MUSEUM & ART GALLERY

19 New Church Road Hove East Sussex BN3 4AB (0273) 779410

Opening times
Tuesday-Friday 10am – 5pm   Sunday 2pm – 5pm
Saturday 10am – 4.30pm   Closed Monday

Admission Free   Museum Shop

Twentieth century paintings and drawings. Eighteenth century pictures, furniture and decorative arts, dolls, toys and dolls houses. New display of Hove history incorporating Hove's pioneer film-makers. Special exhibitions of historic and contemporary art and crafts, housed in one of the town's most impressive Victorian Villas.
Admission: Free

LEWES

ANNE OF CLEVES HOUSE MUSEUM
(Sussex Archaeological Society)
Anne of Cleves House, Southover High Street, Lewes   **Tel:** (0273) 474610
A picturesque half-timbered building. Collection of household equipment, furniture, Sussex ironwork and pottery and a gallery of Lewes History.
Open: April to Oct: Mon to Sat 10-5.30: also Sun 11-5.30.
Admission: Adult £1.60, child 80p.

LEWES LIVING HISTORY MODEL
(Sussex Archaeological Society)
Barbican House, 169 High Street, Lewes   **Tel:** (0273) 486290
Large-scale model of historic Lewes with 25 minute audio-visual programme describing the town's development and with substantial static exhibition.
Open: April to mid Sept, daily 11-5.30; Oct to Mar, Sat and Sun only, 11-5.30.
Admission: £2.50, Child £1.25 (includes admission to Lewes Castle and Museum of Sussex Archaeology).

MUSEUM OF SUSSEX ARCHAEOLOGY
(Sussex Archaeological Society)
Barbican House, 169 High Street, Lewes   **Tel:** (0273) 486290
Large collection of prehistoric, Romano-British, Saxon and medieval antiquities relating to Sussex. Prints and watercolours of Sussex.
Open: Mon to Sat 10-5.30; Sun 11-5.30.
Admission: Adult £2.50, child £1.25 (includes admission to Lewes Castle and Lewes Living History Model).

RYE

LAMB HOUSE
(The National Trust)
West Street, Rye
A dignified early Georgian town house, the home of Henry James from 1898 to 1916. Some of his furniture, pictures and personal possessions are on view. Walled gardens,

staircase, hall and three rooms on the ground flour are shown.
Admission: Fee charged, *no reduction for children or parties.*

RYE HERITAGE CENTRE TOWN MODEL
Son et Lumiere, Strand Quay (at the foot of Mermaid Street), Rye
Rye has a superb new Heritage Centre with Local Exhibition. Come and see the fascinating history of the Town of Rye dramatically brought to life in this theartical combination of a realistic sound and light show and an authentic Town Model.

RYE MUSEUM
Ypres Tower, Rye TN31 7HH   **Tel:** (0797) 226728

RYE MUSEUM
RYE, EAST SUSSEX

Ypres Tower, Gun Garden

The collections illustrate the history of, and life in, Rye and district through the centuries. Arrangements of militaria, shipping, country life, ceramics, glass, toys and dolls are colourfully displayed in a 13th century fortification.

Local collections housed in a 13th century tower. Medieval and other pottery from the Rye kilns. Cinque Ports material, shipping, toys and dolls.
Open: Easter to late October: Mon to Sat 10.30-5.30; Sun 11.30-5.30; Last entry 30 minutes before closing.
Admission: Charge

SEAFORD

SEAFORD MUSEUM OF LOCAL HISTORY
Martello Tower No,74, Esplanade, Seaford   **Tel:** (0323) 899007
'A trip down Memory Lane'. Period shops, TV, radio, domestic appliances, photographs. Seaford Gallery.
Open: Summer: Sun, Wed, Sat: 2.30-4.30 and Sun 11-1. Winter: Suns: 11-1, 2.30-4.30. Bank Hols and Sun all year.
Parties: appointment only.

SHEFFIELD PARK

BLUEBELL RAILWAY
(Bluebell Railway)
Sheffield Park Station, Sheffield Park, Nr Uckfield   **Tel:** (082 572) 2370 (talking timetable) 3777 (enquiries)
The Bluebell Railway - Living Museum. Operates vintage steam trains between Sheffield Park, Horsted Keynes and extension to new Coombe Bridge (2m) in Sussex.
Open: Every Sun, weekends Spring and Autumn, daily June to Sept. Santa Specials in December. Open for limited viewing other dates. Brochure timetable available.
Refreshments: Buffet available.
Museum and shop. Car parking. Special events held annually. 'Golden Arrow Pullman' Dining Train for hire or on regular service with option of overnight sleeping - ask for leaflet.

WILMINGTON

WILMINGTON PRIORY AND LONG MAN
(Sussex Archaeological Society)
   Wilmington Priory   **Tel:** (0323) 870537
Remains of 13th century Benedictine Priory with collection of bygone agricultural implements and farmhouse utensils.
Open: Mar 25 to Oct 31; Mon to Sat (except Tues) 11-5.30. Sun 2-5.30;
Admission: Adults £1.70 child 60p. Details correct at time of going to press.

WINCHELSEA

WINCHELSEA MUSEUM
   Court Hall, Winchelsea
Collection illustrating the history of Winchelsea and the Cinque Ports. Handicrafts, archaeologocal specimens, models, maps, documents.
Open: May to Sept

WEST SUSSEX

AMBERLEY

AMBERLEY CHALK PITS MUSEUM
(Southern Industrial History Centre Trust)
   Houghton Bridge,, Amberley, near Arundel   **Tel:** (0798) 831370

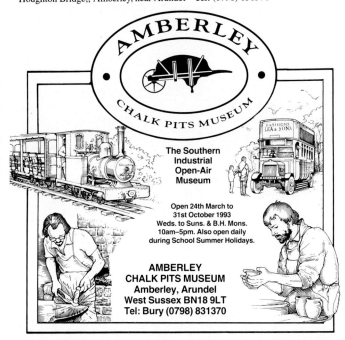

AMBERLEY CHALK PITS MUSEUM

The Southern Industrial Open-Air Museum

Open 24th March to 31st October 1993 Weds. to Suns. & B.H. Mons. 10am–5pm. Also open daily during School Summer Holidays.

AMBERLEY CHALK PITS MUSEUM Amberley, Arundel West Sussex BN18 9LT Tel: Bury (0798) 831370

36 acre open air museum of industrial history featuring working craftsmen, operational narrow gauge industrial railway, early motor buses, stationary engines, chalk pits and lime kilns, timber yard with steam crane, metal working shop, forge, pottery, printshop, boat builder's shop, brick display, wireless exhibition, ironmongers shop, domestic display, steam traction engines and rollers, etc. The South Eastern Electricity Board's Milne Museum due to open at Amberley during 1993.
Open: Beginning of Apr to end Oct, Wed to Sun, plus Bank Hol Mons. Open daily during school summer hols 10-5.

ARUNDEL

ARUNDEL TOY AND MILITARY MUSEUM
   23 High Street, Arundel   **Tel:** (0903) 883101/882908

MUSEUM AND HERITAGE CENTRE
   61 High Street, Arundel   **Tel:** (0903) 882344
Old Arundel on view in nine galleries.
Open: Easter to Oct: Open every weekend; also open Tues to Fri and Bank Hols in High Season.
Admission: £1, Child 50p
Parties any time by arrangement.

BRAMBER

ST. MARY'S HOUSE
   Bramber   **Tel:** (0903) 816205

CHICHESTER

CHICESTER DISTRICT MUSEUM
(Chichester District Council)
   29 Little London, Chichester   **Tel:** (0243) 784683
Discover the life and work of the people of Chichester and the local countryside. Temporary exhibitions.
Open: Tues to Sat 10-5.30 *Closed* Sun and Mon.
Admission: Free
Shop, Quiz sheets

GUILDHALL MUSEUM
(Chichester District Council)
   Priory Park, Chichester   **Tel:** (0243) 784683
13th century church, later the Town Hall and Law Court. Explore this fine building and discover monks, smugglers and William Blake.
Open: June to Sept: Tues to Sat 1-5. *Closed* Sun and Mon
Admission: Free

MECHANICAL MUSIC AND DOLL COLLECTION
   Church Road, Portfield, Chichester   **Tel:** (0243) 785421
Music boxes, barrel organs, street pianos, dance organs etc., all fully restored and playing for the visitors. Also fine display of Victorian china dolls.
Open: Easter to Sept 30: Daily 10-5. Oct to Easter: Weekends only. Closed Dec.

PALLANT HOUSE
(Pallant House Gallery Trust)
   9 North Pallant, Chichester   **Tel:** (0243) 774557
British Art at Home - excellent collections of Modern British Art (Moore, Sutherland, Piper, Hitchens, etc.) in the setting of a meticulously restored Queen Anne townhouse. Added attractions include the Geoffrey Freeman Collection of Bow Porcelain (the finest in the world), the lively programme of loan exhibitions, and the peaceful walled formal garden.
Open: All year: Tues to Sat 10-5.30. *Closed* Sun, Mon and Bank Hols.
Admission: Fee charged.

WEALD AND DOWNLAND OPEN AIR MUSEUM
   Singleton, Chichester   **Tel:** (024 363) 348

WEALD AND DOWNLAND OPEN AIR MUSEUM

Singleton, nr. Chichester, Sussex

The Museum rescues and reconstructs vernacular buildings from S.E. England threatened with destruction. So far more than 30 buildings have been re-erected on the Museum's beautiful 40 acre Downland site. These include Medieval Houses, Farm Buildings, a Tudor Market Hall, a 17th century Treadwheel, a Blacksmith's Forge, a 19th century Village School and a working Watermill.
A Medieval Farmstead and History of Farming Exhibition is centred around the Bayleaf Farmhouse (above).

A fascinating collection of rescued historic buildings reconstructed in attractive Downland setting. Exhibits include Medieval farmstead, houses and rural craft workshops. The Lurgashall Mill is in daily operation during the main season producing stone ground flour. The museum is continuously developing and new buildings are regularly being re-erected.
Open: Mar 1 to Oct 31: Daily 11-5. Nov 1 to Feb 29: Wed, Sun and Bank Hols only 11-4.
Refreshments: Light only, available Apr to Oct.
Parties by arrangement.

CUCKFIELD

CUCKFIELD MUSEUM
Queen's Hall, High Street, Cuckfield

DITCHLING

DITCHLING MUSEUM
Church Lane, Ditchling   **Tel:** (0273) 844744
History comes alive with dioramas and costume tableaux. Country crafts; work by famous local artists; wide-ranging special exhibitions.
Open: Easter to late Oct: weekdays 11-5; Sun 2-5. Winter weekends only to 4.30.
Admission: £1.50; first accompanied Child free, others £1. 10% reduction for groups of more than ten.
Free parking nearby (disabled drivers on-site). Wheelchairs welcome.

EAST GRINSTEAD

EAST GRINSTEAD TOWN MUSEUM
East Grinstead Mansion, East Grinstead
A small collection devoted to the town of East Grinstead; occupies part of the East Court Mansion (1769).
Open: Wed 2-4 and Sat 2-5 (2-4 in winter) and some Bank Hols. Parties at other times on application to the Curator.

FISHBOURNE

FISHBOURNE ROMAN PALACE
(Sussex Archaeological Society)
Salthill Road, Fishbourne

FISHBOURNE
ROMAN PALACE
AND MUSEUM

SALTHILL ROAD,
FISHBOURNE,
nr CHICHESTER,
WEST SUSSEX PO19 3QR
Telephone: 0243 785859

Remains of a Roman Palace with superb mosaic floors, which are preserved and displayed inside a modern cover building. Displays of Roman everyday items. Audio-visual theatre. Re-planted Roman garden. Cafeteria, picnic area, large coach and car parks. Good facilities for the disabled.

A property of the SUSSEX ARCHAEOLOGICAL SOCIETY

Remains of the first century Palace with many fine mosaic floors including some of the earliest in the country. Finds from the excavations. Re-planted Roman Garden.
Open: Daily mid-Feb, Mar, Apr, Oct: 10-5. May-Sep:10-6. Nov-mid-Dec: 10-4. Open Sun only: Dec, Jan, Feb: 10-4
Admission: £3.20 adult, £1.50 child

HENFIELD

LOCAL HISTORY MUSEUM
Village Hall, High Street, Henfield   **Tel:** (0273) 492546
Archaeology and geology of the area. Domestic objects, costume, agricultural tools, local paintings, and photographs.
Open: Mon, Tues, Thurs, Sat 10-12, Wed 2.30-4.30. Other times by appointment.

HORSHAM

HORSHAM MUSEUM
9 The Causeway, Horsham   **Tel:** (0403) 54959
Many visitors have told us how attractive the museum is, find out why! It has, if anything, improved with new displays on Prehistory, Geology, the Poet Shelley, costume, ceramics, bicycles, saddlery as well as an enchanting garden lying behind a timber framed Tudor House. Throughout the year attractive, and informative temporary exhibitions draw on the extensive collections of this 100 year old Museum.
Open: Tues to Sat 10-5
Admission: Free

LITTLEHAMPTON

LITTLEHAMPTON MUSEUM
(Arun District Council)
Manor House, Church Street, Littlehampton   **Tel:** (0903) 715149

LITTLEHAMPTON MUSEUM
WEST SUSSEX

★ **Fine ship paintings**
★ **Local history & archaeology**
★ **Temporary exhibitions ★ Free entry**

Maritime paintings, bygones, photographs of the district, local archaeology and history and temporary exhibitions.
Open: Tues to Sat 10.30-4.30. and Summer Bank Hol Mons
Admission: Free

MIDHURST

RICHARD COBDEN COLLECTION
(National Council of Y.M.C.As.)
Dunford, Midhurst
Portraits and library of Richard Cobden and family.

PULBOROUGH

PARHAM ELIZABETHAN HOUSE & GARDENS
Parnham Park, Pulborough   **Tel:** (0903) 742021

SHOREHAM-BY-SEA

MARLIPINS MUSEUM
(Sussex Archaeological Society)
   High Street, Shoreham-by-Sea   **Tel:** (0273) 462994
The building dates from the early 12th century; Maritime and Local History Museum.
Open: May to mid-Sept: Tues to Sat: 10-1, 2-4.30; Sun 2-4.30.
Admission: Free (donations welcome)

STEYNING

STEYNING MUSEUM
   Church Street, Steyning   **Tel:** (0903) 813333
Steyning from the Romans to the railway, from Saxon Saint to 400 year old school; its traditions, industry and artistic vitality. Plus regular special exhibitions.
Admission: Free

TANGMERE

TANGMERE MILITARY AVIATION MUSEUM TRUST
   Tangmere Airfield PO20 6ES   **Tel:** (0243) 775223

TANGMERE
MILITARY AVIATION MUSEUM
Telephone: Chichester 775223

Tangmere Airfield, 3 miles east of Chichester, signposted off the A27

Famous Battle of Britain airfield now the home of a museum that will interest all ages. A superb collection of exhibits related to 70 years of flying. Personal belongings, relics of wartime air battles, maps, paintings, photos, medals, uniforms, dioramas, static and working models, a Spitfire flight simulator and more besides. New exhibits always being added. Well worth a visit.

Open Daily 10.00 to 5.30p.m.
February – November

Free Parking ● Picnic Area ● Souvenir Shop

Well worth a visit. Tangmere Aeromart - 80 stalls - normally last Sat in Sept.
Admission: Adults £2.50, Child £1. Party rates by arrangement.
Location: 3m E of Chichester off A27.
Refreshments: Snack bar
A bus service from Chichester passes the entrance. Free parking. Picnic area. Souvenir shop. Suitable for disabled.

WEST HOATHLY

PRIEST HOUSE
(Sussex Archaeological Society)
   West Hoathly   **Tel:** (0342) 810479
15th century Clergy House, later converted into a dwelling-house, containing furnished rooms and collection of general bygones, toys, samplers and costume.
Open: Mar 25 to Oct 31 Mon to Sat (except Tues) 11-5.30; Sun 2-5.30.
Admission: £1.70 adult, 60p child. Details correct at time of going to press.

WORTHING

WORTHING MUSEUM AND ART GALLERY
(Worthing Borough Council)
   Chapel Road, Worthing   **Tel:** (0903) 239999 Ext 2528 (Sats (0903) 204229)

'Best Museum of Archaeological or Historical Interest' – Museum of the Year Awards 1987

Shepherding on the South Downs is one of the themes with which the museum deals. Others are the archaeology of the area and the history of the town of Worthing itself, with its seaside life. Other popular features include the Costume Galleries and displays of toys and dolls. The art collections comprise English paintings, pottery and glass. There are frequent exhibitions–current programme on request.
Open daily except Sundays 10 a.m.–6 p.m. April-September: 10 a.m.-5p.m. October-March. Admission Free. Parties by arrangement. Tel. Worthing 239999 Ext. 2528 (Sats 204229).

Collections include regional archaeology and local history, Sussex bygones, dolls and toys, English paintings, pottery and glass.
Admission: Free
Easy access for disabled visitors.

TYNE & WEAR

GATESHEAD

BOWES RAILWAY
   Springwell Village, Gateshead

SHIPLEY ART GALLERY
(Tyne and Wear Museums)
   Prince Consort Road South, Gateshead   **Tel:** 091-4771495

JARROW

BEDE MONASTERY MUSEUM
(St. Paul's Jarrow Development Trust)
Jarrow Hall, Church Bank, Jarrow NE32 3DY   **Tel:** 091-4892106

BEDE MONASTERY MUSEUM
JARROW, TYNE & WEAR

The Museum is housed in Jarrow Hall (c. 1800) and tells the story of the monastery of St. Paul's, Jarrow, home of the Venerable Bede (AD 673-735), the foremost scholar of his age and author of "The Ecclesiastical History of the English People". The monastery has been excavated, and many finds – the earliest coloured window glass, sculpture, metalwork and pottery – are displayed, alongside a model of the monastery and an audio-visual about the life of a monk. The Museum also has temporary exhibitions, a craft shop, Tourist Information Centre, cafe, herb garden and full educational facilities.

The Museum on the south bank of the River Tyne. Permanent exhibition of material from archaeological excavations includes Anglo-Saxon window glass and stone sculpture and a model of the 7th century monastery. An audio-visual display about the life of the monk. To book school visits, contact Educational Officer. Oval Room. Craft shop specialising in Anglo-Saxon related and herbal products.
Open: Apr to Oct: Tues to Sat 10-5.30; Sun 2.30-5.30. Nov to Mar: Tues to Sat 11-4.30; Sun 2.30-5.30. *Closed* Mon (except Bank Hols); between Christmas and the New Year, and Good Friday.
Admission: Small fee charged.
Refreshments: Tea room serving coffee, lunches and teas.
Curator: Miss S.A. Mills

NEWCASTLE UPON TYNE

THE CASTLE KEEP MUSEUM
St. Nicholas Street, Newcastle upon Tyne
The keep of the 'New Castle' built by Henry II in 1170. Interpretation of the history of the Castle site.
Open: Apr to Sept: Tues to Sun 9.30-5. Oct to Mar: Tues to Sun 9.30-4. *Closed* Christmas Day, Boxing Day, New Year's Day and Good Friday.

THE GREEK MUSEUM
Percy Building, The Quadrangle, Newcastle Upon Tyne   **Tel:** 091-2226000 Ext. 7966
Collection of ancient Greek and Etruscan art ranging from Minoan to Hellenistic times; vases, terracottas, bronzes, gems and armour.
Open: Normally Mon to Fri 10-4.30, and by appointment.

HATTON GALLERY
(situated within the Department of Fine Art)
Newcastle Upon Tyne   **Tel:** 091-2226057
Hosts a programme of temporary exhibitions of contemporary and historical art. The gallery frequently displays items from its own Permanent Collection including British and European paintings, drawings, sculptures and prints from the 16th-17th centuries. On permanent display are the 'Elterwater Merzbarn' a large installation by Dada Artist Kurt Schwitters and the Uhlman Collection of African Sculpture.
Open: The Gallery is open during exhibition periods Mon to Fri 10-5.30 and Sat (term time) 10-4.30.

JOHN GEORGE JOICEY MUSEUM
Tyne and Wear Museum Service)
City Road, Newcastle upon Tyne NE1 2AS
Situated a few minutes from the Tyne Bridge in distinguished 17th century almshouse and adjoining 19th century soup kitchen. Displays include local art, period rooms, regimental collections of the 15th/19th King's Royal Hussars.

LAING ART GALLERY
(Tyne and Wear Museums)
Higham Place, Newcastle Upon Tyne NE1 8GA   **Tel:** 091-2327734

MUSEUM OF ANTIQUES
(jointly with the Society of Antiquaries)
The Quadrangle, Newcastle Upon Tyne   **Tel:** 091-2226000 Ext. 7844
Prehistoric, Roman, Anglo-Saxon and Medieval antiquities, chiefly from Northumberland. Scale models of Hadrian's Wall and reconstructions of Roman arms and armour and of a temple of Mithras.
Open: Weekdays 10-5. *Closed* Dec 24,25,26, New Year's Day and Good Friday.

MUSEUM OF SCIENCE AND ENGINEERING
(Tyne and Wear Museums)
Blandford House, Blandford Square, Newcastle Upon Tyne   **Tel:** 091-2326789

TRINITY MARITIME CENTRE
(Captain G.W.Clark, MBE, Chairman of Trustees)
29 Broad Chare, Quayside, Newcastle Upon Tyne NE1 3DQ   **Tel:** 091-2614691

TURBINIA HALL
(Tyne and Wear Museums Service)
Exhibition Park, Newcastle Upon Tyne

The University of Newcastle upon Tyne: MUSEUMS

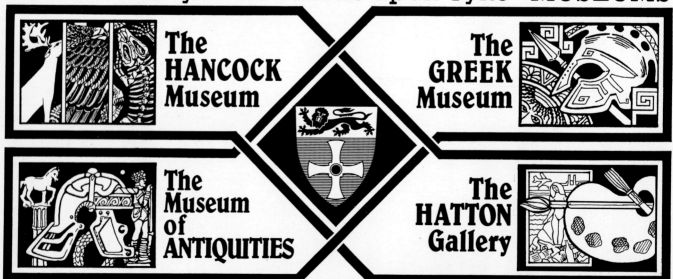

UNIVERSITY OF NEWCASTLE UPON TYNE HANCOCK MUSEUM
(jointly with the Natural History Society of Northumbria)
Barras Bridge, Newcastle Upom Tyne   **Tel:** 091-2227418
Comprehensive collections of natural history. Rich ethnographical section. Major modernisation of displays completed recently, new look for birds, geology and mammals. Major temporary exhibition until March 1993 'Monsters of the Deep'.
Open: Mon to Sat 10-5; Sun 2-5
Admission: £1.50, OAPs and unwaged 75p/

NORTH SHIELDS

STEPHENSON RAILWAY MUSEUM
(Tyne and Wear Museums)
Chirton Industrial Estate, North Shields   **Tel:** 091-2522627

SOUTH SHIELDS

ARBEIA ROMAN FORT
(Tyne and Wear Museums)
Baring Street, South Shields   **Tel:** 091-4561369

MUSEUM AND ART GALLERY
(Tyne and Wear Museums)
Ocean Road, South Shields   **Tel:** 091-4568740

SUNDERLAND

GRINDON MUSEUM
(Tyne and Wear Museums)
Grindon Lane, Sunderland   **Tel:** 091-5284042

MONKWEARMOUTH STATION MUSEUM
(Tyne and Wear Museums)
North Bridge Street, Sunderland   **Tel:** 091-5677075

MUSEUM AND ART GALLERY
(Tyne and Wear Museums)
Borough Road, Sunderland   **Tel:** 091-5141235

RYHOPE ENGINES MUSEUM
Sunderland

WALLSEND

WALLSEND HERITAGE CENTRE
(Tyne and Wear Museums)
Buddle Street, Wallsend   **Tel:** 091-2620012

WASHINGTON

WASHINGTON 'F' PIT INDUSTRIAL MUSEUM
(Tyne and Wear Museums)
Albany Way, Washington   **Tel:** 091-4167640

WASHINGTON OLD HALL
(The National Trust)
Washington   **Tel:** 091-4166879
The ancestral home of the first President of the United States from which the family took its name. The Hall contains 17th century furniture, Delft ware and many Washington relics.

WARWICKSHIRE

EDGE HILL

UPTON HOUSE
(The National Trust)
near Banbury, Edge Hill   **Tel:** (029 587) 266
The mellow stone house dating from 1695 contains superb collections of Old Master paintings, Brussels tapestries, outstanding 18th century furniture and Sevres porcelain. The large garden includes lakes, woodland and lovely views.
Location: near Banbury (Oxon) on A422
Parties by written arrangement.

GAYDON

HERITAGE MOTOR CENTRE
(The British Motor Industry Heritage Trust)
Banbury Road, Gaydon CV35 OBJ   **Tel:** (0926) 641188   **Fax:** (0926) 641555
The finest collection of uniquely British Cars. 250 vehicles representing the history of the British Motor Industry.
Open: Daily 10-5.30. (except Christmas & Boxing Day). Nov to Feb 10-4.
Admission: Fee charged. Discounts for group bookings.
Refreshments: Available
Suitable for disabled persons. Conference Centre, Education Centre. Opening Spring 1993.

LEAMINGTON SPA

LEAMINGTON SPA ART GALLERY AND MUSEUM
(Warwick District Council)
Avenue Road, Leamington Spa   **Tel:** (0926) 426559
Paintings by Dutch and Flemish masters; 19th and 20th century oils and watercolours, mainly English, Sixteenth-nineteenth century pottery and porcelein; 18th century English glass. Local history displays.
Open: Mon, Tues, Thurs to Sat 10-1, 2-5.(also Thurs evening 6-8) *ClosedD Wed and Sun.*

NUNEATON

NUNEATON MUSEUM AND ART GALLERY
Riverley Park, Nuneaton   **Tel:** (0203) 350720
Local history, major displays on local authoress George Elliot, Art Exhibitions.
Open: Tues to Sat: 10.30-4.30; Sun: 2pm-4.30pm; Tearoom only: Mon 10.30-4.30
Refreshments: Tea room
Toilets. Disabled access/lift.

RUGBY

RUGBY LIBRARY AND EXHIBITION GALLERY
St. Mathew's Street., Rugby   **Tel:** (0788) 542687 or 571813
Exhibitions by local artists and societies.
Open: Mon, Tues, Thurs and Fri 9.30-8; Wed 9.30-5; Sat 9.30-4.

STRATFORD-UPON-AVON

THE SHAKESPEARE BIRTHPLACE TRUST'S PROPERTIES
The Shakespeare Centre, Henley Street, Stratford-upon-Avon .   **Tel:** (0789) 204016
Shakespeare's Birthplace, Anne Hathaway's Cottage, New Place/Nash's House, Hall's Croft and the Shakespeare Countryside Museum at Mary Arden's House; the five beautifully preserved Tudor houses in and around Stratford connected with the dramatist and his family. Outstanding period furniture, museum and folk-life collections and delightful gardens.
Send sae for adm details to the Director.

THE TEDDY BEAR MUSEUM
(Gyles Brandreth)
19 Greenhill Street, Stratford-Upon-Avon CV37 6LF   **Tel:** (0789) 293160

Old bears - new bears - giant bears - tiny bears - mechanical bears - musical bears - amazing bears - amusing bears - famous bears and bears of the famous - you'll find them all at Stratford's award-winning Teddy Bear Museum, home of William Shakesbear, his family and friends.
Admission: £1.90. Child (under 14) 95p.

WARWICK

DOLL MUSEUM
(Warwickshire County Council)
   Oken's House, Castle Street, Warwick   **Tel:** (0926) 495546
Displays on dolls and their houses, puzzles and games.
Open: Easter to end Sept: Mon to Sat 10-5; Sun 2-5.

ST. JOHN'S HOUSE
(Warwickshire County Council)
   St. John's, Warwick   **Tel:** (0926) 412132
Warwickshire bygones and period costume. Victorian classroom, kitchen and parlour.
Open: Tues to Sat 10-12.30, 1.30 to 5.30. *Closed* Mon (except Bank Hols).Sun (May to Sept) 2.30-5

WARWICKSHIRE MUSEUM
(Warwickshire County Council)
   Market Place, Warwick   **Tel:** (0926) 412500; Sat 412501
Wildlife, geology, archaeology and history of Warwickshire including the famous Sheldon tapestry map and giant fossil plesiosaur.
Open: Mon to Sat 10-5.30; Sun (May to Sept) 2.30-5

WEST MIDLANDS

BICKENHILL

NATIONAL MOTORCYCLE MUSEUM
   Coventry Road, Bickenhill   **Tel:** (0675) 443311

Hundreds of beautifully restored motorcycles create a colourful evocation of the history of British motorcycling. Vintage motorcycles, racing machines, many unusual exhibits. Giant poster boards. Historic documentation of the machines and their riders.
Open: Daily 10-6 (except Christmas Eve, Christmas Day and Boxing Day)
Admission: £3.75, Child/OAPs £2.50. Reduction for parties on application.
Refreshments: Restaurant and snack bar.
Gift and book shop. Conference facilities available. Free coach and car park.

BIRMINGHAM

ASTON HALL
   Trinity Road, Aston, Birmingham   **Tel:** 021-327 0062
Birmingham's major 17th century building is a large country house standing in the remaining acres of its park. Over 18 rooms are on view to the public, filled with furnishing from the various periods of its history in the 17th, 18th and 19th centuries. The particularly fine Jacobean oak staircase and the magnificent Long Gallery are substantially unaltered since the Holte family built the house in the 1620s and 30s. Many of the interiors are distinguished for their elaborate plaster ceilings and large

Jacobean chimneypieces.
Open: Mid March to end October daily 2-5.
Admission: Free
Educational and group visits by arrangement.

BIRMINGHAM MUSEUM AND ART GALLERY
   Chamberlain Square, Birmingham B3 3DH   **Tel:** 021-235 2834
The Department of Fine Art: Birmingham possesses a representative selection of British and European painting and sculpture from the 14th to the 20th century. Of particular significance are the Italian 17th century paintings and the English Pre-Raphaelite Collection, which is considered to be the finest in the world. There is also an outstanding Collection of English 18th and 19th century drawings and watercolours which may be viewed by prior arrangement. *The Department of Applied Arts:* The Applied Arts are well represented with collections of ceramics, glass, stained glass, silver, textiles, jewellery, non-precious metalwork, Oriental, Indian and Middle Eastern artefacts and English costume. Much of this material is on display for the first time in the newly refurbished Industrial Gallery. A gallery devoted to items of contemporary craft was established in 1980 with assistance from West Midland Arts. *The Department of Archaeology and Ethnography:* The collections include archaeological objects from the West Midlands and other parts of Britain the Near East, Egypt, Mediterranean area, Indian South and Central America as well as ethnographic material from North America, Africa and the Pacific. There are also collections of ancient and Medieval coins with special emphasis on those stuck in the West Midlands. Gallery 33, a new permanent display opened in 1990, is devoted to values, customs and art from around the world. *The Department of Social History* The department of Social History collects documents and makes available material evidence depicting the origins and growth of Birmingham and its suburbs from the end of the Middle Ages to the present day. Its collections cover social and domestic history, civic life, crafts, trades and industries, local worthies, topographical views and numismatics. The department is also responsible for the Pinto Collection of wooded bygones. *The Department of Natural History* The department of Natural History has fine collections of British and foreign bird specimens, lepidoptera, minerals, molluscs and plants; also a good series of British fossils and a unique collection of gemstones. The Zoology galleries display several habitat dioramas of European wildlife, the biology of vertebrate animals, including fishes, amphibians, reptiles, birds and mammals, and the Beale gallery of British birds in natural settings. The fossil gallery has a life-size model of a carnivorous dinosaur as well as the actual skull of another - the plant-eater Triceratops from Montana. *The Department of Conservation:* Conservation and restoration work is under-taken on the material from the collections, primarily in archaeology, applied art, furniture, paintings, paper and textiles. *Schools Liaison:* The Schools Liaison assists teachers wishing to use the museum's collections in their work. It organises courses for serving and student teachers and provides facilities for practical sessions for group visits. It arranges events for all ages including leisure courses, craft demonstrations, talks and exhibitions. During major school holidays a full programme of events is provided for everyone.
Open: Mon to Sat 9.30-5; Sun 2-5. *Closed* Christmas Day, Boxing Day, and New Year's Day.
Admission: Free
Lift to all floors.

BIRMINGHAM NATURE CENTRE
   Edgbaston, Birmingham   **Tel:** 021-472 7775
The Nature Centre displays living animals of the British Isles and Europe in both outdoor and indoor enclosures, including lynx, fox, badger, polecats, otters and beavers, owls and many others. Conditions have been created to resemble natural habitats and to attract wild birds, butterflies etc. Its grounds of six acres include fishponds, duckponds, stream, rock outcrops, aviaries and beehives.
Open: Mid March end October daily 10-5. Last admission 4.30. Winter weekends 10-dusk. *Closed* Christmas Day, Boxing Day and New Year's Day.

Market Hall
Mon–Sat 10.00–5.30
Sun (May–Sept) 2.30–5.00

St John's House Museum
Tues–Sat 10.00–12.30 1.30–5.30
Sun (May–Sept) 2.30–5.00

Warwickshire
County Council

The Doll Museum
Easter–Sept and school holidays
Mon–Sat 10.00–5.00
Sun 2.00–5.00

Warwickshire's Museum
Telephone: (0926) 412500

Admission: Free
Location: At south-west entrance to Cannon Hill Park (opposite Pebble Mill Road)

BLAKESLEY HALL
Blakesley Road, Yardley, Birmingham   **Tel:** 021-783 2193
Timber-framed yeoman's farmhouse built 1590, furnished as a period house supporting displays on local history.
Open: Daily 2-5 from mid March to end October.
Admission: Free
Educational and group visits by arrangement.

JEWELLERY QUARTER DISCOVERY CENTRE
77-79 Vyse Street, Hockley, Birmingham B18 6HA   **Tel:** 021-554 3598
Birmingham's latest heritage attraction tells the story of the Jewellery Quarter and allows visitors the opportunity to explore a 'time capsule' jewellery factory left undisturbed after closure in 1981.
Open: Mon-Sat 10.00-17.00.
Admission: Charge.

THE LAPWORTH MUSEUM
(School of Earth Sciences)
The University of Birmingham, Edgebaston B15 2TT   **Tel:** 021-414 4173/6751
Collections of fossils, minerals, rocks and stone implements from UK and around the world.
Open: Mon to Fri 9-5, at other times by arrangement.

THE MUSEUM OF SCIENCE AND INDUSTRY
Newhall Street, Birmingham B3 1RZ   **Tel:** 021-235 1661
The museum preserves and exhibits a wide range of items of general industrial and scientific interest including steam engines, machine tools, small arms, transport, aircraft and scientific instruments. These are supplemented by temporary exhibitions.
Open: Mon to Sat 9.30-5; Sun 2-5. First and third Wed of each month engines on steam.
Closed Christmas Day, Boxing Day and New Year's Day
Admission: Free

THE PATRICK COLLECTION
(J.A. Patrick - (Chairman of the Trustees of 'The Patrick Foundation'))
Patrick House, 180 Lifford Lane, Birmingham

SAREHOLE MILL
Cole Bank Road, Hall Green, Birmingham   **Tel:** 021-777 6612
An 18th century water-powered corn mill which ceased production in 1919. The mill was also used for blade grinding and has now been restored to working order.
Open: Mid March-end October daily 2-5.
Admission: Free
Educational and group visits by arrangement.

WEOLEY CASTLE
Alwold Road, Birmingham   **Tel:** 021-427 4270
The ruins of a fortified manor house dating in its present form from the late 13th century. Excavations have revealed evidence of earlier occupation and the finds are exhibited in

a small museum on the site.
Open: Mid March to end October, Tues to Fri 2-5.
Admission: Free
Educational and group visits by arrangement.

BRIERLEY HILL

ROYAL BRIERLEY MUSEUM
(Royal Brierly Crystal)
North Street, Brierley Hill   **Tel:** (0384) 70161
A fine collection of early glass and crystal, all hand made. One large section includes only fine pieces created over 150 years at Royal Brierley Crystal Ltd (formerly known as Stevens and William Limited)
Admission: Free
Location: 20 minutes from junc. 2, M5.
Parties by arrangement. Plenty of car parking.

COVENTRY

HERBERT ART GALLERY AND MUSEUM
Jordan Well, Coventry   **Tel:** (0203) 832381
Archaeology, natural and local history, visual and decorative arts.
Open: Mon to Sat 10-5.30; Sun 2-5. *Closed* Good Friday and part of Christmas period.
Admission: Free

LUNT ROMAN FORT (RECONSTRUCTION)
Baginton, near Coventry   **Tel:** (0203) 832381/832433
Rampart, gateway, gyrus and granary displaying finds from the site and the life of the soldiers in the fort.
Open: May to Oct: Tues, Wed, Fri, Sat and Sun 12-6.
Admission: £1, Child/OAPs 50p

MIDLAND AIR MUSEUM
Coventry Airport, Baginton   **Tel:** (0203) 301 033
Over 20 aircraft from diminutive Gnat jet fighter to giant Vulcan bomber and Argosy freighter. Sir Frank Whittle Jet Heritage Centre - exhibition building contains display on work of Coventry born jet pioneer.
Open: Apr to Oct: Mon to Sat, 10.30-5; Sun 11-6; Winter: Sat and Sun only 11-5.
Admission: £2 child £1.50 OAP's £1.75 family ticket £7. Reductions for parties.
Refreshments: Available.
Free car parking. Suitable for disabled persons. Souvenir shop, picnic area.

MUSEUM OF BRITISH ROAD TRANSPORT
Coventry   **Tel:** (0203) 832425   **Fax:** (0203) 832465
Over 400 exhibits on display including cars, cycles, motor cycles and commercial vehicles.
Open: Daily 10-5.
Admission: £2, Child/OAPs £1. Pre-booked party concessions available.
For further information telephone the above number.

COVENTRY'S MUSEUMS–Where Past Meets Present

City of Coventry

HERBERT Art Gallery & Museum

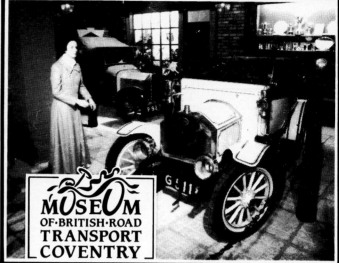

MUSEUM OF·BRITISH·ROAD TRANSPORT COVENTRY

WHITEFRIARS MUSEUM
London Road, Coventry   **Tel:** (0203) 832381 (for information)
The cloister and dormitory of a fourteenth century Carmelite Friary. Built in beautiful pink sandstone, now restored and a regular venue for sculpture exhibitions.
Open: Thurs to Sat 10-5
Admission: Free

DUDLEY

BLACK COUNTRY MUSEUM
Tipton Road, Dudley   **Tel:** 021-557 9643

THE BLACK COUNTRY MUSEUM

The open air Museum for the heart of industrial Britain which reflects the unique character of an area famous for its wide range of manufactured products. With the working replica of the world's first Steam Engine, the Chainmaker at his Forge, the Electric Tramcar, The Ironmonger in his shop, the Underground Coal Mine and the Publican in the Bottle & Glass, the Museum combines careful preservation with living interpretation.

Open every day from 10.00am to 5.00pm
March 1st to October 31st.

November to February, Open Wednesday to Sunday
10.00am to 4.00pm, Closed Christmas Day.

**TIPTON ROAD, DUDLEY, WEST MIDLANDS
Telephone: (021) 557 9643**

On a 26 acre site in the heart of the Industrial West Midlands buildings and machines from throughout the area create a living tribute to the skills and enterprise of the people of the Black Country. An electric tramcar carries visitors past a unique underground coal mining display 'Into the Thick' and a working replica of the world's first steam engine to the village where carefully reconstructed shops and houses cluster around a chapel and pub next to ironworks and manufactories. Nailmaking and chainmaking, glass cutting, baking, boatbuilding and ironworking are demonstrated regularly providing an educational and entertaining glimpse of times past.
Open: Daily 10-5, Mar 1 to Oct 31; Wed to Sun 10-4, Nov to Feb. *Closed* Christmas Day.

BROADFIELD HOUSE GLASS MUSEUM
(Dudley Metropolitan Borough)
Barnett Lane, Kingswinford, Dudley   **Tel:** (0384) 273011

BROADFIELD HOUSE GLASS MUSEUM

Internationally famous collection of 19th and 20th century Stourbridge Glass

Opening times ~
Tues - Fri, Sun & Bank Holiday Mondays 2 - 5 pm;
Sat 10 am - 1 pm, 2 - 5 pm

❖ **ADMISSION FREE**

'The Pearl Necklace' cameo glass plaque carved by George Woodall, Thomas Webb & Sons Stourbridge c. 1910

Broadfield House Glass Museum, Barnett Lane, Kingswinford, West Midlands DY6 9QA.
Telephone (0384) 273011

Internationally famous collection of 19th and 20th century glass concentrating on the spectacular cut, engraved, etched, cameo and rock crystal glass made in Stourbridge during the Victorian period. Glass making studio at the rear of the museum.
Open: Tues to Fri 2-5, Sat 10-1 and 2-5, Bank Holiday Mon 2-5.
Admission: Free
Museum shop selling modern glass and glass publications.

DUDLEY MUSEUM AND ART GALLERY
(Dudley Metropolitan Borough)
St. James's Road, Dudley   **Tel:** (0384) 453570
Fine Geological displays, especially of local Silurian (Wenlock Limestone) and Coal Measure fossils. The Brooke Robinson Collection of 17th, 18th and 19th century European paintings, Japanese netsuke and inro, enamels, furniture, Greek, Roman, Chinese and European ceramics. Permanent art collection (in store) and a wide variety of temporary exhibitions throughtout the year.
Open: Mon to Sat 10-5. *Closed Sun and Bank Hols.*

THE GARMAN-RYAN COLLECTION...

...formed by Lady Kathleen Epstein (nee Garman) with the assistance of American sculptress Sally Ryan, was donated to the town by Lady Epstein.

This important collection of 360 works of art contains one of the most representative samples of the work of Jacob Epstein. Alongside these are works by artists as diverse as Rembrandt, Constable, Van Gogh, Modigliani, Matisse and work from classical Greece and Rome, Africa, Asia, and the Pacifics.

Walsall Museum & Art Gallery, Lichfield Street, Walsall WS1 1TR. Telephone: 0922 653135

WALSALL

BIRCHILLS CANAL MUSEUM
(Walsall Metropolitan Borough Council)
Old Birchills **Tel:** (0922) 653116
Open: Tues,Wed 9.30-12.30; Thurs, Fri, Sat, Sun 1.00-4.00; March by appointment only tel above number.
See separate entries for Walsall Museum and Art Gallery, Willenhall Museum, Jerome K. Jerome Birthplace Museum, Walsall Leather Centre Museum and Garman Ryan Collection.

GARMAN RYAN COLLECTION
(Walsall Metropolitan Borough Council)
Lichfield Street, Walsall **Tel:** (0922) 653135
Amazing collection of works by major artists, including Matisse, Modigliani, Lucien Freud, Degus, Pissarro, Manet, Augustus John, Constable, Van Gogh and many more. At the core of the Collection are 43 works by Jacob Epstein, representing every aspect of his career. The Collection was formed by Lady Epstein (nee Kathleen Garman), with the assistance of the American sculptor Sally Ryan. Lady Epstein bequeathed the Collection to Walsall in 1974 as she was born and brought up in the area.
Open: Mon to Fri 10-6, Sat 10-4.45. *Closed* Sun and Bank Holidays.
See separate entries for Willenhall Museum, Walsall Leather Museum,Walsall Museum & Art Gallery, Jerome K. Jerome Birthplace Museum and Birchills Canal Museum.

JEROME K JEROME BIRTHPLACE MUSEUM
(Walsall Metropolitan Borough Council)
Belsize House, Bradford Street, Walsall
Open: Sat 10-1
See separate entries for Walsall Leather Centre Museum, Walsall Museum and Art Gallery, and Garman Ryan Collection, Willenhall Museum and Birchills Canal Museum.

MUSEUM AND ART GALLERY
(Walsall Metropolitan Borough Council)
Lichfield Street, Walsall **Tel:** (0922) 653135

Walsall Museum & Art Gallery

Home of the two Galleries detailed below – also the Garman-Ryan Collection.

Local History Gallery
Depicts Walsall's fascinating history and development. Special emphasis on people, including Sister Dora, Walsall's celebrated 19th cent. heroine.

Temporary Exhibition Gallery
Exciting programme of events contains something for everyone. Also regular arts-related activities including videos, children's workshops, dance and music.

ADMISSION FREE

Location: Walsall Museum and Art Gallery, Lichfield Street, Walsall. Tel: (0922) 653135
Opening Hours: Mon–Fri 10am–6.00pm
Saturday 10am–4.45pm
Closed Sundays & Bank Holidays.

JEROME K. JEROME BIRTHPLACE MUSEUM
'Three Men in a Boat' author's birthplace is now a museum containing much Jerome memorabilia.
Location: Belsize House, Bradford Street, Walsall. Tel: (0922) 653135.
Opening Hours: Mon–Fri 9.00am–5.00pm
Saturday 10.00am–1.00pm
Closed Sundays and Bank Holidays

WILLENHALL MUSEUM
Dedicated to the community and people of the Lock capital of Britain.
Location: Above Willenhall Library, Walsall Street, Willenhall. Tel: (0922) 653135.
Opening Hours: Mon., Tues., Thurs. & Fri. 9.30am–6.00pm.
Sat 9.30am–12.30pm and 2.00pm–4.30pm.
Closed Sundays and Bank Holidays

BIRCHILLS CANAL MUSEUM
Community museum set up by local enthusiasts in original Boatmen's Mission building of 1900.
Location: Old Birchills, Walsall. Tel: (0922) 653135.
Opening Hours:
Tues 9.30am–12.30pm
Weds, Thurs, Sat, Sun 12.00 noon–3.00pm.

Contains the History Gallery and a Temporary Exhibition Gallery, which houses an exciting and innovative programme of exhibitions and events.
Open: Mon to Fri 10-6, Sat 10-4.45. *Closed* Sun and Bank Holidays.
Access for disabled. Small shop. See separate entries for Willenhal Museum and Jerome K Jerome Birthplace Museum, Walsall Leather Centre Museum, Garman Ryan Collection and Birchills Canal Museum.

West Midlands

WALSALL LEATHER CENTRE MUSEUM
(Walsall Metropolitan Borough Council)
56-57 Wisemore, Walsall WS2 8EQ **Tel:** (0922) 721153

See Traditional English Leather Craftsmanship – in the making

See the history of English leatherworking unfold before your eyes at a working museum dedicated to this ancient craft industry.

Time-served craftsmen and women demonstrate their remarkable skills in working with one of nature's most versatile materials.

Fascinating displays, exhibitions and workshops are located in an original Victorian factory building close to the centre of Walsall – the leather capital of Britain.

And don't miss Tanners Coffee Shop or the Souvenir Shop.

Opening times:
Tues–Sat 10am–5pm
Sundays 12 noon–5pm
(Nov–March 10am–4pm)
Open Bank Holiday Mondays
ADMISSION FREE
56–57 Wisemore
Walsall WS2 8EQ
Tel: (0922) 721153

WALSALL LEATHER CENTRE MUSEUM

A Working Museum

Walsall Leisure for all

Industrial/Social History 'MUSEUM OF THE YEAR' 1990 – National Heritage

A fascinating working museum depicting all aspects of the leather industry and its history in Walsall, the leather capital of Britain. Housed in a Victorian factory with displays showing all the various stages of leather production from tanning to finishing, together with fine displays of historic and contemporary products, tools and artefacts. See demonstrations of the leather worker's craft in faithfully reproduced workshops.
Admission: Free
Refreshments: Care
Gift shop. Facilities for the disabled. Parking facilities opposite. Winner National Heritage Museum of the Year Awards 1990. Best Museum of Industrial or Social History. See separate entries for Walsall Museum and Art Gallery, Garman Ryan Collection, Willenhall Museum, Jerome K. Jerome Birthplace Museum and Birchills Canal Museum.

WILLENHALL MUSEUM
(Walsall Metropolitan Borough Council)
Walsall Street, Willenhall, Walsall
Open: Mon, Tues, Thurs, Fri 10.00-6. Sat 9.30-12.30 and 2-4.30.*Closed* Sundays Wednesdays and Bank Holidays
Location: Above Willenhall Library.
See separate entries for Walsall Leather Museum, Walsall Museum and Art Gallery and Garman Ryan Collection.

WARLEY

AVERY HISTORICAL MUSEUM
Smethwick, Warley B66 2LP **Tel:** 021-558 1112
A collection of weighing machines, weights, records relating to the history of weighing.
Open: During factory hours by appointment.

WEDNESBURY

ART AND GALLERY MUSEUM
(Sandwell Corporation)
Holyhead Road, Wednesbury

WEST BROMWICH

OAK HOUSE MUSEUM
(Sandwell Corporation)
Oak Road, West Bromwich

WILLENHALL

THE LOCK MUSEUM
(Lock Museum Trust)
54 New Road, Willenhall **Tel:** (0902) 634542
A museum of licks situated in a Victorian locksmith's house and workshop.
Open: All year except Christmas 10-5. Last admission 4 pm. Evening visits if booked in advance.
Admission: Adults 80p unwaged 50p.
Activity days for schools: hands on experience.

WOLVERHAMPTON

BANTOCK HOUSE
(Wolverhampton Borough Council)
Bantock Park, Bradmore, Wolverhampton

BILSTON MUSEUM AND ART GALLERY
(Wolverhampton Borough Council)
Mount Pleasant, Wolverhampton

CENTRAL ART GALLERY AND MUSEUM
(Wolverhampton Borough Council)
Lichfield Street, Wolverhampton

WILTSHIRE

AVEBURY

ALEXANDER KEILLER MUSEUM
(English Heritage)
Avebury **Tel:** (067 23) 250
Avebury Stone Circles are thought to have been constructed over 4,000 years ago. However, in more recent times Alexander Keiller investigated the area and his finds, including a prehistoric child called Charlie, can be found in the museum, one of the most important archaeological collections in Britain. Refurbished in 1991 with new displays.
Open: Apr 1 to Sept 30, daily 10-6. 1 October-March 31, daily 10-4. *Closed* 24-26 December and 1 January.
Admission: £1.20, Concessions 90p, Child 60p (1992 prices).

THE GREAT BARN MUSEUM OF WILTSHIRE RURAL LIFE
Avebury **Tel:** (067 23) 555
A large aisled and thatched barn of the 17th century, housing displays on the rural and agricultural history of Wiltshire. There are regular craft demonstrations each Sun in season.
Open: Mar to Nov: Daily 10-5.30. Open most weekends at other times.
Admission: Fee charged.

BLUNSDON

SWINDON & CRICKLADE RAILWAY
Blunsdon Station, Nr. Swindon, Blunsdon **Tel:** (0793) 771615
Operating steam and diesel locomotives. When completed 4 1/2 miles of M. & S.W.J.R. will be restored.
Open: For Steam and diesel locomotives viewing April to October. Open every weekend to view restoration work.
Refreshments: Restaurant available.
Shop and free parking, Bar-B-Q and picnic area.

CHIPPENHAM

YELDE HALL MUSEUM
Market Place, Chippenham

CORSHAM

BATH STONE QUARRY MUSEUM
Bradford Road, Corsham **Tel:** (0249) 716288

DEVIZES

DEVIZES MUSEUM
(Wiltshire Archaeological and History Society)
41 Long Street, Devizes SN10 1NS **Tel:** (0380) 727369
Prehistoric collections of international standing. Weapons, exotic ornaments and personal finery. Henge Monument Room, galleries for Roman, Saxon and Medieval periods. Art gallery; natural history displays. Local history gallery. New Bronze Age gallery. Library for study of local history.
Open: All year, Mon to Sat 10-5 (excluding public holidays).
Admission: £1.75, Students, OAPs £1.25, Child 40p. Special arrangements for pre-arranged parties.
Shop.

KENNET AND AVON CANAL
Canal Centre, Couch Lane, Devizes **Tel:** (0380) 721279/729489
The exhibition tells of the building, deterioration and restoration of the canal now linking London and Bristol by water.

LACOCK

FOX TALBOT MUSEUM
(The National Trust)
Lacock   **Tel:** (0249) 730459
Museum of the history of photography with changing exhibitions.

LACKHAM GARDENS AND MUSEUM
Lacock   **Tel:** (0249) 443111
Agricultural implements and tools housed in reconstructed farm buildings.
Open: Apr-Oct 11-5.

MALMESBURY

ATHELSTAN MUSEUM
Malmesbury   **Tel:** (0666) 822143
Articles concerned with the town and locality - Malmesbury penny (William II) and other coins, Thomas Girtin drawing of Malmesbury Cross, Malmesbury lace making, portraits and photographs, household articles and an 18th century fire engine.
Admission: Free

MERE

MERE CHURCH MUSEUM
The Vicarage, Angel Lane, Mere

MERE MUSEUM
Barton Lane,, Mere

POTTERNE

FIRE DEFENCE COLLECTION
Manor House, Potterne

PURTON

PURTON MUSEUM
Purton Library, High Street, Purton

SALISBURY

SALISBURY AND SOUTH WILTSHIRE MUSEUM
The King's House, 65 The Close, Salisbury   **Tel:** (0722) 332151

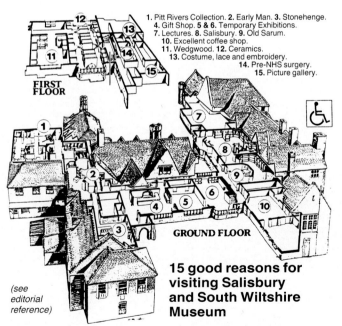

1. Pitt Rivers Collection. **2.** Early Man. **3.** Stonehenge. **4.** Gift Shop. **5 & 6.** Temporary Exhibitions. **7.** Lectures. **8.** Salisbury. **9.** Old Sarum. **10.** Excellent coffee shop. **11.** Wedgwood. **12.** Ceramics. **13.** Costume, lace and embroidery. **14.** Pre-NHS surgery. **15.** Picture gallery.

FIRST FLOOR

GROUND FLOOR

(see editorial reference)

15 good reasons for visiting Salisbury and South Wiltshire Museum

Beautifully designed galleries include the only one in the country devoted to Stonehenge, the story of the earliest settlers in South Wiltshire from the Stone Age to the Saxons, the history of Old Sarum and Salisbury, the renowned Pitt Rivers Collection, ceramics, Wedgwood, pre-NHS surgery and pictures. Temporary exhibitions throughout the year. The newest gallery 'Stitches in Time' displays the historical costume, lace and embroidery of Wiltshire. **Winner of five awards including Museum of the Year Special Judges Award**.
Open: All year Mon to Sat 10-5, Suns in July, Aug and Salisbury Festival 2-5. *Closed* Christmas
Admission: £2.25, Child 50p, Concessions £1.50. Ticket gives unlimited visits throughout the calendar year
Location: Located in the Cathedral Close opposite the west front. Station: Salisbury
Refreshments: Coffee Shop
Gift Shop

SWINDON

GREAT WESTERN RAILWAY MUSEUM
(Thamesdown Borough Council)
Faringdon Road, Swindon   **Tel:** (0793) 526161. Ext. 3189.
Historic G.W.R. locomotives, wide range of name-plates, models, illustrations, posters, tickets etc.
Open: Mon to Sat 10-5; Sun 2-5.
Admission: £1.80, Child and OAPs 90p (admits also to Railway Village Museum). Party rates

LYDIARD HOUSE
Lydiard Tregoze, Swindon   **Tel:** (0793) 770401
18th Century house, former home of St John family, set in parkland. Fine furniture, portrait collections, original wallpaper and fascinating painted window. Adjacent Parish Church contains exceptional monuments to the St John Family.
Open: Mon-Sat 10-1, 2-5.30. Sun 2-5.30. Early Closing Nov-Feb 4.
Admission: £1.40, Child/OAPs 70p. Party rates.

MUSEUM AND ART GALLERY
(Thamesdown Borough Council)
Bath Road, Swindon   **Tel:** (0793) 526161, Ext. 3188
Archaeology, geology and social history of Swindon and N.E. Wiltshire, the Manners collection of pot lids and ware. Permanent 20th century British art and ceramic collection.
Open: Mon to Sat 10-5.30; Sun 2-5.00.
Admission: Free

RAILWAY VILLAGE MUSEUM
(Thamesdown Borough Council)
34 Faringdon Road, Swindon   **Tel:** (0793) 526161, Ext. 3189
A foreman's house in the original G.W.R. Village refurbished as it was at the turn of the century.
Open: Mon to Sat 10-1, 2-5; Sun 2-5.
Admission: 75p, Concessions 35p.

RICHARD JEFFERIES MUSEUM
(Thanesdown Borough Council)
Coate, Swindon   **Tel:** (0793) 526161, Ext. 4526
Reconstruction of Jefferies' study and cheese room, with personal items, manuscripts, first editions, natural history displays and historical photographs relating to Richard Jefferies and Alfred Williams.
Open: Restricted. Telephone to confirm.
Admission: Free

TROWBRIDGE

THE TROWBRIDGE MUSEUM
(Trowbridge Town Council)
The Shires, Court Street, Trowbridge   **Tel:** (0225) 751339
A new museum opened in July 1990. Displays on the West of England woollen industry with working textile machinery and various room settings, including a weaver's cottage, shearing workshop and draper's shop. Other displays trace the history of the town and its surroundings up to the present day. Also a temporary exhibition programme; schools/meeting room.
Open: Tues to Fri 12-4, Sat 10-5, all day by appointment
Full disabled access. Shop

WROUGHTON

SCIENCE MUSEUM
Wroughton Airfield, Wroughton   **Tel:** (0793) 814466 or 071-938 8000
Open: Selected days throughout the summer period. For further details telephone as above.

NORTH YORKSHIRE

ALDBOROUGH

THE ALDBOROUGH ROMAN MUSEUM
(English Heritage)
Aldborough   **Tel:** (0423) 322768
The museum contains Roman finds, including pottery, glass, metalwork and coins from the Roman town.
Open: Apr 1 to Sept 30, daily 10-6.
Admission: £1.10, Concessions 85p, Child 55p (1992 prices)

AYSGARTH

THE YORKSHIRE MUSEUM OF CARRIAGES & HORSE DRAWN VEHICLES
Yore Mill, By Aysgarth Falls, Aysgarth

CASTLE HOWARD

CASTLE HOWARD COSTUME GALLERIES
Castle Howard, York   **Tel:** (065 384) 333

EMBSAY STATION

EMBSAY STEAM RAILWAY
(Yorkshire Dales Railway Museum Trust)
Near Skipton, Embsay Station

HARROGATE

HARLOW CARR MUSEUM OF GARDENING
(Northern Horticultural Society)
Crag Lane, Harrogate HG3 1QB   **Tel:** (0423) 565418
Small museum of gardening implements and history, set within 68 acres of beautiful gardens and woodland.
Open: Daily 9.30-4.30 except Christmas Day and New Year's Day.
Admission: Fee charge to gardens includes museum.
Refreshments: Restaurant
Plant sales, shop

THE MERCER GALLERY
(Harrogate District Council)
Swan Road, Harrogate   **Tel:** (0423) 503340
Details of exhibitions on request.

NIDDERDALE MUSEUM
Council Offices, King Street, Pateley Bridge, Harrogate   **Tel:** (0423) 711225

ROYAL PUMP ROOM MUSEUM
(Harrogate District Council)
Opposite Valley Gardens, Harrogate   **Tel:** (0423) 503340
The museum of spa history now restored to its former splendour.
Location: Opposite Valley Gardens

HAWES

DALES COUNTRYSIDE MUSEUM
(North Yorkshire County Council)
Station Yard, Hawes   **Tel:** (096 97) 494

HELMSLEY

RIEVAULX TERRACE AND TEMPLES
(The National Trust)
Helmsley
Examples of English landscape design in the 18th century with permanent exhibition of Landscape Design; photographs from the Victorian family album of the Duncombes, owners of the Terrace for two centuries.
Open: Apr 1 to Nov 1: Daily 10.30-6 or dusk if earlier (last admission 5.00). Ionic Temple closed 1-2.
Admission: £2.10, Child 90p; Adult parties £1.70, Child 80p. NT members free.
Free car and coach park. Note: Electric 'Runaround' for disabled visitors.

HUTTON-LE-HOLE

RYEDALE FOLK MUSEUM
(Crosland Foundation)
Hutton-Le-Hole   **Tel:** (075 15) 367

HUTTON-LE-HOLE, YORK Y06 6UA

The museum has rescued and re-erected interesting buildings from the area on its attractive two-and-a-half acre site set behind the 18th century farm building, which forms the entrance, fronting on to the village green. You can walk through a medieval long-house complete with a witch-post, an Elizabethan manor house or a furnished 18th/19th century cottage, all with traditional thatched roofs. The latest building is the oldest daylight photographic studio in the U.K. The displays in these, and seven other buildings, illustrate the origins, superstitions, everyday tasks and crafts of the people of Ryedale from prehistoric to recent times. Open daily end of March to beginning of November, 10.00am to 5.30pm last admission 4.30pm. Admission charge. For party bookings: Tel: (075 15) 367.

Open air museum with interesting collection of rescued buildings rebuilt on an attractive 2 1/2 acre site. Includes a medieval long-house with a witch-post and a 16th century manor house, both cruck-framed and thatched; an 18th/19th century furnished cottage; an Elizabethan glass furnace; workshops with extensive collections of tools of many 19th century crafts. The oldest complete daylight photographic studio in the UK. Varied collections illustrating the folk life of Ryedale.
Admission: Charge

KNARESBOROUGH

KNARESBOROUGH CASTLE AND OLD COURTHOUSE MUSEUM
(Harrogate District Council)
Castle Grounds, Knaresborough   **Tel:** (0423) 503340
Local history

MALTON

EDEN CAMP - MODERN HISTORY THEME MUSEUM
Eden Camp, Malton   **Tel:** (0653) 697777
A visit to our unique museum at Eden Camp will transort you back to Wartime Britain. This is no ordinary museum - it is a series of reconstructed scenes, telling the story of civilian life during World War II.
Open: Daily Feb 14 to Dec 23, 10-5.
'Yorkshire & Humberside visitor attraction of The Year 1992'

MALTON MUSEUM
Town Hall, Market Place, Malton   **Tel:** (0653) 695136 or 692610

PICKERING

BECK ISLE MUSEUM OF RURAL LIFE
Pickering   **Tel:** (0751) 73653
Regency residence of William Marshall, a noted agriculturist of the late 18th and early 19th centuries. Situated in the centre of an historic town, the many rooms house a considerable collection illustrating the work, social life and customs of the rural community during the past 200 years. Of educational interest to all ages.
Open: 28 March-Oct 31: Daily to Oct 31: 10-5.
Admission: Fee charged.
Parties by arrangement. Phone (0751) 73548

REETH

SWALEDALE FOLK MUSEUM
Reeth, near Richmond   **Tel:** (0748) 84517
Depicts how leadmining and sheep farming shaped life in this remote and beautiful Dale.

RICHMOND

GEORGIAN THEATRE ROYAL
Victoria Road, Richmond   **Tel:** (0748) 823710
Built in 1788. The country's oldest theatre in original form; also Theatre Museum.
Open: Easter Sat to Oct 31: Mon to Sat 11-4.45; Sun 2.30-4.45.
Admission: Fee charged
Parties all year round on application to the Manager.

THE GREEN HOWARDS MUSEUM
Trinity Church Square, Richmond   **Tel:** (0748) 822133
Uniforms, medals, campaign relics, contemporary MSS, pictures and prints, headdress, buttons, badges and embellishments from 17th century onwards.
Open: Apr to Oct: Weekdays 9.30-4.30; Sun 2-4.30. Nov, Feb and Mar: Weekdays 10-4.30. *Closed* Sat and Sun Feb, Sun Mar and Nov and throughout Dec and Jan.

THE RICHMONDSHIRE MUSEUM
(The Richmondshire Museum Trust)
Ryders Wynd, Richmond   **Tel:** (0748) 825611
The history of Richmond. Lead mining, local crafts, agriculture, cruck house, model of Richmond railway complex, costume and needlecraft, toys, archaeology. Vet's surgery set from Herriot TV series.
Open: Daily Good Friday to autumn half-term, 11-5.
Admission: 70p, Child/Students/OAPs 50p. Family groups £2.
Parties by appointment.

RIPON

FOUNTAINS ABBEY AND STUDLEY ROYAL
(The National Trust)
Ripon
Awarded World Heritage status, the largest monastic ruin in Britain, founded by Cistercian monks in 1132. Landscape garden laid out 1720-40 with large, formal water garden and temples; deer park. St. Mary's Church built by William Burges 1871-8. A small museum; exhibition in Fountains Hall.
Open: Deer Park open all year during daylight hours, admission free. Fountains Hall: Apr-Sept 11-6, Oct-Mar 11-4pm, admission free. Abbey and Gardens open daily except 24 and 25 Dec & Fridays in Jan, Nov & Dec. Jan-Mar, Oct-Dec 10-5 or dusk if earlier.
Admission: Jan-Mar Adult £3.00, child £1.50, family £7.50. Group min 15 £2.50, child £1.30. April-Oct £3.80, child £1.90, family £9.00. Group min 15 £3.40, child £1.70. Nov-Dec £3.30, child £1.60, family £8.00. Group min 15 £2.80, child £1.40. Parking: Free at Visitor Centre Car Park (Studley park £1.70)
Refreshments: Light lunches, sandwiches, soup & cakes etc. Visitor Centre Restaurant: Daily Jan-March Oct-Dec 10-5, April-Sept 10-6. Studley Royal Tearoom Weekends Jan-March & Oct-Dec 10-5, Daily April-Sept 10-6.

RIPON MUSEUM AND POLICE MUSEUM
St. Marygate, Ripon   **Tel:** (0765) 690799
A former Victorian prison with cells converted to museum use. the displays deal with crime, punishment, imprisonment and law enforcement over recent centuries.
Open: Easter to Oct: weekdays (except July & Aug) 1-5; July, Aug; 11-5; Sun 1-5.
Parties by arrangement at amy time. Car park opposite.

SCARBOROUGH

ROTUNDA MUSEUM
(Scarborough Council)
Vernon Road, Scarborough   **Tel:** (0723) 374839
Fine example of Georgian purpose-built museum opened 1829. The Upper Galleries are lined with original display cabinets and the 'Moveable Stage', as seen on television's 'Cabinet of Curiosities'. Exhibitions illustrate life and activities of people living in the area from the early prehistoric to the development of the seaside spa resort.
Books and cards for sale.

SCARBOROUGH ART GALLERY
(Scarborough Borough Council)
The Crescent, Scarborough   **Tel:** (0723) 374753
Victorian villa, built 1835 in Italianate style, houses the Laughton Collection, fine works of art from leading artists from 17th to 20th centuries and an extensive local collection of watercolours by Scarborough artists. Monthly exhibitions show a varied range of contemporary and art historical works, crafts, ceramice, sculpture and photography.
Refreshments: New coffee room.
Books, cards and prints for sale.

WOOD END MUSEUM
(Scarborough Borough Council)
The Crescent, Scarborough   **Tel:** (0723) 367326
Built 1835 and former home of the Sitwells, contains an almost complete collection of their published works, together with portraits and paintings connected with their writings, in the restored West Wing. A double-stored Victorian conservatory, housing tropical plants and aquarium, links with the Main Building where there are displays on local geology and natural history.
Open: Tues to Sat 10-1, 2-5; Sun (Spring Bank Hol to end Sept) 2-5. *Closed Mondays but open Bank Holiday Mondays.*

SKIPTON

CRAVEN MUSEUM
Town Hall, High Street, Skipton   **Tel:** (0756) 794079
Craven antiques, social history, natural history, geology specimens.
Open: Apr to Sept: Mon, Wed, Thurs and Fri 11-5; Sat 10-12, 1.00-5.00; Sun 2.00
Admission: Free

THIRSK

THIRSK MUSEUM
14-16 Kirkgate, Thirsk YO7 1PQ   **Tel:** (0845) 522755
Folk museum, local history. See infamous 'death chair'. Birthplace of Thomas Lord, founder of Lord's Cricket Ground.
Open: Daily. Easter to end of Oct.
Admission: Fee charged
Free car parking nearby

SCARBOROUGH MUSEUMS & ART GALLERY

SCARBOROUGH ART GALLERY
'Scarborough Spa at night'
F. Sydney Muschamp. 1879

ROTUNDA MUSEUM
Interior view of original Georgian Circular Gallery

WOOD END, MUSEUM OF NATURAL HISTORY
Former home of the literary Sitwell family

WHITBY

WHITBY MUSEUM
(Whitby Literary and Philosophical Society)
 Pannett Park, Whitby   **Tel:** (0947) 602908

WHITBY MUSEUM

● A treasure trove of Whitby's past

● From giant fossils to model ships, from Maori war-clubs to intricately carved Whitby jet, Whitby Museum is full of fascinating things.

● Sections on Captain Cook and William Scoresby Jr, renowned Arctic scientist, whaling captain and clergyman, and relics of the whaling industry.

Pannett Park, Whitby, North Yorkshire YO21 1RE

Nationally-important collections of fossils, Whitby jet jewellery, model ships. Fine ethnographic collection. Local archaeology, geology, natural history. Bygones, costumes, dolls and toys.
Open: May to Sept: Weekdays 9.30-5.30, Sun 2-5. Oct to Apr: Mon, Tues 10.30-1, Wed to Sat 10.30-4, Sun 2-4.
Admission: Fee charged

YORK

THE ARC
 Archaeological Resource Centre, St. Saviourgate, York   **Tel:** (0904) 654324

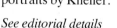
Archaeological Resource Centre, St. Saviourgate, York. Telephone (0904) 654324
Student Concessionary Price

The ARC is 'state of the art' for visitor involvement in archaeology. Whether handling actual artefacts such as pottery sherds, bone, sieved soil samples or experimenting with ancient craft technologies in stitching a Roman shoe, or weaving on a Viking loom, visitors will find themselves in touch with the past. Excavation can be explored with the use of interactive videos, and computers can be used, just as the modern archaeologist does, to record and process details. Visitors can also watch archaeologists at work examining objects and entering data. The ARC dispels the 'backroom' image of archaeological research in an innovative and absorbing way.

Open: Mon to Fri 10-5, Sat and Sun 1-5. *Closed* Good Friday, 18th Dec - 1st Jan inclusive.
Admission: Fee charged.
National Heritage Museum of the Year Awards - voted 'Best Museum of Archaeological and Historical Interest', sponsored by BBC.

THE BAR CONVENT MUSEUM
 17 Blossom Street, York YO2 2AH   **Tel:** (0904) 643238
Museum and Education Centre based in the oldest active convent in the country. The Museum, based in an impressive Georgian town house, features a display telling the story of the Sisters against the background of the spread of Christianity in the North of England. The building houses an elegant neo-classical Chapel, hidden from the outside world. A lively programme of exhibitions in the exhibition gallery. Education programme includes courses and workshops in History of Art and Design, Calligraphy, and Embroidery.
Open: Feb to Dec: Tues to Sat 10-5
Refreshments: Cafe

BENINGBROUGH HALL
(The National Trust)
 Near Shipton, York

THE NATIONAL TRUST
BENINGBROUGH HALL
near York

Beautifully restored early Georgian country house of grand proportions with exceptionally fine wood carving and plasterwork. The rooms are hung with over 100 portraits on loan from the National Portrait Gallery. The Dining Room displays some of the famous Kit-cat Club portraits by Kneller.

See editorial details

A beautifully restored early Georgian country house built originally for John Bourchier. In a tour of the principal rooms, stable and grounds the visitor will experience much of the atmosphere and life of the 18th century. Paintings of famous people of the period 1688-1760 are on permanent loan from the National Portrait Gallery. Exhibitions.
Open: Apr 3 to Sept 30: Mon, Tues, Wed, Sat, Sun & Good Friday. Also Fridays in July & August. House 11-5pm (last adm 4.30). Grounds, shop & restaurant 11-5.30pm (last adm 5.00pm)
Admission: House, Garden & Exhibitions: £4.40, Child £2.20, Family £11. Parties £3.40, Child party £1.70. Garden & Exhibition: £2.80, Child £1.40, Family £7.00. (Family ticket - 2 adults, 2 children) *Closed in October for essential building work*
Location: 2m W of Shipton, 8m NW of York off A19
Refreshments: Restaurant available.
Shop. Garden. Victorian laundry and potting shed. Picnic area. Wilderness play area.

FAIRFAX HOUSE
(York Civic Trust)
Castlegate, York YO1 1RN

An 18th century house designed by John Carr of York and described as a classic architectural masterpiece of its age. Certainly one of the finest townhouses in England and saved from near collapse by the York Civic Trust who restored it to its former glory during 1982/84. In addition to the superbly decorated plasterwork, wood and wrought iron, the house is now home for an outstanding collection of 18th century Furniture and Clocks, formed by the late Noel Terry. Described by Christie's as one of the finest private collections of this century, it enhances and complements the house and helps to create a very special 'lived in' feeling. The gift of the entire collection by Noel Terry's Trustees to the Civic trust has enabled it to fill the house with the appropriate pieces of the period and has provided the basis for what can now be considered a fully furnished Georgian Townhouse. Annual exhibitions on aspects of 18th century life.
Open: Mar 1 to Dec 31: Mon to Thurs and Sat 11-5; Sun 1.30-5 (last adm 4.30) *Closed Fri.*
Admission: £3.00, Child £1.50, OAP £2.50 Parties, Adult (prebooked 15 or more) £2.50 Child £1.00.
Public car park within 50 yards. Suitable for disabled persons only with assistance (by telephoning beforehand staff can be available to help). A small gift shop offers selected antiques, publications and gifts. Opening times are the same as the house.

IMPRESSIONS GALLERY
(Paul Wombell - Director)
29 Castlegate, York   **Tel:** (0904) 654724
Impressions was the first photographic gallery to open outside London, in 1972. There are three gallery areas showing a wide range of photographic exhibitions, both contemporary and historical, also darkroom with courses and workshops.
Open: Mon to Sat 10.30-5.30.
Admission: Free

Location: Entrance on York Castlewalk.
Refreshments: Cafe
The gallery has an exciting photographic bookshop selling a variety of posters and postcards. Unsuitable for disabled persons.

JORVIK VIKING CENTRE
(York Archaeological Trust)
Coppergate, York   **Tel:** (0904) 643211

Uncovered by archaeologists Jorvik is the Viking city untouched since the Vikings lived in York a thousand years ago. Cooking-ware, shoes, fragments of clothing. A market, busy wharf, houses re-created in accurate detail. The Viking Dig, reconstructed where it took place, with the preserved 10th century buildings replaced where they were found.
Open: Apr to Oct: Daily 9-7. Nov to Mar: Daily 9-5.
Admission: Fee charged.

MUSEUM OF AUTOMATA
9 Tower Street, York YO1 1SA   **Tel:** (0904) 655550
The Museum of Automata opened on in 1990. The story of automata is traced from the simple articulated figurines of ancient civilisations through to modern robotics. A video wall display at the start of the visit introduces the subject and provides a potted history. As automata need to be seen in action to be fully appreciated, computer graphics and video aids have been used to bring to life a selection of those exhibits which are too old or fragile to be put in motion regularly. The core of the museum collection is 19th century French. The contemporary gallery contains a growing, changing collection that can be activated by visitors.
Open: 7 days a week all year round 9.30-5.30.
Admission: Fee charged
Location: Just across the road from Clifford's Tower in Tower Street.

Party bookings on (0904) 628070. Car Park adjacent. Suitable for the disabled (wheelchair available). Parties may disembark immediately outside the museum. Map for coach parking available. Toilets (including those for the disabled) inside the museum.

NATIONAL RAILWAY MUSEUM
(Science Museum)
    Leeman Road, York **Tel:** (0904) 621261
At the new National Railway Museum you will see nearly two hundred years' history of the technical and social changes that were brought about by the British invention of railways and their immense contribution to civilisation.
Open: Mon to Sat 10-6; Sun 11-6, (last adm 5). *Closed* 24,25,26 December and 1 January.
Refreshments: Restaurant
Education service, reference library, conference facilities, corporate hire. Museum shop, car park, free coach parking for pre-booked parties. Facilities for the disabled.

THE YORKSHIRE MUSEUM
(North Yorkshire County Council)
    Museum Gardens, York
Contains extensive Roman, Anglo-Saxon and Viking collections, Yorkshire pottery and important medieval architectural sculptures.

TREASURER'S HOUSE
(The National Trust)
    York
The home of the Treasurer of York Minster from the time of William the Conqueror until the reign of Henry VIII. Most of the present house dates from the early 17th century. Exhibitions and video show illustrates some of the personalities and traditions associated with Treasurer's House.
Open: Apr 1-Oct 31 Daily 10.30-5 (last adm 4.30)
Admission: £2.80, Child £1.40, Adult party £2.40, Child party £1.20. (no reduction for Sun or Bank Hols). NT members free.
Location: Behind York Minster
Refreshments: Tearoom and Shop open as house.

YORK CASTLE MUSEUM
(York City Council)
    Eye of York, York YO1 1RY **Tel:** (0904) 653611
An outstanding social history museum based on the Kirk collection of bygones and including period rooms, a cobbled street, domestic and agricultural equipment, costumes, toys, arms and armour, an Edwardian street park and a water-driven corn mill. New special exhibition gallery: 'The Music Show' until Dec 1992.
Open: Apr to Oct: Mon to Sat 9.30-last admission 5.30; Sun 10-last admission 5.30; Nov to Mar: Mon to Sat (9.30-last admission 4; Sun 10-last admission 4. Last admission one hour before closing.
Admission: Adults £3.50, Child/OAPs/Students/Unemployed £2.50. Party rate:10 or more £3.00 adult, £2.00 Child/OAPs/Students/Unemployed
Refreshments: Cafe
Shop

YORK CITY ART GALLERY
(York City Council)
    Exhibition Square, York **Tel:** (0904) 623839

YORK CITY ART GALLERY
Exhibition Square

Strigel   *Sleeping Soldier*

A treasure-house of European and British paintings

Outstanding collections of European and British paintings including the Lycett Green collection of Old Masters and works by York artists, notably William Etty; water-colours, drawings and prints mostly devoted to the topography of York; unrivalled

collection of pioneer studio pottery. Lively and varied programme of changing exhibitions and events.
Open: Mon to Sat 10-5, Sun 2.30-5 (last adm 4.30). *Closed* Dec 25,26, Jan 1 and Good Friday.
Admission: Free
Gallery News Leaflet available on request. Gallery shop. Facilities for the disabled.

YORK STORY
(York City Council)
    The Heritage Centre, Castlegate, York **Tel:** (0904) 628632
Britain's finest Heritage Centre, set up in 1975 to interpret the social and architectural history of the City of York. The exhibitions, which include many notable pieces by modern artists and craftsmen, is equipped with a new audio-visual presentation which shows the history of York, highlighting the surviving buildings and objects. Models and dioramas.
Open: Mon to Sat 10-5; Sun 1-5.
Admission: £1.30, Child OAPs, Students and Unemployed 80p (prices apply to Mar 31 1992)
Shop

YORKSHIRE MUSEUM OF FARMING
(Yorkshire Museum of Farming Ltd)
    Murton, York **Tel:** (0904) 489966
Set in 8 acres of country park.
Location: 3 miles from York.

SOUTH YORKSHIRE

BARNSLEY

CANNON HALL MUSEUM
(Barnsley Metropolitan Council)
    Cawthorne, Barnsley S75 4AT **Tel:** (0226) 790270
Cannon Hall is a late 17th century house remodelled by John Carr of York in the 1760s. The museum has a fine collection of furniture, paintings, glassware and pottery, some of which is displayed in period rooms. It also houses the Regimental Museum of the 13th/18th Royal Hussars (Queen Mary's Own). The museum is situated in Cannon Hall Country Park, which, with its landscaped grounds, provides an ideal setting for a family day out.
Open: Tues, Wed, Thurs, Fri, Sat 10.30-5; Sun 2.30-5. *Closed* Mon

CANNON HALL

COOPER GALLERY

COOPER GALLERY
(Barnsley Metropolitan Borough Council)
    Church Street, Barnsley SA70 2AH **Tel:** (0226) 242905
The Cooper Gallery presents a continuous programme of temporary exhibitions and related activities, focusing on contemporary art and craft and including thematic exhibitions from the permanent collection. The Cooper Gallery Collections include 17th Century Dutch, 18th and 19th Century French and European paintings and a fine collection of English drawings and watercolours from the Michael Sadler Bequest. Specific examples from the permanent collection may be viewed by prior appointment with the Curator.
Open: Tues 1-5.30; Wed to Sat 10-5.30 *Closed* Sun and Mon

VICTORIA JUBILEE MUSEUM
Cawthorne, Barnsley   **Tel:** (0226) 791273
Natural history, geology and objects of local interest.

WORSBROUGH MILL MUSEUM
(Barnsley Metropolitan Borough Council)
Worsbrough Bridge, Barnsley S70 5LJ   **Tel:** (0266) 203961
17th and 19th century corn mills restored to working condition. Daily demonstrations of water-powered machinery. Programme of milling days and craft weekends. Various stoneground flours produced for sale. Set in 200 acre country park. Including Open Farm.
Open: Wed to Sun 9-5.00. *Closed* Mon and Tues

DONCASTER

DONCASTER MUSEUM AND ART GALLERY
(Doncaster Metropolitan Borough Council)
Chequer Road, Doncaster DN1 2AE   **Tel:** (0302) 734293
Natural history, prehistoric, Roman and medieval archaeology and local history, militaria, costume, paintings, sculpture, silver, ceramics and glass. The Regimental Collection of the King's Own Yorkshire Light Infantry.
Open: Mon to Sat 10-5; Sun 2-5.

MUSEUM OF SOUTH YORKSHIRE LIFE
(Doncaster Metropolitan Borough Council)
Cusworth Park, Doncaster DN5 7TU   **Tel:** (0302) 782342
Social history collections, agriculture, industry, costume and toys.
Open: Mon to Sat 11-5; Sun 1-5. *Closes* at 4 in winter.

DONCASTER METROPOLITAN BOROUGH
MUSEUMS AND ARTS SERVICE

MUSEUM AND ART GALLERY
CHEQUER ROAD

Established 1908, moved to the present building in 1964. Regional collections of Archaeology, Natural History, Geology and Art. Frequent temporary Exhibitions. Admission Free.

MUSEUM OF SOUTH YORKSHIRE LIFE
CUSWORTH HALL

The 18th Century mansion of the Wrightson family used to depict everyday life of local people during the past two centuries. Programme of temporary exhibitions and family activities. Admission Free.

South Yorkshire

ROTHERHAM

ART GALLERY
(Rotherham Metropolitan Borough Council)
   Brian O'Malley Library and Arts Centre, Walker Place, Rotherham   **Tel:** (0709) 382121, Ext. 3628/3635
Continuous programme of temporary exhibitions including, at times, 19th and 20th century paintings from the museum collections.
Open: Tues to Sat 10-5. *Closed* Sun, Mon and Bank Hols.

CLIFTON PARK MUSEUM
(Rotherham Metrepolitan Borough Council)
   Clifton Park, Rotherham   **Tel:** (0709) 382121, Ext. 3628 or 3635

CLIFTON PARK MUSEUM
ROTHERHAM, SOUTH YORKSHIRE

The museum is housed in a late 18th century mansion, reputedly by John Carr of York. It contains 18th century furnished rooms, family portraits, period kitchen, displays of Victoriana, local history, local Roman antiquities, glass and glassmaking. Church silver, 19th and 20th century paintings, British ceramics including Rockingham, local geology and natural history. There are periodic temporary exhibitions.

Open: Apr to Sept: Weekdays (excluding Fri) 10-5; Sun 2.30-5. Oct to Mar: Weekdays (excluding Fri) 10-5; Sun 2.30-4.30.
Activities for Schools and other Educational Groups.

THE YORK AND LANCASTER REGIMENT MUSEUM
   Brian O'Malley Library and Arts Centre, Walker Place, Rotherham   **Tel:** (0709) 382121, Ext. 3625
Uniforms, medals (including V.C.'s), campaign relics and insignia covering the history of the Regiment and its forebears, the 65th, and 84th. Foot, from 1758 to 1968.
Open: For times see Art Gallery entry.
Admission: Free

SHEFFIELD

ABBEYDALE HAMLET
(Sheffield Metropolitan District Council)
   Abbeydale Road South, Sheffield   **Tel:** (0742) 367731

BISHOPS' HOUSE
(Sheffield Metropolitan District Council)
   Meersbrooke Park, Sheffield   **Tel:** (0742) 557701

GRAVES ART GALLERY
(Sheffield Metropolitan District Council)
   Surrey Street, Sheffield   **Tel:** (0702) 735158

KELHAM ISLAND INDUSTRIAL MUSEUM
(Sheffield Metropolitan District Council)
   Alma Street, Sheffield S3 8RY   **Tel:** (0742) 722106

MAPPIN ART GALLERY
(Sheffield Metropolitan District Council)
   Weston Park, Sheffield   **Tel:** (0702) 726281

RUSKIN GALLERY
(Sheffield Metropolitan District Council)
   101 Norfolk Street, Sheffield S1 2JE   **Tel:** (0742) 735299

SHEFFIELD CITY MUSEUM
(Sheffield Metropolitan District Council)
   Weston Park, Sheffield   **Tel:** (0742) 768588

SHEPHERD WHEEL
(Sheffield Metropolitan District Council)
   Whiteley Wood, Hangingwater Road, Sheffield   **Tel:** (0742) 367731

WEST YORKSHIRE

BATLEY

BAGSHAW MUSEUM
(Kirklees Metrolitan Council)
   Wilton Park, Batley   **Tel:** (0924) 472514
Exotic Victorian building housing local collections, natural history, ethnography, egyptology and Oriental arts.

BATLEY ART GALLERY
(Kirklees Metropolitan Council)
   Market Place, Batley   **Tel:** (0924) 473141
Temporary exhibitions

YORKSHIRE FIRE MUSEUM
   Bradford Road, Batley

BIRSTALL

OAKWELL HALL
(Kirklees Metropolitan Council)
   Nutter Lane, Birstall   **Tel:** (0924) 474926
16th century working manor house furnished as the Batt house of the 1690's. Regular events and activities. Set in extensive Country Park. Bronte connections.

BRADFORD

BOLLING HALL
(Bradford Metropolitan Council)
   Bowling Hall Road, Bradford BD4 7LP   **Tel:** (0274) 723057
A fine example of West Yorkshire domestic architecture, ranging in date from the Pele Tower (c. 1450) to the Carr Wing (1779-80). There are very good ceilings in the Ghost Room (early 17th cerntury) and the Carr drawing room. Fine 17th and 18th century furniture. The rooms are furnished appropriately for their period.
Open: Tues to Sun 10-6 (Oct to Mar 10-5). *Closed* Mon (Except Bank Hols) and Christmas Day, Boxing Day and Good Friday.

BRACKEN HALL
BOLLING HALL
CARTWRIGHT HALL
INDUSTRIAL MUSEUM
and Horses at Work
CLIFFE CASTLE
MANOR HOUSE
METRO ARTS

Cartwright Hall

BRACKEN HALL COUNTRYSIDE CENTRE
(Bradford Metropolitan Council)
Glenn Road, Baildon, Bradford BD17 5EA   **Tel:** (0274) 584140
Situated at the local beauty spot of Shipley Glen, housing displays and exhibits relating to the natural history, geology and local history of the area. Please phone for details of events.
Open: Wed to Sun 11-5 and Bank Holidays.

BRADFORD INDUSTRIAL MUSEUM AND HORSES AT WORK
(Bradford Metropolitan Council)
Moorside Road, Bradford BD2 3HP   **Tel:** (0274) 631756
Sited in a former spinning mill, the collections preserve the industrial heritage of the City and District. Displays feature engineering, textiles and transport, with the mill owners house, and back to back cottages reflecting domestic life at the turn of the century.
Open: Tues to Sun 10-5. *Closed* Mon (except Bank Hols) and Good Friday, Christmas Day, Boxing Day.

CARTWRIGHT HALL ART GALLERY
(Bradford Metropolitan Council)
Lister Park, Bradford BD9 4NS   **Tel:** (0274) 493313
The permanent collections of important late Victorian and Edwardian art include Rossetti, Ford Madox Brown, Clausen, Wadsworth, Eurich, Hockney and 20th century British art, and contemporary prints. There is a lively programme of touring exhibitions and events.
Open: Tues to Sun 10-6 (Oct to Mar 10-5). *Closed* Mon (except Bank Hols), Good Friday, Christmas Day and Boxing Day.

COLOUR MUSEUM
(The Society of Dyers and Colourists)
82 Grattan Road, off Westgate, Bradford   **Tel:** (0274) 390955
Step into the world of colour. This award winning museum has many interactive exhibits which allow you to experience colour, see how we react to it and to discover some of its many uses. You can even use some of the latest technology to take charge of a modern dye making factory and to test the colour of any material.
Open: Tues to Fri 2-5, Sat 10-4. School and other parties can visit on Tues to Fri mornings by prior arrangement.
Admission: Small fee charged.

MANOR HOUSE MUSEUM AND ART GALLERY
Bradford   **Tel:** (0943) 600066
See Ilkley. Further information from the Assistant Keeper, Education or Assistant Keeper, History.

METRO ARTS
(Bradford Metropolitan Council)
17-21 Chapel Street, Little Germany, Bradford BD1 5DT   **Tel:** (0274) 721372
Community Arts Centre in an old Quaker school. Good physical access, ramp and lift to all floor, loop systems and braille signs. The centre offers skills, equipment, workshops, exhibitions and meeting space.
Open: Mon to Fri 10-4.30. Sat 1-4 only during exhibitions. Special opening during events.

NATIONAL MUSEUM OF PHOTOGRAPHY, FILM AND TELEVISION
Pictureville, Bradford BD1 1NQ   **Tel:** (0274) 727488
Opened in 1983, NMPFT is now the most popular national museum outside London. An outstation of the National Museum of Science and Industry in London, it is its fastest growing offshoot. Its six floors of interactive displays, special exhibitions, theatre and education attract around 750.000 visitors annually. Permanent displays include: **The Story of Popular Photography (the Kodak Museum)**. Relocated from Kodak Limited in Harrow, this important collection of over 50,000 objects and images has been theatrically re-interpreted to tell the history of photography from the point of view of the man and woman in the street. **Photography is news** explores the techniques and history of photojournalism and includes a 1930s news cinema and displays from the Daily Herald Archive, 1.3 million images from this newpaper's history, now held by the NMPTF. **Television Galleries:** two floors devoted to the history and practice of the craft of television. Visitors can read the news, operate a camera or fly our chromakey magic carpet. In **The IMAX Cinema** is the UK's largest cinema screen, projector and film format. **Pictureville Cinema**, alongside the main building, shows the best in world cinema, old and new. **Special Exhibitions:** two floors of temporary exhibitions showing both still and moving pictures.
Open: Tues-Sun 10.30-6, special exhibitions open until 8pm. *Closed* Mondays.
Admission: Free. Booking details for cinema on (0274) 732277.
Refreshments: Wine and coffee bars open daily 10.30-6.
Disabled access.

WEST YORKSHIRE TRANSPORT MUSEUM
Ludlam Street Depot, Mill Lane, Bradford BD5 0HG   **Tel:** (0274) 736006
An interesting and unique collection of 60 historic vehicles including restored trams, trolleybuses, motorbuses and service vehicles. Monthly operating days including free historic vehicle rides, demonstrations, vehicle restoration, bus similator, stalls, memorabilia and other special attractions.
Open: Sun 11-5. Operating days - first Sunday in the month, special events.
Admission: 50p, concessions 25p, Family £1.25
Refreshments: Cafe
Shop. Free car parking. Full details of the programme can be obtained by contacting the Museum's offices. Visits by school parties and other organised groups can be organised at other times by prior arrangement. Suitable for the disabled.

CASTLEFORD

CASTLEFORD MUSEUM
(Wakefield Metropolitan District Council)
Carlton Street, Castleford   **Tel:** (0977) 559552
Castleford Museum Room has changing displays of Roman finds, local pottery etc.
Open: Mon to Fri 2-5. *Closed* weekends and local government and public holidays.
Location: Room in Castleford library.

CLECKHEATON

RED HOUSE
(Kirklees Metropolitan Council)
Oxford Road, Gomersal, Cleckheaton   **Tel:** 0274) 872165
Regency house with strong associations with the Bronties. Completely re-furbished as the Taylor home of the 1830s for the 1990 season.

West Yorkshire

DEWSBURY

DEWSBURY MUSEUM
(Kirklees Metropolitan Council)
Crow Nest Park, Heckmondwike Road, Dewsbury   **Tel:** (0924) 468171
Devoted to the theme of 'Childhood'. Temporary exhibitions throughout the year.

HALIFAX

BANKFIELD MUSEUM
(Calderdale Metropolitan Borough Council)
Akroyd Park,, Halifax   **Tel:** (0422) 354823/352334
Textiles, military costume, art and military history. The Duke of Wellington's Regimental Museum is also at Bankfield. Lively programme of temporary exhibitions.
Open: Tues to Sat 10-5; Sun 2-5. Open Bank Holidays.
Admission: Free

CALDERDALE INDUSTRIAL MUSEUM
(Calderdale Metropolitan Borough Council)
Entrances Piece Hall and Winding Road, Halifax   **Tel:** (0422) 358087
150 years of Calderdale's Industrial history with working machinery.
Open: Tues to Sat 10-5; Sun 2-5.
Admission: £1, Child/OAPs and unwaged 50p.

EUREKA! THE MUSEUM FOR CHILDREN
The Museum for Children, Discovery Road, Halifax HX1 2NE   **Tel:** (0422) 330275 Information line: (0422) 344444   **Fax:** (0422) 330275
Eureka! is the first museum in Britain designed especially for children between the ages of 5 and 12. Wherever you go in Eureka! you can touch, taste and smell as well as look.
Open: Mon Tues 10am-2pm; Weds 10am-7pm; Thurs-Sun 10am-5pm.
Admission: Children (3-12) £2.50. Adults (over 12) £3.50. Family ticket £10. Under 3 free.

THE PIECE HALL
(Calderdale Metropolitan Borough Council)
Halifax
A handsome Italian Piazza style building with an Art Gallery. A varied programme of exhibitions and entertainment.
Open: Mon to Sun 10-5. Also open Bank Holidays.
Admission: Free
Refreshments: Cafe
50 speciality shops.

SHIBDEN HALL
(Calderdale Metropolitan Borough Council)
Shibden Park, Halifax   **Tel:** (0422) 352246
1420 half-timbered hall with 17th century furniture; a 17th century barn; early agricultural implements; coaches and harness; craft workshops.
Open: Mar to Nov: Mon to Sat 10-5, Sun 12-5. Feb: Sun 2-5. *Closed* Dec and Jan.
Admission: £1.50, Child/OAPs, unwaged 75p.
Refreshments: Cafe

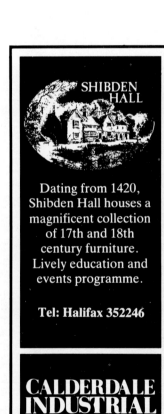

SMITH ART GALLERY
(Calderdale Borough Council)
Halifax Road, Brighouse, Halifax
Permanent collection of about 450 pictures, oils and water-colours - and a changing programme of temporary exhibitions.
Open: Mon to Sat 10-5, Sun 2-5.*Closed* Wed
Admission: Free

HAWORTH

BRONTË PARSONAGE MUSEUM
Haworth
The collection consists of Brontëana and includes many drawings, manuscripts etc., also a permanent exhibition 'The Brontës - a family history'.

HEBDEN BRIDGE

AUTOMOBILIA
(Transport Museum)
Billy Lane, Old Town, Wadsworth, Hebden Bridge **Tel:** (0422) 844775 **Fax:** (0422) 842884
A restored stone built 19th century cloth warehouse housing a superb collection of cars, motorcycles and bicycles.

HEPTONSTALL

HEPTONSTALL
(Calderdale Metropolitan Borough Council)
Heptonstall **Tel:** (0422) 843738
17th century stone school building with local history display and old grammar school furniture.
Open: Weekends and Bank Holidays 1-5, mid-week visits by appointment.
Admission: 50p, Child/OAP/Unwaged 25p.

HOLMFIRTH

HOLMFIRTH POSTCARD MUSEUM
(Kirklees Metropolitan Council)
Huddersfield Road, Holmfirth **Tel:** (0484) 682231
Britain's first Postcard Museum entertains and tells the story of the local firm Bamforth and Co. through their saucy and sentimental postcards, lantern slides and pioneering silent films.

HUDDERSFIELD

HUDDERSFIELD ART GALLERY
(Kirklees Metropolitan Council)
Princess Alexandra Walk, Huddersfield **Tel:** (0484) 513808

TOLSON MUSEUM
(Kirklees Metropolitan Council)
Ravensknowle Park, Wakefield Road, Huddersfield **Tel:** (0484) 530591
Natural sciences, archaeology, social history, industry, farming and transport particularly relating to the Huddersfield area.

ILKLEY

MANOR HOUSE MUSEUM AND ART GALLERY
(Bradford Metropolitan Council)
Castle Yard, Ilkley LS29 9TD **Tel:** (0943) 600066
A small Manor House dating from the 16th century with local history displays including craft shows in upper gallery.
Open: Tues to Sun 10-6 (Oct to Mar 10-5). *Closed* Mon. (Open Bank Holidays) and Good Friday, Christmas Day, Boxing Day.

KEIGHLEY

CLIFFE CASTLE MUSEUM AND ART GALLERY
(Bradford Metropolitan Council)
Spring Gardens Lane, Keighley BD20 6LH **Tel:** (0274) 758230
A former Victorian mansion housing a wide range of natural history and folk life material. Victorian reception rooms, the Airdale gallery, Molecule to Minerals and temporary exhibition areas.
Open: Tues to Sun 10-6 (Oct to Mar 10-5). *ClosedD* Mon (except Bank Hols) and *Christmas Day, Boxing Day and Good Friday.*

KEIGHTLEY & WORTH VALLEY RAILWAY
Haworth Station, Keighley

VINTAGE RAILWAY CARRIAGE MUSEUM
Ingrow Station Yard, Ingrow, Keighley **Tel:** (0535) 680425
Award-winning museum housing a unique collection of historic railway carriages.
Open: Every weekend and Bank Holiday throughout the year. Also Daily Easter Week and Spring Bank Holiday to mid-Sept 11.30-5 (winter 12-4).
Admission: 80p, Child/OAP 40p. Party 15+ 50p, Child 30p. Adults accompanying school party free.
Car parking. Not suitable for disabled persons.

LEEDS

ABBEY HOUSE
(Kirkstall), Leeds
The 12th century abbey gatehouse now houses a folk museum showing the life of Leeds people and includes three full-size streets of local shops and cottages. See entries for The Museum opf Leeds Armley Mills and Kirstall Abbey.

ARMLEY MILLS
Canal Road, Armley, Leeds **Tel:** (0532) 637861
Once the world's largest woollen mills, this museum is housed in a unique fireproof building of 1806 on an impressive island site in the River Aire.

KIRSTALL ABBEY
Kirstall, Leeds **Tel:** (0532) 755821
Britain's finest early monastic ruin, founded by Cistercian monks in 1152.

LEEDS CITY ART GALLERY
The Headrow, Leeds LS1 3AA
Collection Victorian Paintings, early English Watercolours, 20th century British paintings and sculpture; Henry Moore Study Centre. Temp exhibition programme.
Open: Mon to Fri 10-5.30 (Wed until 9pm) Sat 10-4 *Closed* Sunday
Admission: Free
Refreshments: Restaurant 10-3.30. (*closes* Sun)

LEEDS CITY MUSEUM
(City of Leeds)
Municipal Buildings, Leeds LS1 3AA **Tel:** (0532) 478275
Collections illustrating nearly every aspect of natural history, ethnograpohy and archaeology. Although their scope is worldwide, they particularly concern the Yorkshire region.

MUSEUM OF LEEDS
(City of Leeds)
Leeds
Industrial Museum of the Year 1983. This canalside footpath trail follows six miles of the Aire Valley from the centre of Leeds to the Village of Rodney, linking the museum with over 40 historical sites.
Guidebook available from local museums and bookshops. See entries for Armley Mills, Kirstall Abbey and Abbey House.

OTLEY

OTLEY MUSEUM
Civic Centre, Cross Green, Otley

PONTEFRACT

PONTEFRACT CASTLE
(Wakefield Metropolitan District Council)
Castle Chain, Pontefract **Tel:** (0977) 600208/797289
Ruins of important castle dating back to the 11th century. Scene of Richard II's death and Royalist stronghold in the Civil War. Visitor Centre houses an exhibition on the castle's history.
Open: Mon to Fri 8.30-7 (dusk), Sat and Sun 10.30-7 (dusk). Open all Bank Holidays except Christmas and New Year.
Admission: Free

PONTEFRACT MUSEUM
(Wakefield Metropolitan District Council)
Salter Row, Pontefract **Tel:** (0977) 797289
Displays on the history of Pontefract, including the fine early 17th century painting of Pontefract Castle. Temporary exhibition programme.
Open: Mon to Sat 10.30-5, Sun 2.30-5. Open all Bank Holidays except Christmas and New Year.
Admission: Free

SALTAIRE

MUSEUM OF VICTORIAN REED ORGANS & HARMONIUMS
(Phil & Pam Fluke)
Victoria Hall, Victoria Road, Saltaire **Tel:** (0274) 585601 After 5pm.

WAKEFIELD

ELIZABETHAN GALLERY
(Wakefield Metropolitan District Council)
   Brook Street, Wakefield   **Tel:** (0924) 295797
An attractive Elizabethan building converted to a spacious gallery. A changing and varied programme of temporary exhibitions covers all arts and crafts, as well as history and archaeology.
Open: Mon to Sat 10.30-5, Sun 2.30-5 and Spring and Summer Bank Holidays during exhibitions only.
Admission: Free

NOSTELL PRIORY
(The National Trust)
   Near Wakefield   **Tel:** (0924) 863892
Home of the Winn family since 1654, the present house was built in 1733 for Sir Rowland Winn by James Paine with additions in 1766 by Robert Adam. Famous collections of Chippendale furniture specially designed for the house.
Open: Apr 3 to Oct 31: Apr, May, June. Sept and Oct: Sat 12-5, Sun 11-5. July and Aug every day except Fri 12-5, Sun 11-5, Bank Hol openings: Good Friday, Easter Mon & Tues, May day Mon, Spring Bank Hol Mon & Tues, Aug Bank Hol Mon, Mons 11-5pm, Tues 12-5pm.
Admission: House & Grounds: £3.50, child £1.80, parties £3.00, child party £1.50. Grounds: £2.20, child £1.10. NT members free.
Location: 6m SE of Wakefield on A638
Free parking.

SANDAL CASTLE
(Wakefield Metropolitan District Council)
   Manygates Lane, Sandal, Wakefield   **Tel:** (0924) 295351
Ruins of 13th century stone castle of the Warennes. Finds from excavations on display in Wakefield Museum.
Open: Daily
Admission: Free

WAKEFIELD ART GALLERY
(Wakefield Metropolitan District Council)
   Wentworth Terrace, Wakefield   **Tel:** (0924) 375402 or 295796
Significant early works by Henry Moore and Barbara Hepworth and important work by other major British modern artists form the core of this collection. Works from other periods and European schools are also on display. There is a changing programme of touring exhibitions and displays from the permanent collections.
Open: Mon to Sat 10.30-5, Sun 2.30-5. Open all Bank Holidays except Christmas and New Year.
Admission: Free

WAKEFIELD MUSEUMS, GALLERIES AND CASTLES

Wakefield Art Gallery, Wakefield Museum,
Elizabethan Exhibition Gallery,
Pontefract Museum,
Castleford Museum Room,
Pontefract and Sandal Castles

For details of exhibitions
and events,

Telephone 0924 375402

Admission Free

WAKEFIELD MUSEUM
(Wakefield Metropolitan District Council)
   Wood Street, Wakefield   **Tel:** (0294) 295351
Wakefield museum is full of objects and images which depict Wakefield's long and complex history. Visitors will find everything from flint axes and Roman pottery to model locomotives and plastic tea cups! We also house the exotic and eccentric natural history collections of the Victorian emplorer, Charles Waterton. You will see nothing like these anywhere else in Yorkshire! There are also about six temporary exhibitions each year, on topics as diverse as tin toys, antique shoes and wildlife photography.
Open: Mon to Sat 10.30-5, Sun 2.30 to 5. Open all Bank Holidays except Christmas

and New Year.
Admission: Free

YORKSHIRE MINING MUSEUM
   Caphouse Colliery, New Road, Overton, Wakefield WF4 4RH   **Tel:** (0924) 848806
Award-winning museum of the Yorkshire coalfield includes an exciting guided tour 450 feet underground. An experienced miner takes visitors through authentic workings where methods and conditions of mining from 1820 to the present day have been reconstructed. On the surface there are indoor and outdoor displays, train rides, genuine pit ponies, steam winder, nature trail and adventure playground.
Open: 10-5 except Dec 25, 26 and Jan 1.
Refreshments: Licensed cafeteria.
Film show, shop. Access for disabled and ample free parking.

YORKSHIRE SCULPTURE PARK
   Bretton Hall, West Bretten, Wakefield

WALES

CLWYD

CHIRK

CHIRK CASTLE
(The National Trust)
   Nr Wrexham, Chirk,
The castle is an outstanding example of a Marcher Fortress, built 1295-1310 and is still inhabited. The interior provides examples of 16th, 17th, 18th and 19th century decorations. The park was landscaped by Emes in the mid 18th century. Extensive gardens with fine views.
Admission: Fee charged.

HOLWAY

GRANGE CAVERN MILITARY MUSEUM
(A. Pearce)
   Grange Lane, Holway,

LLANGOLLEN

PLAS NEWYDD MUSEUM
(Glyndwr District Council)
   Hill Street, Llangollen

RUTHIN

RUTHIN CRAFT CENTRE
   Park Road, Ruthin, LL15 1BB   **Tel:** (08242) 4774/5675
A Craft Council selected Gallery, housed within a purpose-built Craft Centre in the beautiful Vale of Clwyd, specialises in work by top British artists and designer-makers, but also reflects the wealth of talent within the principality. Our programme of changing exhibitions shows a constant variety of excellence. There are also thirteen independent studios where craftsmen work on a daily basis, situated around a landscaped courtyard. Craft library also workshops for adults and children throughout the year.
Open: 10-5 seven days a week (Sunday 12-5 in the winter).
Admission: Free
Refreshments: Licensed restaurant.
Parking. Advanced notice for parties. Suitable for disabled persons - all areas have access ramps for wheelchairs.

ST. ASAPH

BODELWYDDAN CASTLE
(Clwyd County Council)
    Bodelwyddan, St. Asaph, LL18 5YA   **Tel:** (0745) 583539

Bodelwyddan Castle has been authentically restored as a Victorian Country House and contains a major collection of portraits and photography on permanent loan from the National Portrait Gallery. The codllection includes works by many eminent Victorian Portraitists such as G.F.Watts, William Holman Hunt, John Singer Sargeant, Sir Edwin Landseer and Sir Thomas Lawrence. The portraits are complemented by furniture from the Victorian & Albert Museum and sculptures from the Royal Academy. The castle is situated in beautiful countryside and is a member of the National Garden Scheme. The extensive formal gardens have been restored to their former glory and provide a magnificent display of flowering plants, water features, maze, aviary and woodland walks. For children there is an adventure woodland and play areas.
Open: Easter to June 30 and Sept 1 to Nov 1: Daily except Fri; July 1 to Aug 31: Daily 10-5. Williams Hall opens 10.30. Last admission one hour before closing. For details of winter opening please ring.
Admission: Fee charged. Discount rates available for groups of 20 or more.
Location: Just off the A55 near St. Asaph (opposite the Marble Church).
Refreshments: Victorian Tea Room, Pavilion Restaurant, Cafeteria.
Suitable for disabled persons (wheelchairs available). Giftshop. Picnic area. Woodland walk. Maze and Aviary.

WREXHAM

BERSHAM INDUSTRIAL HERITAGE CENTRE
(Clwyd County Council)
    Bershaw, Near Wrexham, LL14 4HT   **Tel:** (0978) 261529

ERDDIG
(The National Trust)
    Wrexham
A late 17th century house with 18th century additions that contains much of the original furniture. The outbuildings, including laundry, bakehouse, sawmill and smithy, are in working order. The garden has been restored to its 18th century design and contains varieties of fruit known to have been grown there during that period. The Country Park Visitor Centre containing early farm implements and local farm machinery dating from the later half of the 19th century.
Open: Weekends only.
Admission: Fee charged.

KING'S MILL VISITOR CENTRE
(Wrexham Maelor Borough Council)
    King's Mill Road, Wrexham   **Tel:** (0978) 362967
Restored mill housing 'The Miller's Tale' - what it was like to live and work in an 18th century mill. Also waterwheel and video presentation.
Open: Easter to Sept: Tues to Sun 10-5; Oct, Feb and Mar weekends 10-5.
Admission: Fee charged

WREXHAM MAELOR HERITAGE CENTRE
(Wrexham Maelor Borough Council)
    47/49 King Street, Wrexham, LL11 1HR   **Tel:** (0978) 290048
Permanent exhibition on the local, social and industrial history of the Wrexham area especially the brick, tile and terracota industry. Changing temporary exhibition

programme.
Open: Mon to Sat 10-5.
Admission: Free

DYFED

ABERYSTWYTH

ABERYSTWYTH ARTS CENTRE EXHIBITIONS
    University College of Wales, Aberystwyth, SY23 3DE   **Tel:** (0970) 622887/2
Fax: (0970) 622883

The Arts Centre is situated on the university campus and has panoramic views over Cardigan Bay. Purpose built in 1972 it has steadily gained recognition as a major arts venue in Wales consisting of four galleries, concert hall, theatre and studio. The Arts Centre has an extensive exhibition programme which includes the work of (mainly contemporary) artists, makers and photographers. There are approximately forty shows a year in all, some of which originate here and tour U.K. An education service for adults and children includes talks, residential courses, workshops, demonstrations etc. The Arts Centre also hosts a Bi-annual Potters' Festival. Part of the College Ceramics Collection (numbering approx 1,500 pieces) is always on display in the Ceramics Gallery with regular 'Ceramic Series' contemporary ceramics exhibitions opposite. To view the whole collection it is necessary to make an appointment. Tel: (0970) 623339
Open: Daily Mon to Sat 10-5 and during evening performances 7-9. *Closed* mid

May-end June for university exams.
Refreshments: Cafe
Bookshop and craftshop. (Crafts Council listed). 'Collectorplan' no interest credit scheme available for purchasing art works. Disabled access to lower gallery and cafe.

THE CATHERINE LEWIS PRINT ROOM
(The Hugh Owen Library, The University College of Wales)
Aberystwyth **Tel:** (0970) 62339/623591

From *Spirit of Jem* by Keith Vaughan 1912-1977

THE CATHERINE LEWIS PRINT ROOM

The University College of Wales, Aberystwyth SY23 1HB
See editorial for details

Permanent collection of graphic art from 15th-20th century particularly 1860's illustration, 1920's/30's and contemporary prints, 20th century Italian and British photography. Changing exhibitions from the collection and special exhibitions of graphic art (see posters or telephone). Reference available by appointment.
Open: Mon to Fri 9.30-5; Sat (College Term only) 9.30-12.30 (except for Christmas, Easter and Bank Hols).
Admission: Free
Parties by arrangement. Car parking. Suitable for disabled persons.

CEREDIGION MUSEUM
(Ceredigion District Council)
Coliseum, Terrace Road, Aberystwyth SY23 2AQ **Tel:** (0970) 617911
Local Museum housed in a restored Edwardian Theatre. Displays illustrate the history and artifacts of Ceredigion including archaeology, geology, agriculture, seafaring, lead mining. Fine collection of furniture and clocks. Many folk life exhibits. Temporary art and other exhibitions throughout the year.
Open: Mon to Sat 10-5. Sundays in school holidays.
Admission: Free

LLYWERNOG SILVER-LEAD MINE MUSEUM
Potterwyd, Aberystwyth, **Tel:** (097085) 620
An award winning restoration of a Victorian water-powered metal-mine which captures the spirit and atmosphere of the 'boom-days'.

THE NATIONAL LIBRARY OF WALES
Aberystwyth SY23 3BU

CARMARTHEN

THE CAMARTHEN MUSEUM
(Dyfed County Council)
Aberwili, Carmarthen, **Tel:** (0267) 231691
Situated in the former Palace of the Bishop of St. David's, the museum is surrounded by seven acres of beautiful parkland. Displays cover the history and natural history of the region and include archaeology, costume and folk life material.
Open: Mon to Sat 10-4.30.
Admission: 50p. Reductions for parties, OAPs, Students and the unemployed.

DRE-FACH FELINDRE

MUSEUM OF THE WOOLLEN INDUSTRY
Dre-Fach Felindre, Near Newcastle Emlyn **Tel:** (0559) 370929
The **Museum of the Welsh Woollen Industry** is located at Dre-Fach Felindre which was once the most important wool producing area in wales and supplied flannel to the mining communities of the South Wales valleys. Located alongside a working woollen mill and other craft workshops, the Museum houses working exhibitions with

demonstrations tracing woollen cloth from fleece to fabric. Attention is also focused upon the contemporary products of the Welsh mills.
Open: Apr 1 to Sept 30: Mon to Sat 10-5. Oct 1 to Mar 31: Mon to Fri 10-5. *Closed* Sun, Christmas Eve, Christmas Day, Boxing Day, New Year's Day, Boxing Day, Good Friday.
Admission: £1, OAPs 75p, Chld (under 16) 50p. 20% discount for pre-booked travel trade parties of more than 20 in number. 10% discount if not pre-booked.
Location: 4m east of Newcastle Emlyn off the A484 Carmarthen to Cardigan road.
Refreshments: Snack bar. Picnic area.
Bookings contact officer in charge. Coaches: ample free parking. Gift/book shop. Toilets, toilets for the disabled.

HAVERFORDWEST

HAVERFORDWEST CASTLE MUSEUM AND ART GALLERY
The Castle, Haverfordwest, **Tel:** (0437) 763708
Open: All year Mon to Sat 10-4.30.*Closed* Good Friday and from Christmas to New Year.
Admission: Small fee charged. Child free.
Car park. Museum shop.

PENRHOS COTTAGE
Llanycefn, near Maenclockog, Haverfordwest
Traditional furnished Welsh Cottage near Preseli Hills.
Open: Easter to end Sept, Tues to Sat and Sun afternoon, 10-1 and 2-5.
Admission: Small fee charged. Child free,
Enquiries to Scolton Manor Museum

SCOLTON MANOR MUSEUM
Spittal,, Near Haverfordwest **Tel:** (0437) 731328
A Museum about Pembrokeshire set in a 60 acre Country Park. Countryside Centre, woodland nature trail, picnic sites.
Open: Museum, May to Sept, Tues to Sun 10-4.30. Country park, all year *closed* Mon.
Admission: Small fee charged. Child free.
Location: On B4329
Refreshments: Tea room (high season only)

GRAHAM SUTHERLAND GALLERY
Picton Castle, Rhos, Haverfordwest **Tel:** (0437) 751296
This Gallery was specially created for the important collection of paintings, drawings and prints donated by the artist himself. The works on display are inspired largely by the lanes and estuaries of the surrounding areas. There is an excellent temporary exhibition programme throughout the season.
Open: Mar to Oct: Daily (*except Mon but open Bank Hol Mons*) 10.30-12.30, 1.30-5.

KIDWELLY

KIDWELLY INDUSTRIAL MUSEUM
(Kidwelly Heritage Centre and Tinplate Museum Trust/Llanelli Borough Council)
Kidwelly

LLANELLI

PARC HOWARD MUSEUM AND ART GALLERY
(Llanelli Borough Council)
Llanelli **Tel:** (0554) 773538
Collection of Llanelli pottery. Exhibits of Welsh artists. Items of local interest. Travelling exhibitions.

PUBLIC LIBRARY GALLERY
(Llanelli Borough Council)
Tel: (0554) 773538
Collection of local artists, travelling and other exhibitions.
Open: Mon-Sat 10-6

PEMBROKE

NATIONAL MUSEUM OF GYPSY CARAVANS, ROMANY CRAFTS AND LORE
Commons Road, Pembroke **Tel:** (0646) 681308
An outstanding collection of Gypsy caravans and representation of Gypsy life.

TENBY

TENBY MUSEUM AND PICTURE GALLERY
Castle Hill, Tenby,   Tel: (0834) 842809

AND PICTURE GALLERY

**CASTLE HILL,
TENBY, PEMBROKESHIRE**
Tel: Tenby (0843) 842809

An independent community museum since 1878, within the castle site, interpreting Tenby's heritage from prehistory to the present; the picture gallery features artists and works with local associations.

Winifred John by Gwen John.

An outstanding display of the geology, archaeology and natural history of Pembrokeshire. The maritime gallery commemorates Tenby's seafaring past and its achievements as a lifeboat station; there are special exhibitions of local history. Pictures of local interest and by artists with local connections, including Augustus and Gwen John and Nina Hamnett are on view in the gallery.
Open: Daily Easter to Oct: 10-6. Winter times from Nov 1: Mon to Fri 10-12, 2-4.
Admission: 70p, reductions for Child/OAPs. School parties by appointment, free.

MID GLAMORGAN

BRIDGEND

SOUTH WALES POLICE MUSEUM
Cowbridge Road, Bridgend, Mid Glamorgam CF31 3SU   Tel: (0656) 655555, Ext 427.
From truncheons to typewriters, buttons to a 1940s bicycle, this collection of police memorabilia from Glamorgan is the most extensive in Wales.
Open: Mon to Thurs 10-2, 2-4,30; Fri 10-1, 2-4. *Closed* Bank Hols. Open by appointment only.
Admission: Free
Parties by appointment. Souvenir shop. School's service. Car parking. Not suitable for disabled persons.

LLANTRISANT

MODEL HOUSE GALLERY
Bull Ring, Llantrisant, CF7 8EA   Tel: (0443) 237758
A superb, contemporary visitor centre. The Craft Council listed Gallery Shop sells quality work from top UK makers, with a variety of exhibitions each year. Open craft studios are situated on the second floor along with the Royal Mint display and a conference facility.
Open: May 1 to Dec 22, Tues to Sun 10-5. Jan 2 to Apr 30, Wed to Sun 12-5.
Admission: Free
Refreshments: Coffee shop.
Guided tours arranged by appointment. Full facilities for disabled persons.

MERTHYR TYDFIL

CYFARTHFA CASTLE MUSEUM AND ART GALLERY
Merthyr Tydfil   Tel: (0685) 723112
Situated in the ironmasters gothic mansion the collections cover paintings, ceramics, silver furniture and decorative art. There are displays on local history, industrial history, enthnography, archaeology and Egyptology. New Social History galleries now open, entitled 'Merthyr - 3000 years of History'. Programme of temporary exhibitions throughout the year.
Open: Weekdays 10-6 (Fri close 5). Sun 2-5. During winter Oct 1 to Apr 1 close one hour earlier. *Closed* Christmas and Good Friday.
Admission: 50p, Child 30p. Educational groups free.
Schoolroom available. Access for disabled.

JOSEPH PARRY'S BIRTHPLACE
(Merthyr Tydfil Heritage Trust)
4 Chapel Row, Georgetown, Merthyr Tydfil CF48 1BN   Tel: (0685) 383704
The ground floor of the cottage has now been restored to the way it appeared in the 1840s when Dr. Joseph Parry, the musician and composer, lived here as a boy. Upstairs are exhibitions on Parry's life and works plus brief history of Merthyr.
Open: Easter to Oct 30: Mon to Sun 2-5, including Bank Holidays. Winter: by arrangement.
Admission: Nominal fee charged.
Parking adjacent.

YNYSFACH ENGINE HOUSE
(Merthyr Tydfil Heritage Trust)
Ynysfach Road, Merthyr Tydfil, CF48 1AG   Tel: (0685) 721858 & 383704
Winner of a Prince of Wales award in 1989, this Heritage Centre contains exhibitions introducing the fascinating history of Merthyr's once world famous Iron Industry. Includes 18 minute a/v programme (Narrator: Philip Madoc).
Open: Easter to Oct 31: Mon to Fri 11-5, Sat. Sun and Bank Holidays 2-5; Nov 1 to Easter: Mon to Fri 10-4, Sat & Sun 1-4.
Admission: Fee charged to exhibitions. Free entry to coffee shop and gift shop (local history, crafts and souvenirs).
Refreshments: Coffee shop.
Parking close by. Guided walks around Merthyr Tydfil covering different aspects of industrial history may be booked.

SOUTH GLAMORGAN

CARDIFF

BURGES DRAWINGS COLLECTION
The Burges Room, Cardiff Castle, Cardiff

THE NATIONAL MUSEUM OF WALES
Main Building, Cathays Park. (Cymru Amgueddfa Genedlaethol), Cardiff
Treasurehouse of Wales, the **National Museum of Wales** main building at the heart of Cardiff's elegant civic centre is proud of its excellent collections including paintings, silver and ceramics, coins and medals, fossils, minerals, shells, archaeological artefacts and even dinosaur skeletons. The recent refurbishment of the East Wing has provided a splendid new setting for the museum's impressive art collection showing them in their Welsh and European context. A major development currently under way will provide further new galleries for displaying unique collections including French Impressionist paintings. Special exhibitions of world-wide interest contribute to the museum's popularity as one of Wales' foremost tourist attractions. An exciting schedule of events and temporary exhibitions enhances the museum's visitor appeal.
Open: Tues to Sat 10-5 & Bank Hol. Mon ; Sun 2.30-5. *Closed* Mon. Christmas Eve, Christmas Day, Boxing Day, New Year's Day, Good Friday.
Admission: £2, OAPs £1.50, Child (under 16)£1 20% discount for pre-booked travel trade parties over 20 in number. 10% discount if not pre-booked.
Refreshments: Restaurant, Snack bar.
Parties can be dropped at the main entrance to the museum. **Bookings contact:** Dept. of Public Services. Museum gift/book shop. Toilets, Toilets for the disabled.

WELSH INDUSTRIAL AND MARITIME MUSEUM
Bute Street, Cardiff   Tel: (0222) 481919
In Cardiffs dockland, among the world's most famous maritime districts, the **Welsh Industrial and Maritime Museum** stands at the heart of the Cardiff Bay Development area and tells visitors the story of industrial and maritime Wales. Within the Hall of Power, working exhibits show the evolution of methods of driving machinery, with the waterwheel, steam engine, gas engine, steam turbine and Rolls Royce jet engine. A transport gallery includes a working replica of Trevithick's Locomotive, and the Railway and Shipping galleries complete the picture of how Wales communicated with the world. The newest attraction is a miniture passenger-carrying Railway which takes visitors around the site. Pulling the train is a scaled down model of the world's first steam locomotive. Branches of this particular museum included 126 Bute Street with displays illustrating Cardiff's growth from small town quay to coal metropilis of the world, the Railway Gallery with its story of the Welsh Railway Companies and Q-Shed, the museum events centre.
Open: Tues to Sat 10-5, Sun 2.30-5. *Closed* Mon (except Bank Hols), Christmas Eve, Christmas Day, New Year's Day, Good Friday.
Admission: £1, OAPs 75p, Chld (under 16) 50p. 20% discount for pre booked travel trade parties. 10% discount if not pre-booked.
Bookings contact: Administrative officer. Gift/book shop. Toilets, toilets for the disabled.

PENARTH

TURNER HOUSE
Plymouth Road, Penarth   Tel: (0222) 569441
A small gallery holding temporary exhibitions of pictures and objects d'art from the National Museum of Wales and other sources.
Open: Tues to Fri 11-12.45, 2-5. Also Bank Holiday Mon. *Closed* Sat, Mon (other than Bank Holidays), Christmas Eve, Christmas Day, Boxing Day, New Year's Day, Good Friday.
Admission: Free
For booking contact: Principal Officer. Coaches: Parking nearby. Museum Gift/book shop.

National Museum of Wales

bringing to you the rich heritage of Wales in lively and exciting presentations

● **The Main Building**
Cathays Park, Cardiff. Tel. 0222 397951

● **Welsh Folk Museum**
St Fagans, Cardiff. Tel. 0222 569441

● **Welsh Industrial and Maritime Museum**
Bute Street, Cardiff. Tel. 0222 481919

● **Roman Legionary Museum, Caerleon**
Caerleon, Gwent. Tel. 0633 423134

● **Turner House**
Plymouth Road, Penarth, South Glamorgan.
Tel. 0222 708870

● **Museum of Welsh Woollen Industry**
Dre-fach Felindre, Llandysul, Dyfed.
Tel. 0559 370929

● **Graham Sutherland Gallery**
The Rhos, Haverfordwest. Tel. 0437 751296

● **Museum of the North**
Llanberis, Gwynedd. Tel. 0286 870636

● **Welsh Slate Museum**
Llanberis, Gwynedd. Tel. 0286 870630

● **Segontium Roman Fort Museum**
Caernarfon, Gwynedd. Tel. 0286 5625

ST. FAGANS

WELSH FOLK MUSEUM
St. Fagans   **Tel:** (0222) 569441

One of Europe's foremost open-air museums, the **Welsh Folk Museum** features everything from a castle to the humble moorland cottage of a slate quarry worker among its unique collection of furnished re-erected buildings. Reflecting the lifestyle of the past both at home and at work, the buildings have been brought from all over Wales and re-erected within the museum's 100 acre parkland. As well as farmhouses, a terrace of six cottages and a victorian shop complex from the industrial valleys of south Wales, there is a tollhouse, tannery, smithy, corn mill, woollen mill, bakehouse and a pottery. The museum is brought to life by the craftmen who provide displays of traditional skills for the visitors. Galleries at the museum focus on agriculture, costume and material culture, and special events, demonstrations and temporary exhibitions are held regularly. Major annual seasonal festivals include May Fair, Mid summer Festival, Harvest Festival and Christmas Tree.

Open: Apr 1 to Oct 31, Daily 10-5. Nov 1 to Mar 31, Mon to Sat 10-5. *Closed* Sun between Nov 1 and Mar 31, Christmas Eve, Christmas Day, Boxing Day, New Year's Day, Good Friday.

Admission: £3.50, OAP £2.60, Chld (under 16) £1.75. 20% discount for pre-booked travel trade parties over 20 in number. 10% discount if not pre-booked.

Location: 4 miles west of Cardiff City Centre in the beautiful Vale of Glamorgan. The Welsh Folk Museum is clearly signposted from junction 33 of the M4 Motorway. Direct access from the A4232 into the museum.

Refreshments: Self service restaurant, waitress service restaurant. Coffee tavern. Picnic area.

Bookings contact: Travel and Trade Officer. Tel (0222) 555105. Guide books available. Ample free car parking. Free adm for coach driver. Gift/book shop. Toilets, toilets for disabled. Access to almost all areas for the disabled.

WEST GLAMORGAN

NEATH

CEFN COED COLLIERY MUSEUM
(West Glamorgan County Council)
Blaenant Colliery, Crynant, Neath,   **Tel:** (0639) 750556
The museum vividly portrays the story of men and machines involved in the mining of coal at the former Cefn Coed Colliery.

SWANSEA

CERI RICHARDS GALLERY
(University College Swansea)
Taliesin Arts Centre, University College, Singleton Park, Swansea. SA2 8PZ
Tel: (0792) 295438 (admin)

GLYNN VIVIAN ART GALLERY
(Leisure Services Department, Swansea City Council)
Alaxandra Road, Swansea,   **Tel:** (0792) 655006/651738

Pictures, sculpture, glass and Swansea china. All year exhibitions programme and many other activities.
Open: Tues-Sun 10.30-5.30.
Admission: Free

MARITIME AND INDUSTRIAL MUSEUM
(Swansea City Council)
Museum Square, Maritime Quarter, Swansea, **Tel:** (0792) 470371/650351

SWANSEA LEISURE SERVICES DEPT.
MARITIME AND INDUSTRIAL MUSEUM
Maritime Quarter, Swansea. Tel: (0792) 650351

* Step aboard the largest collection of historic vessels in Wales
* Visit a fully operational traditional Woollen Mill
* Tramshed annexe with Mumbles railway displays
* Full programme of touring exhibitions
Closed Mondays (Bank Holidays Excepted)
Admission Charged April – September
Open 10-30 – 5.30 Last admission 5-15 DISABLED ACCESS

See the working woollen mill; transport, maritime and industrial displays. Step aboard the boats floating alongside museum. Activities for all.
Open: Daily 10.30-5.30. Closed Monday (Bank Holidays excepted)

SWANSEA MUSEUM
Swansea City Council
Victoria Road, Swansea SA1 ISN **Tel:** (0792) 653763
Wales oldest Museum in its original building. Collections:- local social history and archaeology, natural history, Egyptology, ceramics, fine art, photography, costume and library. Visiting exhibitions.
Open: Tues to Sun all year
Admission: Summer admission charges: Adults £1
Refreshments: Available

GWENT

ABERGAVENNY

ABERGAVENNY AND DISTRICT MUSEUM
(Monmouth District Council)
The Castle, Castle Street, Abergavenny

BLAENAVON

BIG PIT MINING MUSEUM
Blaenavon

CAERLEON

ROMAN LEGIONARY MUSEUM
Caerleon **Tel:** (0633) 423134
At the **Roman Legionary Museum**, Caerleon, the history of Roman Caerleon and the daily life of its garrison are featured in the displays of exciting finds from the area. Highlights include life-size Roman Soldiers - a centurion standard bearer and legionary - arms, armour and equipment of the Roman Soldier, a labyrinth mosaic, a remarkable collection of engraved gemstones from the Fortress baths and early Roman finds from the logionary base at Usk. Nearby are other impressive remains of the town's history - the amphitheatre designed to seat 5000 spectators, the Fortress Baths which served as the main leisure and social centre for the soldiers and was one of the largest baths in the Roman province, the Roman defences and the only remains of the legionary barracks on view in Europe.
Open: Mar 15 to Oct 15: Mon to Sat 10-6, Sun 2-6. Oct 16 to Mar 14: Mon to Sat 10-4.30, Sun 2-4.30. *Closed* Christmas Eve, Christmas Day, Boxing Day, New Years Day, Good Friday.
Admission: £1.25, OAPs 75p, Chld (under 16) 75p. Also joint tickets available with Roman Baths and Amphitheatre, administered by 'CADW' Welsh Historic Monuments. 20% discount for pre-booked travel parties over 20 in number. 10% if not pre-booked. For bookings, contact the curator. Coaches can park at the nearby Roman Amphitheatre. Gift shop and book shop. Toilets, toilets for the disabled.

CALDICOT

CALDICOT CASTLE MUSEUM
(Manmouth District Council)
The Castle, Caldicot

CHEPSTOW

CHEPSTOW MUSEUM
(Monmouth District Council)
Bridge Street, Chepstow
Recently moved to this elegant late 18th century town house, the museum's collections illustrate the history and development of Chepshow and the surrounding area.

CWMBRAN

LLANTARNAM GRANGE ARTS CENTRE
St. Davids Road, Cwmbran **Tel:** (06333) 483321

Llantarnam Grange Arts Centre

Early Victorian farmhouse with warm, gracious atmosphere. Tastefully converted with two galleries (monthly exhibitions: mainly craft - some fine art).
Open: Mon to Sat 10-4.
Admission: Free
Location: Off St. Davids Road next to car park 2 near Cwmbran town centre.
Refreshments: Coffee shop with gallery. Group buffet lunches bao.
Originals craft shop, year round programme of workshops, lectures and events. Free parking. Contact Ms. Sara Bowie.

MONMOUTH

NELSON COLLECTION AND LOCAL HISTORY CENTRE
Priory Street, Monmouth

NEWPORT

MUSEUM AND ART GALLERY
(Borough of Newport)
John Frost Square, Newport, **Tel:** (0633) 840064
Natural science displays including geology; fine and applies art, specialising in early English watercolours, teapots and contemporary crafts; Prehistoric and Romano-British remains from Caerwent; local history including the Chartist movement. Regular exhibitions and associated activities.
Open: Mon to Thurs 9.30-5; Fri 9.30-4.30; Sat 9.30-4.
Admission: Free

PONTYPOOL

THE VALLEY INHERITANCE
(Torfaen Museum Trust)
Pontypool **Tel:** (0495) 752036

NEWPORT MUSEUM & ART GALLERY, GWENT

John Frost Square, Newport, Gwent. Tel: (0633) 840064

A hunter in the Severn Estuary. Circa 5,000 B.C.

Newport Museum and Art Gallery, housed in a modern purpose-built building, overlooks John Frost Square in the Town Centre and is close to main line rail and bus stations. The archaeology department includes material excavated from the Romano-British town of Caerwent. Other displays portray the 19th century growth of Newport, John Frost and the Monmouthshire Chartist uprising of 1839 and a wide range of objects depicting domestic and working life in town and country. Newport has a fine collection of early English water-colours, oil paintings by British artists, notably those of Welsh origin, and an exhibition of teapots. The new natural history displays cover freshwater life, wildlife in the home, geology and the weather. Continuous programme of exhibitions.

1930's Room setting in John Wait Teapot display.

USK

GWENT RURAL LIFE MUSEUM
The Malt Barn, New Market Street, Usk,   **Tel:** (0291) 673777
Agricultural and craft tools, wagons, vintage machinery, farmhouse, kitchen, laundry, dairy. Winner of the Prince of Wales Award.
Open: Apr 1 to Oct 31: Mon to Fri 10-5; weekends 2-5. Nov to Mar: please telephone museum.
Admission: Fee charged.
Parties by arrangement.*An Independent Museum*

GWYNEDD

BEAUMARIS

BEAUMARIS GAOL AND COURTHOUSE
(Culture & Leisure: Archives & Museums)
Beaumaris, Isle of Anglesey   **Tel:** (0248) 750262 ext 269
Built in 1829 the Gaol is a grim reminder of the harshness of justice in Victorian Britain. Visitors can see the cells, including the punishment and condemned cells, the unique treadwheel and a condemned man's final walk to the scaffold. In the Court you can stand in the dock from which prisoners found guilty of murder received the death sentence. A Time Machine Walkman tape tour is available at both locations.
Open: Easter, weekends in May, end May - end Sept: Daily 11-6. (except when court is in session). Other times by appointment.

MUSEUM OF CHILDHOOD
1 Castle Street, Beaumaris LL58 8AP   **Tel:** (0248) 810448
The museum is housed in 9 rooms of a Georgian building opposite Beaumaris Castle with over 2000 items on display which brings back nostalgic childhood memories. Winner of the National Heritage and British Tourist Authority Awards.

BEDDGELERT

SYGUN COPPER MINE
Beddgelert   **Tel:** (0766 86) 595
A Prince of Wales and British Tourist Authority Award winning family attraction in the heart of the stunning Snowdonia National Park. Guided tours take the visitor into the underground world of the 19th century copper miner. Magnificent stalactite and stalagtite formations.
Admission: £3.60, OAP £3, Child £2.25. Special group rates.
Free parking. Unsuitable for the disabled.

BLAENAU FFESTINIOG

LLECHWEDD SLATE CAVERNS
Blaenau Ffestiniog   **Tel:** (0766) 830306
Preserved section of a slate mine offering mine tours to visitors. Slate mine and associated buildings and equipment. Surface attractions include the Slate Mill and Victorian Village (includes Miners Arms Pub, Victorian Shops, Bank, Lock-up, Printers & Cobblers workshops and working Smithy).
Open: All year 10.00 - last tours 5.15. (4.15 October - February)
Admission: 1992 Tour Prices: Both tours Adult £6.50, Child £4.50, OAPs £5.25. Either tour Adult £4.25, Child £3.00, OAPs £3.75. Free admission to surface attractions. Reductions for parties of 20+.
Free car parking. Only partly suitable for disabled persons.

CAERNARFON

THE ROYAL WELCH FUSILIERS
Queen's Tower, Caernarfon Castle, Caernarfon
Hat ribbon worn by King William of Orange in 1690, Key of Corunna, Officer's Mitre Cap 1750, ten V.C.s, Gold Peninsular War medals; large collection of Campaign medals, full size Tableau and Royal and other portraits by Dennis Fields, Oswald Birley and Gerald Kelly.
Open: End-Mar to end-Oct: Weekdays 9.30-4; Sun 2-4.
Admission: To Castle £3, Child/OAPs £2. Regimental museum free.

SEGONTIUM ROMAN FORT MUSEUM
Caernarfon   **Tel:** (0286) 5625
The Roman Fort Museum is an archaeological branch gallery of the National Museum of Wales. Remains of the Roman Fort of Segontium and a museum of excavated relics are on display here.
Open: 9.30-6, Daily Apr to Sep. 9.30-4, Daily Oct to Mar. *Closed* Christmas Eve, Christmas Day, Boxing Day, New Year's Day, Good Friday.
Admission: Free
Coaches: Ample parking nearby. Museum gift/book shop.

SEIONT II MARITIME MUSEUM
Victoria Dock, Caernarfon
Step back in time when you board the Museum's operational centrepiece, the steam dredger *Seiont II* and in the Museum itself absorb the development, hardships and drama of the area's maritime history.
Open: Easter, May to Sept: Daily 1-5 (often open to dusk during the summer holidays).

CONWY

PLAS MAWR
High Street, Conwy

CRICCIETH

THE NEW LLOYD GEORGE MUSEUM AND HIGHGATE HIS BOYHOOD COTTAGE HOME WITH VICTORIAN COTTAGE GARDEN
(Culture & Leisure: Archives & Museums)
Llanystumdwy, Criccieth   **Tel:** (0766) 522071 & (0286) 679098
The museum outlines the life and times of the statesman. His boyhood home is recreated as it would have been when he lived there between 1864-1880 as is his Uncle Lloyd's shoemaking workshop. A **New Attraction** is Highgate Cottage's Victorian Garden.
Open: Easter to Sept: Daily 10-5 & Oct Mon-Fri 11-4. Other times by appointment.

Explore Gwynedd's Heritage visit . . .

● **THE NEW LLOYD GEORGE MUSEUM & HIGHGATE, HIS BOYHOOD COTTAGE HOME, LLANYSTUMDWY, CRICCIETH.**
Explore the life and times of the famous statesman at the newly extended museum with its improved exhibitions, costumes, 'talking head', new audio visual theatre and Victorian schoolroom.

● **BEAUMARIS GAOL & COURTHOUSE.**
Experience the grim gaol, with its unique treadwheel, various cells and exhibitions. The court, with its 17th century origins, is a unique survival of a Victorian court room.

● **HAULFRE STABLES, LLANGOED, NEAR BEAUMARIS.**
Visit the 19th century stables and tackroom with their original fittings and contents. They represent the landed gentry's way of life in the last century.

CULTURE & LEISURE: Archives & Museums

See editorial for further information.

HOLYHEAD

HOLYHEAD MARITIME MUSEUM
Rhos-y-Gaer Avenue, Holyhead
Open: May to Sept: Daily 1-5, but *closed* Mon (except Bank Hols).
Location: Close to Railway Station

ISLE OF ANGLESEY

PLAS NEWYDD
(The National Trust)
Llanfairpwll, Isle of Angelsey
The 16th century house was extended and redecorated in the 18th century with gothic and neo-classical interiors designed by James Wyatt. The house contains Rex Whistler's finest mural painting, and an exhibition of his work; a Military Museum with relics of the 1st Marquess of Anglesey, and the Ryan collection of uniforms and headgear. Park and gardens by Repton, in an unrivalled position beside the Menai Strait.
Admission: Fee charged.

LLANBERIS

MUSEUM OF THE NORTH
Llanberis   **Tel:** (0286) 870636
The **Museum of the North/Power of Wales** is the National Museum of Wales' main centre in North Wales and is located in Llanberis, Gwynedd in an attractive setting overlooking Lake Padarn at the foot of Snowdon. Your host is Merlin, the Welsh Wizard who, with the aid of a multi media presentation, takes you on a fascinating journey through time and reveals to you the 'Power of Wales'. To complete your experience, there's an insight into how the natural power of water has been harnessed to produce electricity at Dinorwig Pumped Storage Power Station. There is also a continuing programme of splendid temporary exhibitions.
Open: June-Sept 9.30-6. Daily Apr to May, Oct 10-5. Nov to Mar: groups only by appointment.
Admission: £3.50, Child (under 16) £1.75, Pensioner £2.60. 20% discount for pre-booked travel trade parties of more than 20 in number. 10% discount if not pre-booked.
Ample free parking. Museum gift/book shop. Toilets. Toilets suitable for the disabled.

WELSH SLATE MUSEUM
Llanberis   **Tel:** (0286) 870630
When the extensive Dinorwig Quarry at Llanberis, Gwynedd was closed in 1969 the workshops, most of the machinery and plant were preserved and the **Welsh Slate**

Museum was established. Much of the original atmosphere remains in the fitting and erecting shops, repair shops, smithy, dressing and sawing sheds, foundry office, mess room and yard. There are also demonstrations of many traditional slate crafts.
Open: 9.30-5. Daily Apr to Sept *Closed* Nov to Mar.
Admission: £1.50, Child (under 16) 90p, OAPs 90p. 20% discount for pre-booked trade parties of 20 or more. 10% discount if not pre-booked.
Ample free coach and car parking.

LLANDUDNO

LLANDUDNO MUSEUM
17-19 Gloddaeth Street, Llandudno   **Tel:** (0492) 76517

ORIEL MOSTYN
12 Vaughan Street, Llandudno   **Tel:** (0492) 879201

Oriel Mostyn

12 Vaughan Street, Llandudno, Gwynedd

A purpose-built Victorian building, Oriel Mostyn, can justifiably lay claim to being the most beautiful gallery in Wales.

EXHIBITIONS A changing programme of exhibitions that includes a wide range of contemporary and historical fine and applied arts.

CRAFT SHOP Selling the best from Wales and the U.K.

BOOKSHOP Specialising in fine art books, postcards, posters, artists' prints and a

changing selection of paintings by regional artists. The Gallery is also the centre for day and evening classes in painting, photography and weekly life classes.

OPEN Monday to Saturday 10.30–5.00

Tel: 0492 879201
870875
Fax: 0492 878869

ADMISSION FREE. Easy access and toilet facilities for the disabled.

This major public gallery organises temporary exhibitions covering a wide range of the contemporary arts from Britain and abroad, work by artists working in Wales as well as historical exhibitions of the fine and applied arts which are of particular regional interest.
Open: During exhibitions Mon to Sat: all year 10.30-5.
Admission: Free
Easy access for disabled. Bookshop, postcards, crafts, prints.

LLANGOED

HAULFRE STABLES
(Culture & Leisure: Archives & Museums)
Llangoed, Nr. Beaumaris, Anglesey   **Tel:** (0248 878) 709
The Stables represent the landed gentry's way of life in the last century. this venture is run in co-operation with the 'All Wales Strategy/Mental handicap (Social Services)', who also care for the gardens where fresh produce may be bought.
Open: Throughout the year. Mon-Fri 9-4.30. Weekends by Appointment.
Admission: Free

NEFYN

LLEYN HISTORICAL AND MARITIME MUSEUM
Old St. Mary's Church, Church Street, Nefyn

PORTHMADOG

FESTINIOG RAILWAY MUSEUM
(Festiniog Railway Co.)
Harbour Station, Porthmadog
Museum in part of former Goods Shed illustrating the Railway's history from the 1830s to the present day.
Open: Daily during train service hours.

PORTHMADOG MARITIME MUSEUM
Porthmadog
Situated on one of the old wharves of Porthmadog harbour, the last remaining slate shed houses a display on the maritime history of Porthmadog. Re-opened during 1992 with the building vastly improved and containing a new display.

PWLLHELI

ORIEL PLAS GLYN-Y-WEDDW GALLERY
Llanbedrog, Pwllheli LL53 7TT   Tel: (0758) 740763

Oriel–Plas Glyn-y-Weddw–Gallery

A fine Victorian Mansion standing in beautiful grounds at the end of Llanbedrog Bay.
One of the most charming and picturesque locations in Wales.
The art gallery has monthly changing exhibitions of a wide range of contemporary arts throughout the year.
The gallery is also a centre for day and residential art courses.

Opening times: Daily from 10.00am to 6.00pm.

Llanbedrog, Pwllheli, Gwynedd, LL53 7TT
Tel: (0758) 740763

POWYS

BRECON

BRECKNOCK MUSEUM
(Powys County Council)
Captain's Walk, Brecon   Tel: (0874) 624121
Collections illustrating the local and natural history of Brecknock. Archaeological, agriculture and domestic material, pottery, porcelain and lovespoons. Assize Court reconstruction, library and archives collection.
Open: Mon to Sat 10-5. Also open Suns Apr to Sept. *Closed* Christmas Day to New Year's Day incl. and Good Friday.

LLANDRINDOD WELLS

LLANDRINDOD MUSEUM
(Powys County Council)
Temple Street, Llandrindod Wells   Tel: (0597) 824513
The local history of Radnorshire seen through displays of archaeology, natural history and social history. Includes a gallery depicting the town's heyday as a Victorian spa, a fine collection of samplers and a photographic archive.
Open: Mon, Tues, Thurs, Fri (and weekends May-Oct) 10-1, 2-4.
Admission: Free

LLANIDLOES

MUSEUM OF LOCAL HISTORY AND INDUSTRY
(Powys County Council)
Market Hall, Llanidloes,
Displays iillustrating the social and industrial history of the area housed in a unique 16th century Market Hall.
Open: Easter week and Spring Bank Holiday to Sept 11-1, 2-5.

MACHYNLLETH

CENTRE FOR ALTERNATIVE TECHNOLOGY
Machynlleth SY20 9AZ   Tel: (0654) 702400
A futuristic centre with 16 years experience at working with and displaying technologies for a sustainable future: solar energy; wind-turbines; wave-power; re-cycling; water-power; amazing organic gardens; adventure playground; newest feature: a unique water-powered cliff railway.
Admission: £3.50 (including return trip in cliff railway). 10% reduction for groups of over 20.
Refreshments: Restaurant
Shop. Book in advance for guided tours or full meals. Suitable for disabled persons.

NEWTOWN

ROBERT OWEN MUSEUM
(Independent)
The Cross, Broad Street, Newtown   Tel: (0686) 626345
Robert Owen (1771-1858), model employer, social reformer, inspirer of the Co-operative movement.
Open: Mon to Fri 9.45-11.45, 2-3.30. Sat 10-11.30.
Admission: Free

W H SMITH MUSEUM
24 High Street, Newtown   Tel: (0686) 626280
The museum is on the first floor of the Newtown branch of W H Smith. The shop has been completely restored to its 1927 appearance, when the branch first opened. It has the original oak-shop front, tiling and mirrors, plaster relief decoration and other details. Storyboards show how the history of the company, founded in 1792, is inextricably linked with the changes in social patterns, transport and printing.
Open: Mon to Sat 9-5. *Closed* Sun and Bank Hols
Admission: Free
Some street parking and public car park approx 0¼ mile away. Not suitable for disabled persons.

WELSHPOOL

POWIS CASTLE
(The National Trust)
Welshpool
The castle of c. 1300 with some later reconstruction. The interior has fine plasterwork of the late 16th century; tapestries, paintings and furniture of the 17th centuries; collected by the 1st Lord Clive. Superb late 17th century terraced garden.
Admission: Fee charged.

POWYSLAND MUSEUM & MONTGOMERY CANAL CENTRE
(Powys County Council)
The Canal Wharf, Welshpool   Tel: (0938) 554656
The museum displays archaeological collections, the history of the railways and the canal, agricultural development and folk life material. The collections are housed in a converted and restored warehouse by the Montgomeryshire Canal.
Open: From Spring Bank Holiday to Sept 30: Mon, Tues, Thurs, Fri 11-1, 2-5. *Closed* Wed. Open Sat, Sun 10-1, 2-5. Oct to Spring Bank Holiday : Mon, Tues, Thurs, Fri 11-1, 2-5; Sat 2-5. *Closed* Wed, Sat am, Sun. Also *closed* Dec 25 to Jan 2.

IRELAND

IRELAND

CLONMEL

TIPPERARY (S.R.) CO. MUSEUM
(Patrick Holland M.A. Curator)
Parnell Street, Clonmel   Tel: (052) 21399
Tipperary (S.R.) County Museum collects records, preserves and displays objects which show the history of South Tipperary. An extended and completely renovated display incorporating many recent acquisitions has been set up. Temporary and touring exhibitions are also hosted. In 1985 the museum received a special commendation in the Irish 'Museum of the Year' award.
Open: Tues to Sat 10-1, 2-5. *Closed* Bank Holidays etc.
Admission: Free
Parties welcome by prior arrangement. Car park nearby. Unsuitable for disabled persons.

DUBLIN

ARCHBISHOP MARSH'S LIBRARY
(Muriel McCarthy M.A., Keeper)
St. Patrick's Close, Dublin   **Tel:** 01-543511

CHICHESTER BEATTY LIBRARY AND GALLERY OF ORIENTAL ART
20 Shrewsbury Road, Dublin

DUBLIN CIVIC MUSEUM
City Assembly House, South Williams Street, Dublin

GUINNESS MUSEUM
(Arthur Guinness, Son & Co. (Dublin) Ltd.)
The Old Hop Store, Crane Street, Dublin

THE HUGH LANE MUNICIPAL GALLERY OF MODERN ART
(Dublin Corporation)
Charlemont House, Parnell Square, Dublin   **Tel:** 01 741903
Large representative collection of modern European painting and sculpture including contemporary Irish art. Artists represented include Monet, Degas, Jack B. Yeats, William Scott and Louis le Brocquy. Regular temporary exhibitions.
Open: Tues to Fri 9.30-6, Sat 9.30-5, Sun 11-5. *Closed* Monday.

DOUGLAS HYDE GALLERY OF CONTEMPORARY ART
Trinity College, Nassau Street, Dublin

NATIONAL GALLERY OF IRELAND
Merrion Square (West), Dublin   **Tel:** 01-615133   **Fax:** 01-615372

NATIONAL GALLERY OF IRELAND

MERRION SQUARE, DUBLIN, 2

Old Master Paintings and Drawings of the Continental, Irish and British Schools.
Open each weekday 10-6 (Thursday 10-9); Sunday 2-5.

Admission free

Pierrot by Juan Gris

Paintings, drawings and sculptures of all European schools from 1300-1920s, also major Irish collection.
Open: Mon, Tues, Wed, Fri and Sat 10-6; Thurs 10-9; Sun 2-5.
Refreshments: Restaurant
Bookshop. Conducted tours of the Gallery, and lectures weekly.

NATIONAL MUSEUM OF IRELAND
(The National Museum)
Dublin   **Tel:** 01-618811
Contains the National collections of archaeology, the decorative arts, history, folk life, zoology and geology. Outstanding exhibitions of Prehistoric gold and Early Christian metalwork. Exhibitions of silver, ceramics and textiles. Special display of Japanese decorative art. Historical exhibition focuses on Irish history 1900-1921. Archaeological, historical and decorative arts collections located at Kildare Street, Zoological collections in the Natural History Museum at Merriton street. Geological exhibitions at the Exhibition Centre, 7-9 Merrion Row.
Open: Tues, Thurs and Sat 10-5, Fri 10.30-5; Sun 2-5
Admission: Free

KILKENNY

ROTHE HOUSE MUSEUM
(Kilkenny Archaeological Society)
Parliament Street, Kilkenny   **Tel:** 056-22893

KILMORE QUAY

KILMORE QUAY MARITIME MUSEUM, 'THE GUILLEMOT LIGHT SHIP'
Kilmore Quay
The Museum is displayed on board the last complete Irish Lightship and contains maritime pictures, models and a history of the Irish Navy as well as the fully fitted out 1922 built Lightship.

KINSALE

KINSALE REGIONAL MUSEUM
Kinsale   **Tel:** 021-772044
17th century Market House, Charters and general collection depicting life in town and port through the centuries.
Open: Daily at reasonable times.
Admission: 40p, child 10p.

LOUGHREA

LOUGHREA MUSEUM
St. Brendan's, Loughrea, Galway   **Tel:** 091-41212
Ecclesiastical Museum, vestments, chalices, statues. 13th century.
Open: All year by request.

MONAGHAN

MONAGHAN COUNTY MUSEUM
(Monaghan County Council)
1-2 Hill Street, Monaghan   **Tel:** 047-82928
Heritage and contemporary arts. New permanent exhibitions on archaeology, local history, folklife crafts and lace. Awarded 1980 Council of Europe Museum Prize.
Open: Tues to Sat 11-1. 2-5. *Closed* public hols.

VALENTIA ISLAND

KNIGHTSTOWN
(Valentia Heritage Society)
Valentia Island, Kerry

WEXFORD

IRISH AGRICULTURAL MUSEUM
(The Irish Agricultural Museum (J.C.) Ltd)
Johnstown Castle, Wexford   **Tel:** 053-42888   **Fax:** 053-42004
National museum of agricultural and Irish rural life. Housed in estate farmyard set in the 50 acre gardens of Johnstown Castle. Specialist sections on rural transport, country furniture and rural crafts. New exhibitions being added annually.

NORTHERN IRELAND

NORTHERN IRELAND

ARDRESS

FARMYARD DISPLAY
(The National Trust)
Ardress
Display in the farmyard of a 17th century house, covering agricultural life in the area during the 19th/20th centuries.

ULSTER – AMERICAN FOLK PARK

CAMPHILL, OMAGH, CO. TYRONE, BT785QY
TEL. 0662 243292/3

The Ulster-American Folk Park tells the story of the great migrations of Ulster people to the New World and of the contribution they made to the U.S.A. throughout the whole period of its birth and growth. Through the medium of restored or recreated buildings similar to those they left behind in Ulster and log dwellings of the type they constructed when they first set up their home in America a fascinating insight is given into the everyday life of the emigrant. There is also a modern exhibition building and a new Ship and Dockside Gallery.

Easter – Late September – Monday to Saturday 11.00-6.30. Sundays & Public Holidays 11.30 – 7.00

October – Easter – Open Monday – Friday 10.30-5.00 (except Public Holidays)

Closed weekends and Public Holidays from late September to Easter.

ARMAGH

ARMAGH COUNTRY MUSEUM
(County of Armagh)
The Mall East, Armagh
Local antiques, Prehistoric weapons, implements. Period costumes, uniforms. Natural History and bygones.
Open: Mon to Sat 10-1, 2-5. *Closed* certain Public Hols.

BANGOR

NORTH DOWN HERITAGE CENTRE
(North Down Borough Council)
Town Hall, Bangor Castle, Bangor   **Tel:** (0247) 270371
Local History and works of art reflecting aspects of North Down's historical and cultural past. Audio-visual shows; varying temporary exhibitions.
Open: Tues to Sat 10.30-4.30; Sun 2-4.30. July and Aug 10.30-5.30; Sun 2-5.30.
Admission: Free.
Refreshments: Castle Garden Room Restaurant.
Parties by prior arrangement.. Suitable for disabled persons. Curator I.A. Wilson B.A., Dip. Ed.

BELFAST

ULSTER MUSEUM
Botanic Gardens, Belfast BT9 5AB   **Tel:** (0232) 381251

Irish archaeology and local history, industrial archaeology including linen textile machinery. Coins and ethnography. Geology including the Dinosaur Show, featuring a complete anatosaurus skeleton and the natural history of Ireland with the unique feature on the 'Living Sea'. Irish and European Art.
Open: Free
Refreshments: Cafe
Shop

DOWNPATRICK

DOWN COUNTY MUSEUM
(Down District Council)
   The Mall, Downpatrick   **Tel:** (0396) 615218
The archaeology, history and natural history. Housed in 18th century country gaol.
Open: Tues-Fri 11-5, Sat 2-5, Sun afternoon and Mon opening from July to mid-Sept.
Open St. Patrick's Day, Easter Mon and May Bank Holidays.
Admission: Free
Car Parking. Partly suitable for disabled persons.

ENNISKILLEN

ENNISKILLEN CASTLE: MUSEUMS
   Enniskillen   **Tel:** (0365) 325000
Fermanagh County Museum (Fermanagh District Council) and Royal Inniskilling
Fusiliers Museum. The story of Fermanagh: Its landscape and people. Audio visual
programmes and special exhibitions.
Open: Tues to Fri 10-5; May to Sept: Sat 2-5; July & Aug: Sun Mon 2-5.
Admission: Free
Shop. Car parking nearby. Partly suitable for disabled.

NEWRY

NEWRY ARTS CENTRE
   1A Bank Parade, Newry BT35 6HP

NEWRY MUSEUM
   1a Bank Parade, Newry BT35 HHP   **Tel:** (0693) 66232
Housing and panelled room from Newry's commercial greatness.
Open: Weekdays 11-5. Sats on request.

OMAGH

ULSTER-AMERICAN FOLK PARK
   Camphill, Co. Tyrone, Omagh
The Ulster-American Folk Park tells of the story of migrations of Ulster people to the
New World and of the contribution they made to the U.S.A. over 200 years. Restored
and recreated buildings, log dwellings, Ship and Dockside Gallery linking the Old and
New World exhibits, craft demonstrations, modern exhibitions.
Open: Easter to late Sept: Mon to Sat 11-6.30; Sun and Public Bank Hols 11.30-7. Oct
to Easter: Mon to Fri 10.30-5 (except Public Hols).
Admission: £2.60, Child/OAPs and disabled £1.30. Reductions for parties of 20 or
more.
Education service.

SPRINGHILL

SPRINGHILL
(The National Trust)
   Co. Londonderry, Springhill
Costume Museum housed in an ancillary building to the 17th century Manor house.

SCOTLAND

BORDERS

COLDSTREAM

THE HIRSEL HOMESTEAD MUSEUM
   Coldstream   **Tel:** (0890) 2834/2965/3160/2629/2977/3215
Tools from the Estate's past - archaeology, agriculture, forestry, jioners, blacksmiths,
natural and family history, Craft House and Workshops.
Open: All reasonable daylight hours throughout the year.
Admission: Adult admission charge.
Refreshments: Available.
Walks, Picnic area, Car Park, Playground.

EYEMOUTH

EYEMOUTH MUSEUM
   Auld Kirk, Market Place, Eyemouth   **Tel:** (08907) 50678

GALASHIELS

OLD GALA HOUSE
(Ettrick and Lauderdale District Council)
   Scott Cresent, Galashiels   **Tel:** (0750) 20096

Halliwell's House Museum
Market Place, Selkirk
(Ironmongers shop, Videos, Social History,
Temporary Exhibitions)
OPEN SEVEN DAYS A WEEK MID MARCH–DECEMBER

Old Gala House
Scott Crescent, Galashiels
(Painted Ceiling (1635), Wall Mural, Exhibitions)
OPEN SEVEN DAYS A WEEK MID MARCH–OCTOBER

For further information telephone Selkirk (0750) 20096

ADMISSION FREE

This historic house, dating from 1593, once the home of the Lairds of Gala, was
re-opened as an interpretive centre in 1988. Displays tell the story of the House, the
Lairds of Gala and their involvement in the development of the town. Particularly
memorable are the painted ceiling (1635) and painted wall (1988). Temporary
Exhibition Galleries. A visit to Old Gala House now includes a walk through the 'old
town' to the recently restored seventeenth century Gala Aisle.
Open: Mid Mar to end of Oct: Mon to Sat 10-4; Sun 2-4. Nov to Easter: limited opening,
telephone for times.
Admission: Free
Refreshments: Tearoom.

HAWICK

MUSEUM AND THE SCOTT ART GALLERY
(Roxburgh District Council)
   Wilton Lodge Park, Hawick
Social history, local industries (particularly knitwear), natural history and fine local
collections. Scottish paintings and temporary exhibitions in the Scott Gallery.
Open: Apr-Sept: Mon to Sat 10-12, 1-5; Sun 2-5. Oct to Mar: Mon to Fri 1-4 Sun 2-4.
Closed Sat.
Admission: Adm. 70p, Chld/OAPs/students and the unemployed 35p. Roxburgh
district residents and Borders Regiinal schools free.

INNERLEITHEN

NATIONAL TRUST FOR SCOTLAND
   Innerleithen
**Open: Please note, that with this property, and all other NTS properties, last
admissions are 45 minutes before the advertised closing times.**
**Admission: OAPs/students/unemployed are admitted at half the standard adult
rate on production of their cards.**
Only guide dogs are permitted

ST. RONAN'S WELLS INTERPRETIVE CENTRE
(Tweeddale District Council)
   Innerleithen   **Tel:** (0721) 20123
History of site interpreted through objects, photographs and documents.
Open: Daily 2-5pm Easter-October
Refreshments: Available

ROBERT SMAIL'S PRINTING WORKS
(National Trust for Scotland)
   Innerleithen
This 130-year-old printing works, a time-capsule of local history, and the printing
methods of yesteryear, has a water-wheel and working machinery. All machinery has
been restored to full working order and the printer may be viewed at work.
Open: Apr 1 to Oct 31: Mon to Sat 10-1, 2-5; Sun 2-5.
Admission: £2.00, Child £1.00 Adult parties £1.60, Schools 80p
Restored Printing Works and Shop.

JEDBURGH

CASTLE JAIL
(Roxburgh District Council)
Castlegate, Jedburgh
A Howard reform jail, built in 1823, on the site of the former Jedburgh Castle and
gallows. Contains articles associated with prison life and the history of the Royal Burgh.
Open: Apr to Sept: Mon to Sat 10-12, 1-5; Sun 1-5
Admission: Adults 70p, Chld/OAPs/students and the unemployed 35p.
Reductions for pre-booked parties over 20. Roxburgh district residents and Borders
regional schools free.

MARY, QUEEN OF SCOTS' HOUSE
(Roxburgh District Council)
Queen Street, Jedburgh

ROXBURGH DISTRICT MUSEUMS

Where the only thing gathering dust is the hoover!

MARY QUEEN of SCOTS HOUSE (illustrated) & the
CASTLE JAIL, JEDBURGH.
★
HAWICK MUSEUM & The SCOTT GALLERY
★
KELSO MUSEUM. *See entries for opening times*

Recently refurbished to an exceptional standard, the house tells the story of the life of the tragic queen, who herself visited Jedburgh in 1566.
Open: Apr to Oct: Daily 10-5
Admission: Adm £1.10 Chld/OAPs students and the unemployed 55p. 5% discount for parties over 20. Roxburgh district residents and Borders Regional schools free.

KELSO

KELSO MUSEUM
(Roxburgh District Council)
Turret House, Abbey Court, Kelso   **Tel:** (0573) 25470
A new award winning museum in a charming 18th century building owned by the National Trust for Scotland. Once used as a skinner's workshop, the house has displays reconstructing a skinner's business as well as areas reflecting Kelso's growth as a market town and about Kelso Abbey.
Open: Apr-Oct Mon-Sat 10-12 & 1-5 Sun 2-5
Admission: Adults 70p Chld,OAPs, students, unemployed 35p. Parties over 20, 5% discount. Roxburgh district residents and Borders Regional schools free.
There is also a Victorian School Room.Car park nearby (200 yds). Only grounhd floor display suitable for disabled.

LAUDER

THIRLESTANE CASTLE
Lauder
Incorporating Border Country life exhibitions.
Location: A68, 28m South of Edinburgh

PEEBLES

TWEEDDALE MUSEUM
(Tweeddale District Council)
Chambers Institute, High Street, Peebles   **Tel:** (0721) 20123
Local museum which has displays relating mainly to Tweeddale District, its history, environment and culture. Picture gallery showing monthly programme of contemporary art and craft.
Open: All year Mon to Fri 10-1, 2-5; Apr-Oct: Sat and Sun 2-5.

SELKIRK

HALLIWELL'S HOUSE MUSEUM
(Ettrick and Lauderdale District Council)
Halliwell's Close, Market Place, Selkirk   **Tel:** (0750) 20096
Selkirk's oldest surviving dwelling house now creates for the present day visitor its past role as a home and ironmonger's shop. First floor galleries tell the tale of the development of the historic Royal Burgh of Selkirk. The stories are told by objects, text, drawings, videos and a talking post and the Museum was a winner in the British Tourist Authority's 'Come to Britain' Awards for 1984. A temporary Exhibition Gallery (displays changing monthly)
Open: Mid Mar to Oct: Daily 10-5; Sun 2-4. Nov to Dec: daily 2-4.

Admission: Free
Free parking. Tourist Information Centre and shop.

WALKERBURN

SCOTTISH MUSEUM OF WOOLLEN TEXTILES
(Clan Royal of Scotland)
Tweedvale Mill, Walkerburn EH43 6AH   **Tel:** (089 687) 281/3
A history of the woollen industry.
Open: Easter to Oct Daily. Arrangements can be made for school parties all year.
Admission: Fee charged.

CENTRAL

ALLOA

ALLOA MUSEUM AND GALLERY
(Clackmannan District Council)
Speirs Centre, Primrose Street, Alloa, Central   **Tel:** (0259) 213131
Local history and art exhibitions. Imaginary exhibitions changed monthly. Community involvement, school projects and regular lectures.
Open: Mon to Fri 10-4, Sat 10-12.30. *Closed* Public Hols.
Admission: Free
Refreshments: Vending machines.
Parties by prior arrangement. Car parking. Suitable for disabled persons.

BANNOCKBURN

BANNOCKBURN
(National Trust for Scotland)
Bannockburn, Central   **Tel:** (0786) 812664
Borestone site from where King Robert the Bruce commanded the battle of 1314 which gave the Scots their freedom and independence from English domination. Equestrian statue. Bannockburn is a Heritage Centre, with an exhibition 'The Kingdom of the Scots' tracing the history of Scotland by an imaginative series of displays from the Wars of Independence up to the Union of the Crowns in 1603.
Open: Apr 1 to Oct 31, daily 10-6 (Last audio-visual show 5.30)
Admission: £1.50, Child 80p. Adult parties £1.20, Schools 60p
Heritage Centre and Shop.

DOUNE

DOUNE MOTOR MUSEUM
Carse of Cambus, Doune   **Tel:** (0786) 841203

A unique collection of vintage and post vintage throughbred cars. The display includes examples of Hispano Suiza, Bentley, Jaguar, Aston Martin, Lagonda and many others, including the second oldest Rolls-Royce in the world.
Open: Apr to Oct. Daily.
Admission: Fee charged.
Location: On the A84
Refreshments: Cafeteria
Gift shop. Free car parking.

DUNBLANE

DUNBLANE CATHEDRAL MUSEUM
(Society of Friends of Dunblane Cathedral)
   The Cross, Dunblane, Central   **Tel:** (0786) 824254
Collection of artefacts, archives and pictures concerning the history of Dunblane and its Cathedral. Large collection of Communion Tokens. Library.
Open: Late May to early Oct: 10.30-12.30, 2.30-4.30. Other times on request.

FALKIRK

FALKIRK MUSEUM
   15 Orchard Street, Falkirk, Central FK1 1RF   **Tel:** (0324) 24911 Ext. 2472
Displays trace the history and development of Falkirk District from earliest times. Roman, medieval and Victorian pottery and local cast iron products.
Open: Mon to Sat 10-5.
Shop

GRANGEMOUTH MUSEUM
   Victorian Library, Bo'ness Road, Grangemouth, Falkirk, Central
Tells the story of one of Scotland's earliest planned industrial towns, from its origins as the east terminal port of the Forth and Clyde Canal to its present internal status as a centre for the petro-chemical industry.
Open: Mon to Sat 2-5.
Shop

KINNEIL MUSEUM AND ROMAN FORTLET
   Kinneil Estate, Bo'ness, Falkirk, Central
Social history, particularly the Bo'ness pottery industry. Special exhibition and audio-visual '2,000 years of History' tells the story of Kinneil Estate from Roman times. The Emperor, Antonius Pius, St. Serf, Mary Queen of Scots and James Watt are among many historical characters associated with the Estate. A short walk from the museum is Kinneil Roman Fortlet, consolidated for public viewing. History tours with costumed 18th century guides are provided in Summer.
Open: Apr to Sept: Mon to Sat 10-5. Oct to Mar: Sat only 10-5.
Shop

DUMFRIES & GALLOWAY

CASTLE DOUGLAS

CASTLE DOUGLAS ART GALLERY
   Castle Douglas
Temporary exhibition programme throughout the year, including touring exhibitions and the work of the local art and craft groups.

DUMFRIES

ROBERT BURNS CENTRE
(Nithsdale District Council)
   Mill Road, Dumfries   **Tel:** (0387) 64808
Exhibition on Burns and his life in Dumfries. AV theatre. Quality feature films 5 evenings a week.
Open: Apt to Sept: Mon to Sat 10-8; Sun 2-5. Oct to Mar: Tues to Sat 10-1, 2-5.
Admission: Free except to AV theatre, 70p, concessions 35p. *Combined ticket for Camera Obscura, Burns House and Burns Centre AV theatre £1.40 only. Concessions 70p.*
Refreshments: Cafe
Shop

BURNS HOUSE
(Nithsdale District Council)
   Burns Street, Dumfries   **Tel:** (0387) 55297
House in which Robert Burns lived for the three years prior to his death.
Open: Times as Dumfries Museum.
Admission: 70p, concessions 35p.

DUMFRIES MUSEUM
(Nithsdale District Council)
   The Observatory, Dumfries   **Tel:** (0387) 53374

Natural history, archaeology and folk collections.
Open: Weekdays 10-1, 2-5; Sun 2-5. *Closed* Sun and Mon, Oct to Mar
Admission: Free. Camera obscura 70p, concessions 35p. Obscura *Closed* Oct to Mar.

GRACEFIELD - THE ARTS CENTRE FOR SOUTH WEST SCOTLAND
   28 Edinburgh Road, Dumfries   **Tel:** (0387) 62084

Situated in beautiful grounds overlooking the river Nith, the Centre has a collection of over 400 Scottish paintings. Regular exhibitions of contemporary art. Dark room. Pottery, studios.
Open: All year: Studios Tues to Fri 9-5 Galleries Tues to Fri 10-5 summer, 12-5 winter. Galleries and Studio: Sat 10-5, Sun 12-5.
Refreshments: Bar/Cafe
Ample car parking.

OLD BRIDGE HOUSE MUSEUM
(Nithsdale District Council)
Dumfries   **Tel:** (0387) 56904
Seventeenth century house with six period and historical rooms.
Open: As Dumfries Museum, *Closed* Oct to Mar.
Admission: Free

SANQUHAR MUSEUM
(Nithsdale District Council)
Dumfries
1735 Adam-designed town house; covers local history, geology etc.
Open: Apr to Sept: Tues to Sat 10-1, 2-5; Sun 2-5.

SAVINGS BANK MUSEUM
Ruthwell, Dumfries

ECCLEFECHAN

CARLYLE'S BIRTHPLACE
(National Trust of Scotland)
The Arched House, Ecclefechan   **Tel:** (057 63) 666
House in which Carlyle was born in 1795 containing personal relics and manuscript letters.
Open: Apr 1 to Oct 31: Daily 12-5 (last tour 4.30). Also by arrangement.
Admission: £1.50, Child 80p, adult parties £1.20, Schools 60p

KIRKCUDBRIGHT

BROUGHTON HOUSE
(Trustees of the late E.A.Hornel)
Kirkcudbright   **Tel:** (0557) 31217
A large reference library with a valuable Burns collection.

THE STEWARTRY MUSEUM
Kirkcudbright
Displays the archaeology, history and natural history of the Stewartry District.
Open: Easter to Oct: Mon to Sat, Apr and Oct 11-4, May, June and Sept 11-5, July and Aug 11-7.30 and Sun 2-5.
Admission: £1, OAPs 50p, Child free.

STRANRAER

CASTLE OF ST JOHN
(Wigtown District Council)
Castle Street, Stranraer   **Tel:** (0776) 5088
16th century towerhouse with display on the Castle, the Covenanters and the 19th century town jail.
Open: Apr to mid-Sept: Mon to Sat 10-1, 2-5.
Shop and information point.

STRANRAER MUSEUM
(Wigtown District Council)
The Old Town Hall, George Street, Stranraer   **Tel:** (0776) 5088
Permanent exhibition on Farming, Archaeology and Polar Explorers, John and James Clark Ross, Temporary exhibition programme.
Open: All year: Mon to Sat 10-5.
Admission: Free
Disabled access throughout. Shop and information point.

WANLOCKHEAD

MUSEUM OF LEAD MINING
(Wanlockhead Museum Trust)
Goldscaur Row, Wanlockhead   **Tel:** (0659) 74387
Set in Scotland's highest village in the beautiful Lowther Hills. Period cottages, visitor centre and trail. Guided tours of lead mine.
Open: Daily: Easter to Oct 11-4.30 (mine 4). Enquire for times Oct-March.
Admission: Fee charged. Party discounts.
Refreshments: Tea room
Wheelchairs welcome. Shop

WIGTOWN

WIGTOWN MUSEUM
(Wigtown District Council)
County Hall, Main Street, Wigtown   **Tel:** (0776) 5088
Changing displays on local history and Wigtown area including Wigtown Martyrs.
Open: May to mid-Sept: Afternoons 2-4, Mon to Fri
Sales and information point. Disabled access.

FIFE

ANSTRUTHER

THE SCOTTISH FISHERIES MUSEUM
St. Ayles, Harbourhead, Anstruther   **Tel:** (0333) 310628
16th to 19th century buildings housing marine aquarium, fishing and ships' gear, model and actual fishing boats, period fisher-home interiors, reference library.
Open: Apr to Oct: Weekdays 10-5.30, Sun 11-5. Nov to Mar: weekdays 10-4.30. Sun 2-4.30.
Admission: £1.80, Child/OAPs £1 (1992 rates).*Reduced rates for parties.*
Refreshments: Tea room
Shop. Wheelchair friendly.

CERES

FIFE FOLK MUSEUM
Ceres
A varied local exhibition displayed in a unique setting.

CULROSS

DUNIMARIE MUSEUM
Culross   **Tel:** (0383) 229
Napoleonic furniture, oil paintings, library, ceramics, glass, silver and objets d'art.
Admission: Fee charged.

DUNFERMLINE

ANDREW CARNEGIE BIRTHPLACE MUSEUM
Junction of Moodie Street and Priory Lane, Dunfermline   **Tel:** (0383) 724302
'The man who dies rich dies disgraced'. Born in a humble weaver's cottage, Andrew Carnegie became the greatest steelmaster in 19th century America - and gave away $350 million. Exciting displays in his Birthplace Cottage and the adjoining Memorial Hall tell his fascinating story and illustrate the work of the major Trusts and Foundations he established in Britain, Europe and America. Audio-visual programme. Guided tours available during summer weekends.
Open: Apr to Oct: Mon to Sat 11-5; Sun 2-5. Nov to Mar: Daily 2-4
Admission: Free
Provision for disabled. Shop. Classroom/Seminar Room available for school and group visits. Car parking at museum.

DUNFERMLINE DISTRICT MUSEUM AND THE SMALL GALLERY
(Dunfermline District Council)
Viewfield, Dunfermline   **Tel:** (0383) 721814
Local history and natural history of the district. Small gallery: monthly art and craft exhibitions.
Open: Mon to Sat 11-5.*Closed* Sun and public holidays.
Admission: Free

PITTENCRIEFF HOUSE MUSEUM
(Dunfermline District Council)
Pittencrieff Park, Dunfermline   **Tel:** (0383) 722935/721814
Local history and costume displays; temporary paintings and photographic exhibitions.
Open: May 1 to Oct 31. Daily (except Tues) 11-5.

INVERKEITHING

INVERKEITHING MUSEUM
(Dunfermline District Council)
Queen Street, Inverkeithing   **Tel:** (0383) 413344/721814
Small local history museum with changing Social History exhibitions.
Open: Wed to Sun 11-5.*Closed* Mon and Tues, 25 and 26 Dec, 1 and 2 Jan.
Admission: Free
Car parking outside museum. Unsuitable for disabled persons.

KIRKCALDY

BURNTISLAND EDWARDIAN FAIR
(Kirkcaldy District Museums)
High Street, Kirkcaldy   **Tel:** (05892) 260732
New displays bring back the fun, colour and noise of an Edwardian fairground. Visit the Burntsland Lion**1990 Scottish Museum of the Year Award Winner**.
Open: Daily during library hours. (*Closed* 1-2)
Location: Entrance in Burntisland Library.

Fife

KIRKCALDY MUSEUM AND ART GALLERY
(Kirkcaldy District Museums)
Kirkcaldy   **Tel:** (0592) 260732

KIRKCALDY MUSEUM & ART GALLERY
FIFE

"A Lowland Lassie" Thomas Faed.

Scottish Art from 1800 to present day.
Changing Exhibitions.   A Museum of the Year Award Winner,
Café Wemyss, Shop, Disabled Access to ground floor.
Open: 11 – 5 Mon. – Sat.   2 – 5 Sun.   Admission Free

A Scottish Museum of the Year Award winner 1989. A unique collection of paintings including works by the Scottish Colourists, the Camden Town Group and contemporary artists. Fascinating historical displays and a lively changing exhibition programme.
Open: Mon to Sat 11-5, Sun 2-5.
Admission: Free
Location: By Kirkcaldy Railway Station
Refreshments: New Cafe incorporating Wemyss pottery displays.
Gallery shop for crafts, cards and local publications. Special enquiry and Outreach Service available.

MCDOUALL STUART MUSEUM
(Kirkcaldy District Museums)
Rectory Lane, Dysart, Kirkcaldy   **Tel:** (0592) 260732
This small museum occupies one of Dysart's many National Trust for Scotland restored 'little houses' which form the 18th century burgh with its historic harbour. The house is the birthplace of John McDouall Stuart, first explorer to cross Australia 1861-2 and displays describe his harrowing journeys, the Australian wilderness and the Aborigines. Sales area and starting point for self-guided tours around this attractive burgh.
Open: June 1 to Aug 31: Daily (incl. Sun) 2-5.

HERITAGE EDUCATION TRUST

ETHA
Education Through Heritage and the Arts

sponsored for HET by one of the Sainsbury Family Trusts

ETHA will • encourage schools throughout the country to turn to the resources of the heritage for inspiration
• be of interest to property owners/administrators education officers, advisers and teachers' of many subjects

All enquiries to
Heritage Education Trust, Burn House, Moor Road, Askrigg, nr. Leyburn, N. Yorkshire   Tel: 0969 50294

ST. ANDREWS

BRITISH GOLF MUSEUM
(Royal & Ancient Golf Club of St. Andrews Trust)
Bruce Embankment, St. Andrews   **Tel:** (0334) 78880 **Fax:** (0334) 73306

Trace the game's history, stroke for stroke, with visual and touch-screen displays. Re-live famous moments and enjoy all the history and atmosphere of the game's 500 years.

The British Golf Museum, Bruce Embankment, St Andrews, Fife KY16 9AB
Tel: 0334 78880 Fax: 0334 73306
Call for details of opening times and charges. Group rates available.

Everything that's best of the game's 500 year history is on display at the award winning British Golf Museum in St. Andrews; walk around the galleries and trace the development of golf. Re-live the famous golfing moments - stroke for stroke. The museum is home to the most innovative multi-media system in the UK. Thanks to Compact Disk Interactive (CDI) technology, specially designed, developed and supplied by Philips Electronics, you can listen to commentaries and see biographies of the players accompanied by video and photographs. You can even test your knowledge of the game - all at the touch of a screen.
Open: 0n application for 1993.
Admission: Fee charged. Special reductions for parties.
Car parking. Suitable for the disabled.

CRAWFORD ARTS CENTRE
93 North Street, St. Andrews   **Tel:** (0334) 74610
Monthly programme of temporary exhibitions including contemporary and historical Scottish and international art, photography, architecture, crafts etc. Also dramas and music performances and workshops.
Open: All year Mon to Sat 10-5, Sun 2-5.*Closed* Christmas and New Year.
Admission: Free
Main Gallery suitable for disabled persons.

GRAMPIAN

ABERDEEN

ABERDEEN ART GALLERY
(Aberdeen District Council)
Schoolhill, Aberdeen,   **Tel:** (0224) 646333
Permanent collection of 18th, 19th and 20th century art with emphasis on contemporary art - oil paintings, watercolours, prints, drawings, sculpture, decorative arts. Full programmme of special exhibitions. Music, Dance Poetry.
Open: Mon to Sat 10-5 (Thur 10-8); Sun 2-5.
Admission: Free
Refreshments: Cafeteria
Museum shop. Access for disabled. Parking (50m) 400 places.

ABERDEEN MARITIME MUSEUM
(Aberdeen District Council)
Provost Ross's House, Shiprow, Aberdeen,   **Tel:** (0224) 585788
Display themes on local shipbuilding, fishing, North Sea Oil, ship models and paintings within the restored 16th century building. Special Exhibitions.
Open: Mon to Sat 10-5.
Admission: Free
Museum shop. Parking (50m) 400 places.

ABERDEEN UNIVERSITY MARISCHAL MUSEUM
Aberdeen, Fife **Tel:** (0224) 273131 or 273132
General archaeological and ethnographical museum with Classical, Oriental, Egyptian, American and Pacific collections and local antiquities
Open: Mon to Fri 10-5; Sun 2-5. *Closed* Sat

ABERDEEN UNIVERSITY NATURAL HISTORY MUSEUM
Zoology Department, Tillydrone Avenue, Aberdeen, **Tel:** (0224) 272850
Teaching and study collections of natural history.
Open: By appointment.

JAMES DUN'S HOUSE
61 Schoolhill, Aberdeen, **Tel:** (0224) 646333
18th century town house renovated for use as a museum with permanent displays and special exhibitions.
Open: Mon to Sat 10-5.
Admission: Free
Parking (300m) 250 places.

PROVOST ROSS'S HOUSE
(National Trust for Scotland)
Shiprow, off Castle Street, Aberdeen, **Tel:** (0224) 572215
Houses the Aberdeen Maritime Museum, operated by the City of Aberdeen District Council, in one of the oldest surviving houses in Aberdeen, built 1593.
Open: All year, Mon to Sat 10-5. NTS Visitor Centre, video programme and shop open May 1 to Sept 30, Mon to Sat 10-4
Admission: Free

PROVOST SKENE'S HOUSE
(Aberdeen District Council)
Guestrow (off Broad Street), Aberdeen, **Tel:** (0224) 641086
17th century furnished house with period rooms and displays of local history and domestic life. Video programme showing daily.
Open: Mon to Sat 10-5.
Admission: Free
Refreshments: Provost Skene's Kitchen has been restored and serves coffee, tea and light meals.
Parking (25m) 35 places.

ALFORD

GRAMPIAN TRANSPORT MUSEUM
(Grampian Transport Museum Trust)
Alford AB33 8AD **Tel:** (09755) 62292 **Fax:** (09755) 62180

Grampian Transport Museum
ALFORD, ABERDEENSHIRE
A Bentley Works Racer at speed on the Museum Circuit
BRINGING HISTORY TO LIFE!
Open Daily 28th March-31st Oct, 10.00a.m.-5p.m.

**THE GRAMPIAN TRANSPORT MUSEUM
ALFORD, ABERDEENSHIRE AB33 8AD
TEL: 09755 62292   FAX: 09755 62180**

An extensive collection of road transport vehicles and items housed in purpose built exhibition hall. All types of vehicle are represented including steam and horse drawn. Most of vehicles have strong local associations. Regional road transport history is reflected by photographs and displays. Extensive summer events programme strongly boosted by new tarmac circuit facility allowing demonstration of vehicles in a suitable road environment. Also allows for motorsport events such as the Grampian Classic Car sprint on Sun Aug 8 1993. Alford Cavalcade July 25 1993, a monumental gathering of the region's preserved transport. A separate railway exhibition is housed in the reconstructed GNSR village station which also acts as a terminus of the Alford Valley Railway, a two foot gauge passenger carrying railway.
Open: Mar 28 to Oct 31: daily 10-5.
Admission: Fee charged. Special reduction for parties.
Extensive free parking. Suitable for disabled persons.

BANCHORY

BANCHORY MUSEUM
(North East of Scotland Museum Service)
The Square, Banchory **Tel:** (0779) 77778
Local history and bygones featuring relics of J. Scott Skinner the 'Strathspey King' who was a native of Banchory.
Open: June to Sept.

BANFF

BANFF MUSEUM
(North East of Scotland Museum Service)
High Street, Banff **Tel:** (0779) 77778
Local history including silver display, award winning natural history display and geology display; James Ferguson relics.
Open: June to Sept

BUCKIE

BUCKIE MARITIME MUSEUM
(Moray District Council)
Cluny Place, Buckie **Tel:** (0309) 673701
Fishing, lifeboats, coopering, local history. Peter Anson paintings.
Open: Mon to Fri 10-8; Sat 10-12.

DUFFTOWN

DUFFTOWN MUSEUM
(Moray District Council)
The Tower, Dufftown **Tel:** (0309) 673701
Local history. Mortlach Kirk. Temporary exhibitions.
Open: Daily Apr to Oct: 10-6.

MORAY DISTRICT COUNCIL
MUSEUMS DIVISION

Oldmills Working Mill, Elgin

Museums at Buckie, Dufftown, Elgin, Forres, Tomintoul, Tugnet

ELGIN

OLDMILLS WORKING MILL & VISITOR CENTRE
(Moray District Council)
Oldmills Road, **Tel:** (0309) 673701
Working watermill, visitor centre. lakeside trail.
Open: April-September, Tuesday - Sunday 9 - 5.

FOCHABERS

FOCHABERS FOLK MUSEUM
Fochabers

FORRES

FALCONER MUSEUM
(Moray District Council)
Forres   **Tel:** (0309) 73701
Local history 'The Story of Forres'; Natural history; Exhibits on Hugh Falconer and other prominent local people. Temporary exhibitions.
Open: Mid May to Sept: Daily 9.30-5.30. Other periods from Mon to Fri 10-12.30, 1.30-4.30.

NELSON TOWER
(Moray District Council)
Grant Park   **Tel:** (0309) 673701
Historic viewpoint with temporary exhibitions.
Open: May - August Tuesday - Sunday 2pm-4pm

FYVIE

FYVIE CASTLE
(National Trust for Scotland)
Fyvie   **Tel:** (0651 891) 266
Probably the grandest example of Scottish baronial architecture, reflecting the opulence of the Edwardian era. Contains an exceptionally important collection of portraits including works by Batoni, Raeburn, Ramsey, Gainsborough, Opie and Hoppner. In addition there are arms and armour and 16th century tapestries. Castles of Mar exhibition.
Open: Castle Apr 3-25 and Oct 2-31; Sat/Sun 2-5, May 1-31 and Sept 1-30, daily 2-6; June 1-Aug 31, daily 11-6. Grounds open all year, daily 9.30-sunset.
Admission: £3.30, Child £1.70 Adult parties £2.60, schools £1.30. Grounds 50p.
Refreshments: Tearoom.

HUNTLY

BRANDER MUSEUM
(North East of Scotland Museum Service)
Public Library Building, Huntly   **Tel:** (0779) 77778
Small display of local bygones; interesting display of Scottish Communion Tokens. Special temporary exhibitions.
Open: All year.

INVERURIE

INVERURIE MUSEUM
(North East of Scotland Museum Service)
Public Library Building, The Square, Inverurie   **Tel:** (0779) 77778
Collection of Prehistoric material from locality. Railway and canal memorabilia. Special temporary exhibitions.
Open: All year.

KEITH

THE GLENFIDDICH DISTILLERY
(The Grant Family)
Dufftown, Keith

KENNETHMONT

LEITH HALL
(National Trust for Scotland)
Kennethmont   **Tel:** (046 43) 216
Unusual house, built round a central courtyard. Home of the Leith family from 1650. House contains personal possessions of successive Laird's, Jacobite relics. Major exhibition - 'For Crown and Country: The Military Lairds of Leith Hall'.
Open: May 1 to Sept 30: Daily 2-6. Sat and Sun in Oct 2-5.
Admission: £3.30, Child £1.70, Adult parties £2.60, Schools £1.30
Refreshments: Tearoom.

MINTLAW

NORTH EAST OF SCOTLAND AGRICULTURAL HERITAGE CENTRE
(Leisure and Recreation Dept., Banff and Buchan District Council)
Aden Country Park, by Peterhead, Mintlaw AB4 8LD

PETERHEAD

ARBUTHNOT MUSEUM
(North East of Scotland Museum Service)
St. Peter Street, Peterhead   **Tel:** (0779) 77778
Collections illustrating local history; whaling, Arctic and fishing section; coins. Large local photograph collection; lively temporary exhibitions programme.
Open: All year.

PITMEDDEN

PITMEDDEN MUSEUM OF FARMING LIFE
(National Trust for Scotland)
Gordon, Pitmedden   **Tel:** (06513) 2352
Collection of Agricultural and domestic artifacts.
Open: May 1 to Sept 30: 10-6.
Admission: £2.80, Child £1.40, Adult parties £2.20, Schools £1.10
Location: On A920, 1m W of Pitmedden village and 14m N of Aberdeen.
Refreshments: Tea room.

SPEY BAY

TUGNET ICE HOUSE
(Moray District Council)
Spey Bay   **Tel:** (0309) 673701
Exhibition of Salmon fishing and the River Spey.
Open: June to Sept: Daily 10.00-4.00

STONEHAVEN

TOLBOOTH MUSEUM
(North East of Scotland Museum Service)
The Harbour, Stonehaven   **Tel:** (0779) 77778
Housed in one of the town's oldest buildings on the old quay, the museum has local history and fishing displays.
Open: June to Sept

TOMINTOUL

TOMINTOUL VISITOR CENTRE
(Moray District Council)
The Square, Tomintoul, Grampian   **Tel:** (0309) 673701
Wildlife, landscape, geology, climate, local history, reconstructed farm kitchen and village smithy.
Open: Easter to Oct: Daily 9.30-6.

HIGHLANDS

AVIEMORE

STRATHSPEY STEAM RAILWAY
(Strathspey Railway Co. Ltd.)
Aviemore

BETTYHILL

STRATHNAVER MUSEUM
Clachan, Bettyhill, by Thurso, Sutherland
An expansive collection of local antiquities revealing the life and times of bygone days. Special features include the Farr Stone (9th century B.C.), the Highland Clearances of Strathnaver (1812-1819) Clan Mackay memorial room.

CAITHNESS

LHAIDHAY CROFT MUSEUM
Dunbeath, Caithness

CROMARTY

HUGH MILLER'S COTTAGE
(National Trust for Scotland)
Cromarthy   **Tel:** (038 17) 245
Birthplace of the renowned geologist, editor and writer, containing relics and geological specimens.
Open: Apr 1 to Sept 26, Mon to Sat 10-1 and 2-5, Sun 2-5
Admission: £1.50, Child 80p. Adult parties £1.20, Schools 60p

CULLODEN

CULLODEN
(National Trust for Scotland)
Culloden   **Tel:** (0463) 790607
Site of defeat in 1746 of Prince Charles Edward Stuart and the end of the 1745 Jacobite Rising. Graves of the Clans, Well of the Dead, Memorial Cairn. Colourful historical display. Visitor centre including A/V and Old Leanach Cottage.
Open: Feb 6 to Mar 31 and Nov 1 to Dec 30: 10-4 (*except* Christmas and Boxing Day); Apr 1 to May 21 and Sept 13 to Oct 30: 9.30-5; May 22 to Sept 12: 9.30-6 Audio-visual show and restaurant close 30 mins before Visitor Centre.
Admission: £1.50, Child 80p. Adult parties £1.20, Schools 60p
Refreshments: Restaurant

DINGWALL

DINGWALL MUSEUM
(Dingwall Museum Trust)
Town House, High Street, Dingwall IV15 9RY   **Tel:** (0349) 65366
Collection of objects, militaria and photographs relating to the Dingwall area. Temporary exhibitions throughout the season.
Open: Mon to Sat 10-5
Admission: 50p, Chd/OAP 25p.

FORT WILLIAM

THE WEST HIGHLAND MUSEUM
Cameron Square, Fort William   **Tel:** (0397) 702169
Historical, natural history and folk exhibits. Prince Charles Edward Stuart and the '45 Rising. Items of local interest from pre-history to modern industry. Tartans.
Open: Mon to Sat, Sept to June: 10-5, (may be closed 1-2 in wintertime); July to Aug: 9.30-6; Sun 2-5. (please telephone to check Sunday opening).
Admission: Small fee charged.

GAIRLOCH

GAIRLOCH HERITAGE MUSEUM
Gairloch   **Tel:** (044 583) 243
Local history museum illustrating all aspects of past life in a West Highland Parish.

GLENCOE

GLENCOE AND NORTH LORN FOLK MUSEUM
Glencoe
Thatched restored 'Cruck' cottage in Glencoe village. Exhibits include domestic bygones, costume, weapons. Jacobite relics, agricultural implements and natural history.
Open: Late May to end of Sept: Mon to Sat 10-5.30.

INVERNESS

INVERNESS MUSEUM AND ART GALLERY
(Inverness District Council)
Castle Wynd, Inverness   **Tel:** (0463) 237114
Interprets the human and natural history of the highlands. Displays of highland weapons, musical instruments, costume and Jacobite memorabilia. There is a reconstruction of the highland taxidermist's workshop and a silversmith's workshop which compliments the important display of local silver. There is a growing art collection and an active programme of temporary exhibitions and events.
Open: Mon to Sat 9-5, Sun 2-5 July and Aug *only*
Admission: Free
Refreshments: Coffee shop
Disabled access to all galleries. Museum shop stocks gifts, books and souvenirs.

ISLE OF SKYE

THE MUSEUM OF THE ISLES
Clan Donald Centre, Armadale, Isle of Skye   **Tel:** (047 14) 305/227

KINGUSSIE

THE HIGHLAND FOLK MUSEUM
Kingussie   **Tel:** (0540) 661307
A comprehensive collection of old Highland artefacts including examples of craft-work and tools, household plenishings, tartans etc. In the grounds there is a furnished cottage with a mill and an extensive farming museum.

ROSEMARKIE

GROAM HOUSE MUSEUM
High Street, Rosemarkie   **Tel:** (0381) 20961
An award-winning Pictish Centre for Ross & Cromarty with original sculptured stones, colourful impressions and video programmes.
Open: May 1 to Oct 1 and winter weekends: Daily 11-5, Suns 2.30-4.30.
Admission: £1.50, OAPs 75p, Child free.

STORNOWAY

MUSEUM NAN EILEAN
Town Hall, Stornoway

STRATHPEFFER

HIGHLAND MUSEUM OF CHILDHOOD
The Old Station
Displays illustrate the social history of childhood in the Highlands.
Open: All year July-September Mon to Fri 9-6 7.30-9.30 Sat 10-6, Sun 1-6. November-February Tue-Sun 1-4 closed Mon, rest of year open Mon-Sat 9-4 and Sun 1-4.
Admission: Charged

LOTHIAN

ABERLADY

MYRETHON MOTOR MUSEUM
East Lothian, Aberlady   **Tel:** (087 57) 288

BO'NESS

BIRKHILL CLAY MINE
(Bo'ness Heritage Trust)
Birkhill, Bo'ness

BO'NESS & KINNEIL RAILWAY
(Scottish Railway Preservation Society)
Bo'ness Station, Union Street, Bo'ness

EDINBURGH

BIGGAR GASWORKS MUSEUM
(National Museums of Scotland)
Biggar, Lanarkshire, Edinburgh   **Tel:** 031-225 7534
Museum of the Gas Industry. Selection of gas lights and domestic appliances on display. Working steam engines on some Suns in mid-season.
Open: End May to end Sept: daily 2-5.

BRAIDWOOD AND RUSHBROOK MUSEUM
Lauriston Place, Edinburgh

BRASS RUBBING CENTRE
(City of Edinburgh)
Trinity Apse, Chalmers Close, High Street, Edinburgh   **Tel:** 031-556 4634
Display of replica brasses and Scottish carved stones. Facilities for making rubbings.
Open: Mon to Sat 10-5 (June to Sept 10-6). During Festival period open Sun 12-5.
Admission: Free
Location: Opposite the Museum of Childhood.

NO.7 CHARLOTTE SQUARE 'THE GEORGIAN HOUSE'
(National Trust for Scotland)
Edinburgh   **Tel:** 031-225 2160
The lower floors of this Georgian House are furnished as it might have been by its first owners, showing the domestic surroundings and reflecting the social conditions of that age.
Open: Apr 1 to Oct 31: Daily 10-5; Sun 2-5.
Admission: Including audio-visual presentation £2.80, Child £1.40. Adult parties £2.20 Schools £1.10

CITY ART CENTRE
(City of Edinburgh)
2 Market Street, Edinburgh   **Tel:** 031-225 2424, Ext 6650
Art collections of works by late 19th and 20th century artists, mostly Scottish. Frequent temporary exhibitions.
Open: Mon to Sat 10-5 (June to Sept 10-6). During Festival period open Sun 2-5.

Lothian

Admission: Free
Recently re-opened after major expansion and re-development.

THE FRUITMARKET GALLERY
29 Market Street, Edinburgh EH1 1DF **Tel:** 031-225 2383

GLADSTONE'S LAND
(National Trust for Scotland)
477B Lawnmarket, Edinburgh **Tel:** 031-226 5856
Built 1620. Remarkable painted wooden ceilings.
Open: Apr 1 to Oct 31; Mon to Sat 10-5; Sun 2-5
Admission: £2.40, Child £1.20, Adult parties £1.90, Schools £1.00. Combined ticket for Georgian House and Gladstone's Land Adm £5.00, Child £2.50, Adult parties £4.00, Schools £2.00

HUNTLY HOUSE
(City of Edinburgh)
142 Canongate, Edinburgh **Tel:** 031-225 2424 Ext.6689
Local history and topography; important collections of Edinburgh silver, glass and Scottish pottery. Reconstruction of an old Scots kitchen. Original copy of the 'National Covenant' of 1638. Also personal collections of Field Marshal Earl Haig.
Open: Mon to Sat 10-5 (June to Sept 10-6). During Festival period Sun 2-5.
Admission: Free

MALCOLM INNES GALLERY
67 George Street, Edinburgh EH2 2JG **Tel:** 031-226 4151
19th and 20th Century Scottish landscape, sporting and military pictures - oil paintings, watercolours and prints.
Open: Mon to Sat 9.30-6, most Sats 10-1. *Closed* Bank Hols.

JOHN KNOX HOUSE MUSEUM
Royal Mile, Edinburgh **Tel:** 031-556 6961

LAURISTON CASTLE
(Trust-City of Edinburgh)
Cramond Road South, Edinburgh **Tel:** 031-336 2060
16th century with 19th century additions. Period furniture, tapestries, Blue-John, wool mosaics.
Open: Apr to Oct: Daily (except Fri) 11-1, 2-5; Nov to Mar: Sat and Sun only 2-4.
Admission: £2; Child £1.

MUSEUM OF CHILDHOOD
(City of Edinburgh)
42 High Street, (opposite John Knox's House), Edinburgh **Tel:** 031-225 2424 Ext. 6645
Re-opened 1986 following complete re-display and extension. Still the noisiest museum in the world!
Open: Mon to Sat 10-5; (Jun to Sept 10-6); during Festival period open Sun 2-5.
Admission: Free

MUSEUM OF COMMUNICATION
(C.H.C. Matthews)
University of Edinburgh, Mayfield Road, Edinburgh **Tel:** (0506) 824507
A collection of telephones, spark transmitters, crystal sets, early valve sets, communication receivers, transmitters, Fultophone, teleprinters, hearing aids, wire and tape recorders, television radar, valves from midgets to giants.

MUSEUM OF FLIGHT
(National Museums of Scotland)
East Fortune Airfield, nr. North Berwick, Edinburgh **Tel:** 062-088 308 or 031-225 7534
Over 30 aircraft and aero engines including a Comet 4C and Vulcan.
Open: Daily Apr to Sept 10.30-4.30.
Refreshments: Tearoom
Shop

MUSEUM OF THE ROYAL COLLEGE OF SURGEONS OF EDINBURGH
Nicolson Street, Edinburgh
Exhibits of surgical, dental, pathological and historical interest.
Open: By appointment.

NATIONAL GALLERY OF SCOTLAND
The Mound, Edinburgh EH2 2EL **Tel:** 031-556 8921

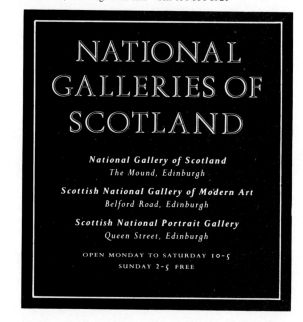

A late 16th century tower - house with extensive 19th century additions. It has a fine Edwardian interior containing 18th and 19th century furniture, impressive collections of Derbyshire Blue John, Crossley wool mosaics and objets d'art. Visitors are taken on a guided tour lasting approximately 40 minutes. There is a free car park. Opening hours - April to October, Daily (except Friday) 11am - 1pm, 2 - 5pm, last tour starts at approximately 3.20pm. Telephone 031 336 2060.

Admission Charges Adults: £2.00 Children, UB40's, Benefit recipients and Leisure Access card holders: £1.00. Free admission to the Castle grounds.

Bus no 41 from George Street to Lauriston Castle gates, and Bus no 40 from the Mound, Princes Street to Davidson Mains.

An outstanding collection of paintings, drawings and prints by the greatest artists from the Renaissance to Post Impressionism, including Velázquez, El Greco, Rembrandt, Vermeer, Gainsborough, Turner, Constable, Degas, Monet and Van Gogh. Also the national collection of Scottish art including Ramsay, Raeburn, Wilkie and McTaggart.
Open: Mon to Sat 10-5, Sun 2-5. *Closed* Dec 25, 26, 31, Jan 1, 2 and May Day Holiday.
Admission: Free except for some loan exhibitions

NATIONAL MONUMENTS RECORD OF SCOTLAND
(Royal Commission on the Ancient and Historical Monuments of Scotland)
   6-7 Coates Place, Edinburgh EH3 7AA   **Tel:** 031-225 5994 **Fax:** 031-220 6851
Collection of about 450,000 drawings, 600,000 photographs, 12,000 maps and 15,000 printed books relating to Scottish archaeology and architecture of Scotland.
Open: Mon to Thurs 9.30-4.30; Fri 9.30-4.00 or by appointment.

THE PEOPLE'S STORY
(City of Edinburgh)
   Canongate Tolbooth, 163 Canongate, Edinburgh   **Tel:** 031-225 2424, Ext 6638
Housed in the 16th century Tolbooth, this exciting new museum tells the story of the life and work of Edinburgh's people over the past 200 years.
Open: Mon to Sat 10-5 (June to Sept 10-6). During Festival period open Sun 2-5.
Admission: Free

QUEENSFERRY MUSEUM
(City of Edinburgh)
   Edinburgh   **Tel:** 031-331 1590
Situated between the two Forth bridges in the Council Chambers of the former Royal Burgh of Queensferry. Local history collections.
Open: Thurs to Sat and Mon 10-1, 2.15-5. Sun 12-5.
Admission: Free

ROYAL MUSEUM OF SCOTLAND
(National Museums of Scotland)
   Chambers Street, Edinburgh EH1 1JF   **Tel:** 031-225 7534
Houses the national collections of decorative arts of the world, ethnography, natural history, geology, technology and science. Displays range from primitive art to space material, from ceramics to fossils, from birds to working models in the hall of power. Items of importance in all fields. Additional major displays in course of preparation. Main Hall of architectural interest. Temporary exhibitions. Lectures and films at advertised times.
Open: Mon to Sat 10-5; Sun 12noon-5.
Admission: Free
Refreshments: Tea room.
Shop

ROYAL MUSEUM OF SCOTLAND
(National Museums of Scotland)
   Queen Street, Edinburgh EH2 1JD   **Tel:** 031-255 7534
Collections cover the whole of Scotland from the Stone Age to recent times; prehistoric and Roman objects, sculptured stones, relics of the Celtic church, Scottish coins and medals, Stuart relics, Highland weapons, domestic life, costumes and textiles; also reference library. Special exhibition 'Dynasty: The Royal House of Stewart'.
Open: Mon to Sat 10-5; Sun 2-5.
Admission: Free

RUSSELL COLLECTION OF EARLY KEYBOARD INSTRUMENTS
(University of Edinburgh)
   St. Cecilia's Hall, Niddry Street, Cowgate, Edinburgh   **Tel:** 031-650 2805
Forty-seven keyboard instruments, including harpsichords, clavichords, fortepianos, regals, spinets, virginals and chamber organs. Pictures (Pannini etc.). Tapestries and textiles.
Open: Sat and Wed 2-5 throughout the year. Daily during Edinburgh Festival (mornings)
Admission: £1

SCOTCH WHISKY HERITAGE CENTRE
   354 Castlehill, Royal Mile, Edinburgh EH1 2NE   **Tel:** 031-220-0441
The Scotch Whisky Heritage Centre provides an entertaining explanation of the making of Scotch Whisky from the barley to the bottle. Travel through 300 years of Scotch Whisky history in a Barrel Car, with commentary in English or six other languages.
Open: Daily from 10-5 all year. Extended hours in summer.
Admission: Charge

SCOTTISH AGRICULTURAL MUSEUM
(National Museums of Scotland(Outstation))
   Ingliston, Newbridge, Edinburgh   **Tel:** 031-225 7534 or 031-333 2674
Illustrates the history of agriculture in Scotland. Room settings, crafts, animal husbandry etc.
Open: May, June, July and Aug: Mon to Fri 10-4.30. Sat (mid-season only) 10-4.30. *Closed* Sun
Location: In Royal Highland Showground

SCOTTISH NATIONAL GALLERY OF MODERN ART
   Belford Road, Edinburgh EH4 3DR   **Tel:** 031-556-8921
Scotland's finest collection of 20th-Century painting, sculpture and graphic art. The work of such established masters as Picasso, Matisse, Ernst, Kirchner, Dix, Moore; major Scottish artists including Alan Davie, John Bellany and Stephen Conroy and the leading figures of the contemporary international scene.
Open: Mon to Sat 10-5, Sun 2-5. *Closed* Dec 25, 26, 31, Jan 1, 2 and May Day Holiday.
Admission: Free except for some loan exhibitions
Study Rooms: The **Department of Prints and Drawings** at the National Gallery, and the **Print Room and Reference Section** at the Portrait Gallery are open to visitors by arrangement at the front desk of the Galleries: Mon to Fri 10-12.30, 2-4.30. **The Prints and Drawings Study Room** at the Gallery of Modern Art is open by prior appointment only: Mon to Fri 10-1. **Further information** about the Galleries, the collections and activities is available from the Information Department. Tel 031-556-8921.

SCOTTISH NATIONAL PORTRAIT GALLERY
   1 Queen Street, Edinburgh EH2 1JD   **Tel:** 031-556 8921
Portraits in all media of people who have played a significant role in Scottish history from the 16th century to the present, recorded by the most famous artists of the day. Subjects include Mary, Queen of Scots, Robert Burns and the Queen Mother. Also the national collection of photography.
Open: Mon to Sat 10-5, Sun 2-5. *Closed* Dec 25, 26, 31, Jan 1, 2 and May Day Holiday.
Admission: Free except for some loan exhibitions

SCOTTISH UNITED SERVICES MUSEUM
(National Museums of Scotland)
   Edinburgh Castle, Edinburgh   **Tel:** 031-225 7534
Illustrates by its display of uniform, head dress, arms and equipment, medals, portraits and models, the history of the armed forces of Scotland. Extensive library and comprehensive collection of prints of uniforms.
Open: Times as for Edinburgh Castle
Shop

SHAMBELLIE HOUSE MUSEUM OF COSTUME
(National Museums of Scotland)
   New Abbey, Dumfries, Edinburgh   **Tel:** 031-225 7534/038-785 375
Open: Re-opens Summer '93

LADY STAIR'S HOUSE
(City of Edinburgh)
   Lady Stair's Close, Lawnmarket, Edinburgh   **Tel:** 031-225 2424, Ext. 6593
A reconstructed town house dating from 1622. Relics connected with Robert Burns, Sir Walter Scott and R.L.Stevenson.
Open: Mon to Sat 10-5 (June to Sept 10-6). During Festival period open Sun 2-5.
Admission: Free.

LIVINGSTON

THE ALMOND VALLEY HERITAGE CENTRE, LIVINGSTON MILL
(The Almond Valley Heritage Trust)
   Livingston Mill, Millfield, Livingston   **Tel:** (0506) 414957
Heritage Centre containing the Scottish Shale Oil Museum, local history displays and other exhibitions; plus a working farmstead with traditional livestock and fully operational 18th century watermill.
Open: Daily throughout the year 10-5.
Admission: Fee charged. Party discounts by arrangement.
Refreshments: Available
Ample parking, museum shop, suitable for disabled persons.

NEWTONGRANGE

SCOTTISH MINING MUSEUM
   Lady Victoria Colliery, Newtongrange EH22 4QN

NORTH BERWICK

NORTH BERWICK MUSEUM
   School Road, North Berwick   **Tel:** (0620) 3470
Local history, wildlife and golf.

PRESTONGRANGE

SCOTTISH MINING MUSEUM
   Prestongrange, Nr Prestonpans

SOUTH QUEENSFERRY

HOPETOUN HOUSE
South Queensferry
Ancestral home of the Marquess of Linlithgow. Magnificant interiors. 18th century furniture and outstanding collection of pictures. Also three exhibitions, deer parks, nature trails, rooftop viewing platform.
Admission: Fee charged.

ORKNEY ISLES

HARRAY

THE ORKNEY FARM AND FOLK MUSEUM
(Ortney Islands Council)
Harray
Two restored farmsteads illustrating tradition and change in island life, at **Kirbuster** and **Corrigall**.
Open: Mar to Oct: Mon to Sat 10.30-1, 2-5; Sun 2-7.
Admission: Fee charged.

ST. MARGARET'S HOPE

ORKNEY WIRELESS MUSEUM
Church Road, St. Margaret's Hope, Ortney Isles
Featuring domestic radio and defences at Scapa Flow.
Open: Apr to Sept.

STROMNESS

THE PIER ARTS CENTRE
(The Pier Arts Centre Trust)
Stromness
Permanent collection of 20th century British art; also a programme of changing exhibitions.
Admission: Free

STROMNESS MUSEUM
(Ortney Natural History Society)
Stromness
Ortney Maritime and natural history displays; Scapa Flow and the German Fleet.
Open: Mon to Sat 10.30-12.30, 1.30-5.*Closed* Sun
Admission: Fee charged.

SHETLAND ISLES

DUNROSSNESS

SHETLAND CROFT HOUSE MUSEUM
(Shetland Islands Council)
c/o Shetland Islands Museum, Lerwick, Dunrossness, Shetland Islands ZE1 OEL
Tel: (0595) 5057 **Fax:** (0595) 6729
A restored (c. 1870s) Croft house, Steading and Water Mill, at Voe, Dunrossness.
Open: May 1 to Sept 30: Daily 10-1, 2-5.
Admission: 75p, Child 25p.

LERWICK

BÖD OF GREMISTA
Lerwick **Tel:** (0595) 4386 (when open); (0595) 4632 at other times.
Birthplace of Arthur Anderson, co-founder and main developer of P & O Company.
Open: 1st May-31st Sept.
Admission: Fee charged
Further information contact Shetland Museum (0595) 5057

SHETLAND MUSEUM
(Shetland Islands Council)
Lerwick ZE1 OEL **Tel:** (0595) 5057 **Fax:** (0595) 6729
The theme of the museum is 'Life in Shetland through the Ages'. Our disciplines comprehend local archaeology. folk life, history, a large maritime section complete with the fine ship and boat models and a growing natural history collection. We also hold an extensive photographic collection, c.30,000 negatives and a growing archive.
Open: All year: Mon, Wed and Fri 10-7; Tues, Thurs and Sat 10-5.
Admission: Free
Location: Town centre
Adjacent car parking.

STRATHCLYDE

ALLOWAY

BURN'S COTTAGE AND MUSEUM
(Burns' Monument Trust)
Alloway
Thatched cottage in which Robert Burns was born, 1759. Museum with Burns' relics. (includes entry to Burns' Monument).
Open: Summer: Weekdays 9-7; Sun 10-7. Winter: Weekdays 10-4. *Closed* Sun
Admission: £1.80, Child and OAPs 90p.

APPIN

APPIN WILDLIFE MUSEUM
Appin Home Farm, Appin

AYR

AYR CARNEGIE LIBRARY
(Kyle and Carrick District Council)
12 Main Street, Ayr **Tel:** (0292) 269141, Ext. 5227
Occasional Exhibitions.
Open: Mon, Tues, Thurs, Fri, 9-7. Wed, Sat 9-5.

MACLAURIN GALLERY AND ROZELLE HOUSE
(Kyle and Carrick District Council)
Rozelle, Ayr **Tel:** (0292) 45447
Variety of exhibitions 3 to 5 weeks' duration. Fine art, craft, photography, contemporary art. Local history and military exhibits in house.
Open: Mon to Sat 11-5; Sun 2-5 (Apr to Oct only)

TAM O'SHANTER MUSEUM
High Street, Ayr

BIGGAR

ALBION ARCHIVE
17 North Back Road, Biggar
Records of Scotland's most successful commercial motor.

BIGGAR GAS WORKS MUSEUM
Biggar
See entry under Royal Museum of Scotland, Edinburgh.

JOHN BUCHAN CENTRE
Biggar
Life and times of the author of 'The 39 Steps'.
Location: 6 miles from Broughton

GLADSTONE COURT
North Back Road, Biggar
Small indoor street of shops, workshops, a bank, telephone exchange and village library.

GREENHILL COVENANTER'S HOUSE
Burn Braes, Biggar
Two-storey farmhouse, rescued in ruinous condition in upper Clyde Valley and re-erected at Biggar.

MOAT PARK HERITAGE CENTRE
Burn Braes, Biggar
Flagship of a growing number of local museums. Moat Park was opened by HRH The Princess Royal in 1988.

BISHOPBRIGGS

THOMAS MUIR MUSEUM
(Strathkelvin District Council)
Bishopbriggs Library, Bishopbriggs **Tel:** (041 775) 1185
Display illustrating the life of Thomas Muir.
Open: Mon to Fri 9.45-8. Sat 10-1.

BLANTYRE

THE DAVID LIVINGSTONE CENTRE
Blantyre
Includes 'THE LIVINGSTONE MEMORIAL'. The birthplace of David Livingstone (1813) containing personal relics, tableaux and working models.

CAMPBELTOWN

CAMPBELTOWN MUSEUM
(Argyll and Bute District Council)
Campbeltown

CLYDEBANK

CLYDEBANK DISTRICT MUSEUM
Old Town Hall, Dumbarton Road, Clydebank   **Tel:** 041-941 1331, Ext. 402.
A small museum situated beside the shipyard where some of the world's greatest liners were built. Displays tell the story of the shipbuilders and the town which grew up round their yards. Also on show is part of the museum's large and very fine collection of sewing machines.
Open: Mon and Wed 2-4.30; Sat 10-4.30 and other times by prior arrangement.

COATBRIDGE

SUMMERLEE HERITAGE TRUST
West Canal Street, Coatbridge ML5 1QD   **Tel:** (0236) 431261
Winner of the award Scottish Museum of the Year 1990. Museum of social and industrial history with indoor and open air exhibits including recently extended working tramway, belt driven machinery, 19th century coal mine, miners' rows and other social history exhibitions. Ironworks gallery, regularly changing exhibitions and special events.
Open: 10-5 daily. *Closed* Dec 25, 26, Jan 1, 2.
Admission: Free
Refreshments: Tea room
Gift shop. Wheelchair accessible. Free car parking. Convenient access from BR Sunnyside and Coatbridge stations.

CULZEAN BAY

CULZEAN CASTLE
(National Trust for Scotland)
Culzean Bay
Built 1772-1792 by Robert Adam on a spectacular cliff top site. Superb furnishings, magnificent Oval Staircase and Round Drawing Room. Eisenhower presentation explains the General's association with Culzean.
Open: Castle, licenced caféteria, visitor centre and shop open Apr 1 to Oct 31; daily 10.30-5.30.
Admission: £3.30, Child £1.70, Adult parties £4.00, Schools £2.00 (last two prices include coach entry to Country Park). Other times by appointment.
Location: 12 miles south of Ayr.
Refreshments: Licensed caféteria.
Visitor centre and shop.

CUMBERNAULD

CUMBERNAULD & KILSYTH DISTRICT MUSEUM
Ardenlea House, The Wynd, Cumbernauld, Strathclyde

CUMNOCK

BAIRD INSTITUTE MUSEUM
Lugar Street, Cumnock   **Tel:** (0290) 22111
A local history museum featuring local pottery and wooden ware, in conjunction with a programme of temporary exhibitions.
Open: Fri 9.30-1, 1.30-4; Sat 11-1.
Admission: Free

DALMELLINGTON

SCOTTISH INDUSTRIAL RAILWAY CENTRE
(Ayrshire Railway Preservation Group)
Minnivey Colliery, Burnton, Dalmellington
Steam and diesel locomotives, rolling stock and cranes.
Location: 12 miles South East of Aye, just off the A713.

DUMBARTON

THE DENNY TANK
Castle Street, Dumbarton G82 1QS   **Tel:** (0389) 63444

DENNY SHIP MODEL EXPERIMENT TANK

See editorial reference

The Denny Tank occupies a unique place in maritime history. Established in 1883 by Wm. Denny III, it was the first commercial ship model testing Tank in the world. Through the years, it has been the origin of many outstanding innovations in ship design; eg: the Denny/Brown Ship Stabilizing System. Hydrofoils, and Side-wall Hovercraft. Also the Tank, ships as diverse as P&O liner 'Canberra', and Sir Thomas Lipton's 'Shamrock III' have been tested. Presently, the Tank is a working artifact, owned by Scottish Maritime Museum, and visitors can see in the Tank, a memorial to the Clyde's originality in shipbuilding science.
Open: Mon to Sat 10-4.
For advanced bookings and further information contact the Education Officer at the above address or telephone number.

EASDALE ISLAND

EASDALE ISLAND FOLK MUSEUM
By Oban, Argyll, Easdale Island   **Tel:** (08523) 370 (evenings)

GLASGOW

ART GALLERY AND MUSEUM
Kelvingrove, Glasgow G3 8AG   **Tel:** 041-357 3929
Fine Art: Collection includes great paintings by Giorione, Botticelli, Rembrandt, Millet, Monet, Van Gogh, Derain and Dali as well as works from all major European schools, notable the Dutch 17th century and French Barbizon, Impressionist and Post-Impressionist periods. Also British painting 17th to 20th centuries with emphasis on Scottish art, especially Glasgow Boys and Scottish Colourists. Decorative Art: Collections include important specimens of Western European ceramics, glass, silver and furniture. Recently opened gallery displays Glasgow decorative arts 1880-1920. Armour: The Scott Collection of arms and armour including the Milanese Armour c.1450, the Whitelaw Collection of Scottish arms. Archaeology and History: Neolithic, Bronze and Iron Age material; items from the Egyptian, Greek and Cypriot collecctions. Ethnography: tools, clothing, weapons, religious and ceremonial objects relating to non-European societies. Natural History: Collection contains important botanical, geological and zoological material, being particularly strong in Scottish fossils, worldwide non-flowering plants (Stirton Collection), birds, fish, molluscs, for example. There are many historically interesting specimens, including type specimens.
Open: Weekdays: 10-5, Sun 11-5.
Refreshments: Self-service restaurant and coffee bar.

BURRELL COLLECTION
Pollok Country Park, Glasgow G45 1AT   **Tel:** 041-649 7171
Housed in new building opened in 1983. World famous collection of textiles, furniture, ceramics, stained glass, silver, art objects and pictures including major works by Cracach, Rembrandt, Courbet, Manet, Degas, Cezanne, gifted to Glasgow in 1944 by Sir William and Lady Burrell.
Open: Weekdays: 10-5, Sun 11-5.
Refreshments: Self-service restaurant.

Glasgow Museums & Art Galleries

ART GALLERY & MUSEUM
Kelvingrove Glasgow G3 8AG Tel: 041-357 3929
Open: Mon-Sat 10-5 Sun 11-5
THE BURRELL COLLECTION
2060 Pollokshaws Road Glasgow G43 1AT Tel: 041-649 7151
Open: Mon-Sat 10-5 Sun 11-5
HAGGS CASTLE
100 St Andrews Drive Glasgow G41 4RB Tel: 041-427 2725
Open: Mon-Sat 10-5 Sun 11-5
MUSEUM OF TRANSPORT
Kelvin Hall 1 Bunhouse Road Glasgow G3 8DP Tel: 041-357 3929
Open: Mon-Sat 10-5 Sun 11-5
PEOPLE'S PALACE
Glasgow Green Glasgow G40 1AT Tel: 041-554 0223
Open: Mon-Sat 10-5 Sun 11-5
POLLOK HOUSE
2060 Pollokshaws Road Glasgow G43 1AT Tel: 041-632 0274
Open: Mon-Sat 10-5 Sun 11-5
PROVAND'S LORDSHIP
3 Castle Street Glasgow G4 0RB Tel: 041-552 8819
Open: Mon-Sat 10-5 Sun 11-5
RUTHERGLEN MUSEUM
King Street Glasgow G73 1DQ Tel: 041-647 0837
Open: Mon-Sat 10-5 Sun 11-5
Open all year except Christmas Day and New Year's Day
Admission Free
McLELLAN GALLERIES
270 Sauchiehall Street Glasgow G2 2EH Tel: 041-331 1854
Open: Mon-Sat 10-5 Sun 11-5
For exhibition dates and admission prices see press.

HAGGS CASTLE
100 St. Andrews Drive, Glasgow G41 4RB   **Tel:** 041-427 2725
A museum of history for children with work space for children's activities.
Open: Weekdays 10-5; Sun 11-5.

HUNTERIAN ART GALLERY
Hillhead Street, Glasgow University, Glasgow   **Tel:** 041-330 5431
Unrivalled collections of C.R.Mackintosh, including reconstructed interiors of the architect's house, and of J.A.M. Whistler. Works by Rembrandt, Chardin, Stubbs, Reynolds, Pissarro, Sisley, Rodin plus Scottish paintings from the 18th century to present. Large collection of Old Master and modern prints, Sculpture Courtyard. Varied programme of temporary exhibitions.
Open: Mon to Sat 9.30-5. (Mackintosh House *closed* Mon to Sat 12.30-1.30). Telephone enquiries to the above number.

HUNTERIAN MUSEUM
Glasgow University, Glasgow G12 8QQ   **Tel:** 041-330 4221
Scotland's oldest public museum, opened in 1807. Situated in Sir George Gilbert Scott's magnificent Victorian Gothic building. Collections include geological, archaeological, historical, ethnographic and numismatic material. New exhibitions include *Giant Steps of Mankind* and *Roman Scotland: Outpost of an Empire*.
Open: Mon to Sat 9.30-5.
Refreshments: Small 18th century coffee shop
Book shop. Enquiries: phone the above number.

MCLELLAN GALLERIES
270 Sauchiehall Street, Glasgow G2 3EH   **Tel:** 041-331 1854
Reopened in January 1990 as part of Glasgow's celebrations as European City of Culture for the display of large temporary exhibitions, this handsome building originally housed Ardchibald McLellan's collection which became the nucleas of Glasgows Museums and Art Galleries fine art holding in 1856.
Open: Weekdays 10-5, Sun 11-5.
For exhibition dates and admission prices see press or telephone the above number.

MUSEUM OF TRANSPORT
Kelvin Hall, 1 Bunhouse Road, Glasgow G3 8DP   **Tel:** 041-357 3929
Opened Spring 1988. A new and considerably enlarged museum of the history of transport, including a reproduction of a typical 1938 Glasgow street. Other new features are a larger display of the ship models and a walk-in Motor Car Showroom with cars from the 1930s up to modern times. Other displays include Glasgow trams and buses, cycles and motorcycles, railway locomotives and a Glasgow Subway station.
Open: Weekdays 10-5, Sun 11-5.
Refreshments: Restaurant, fast food and bar facilities are shared with the adjacent indoor Sports Centre.

PEOPLE'S PALACE
Glasgow Green, Glasgow G40 1AT   **Tel:** 041-554 0223
Museum of Glasgow history from 1175 to the present day. Collections cover early Glasgow, the rise of the tabacco in the 18th century and domestic, social and political life in the 19th and 20th centuries.

The Hunterian Museum, named after the 18th century physician and medical teacher, William Hunter, opened to the public in 1807. The Museum contains important geological and archaeological collections, including Roman finds from the Antonine Wall and ethnographic material from Captain Cook's voyages to the South Seas. Treasures from Hunter's coin cabinet are displayed. The story of Glasgow's University, founded in 1451, is also told.

The purpose-designed Hunterian Art Gallery, opened in 1980, houses important collections of Old Masters, British 18th century portraits, prints, Scottish paintings from the 19th century to the present, and unrivalled holdings of work by James McNeill Whistler and Charles Rennie Mackintosh. The Mackintosh House is a reconstruction of the principal rooms from Mackintosh's home, complete with original fitments and furnishings.

See listings for further details and opening hours

Open: Weekdays 10-5, Sun 11-5.
Refreshments: Snack bar

POLLOK HOUSE
Pollok Country Park, Glasgow G43 1AT   **Tel:** 041-632 0724
House built c.1750 in Palladian style with Edwardian additions. Contains Stirling Maxwell Collection of paintings including works by El Greco, Murillo, Goya, Signorelli and William Blake, and also late 18th and early 19th century furniture and decorative arts. Set in beautiful wooded parkland.
Open: Weekdays 10-5, Sun 11-5.
Refreshments: Tea room

PROVAND'S LORDSHIP
3 Castle Street, Glasgow G4 0RB   **Tel:** 041-552 8819
Facing the Cathedral, the only other surviving medieval building in Glasgow built 1471. Period displays ranging in date from 1500 to 1918.
Open: Weekdays 10-5, Sun 11-5.

PROVANHALL HOUSE
Auchinlea Park, Auchinlea Road, Glasgow G34   **Tel:** 041-771 1538
House dating from 17th century with some period displays, maintained in conjunction with Department of Parks and Recreation.

CHARLES RENNIE MACKINTOSH SOCIETY - QUEEN'S CROSS
Queen's Cross, 870 Garscube Road, Glasgow G20 7EL   **Tel:** 041-946 6600

RUTHERGLEN MUSEUM
King Street, Glasgow G73 1DQ   **Tel:** 041-647 0837
A museum of the history of the former Royal Burgh of Rutherglen with regularly changing displays and temporary exhibitions.
Open: Weekdays 10-5, Sun 11-5.

SPRINGBURN MUSEUM & EXHIBITION CENTRE
(Springburn Museum Trust)
Ayr Street, Glasgow G21 4BW   **Tel:** 041-557 1405
Changing exhibitions about the past and present of an area which was once the greatest centre of steam locomotive manufacture in Europe. Social and Industrial History Museum of the Year Award in 1989.
Open: Mon to Fri 10.30-5, Sun 10-4.30. Enquire for public holiday opening times.
Admission: Free
Suitable for disabled persons though no wheelchairs available.

THE TENEMENT HOUSE
(National Trust for Scotland)
No. 145 Buccleuch Street, Garnethill, Glasgow   **Tel:** 041-333 0183
A restored first floor flat in a Victorian tenement building, built 1892, presents a picture of social significance. A second flat on the ground floor provides reception interpretative and educational facilities.
Open: Weekday morning visits by education and other groups (no more than 15) to be arranged by advance booking only. Open until Mar 28, 1993: Sat & Sun 2-4; Apr 1 to Nov 1: Daily 2-5; Nov 7 to Mar 31, 1993: Sat & Sun 2-4. (last adm 1/2 hr before closing).
Admission: £2.00, Child £1.00, Adult parties £1.60, Schools 80p
Location: N. of Charing Cross

GREENOCK

THE MCLEAN MUSEUM
(Inverclyde District Council)
15 Kelly Street, West End, Greenock   **Tel:** (0475) 23741

HAMILTON

HAMILTON DISTRICT MUSEUM
(Hamilton District Council)

129 Muir Street, Hamilton ML3 6BJ   **Tel:** (0698) 283981
17th century coaching inn now housing a local history collection. Includes 18th century Assembly Room, Fives Court and stable. Contains displays of costume, art, historical photographs, agriculture, handloom weaving, lacemaking, coalmining etc. Also extensive transport gallery and reconstructed Victorian kitchen. Regular temporary exhibition programme.
Open: Mon to Sat 10-5 but closed between 12 and 1 on Wed and Sat.

HELENSBURGH

THE HILL HOUSE

(National Trust for Scotland)
Upper Colquhoun Street, Helensburgh   **Tel:** (0436) 73900
This is one of the finest examples of the domestic architecture of Charles Rennie Mackintosh. His original and highly idiosyncratic sense of design created this 20th century masterpiece. Exhibition.
Open: Apr 1 to Dec 23 and Dec 28-30: Daily 1-5 (Last admission 4.30) Closed for restoration Dec 31 1993 until Mar 31 1994.
Admission: £2.80, Child £1.40, Adult parties £2.20, Schools £1.10
Refreshments: Tea room.

INVERARAY

AUCHINDRAIN TOWNSHIP OPEN AIR MUSEUM
(Auchindrain Museum Trustees)
Inveraray
The domestic and agricultural buildings of the township of Auchindrain in situ restored and awaiting restoration and furnished and equipped to illustrate the lifestyle of its inhabitants in the past.
Location: 5 miles SW of Inveraray on A83.

HAMILTON DISTRICT MUSEUM

Step into the past at Hamilton District Museum, the oldest building in the town. It was originally the Hamilton Arms Inn, built in 1696, and London coaches stopped here daily. Re-live that era in our restored stable and fascinating transport gallery with four-in-hand coach and other early vehicles. Stroll through the elegant 18th century Assembly Room with its original plasterwork and musicians' gallery, and then savour the atmosphere of our reconstructed Victorian kitchen. We also have a wide range of local history displays, including costume, archaeology, lacemaking, handloom weaving, coalmining and much more.

129 MUIR STREET, HAMILTON
Telephone 283981

18th century Assembly Room

Strathclyde

IRVINE

GLASGOW VENNEL MUSEUM AND HECKLING SHOP
(Cunninghame District Council)
   10 & 4 Glasgow Vennel, Irvine
Robert Burns' Heckling Shop and Lodging House where he worked and lived.

SCOTTISH MARITIME MUSEUM
(Scottish Maritime Museum Trust)
   Laird Forge, Gottries Road, Irvine KA12 8QE **Tel:** (0294) 78283

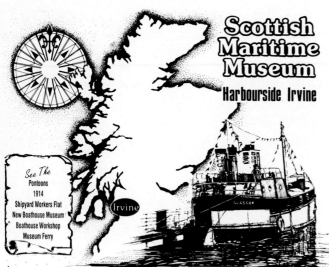

Scottish Maritime Museum
Harbourside Irvine

See The Pontoons 1914 Shipyard Workers Flat New Boathouse Museum Boathouse Workshop Museum Ferry

Open daily 10am-5pm From 1st April to 31st October Groups and other times by arrangement
Charges Adult £1.75 Child OAP 90p Family £3.50
Laird Forge Building Gottries Road Irvine KA12 8QE Tel 0294 78283

The Scottish Maritime Museum contains, on four sites, full size ships, a Boat Shed special exhibition gallery with a new maritime theme display every year, Educational Centre and a restored Tenement Flat. There is also a Workshop and Research Unit and the site of the reconstruction of the 1872 Linthouse Engine Shop which will provide an increase in Museum Display Area over the next decade. Come and discover the world of Scotland and the sea, board the Puffer, 'Spartan', Tug and Lifeboat. Museum vessels operate in the harbour from time to time.
Open: Apr 1 to Oct 31: daily 10-5. Other times by appointment.
Admission: £1.75, Child and Concessions 90p, Family £3.50. Special rates for school and organised parties.
Refreshments: Tea Room
Car park. Suitable for disabled (no wheelchairs available)

ISLE OF ARRAN

BRODICK CASTLE
(National Trust for Scotland)
   Isle of Arran **Tel:** (0770) 2202
This ancient seat of the Dukes of Hamilton was more recently the home of the late Mary, Duchess of Montrose. The contents include superb silver, porcelain, and paintings from the collections of the Dukes of Hamilton, William Beckford and the Earls of Rochford. Sporting pictures and trophies. Castle.
Open: Apr 1-18 and May 2 to Sept 30 daily 1-5; Apr 19 to May 1 and Oct 2-23 Mon/Wed/Sat 1-5. Reception Centre and shop (dates as castle) Mon-Sat 10-5, Sun 11-5. Restaurant (dates as castle) Mon-Sat 10-5, Sun 12-5
Admission: Garden £2, Child £1. House and garden £3.50, Child £1.80, Adult parties £2.80, Schools £1.40
Refreshments: Restaurant
Shop

ISLE OF ARRAN HERITAGE MUSEUM
   Rosaburn, Brodick, Isle of Arran
A collection of traditional buildings: Smithy, cottage furnished in late 19th and early 20th century styles, stable block with displays of local social history, archaeology and geology.
Open: Apr to end Oct: Mon to Sat. Weekends as advertised.
Admission: Fee charged.
Refreshments: Tea room.
Car park, picnic area.

KILBARCHAN

WEAVER'S COTTAGE
(National Trust for Scotland)
   The Cross, Kilbarchan **Tel:** (050 57) 5588
Attractive 18th century craftsman's house containing traditional weaving and domestic exhibits. Weaving demonstrations (check for times)
Open: Apr 1 to May 30 and Sept 2 to Oct 31: Tues, Thurs, Sat, Sun 2-5, May 31 to Aug 31: Daily 1-5 (last admission 4.30)
Admission: Adults £1.50, Child 80p, Adult parties £1.20, Schools 60p

KILMARNOCK

DEAN CASTLE
(Kilmarnock and Loudoun District Council)
   Dean Road, off Glasgow Road, Kilmarnock **Tel:** (0563) 26401 or (0563) 22702
Medieval arms and armour, musical instruments, tapestries.
Open: Daily 12-5. *(Closed* Dec 25, 26 and Jan 1, 2)
Admission: £1, Child, free.
Organised parties must book.

DICK INSTITUTE MUSEUM AND ART GALLERY
(Kilmarnock and Loudoun District Council)
   Elmbank Avenue, Kilmarnock **Tel:** (0563) 26401
Paintings, geology, archaeology, natural history, industry. Frequent temporary exhibitions.

KIRKINTILLOCH

THE AULD KIRK MUSEUM
(Strathkelvin District Council)
   Cowgate, Kirkintilloch **Tel:** (041) 775 1185
Temporary exhibitions only, including art, photography, local history, archaeology and social and industrial history.
Open: Tues, Wed, Fri 10-12, 2-5, Thurs 10-5

THE BARONY CHAMBERS MUSEUM
(Strathkelvin District Council)
   The Cross, Krkintilloch **Tel:** 041-775 1185
Local social and industrial history, weaving, coalmining, transport, shipbuilding, ironfounding, domestic collections on display.
Open: Apr to Oct: Tues, Wed, Thurs and Fri 2-5; Sat 10-1, 2-5. Nov to Mar: Tues, Thurs 2-5; Sat 10-1, 2-5.

KIRKOSWALD

SOUTER JOHNNIE'S COTTAGE
(National Trust for Scotland)
   Kirkoswald **Tel:** (065 56) 603 or 274
The home of John Davidson on whom Burns modelled Souter Johnnie in his narrative poem 'Tam o' Shanter'. Life-sized sculptured figures of Souter, Tam, the housekeeper and his wife are in the restored ale house in cottage garden.
Open: Apr 1 to Oct 25: Daily 12-5. Also by appointment.
Admission: Adults £1.50, Child 80p. Adult parties £1.20, Schools 60p.
Location: 4m SW of Maybole.

LANARK

NEW LANARK CONSERVATION VILLAGE
(New Lanark Conservation Trust)
New Lanark Mills, Lanark ML11 9DB **Tel:** (0555) 661345

NEW LANARK WORLD HERITAGE VILLAGE

Surrounded by the spectacular beauty of the Clyde gorge, this award-winning conservation village was the site of Robert Owen's social experiments. The New Lanark Visitor Centre features 'The Annie McLeod Experience' – a magical history tour of the village in 1820, using the latest laser and hologram technology, as well as working 19th century spinning machinery, other displays, gift and coffee shop.

Open 11am–5pm daily.
Please phone for admission charges.
New Lanark Conservation Trust. 0555-661345

New Lanark Conservation

Award-winning 200 year old Cotton Mill Village, site of Robert Owen's social and educational experiments. Nominated as a World Heritage site, the village is undergoing major restoration. Set in the Clyde Gorge, surrounded by beautiful woodlands and the Falls of Clyde, New Lanark is Europe's premier Industial Heritage Site. Visitor Centre, Exhibitions.
Open: Daily from 11-5.*Closed* Dec 25, 26 and Jan 1, 2.
Admission: Please telephone for charges. Pre-booking advisable - special rates for schools.
Refreshments: Coffee bar.
Gifts. Edinburgh Woollen Mill shop, picnic area, childrens playground. Car parking in visitor car park 'visitor centre' suitable for disabled persons. One wheelchair available. Access to village free at all times. Limited disabled parking in village square.

LANGBANK

FINLAYSTONE DOLL COLLECTION
(Mrs Jane MacMillan)
Langbank **Tel:** (047 554) 285

LOCHWINNOCH

LOCHWINNOCH COMMUNITY MUSEUM
(Renfrew District Council)
Main Street, Lochwinnoch **Tel:** (0505) 842615
A series of changing exhibitions reflecting the historic background of local agriculture, industry and village life.
Open: All year (except Bank Holidays) Mon, Wed, Fri: 10-1, 2-5.
Admission: Free
Limited car parking.

MILLPORT

MUSEUM OF THE CUMBRAES
Garrison House, Millport **Tel:** (0475) 530741
Unique history of the Isles of Cumbrae.
Open: June 1 to Sept 30, Mon to Sat 10-4.30.

ROBERTSON MUSEUM AND AQUARIUM
Marine Station, Millport **Tel:** (0475) 530581/2

MILNGAVIE

HEATHERBANK MUSEUM OF SOCIAL WORK
163 Mugdock Road, Milngavie **Tel:** 041-956 2687

LILLIE ART GALLERY
(Bearsden and Milngavie District Council)
Station Road, Milngavie, Glasgow **Tel:** 041-943 3247
Collections of 20th century Scottish paintings; temporary and loan exhibitions of art and crafts .
Open: Monday-Friday 10am-5pm; Saturday 4 Sunday 2pm-5pm

OBAN

MCGAIG MUSEUM
Corran Halls, Oban

PAISLEY

COATS OBSERVATORY
(Renfrew District Council)
49 Oakshaw Street West, Paisley PA1 2DR **Tel:** 041-889 2031
Dating from 1883, but recently renovated, the observatory plays an important role in the fields of astromomy, metereology and seismology. Displays relate to the history of the building, astronomy, metereology and space flight.
Open: All year (except Bank Holidays). Mon, Tues, Thurs: 2-8. Wed, Fri, Sat: 10-5.
Admission: Free
Limited car parking. Unsuitable for disabled persons.

PAISLEY MUSEUM AND ART GALLERIES
(Renfrew District Council)
High Street, Paisley PA1 2BA **Tel:** 041-889 3151 **Fax:** 041-889 9240
A world famous collection of Paisley shawls. The collections illustrate the local, industrial and natural history of the town and district. The art collection places emphasis on 19th century artists.
Open: All year (except Bank Holidays). Mon to Sat 10-5.
Admission: Free
Unsuitable for disabled persons

ROTHESAY

BUTESHIRE NATURAL HISTORY SOCIETY MUSEUM
Stuart Street, Rothesay
Collections of the natural history, archaeology, geology and history of the island of Bute.

SALTCOATS

NORTH AYRSHIRE MUSEUM
(Cunninghame District Council)
Manse Street, Kirkgate, Saltcoats **Tel:** (0294) 64174

STRATHAVEN

JOHN HASTIE MUSEUM
(East Kilbride District Council)
Threestanes Road, Strathaven, Strathclyde ML10 6DX **Tel:** (0357) 21257
A small local history museum with displays featuring Strathaven Castle, weaving, the Covenanters, the 1820 Uprising, paintings, old photos, and the Burnbrae Collection of ceramics. A programme of temporary displays is being developed.
Open: Easter to 1st November 1992.

TARBOLTON

BACHELORS' CLUB
(National Trust for Scotland)
Tarbolton, Strathclyde **Tel:** (0292) 541940
17th century house named after the literary society founded within by Robert Burns and his friends in 1780. Contains facsimiles of letters and poems from the poet's Lochlea days, and period furnishings.
Open: Apr 1 to Oct 31: Daily 12-5. Also by appointment.
Admission: Adults £1.50, Child 80p Adult parties £1.20, Schools 60p

TAYSIDE

ARBROATH

ARBROATH ART GALLERY
(Angus District Council)
Public Library, Hill Terrace, Arbroath **Tel:** (0241) 75598
Collection of paintings by local artists and local views, in particular the works of J.W. Herald, watercolourist. Also two oil paintings, by Peter Breughell II.
Open: Mon, Wed 9.30-8; Tues, Thurs 9.30-6; Sat 9.30-5.

Inchbrayock Sculptured Stone

Angus District MUSEUMS

Arbroath Museum
Arbroath Art Gallery
Brechin Museum
Forfar Museum and Art Gallery
Montrose Museum and Art Gallery
William Lamb Memorial Studio

All enquiries to the District Curator, Museum and Art Gallery, Meffon Institute, 20 West High Street, Forfar, Angus DD8 1BB   Tel: (0307) 68813

Hugh McDiarmid by W. Lamb A.R.S.A.

ARBROATH MUSEUM
(Angus District Council)
   Signal Tower, Ladyloan, Arbroath   **Tel:** (0241) 75598
Local collections cover the history of Arbroath from Prehistoric Times to the Industrial Revolution. Special features include the Bellrock Lighthouse, Fishing and the Wildlife of Arbroath Cliffs.
Open: Apr to Oct: Mon to Sat 10.30-1; 2-5. July and Aug: Sun 2-5. Nov to Mar5: Mon to Fri 2-5; Sat 10.30-1; 2-5.

BLAIR ATHOLL

ATHOLL COUNTRY COLLECTION
(Mr and Mrs John and Janet Cameron)
   The Old School, Blair Atholl   **Tel:** (0796) 481232
A unique and lively museum with interesting displays of village and glen life. Something for all ages.
Open: Easter then June to mid-Oct.

BLAIR CASTLE
(The Duke of Atholl)
   Blair Atholl   **Tel:** (0796) 481207   **Fax:** (0796) 481487

BRECHIN

BRECHIN MUSEUM
(Angus District Council)
   Public Library, St. Ninian's Square, Brechin
Local collections tell the story of the development of Brechin from the Celtic church of the 10th century to the last days of the Burgh in 1975. There is a small display of some of the works of D.Waterson, etcher and watercolourist.
Open: Mon, Wed 9.30-8; Tues, Thurs 9.30-6; Fri, Sat 9.30-5.
Enquiries: Forfar Museum

DUNDEE

BARRACK STREET MUSEUM
(City of Dundee District Council)
   Barrack Street, Dundee   **Tel:** (0382) 23141
Natural History Museum. There are currently displays on Scottish Wildlife along with the skeleton of the famous Tay Whale, a humpback whale which swam up the Tay in 1883. The Art and Nature Gallery, is devoted to temporary exhibitions exploring the influence of nature on the arts and environmental themes.
Open: Mon to Sat 10-5. *Closed* Sun

BROUGHTY CASTLE MUSEUM
(City of Dundee District Council)
   Broughty Ferry, Dundee   **Tel:** (0382) 76121
A 15th Century estuary fort located by the seashore in Broughty Ferry. Besieged by the English in the 16th Century and attacked by Cromwell's army under General Monk in the 17th Century, it was left as a ruin, but was restored in 1861 as part of Britain's coastal defences. It is now a museum with displays on local history, arms and armour, seashore

life and Dundee's whaling story. The observation area at the top of the castle provides fine views over the Tay Estuary to N.E. Fife.
Open: Mon to Thurs and Sat 10-1, 2-5. Sun (July to Sept) 2-5. *Closed* Fri.
Location: 6m East of Dundee

MCMANUS GALLERIES
(City of Dundee District Council)
   Albert Square, Dundee   **Tel:** (0382) 23141
Built in 1867 and designed by Sir George Gilbert Scott, the McManus Galleries house an art collection of national importance. It includes fine examples of 19th and 20th Century Scottish paintings, prints, drawings, sculpture, furniture, clocks, glass, ceramics and silver. The McManus Galleries also house Dundee's human history collections. Three galleries tell the story of life in Tayside from prehistoric times through to the Industrial Revolution and on into the 20th Century. The costume gallery looks at clothes and customs with thematic displays. The Archaeological Gallery also has a significant display of material from Ancient Egypt. There is a programme of changing exhibitions alongside more permanent displays using the collections.
Open: Mon to Sat 10-5. *Closed* Sun

MILLS OBSERVATORY
(City of Dundee District Council)
   Balgay Hill, Dundee   **Tel:** (0382) 67138
Britain's only full-time Public Observatory. It is located in Balgay Park and houses a 10-inch Cooke Refracting Telescope. During the winter months viewing of the night sky is possible under the supervision of the Resident Astronomer. It is open throughout the year and offers panoramic views across the Tay to Fife. There is a small planetarium (viewing by arrangement), an audio-visual presentation and an exhibition of telescopes and scientific instruments.
Open: Apr to Sept: Mon to Fri 10-5, Sat 2-5; Oct to Mar: Mon to Fri 3-10, Sat 2-5. *Closed* Sun.

ROYAL RESEARCH SHIP DISCOVERY
(Dundee Heritage Trust)
   Victoria Dock, Dundee   **Tel:** (0382) 201175 or 25282

ST. MARY'S TOWER
(City of Dundee District Council)
   Nethergate, Dundee   **Tel:** (0382) 23141
Dundee's oldest building. 15th Century Steeple Tower, restored in 19th Century.
Open: *Closed*
Enquiries to the McManus Galleries. For all City of Dundee Museums, enquiries should be made at the McManus Galleries, Albert Square, Dundee, DD1 1DA. Tel: As above.

FORFAR

FORFAR MUSEUM
(Angus District Council)
   Meffan Institute, 20 West High Street, Forfar DD8 1BB   **Tel:** (0307) 68813
Open: Closed until further notice.
All enquiries to District Curator, Museums and Art Galleries at the above address.

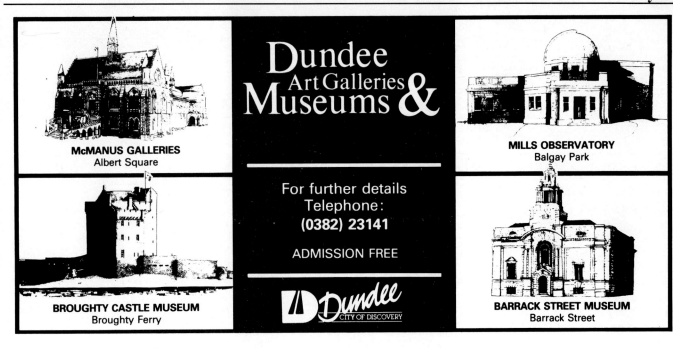

GLAMIS

THE ANGUS FOLK MUSEUM
(National Trust for Scotland)
 Kirkwynd Cottages, Glamis   **Tel:** (030784) 288
Collection of early furnishings, clothing, domestic utensils and agricultural implements from the former County of Angus.
Open: Apr 9-12 and May 1 to Sept 30: Daily 11-5. Last adm 4.30.
Admission: £1.50, Child 80p. Adult parties £1.30, schools 60p.

KIRRIEMUIR

BARRIE'S BIRTHPLACE
(National Trust for Scotland)
 Kirriemuir   **Tel:** (0575) 72646
Contains mementoes and manuscripts of Sir James Barrie. New exhibition features 'Peter Pan' and other of Barrie's works.
Open: Apr 9-12 and May 1 to Sept 30: Mon to Sat 11-5.30; Sun 2-5.30.
Admission: £1.50, Child 80p. Adult parties £1.30 schools 60p.
Refreshments: Tea room.

MONTROSE

HOUSE OF DUN
(National Trust for Scotland)
 Montrose   **Tel:** (067481) 264
Palladian house overlooking the Montrose Basin. Built in 1730 for David Erskine, Lord Dun, to designs by William Adam. Exuberant plasterwork. Exhibition on the architecture of the house & garden.
Open: 9-12 Apr and May 1 to Oct 17: Daily 11-5.30. Garden and grounds open all year daily 10-sunset.
Admission: £3.30, Child £1.70, Adult parties £2.60, schools £1.30.
Refreshments: Restaurant.

WILLIAM LAMB MEMORIAL STUDIO
(Angus District Council)
 24 Market Street, Montrose   **Tel:** (0674) 73232
The working studio of the famous Montrose sculptor includes displays of his sculptures, etchings, paintings and drawings. Also featured are his workroom and tools and his living room with self-styled furniture.
Open: July and Aug: Sun 2-5 or by arrangement.

MONTROSE MUSEUM
(Angus District Council)
 Panmure Place, Montrose   **Tel:** (0674) 73232
Extensive local collections cover the history of Montrose from prehistoric times to local government reorganisation, the maritime history of the port, the Natural History of Angus and local art. Pictish stones, Montrose silver and pottery; whaling artefacts; Napoleonic items (including a cast of his death mask). Paintings by local artists and local views, sculpture by W.Lamb.
Open: Apr to Oct: Mon to Sat 10.30-1, 2-5. July and Aug: Sun 2-5. Nov to Mar: Mon to Fri 2-5; Sat 10.30-1, 2-5.

SUNNYSIDE MUSEUM
(Tayside Health Board)
 Sunnyside Royal Hospital, Hillside, Montrose   **Tel:** (067 483) 361
This museum outlines the history of psychiatry in Scotland. Exhibits include slides, audio/visual shows.
Open: Easter to Sept: every Wed 2-3.30.

PERTH

PERTH MUSEUM AND ART GALLERY
(Perth and Kinross District Council)
 George Street, Perth

SERVICES MUSEUMS

This list of Services Museums gives times of opening, location and telephone numbers. Museums contain displays of uniforms, old arms, awards, campaign medals, regimental colours, pictures, trophies and souvenirs. Special items in the Collection are mentioned. Admission is free unless otherwise stated.

Airborne Forces Museum
Browning Barracks, Aldershot.
Tel: Aldershot (0252) 349619.
The history of the men who trained to go by air to battle. Their story is told using original briefing models, dioramas, tableaux, uniforms, equipment and transport. Tues to Sun 10–4.30. *Closed* Mon except by appt. *Closed* Dec 24–26. Adm £1.25, Chld, OAP, serving and ex members 60p; groups by appt.

Aldershot Military Museum
(Aldershot Military Historical Trust)
Queens Avenue, Aldershot.
Tel: (0252) 314598.
Tells the story of the Home of the British Army from its creation in 1854 to the present day, with photographs, models and displays recording the daily life of the soldier. Features an original Victorian barrack room with period uniforms and equipment. Diorama of pioneer flying machines, balloons and airships depict the birth of British aviation at Farnborough. Canadian gallery recalls the Canadian Army's long association with Aldershot from Queen Victoria's Diamond Jubilee Review to their takeover of the camp as their main UK base for the whole of World War 2. A collection of fabulously decorated uniforms from the Flint-Shipman Yeomanry & Volunteer collection is displayed in a military tailor's shop setting. New Rushmoor local history gallery and temporary exhibitions. External exhibits. Ample parking. Open daily Mar to Oct 10–5; Nov to Feb 10–4.30. *Closed* Jan 1 and Dec 13–26. Adm £1.50, Chld 40p. Reductions for OAPs and parties.

The Argyll & Sutherland Highlanders
Stirling Castle, Stirling.
Display in the King's Old Building. Easter to Sept: Mon to Sat 10–5.30; Sun 11–5; Oct: Mon to Fri 10–4. *Closed* Sat and Sun.

Army Physical Training Corps Museum
A.S.P.T. Queen's Avenue, Aldershot GU11 2LB.
Tel: Aldershot (0252) 347131.
Mon to Fri 9–4. Weekends by appointment.

Army Transport Museum *see* **Museum of Army Transport**

Ayrshire (E.C.O.) Yeomanry
Rozelle House, Alloway, by Ayr.
Tel: (0292) 264091.
All year Mon to Sat, 10–5; open also on Suns from Apr 1 to Oct 30, 2–5.

Battle of Britain Memorial Flight
Royal Air Force
Coningsby
Lincs LN4 4SY
Tel: (0526) 44041
One hour conducted tour of the flying aircraft, five Spitfires, one Hurricane and one of the only two flying Lancasters in company of expert guide. A memorabilia exhibition and souvenir shop. Open Mon to Fri 10–5 (last conducted tour 3.30). *Closed* Weekends, Bank Hols and over Christmas. Adm charge.

The Bedfordshire & Hertfordshire Regiment
c/o Luton Museum, Wardown Park, Luton LU2 7HA.
Tel: (0582) 36941–2.
Opening times see Luton Museum & Art Gallery.

The Black Watch (R.H.R.)
Balhousie Castle, Hay Street, Perth (facing North Inch, entrance and car park by Hay Street Gate).
Tel: Perth (0738) 21281, Ext. 8530.
Mon to Fri 10–4.30 (winter 3.30); Sun and Public Hols (Easter to Sept only) 2–4.30. *Closed* Sat, Public and Military Hols.

The Border Regiment & King's Own Royal Border Regiment
Queen Mary's Tower, The Castle, Carlisle.
Tel: Carlisle (0228) 32774.
Two dioramas, four V.Cs., treasures and battle trophies. Uniforms, records and documents from 1702. Apr 1 to Sept 30: 9.30–6, Sun 10–6; Oct 1 to March 31: 9.30–4; Sun 10–4.

Buffs Regimental Museum
Canterbury, Kent.
Tel: (0227) 452747.
Opening times see The Royal Museum & Art Gallery, Canterbury.

Cambridgeshire Regimental Collection/Ely Museum
High Street, Ely, Cambridgeshire CB7 4HL.
Tel: (0353) 666655.
Unique collection of uniforms, objects and photographs illustrating the history of the Cambridgeshire Regiment. Includes the regimental drums buried at the fall of Singapore and recovered after the war. Open Summer: Sun 2.15–5; Tues to Sat 10.30–1, 2.15–5, *closed* Mon. Winter: Tues to Fri 11.30–3.30, *closed* Mon. Sat 11.30–4, Sun 1–4. Adm charge.

The Cameronians (Scottish Rifles)
Mote Hill, off Muir Street, Hamilton, Lanarkshire ML3 6BY.
Tel: Hamilton (0698) 428688.
For details please telephone above number.

The Cheshire Military Museum
The Castle, Chester, CH1 2DN. 5th Royal Inniskilling Dragoon Guards, 3rd Carabiniers, Cheshire Yeomanry, 22nd (Cheshire) Regiment.
Open Daily 9–5. *Closed* Dec 19 to Jan 3 and Good Friday. Enquiries (0244) 327617. Adm 50p, Chld/OAP/disabled 20p.

Derbyshire Yeomanry Cavalry
Derby Museum & Art Gallery, The Strand, Derby DE1 1BS.
Tel: Derby (0332) 25-5581.
Items illustrating the history of volunteer cavalry in Derbyshire from 1794. Displays include reconstruction Scout car. Opening times see Derby Museum & Art Gallery.

The Dorset Military Museum
The Keep, Bridport Road, Dorchester.
Tel: Dorchester (0305) 264066.
Exhibits of Dorset Regiment, Dorset Militia and Volunteers, Queen's Own Dorset Yeomanry and Devonshire and Dorset Regiment (from 1958). Mon to Fri 9–1, 2–5; Sat 10–1 (Oct to June: *closed* Sat afternoon). Adm £1, Chld/OAPs 50p. Parties by appointment. Free car park.

The Duke of Cornwall's Light Infantry
The Keep, Bodmin, Cornwall.
Tel: Bodmin (0208) 72810.
Mon to Fri 8–4.45. Except Public Hols. Adm £1.

The Duke of Edinburgh's Royal Regiment (Berkshire and Wiltshire Museum)
The Duke of Edinburgh's Royal Regiment, Regimental HQ and Museum. The Wardrobe, 58 The Close, Salisbury SP1 2EX
Tel: (0722) 414536
Mon to Fri 10–5 (Fri 4.30). May to Oct open daily. Apr: Sun to Fri. *Closed* Dec & Jan. Adm £1.50, OAPs/Students £1, Chld (under 16 yrs) 50p. Party rates available on request.

Duke of Lancaster's Own Yeomanry *see* **Lancashire Country and Regimental Museum.**

The Duke of Wellington's Regiment Museum
Bankfield Museum, Akroyd Park, Halifax, W. Yorks
Tel: Halifax (0422) 354823.
Recently re-displayed, the collections cover the history of the regiment from 1702 to the present day. Emphasis is on the uniforms, equipment and relics, often displayed in period settings, and some of them touchable. Along with regimental material, local volunteer and militia items are included, as is a display of relics associated with the Iron Duke himself. Tues–Sat: 10–5; Sun 2–5. The extensive reserve collection and archive can be studied by appointment.

Durham Light Infantry Museum
Aykley Heads, Durham City.
Tel: (0385) 42214.
The history of the D.L.I. from 1758 to 1968 (also Durham Militia and Volunteers) uniforms, medals, weapons, photographs and regimental treasures. Weekdays (except Mon but open Bank Hols) 10–5; Sun 2–5. Adm 75p, Chld/OAPs 35p. Free car park. Suitable for the Disabled.

East Lancashire Regiment Museum
c/o Blackburn Museum, Museum Street, Blackburn.
Tel: (0254) 667130.
Trophies, medals, uniforms, pictures, colours and weapons of the East Lancashire Regiment and its forebears, the 30th (Cambridgeshires) dating from 1689, 59th (2nd Notts) dating from 1775, the 5th Royal Lancashire Militia and local corps of the Lancashire Volunteer Rifles. The popular play, 'The Accrington Pals' has given the museum an extra popularity. Tues to Sat 10–5. Currently being re-displayed. Please enquire for details of present position.

Fleet Air Arm Museum, Royal Naval Air Station.
Yeovilton, Somerset.
Tel: Ilchester (0935) 840565.
Daily 10–5.30 (Apr to Oct), 4.30 (Nov to Mar). *Closed* Dec 24, 25 and 26. Adm charge.

Fusiliers London Volunteers' Museum
Fusilier House, 213 Balham High Road, London SW17 7BQ.
Tel: 081-672 1168.
Exhibits portraying the history of 1st & 2nd Battalions of the London Regiment and Royal Regiment of Fusiliers. Adm only by appointment. Adm free.

The Gloucestershire Regimental Museum *see* **Regiments of Gloucestershire Museum.**

The Gordon Highlanders
Viewfield Road, Aberdeen.
Tel: Aberdeen (0224) 318174.
Open by appointment.

The Green Howards Museum
Trinity Church Square, Richmond, Yorkshire.
Tel: Richmond (0748) 822133.
Feb: Mon–Fri 10–4.30; Mar & Nov: Mon–Sat 10–4.30; Apr–Oct: Mon–Sat 9.30–4.30. Sun 2–4.30. *Closed* Dec & Jan. Adm fee charged.

The Guards Museum
Wellington Barracks, Birdcage Walk, London SW1E 6HQ.
Tel: 071-414 3428.
The story of the Foot Guards, a superb collection of uniforms, weapons and memorabilia illustrating their martial history and service to The Sovereign and The City of London for over three centuries. Open 10–4 inc w/ends & all Bank Hols. *Closed* Fri & Christmas. £2, Child, OAPs, Groups of over 25 £1. Guide can be arranged. Family tickets £4. No parking. Suitable for disabled. Available as a magnificent venue for all types of functions. Details on request.

Herefordshire Regiment/Herefordshire Light Infantry Regimental Museum
Harold Street, Hereford.
Tel: Hereford (0432) 357311, Ext. 2380.
Mon to Fri 9.30–12, 2–4. By appointment only.

Hertfordshire Yeomanry & Artillery
c/o Hitchin Museum, Paynes Park, Hitchin, Herts.
Tel: (0462) 434476.
Opening times see Hitchin Museum.

Honourable Artillery Company
Armoury House, City Road, London EC1Y 2BQ.
Tel: 01-606 4644.
Open by appointment from 12 noon to 6 on weekdays.

The Household Cavalry Museum
Combermere Barracks, Windsor.
Tel: Windsor (075 35) 868222, Ext. 5203.
General exhibits of The Life Guards and Royal Horse Guards (The Blues), and 1st Royal Dragoons. Mon to Fri 10–1, 2–5, last adms 12.30 and 4.30). *Closed* Bank Hols.

Services Museums — *continued*

Inns of Court and City Yeomanry Museum
10 Stone Buildings, Lincolns Inn, London WC2A 3TG.
Tel: (01) 405 8112/831 1693.
Small but interesting display of uniforms, medals and equipment of the Inns of Court Regiment and the City of London Yeomanry (the Rough Riders) which together comprise the Inns of Court and City Yeomanry covering period 1798 to date. Open 10–3.30, Mon to Fri (but visitors are advised to telephone beforehand). Adm free but donations gratefully received. Curator: Major R. J. B. Gentry.

The Intelligence Corps Museum
Templer Barracks, Ashford, Kent.
Tel: Ashford (0233) 657208.
The only museum in Great Britain covering military intelligence in memento, document and pictorial form from Elizabethan times to present day. Open Tues and Thurs 9–12.30, 2–4.30. Other times by appointment only.

Kent and Sharpshooters Yeomanry Museum
Hever Castle, Edenbridge, Kent.
Tel: (0732) 865224.

The King's Own Royal Regiment Museum
Lancaster City Museum, Market Square LA1 1HT.
Tel: Lancaster (0524) 64637.
Uniforms, medals (including 3 VCs), campaign relics, records and documents from 1680 to 1959. Opening times see Lancaster City Museum.

The King's Own Scottish Borderers
The Barracks, Berwick-upon-Tweed.
Tel: Berwick (0289) 307426.
Mon to Fri 9.15–4.30; Sat 9.15–12. Sun by appointment. Adm charge.

The King's Own Yorkshire Light Infantry
Doncaster Museum and Art Gallery, Chequer Road, Doncaster S. Yorks.
Tel: (0302) 734293.
Open Mon to Sat 10–5, Suns 2–5. Adm free.

The King's Regiment Collections
Liverpool Museum, National Museums and Galleries on Merseyside, William Brown Street, Liverpool L3 8EN.
Opening times see Liverpool Museum.

The 14th/20th Kings Hussars *see* Lancashire County and Regimental Museum.

The 15th/19th The King's Royal Hussars and Northumberland Hussars
c/o John George Joicey Museum, City Road, Newcastle upon Tyne NE1 2AS.
Tel: (091) 2324562.
Tues to Fri 10–5.30; Sat 10–4.30. Bank Holidays 10–5.30. *Closed* Sun and Mon (except Bank Holidays).

Lancashire County and Regimental Museum
Stanley St., Preston PR1 4YP.
Tel: Preston (0772) 264075.
This new museum displays collections relating to the Duke of Lancaster's Own Yeomanry, the 14/20th King's Hussars, Queen's Lancashire regiment and the historic Lancashire Hussars. Re-created scenes include a First World War trench, with light, sound and smell effects. Classroom available for schools. Open daily (except Thurs and Sun) 10–5. *Closed* Bank Hols. Adm free. Free car park.

The Lancashire Fusiliers
Lancashire Headquarters, The Royal Regiment of Fusiliers, Wellington Barracks, Bury, Lancs.
Tel: 061-764 2208.
Daily 9.30–4.30 (except Mon and Thurs). Adm 25p, Chld 10p. *Closed* Bank Hols.

Lancashire Hussars *see* Lancashire County and Regimental Museum.

The 17th/21st Lancers
Belvoir Castle, 5 miles SW of Grantham, Lincs.
Tel: Grantham (0476) 67413 Ext. 3252 (Museum Curator)
Grantham (0476) 870262 (Castle Controller).
Exhibition relating story of the 17th, 21st and 17th/21st Lancers from 1759 to present day. Weapons, uniforms, medals, silver, pictures and historical relics etc. Open Apr to Sept inclusive daily 11–5. *Closed* Mon and Fri. Adm (Castle & Museum inclusive) £3.20, Chld £2.20 (subject to increase).

Liverpool Scottish Regimental Museum (T.A.)
Forbes House, Score Lane, Childwall, Liverpool 16.
Tel: (daytime) 051-722 7711.
By appointment.

The Loyal Regiment (NL) *see* The Queen's Lancashire Regiment

Military Vehicle Museum
Exhibition Park Pavilion, Newcastle Upon Tyne NE2 4PZ
Tel: (091) 281 7222.
Over thirty vehicles mostly from World War II including guns and artefacts relating to the war years. Open daily 10–4.30 (last adm). Adm £1, Chld/OAPs 50p. Reductions for parties of chldn by arrangement. Car parking outside park. Exhibition park bus stop on the Great North Road or by Tyne-side Metro to Jesmond or Haymarket stations – if using public transport. Full disabled facilities (including car parking but not wheelchairs).

Mosquito Aircraft Museum
Salisbury Hall, B556, London Colney, St. Albans, Herts
Tel: (0727) 22051.
Display of 16 aircraft featuring the DeHavilland Mosquito prototype. Also extensive displays of Mosquito squadrons memorabilia, and collection of aero engines. Open Sun & Bank Hols 10.30–5.30 from Easter to end of Oct. Thurs 2–5.30 July to end of Sept. Adm £1, chld 40p. Parties of 30+ by appointment. Free car park.

Museum of Army Flying
Middle Wallop, Stockbridge, Hants. SO20 8DY.
Tel: Andover (0264) 384421.
All aspects of Army Flying from the 19th Century to the present. Now double the size. Open daily 10–4.30. *Closed* Christmas period. Shop, free cinema and coffee shop, full disabled facilities. Adm charge.

Museum of Army Transport
Flemingate, Beverley, North Humberside.
Tel: (0482) 860445.
The Royal Corps of Transport Collection of Army road, rail, sea and air transport. Daily 10–5 (except Christmas Eve, Christmas Day and Boxing Day). Adm charge. Free parking. Shop, café, bar and conference centre.

Museum of Artillery
The Rotunda, Repository Road, Woolwich, London SE18.
Tel: 081-316 5402.
Mon to Fri 12–5; Sat and Sun 1–5. *Closed* at 4 in winter.

The Museum of The Manchesters. A Social and Regimental History
(Tameside Metropolitan Borough)
Ashton Town Hall, The Market Place.
Tel: 061-344 3078.
The History of The Manchester Regiment, displayed with the social history of the community in which it was based. Mon to Sat 10–4. *Closed* Sun and Bank Hols. Adm free. Full access and facilities for disabled.

National Army Museum
Chelsea, London SW3.
Tel: 01-730 0717.
The British Army from 1485 and the Indian Army until independence in 1947.

Norfolk & Suffolk Aviation Museum Ltd.
Flixton, Bungay, Suffolk.
16 historic aircraft and unique indoor exhibition of aviation items from the early days of flying to the present day.

The Northamptonshire Regiment
Abington Park, Northampton.
Tel: (0604) 31454.
Abington Museum will be closed for structural work until further notice.

Northamptonshire Yeomanry
Abington Park, Northampton.
Tel: (0604) 31454.
Abington Museum will be closed for structural work until further notice.

The Pembroke Yeomanry Historical Trust
c/o The Castle Museum & Art Gallery, The Castle, Haverfordwest, Dyfed SA61 2EF.
Tel: (0437) 763708.
Opening times Mon–Sat 10–4.30. *Closed* Good Friday and Christmas Day to New Year's Day.

The Prince of Wales's Own Regiment of Yorkshire (West & East Yorkshire Regts.) 4/7 Royal Dragoon Guards.
Tower Street, York.
Tel: York (0904) 642038.
Mon to Sat 9.30–4.30. *Closed* Public Hols. Adm 50p, chld/OAPs 25p.

Queen Alexandra's Royal Army Nursing Corps
The Royal Pavilion, Farnborough Road, Aldershot, Hants.
Tel: Direct dialling (0252) 349301 or 349315.
Mon & Fri by appointment only; Tues & Wed 9–12.30, 2–4.30; Thurs 9–12.30.

1st The Queen's Dragoon Guards
Cardiff Castle, Cardiff.
Tel: 227611 Ext. 8232 (Maindy Barracks, Cardiff).
Collection includes KDG Mounted Officer tableau, Bays Drum Horse tableau, Officers Mess Dinner tableau, Hologram depicting 3 equestrian figures of different periods, VC case, Trench System, 1914–1918 war, and many other attractions.

The Queen's Lancashire Regiment
incorporating **The Loyal Regiment (NL)**
Fulwood Barracks, Preston PR2 4AA.
Tel: Preston (0772) 716543 Ext. 2362.
Open Tues and Thurs 9–12, 2–4 or by appointment. Curator: Major (Retd) A. J. Maher MBE.

Queens Own Cameron Highlanders *see* Queens Own Highlanders.

Queen's Own Highlanders (Seaforth and Camerons)
Fort George, Inverness-shire.
April to Sept: Mon to Fri 10–6; Sun 2–6. Oct to March: Mon to Fri 10–4. *Closed* Sat & Sun. *Closed* Dec 25, Jan 1 & 2 and Easter, Spring & Summer Bank Hol weekends and Civil Service hols.

The Queen's Own Hussars
Lord Leycester Hospital, High Street, Warwick.
Summer: Tues to Sat. 10–6; Mon 2–6. Winter: Tues to Sat 10–4; Mon 2–4. No adm charge to museum. Adm charge to Lord Leycester Hospital £2, Chld (under 14) 80p, OAPs and Students £1.25. Discount for parties of 20 adults or more.

The Queen's Own Royal West Kent Regimental Museum
Maidstone, Kent.
Tel: Maidstone (0622) 754497.
Items from the 50th and 97th Regts, West Kent Militia and The Queen's Own Royal West Kent Regiment. Opening times see Maidstone Museum.

The Queen's Regiment Museum
Dover Castle.
Exhibits include many items from the late Regiments from which the present Queen's Regiment was formed on Dec 31, 1966. i.e. Queen's Royal Regiment (West Surrey); The Buffs (Royal East Kent Regiment); The East Surrey Regiment; The Queen's Own Royal West Kent Regiment; The Royal Sussex Regiment and the Middlesex Regiment (Duke of Cambridge's Own). Summer: daily 10–6; Winter: daily 10–4. Permanent exhibition of the Regiment, 1661–1988.

16th/5th The Queen's Royal Lancers and The Staffordshire Yeomanry (Q.O.R.R.)
Kitchener House, Lammascote Road, Stafford ST16 3TA. Tel: Stafford (0785) 45840.
Mon to Fri 9.30–1, 2–4 or by appointment. Curator, Major D. J. H. Farquharson.

The Queen's Royal Surrey Regiment Museum
(The National Trust) Clandon Park, West Clandon, Guildford, Surrey GU4 7RQ.
Tel: Guildford (0483) 223419.
Historical items of the former Queen's Royal Regiment, The East Surrey Regiment and The Queen's Royal Surrey Regiment. Easter to mid-Oct: Sat, Sun, Mon, Tues & Wed 1.30–5.30. Open Bank Hol Mon. National Trust admission to be paid; no additional charge for the Museum.

Regimental Museum of the South Lancashire Regiment (Pwv)
Peninsula Barracks, Orford, Warrington, Lancs.
Tel: Warrington (0925) 33563.
Mon to Fri 9–2, including the lunch period. At other times by appointment.

Regiments of Gloucestershire Museum
Custom House, Gloucester Docks, Gloucester GL1 2HE
Tel: (0452) 22682.
Award-winning museum telling the story of The Glosters and the Royal Gloucestershire Hussars. Life-size displays with sound effects, small scale models, archive photographs and film. Open Tues to Sun and Bank Hol Mons 10–5. Shop. Facilities for disabled visitors. Admission charge.

Services Museums — *continued*

Royal Air Force Museum
Grahame Park Way, Hendon, London NW9 5LL.
Tel: 081-205 2266.
Britain's national museum of aviation houses one of the world's finest collections of historic aircraft illustrating the development of aviation from before the Wright Brothers to the present day RAF. Over 60 aircraft on display including the legendary Spitfire and Lancaster, plus German and American aircraft. Complex includes Battle of Britain Experience and Bomber Command Hall. Film Shows; art exhibitions; flight simulator; shop; licensed restaurant; large free car park. Open daily 10–6. Adm charge.

RAF Regiment Museum
RAF Regiment Depot, RAF Catterick, Richmond DL10 7NP. Tel: (0748) 811441.
Exhibits from the earliest days of RAF armoured cars. The Iraq Levies and the Aden Protectorate Levies. Displays depicting RAF Regiment operations from 1942 to the present day. Open by appointment. Adm free. Parties by appointment. Car parking. Not suitable for disabled. Entry to RAF Catterick requires "booking-in" formality.

Royal Army Chaplains' Department
Bagshot Park, Bagshot, Surrey GU19 5PL.
Tel: (0276) 71717.
Mon, Tues, Wed, Thurs & Fri 10–4 by appointment only.

Royal Army Dental Corps Museum, HQ and Central Group RADC
Evelyn Woods Road, Aldershot, Hants GU11 2LS
Tel: (0252) 347782.
Instruments and items of professional interest. Mon to Fri 10–12, 2–4.

Royal Army Medical Corps Historical Museum
Keogh Barracks, Ash Vale, Aldershot.
Tel: Aldershot (0252) 24431, Ext. Keogh 5212.
Mon to Fri 8.30–4. Evenings and weekends by appointment. Facilities for disabled.

Royal Army Ordnance Corps Museum
Deepcut, Camberley, Surrey.
Tel: Aldershot (0252) 340515.
Mon to Thurs 8.30–12.30, 1.30–4.30; Fri 8.30–12.30, 1.30–4.

Royal Army Pay Corps
Worthy Down, Winchester, Hants.
Tel: Winchester 880880, Ext. 2435.
Mon to Fri 10–12, 2–4. *Closed* Public Hols.

Royal Army Veterinary Corps Museum
Gallwey Road, Aldershot, Hants. GU11 2DQ.
Tel: Aldershot (0252) 24431, Ext. 3527/28.
Closed w.e.f. Sept 1985, pending relocation.

Royal Artillery Regimental Museum
Old Royal Military Academy, Red Lion Lane, Woolwich, London SE18 4DN.
Tel: 081-781 5628.
Mon to Fri 12.30–4.30; Sat and Sun 2–4.

Royal Berkshire Yeomanry Cavalry
Berkshire Yeomanry Museum, TA Centre, Bolton Road, Windsor, Berks SL4 3JG.
Tel: (0753) 860600.
The Berkshire Yeomanry Museum covers the history of the Regiment from 1794 to the present day. It is run by serving and ex-members of the Berkshire Yeomanry and shows items of uniform, equipment, photographs, prints, documents and ephemera associated with the Regiment over nearly 200 years. Open by appointment.

Royal Corps of Transport Museum
Buller Barracks, Alison's Road, Aldershot, Hants. GU11 2BX.
The history of the Corps and its predecessors from the 18th century. Weekdays 9–12, 2–4. Parties at other times, by appointment.

4th/7th Royal Dragoon Guards
No. 3A Tower Street, York.
Tel: York (0904) 642036.
Opening times Mon to Sat 9.30–5. Adm 50p, Chld and OAPs 25p.

Royal Electrical and Mechanical Engineers (REME) Museum
Isaac Newton Road, Arborfield, Reading, Berks.
Tel: Arborfield Cross (0734) 763567.
Open weekdays less public hols 9–12.30, 2–4.30 (4 on Fris). Restricted space precludes coach parties. Reserved car parking. Displays include life size tableaux, models, photos and artifacts telling the story of REME. Adm free.

Royal Engineers Museum
Prince Arthur Road, Gillingham, Kent.
Tel: (0634) 406397.
Large Museum tracing the lives and work of Britain's soldier engineers from 1066 to 1945. Fine medal rooms with 19 VCs. Wide survey of military and Imperial history. Richly international decorative arts collection. Open Tues to Fri and Spring/Summer Bank Hol Mons 10–5; Sun 11.30–5. Adm £1; Chld/unwaged 50p. Service ID Free.

The Royal Fusiliers
Tower of London, Tower Hill EC3.
Tel: 071-488 5611.
Artifacts and narrative illustrating the history of the Royal Fusiliers from foundation in 1685 to present day. Ten V.C.'s including the original prototype, Peninsular War Gold Medal, etc. Weekdays: summer 9.30–5; winter 9.30–4. Adm 25p.

The Royal Green Jackets
Peninsula Barracks, Romsey Road, Winchester.
Tel: Winchester (0962) 863846.
This splendid and exciting Museum tells the history of The Oxfordshire and Buckinghamshire Light Infantry, The King's Royal Rifle Corps and The Rifle Brigade and the Royal Green Jackets. With the use of graphics, models and artefacts, it tells a compelling story of not only the Regiment's history but also that of the nation's, from 1741 to this present time. For schools it contains much of that history required for the national curriculum, including the Napoleonic periods, the Waterloo period and the 1st and 2nd World Wars. It also contains the largest diorama, measuring 22' × 11', in the country of the Battle of Waterloo; this diorama has some 22,000 model figures on it with sound and lighting effects. Open daily throughout the year except for 14 days at Christmas. Mon to Sat 10–5, Sun 12–4. Adm £2, OAPs & Chld £1. Groups (minimum of 10) £1.25. Family Group £6. Schools very welcome by arrangement.

The Royal Hampshire Regiment and Memorial Garden
Serles House, Southgate Street, Winchester.
Tel: Winchester (0962) 863658.
Easter to Oct 30, Mon to Fri 10–12.30, 2–4, Sat, Sun and Bank Hols 12–4.

The Royal Highland Fusiliers (Princess Margaret's Own Glasgow and Ayrshire Regiment)
518 Sauchiehall Street, Glasgow G2 3LW.
Tel: 041-332 5639.

The 13th/18th Royal Hussars (Queen Mary's Own)
c/o Cannon Hall Museum, Cawthorne, near Barnsley, South Yorks. S75 4AT.
Opening times see Cannon Hall Museum.

The Royal Inniskilling Fusiliers
The Castle, Enniskillen, Co. Fermanagh.
Tel: Enniskillen (0365) 323142.
Mon to Fri 9.30–12.30, 2–4.30. Adm 50p, Chld 10p. Parties (over 20) half-price per person.

The Royal Irish Fusiliers
Sovereign's House, The Mall, Armagh.
Tel: Armagh (0861) 522911.
Mon to Fri 10–12.30, 2–4.30.

The 9th/12th Royal Lancers Regimental Museum
Derby Museum & Art Gallery, The Strand, Derby DE1 1BS.
Tel: Derby (0332) 25-5581.
Items illustrating the history of the regiment and its two predecessors from 1715 to the present day. Replica stable circa 1885, large uniform and medal displays. Opening times see Derby Museums & Art Gallery.

The Royal Leicestershire Regiment
The Magazine, Oxford Street, Leicester.
Tel: (0533) 555889.
Weekdays 10–5.30; Sun 2–5.30.

The Royal Lincolnshire Regiment
Collection on display in the Museum of Lincolnshire Life. Opening times see entry under Lincoln.

Royal Marines Museum
Southsea, Hants.
Tel: Portsmouth (0705) 819385.
Considered one of the finest military Museums in Britain. It is located in spacious grounds adjacent to Southsea beach and outdoor exhibits include a Whirlwind helicopter and a Falklands Landing Craft which visitors can walk into. The Museum tells the story of the Royal Marines from 1664 to the present day in a lively and fascinating way. Popular exhibitions include: the fascinating Falklands audio-visual; a chilled Arctic Display; a new early history gallery featuring a talking head of Hannah Snell, the first female Marine, and live maggots. Plus one of the greatest medal collections in the country. Open daily 10–5.30 Whitsun to Aug; 10–4.30 Sept to Whitsun. Free car parking & seafront entrance. Well stocked shop offers a wide range of quality goods for all ages. Junior Commando Assault course. Adm charge.

Royal Military Police Corps Museum
The Keep, Roussillon Barracks, Broyle Road, Chichester, West Sussex PO19 4BN.
Tel: (0243) 786311 Ext. 4225.
Fully refurbished in 1985, tracing military police history from Tudor times to date – along with cleverly presented aspects of the RMP's role in the modern professional army. Features include historic uniforms, a new medal room, nostalgic 'National Service' kit lay out and Barrack Room, North Africa diorama of desert mine field c1942 and videos. Open Apr to Sept, Tues to Fri, 10.30–12.30, 1.30–4.30. Sat & Sun: 2–6. Oct to Mar: Tues to Fri 10.30–12.30, 1.30–4.30. *Closed* Jan. Adm free. Car parking. Suitable for disabled persons (no wheelchairs). Shop.

Royal Military School of Music
Kneller Hall, Twickenham, London TW2 7DU.
Tel: 081-898 5533/4/5.
By appointment only. Curator: Major (Ret'd) R. G. Swift LRAM, ARCM, LTCL.

Royal Monmouthshire Royal Engineers (Militia) Regimental Museum
The Castle, Monmouth, Gwent NP5 3BS
Tel: (0600) 2935.
Historical record of Monmouth Castle and R Mon RE(M). Open daily from Easter to Aug Bank Hol, weekends only for rest of the year, 2–5. Researchers may visit on weekdays by arrangement with the ADJT. Adm free, donations welcome. Suitable for disabled persons.

Royal Navy Submarine Museum
Haslar Jetty Road, Gosport PO12 2AS.
Tel: Gosport (0705) 529217.
Underwater warfare yesterday and today. Apr to Oct 10–last tour starting 4.30; Nov to Mar 10–last tour starting 3.30. *Closed* Dec 24 to Jan 1. Adm charge. Special rates for groups.

The Royal Norfolk Regimental Museum
Shirehall, Market Avenue, Norwich NR1 3JQ.
The story of a County Regiment and the men who served in it from 1658 to the present day. Mon to Sat 10–5, Sun 2–5.

The Royal Northumberland Fusiliers
The Abbot's Tower, Alnwick Castle, Alnwick, Northumberland.
Tel: Alnwick (0665) 602152.
Open with Alnwick Castle. May to Sept, or by appointment. Adm 25p.

Royal Pioneer Corps Museum
Simpson Barracks, Wootton, Northampton NN4 0HX.
Tel: Northampton (0604) 762742, Ext. 4734.
Mon to Fri 9.30–4. Weekends by prior appointment.

The Royal Regiment of Wales
South Wales Borderers & Monmouthshire Regiment, The Barracks, Brecon, Powys, South Wales.
Tel: Brecon 623111 Ext. 2310.
The Museum portrays the history of the 24th Regiment (The South Wales Borderers), as well as associated Militia and Volunteer Units, from it's inception in 1689 to its amalgamation with the 41st Regiment (The Welch Regiment) in 1969. The new regiment is known as The Royal Regiment of Wales. Uniforms, equipment, paintings, guns, a cinema and many trophies tell the story of nearly 300 years service. Adm 50p per person. Car parking. Suitable for disabled persons. Souvenir stand. Open weekdays, Oct to Mar. *Closed* Suns from Apr to Sept.

The Royal Scots Dragoon Guards
The Castle, Edinburgh, Midlothian EH1 2YT. Scotland.
Tel: 031-225 9366.
Collections relating to the history of the Royal Scots Greys, and 3rd Dragoon Guards (3rd Carabiniers). Open Mon to Fri 9.30–4, Sat 10–4 July to Aug depending on availability of staff. *Closed* Sun, Public Hols and Civil Service Hols. Adm free (Adm to Castle £2, chld/ OAPs £1.50). Car parking Edinburgh Castle.

Services Museums — *continued*

The Royal Scots Regimental Museum
Edinburgh Castle.
Apr to Sept: Daily 9.30–4.30; Oct to Apr: Mon to Fri 9.30–4. *Closed* Sat & Sun. No extra charge to view Regimental Museum.

Royal Signals Museum
Blandford Camp, Dorset, near Blandford Forum.
Tel: Blandford (0258) 482248.
Museum shows history of army communications and the history of the Royal Signals, including Middlesex Yeomanry section. Mon to Fri 10–5; Weekends June to Sept, 10–4.

The Royal Sussex Regiment
Redoubt, Eastbourne.
Tel: (0323) 410300.
Opening times see Sussex Combined Services Museum.

The Royal Ulster Rifles
Waring Street, Belfast.
Tel: Belfast (0232) 232086.
Mon to Fri 10–4 (prior notice may sometimes be necessary). *Closed* Bank Hols.

The Royal Warwickshire Regiment
St. John's House, Warwick.
Tel: (0926) 491653.
Tues to Sat 10–12.30, 1.30–5.30; Sun (May to Sept incl.) 2.30–5. *Closed* Mon. Curator, Brigadier J. K. Chater.

The Royal Welch Fusiliers
Queen's Tower, Caernarfon Castle, Caernarfon.
Tel: (0286) 673362.
Hat ribbon worn by King William of Orange 1690, Keys of Corunna, officer's Mitre cap 1750, 10 V.C.'s, Gold Peninsular War medals; Large collection of campaign medals, full size tableau and Royal and other portraits by Dennis Fields, Oswald Birley, Gerald Kelly. End-March to end-Oct: Daily 9.30–6.30. Mid-Oct to mid-March: Weekdays 9.30–4; Sun 2–4. Adm: Castle £3, chld/OAPs £1.75. Regimental Museum free.

The Royal Wiltshire Yeomanry
c/o Museum & Art Gallery, Bath Road, Swindon.
Tel: (0793) 526161, Ext. 4551.
Weekdays 10–5.30; Sun 2–5.30.

St Peter's Bunker Museum
St. Peter, Jersey, Channel Islands.
Tel: 81048.
Museum of the German occupation of Jersey. Comprehensive collection of German Militaria of WWII including rare 'enigma' decoding machine. Open Mar to end Oct 10–5 daily. Adm £1.40, chld 70p. Parties by arrangement. In the same car park as the Jersey Motor Museum, with Hotel, Pub and Coffee Lounge. Opposite is 11th Century Church of St. Peter.

The Scottish Horse
The Cross, Dunkeld, Perthshire, Scotland.
Easter to Sept: Daily 10–12, 2–5. Adm 50p.

Scottish United Services Museum
The Castle, Edinburgh.
Tel: 031-225 7534. Fax: 031-225 3848.
The Armed Forces at all periods with particular emphasis on Scottish regiments and on the Royal Navy or Royal Air Force in Scotland. Opening times and admission charges to the public galleries as for Edinburgh Castle, basically: Weekdays 9.30–6 (winter 9.30–5); Sun 11–5.50 (winter 12.30–4.20).

Seaforth Highlanders *see* **Queen's Own Highlanders**

Sherwood Foresters (Notts & Derby) Regiment
Derby Museum & Art Gallery, The Strand, Derby DE1 1BS (in addition to main displays at Nottingham Castle Museum).
Tel: Derby (0332) 25-5581.
The story of infantry in Derbyshire from 1689 through to the formation of the Sherwood Foresters in 1881 and amalgamation with the Worcestershire Regiment in 1970. Displays include items from the Militia, Volunteers, Territorials and 95th Derbyshire Regiment. Also First World War trench diorama and sentry box. Opening times see Derby Museum and Art Gallery.

The Sherwood Foresters Museum (45th/95th Foot)
The Castle, Nottingham NG1 6EL.
Tel: (0602) 483504.
The history of the Regiment from formation of the 45th Regiment in 1741 to amalgamation with the Worcestershire Regiment in 1970. Medals, buttons, badges, uniforms, weapons, pictures and Regimental trophies. Opening times see the Castle Museum, Nottingham. Subsidiary displays in the Civic Museums of Derby and Newark, the latter entirely devoted to the 8th Battalion.

The Shropshire Regimental Museum
The Castle, Shrewsbury.
Tel: Shrewsbury (0743) 358516.
A museum containing the collections of The King's Shropshire Light Infantry, The Shropshire Yeomanry, The Shropshire Royal Horse Artillery and the Lieutenancy in the historic surroundings of Shrewsbury's ancient Castle. Daily 10–5. *Closed* Suns in the winter. Adm £1, Chld/OAPs 50p.

The Somerset Military Museum
Somerset County Museum, Taunton Castle.
Tel: (0823) 255504 or 333434.
Mon to Sat 10–5. Adm to the County Museum £1.20, OAPs 80p, Chd (5–15) 30p, Chd under 5 free.

The South Wales Borderers and Monmouthshire Regiment
The Barracks, Brecon.
Tel: Brecon (0874) 623111, Ext. 2310.
April to Sept: Daily 9–1, 2–5. *Closed* Suns. Oct to March: Mon to Fri only 9–1, 2–5. Adm 50p.

Staff College Museum
Camberley, Surrey GU15 4NP.
Exhibits covering the development of Staff officers and the Army Staff College. By appointment only: Mon to Fri 9–5. *Closed* Sat, Sun and Bank Hols. Hon Curator: Col (Ret'd) P. S. Newton MBE, FMA, FRSA.

The Staffordshire Regiment (The Prince of Wales's)
Whittington Barracks, Lichfield, Staffs.
Tel: Whittington 021-311 3240 or 3229.
Collection includes rare embroidered cap c. 1760 and medals of 8 holders of the V.C. Mon to Fri 9–4, weekends and Bank Hols by arrangement. *Closed* Christmas to New Year.

The Suffolk Regiment
Gibraltar Barracks, Out Rishygate St., Bury St. Edmunds, Suffolk.
Tel: Bury St. Edmunds 752394.
Weekdays 10–12, 2–4. *Closed* Bank Hols.

The Sussex Combined Services Museum
Redoubt Fortress, Royal Parade, Eastbourne.
Tel: (0323) 410300.
Includes Royal Sussex Regiment Collection and Queens Royal Irish Hussars collections. Easter to end Oct: Daily 10–5.30. Other times by arrangement. Adm free to Fortress (including battlements and cannons). Separate charges for museum and aquarium.

The Tank Museum (Royal Armoured Corps and Royal Tank Regiment Museums)
Bovington Camp, near Wool, Dorset.
Tel: (0929) 403463 or 403329 or 463953 ansafone.
World's largest collection of armoured fighting vehicles. Daily 10–5. *Closed* two weeks at Christmas and New Year. Five new Exhibition Halls with many new displays and major exhibits. Costume collection, new T. E. Lawrence Exhibition plus new Past & Presents gift shop in addition to our usual military gift shop. Large restaurant, video theatres, picnic area. Free parking. Adm charge. Facilities for disabled.

The Warwickshire Yeomanry Museum
The Court House Vaults, Jury Street, Warwick (entrance in Castle Street).
Tel: Warwick (0926) 492212.
Good Friday to end Sept: Fri, Sat, Sun and Bank Hols 10–1, 2–4.

The Weapons Museum
The School of Infantry, Warminster, Wilts.
Tel: Warminster (0985) 214000, Ext. 2487.
By appointment only.

The Welch Regiment Museum of The Royal Regiment of Wales
The Black and Barbican Towers, Cardiff Castle, Cardiff.
Tel: Cardiff (0222) 229367.
Colours, uniform and appointments of the 41st and 69th Foot, later 1st & 2nd Battalions, The Welch Regiment, as also the Militia and Volunteer Corps of South Wales. Gallantry awards and campaign medals. The national colour of the 4th American Infantry surrendered at Fort Detroit, 1812. May 1 to Sept 30: daily 10–6. Other months 10–4. Adm: Castle Grounds, Roman Wall, Norman Keep, The Welch Regt and Queen's Dragoon Guards Museums £1.85, Chld & OAP 85p.

Westmorland & Cumberland Yeomanry
Dalemain, Penrith, Cumbria CA11 0HB.
Tel: (07684) 86450.
Easter Sun to early Oct: Daily (except Fri and Sat) 11.15–5. Adm to House, Garden and Museum £3.50.

Woman's Royal Army Corps
Queen Elizabeth Park, Guildford, Surrey.
Tel: (0252) 24431, Ext. Guildford 8565.
Open weekdays 9–4. Adm free.

The Worcestershire Regiment
City Museum & Art Gallery, Foregate Street, Worcester.
Tel: Worcester (0905) 25371.
Mon to Fri 9.30–6; Sat 9.30–5. *Closed* Thurs.

The Worcestershire Yeomanry Cavalry Regimental Museum
City Museum and Art Gallery, Foregate Street, Worcester.
Tel: Worcester (0905) 25371.
Mon to Fri 9.30–6; Sat 9.30–5. *Closed* Thurs.

The York & Lancaster Regimental Museum
Brian O'Malley Central Library and Arts Centre, Walker Place, Rotherham, South Yorkshire.
Tel: Rotherham 382121, Ext 3625.
Tues to Sat 10–5. *Closed* Mons, Suns & Bank Hols. Adm free.

SUBJECT INDEX

ADVERTISING, POSTERS AND PACKAGING

Battle – *East Sussex*
Museum of Shops & Social History
Glasgow – *Scotland*
Glasgow Museum and Art Gallery
Burrell Collection
Haggs Castle
People's Palace
Pollock House
Provands Lordship
Gloucester – *Glos.*
Robert Opie Collection
London – *London*
Grange Museum
National Sound Archives

AERIAL PHOTOGRAPHY

Aylesbury – *Bucks.*
Buckinghamshire County Museum
Biggar – *Strathclyde*
Moat Park Heritage Centre
Biggleswade – *Beds*
The Shuttleworth Collection
Cambridge – *Cambs.*
Cambridge University
Colchester – *Essex*
Colchester & Essex Museum
Dorchester – *Dorset*
Dorset County Museum
Dumfries – *Dumfries & Galloway*
Dumfries Museum
Jersey – *Channel Isles*
Jersey Museum
Kirkleatham – *Cleveland*
Kirkleatham Old Hall
Lincoln – *Lincs.*
City & County Museum
London – *London*
National Monuments Record
Middle Wallop – *Hants*
Museum of Army Flying
Paisley – *Strathclyde*
Redcar – *Cleveland*
See Kirkleatham
Swindon – *Wilts.*
Thamesdown Museum Service
Warwick – *Warwicks*
Warwickshire Museum

AERONAUTICS – see TRANSPORT

AIR FORCES – see MILITARY

AGRICULTURE

Abergavenny – *Gwent*
Acton Scott – *Salop*
Ardress – *N. Ireland*
Avebury – *Wilts.*
The Great Barn Folk Life Museum
Aylesbury – *Bucks*
Buckinghamshire County Museum
Banchory – *Grampian*
Banchory Museum
Barnsley – *S. Yorks.*
Worsbrough Mill Museum
Barton-on-Humber – *Humberside*
Batley – *W. Yorks.*
Oakwell Hall
Bedford – *Beds*
Bedford Museum
Beverley – *Humberside*
Skidby Windmill & Museum
Bibury – *Glos.*
Biggar – *Strathclyde*
Greenhill Covenanter's House
Moat Park Heritage Centre
Birmingham – *W. Midlands*
Sarehole Mill
Birstall – *W. Yorks*
Oakwell Hall
Blackburn – *Lancs.*
Witton Park Visitor Centre
Hampshire Farm Museum
Boston – *Lincs.*
Boston Guildhall Museum
Botley – *Hants.*
Bristol – *Avon*
Blaise Castle House Museum
Bromsgrove – *Hereford & Worcs*
Avoncroft Museum of Buildings
Budleigh Salterton – *Devon*
Burnham-on-Crouch – *Essex*
Calderdale – *W. Yorks.*
West Yorkshire Folk Museum,
  Shibden Hall, Halifax

Ceres – *Fife*
Fife Folk Museum
Chalfont St. Giles – *Bucks.*
Chiltern Open Air Museum
Chard – *Somerset*
Chelmsford – *Essex*
Chelmsford & Essex Museum
Cheltenham – *Glos*
Cheltenham Art Gallery & Museum
Chester – *Cheshire*
Grosvenor Museum
Chichester – *West Sussex*
Weald and Downland Open Air
  Museum
Colchester – *Essex*
Colchester & Essex Museum
Coldstream – *Borders*
Hirsel Homestead Museum
Cwmbran – *Gwent*
Darlington – *Co. Durham*
Darlington Museum
Ditchling – *West Sussex*
Ditchling Museum
Doncaster – *S. Yorks*
Doncaster Museum & Art Gallery
Dorchester – *Dorset*
Dorset County Museum
Dre-Fach Felindre – *Dyfed*
Museum of the Woollen Industry
Dumfries – *Dumfries & Galloway*
Dumfries Museum
Edinburgh – *Lothian*
National Museums of Scotland
Elvaston – *Derbys*
Evesham – *Hereford & Worcs*
Almonry Museum
Eyemouth – *Borders*
Farnham – *Surrey*
Old Kiln Agricultural Museum
Ford & Etal Estates – *nr Berwick
  upon Tweed, Borders*
Heatherslaw Mill
Glamis – *Grampian*
Glasgow – *Scotland*
Museum of Transport
Glastonbury – *Somerset*
Somerset Rural Life Museum
Gloucester – *Glos.*
Folk Museum
Grays – *Essex*
Thurrock Local History Museum
Gressenhall – *Norfolk*
Halifax (see Calderdale) – *W. Yorks.*
Harlow – *Essex*
Harlow Museum
Harray (see Orkney Isles)
Hatfield – *Herts*
Old Mill House, museum and mill
Haverfordwest – *Dyfed*
Pembrokeshire Museums
Heathfield – *Sussex*
Sussex Farm Museum
Hereford – *Hereford & Worcs.*
City Museum & Art Gallery
Hitchin – *Herts*
Museum and Art Gallery
Hornsea – *Humberside*
Huntly – *Grampian*
Brander Museum
Hutton-le-Hole – *N. Yorks*
Ryedale Folk Museum
Inverary – *Strathclyde*
Auchindrain Museum
Isle of Arran – *Strathclyde*
Isle of Man – *Isle of Man*
The Grove Rural Life Museum.
  Ramsey
Isle of Wight – *Isle of Wight*
Jersey – *Channel Isles*
La Hougue Bie
Kendal – *Cumbria*
Abbot Hall Museum of Lakeland
  Life & Industry
Kendal Museum of Archaeology &
  Natural History
Kingsbridge – *Devon*
Kingussie – *Highland*
Kirkintilloch – *Strathclyde*
Barony Chambers Museum
Kirkleatham – *Cleveland*
Kirkleatham Old Hall
Livingston – *Lothian*
Livingston Mill Farm
London – *London*
Grange Museum
National Sound Archives
Science Museum
Lyndhurst – *Hants*
New Forest Museum & Visitor
  Centre
Maidenhead – *Berks.*
Courage Shire Horse Centre
Maidstone – *Kent*
Museum of Kent Life

Milton Keynes – *Bucks.*
Mintlaw – *Grampian*
Northeast of Scotland Agricultural
  Heritage Centre
Murton – *N. Yorks*
Yorkshire Museum of Farming
Nelson – *Lancs*
Pendle Heritage Centre
Newbury – *Berks*
Newbury District Museum
Newport – *Gwent*
Newport Museum & Art Gallery
Northleach – *Glos.*
Cotswold Countryside Collection
Norwich – *Norfolk*
Strumpshaw Steam Museum
Oakham – *Leics.*
Rutland County Museum
Orkney Isles – *Orkney Isles*
Corrigall Farm Museum, Harray
Peterborough – *Cambs.*
Sacrewell Watermill, Farming and
  Country Life Centre
Pickering – *N. Yorks.*
Porthtowan – *Cornwall*
Farm Museum
Reading – *Berks.*
Museum of English Rural Life
Redcar (see Kirkleatham) –
  Cleveland
St. Fagans – *S. Glam.*
Welsh Folk Museum
Shebbear – *Devon*
Sheffield – *S. Yorks.*
Abbeydale Industrial Heritage
  Museum
Bishop's House
Shugborough – *Staffs.*
Singleton – *W. Sussex*
Weald and Downland Open Air
  Museum
Skegness – *Lincs.*
Stowmarket – *Suffolk*
Museum of East Anglian Life
Stranraer – *Dumfries*
Stranraer Museum
Swansea – *Wales*
Maritime & Industrial Museum
Tenterden – *Kent*
Tenterden & District Museum
Tewkesbury – *Glos.*
The John Moore Museum
Tiverton – *Devon*
Upminster – *Essex*
Usk – *Gwent*
Wantage – *Oxon.*
Vale & Downland Museum
Warrington – *Cheshire*
Museum & Art Gallery
Walton Hall
Watford – *Herts.*
Watford Museum
Wells-next-the-Sea – *Norfolk*
Wexford – *N. Ireland*
Irish Agricultural Museum
Whitby – *N. Yorks.*
Whitby Museum
Wilmington – *E. Sussex*
Worcester – *Hereford & Worcs.*
Tudor House Museum
Wroughton – *Wilts.*
Science Museum
Wye – *Kent*
Zennor – *Cornwall*
Wayside Museum

ANATOMY – see MEDICAL

ANTHROPOLOGY – see ARCHAEOLOGY or PRIMITIVE ART

ANTIQUITIES – see ARCHAEOLOGY

ARCHAEOLOGY & PREHISTORY

Aberdeen – *Grampian*
University Anthropological Museum
James Dun's House
Provost Skene's House
Abingdon – *Oxon.*
Town Museum
Accrington – *Lancs.*
Aldborough – *N. Yorks.*
Aldborough Roman Museum
Alnwick – *Northumberland*
Alnwick Castle Museum
Alton – *Hants.*
Curtis Museum
Andover – *Hants.*
Andover Museum & Museum of the
  Iron Age

Angus – *Tayside*
Angus District Museum
Armagh – *N. Ireland*
Ashwell – *Herts.*
Avebury – *Wilts.*
Alexander Keiller Museum
Axbridge – *Somerset*
Aylesbury – *Bucks.*
Buckinghamshire County Museum
Banbury – *Oxon*
Banbury Museum
Banff – *Grampian*
Barnard Castle – *Co. Durham*
Barnstaple – *Devon*
Barton-on-Humber – *Humberside*
Bath – *Avon*
Roman Bath Museum
Sally Lunn's House
Basingstoke – *Hants.*
Willis Museum
Batley – *W. Yorks.*
Bagshaw Museum
Oakwell Hall
Battle – *E. Sussex*
Bedford – *Beds.*
Bedford Museum
Belfast – *N. Ireland*
Ulster Museum
Bexhill – *E. Sussex*
Bexhill Museum
Biggar – *Strathclyde*
Moat Park Heritage Centre
Birchington – *Kent*
Birmingham – *W. Midlands*
Museum & Art Gallery, Dept. of
  Archaeology & Ethnography
Blackburn – *Lancs.*
Museum & Art Gallery
Bodiam – *E. Sussex*
Bolton – *Gt. Manchester*
Museum & Art Gallery
Bo'ness – *Central*
Kinneil Museum
Boston – *Lincs.*
Boston Guildhall Museum
Bournemouth – *Dorset*
Rothesay Museum
Russell-Cotes Art Gallery &
  Museum
Bradford – *W. Yorks.*
Brading (see Isle of Wight)
Bramber – *W. Sussex*
St. Mary's
Brechin – *Tayside*
Brecon – *Powys*
Bridlington – *Humberside*
Brighton – *E. Sussex*
Museum & Art Gallery
Bridgwater – *Somerset*
Bristol – *Avon*
City Museum & Art Gallery
Budleigh Salterton – *Devon*
Fairlynch Arts Centre & Museum
Burghead – *Grampian*
Burnham-on-Crouch – *Essex*
Burnley – *Lancs.*
Towneley Hall
Bury St. Edmunds – *Suffolk*
Moyse's Hall
Buxton – *Derbys.*
Caerleon – *Gwent*
Roman Legionary Museum
Caernarfon – *Gwynedd*
Segontium Museum
Camborne – *Cornwall*
Public Library & Museum
Cambridge – *Cambs.*
Fitzwilliam Museum
Scott Polar Research Institute
University Museum of Archaeology
  & Anthropology
University Museum of Classical
  Archaeology
Campbeltown – *Strathclyde*
Canterbury – *Kent*
The Canterbury Centre
The Roman Pavement
Capton – *Devon*
Prehistoric Hill Settlement
Cardiff – *S. Glam.*
National Museum of Wales
Carlisle – *Cumbria*
Tullie House Museum & Art Gallery
Carmarthen – *Dyfed*
Carmarthen Museum
Castleford – *W. Yorks.*
Chalfont St Giles – *Bucks.*
Chiltern Open Air Museum
Cheddar – *Somerset*
Chedworth – *Glos.*
Chelmsford – *Essex*
Cheltenham – *Glos.*
Art Gallery & Museum
Chertsey – *Surrey*
Chester – *Cheshire*
Grosvenor Museum

Subject Index – *continued*

ARCHITECTURE

Durham – *Co. Durham*
Durham Heritage Centre
Letchworth – *Herts.*
First Garden City Heritage
Museum

ARCHIVES – *see* HISTORICAL ASSOCIATIONS

ARMS & ARMOUR

Aberdeen – *Grampian*
University Anthropological
Museum
Aylesbury – *Bucks.*
Buckinghamshire County Museum
Banbury – *Oxon*
Edgehill Battle Museum
Banff – *Grampian*
Bath – *Avon*
Claverton Manor
Bedford – *Beds.*
Bedford Museum
Biggar – *Strathclyde*
Greenhill Covenanter's House
Birchington – *Kent*
Birmingham – *W. Midlands*
Museum of Science & Industry
Blackburn – *Lancs.*
East Lancashire Regimental
Museum
Museum & Art Gallery
Turton Tower
Blair Atholl – *Perthshire*
Blair Castle
Bournemouth – *Dorset*
Rothesay Museum
Russell-Cotes Art Gallery &
Museum
Bradford – *W. Yorks.*
Bolling Hall
Bridgwater – *Somerset*
Burnley – *Lancs.*
Cambridge – *Cambs.*
Fitzwilliam Museum
Canterbury – *Kent*
The Westgate
Chelmsford – *Essex*
Cheltenham – *Glos.*
Cheltenham Art Gallery & Museum
Chertsey – *Surrey*
Chertsey Museum
Chester – *Cheshire*
Grosvenor Museum
Coventry – *W. Midlands*
Herbert Art Gallery & Museum
Dumfries – *Dumfries & Galloway*
Dumfries Museum
Dundee – *Tayside*
Broughty Castle Museum
Edinburgh – *Lothian*
National Museum of Antiquities of
Scotland
Royal Scottish Museum
Evesham – *Hereford & Worcs.*
Almonry Museum
Exeter – *Devon*
Royal Albert Memorial Museum
Fort William – *Highland*
West Highland Museum
Glasgow – *Strathclyde*
Art Gallery & Museum
Burrell Collection
Glencoe – *Highland*
Glenesk – *Grampian*
Guernsey – *Channel Isles*
Castle Cornet
Harlow – *Essex*
Harlow Museum
Harwich – *Essex*
Harwich Redoubt
Havant – *Hants*
Havant Museum & Art Gallery
Haverfordwest – *Dyfed*
Castle Museum & Art Gallery
Henley-on-Thames – *Oxon.*
Hereford – *Hereford & Worcs.*
City Museum & Art Gallery
Hertford – *Herts.*
Holywell – *Clwyd*
Grange Cavern
Inverness – *Highland*
Ilfracombe – *Devon*
Jersey – *Channel Isles*
Elizabeth Castle
Jersey Museum
Mont Orgueil
Kendal – *Cumbria*
Abbot Hall Museum of Lakeland
Life & Industry
Kilmarnock – *Strathclyde*
Dean Castle
Dick Institute

King's Lynn – *Norfolk*
Lynn Museum
Leeds – *W. Yorks.*
Abbey House Museum
Leicester – *Leics.*
Museum of the Royal Leicestershire
Regiment
Lewes – *E. Sussex*
The Military Heritage Museum
Lichfield – *Staffs.*
Lincoln – *Lincs.*
City & County Museum
Llandudno – *Gwynedd*
Llandudno Museum
London – *London*
Bethnal Green Museum of
Childhood
British Museum
Hampton Court Palace
The Heralds' Museum
Imperial War Museum
London Brass Rubbing Centre
The Museum of London
National Army Museum
National Maritime Museum
Royal Artillery Regimental
Museum
St. John's Gate
Tower of London
Victoria & Albert Museum
Wallace Collection
Ludlow – *Salop*
Macclesfield – *Cheshire*
Manchester – *Greater Manchester*
Manchester Museum
Wythenshawe Hall
Market Bosworth – *Leicestershire*
Bosworth Battlefield
Middle Wallop – *Hants.*
Museum of Army Flying
Newcastle-under-Lyme – *Staffs.*
Newcastle upon Tyne – *Tyne & Wear*
John G. Joicey Museum
The Keep Museum
Museum of Antiquities
Newport – *Gwent*
Newport Museum & Art Gallery
Norwich – *Norfolk*
Bridewell Museum
Castle Museum
Strangers Hall
Nottingham – *Notts.*
Castle Museum
Reading – *Berks.*
Museum & Art Gallery
Rochester – *Kent*
Rossendale – *Lancs.*
Rossendale Museum
Rye – *East Sussex*
Rye Museum
St Fagans – *S. Glam.*
Welsh Folk Museum
Sheffield – *S. Yorks.*
City Museum
Southampton – *Hants.*
Tudor House Museum
Southend-on-Sea – *Essex*
Southchurch Hall
South Queensferry – *Lothian*
The Hopetoun House Museum
Stockton-on-Tees – *Cleveland*
Preston Hall Museum
Stockport – *Greater Manchester*
Bramall Hall
Swindon – *Wilts.*
Thamesdown Museum Service
Tenby – *Dyfed*
Tenby Museum
Tiverton – *Devon*
Warrington – *Cheshire*
Warwick – *Warwicks.*
Warwickshire Museum
Whitby – *N. Yorks.*
Whitby Museum
Worcester – *Hereford & Worcs.*
Commandery
York – *N. Yorks.*
Castle Museum

ASTRONOMICAL INSTRUMENTS – *see* SCIENCE

AUTOGRAPHS – *see* HISTORICAL

BELLS AND BELLFOUNDING

Loughborough – *Leics.*
Bellfoundry Museum

BOTANY – *see* NATURAL HISTORY

BYGONES – *see* FOLK COLLECTIONS

CARPETS – *see* TEXTILES

CERAMICS & GLASS

Aberdeen – *Grampian*
University Anthropological
Museum
Art Gallery
Provost Skene's House
Aberystwyth – *Dyfed*
Arts Centre Gallery
Accrington – *Lancs.*
Alton – *Hants.*
Allen Gallery
Armagh – *N. Ireland*
Axbridge – *Somerset*
Aylesbury – *Bucks.*
Buckinghamshire County Museum
Banchory – *Grampian*
Banchory Museum
Barlaston – *Staffs.*
Wedgwood Museum
Barnard Castle – *Co. Durham*
Barnsley – *S. Yorks.*
Cannon Hall Art Gallery
Barton-on-Humber – *Humberside*
Bath – *Avon*
American Museum in Britain
Holburne of Menstrie Museum of
Art
Batley (see Kirklees) – *W. Yorks.*
Bedford – *Beds.*
Cecil Higgins Art Gallery
Belfast – *N. Ireland*
Ulster Museum
Berwick-upon-Tweed – *Northumberland*
Berwick Borough Museum & Art
Gallery
Bideford – *Devon*
Biggar – *Strathclyde*
Gladstone Court
Birchington – *Kent*
Birkenhead – *Merseyside*
Williamson Art Gallery
Birmingham – *W. Midlands*
Museum & Art Gallery – Dept. of
Applied Art
Birstall – *W. Yorks.*
Oakwell Hall
Blackburn – *Lancs.*
Museum & Art Gallery
Blair Atholl – *Perthshire*
Blair Castle
Bolton – *Greater Manchester*
Museum & Art Gallery
Bournemouth – *Dorset*
Rothesay Museum
Russell-Cotes Art Gallery &
Museum
Bradford – *W. Yorks.*
Cartwright Hall Art Gallery
Bramber – *W. Sussex*
St. Mary's
Royal Brierley
Brierley Hill – *W. Midlands*
Brighton – *E. Sussex*
Museum & Art Gallery
Preston Manor
The Royal Pavilion
Bristol – *Avon*
City Museum & Art Gallery
Georgian House
Burnley – *Lancs.*
Towneley Hall
Cambo – *Northumberland*
Cambridge – *Cambs.*
Fitzwilliam Museum
Canterbury – *Kent*
The Royal Museum & Art Gallery
Cardiff – *S. Glam.*
National Museum of Wales
Carlisle – *Cumbria*
Tullie House Museum & Art Gallery
Carmarthen – *Dyfed*
Castleford – *W. Yorks.*
Ceres – *Fife*
Fife Folk Museum
Chelmsford – *Essex*
Cheltenham – *Glos.*
Art Gallery & Museum
Chertsey – *Surrey*
Chertsey Museum
Chester – *Cheshire*
Grosvenor Museum
Chichester – *West Sussex*
Pallant House Gallery
Chorley – *Lancs.*
Cleckheaton – *W. Yorks*
Red House Museum
Coventry – *W. Midlands*
Herbert Art Gallery & Museum
Culross – *Fife*
Dartford – *Kent*
Dartford Borough Museum

Derby – *Derbys.*
Museum & Art Gallery
Royal Crown Derby Museum
Royal Doulton Museum
Doncaster – *S. Yorks.*
Museum & Art Gallery
Dover – *Kent*
Dover Museum
Dudley – *W. Midlands*
Broadfield House Glass Museum
Museum & Art Gallery
Dumfries – *Dumfries & Galloway*
Dumfries Museum
Gracefield Arts Centre
Dundee – *Tayside*
Central Museum & Art Galleries
McManus Galleries
Durham – *Co. Durham*
University of Durham, Oriental
Museum
East Cowes (see Isle of Wight)
Edge Hill – *Warks.*
Edinburgh – *Lothian*
Huntly House
Lauriston Castle
National Museums of Scotland
Royal Scottish Museum
Ely – *Cambs.*
Stained Glass Museum
Exeter – *Devon*
Royal Albert Memorial Museum
Falkirk – *Central*
Falkirk Museum
Fort William – *Highland*
West Highland Museum
Glasgow – *Strathclyde*
Art Gallery & Museum
Burrell Collection
People's Palace
Pollok House
Rutherglen Museum
Gloucester – *Glos.*
City Museum of Art Gallery
Great Yarmouth – *Norfolk*
Elizabethan House Museum
Guernsey – *Channel Isles*
Guernsey Museum & Art Gallery
Harrogate – *N. Yorks.*
Royal Pump Room Museum
Hartlepool – *Cleveland*
Gray Art Gallery
Hastings – *E. Sussex*
Museum & Art Gallery
Hereford – *Hereford & Worcs.*
City Museum
Hertford – *Herts.*
Hove – *E. Sussex*
Huddersfield (see Kirklees) – *W. Yorks.*
Hull – *Humberside*
Archaeology Museum
Posterngate Gallery
University of Hull Art Collection
Wilberforce House & Georgian
Houses
Hutton-le-Hole – *N. Yorks.*
Ryedale Folk Museum
Ipswich – *Suffolk*
Christchurch Mansion
Isle of Wight – *Isle of Wight*
Osborne House, East Cowes
Jersey – *Channel Isles*
Jersey Museum
Keighley – *W. Yorks.*
Kendal – *Cumbria*
Kilmarnock – *Strathclyde*
Dick Institute
King's Lynn – *Norfolk*
Museum of Social History
Kirkcaldy – *Fife*
Kirkcaldy Art Gallery
Kirkleatham – *Cleveland*
Kirkleatham Old Hall
Kirklees – *W. Yorks.*
Bagshaw Museum, Batley
Huddersfield Art Gallery
Tolson Memorial Museum,
Huddersfield
Lancaster – *Lancs*
City Museum
Leamington Spa – *Warks.*
Leeds – *W. Yorks.*
Temple Newsam
Leek – *Staffs.*
Art Gallery
Cheddleton Flint Mill
Leicester – *Leics.*
Museum & Art Gallery
Letchworth – *Herts.*
Museum & Art Gallery
Lincoln – *Lincs.*
Usher Gallery
Lindisfarne – *Northumberland*
Liverpool – *Merseyside*
City Museum
University of Liverpool Art Gallery

Subject Index – *continued*

Subject Index – *continued*

Clun – *Shrops.*
Colchester – *Essex*
Colchester & Essex Museum
Coventry – *W. Midlands*
Herbert Art Gallery & Museum
Cromarty – *Highland*
Cromer – *Norfolk*

Darlington – *Co. Durham*
Darlington Museum
Dartford – *Kent*
Borough Museum
Derby – *Derbys.*
Industrial Museum
Museum & Art Gallery
Devizes – *Wilts.*
Doncaster – *S. Yorks.*
Museum & Art Gallery
Dorchester – *Dorset*
Dinosaur Museum
Dorset County Museum
Dover – *Kent*
Dover Museum
Dublin – *Rep. of Ireland*
Dudley – *W. Midlands*
Museum & Art Gallery
Dumfries – *Dumfries & Galloway*
Dumfries Museum

Edinburgh – *Lothian*
National Museums of Scotland
Royal Scottish Museum
Evesham – *Hereford & Worcs.*
Almonry Museum
Exeter – *Devon*
Royal Albert Memorial Museum

Folkestone – *Kent*
Folkestone Museum
Forfar – *Tayside*
Forres – *Grampian*
Falconer Museum
Fort William – *Highland*
West Highland Museum

Glasgow – *Lothian*
Art Gallery & Museum
Hunterian Museum
Gloucester – *Glos.*
City Museum & Art Gallery
Greenock – *Strathclyde*
Guernsey – *Channel Isles*
Guernsey Museum & Art Gallery

Harlow – *Essex*
Harlow Museum
Hartlepool – *Cleveland*
Gray Art Gallery & Museum
Haslemere – *Surrey*
Hastings – *E. Sussex*
Museum & Art Gallery
Hereford – *Hereford & Worcs.*
City Museum & Art Gallery
Hertford – *Herts.*
Hertford Museum
Holywell – *Clwyd*
Grange Cavern
Huddersfield (see Kirklees) –
  W. Yorks.
Inverness – *Highland*
Museum & Art Gallery
Ipswich – *Suffolk*
Ipswich Museum
Isle of Arran – *Strathclyde*
Isle of Arran Heritage Museum
Isle of Man – *Isle of Man*
Manx Museum
Isle of Wight – *Isle of Wight*
Museum of Isle of Wight Geology,
  Sandown

Jersey – *Channel Isles*
La Hougue Bie Museum

Kendal – *Cumbria*
Kendal Museum of Archaeology &
  Natural History
Keswick – *Cumbria*
Kettering – *Northants.*
Westfield Museum
Kilkenny – *Ireland*
Rothe House Museum
Kilmarnock – *Strathclyde*
Dick Institute
King's Lynn – *Norfolk*
Lynn Museum
Kirkcaldy – *Fife*
Kirkcaldy Art Gallery
Kirkleatham – *Cleveland*
Kirkleatham Old Hall
Kirklees – *W. Yorks.*
Bagshaw Museum
Tolson Memorial Museum,
  Huddersfield

Leeds – *W. Yorks.*
City Museum
Museum of Leeds
Leicester – *Leics.*
Museum & Art Gallery
Lerwick – *Shetland Islands,*
  Grampian
Shetland Museum

Letchworth – *Herts.*
Letchworth Museum & Art Gallery
Lincoln – *Lincs.*
Lincoln City & County Museum
Llanberis – *Gwynedd*
Museum of the North
Llandrindod Wells – *Powys*
Llandrindod Wells Museum
London – *London*
British Museum
Geological Museum
Passmore Edwards Museum
Ludlow – *Shrops.*
Lyme Regis – *Dorset*

Malvern – *Hereford & Worcs*
Malvern Museum
Manchester – *Greater Manchester*
Manchester Museum
Middlesbrough – *Cleveland*
Dorman Museum
Montrose – *Tayside*

Newbury – *Berks.*
Newbury District Museum
Newcastle upon Tyne – *Tyne &*
  Wear
Hancock Museum
Museum of the Dept. of Mining
  Engineering
Newport – *Gwent*
Museum & Art Gallery
Norwich – *Norfolk*
Castle Museum

Oakham – *Leics.*
Rutland County Museum

Paisley – *Strathclyde*
Peebles – *Borders*
Tweeddale Museum
Peterhead – *Grampian*
Arbuthnot Museum
Portland – *Dorset*
Portsmouth – *Hants.*
City Museum

Reading – *Berks.*
Museum & Art Gallery
Redcar (see Kirkleatham) –
  Cleveland
Reeth – *N. Yorks.*
Swaledale Folk Museum
Rochdale – *Lancs.*
Rochdale Museum
Rochester – *Kent*
Rossendale – *Lancs.*
Rossendale Museum
Rotherham – *S. Yorks.*
Clifton Park Museum
Rothesay – *Strathclyde*

Saffron Walden – *Essex*
Saffron Walden Museum
St. Helens – *Merseyside*
St. Helens Museum
Sandown (see Isle of Wight) – *Isle*
  of Wight
Salisbury – *Wilts.*
Wessex Shire Park
Scarborough – *N. Yorks.*
Wood End Museum
Scunthorpe – *Humberside*
Scunthorpe Borough Museum &
  Art Gallery
Selborne – *Hants.*
Oates Memorial Museum & The
  Gilbert White Museum
Sevenoaks – *Kent*
Sevenoaks Museum
Sheffield – *S. Yorks.*
Art Galleries
City Museum
Shrewsbury – *Shrops.*
Rowley's House Museum
Skipton – *N. Yorks.*
South Queensferry – *Lothian*
Burgh Museum
Southend-on-Sea – *Essex*
Southend Central Museum
Southend-on-Sea Museum
Stevenage – *Herts.*
Stevenage Museum
Stirling – *Central*
Stirling Smith Art Gallery &
  Museum
Stockport – *Greater Manchester*
Stockport Museum
Stoke-on-Trent – *Staffs.*
Chatterley Whitfield Mining
  Museum
City Museum & Art Gallery
Stroud – *Glos.*
Sunderland – *Tyne & Wear*
Swindon – *Wilts.*
Museum & Art Gallery

Taunton – *Somerset*
Telford – *Shrops.*
Tenby – *Dyfed*
Thetford – *Norfolk*
Thurso – *Highland*
Tiverton – *Devon*

Tomintoul – *Highland*
Tomintoul Museum
Truro – *Cornwall*
Tunbridge Wells – *Kent*
Tunbridge Wells Municipal
  Museum & Art Gallery

Warrington – *Cheshire*
Museum & Art Gallery
Warwick – *Warks.*
Warwickshire Museum
Wells – *Somerset*
Weybridge – *Surrey*
Weybridge Museum
Whitby – *N. Yorks.*
Whitby Museum
Winchester – *Hants.*
City Museum
College Museum
Wisbech – *Cambs.*
Wookey Hole – *Somerset*
Worcester – *Hereford & Worcs.*
City Museum and Art Gallery
Worthing – *W. Sussex*
Museum & Art Gallery
York – *N. Yorks.*
Yorkshire Museum

GLASS – *see* CERAMICS

GOLDSMITHS' WORK – *see* FINE ARTS *or* JEWELLERY

HERBARIA – *see* NATURAL HISTORY

HISTORICAL & LITERARY ASSOCIATIONS

Aberdeen – *Grampian*
James Dun's House
Provost Skene's House
Aberystwyth – *Dyfed*
National Library of Wales
Alloway – *Strathclyde*
Angus – *Tayside*
Angus District Museums
Anstruther – *Fife*
Scottish Fisheries Museum
Armadale – *Isle of Skye*
Axbridge – *Somerset*

Banbury – *Oxon*
Edgehill Battle Museum
Banchory – *Grampian*
Banchory Museum
Banff – *Grampian*
Banff Museum
Bath – *Avon*
American Museum in Britain
Building of Bath Museum
Huntingdon Centre
Museum of Bookbinding
Batley – *W. Yorks.*
Bagshaw Museum
Oakwell Hall
Battle – *E. Sussex*
Bedford – *Beds.*
Bedford Museum
Bunyan Museum
Elstow Moot Hall
Belfast – *N. Ireland*
Ulster Museum
Berwick-upon-Tweed –
  Northumberland
Berwick Borough Museum & Art
  Gallery
The Cell Block
The Clock Block
Biggar – *Strathclyde*
Greenhill Covenanter's House
John Buchan Centre
Moat Park Heritage Centre
Biggleswade – *Beds.*
Shuttleworth Collection
Birmingham – *W. Midlands*
Aston Hall
Birstall (see Kirklees) – *W. Yorks.*
Blackburn – *Lancs.*
East Lancashire Regimental
  Museum
Lewis 'Textile' Museum
Museum & Art Gallery
Blair Atholl – *Perthshire*
Blair Castle
Blantyre – *Strathclyde*
Bolton – *Greater Manchester*
Hall-i'-th'-Wood Museum
Bo'ness – *Central*
Kinneil Museum
Boston – *Lincs.*
Boston Guildhall Museum
Bournemouth – *Dorset*
Casa Magni Shelly Museum
Bradford – *W. Yorks.*
Bolling Hall
Bramber – *West Sussex*
St. Mary's
Brecon – *Powys*
Brecknock Museum

Bridgwater – *Somerset*
Brighton – *E. Sussex*
Preston Manor
Broadstairs – *Kent*
Dickens House Museum
Bromsgrove – *Hereford & Worcs.*
Bromsgrove Museum
Budleigh Salterton – *Devon*
Fairlynch Arts Centre & Museum
Burnley – *Lancs.*
Towneley Hall
Burwash – *E. Sussex*

Cambridge – *Cambs.*
Fitzwilliam Museum
Scott Polar Research Institute
Canterbury – *Kent*
The Canterbury Centre
Carmarthen – *Dyfed*
Carmarthen Museum
Castletown (see Isle of Man) – *Isle*
  of Man
Ceres – *Fife*
Fife Folk Museum
Chalfont St. Giles – *Bucks.*
Chawton – *Hants.*
Jane Austen's House
Chelmsford – *Essex*
Chelmsford & Essex Museum
Cheltenham – *Glos.*
Art Gallery & Museum
Chertsey – *Surrey*
Chertsey Museum
Chirk – *Clwyd*
Cleckheaton (see Kirklees) –
  W. Yorks.
Clonmel – *Ireland*
Tipperary S.R. Co. Museum
Clydebank – *Strathclyde*
Clydebank District Museum
Criccieth – *Gwynedd*
Cromarty – *Highland*

Dartmouth – *Devon*
Town Museum
Devizes – *Wilts.*
Dewsbury – *W. Yorks.*
Dewsbury Museum
Dorchester – *Dorset*
Dorset County Museum
Dover – *Kent*
Dover Gaol
Dublin – *Rep. of Ireland*
Dumfries – *Dumfries & Galloway*
Dumfries Museum
Dunblane – *Central*
Dundee – *Tayside*
Barrack Street Museum
Central Museum & Art Galleries
McManus Galleries
Dunfermline – *Fife*
Andrew Carnegie Birthplace
Dunwich – *Suffolk*
Dunwich Museum
Durham – *Co. Durham*
Durham Heritage Centre
Cathedral Treasury

East Cowes (see Isle of Wight) –
  Isle of Wight
Eastwood – *Notts.*
D. H. Lawrence Birthplace
Ecclefechan – *Dumfries &*
  Galloway
Edinburgh – *Lothian*
Lady Stair's House
National Museum of Antiquities of
  Scotland
Forfar – *Tayside*
Fort William – *Highland*
West Highland Museum

Glasgow – *Strathclyde*
Collins Gallery
People's Palace
Glencoe – *Highland*
Grantham – *Lincs.*
Grasmere – *Cumbria*
Dove Cottage and Wordsworth
  Museum
Great Yarmouth – *Norfolk*
Old Merchant's House
The Tollhouse
Greenock – *Strathclyde*
Guildford – *Surrey*
Guildford Museum
British Red Cross Historical
  Exhibition and Archives
Harlow – *Essex*
Harlow Museum
Harrow-on-the-Hill – *Harrow*
  School, Middx.
Old Speech Room Gallery
Hartlepool – *Cleveland*
Gray Art Gallery
Maritime Museum
Harwich – *Essex*
Harwich Redoubt
Port of Harwich Maritime Museum
Hastings – *E. Sussex*
Hastings Museum & Art Gallery

Subject Index – *continued*

Selkirk – *Borders*
Halliwell's House
Settle – *N. Yorks.*
Museum of North Craven Life
Sevenoaks – *Kent*
Sevenoaks Museum
Shaftesbury – *Dorset*
Local History Museum
Shaftesbury Abbey & Museum
Sheffield – *S. Yorks.*
Abbeydale Industrial Hamlet
Bishops House
City Museum
Kelham Island
Shetland – *Shetland Croft &*
Shetland
Shetland Museum
Shoreham-by-Sea – *W. Sussex*
Shrewsbury – *Shrops*
Radbrook Culinary Museum
Shugborough – *Staffs.*
Staffordshire County Museum
Skegness – *Lincs.*
Slough – *Berks*
Slough Museum
Southend-on-Sea – *Essex*
Beecroft Art Gallery
Prittlewell Priory Museum
Southchurch Hall
Southend Central Museum
South Molton – *Devon*
Southport – *Merseyside*
Botanic Gardens Museum
South Queensferry – *Lothian*
Burgh Museum
South Shields – *Tyne & Wear*
South Shields Museum & Art
Gallery
Stafford – *Staffs.*
Stafford Art Gallery
Stamford – *Lincs.*
Stevenage – *Herts.*
Stevenage Museum
Stirling – *Central*
Stirling Smith Art Gallery &
Museum
Stockport – *Greater Manchester*
Bramall Hall
Stockport Museum
Stockton-on-Tees – *Cleveland*
Green Dragon Heritage Centre
Stoke Bruerne – *Northants.*
Stoke-on-Trent – *Staffs.*
Chatterley Whitfield Mining
Museum
City Museum & Art Gallery
Ford Green Hall
Stonehaven – *Grampian*
Tolbooth Museum
Stowmarket – *Suffolk*
Museum of East Anglian Life
Stranraer – *Dumfries & Galloway*
Castle of St. John
Stranraer Museum
Strathaven – *Strathclyde*
John Hastie Museum
Stromness (see Orkney Isles) –
Orkney Isles
Stroud – *Glos.*
Styal – *Cheshire*
Sunderland – *Tyne & Wear*
Grindon Museum
Monkwearmouth Station Museum
Sunderland Museum and Art
Gallery
Swansea – *W. Glam.*
Maritime & Industrial Museum
Swindon – *Wilts.*
Great Western Railway Museum
Lydiard Park
Museum & Art Gallery
Richard Jefferies Museum

Tamworth – *Staffs.*
Tamworth Castle Museum
Telford – *Shrops.*
Tenby – *Dyfed*
Tenterden – *Kent*
Tenterden & District Museum
Tewkesbury – *Glos.*
The Little Museum
Tewkesbury Museum
Thetford – *Norfolk*
Thirsk – *N. Yorks.*
Thirsk Museum
Thurso – *Highland*
Strathnaver Museum
Tiverton – *Devon*
Tomintoul – *Highland*
Tomintoul Museum
Torquay – *Devon*
Torre Abbey
Totnes – *Devon*
The Elizabethan House
Trowbridge – *Wilts.*
Tunbridge Wells – *Kent*
Tunbridge Wells Municipal
Museum & Art Gallery

Usk – *Gwent*
Gwent Rural Life Museum
Wakefield – *W. Yorks.*
City Museum
Walkerburn – *Borders*
Wallingford – *Oxon.*
Walsall – *W. Midlands*
Walsall Museum & Art Gallery
Walsingham – *Norfolk*
Waltham Abbey – *Essex*
Epping Forest District Museum
Wantage – *Oxon.*
Vale & Downland Museum Centre
Wareham – *Dorset*
Wareham Town Museum
Warrington – *Cheshire*
Walton Hall
Warrington Museum & Art Gallery
Warwick – *Warwickshire*
Warwickshire Museum
Watford – *Herts.*
Watford Museum
Wednesbury – *W. Midlands*
Art Gallery & Museum
Wells-next-the-Sea – *Norfolk*
Welshpool – *Powys*
Powysland Museum
West Bromwich – *W. Midlands*
Oak House
Weston-super-Mare – *Avon*
Woodspring Museum
Weybridge – *Surrey*
Weybridge Museum
Whitby – *N. Yorks.*
Whitby Museum
Whitehaven – *Cumbria*
Whitehaven Museum
Wick – *Highland*
Wigan – *Greater Manchester*
Wigan Pier
Willenhall – *W. Midlands*
The Lock Museum
Wimborne Minster – *Dorset*
Winchelsea – *E. Sussex*
Winchester – *Hants.*
Westgate Museum
Winchester City Museum
Wisbech – *Cambs.*
Wolverhampton – *W. Midlands*
Bantock House
Bilston Museum & Art Gallery
City Museum & Art Gallery
Woodstock – *Oxon.*
Oxfordshire County Museum
Worcester – *Hereford & Worcs.*
Tudor House Museum
Workington – *Cumbria*
Workington Hall
Worksop – *Notts.*
Workshop Museum
Worthing – *W. Sussex*
Wye – *Kent*

Yeovil – *Somerset*
York – *N. Yorks.*
Jorvik Viking Centre
Treasurer's House
Zennor – *Cornwall*
Wayside Museum

LOCKS AND KEYS

Brierfield – *Lancs.*
Neville Blakey Museum of Locks,
Keys and Safes

MACHINERY – *see* SCIENCE

MAGIC – *see* WITCHCRAFT

MANUSCRIPTS – *see* HISTORICAL ASSOCIATIONS

MARINE MODELS – *see* SHIPPING

MARITIME – *see* SHIPPING

MEASURING INSTRUMENTS – *see* SCIENCE

MEDALS – *see* COINS *or* MILITARY

MEDICAL

Aberdeen – *Grampian*
Aberdeen University
Bedford – *Beds.*
Bedford Museum
Dumfries – *Dumfries & Galloway*
Dumfries Museum
Edinburgh – *Lothian*
Museum of Childhood
National Museums of Scotland
Royal College of Surgeons of
Edinburgh

Guildford – *Surrey*
British Red Cross Historical
Exhibition and Archives
Haverfordwest – *Dyfed*
Scolton Manor Museum
Hornsea – *Humberside*
Huddersfield – *W. Yorks.*
Tolson Museum
Jersey – *Channel Isles*
Jersey Museum
King's Lynn – *Norfolk*
Lynn Museum
Kingsbridge – *Devon*
Cookworthy Museum
Liverpool – *Merseyside*
Dental Hospital Museum
London – *London*
British Dental Association
Museum
Freud Museum
Hunterian Museum
The Museum of London
Pharmaceutical Society's Museum
St. Bart's Hospital Pathological
Museum
St. John's Gate
Science Museum
Middlesbrough – *Cleveland*
Dorman Museum
Montrose – *Tayside*
Sunnyside Museum
Newport – *Gwent*
Museum & Art Gallery
Norwich – *Norfolk*
Strangers' Hall
Nottingham – *Notts.*
Brewhouse Yard Museum
Oxford – *Oxon.*
Museum of the History of Science
Redhill – *Surrey*
Salford – *Greater Manchester*
Museum & Art Galley
Sheffield – *S. Yorks.*
City Museum
Shugborough – *Staffs.*
Staffordshire County Museum
Swansea – *W. Glam.*
Maritime & Industrial Museum
Thirsk – *N. Yorks.*
Thirsk Museum
Tiverton – *Devon*
Warrington – *Cheshire*
Museum & Art Gallery
Winchester – *Hants.*
City Museum

METALWORK – *see* JEWELLERY

MILITARY (Note: *Military Services Museums* are shown in a separate section, following the County listings).

Aberdeen – *Grampian*
James Dun's House
Aberlady – *Lothian*
Myreton Motor Museum
Aldershot – *Hants.*
Military Museum
Angus – *Tayside*
Angus District Museums
Armagh – *N. Ireland*
Arundel – *W. Sussex*
Toy and Military Museum
Axbridge – *Somerset*
Banbury – *Oxon*
Edgehill Battle Museum
Barnsley – *S. Yorks.*
Cannon Hall Art Gallery &
Museum
Barton-on-Humber – *Humberside*
Baysgarth Museum
Batley – *W. Yorks.*
Bagshaw Museum
Battle – *E. Sussex*
Bedford – *Beds.*
Bedford Museum
Belfast – *N. Ireland*
Ulster Museum
Berwick-upon-Tweed –
Northumberland
The Cell Block
The Clock Block
Biggleswade – *Beds.*
Shuttleworth Collection
Biggar – *Strathclyde*
John Buchan Centre
Moat Park Heritage Centre
Birmingham – *W. Midlands*
Museum of Science & Industry
Blackburn – *Lancs.*
East Lancashire Regimental
Museum
Museum & Art Gallery
Blair Atholl – *Perthshire*
Blair Castle

Bolton – *Greater Manchester*
Museum & Art Gallery
Boston – *Lincs.*
Boston Guildhall Museum
Bournemouth – *Dorset*
Rothesay Museum
Russell-Cotes Art Gallery &
Museum
Bovington Camp – *Dorset*
The Tank Museum
Bradford – *W. Yorks.*
Burnley – *Lancs.*
Towneley Hall
Caernarfon – *Gwynedd*
Royal Welch Fusiliers Museum
Segontium Roman Fort Museum
Calderdale – *W. Yorks.*
Bankfield Museum
Caldicot – *Gwent*
Cambridge – *Cambs.*
Scott Polar Research Institute
Canterbury – *Kent*
The Royal Museum & Art Gallery
The Westgate
Cardiff – *S. Glam.*
The National Museum of Wales
Carmarthen – *Dyfed*
Carmarthen Museum
Ceres – *Fife*
Fife Folk Museum
Chelmsford – *Essex*
Chelmsford & Essex Museum
Cheltenham – *Glos.*
Art Gallery & Museum
Chester – *Cheshire*
Chichester – *W. Sussex*
Tangmere Military Aviation
Chorley – *Lancs.*
Astley Hall Museum & Art Gallery
Colchester – *Essex*
Colchester & Essex Museum
Colne – *Lancs.*
British in India Museum
Coventry – *W. Midlands*
Lunt Roman Fort
Derby – *Derbys.*
Derby Industrial Museum
Museum & Art Gallery
Regimental Museum
Doncaster – *S. Yorks.*
Museum & Art Gallery
Dorchester – *Dorset*
Dorset Military Museum
Dover – *Kent*
Dover Museum
Dumfries – *Dumfries & Galloway*
Dumfries Museum
Dundee – *Tayside*
Broughty Castle Museum
Durham – *Co. Durham*
Light Infantry Museum & Arts
Centre
Duxford – *Cambs.*

East Tilbury – *Essex*
Coalhouse Fort
Eastbourne – *E. Sussex*
Sussex Combined Services
Museum – Redoubt Fortress
Tower 73
Edinburgh – *Lothian*
Canongate Tolbooth
Huntly House
National Museum of Antiquities of
Scotland
Scottish United Services Museum
Evesham – *Hereford & Worcs.*
Almonry Museum
Exeter – *Devon*
Rougemont House Historical
Museum
Farleigh Hungerford – *Somerset*
Fort William – *Highland*
West Highland Museum
Glasgow – *Strathclyde*
Art Gallery & Museum
Gosport – *Hants.*
Royal Navy Submarine Museum
Great Yarmouth – *Norfolk*
Maritime Museum
Guernsey – *Channel Isles*
Castle Cornet
German Occupation Museum
Guildford – *Surrey*
Guildford Museum
British Red Cross Historical
Exhibition and Archives
Halifax (see Calderdale) –
W. Yorks.
Harlow – *Essex*
Harlow Museum
Hartlepool – *Cleveland*
Gray Art Gallery
Harwich – *Essex*
Harwich Redoubt
Port of Harwich Maritime Museum
Haverfordwest – *Dyfed*
Castle Museum & Art Gallery

Subject Index – *continued*

Subject Index – *continued*

PRINTING

Innerleithan – *Borders*
Robert Smail's Printing Works
Yeovilton – *Somerset*
Museum of South Somerset

PRINTS & ENGRAVINGS – *see* FINE ARTS

RAILWAYS – *see* TRANSPORT

REGIMENTAL – *see page 164*

RELIGION

Bath – *Avon*
American Museum
Burnley – *Lancs.*
Towneley Hall
Dublin – *Ireland*
National Gallery of Ireland
Durham – *Co. Durham*
Durham Heritage Centre
Glasgow – *Strathclyde*
Glasgow Art Gallery
Burrell Collection
London
Ben Uri Art Society
Southend-on-Sea – *Essex*
Prittlewell Priory
Tre'r-Ddôl – *Dyfed*
Yr Hen Gapel
York – *N. Yorks.*
Bar Convent Museum

RELIGIOUS ART

London
London Brass Rubbing Centre

ROCKS – *see* GEOLOGY

ROMAN ANTIQUITIES – *see* ARCHAEOLOGY

SCIENCE & INDUSTRY

Aberdeen – *Grampian*
University Anthropological
  Museum
Aberystwyth – *Dyfed*
Llywernog Silver-Lead Mine
Amberley – *W. Sussex*
Anstruther – *Fife*
Scottish Fisheries Museum
Ashton-under-Lyne – *Greater
  Manchester*
Portland Basin
Banff – *Grampian*
Banff Museum
Bath – *Avon*
Building of Bath Museum
Camden Works
Batley (see Kirklees) – *W. Yorks.*
Beamish – *Co. Durham*
Beccles – *Suffolk*
Bedford – *Beds.*
Bedford Museum
Beetham – *Cumbria*
Heron Corn Mill
Belfast – *N. Ireland*
Ulster Museum
Birmingham – *W. Midlands*
Museum of Science & Industry
Blackburn – *Lancs.*
Lewis Textile Museum
Witton Country Park Visitor Centre
Blaenau Ffestiniog – *Gwynedd*
Llechwedd Slate Caverns
Bolton – *Greater Manchester*
Bolton Steam Museum
Museum & Art Gallery
Tonge Moore Textile Museum
Bradford – *W. Yorks*
Cartwright Hall
Colour Museum
Bristol – *Avon*
The Exploratory Hands-on Science
  Centre
Harvey's Wine Museum
Industrial Museum
Bromsgrove – *Hereford & Worcs.*
Avoncroft Museum of Buildings
Burnley – *Lancs.*
Canal Toll House
Towneley Hall
Weavers' Triangle Visitor Centre
Burton-on-Trent – *Staffs.*
Bass Museum
Heritage Brewery Museum
Camborne – *Cornwall*
Cornish Engines
Cambridge – *Cambs.*
Scott Polar Research Institute

Whipple Museum of the History of
  Science
Cardiff – *S. Glam.*
The National Museum of Wales
Welsh Industrial and Maritime
  Museum
Ceres – *Fife*
Fife Folk Museum
Chelmsford – *Essex*
Chelmsford & Essex Museum
Chester – *Cheshire*
Grosvenor Museum
Cinderford – *Glos.*
Clydebank – *Strathclyde*
Clydebank District Museum
Coatbridge – *Strathclyde*
Summerlea Heritage Trust
Darlington – *Co. Durham*
Darlington Museum
Dartmouth – *Devon*
Derby – *Derbys.*
Industrial Museum
Doncaster – *S. Yorks.*
Cusworth Hall Museum
Dre-Fach Felindre – *Dyfed*
Museum of the Woollen Industry
Dublin – *Ireland*
Guinness Museum
Dufftown – *Grampian*
The Glenfiddich Distillery
Durham – *Co. Durham*
Durham Heritage Centre
Dumfries – *Dumfries & Galloway*
Dumfries Museum
Dundee – *Tayside*
Barrack Street Museum
McManus Galleries
Mills Observatory
RRS Discovery
Dunfermline – *Fife*
Dunfermline Dist. Museum and the
  Small Gallery
Edinburgh – *Lothian*
Museum of Communications
National Museums of Scotland
Royal Scottish Museum
Ford & Etal Estates – *nr Berwick-
  upon-Tweed, Borders*
Heatherslaw Mill
Glasgow – *Strathclyde*
Collins Gallery
Hunterian Museum & Art Gallery
Museum of Transport
People's Palace
Rutherglen Museum
Springburn Museum
Gressenhall – *Norfolk*
Halifax – *W. Yorks.*
Calderdale Industrial Museum
The Piece Hall
Hartlepool – *Cleveland*
Gray Art Gallery & Museum
Maritime Museum
Hatfield – *Herts.*
Old Mill House Museum
Helmshore – *Lancs.*
Helston – *Cornwall*
Poldark Mining & Wendron Forge
Hereford – *Hereford & Worcs.*
Museum of Cider
Hertford – *Herts.*
Hove – *E. Sussex*
The British Engineerium
Huddersfield (see Kirklees) –
  W. Yorks.
Huntly – *Grampian*
Brander Museum
Inverkeithing – *Fife*
Inverkeithing Museum
Keighley – *W. Yorks.*
Kendal – *Cumbria*
Abbot Hall Museum of Lakeland
  Life & Industry
Kidderminster – *Hereford & Worcs.*
  Museum
Kidwelly – *Dyfed*
Industrial Museum
Kilmarnock – *Strathclyde*
Dick Institute
Kingsbridge – *Devon*
King's Lynn – *Norfolk*
Lynn Museum
Kirkcaldy – *Fife*
Kirkcaldy Art Gallery
Kirkleatham – *Cleveland*
Kirkleatham Old Hall
Kirklees – *W. Yorks.*
Bagshaw Museum
Tolson Memorial Museum,
  Huddersfield
Lacock – *Wilts.*
Leeds – *W. Yorks.*
Museum of Leeds
Leek – *Staffs.*
The Brindley Mill

Leicester – *Leics.*
Gas Museum
Museum of Technology
Leiston – *Suffolk*
Long Shop Museum
Lewes – *E. Sussex*
Museum of Local History
Lincoln – *Lincs.*
Museum of Lincolnshire Life
Llanberis – *Gwynedd*
Museum of the North
Welsh Slate Museum
Llanidloes – *Powys*
Llanidloes Museum
London – *London*
Chartered Insurance Institute's
  Museum
Darwin Museum
Kew Bridge Steam Museum
Markfield Beam Engine and
  Museum
Michael Faraday's Laboratory &
  Museum
The Museum of London
National Maritime Museum
National Sound Archives
Royal Artillery Regimental
  Museum
Science Museum
Telecom Technology Showcase
  (The)
Thames Barrier Visitor Centre
Tower Bridge
Loughborough – *Leics.*
Bellfoundry Museum
Macclesfield – *Cheshire*
Jodrell Bank
Machynlleth – *Powys*
Centre for Alternative Technology
Manchester – *Greater Manchester*
Museum of Science & Industry
  Manchester
Museum of Transport
Matlock – *Derbyshire*
Caudwell's Mill
Middlesbrough – *Cleveland*
Dorman Museum
Middleton-by-Wirksworth –
  Derbys.
Middle Wallop – *Hants.*
Museum of Army Flying
Neath – *W. Glam.*
Cefn Coed Museum
Newcastle upon Tyne – *Tyne &
  Wear*
Museum & Art Gallery
Museum of Science & Engineering
Turbinia Hall
Northwich – *Cheshire*
Lion Salt Works
Salt Museum
Norwich – *Norfolk*
Bridewell Museum
Colman's Mustard Museum
Strangers' Hall
Nottingham – *Notts.*
Green's Mill
Industrial Museum
Overton – *W. Yorks.*
Caphouse Colliery Mining
  Museum
Oxford – *Oxon.*
Museum of the History of Science
Paisley – *Strathclyde*
Paisley Museum and Art Gallery
Coats Observatory
Peterborough – *Cambs.*
Peterhead – *Grampian*
Arbuthnot Museum
Porthmadog – *Gwynedd*
Festiniog Railway Museum
Portsmouth – *Hants.*
City Museum
Prescot – *Merseyside*
Prescot Museum
Reading – *Berks.*
Blake's Lock Museum
Museum of English Rural Life
Redcar (see Kirkleatham) –
  Cleveland
Redditch – *Hereford & Worcs.*
The National Needle Museum,
  Forge Mill
Rothbury – *Northumberland*
Rotherham – *S. Yorks.*
Clifton Park Museum
Royston – *Herts.*
St. Helens – *Merseyside*
Salford – *Greater Manchester*
Monks Hall Museum
Museum of Mining
Sheffield – *S. Yorks.*
Abbeydale Industrial Hamlet
Industrial Museum
Kelham Island
Shepherd Wheel

Shrewsbury – *Shrops.*
Coleham Pumping Station
Southend-on-Sea – *Essex*
Southend-on-Sea Museum
Stamford – *Lincs.*
Starcross – *Exeter, Devon*
The Brunel Atmospheric Railway
Stockport – *Greater Manchester*
Stockport Museum
Stoke-on-Trent – *Staffs.*
Chatterley Whitfield Mining
  Museum
Stowmarket – *Suffolk*
Museum of East Anglian Life
Street – *Somerset*
Stroud – *Glos.*
Styal – *Cheshire*
Swansea – *W. Glam.*
Maritime & Industrial Museum
Telford – *Shrops.*
Tenterden – *Kent*
Tenterden & District Museum
Tiverton – *Devon*
Tonbridge – *Kent*
Milne Museum
Totnes – *Devon*
Elizabethan House
Walkerburn – *Borders*
Wanlockhead – *Dumfries &
  Galloway*
Museum of Lead Mining
Warley – *W. Midlands*
Warrington – *Cheshire*
Museum & Art Gallery
Washington – *Tyne & Wear*
Washington 'F' Pit Industrial
  Museum
Watford – *Herts.*
Whitby – *N. Yorks.*
Whitby Museum
Wigan – *Greater Manchester*
Wigan Pier
Willenhall – *W. Midlands*
The Lock Museum
Winchester – *Hants.*
Westgate Museum
Wolverhampton – *W. Midlands*
Bilston Museum & Art Gallery
Wroughton – *Wilts.*
Science Museum
Wye – *Kent*
York – *N. Yorks*
National Railway Museum

SCULPTURE – *see* FINE ARTS

SERVICES MUSEUMS – *see* separate section

SHIPPING, SHIPBUILDING & MARINE MODELS

Aberdeen – *Grampian*
Art Gallery
Maritime Museum
Angus – *Tayside*
Angus District Museums
Anstruther – *Fife*
Scottish Fisheries Museum
Appledore – *Devon*
Arbroath – *Tayside*
Arbroath Museum
Barton-on-Humber – *Humberside*
Baysgarth Museum
Bath – *Avon*
American Museum in Britain
Beaulieu – *Hants.*
Maritime Museum
Bideford – *Devon*
North Devon Maritime Museum
Birkenhead – *Merseyside*
Williamson Art Gallery
Birmingham – *W. Midlands*
Museum of Science & Industry
Blackburn – *Lancs.*
Museum & Art Gallery
Boston – *Lincs.*
Boston Guildhall Museum
Bournemouth – *Dorset*
Rothesay Museum
Russell-Cotes Art Gallery &
  Museum
Bridgwater – *Somerset*
Bridlington – *Humberside*
Brighton – *E. Sussex*
Museum & Art Gallery
Bristol – *Avon*
City Museum & Art Gallery
Industrial Museum
Brixham – *Devon*
Brixham Museum
Buckie – *Grampian*
Buckie Maritime Museum
Bucklers Hard (see Beaulieu) –
  Hants.
Calstock – *Cornwall*

181

Subject Index – *continued*

INDEX TO LOCALITIES

Kettering, *Northamptonshire*
Kidwelly, *Dyfed*
Kilbarchan, *Strathclyde*
Kilkenny, *Ireland*
Kilmarnock, *Strathclyde*
Kilmore Quay, *Ireland*
King's Lynn, *Norfolk*
Kingsbridge, *Devon*
Kingston upon Thames, *Greater London*
Kingussie, *Highlands*
Kinsale, *Ireland*
Kirkcaldy, *Fife*
Kirkcudbright, *Dumfries & Galloway*
Kirkintilloch, *Strathclyde*
Kirkleatham, *Cleveland*
Kirklees, *West Yorkshire*
Kirkoswald, *Strathclyde*
Kirriemuir, *Tayside*
Knaresborough, *North Yorkshire*
Knutsford, *Cheshire*

Lacock, *Wiltshire*
Lamberhurst, *Kent*
Lanark, *Strathclyde*
Lancaster, *Lancashire*
Langbank, *Strathclyde*
Langton Matravers, *Dorset*
Lauder, *Borders*
Lavenham, *Suffolk*
Laxey, *Isle of Man*
Leamington Spa, *Warwickshire*
Leeds, *West Yorkshire*
Leek, *Staffordshire*
Leicester, *Leicestershire*
Leigh, *Greater Manchester*
Leiston, *Suffolk*
Leominster, *Hereford & Worcester*
Lerwick, *Shetland Isles*
Letchworth, *Hertfordshire*
Levisham, *North Yorkshire*
Lewes, *East Sussex*
Leyland, *Lancashire*
Lichfield, *Staffordshire*
Lincoln, *Lincolnshire*
Lindisfarne, *Northumberland*
Liskeard, *Cornwall*
Littlehampton, *West Sussex*
Liverpool, *Merseyside*
Livingston, *Lothian*
Llanberis, *Gwynedd*
Llandrindod Wells, *Powys*
Llandudno, *Gwynedd*
Llanelli, *Dyfed*
Llangoed, *Gwynedd*
Llangollen, *Clwyd*
Llanidloes, *Powys*
Llantrisant, *Mid Glamorgan*
Lochwinnoch, *Strathclyde*
London, *Greater London*
London Colney, *Hertfordshire*
Long Wittenham, *Oxfordshire*
Loughborough, *Leicestershire*
Loughrea
Louth, *Lincolnshire*
Lower Hillhead, *Shetland Isles*
Lowestoft, *Suffolk*
Ludlow, *Shropshire*
Luton, *Bedfordshire*
Lutterworth, *Leicestershire*
Lyme Regis, *Dorset*
Lyndhurst, *Hampshire*

Macclesfield, *Cheshire*
Machynlleth, *Powys*
Maidenhead, *Berkshire*
Maidstone, *Kent*
Maldon, *Essex*
Malmesbury, *Wiltshire*
Malton, *North Yorkshire*
Malvern, *Hereford & Worcester*
Manchester, *Greater Manchester*
Mansfield, *Nottinghamshire*
Margate, *Kent*
Market Bosworth, *Leicestershire*
Market Harborough, *Leicestershire*
Maryport, *Cumbria*
Matlock, *Derbyshire*
Mauchline, *Strathclyde*
Melport, *Ayrshire*
Melton Mowbray, *Leicestershire*
Mere, *Wiltshire*
Merthyr Tydfil, *Mid Glamorgan*
Mevagissey, *Cornwall*
Middle Wallop, *Hampshire*
Middlesbrough, *Cleveland*
Middleton-by-Wirksworth, *Derbyshire*
Midhurst, *West Sussex*
Millom, *Cumbria*
Millport, *Strathclyde*

Milngavie, *Strathclyde*
Milton Keynes, *Buckinghamshire*
Minster, *Kent*
Mintlaw, *Grampian*
Mold, *Clwyd*
Monaghan, *Ireland*
Monmouth, *Gwent*
Montrose, *Tayside*
Morpeth, *Gwent*
Morpeth, *Northumberland*
Morwellham Quay, *Devon*
Much Wenlock, *Shropshire*

Nantwich, *Cheshire*
Neath, *West Glamorgan*
Nefyn, *Gwynedd*
Newark-on-Trent, *Nottinghamshire*
Newbury, *Berkshire*
Newcastle upon Tyne, *Tyne & Wear*
Newcastle-under-Lyme, *Staffordshire*
Newent, *Gloucestershire*
Newlyn, *Cornwall*
Newmarket, *Suffolk*
Newport, *Gwent*
Newport, *Isle of Wight*
Newry
Newton Abbot, *Devon*
Newtongrange, *Lothian*
Newtown, *Powys*
North Berwick, *Lothian*
North Shields, *Tyne & Wear*
Northampton, *Northamptonshire*
Northleach, *Gloucestershire*
Northwich, *Cheshire*
Norwich, *Norfolk*
Nottingham, *Nottinghamshire*
Nuneaton, *Warwickshire*

Oakham, *Leicestershire*
Oban, *Strathclyde*
Okehampton, *Devon*
Old Trafford, *Greater Manchester*
Old Warden, *Bedfordshire*
Oldham, *Greater Manchester*
Ollerton, *Nottinghamshire*
Olney, *Buckinghamshire*
Omagh
Ombersley, *Hereford & Worcester*
Otley, *West Yorkshire*
Oxford, *Oxfordshire*

Paddock Wood, *Kent*
Padiham, *Lancashire*
Paignton, *Devon*
Paisley, *Strathclyde*
Peebles, *Borders*
Peel, *Isle of Man*
Pembroke, *Dyfed*
Penarth, *South Glamorgan*
Penrith, *Cumbria*
Penzance, *Cornwall*
Perth, *Tayside*
Peterborough, *Cambridgeshire*
Peterhead, *Grampian*
Petersfield, *Hampshire*
Pickering, *North Yorkshire*
Pitmedden, *Grampian*
Plymouth, *Devon*
Pontefract, *West Yorkshire*
Pontypool, *Gwent*
Poole, *Dorset*
Port St. Mary, *Isle of Man*
Port Sunlight, *Merseyside*
Porthmadog, *Gwynedd*
Portland, *Dorset*
Portsmouth, *Hampshire*
Potterne, *Wiltshire*
Prescot, *Merseyside*
Preston, *Lancashire*
Prestongrange, *Lothian*
Pulborough, *West Sussex*
Purton, *Wiltshire*
Pwllheli, *Gwynedd*

Ramsey, *Isle of Man*
Ramsgate, *Kent*
Reading, *Berkshire*
Redditch, *Hereford & Worcester*
Redhill, *Surrey*
Reeth, *North Yorkshire*
Repton, *Derbyshire*
Retford, *Nottinghamshire*
Rhyl, *Clwyd*
Ribchester, *Lancashire*
Richborough, *Kent*
Richmond, *North Yorkshire*
Ripon, *North Yorkshire*
Rochdale, *Greater Manchester*
Rochester, *Kent*
Rolvenden, *Kent*

Romsey, *Hampshire*
Rosemarkie, *Highlands*
Rossendale, *Lancashire*
Rothbury, *Northumberland*
Rotherham, *South Yorkshire*
Rothesay, *Strathclyde*
Royston, *Hertfordshire*
Ruddington, *Nottinghamshire*
Rufford, *Lancashire*
Rugby, *Warwickshire*
Runcorn, *Cheshire*
Ruthin, *Clwyd*
Rutland Water, *Leicestershire*
Ryde, *Isle of Wight*
Rye, *East Sussex*

Saffron Walden, *Essex*
St. Albans, *Hertfordshire*
St. Andrews, *Fife*
St. Asaph, *Clwyd*
St. Austell, *Cornwall*
St. Fagans, *South Glamorgan*
St. Helens, *Merseyside*
St. Ives, *Cambridgeshire*
St. Ives, *Cornwall*
St. Margaret's Hope, *Orkney Isles*
Salcombe, *Devon*
Salford, *Greater Manchester*
Salisbury, *Wiltshire*
Saltaire, *West Yorkshire*
Saltash, *Cornwall*
Saltburn, *Cleveland*
Saltcoats, *Strathclyde*
Sandown, *Isle of Wight*
Sandwich, *Kent*
Scarborough, *North Yorkshire*
Scunthorpe, *Humberside*
Seaford, *East Sussex*
Selborne, *Hampshire*
Selkirk, *Borders*
Sevenoaks, *Kent*
Shackerstone, *Leicestershire*
Shaftesbury, *Dorset*
Sheffield, *South Yorkshire*
Sheffield Park, *East Sussex*
Shepton Mallet, *Somerset*
Shetland Isles, *Grampian*
Shifnal, *Shropshire*
Shoreham-by-Sea, *West Sussex*
Shrewsbury, *Shropshire*
Shugborough, *Staffordshire*
Sidmouth, *Devon*
Silchester, *Hampshire*
Skegness, *Lincolnshire*
Skipton, *North Yorkshire*
Slough, *Buckinghamshire*
Soho, *London*
South Molton, *Devon*
South Queensferry, *Lothian*
South Shields, *Tyne & Wear*
Southampton, *Hampshire*
Southend-on-Sea, *Essex*
Southport, *Merseyside*
Southport, *Lancashire*
Southwold, *Suffolk*
Spalding, *Lincolnshire*
Sparkford, *Somerset*
Spey Bay, *Grampian*
Springhill
Stafford, *Staffordshire*
Stalybridge, *Greater Manchester*
Stamford, *Lincolnshire*
Staplehurst, *Kent*
Stevenage, *Hertfordshire*
Steyning, *West Sussex*
Sticklepath, *Devon*
Stockport, *Greater Manchester*
Stocksfield, *Northumberland*
Stockton-on-Tees, *Cleveland*
Stoke Bruerne, *Northamptonshire*
Stoke-on-Trent, *Staffordshire*
Stonehaven, *Grampian*
Stornoway, *Highlands*
Stowmarket, *Suffolk*
Stranraer, *Dumfries & Galloway*
Stratford-upon-Avon, *Warwickshire*
Strathaven, *Strathclyde*
Strathpeffer, *Highlands*
Street, *Somerset*
Stretton, *Cheshire*
Stromness, *Orkney Isles*
Stroud, *Gloucestershire*
Styal, *Cheshire*
Sudbury, *Suffolk*
Sudbury, *Derbyshire*
Sunderland, *Tyne & Wear*
Swalcliffe, *Oxfordshire*
Swansea, *West Glamorgan*
Swindon, *Wiltshire*

Tamworth, *Staffordshire*
Tangmere, *West Sussex*
Tarbolton, *Strathclyde*
Tattershall, *Lincolnshire*
Taunton, *Somerset*
Teffont Magna, *Wiltshire*
Telford, *Shropshire*
Tenby, *Dyfed*
Tenterden, *Kent*
Tewkesbury, *Gloucestershire*
Thetford, *Norfolk*
Thirsk, *North Yorkshire*
Tiverton, *Devon*
Tomintoul, *Grampian*
Tonbridge, *Kent*
Topsham, *Devon*
Torquay, *Devon*
Totnes, *Devon*
Tre'r-Ddôl, *Dyfed*
Tring, *Hertfordshire*
Trowbridge, *Wiltshire*
Truro, *Cornwall*
Tunbridge Wells, *Kent*
Turton, *Lancashire*

Uffcolme, *Devon*
Ulverston, *Cumbria*
Upminster, *Essex*
Usk, *Gwent*

Valentia Island, *Ireland*

Wakefield, *West Yorkshire*
Walkerburn, *Borders*
Wall, *Staffordshire*
Wallasey, *Merseyside*
Wallingford, *Oxfordshire*
Wallsend, *Tyne & Wear*
Walsall, *West Midlands*
Walsingham, *Norfolk*
Waltham Abbey, *Essex*
Wanlockhead, *Dumfries & Galloway*
Wantage, *Oxfordshire*
Ware, *Hertfordshire*
Wareham, *Dorset*
Warley, *West Midlands*
Warrington, *Cheshire*
Warwick, *Warwickshire*
Washington, *Tyne & Wear*
Watford, *Hertfordshire*
Wednesbury, *West Midlands*
Wells, *Somerset*
Wells-next-the-Sea, *Norfolk*
Welshpool, *Powys*
Welwyn Garden City, *Hertfordshire*
West Bromwich, *West Midlands*
West Hoathly, *West Sussex*
West Wycombe, *Buckinghamshire*
Westcott, *Surrey*
Weston-Super-Mare, *Avon*
Wexford
Weybourne, *Norfolk*
Weybridge, *Surrey*
Weymouth, *Dorset*
Whitby, *North Yorkshire*
Whitehaven, *Cumbria*
Widnes, *Cheshire*
Wigan, *Greater Manchester*
Wigtown, *Dumfries & Galloway*
Willenhall, *West Midlands*
Willenham, *Wiltshire*
Wilmington, *East Sussex*
Wilton, *Wiltshire*
Wimborne Minster, *Dorset*
Winchcombe, *Gloucestershire*
Winchelsea, *East Sussex*
Winchester, *Hampshire*
Windermere, *Cumbria*
Wisbech, *Cambridgeshire*
Witney, *Oxfordshire*
Wolverhampton, *West Midlands*
Woodhall Spa, *Lincolnshire*
Woodstock, *Oxfordshire*
Wookey Hole, *Somerset*
Worcester, *Hereford & Worcester*
Workington, *Cumbria*
Worksop, *Nottinghamshire*
Worthing, *West Sussex*
Wrexham, *Clwyd*
Wroughton, *Wiltshire*
Wroxeter, *Shropshire*
Wye, *Kent*

Yeovil, *Somerset*
Yeovilton, *Somerset*
York, *North Yorkshire*

Zenor, *Cornwall*

ALPHABETICAL LIST OF MUSEUMS AND ART GALLERIES
(SEE SEPARATE INDEX FOR SERVICES MUSEUMS)

Alphabetical List

Alphabetical List

Alphabetical List

Alphabetical List

Alphabetical List

ALPHABETICAL LIST OF SERVICES MUSEUMS

NOTES

NOTES

NOTES

NOTES

NOTES

NOTES